National Intelligencer Newspaper Abstracts 1814-1817

Joan M. Dixon

HERITAGE BOOKS
2006

HERITAGE BOOKS
AN IMPRINT OF HERITAGE BOOKS, INC.

Books, CDs, and more—Worldwide

For our listing of thousands of titles see our website at
www.HeritageBooks.com

Published 2006 by
HERITAGE BOOKS, INC.
Publishing Division
65 East Main Street
Westminster, Maryland 21157-5026

Copyright © 1997 Joan M. Dixon

All rights reserved. No part of this book may be reproduced or transmitted in any form or by any means, electronic or mechanical, including photocopying, recording or by any information storage and retrieval system without written permission from the author, except for the inclusion of brief quotations in a review.

International Standard Book Number: 978-0-7884-0707-4

NATIONAL INTELLIGENCER NEWSPAPER
WASHINGTON, D C
1814-1817

TABLE OF CONTENTS

Daily National Intelligencer-1814--1
Daily National Intelligencer-1815---75
Daily National Intelligencer-1816--164
Daily National Intelligencer-1817--250

Americans killed in action between Gen Floyd & Creek Indians--8-9
American prisoners at St Jago de Cuba--268
Americans to be exchanged--52
Appointments by the President --11-12; 25; 89; 141; 264; 330
Army promotions & appointments--202; 213; 220-221; 25; 325-327
Army Register--111
Association of Cumberland Co--213-214
Biog of Daniel D Tompkins--199
Bourbon family--30
Brig Argus-killed--51
Citizens of Fayetteville--213-214
Citizens of Washington City--102-103
College of New Jersey-students--144-145
Court Martial of Maj Gen James Wilkinson--65-66
Deserters--55; 56; 81-82; 177-178
Dickerson College-students--145
Directors of Union Bank of Georgetown--19-20
Distressed seamen--271
French Mills-killed & wounded--30-31
Frig Essex-killed & wounded--39-40
Georgetown College, D C-students--44; 133; 212; 304
Invalid Pensioners--191-193; 267-268
Killed on Lake Champlain--54
Killed on the Wasp--67

Ladies with letters in the Post Ofc--2; 20; 38-39; 58; 76-77; 99-100; 124; 146; 164; 183-184; 208; 224-225; 252; 272; 296; 318-319; 334

Leonard Town, Md-meeting--338
Loss of the schooner Alligator-drowned--41
Marine Corps appointments & promotions--47; 93-95
Massacre at Dartmoor--117
Military Academy-West Point--106-107
Nashville fire sufferers--19
Navy promotions--197-198; 264
Officers retained--118-119; 279-280
Pension list--22-23; 90-91
Post Office changes--3-4; 12-13
Prisoners exchanged--59
Prisoners taken at Balt, Md--53

i

Proprietors of the town of Alabama--310
Schooner Surprise shipwreck--101
St Mary's Co, Md-taxes due--207
Troops supplied by Joseph Wheaton--26
U S Army-brevetts--51; 69-70; 77-78
University of Maryland--277-278
Virginia Legislature-nominations--173
Virginia Militia-60th Regt--136-137

Washington City appointments--205
Washington City-taxes due--239-249; 339-340
Washington City-tax sale--23; 40-41; 129; 130; 272-277; 280-281; 298-299; 301

Index--342

Dedicated to my husband of fifty-four years-2005
Roland Campbell Dixon

PREFACE
Daily National Intelligencer Newspaper Abstracts
1814-1817
Joan M Dixon

The National Intelligencer & Washington Advertiser is hereafter the Daily National Intelligencer. It was the first newspaper printed in Washington, D C; Samuel H Smith, the originator. The same was transferred to Jos Gales, jr on Aug 31, 1810; on Nov 1, 1812, the paper was under the firm of Jos Gales, sr, & Wm W Seaton. The Library of Congress has microfilm of the paper from the first issue of Oct 31, 1800 thru Jan 8, 1870, the final paper. The Evening Star Newspaper of Jan 10, 1870 reports: The Intelligencer is discontinued: the proprietor, Mr Alex Delmar, says that having lost several thousand dollars, & being in poor health, he has resolved to discontinue its publication.

Included in the abstracts are advertisements; appointments by the President; Hse o/Rep petitions; passed Acts; legal notices; marriages; deaths; mscl notices; social events; tax lists; military promotions; court cases; deaths by accident; prisoners; & maritime information-crews. Items or events which might be a clue as to the location, age or relationship of an individual are copied.

No attempt has been made to correct the spelling. Due to the length of some articles, it was necessary to present only the highlights of same. Chancery and Equity records are copied as written.

The index contains all surnames and *tracts of lands/places.*

ABBREVIATIONS:
AA CO	ANNE ARUNDEL COUNTY
CO	COMPANY/COUNTY
CMDER	COMMANDER
CMDOR	COMMODOR
D C	DISTRICT OF COLUMBIA
ELIZ	ELIZABETH
ELIZA	ELIZA
MONTG CO	MONTGOMERY COUNTY
PG CO	PRINCE GEORGES CO
WASH	WASHINGTON

BOOKS IN THE NATIONAL INTELLIGENCER NEWSPAPER SERIES: 1800-1805/1806-1810/1811-1813/1814-1817/1818-1820/1821-1823/1824-1826/1827-1829/1830-1831/1832-1833/1834-1835/1836-1837/1838-1839/1840/1841/1842/1843/1844/1845/1846/
SPECIAL: CIVIL WAR 2 VOLS, 1861-1865

DAILY NATIONAL INTELLIGENCER
WASHINGTON, D C

1814

SAT JAN 1, 1814
Abraham Bradley, jr, Assist P O Genr'l, appt'd Pres of the Union Bank, of Gtwn, v Thos Beall, rsgnd.

Being about to remove into the country, I will sell or lease the hse in which I reside, on Capitol Hill, Wash City. -B Thruston

Wash Co, D C. Case of Geo Maxwell, insolvent debtor, confined in the prison of Wash Co, for debt. -Wm Brent, clk.

MON JAN 3, 1814
Rpblcn meeting in Saratoga Co, Dec, 1813, at Benj Burton's in Greenfield; Chas Drake, chrmn; Dr Darius Johnson, sec. Committee: Asa C Barney, Howel Gardner, John Prior, Mark A Child, Jacob Weed & Jonathan Lapham. Subj-patriotic proceedings.

Died: at Marietta, Ohio, on Dec 21, of a lingering consumption, David Everitt, aged 44 yrs, Editor of the *American Friend*.

TUE JAN 4, 1814
Orphans Crt of Wash Co, D C. Prsnl est of Mary Ann M'Nantz, late of said city, dec'd. -W Matthews, exc. Sale at the late dwlg of Mrs Mary Ann M'Nantz, dec'd, all the hsehld & kitchen furn, window sashes, a good milch cow, etc, of the dec'd. -N L Queen, auctioneer.

Sale by auction of featherbeds, furn, etc, being the furn of Augustine Serra, belonging to his boarding establishment, to be sold at his hse nr the Navy Yd, as he has declined the brdg business. -David Bates, auctioneer.

For sale-the Wash Hotel, on Pa av. Also the hse occupied by the subscriber, 5 lots of ground attached to the same, on I & 18th st west; desirable residence. -Toppan Webster.

WED JAN 5, 1814
Hse o/Reps. Petition of John Minor, sr, praying comp for svcs by his brother, Reuben Minor, dec'd, as sldr in the Rev; referred. 2-The petition of Philip Mary Leduc, by Mr Leduc, of Md, was twice read & committed.

THU JAN 6, 1814
Mrd: in Raleigh, on Dec 28, by Rev Pres Chapman, the Rev Anthony Forster, of S C, to Miss Altona Holstein Gales, d/o Jos Gales, of Raleigh.

FRI JAN 7, 1814
Hse o/Reps. 1-Mr Ingersoll, of Pa presented the petition of Cath Robertson, late

wid/o Jacob Ritter, praying comp for his Rev svcs; referred. 2-The petition of Jacob Clement was agained referred to the ways & means cmtee.

SAT JAN 8, 1814
John Peter is re-elected Mayor of Gtwn for the ensuing yr.

Mrd: at Balt, on Jan 4, by Rev Arch Carroll, Robt Y Brent, of Wash City, to Miss Eliza L Carrere, d/o John Carrere, of Balt.

Mrd: recently at N Y, by Rev Dr Ruypers, Mr Silas Butler, merchant of Wash City, to Miss Phebe Waldron, of N Y.

MON JAN 10, 1814
Died: on Dec 31, in his 32d yr, Dr Benj Tabbs, of St Mary's Co, Md.

Ltr to the Editor of the *Albany Argus*, dated Buffalo, Dec 26. Re-Sunday morning last, the British troops crossed the rvr above Ft Niagara & tk the Ft by surprize; the Indians then began their hellish work. On Fri I proceeded to Lewiston; found the bodies of Wm Gardner, deputy shrf, John M Low & Ezra St John, [whose families cannot be found] attorneys, Dr Alvord & others. -Amos Hall

For sale-427 acs in Hardy Co, Va, with dwlg hse. -Saml Burch.

The subscriber, now at an advanced time of life, is desirous of taking into partnership, a young man of good character, well qualified & licenced to practice Physic & Surgery in the state of Md. -Barton Tabbs, St Mary's Co, Md.

Potomac Steam Boat Co meeting, Jan 3, at Triplett's Tavern, in Alexandria; John Dawson elected Pres; John Davis, Robt Lewis, Carey Selden, John Withers, elected Dirs. -Sidney Wishart, sec.

TUE JAN 11, 1814
Ladies with ltrs in the P O at Wash City, Jan 1, 1814:

Miss M G Addison	Eliz Burnel	Miss Eliza Brown-2
Miss E T Beall	Mrs Anne Brooke	Dolly Brown
Mrs Mrs Mary Belt	Nelly Baker	Mrs Jane Baker
Miss Maria Clarke	Eliza Dill	Matilda Dixon
Miss Eliza Duvall-2	Rachael Derrick	Mary Davis
Eliza Ellicott	Mrs Green	Charity Hutchins
Mrs A Hunter	Jane Johnson	Susan Johnson
Ann Kelly	Eliza Kendreb	Miss Ann Lee
Mrs Lane	Hannah Myers	Mrs Middleton
Cath Marquart	Mrs Eliza Nowland-3	Cath Pumroy
Nelly G Queen	Mary A Rowland-2	Mrs S Rose
Mrs Anne Stewart	Miss Hess Scoval	Kitty Skinner
Miss Anne Tootell	Mary Thompson	Miss Stewart c/o Dr Shoaff-3
Mrs B A Talbott	Eleanor Windsor	Mgt Watkins
Eliza Walker		

Orphans Crt of Montg Co, Md. Prsnl est of John Selby, late of said co, dec'd.
-Robt Edmonston, adm

WED JAN 12, 1814
P O changes in Dec, 1813:
Aquia Run Mills, Va, John Tacket v Aaron Halloway, rsgnd.
East Chester, N Y, Geo Fail, v Jas Armstrong, do.
Ft Defiance, N C, Edmund Jones v Wm Davenport, do.
Mitchell's store, Va, Peter Moreton v Thos Mitchell, do.
Cambridge, Vt, Israel P Richardson v Isaac Warner, do.
Marblehead, Mass, Richard Prince v W Abraham, dec'd.
Hardenburg, Ky, Saml M'Clarty v J M'Clarty, rsgnd.
West Cambridge, Mass, Amos Whittemore, jr v Thos Russell, mvd away.
Clay C H, Ky, Thos Murphy v Jas Rice, rsgnd.
Yellow Springs, Pa, Maxwell Kincaid v D Moore, do.
Upper Blue Lick, Ky, Fielding Belt v Jno Finley, do.
Machias, Me, Wm O'Brian v Ralph H Bowles, dec'd.
Lexington, Ky, Jno Fowler v John Jordan, dec'd.
Petersburg, Ga, John Watkins, sen v Alexander Pope, rsgnd.
Canoe Camp, Pa, Amos Spencer v Micah Spencer, do.
Beard's Mill, N C, Smith Blair v John S Travis, do.
Warrentown, Ohio, Robt Blair v Arthur Patterson, do.
Greenville, N C, David A Telfair v Redding Sheppard, do.
North End, Va, Wm Blake, jr v Jasper S Clayton, do.
Queenstown, Md, Peregrine Betton v Chas Hobbs, mv'd away.
Centreville, Md, Wm Elbert v Wm Hindman, rsgnd.
Dagsboro, Del, Thos Smith v Geo Truitt, do.
Millville, Va, Wm Smith v Enoch Arnold, do.
Bridgewater, N Y, Timothy Dorland v Isaiah Bunce, do.
N Y, Va, John Hays v Nathaniel Landraft, do.
Willington, S C, Moses Waddle v Jas Gamble, do.
Wmsburg, Va, Jesse Cole v Jesse Cole, sen, dec'd.
Stroudsburg, Pa, Saml Brooke v Saml Gummore, rsgnd.
Fairfax, Me, Joel Willington v Nathan Haywood, do.
Berlin, Ct, Saml Porter 2d, v Geo Hubbard, jr, rsgnd.
Phillipsburg, Pa, Wm P Dewees v John Lorain, do.
Canandaigua, N Y, Jno C Spencer v Oliver L Phelps, dec'd.
Edgefield C H, S C, Henry Lowe v Jno Simpkins, rsgnd.
Chetauga, N Y, Amasa Fairman v Jas Ormsby, rsgnd.
Cresapsburg, Md, John P Hider v Wm Bruce, dec'd.
Eastport, Me, John Burgain v Oliver Shead, dec'd.
Hancockown, N J, Morris Hancock v Walker Beesley.
Montagues, Va, Robt Dobbins v Saml Foster, dec'd.
Redfield, N Y, Wm West v Aaron Butler, rsgnd.
Chester, Pa, M Davenport v Thos A Anderson, mv'd away.
Harrisburg, S C, Banks Meacham v Wilson Crocket, rsgnd.
Pedlar Mills, Va, Jas Ware v John Ellis, do.

New ofcs est'd in Dec 1813, & postmstrs:
Harford, Susquehanna Co, Pa, Labron Capron.
Jefferson, Lincoln Co, Me, Elijah H Ford.
Newton Lower Falls, Middlesex Co, Mass, Amos Allen.
Hazelton's Ferry, Knox Co, Ind Ter, Gewase Hazelton
Vance's Ferry, Orange dist, S C, Wm Vance.
Tanner's Hill, Newberry dist, S C, John Folk.
Garysville, PG Co, Va, Sterling Gary.
Shelburn, Chittenden Co, Vt, Isaac R Harrington.
Fisher's, Mississippi Terr, Geo Fisher.
Chickesawha, Mississippi Terr, John Brewer.
Green C H, Green Co, Miss Terr, Jas B M'Connell.
Bolle's store, Pendleton dist, S C, G A Bolles.
New Albany, Ind Terr, Joel Scribner.
Sidney, Delaware Co, N Y, Abraham G Siverly.
Whiteland, Chester Co, Pa, Campbell Harris.
Middle Ground, Miss Terr, Hugh W Cooper.
Warminster x Rds, Montg Co, Pa, Wm Hart, jr.
Hancock's, Union dist, S C, Thos Hancock.
Bentley's, Va, Thos M'Cargo.
Huntsville, Lawrens Co, S C, Isaac Underwood.
Thompson's store, Hanover Co, Va, Galland Thompson.
Bradon's store, London Co, Robt Bradon. [probably Va]
Deep Creek, Passquatank Co, N C, Saml Proctor.
Hamilton's Mill, London Co, Va, John Hamilton.
Carrollsville, Montg Co, Md, Wm Carroll.
Rappahannock Academy, Caroline Co, Va, Alex Keech.

For sale-the farm & land on which I reside; 340 acs within one mile of the Pres' Hse; small but convenient dwlg hse. -John Holmead

THU JAN 13, 1814
Wash Co, D C. Case of Wm Hutchinson, insolvent debtor, confined in Wash Co prison for debt. -Wm Brent, clk.

FRI JAN 14, 1814
Died: on board the U S brig *Argus*, Capt Allen, on Aug 14, 1813, of the wound he rec'd in the action with the British ship *Pelican*, Midshipman Wm W Edwards, s/o Mr Lewis Edwards, of Wash City; a youth of uncommon promise.

Pblc sale: order of Orphans Crt of Montg Co, Md, the whole of the est of Wm Veirs, sen, late of said co, dec'd. -Levi Veirs, exc.

SAT JAN 15, 1814
Mrd: in Wash City, on Jan 13, by Rev Mr McCormick, Wm B Branch, of Dinwiddie Co, Va, to Miss Louisa A Magruder, d/o Patrick Magruder.

Drowned: at Charleston, S C, on Dec 23, Midshipman Rousseau, aged 14 yrs, known & esteemed by many in this city, & by his early death, the U S Navy has been bereft of one of its most promising ofcrs.

MON JAN 17, 1814
Orphans Crt of Chas Co, Md. Prsnl est of Jos Padgitt, late of said co, dec'd. -Thos J Reeves, John C Reeves, excs.

TUE JAN 18, 1814
Pblc dinner was given at Tammany Hall, N Y, on Tue, for Cmdor Oliver H Perry; Jas Fairlie presided, assisted by Augustus Wright, Jonathan Lawrence, Thos Farmar, John Bingham, Wm Irving & Geo Buckmaster.

Ranaway-negro man, Joe Mason, aged 28 yrs; lived for some time with Capt Carson & with Mr O'Neale. -Ann Ray.

Subscriber wishing to remove to the Great Kenhaway, offers for sale or exchange for lands in the country & negroes, the farm on which he now resides in Pr Wm Co, Va; about 6 to 700 acs, with new log dwlg hse 30' x 20'. -Philip Alexander, nr Dumfries, Pr Wm Co, Va.

For sale: two story brick hse on F st, Wash City, now occupied by Mr Jas Watson. -Chas Vinson

Merino sheep for sale. -Wm Brooks, C H Smith, Fredericksburg, Va.

WED JAN 19, 1814
Green Spring for sale; the residence of the late Wm L Lee, in Jas City Co, Va, containing 2934 1/2 acs; with saw mill & mansion hse all of brick. Shown by Wm Coleman, of Wmsburg; or Mr Wm M'Candlish of that city. -J H Hooe, lvg nr Alexandria.

Pblc sale at the residence of the late Dr Jas Edelen, on Feb 15, all prsnl est of dec'd. -Jos Edelen, N S Stonestreet, excs.

Wash Co, D C. Case of Andrew Thompson, insolvent debtor, confined in Wash Co prison. -Wm Brent, clk.

THU JAN 20, 1814
Died: at Phil, a few days ago, Gen Ira Allen, of Vt, a distinguished Rev vet.

FRI JAN 21, 1814
Grey Mare stolen nr Mason's Ferry, Gtwn, on Jan 18th. Deliver same to Mr Sewell, at the ferry, or to me, nr the Falls Chr, Fairfax Co, Va. -Musty Fahy

Hse o/Reps. Mr Hubbard, of Mass, presented the petition of Joanna Nash, wid/o Wm Nash, dec'd, late a lt in the army, killed in the line of his duty, praying for a pension. Referred to the cmtee on Rev claims.

$500 reward for British p o ws, who escaped on Jan 12, from the goal in Worcester: Chas De Vilette, Maj, aged 40 yrs; Wm A Steel, Lt, aged 24 yrs; Arthur Carter, Lt, aged 21 yrs; Hector M'Lean, Lt, aged 42 yrs; Francis Decenta, Lt, aged 33 yrs, Fred'k Zechinder, Capt, aged 38 yrs; David Duval, Lt, aged 18 yrs; Albert Manuel, Lt, aged 23 yrs; Chas Morris, Lt, aged 24 yrs. -Jas Prince, Mrshl Mass Dist.

SAT JAN 22, 1814
Mrd: on Jan 18, by Rev Mr Wilmer, Clacgett Lyles, of Gtwn, to Miss Rebecca Seaton, of Alexandria.

Info wanted of waggoner, John Day, of Fairfax Co, Va, who rec'd 2 hogshead of sugar in Balt, of John Oakley, to be delivered to me without delay in this place. Any info will be rec'd & rewarded by T W Peyton, Alexandria.

Pvt sale of farm in Montg Co, Md; 672 1/2 acs; with dwlg hse; originally owned by Sam'l Turner. Mr Wade is the tenant. -Daniel Schnebley, Hagers Town, Md.

MON JAN 24, 1814
$100 reward for run away, Bartlet Shanklin, a black man, blacksmith by trade, aged about 30 yrs. He has a wife at Mr Foots' in PG Co, Md, & is bro to Phillip Alexander's servant, Dick, of Stafford Co. -Abrahm B Hooe, King Geo Co, Va.

TUE JAN 25, 1814
Doct Geo W May tenders his professional svcs to the inhabitants of Wash. His residence is in Pairo's new bldg on Pa av, Wash.

WED JAN 26, 1814
For sale-tract of land in Fairfax Co, Va, cld *Cameron*, the prop of Thos Herbert, about 500 acs. -N Herbert, Alexandria.

THU JAN 27, 1814
Dr J H Blake & Dr Geo A Carroll have this day entered into partnership in the practice of medicine. Wash Item.

FRI JAN 28, 1814
Sulphur Springs, Berkeley Co, Va, for sale or rent; enquire of Jacob Morgan, Alexandria. -H S G Tucker, Winchester, Va.

SAT JAN 29, 1814
For sale, lease, rent or barter; large 3 story brick hse on Water st, lately occupied by Dr John W Beatty. -Robt Ober, Gtwn.

MON JAN 31, 1814
Orphan's Crt of PG Co, Md. Ordered by the Crt, that Thos Ewell, adm of Benj Stoddert, late of said co, dec'd, sell the whole of the deceased's prsnl est. -Truman Tyler, reg.

TUE FEB 1, 1814
Died: at Roxbury, Mass, a few days ago, Maj Gen Wm Heath, a vet of the Rev, aged 77 yrs.

$30 reward for runaway, Alice, negro woman, from the employment of Abraham Dawes, nr Paris, about Jul 12th last. Her hsbnd is Jim Buck & she has a free bro, Jim, who for some time has lived with Mr Forrest, in Gtwn. -Jas Currell, Snicker's Gap, Loudon Co, Va.

$30 reward for runaway, Isaac, negro man, about 23yrs old, from Gtwn College. He was raised at Mrs Johnson's nr Bryantown, Chas Co, Md. -John McElroy, clk of Gtwn College, D C.

WED FEB 2, 1814
Mrd: on Jan 11, at Shoal Creek, Dorchester Co, Md, by Rev Mr Bain, Wm H Fitzhugh, of Va, to Miss Anna Maria Goldsborough, d/o Hon Chas Goldsborough.

Garden to rent in Wash City; & for sale, a healthy negro boy aged 13 yrs, on Mar 4 next. -Thos Tingey, Navy Yd.

THU FEB 3, 1814
Notice-I request all who are indebted to me to make payment immediately as I am going to leave town shortly. -Jacob Baltzers

FRI FEB 4, 1814
Plain seamstress, hsekpr, or nurse, a middle aged woman, is seeking employment. Apply to Jos Russell's next to Mr Lewis Debois', nr the Marine Barracks, Wash.

Licenses given at my ofc in Wash City for owners of carriages. -Jas H Blake, Coll Rev, D C, Jan 15.

Alex'r Parker of Westmoreland Co, elected Maj Gen of the militia of Va, to fill the vacancy occasioned by the absence of Maj Gen H Lee from Va.

SAT FEB 5, 1814
Chas K Mallory, Lt Gov of Va, appt'd Coll of the port of Norfolk, v Col Larkin Smith, dec'd.

Land for sale-about 200 acs in Loudoun Co, Va, the residence of the late Judge Jones; shown by my bro who resides there. -Jas Monroe, Wash City.

For sale, land on Ten mile Crk, Montg Co, Md, 307 acs; also bet 150 & 200 acs on Cubb Run, Fairfax Co, Va, descended to my wife, as one of the heirs of Hardage Lane. -Ninian Edwards.

MON FEB 7, 1814

Killed at Black Rock, in the battle of the 30th ult, Lt Col Seymor Boughton, aged 44. Remains have been remv'd to his late residence in Avon, & interred. On Feb 1, in a skirmish with the British nr Buffalo, Joshua B Tolman, formerly of Colrain, Mass, killed, Lt & Adj in Col Willcocks' corps of vols. At Sclosser, on the 21st ult, fighting in defence of his country, John M Lowe, 1st Lt in the 23d U S Infty.

TUE FEB 8, 1814

Mrd: on Feb 3, by Rev Mr Gibson, the Rev Walter D Addison to Mrs Rebecca Mackall, d/o Wm Bayly, of PG Co, Md.

Dissolution of the partnership of G C Grammer & Henry Mayer, by mutual consent. Grammer will continue the bus in his hse, F & 13th sts; groceries.

WED FEB 9, 1814

Orphans Crt of PG Co, Md. Prsnl est of Walter Truman Greenfield, late of said co, dec'd. -Gerrard T Greenfield, adm.

THU FEB 10, 1814

Geo Wash Campbell, of Tenn, appt'd Sec of the Treas of the U S. Mich'l Leib, sen, from Pa, appt'd Post Mstr of Phil City, vice Robt Patton, dec'd.

$20 reward for run away, Isaac Smothers, negro man, formerly the prop of Miss Eliz Birckhead, in lower A A Co, Md, nr Herring Bay; age about 28 yrs. -Henry Dowel, Calvert co nr Lower Marlborough, Md.

Wash Co, D C. Case of Erasmus Tuell, insolvent debtor, confined in Wash Co, prison. -Wm Brent, clk.

FRI FEB 11, 1814

Hse o/Reps. Petition of Sanders Glover, comp for his svcs as principal assessor of the Dist tax laid in 1798, for a dist in S C, was presented.

Died: at his residence in Fairfax Co, Virg, on Feb 6, in his 84th yr, Dr Jas Craik, formerly Physician Genr'l to the armies of the U S.

For sale-fashionable light coach, with glasses & real Venetian blinds. Enquire of Robt Fielding, coachmkr, 10 So 8th st, Phil, Pa.

Americans killed in the action of Jan 27 bet Gen Floyd & the Creek Indians; Patrick Ward & Alexander D M'Farlan, of Capt Thos' Artl. Sgt Littleton & John Thornton, killed, of Capt Lee's company. Walter T Brockman, of Capt Myrick's Co, was killed. Jos Thompson of Capt Henry's co was killed. Wm Dillon of Capt Owen's Co, was killed. John Whitehead of Brodnax's co was killed; Joel Dixon was severly wounded; Jeremiah Clark, Wm Whitehead, Wm Fitch, Wm Mathews, Edw Cavender, Jas Greer, Isaac Riafs, & John Brown, of same, slightly wounded. Wm Bailey of John Cunningham's Camp was killed. Reuben Goldsby, Anderson Hicks, Abner Jackson of Smith's Co, were wounded severely; John H Greer, of same, wounded slightly. D Blaylock, J Cooper, D Anderson, Greene Berry, Wm Blaylock, of Adams' Co, were killed. -Chas Williamson, Hosp Surgeon.

SAT FEB 12, 1814
Commandants & Ofcrs of Regts desirous of forming bands; music composed & arranged by Jas H Hoffman. Apply to Capt M'Kee, Navy Yd, Wash.

Stock-breeders-thorough bred horse, *Telegraph*, prop of Maj Ch S Ridgely, will stand the ensuing season at the farm of N Lufborough, in the *Forest*, PG Co, Md.

MON FEB 14, 1814
Died: on Feb 8, after a lingering illness, Mrs Ann Peter, w/o Capt Geo Peter, of Gtwn, in her 23d yr.

Hse o/Reps. Petitions: 1-of Ludwig Deitrick, for comp for svcs as sldr in Rev army, presented by Mr Rea of Pa. 2-Pet of Zubulon Whippey, of Balt, for comp for svcs as a staff ofcr in Md Militia, presented by Mr M'Kim of Md. 3-Pet of John Dashner to be on the pension list bec of wound rec'd whilst in a corps of Va in svc of the U S, presented by Mr Cafterton of Va. 4-Pet of Benj Baldwin for a grant of land for svcs in the Rev army, presented by Mr Jackson, of Va.

Orphans Crt of Chas Co, Md. Excs of Joshua Mudd, dec'd, to insert notice of death of same in Alex Gaz & Ntl Intel. -H Darnes [Notice followed-signed by Francis L Mudd, Ann Mudd, excs.]

Wash Library-$3 per share. -Jas Laurie, Pres.

TUE FEB 15, 1814
For sale-land on which I reside, bet 750 & 800 acs, in PG Co, Md; with good frame dwlg hse, cattle, furn, bks, etc. -Ann Sprigg

Hse o/Reps. Cmtee reported unfavorable to the petition of Mary Cheevers, the mthr/o 2 of her own name, seamen on the frig *Constitution*, both of whom were killed in the engagement bet that vessel & the British frig *Java*, on whom she, as well as her dght, was entirely dependent for support.

WED FEB 16, 1814
Pr Wm co [Va] Crt, Jan 7, 1814, in Chancery. Chas Ewell, Jos Smith, Henry Dogan, Francis Montgomerie, Rich'd Cole, & Sam'l Jackson, Overseers of the Poor of Pr Wm Co, successors of Thos Lee, Thos Harrison, Philip Dawe, John M'Millain, Gerrard Alexander, & Alexander Bruce, former Overseers, of said co, plntfs, against, Robt Chesley, John Chesley, Alex Chesley, Wm Chesley, Geo Chesley, Harriet Chesley, Charlotte Short, late Charlotte Chesley, & John C Short, her hsbnd, Cath Bumbury, late Cath Chesley, & Wm Bumbury, her hsbnd, Clarissa Powell, late Clarissa Chesley, & Wm Powell, her hsbnd, Eliz Bourne, late Eliz Chesley, & Wm Bourne, her hsbnd, Louisa Chesley, & Caroline Chesley, chldrn & reps of John Chesley, dec'd, dfndnts. Ordered that Wm Bourne be Grdn of the infant dfndnts; & the sale of land-400acs, under the last will of John Chesley, the

elder, dec'd. -Philip D Dawe, clk. Philip Alexander, Gerard Alexander, jr, Richard Foote, com'rs, Pr Wm Co, Md.

THU FEB 17, 1814
On Monday last, Abijah Bigelow, of Barre, & Oliver Bigelow, his son, were arrested in the name of the U S, on suspicion of assisting in the escape of the British prisoners lately in this town. They passed thru this town on their way to Boston, in custody of Mr Thaxter, Dep Mrshl. -Worcester Aegis.

I will sell about 160 acs of good land lying in Fairfax Co, Va. -Coleman Lewis, lvg in Centreville, Va.

FRI FEB 18, 1814
Act of relief of Daniel Boone; enacted by the Senate & Hse o/Reps of the U S. Daniel Boone is confirmed in his title to 1,000 arpens of land, claimed by him by virtue of a concession made to him under the Spanish government, dated Jan 28, 1798; duty of the recorder of land titles for Mo terr, to issue to the said Daniel Boone, or to his heirs, a certificate of same. -Langdon Cheves, spkr of Hse o/Reps.

The most delicious & wholesome of all animals, the Bear, will be for sale in Gtwn Mkt on Feb 21, at my stall. -Nathan Gray, Gtwn.

Birthnight Ball-Wash City. Mgrs: Thos Tingey, J P Van Ness, John Graham, Thos Sim, Edw Coles, Henry Huntt, Edmund B Duval, Chas Hill. -Local Item

SAT FEB 19, 1814
A Crt Martial was held at Portsmouth, N H, for the trial of Sailing Mstr Wm Harper, U S Navy, on chg of cowardice in action bet the U S brig *Enterprize* & the British sloop of war *Boxer*, preferred against him by Lt R M'Call; on Jan 22. Harper found not guilty. Signed: Isaac Hull-pres, John Smith, Johnston Blakely, John H Elton, Jas P Oellers, Geo W Prescott-Judge advocate.

Notice-present claims against Wm M'Gee, late of Wash City, insolvent debtor, within 10 days. -Geo Moore.

MON FEB 21, 1814
For sale-green oak wood for $1 per cord. -Chas Eversfield, jr, PG Co, Md.

Dissolution of partnership bet Jos Thomas & John M Wright, lumber merchants, by mutual consent. [Great difficulty in procuring materials in their line.]

TUE FEB 22, 1814
Hse & lot for sale in Wash City, on 8th st; hse is 30 x 30, ground is 51 x 100. -Jos L Scholfield, lvg in Wash City.

Dissolution of partnership bet Dan'l Renner & Dan'l Bussard, by mutual consent. Fresh clover seed & new bacon-business cont'd by Dan'l Bussard.

Hse o/Reps. Petition of John Bartlett, of Mass, praying permission to remove his family & property from Portland to Eastport in said state; referred to cmtee on Foreign Relations.

Notice-I have taken up a stray bay mare & a grey colt. -Isaac Riley, residing about 3 miles below Rockville, Md.

For sale-lot on Pa av, nr 12th, with brick hse, Wash City. -John M'Clelland

Reward-$100 for runaway, Tom, negro, who has adopted the surname of Marshall. He went to the pblc stage with a white woman, whose real name is Eliz Lowe, but entered her name on the way bill as Miss Sutton. Eliz is about 35 yrs old, fair skin, blue eyes, dark hair, her fore upper teeth out, & speaks quick; she is of middle stature. An attachment subsists bet them, & she is pregnant. Tom is about 35 yrs of age. -Eliz M'Pherson, lvg in Chas Co, Md.

Orphans Crt of Wash Co, D C. Case of Bennet Murrel, insolvent debtor, confined in Wash Co prison. -Wm Brent, clk.

WED FEB 23, 1814
Runaway, a negro man, Arnold, about 45 yrs old, committed to the Fred'k Co, Md, goal, on Jan 18; says he belongs to Mr Edw Clouden, about 12 miles from Leonard Town, St Mary's Co, Md. -Morris Jones, shrf, Fred'k Co, Md.

Mrd: in PG Co, Md, on Feb 15, by Rev Wm H Wilmer, Mr Henry O Middleton of Gtwn, to Miss Ann H Tolson, d/o Francis Tolson, sen.

Notice-gentlemen who want clothes made, can have them done expeditiously, neat, & fashionable. -Richard Davis, High st, Gtwn.

Norfolk, Feb 18. A lad about 15 yrs old, belonging to Gun Boat 155, was run thru the body with a sword, a few days ago, by Wm Kripgans, mstr's mate of the same boat, & died instantly. Act was done without provocation, Kripgans is delivered into the custoday of the civil authorities.

THU FEB 24, 1814
Killed & wounded on board the privateer *Gov Tompkins* in the action of Dec 25: killed-John Johnson, & John Davis, black men; wounded-John O Farnum, 1st lt, slightly; Thos Davis, since dead; Thos Loveland, severely; Jas Dougherty, John Parker, & John Lundholm, slightly.

Appointments by the Pres of the U S:
Anthony Butler, Lt Col of 28th Regt of infty, to be Col of 2d regt of riflemen.
Geo Croghan, Maj, 17th regt o/infty, Lt Col by brvt, to Lt Col-2d regt of riflemen.
David Gwynne, Capt 19th regt of infty, to Maj in 2d regt of riflemen.
Wm H Puthuff, Capt in 26th regt of infty, to Maj in 2d regt of riflemen.
Wm King, Maj in 16th regt of infty, to Col of 3d regt of riflemen.
Wm S Hamilton, Maj in 10th regt of infty, to Lt Col of 3d regt of riflemen.

Walter H Overton, Capt in 7th regt of infty, to Maj in 3d regt of riflemen.
Jos Selden, Capt in 2d regt of light dragoons, to Maj in 3d regt of riflemen.
Jas Gibson, Capt in regt of light artl & Col by brvt, to Col of 4th regt of riflemen.
Josiah Snelling, Inspec Gen, Maj by brvt & Capt in 4th regt of infty, to be Lt Col of 4th rifle regt.
Talbot Chembers, Capt in 5th regt of infty, to Maj in 4th rifle regt.
Daniel Turney, of Ohio, to be Regt Surgeon in 2d regt of riflemen.
-by order, J B Walbach.

FRI FEB 25, 1814
Mrshl's sale-all right & title, etc, of John A Burford to part of lot 5 in sq 771, in Wash City; at suit of Moses Young, & suit of Jos Mandeville. -Wash Boyd, Mrshl.

P O changes in Jan, 1814:
Swanton, Vt, David M Camp v Wm Brayton, rsgnd.
New Rochelle, N Y, John B Underhill v John Bonnell, jr, do.
Liberty, Ky, David M Rice v Moses Rice, do.
Smithville, N C, Saml Russell v B Blaney.
Lawsville, Pa, Zenas Barnham v Richard Barnham, rsgnd.
Allentown, N C, John M'Auley v Fred'k Randall, do.
Franklin, N Y, Simeon Goodman v Sam'l Hutchinson, do.
Annsville, Va, John Crawford v Wm B Pryor, do.
St Martinsville, La, Wm L Brent v Jas Miller, do.
Boone C H, Ky, Robt Chambers v Joshua Whittington, do.
Rutledge, Ten, John Brown v Wm Keith, do.
Ma_sfield, N Y, John Robins v Wm H_narie, do.
Sudbury, Vt, Jos Munson v Thos White, do.
Dalton, N H, Edw Reid v E Reid.
Wmsburg, Pa, Wm Spear v W W Harris, rsgnd.
Jefferson, Ga, Isaac Crews v Timothy Hopkins.
Barbourville, Ky, Wade N Woodson v Wm Patton, rsgnd.
Hardenburg, Ky, Eli Houston v Saml M'Clarthy, do.
New Canton, Va, Wm Woodson v Thos P_tman, do.
Durham, N Y, Platt Adams v L Hotchkess, mv'd away.
Bridgetown, N Y, Sam'l Seely v Abijah Harris, rsgnd.
Pultneyville, N Y, Sam'l Ledyard v Jacob W Hallett, mv'd.
Frankfort, Va, Jacob Stockslagel v Silas Price, dec'd.
Opelousas, La, Levin Wailes v Sam'l M'Intire, rsgnd.
Pittsboro, N C, Zachariah Harmon v John A Mebane, do.
Irwinton, Ga, Ranson Hornell v Daniel S Pierce.
Shawangunk, N Y, Simon Mullon v Harman Ruggles, mv'd away.
Chester, Vt, Sam'l Sergent, jr v Thos Robinson.
Bridge Branch, Del, Wm Hudson v J Jeffries, rsgnd.
Shawanoetown, Ill Ter, Jos M Street v G Robinson, mv'd away.
Chatham, N Y, David S Osborn v Sam'l Crane.
Angelica, N Y, Geo Renwick v J Mullender, dec'd.
Ne_-York, Va, Jas Hays v John Hays, rsgnd.
Bound Brook, N J, John H Voorhees v J Mollison, do.

Jones' Store, N C, Lewis King v Benj Riggen, do.
Highwasse Garrison, Ten, Timothy Meigs, jr, v Geo Smith.
Warehse Point, Ct, Chas L Phelps v Noah Smith, rsgnd.
Hermitage, Va, B S Pryor v Philip G Tod, do.
Ellis' Ferry, Miss Ter, S Duncan v R Carson, do.
Eaton, N H, Alden Snell v Elisha Hanson, do.
Dixon's Springs, Ten, Robt Black v D Cochran, rsgnd.
New ofc est'd in Jan 1814 & postmstrs:
Skanando, Oneida Co, _, Saml Sidney Breese.
New Iberia, Attakapas Co, La, Jas Miller.
Freeport, Harrison Co, Ohio, John Cadwallader.
Fairfield, Greenville dist, S C, Wm D Thomas.
Martinsburg, Surry Co, N C, Rich'd Conningham.
Tuckersville, Wayne Co, Ga, John Tucker.
Humphreysville, Union dist, S C, Rich'd Humphreys.
Coffee's Ferry, Pulaski Co, Ky, Joel Whitesides.
East Guilford, New Haven Co, Ct, Custis Wilcos.
Gerry, Worcester Co, Mass, Ezekiel L Bascom.
St Helena C H, St Helena Co, La, David Wright.
Bradleyville, Sumpter Co, S C, Robt Muldrow.

SAT FEB 26, 1814
Mrd: on Feb 24, by Rev Mr Brown, Mr Greenbery Griffith, of Alexandria, to Miss Prudence Jones, of this place.

MON FEB 28, 1814
Died: at an advanced age, on Feb 24, at New Mills, Burlington Co, N J, Gen John Lacey, a patriot of the Rev. He served in the Pa line; a kind hsbnd & father.

Died: in Princeton, N J, on Feb 17, after a lingering illness, Dr John Maclean, formerly of Glasgow, Scotland, & for many yrs a Prof in the college of N J.

$100 reward for runaway, Sam Fitzham, negro, age about 18 yrs; has a fr lvg in Phil. -Richard Lamar, PG Co, Md.

Orphans Crt of A A Co, Md. Sale of the prsnl est of the late Bennett Dornall, of *Portland Manor*: foxhounds, chariot, furn, stock, & negroes. Negroes to be sold in families & not carrried out of the state. -J T Shaaff, exc.

Pblc sale of the grocery store goods of Jno E Green. The Trustees. Wash item.

TUE MAR 1, 1814
Died: at Grantham, Eng, John Jackson, aged 70 yrs. He complained of poverty but left 520 pds sterl. -London

Died: at Sutteron, Lincolnshire, Mr Craybourn, whitesmith, aged 75 yrs; left 20,000 pds sterling to his offspring. -London

Land for sale-bet 12 & 1500 acs in Chas Co, Md. Apply to John B Morris or Daniel of St Thos Jenifer, nr Port Tobacco, Md, or Mr Alex Moore, of Alexandria, or the subscriber. -Walter H Jenifer, Port Tobacco, Md.

Gardener wanted-Edgar Patterson, nrly oppo the Bank of Columbia. -Local Item.

WED MAR 2, 1814

The subscriber has obtained a patent for an elevator for raising fluids, grain & flour. -Robt Christy, Berkely Co, Va.

THU MAR 3, 1814

Died: suddenly, on Feb 23, at John Minitree's Tavern, Sign of the Eagle on the Globe, 8th st, Wash City, nr the Navy Yd Gate, Jos Gamble, Sailing Mstr, who has a family in Phil.

Died: at his seat, in Halifax Co, Va, on Feb 10, Gen John B Scott, aged 53 yrs.

Died: in Frankford, Sussex Co, N J, on Feb 14, Matthew *Wiliams, at age 124 yrs; born in Wales, [Europe,] in Jan 1690. Losing his wife, by whom he had 2 sons, he at the late revolution in America, joined the svc, in which he continued until the close of the war. [*as copied]

$100 reward for Sargent Bibb, negro man, age 30 yrs, who eloped from Lynchburg, Va. -Joel Yancey, Bedford, Va.

Mrd: on Feb 25, by Rev Mr Norris, Spencer Ball, of Ky, to Mrs Eliza G Luke, of Alexandria.

FRI MAR 4, 1814

Mrd: on Feb 26, by Rev Mr Brown, Jacint Laval, Col of the First Light Dragoons, to Miss Sophie Villard, d/o Mr S J Villard, of Wash City.

$30 reward for 2 apprentices who absconded from the subscriber on Feb 27; Christopher Mines & John Burneston, both age 18 yrs. -Jacob Shinnick, Balt, Md.

SAT MAR 5, 1814

Hse o/Reps. Petition of Sarah Wheaton, w/o & agent/o Jos Wheaton, of Wash City, to credit the acc't of her said hsbnd with a quantity of whiskey furnished for the use of the U S Navy-referred to the cmtee of claims.

MON MAR 7, 1814

Hse o/Reps. Mr Archer of Md presented the petition of Walter Finney, praying payment of 2 final certificates obtained by him for svcs in the Rev Army.

Montg Co, Md land for sale; 420 acs, part of my estate in Montg co on which I reside. -Wm Carroll

TUE MAR 8, 1814
Mineral water machinery for sale. Apply to Jos Bringhurst, Wilmington, Dela.

Notice-Geo, negro boy, committed to PG Co, [Md] jail; says he belongs to Domendigo Gambray, of Chas Co. -Geo Simmes, shrf, PG Co, Md.

WED MAR 9, 1814
Election of dirs of the Mechanics' Bank of Alexandria, on Mar 14. -Wm Paton, cashier, Alexandria.

THU MAR 10, 1814
The 4 yr old d/o John Doyle, of Doylestown, Pa, died suddenly on Feb 20.

Died: on Feb 27, Miss Cath Simmons, eldest d/o Wm Simmons, Accountant of the War Dept.

On Feb 22, the eldest d/o Mr Ebenezar Senter, of Salem, Mass, aged 3 yrs & 8 mos, was burnt to death.

FRI MAR 11, 1814
Horses Wanted-at my livery stable, Gtwn. -Pendleton Heronimus.

Promoted by the Pres: Daniel Bissell, Col of 5th Infty, & Edmund P Gaines, Col of 25th Infty, & Winfield Scott, Col of 2d Artl, to Brig Genr'ls in svc of U S.

SAT MAR 12, 1814
Died: in Standish, Me, Eleazer H Parker, aged 44 yrs. He was bitten in the arm by a mad cat on Feb 24 last, attempting to rescue his dght, whom the cat seized by the nose. The dght died about 9 wks later; Mr P died on Jan 30th.

MON MAR 14, 1814
For sale-an undivided moiety of the Anti Etam iron works estate, on the Potomac rvr, with lg mansion hse; 15,000 acs. -Jno Breem

TUE MAR 15, 1814
Died: on Feb 23, at Ft Fayette, [Pittsburg,] of wounds rec'd in the action of Sep 10th last, on Lake Erie, Capt Edw Wise Buchan, a p o w at that place, & late cmder of the British vessel of war *Lady Prevost*. Remains interred in the Episcopal burial ground, on Thu, with honors of war.

$20 reward. Deserted from the rendezvous in this place, on Mar 8, David Ambaruse, born in Bedford Co, Va, tho suspected he is a ntv of New Eng; aged 22 yrs. He may be readily recognized by an excrescence, at first sight resembling a tooth, in his right nostril. -Jno Macrae, Capt 20th infty, Dumfries, Va.

$50 reward for Henry Bollinger, who on Feb 17th last, passed counterfeit bank notes to subscriber. He was with his uncle, Jacob Bollinger, & his son, Henry Bollinger. -Theophilus Turton, PG Co, Md.

Land to be sold or rented; 711 acs about 9 miles from Gtwn, on the post rd to Fredericktown, Md; home farm, orchards, etc. -Wm Blanchard, Montg Co, Md.

WED MAR 16, 1814
New publication-The *Life of Field Marshal Souvarof*, by L M P De Laverre, formerly an ofcr of Dragoons, price $1.50. Richards & Mallory, Gtwn.

THU MAR 17, 1814
Ltr from Capt Chas Gordon to Sec of the Navy, dt'd Constellation, of Crany Island, Mar 10, 1814; reporting the loss of midshipman, Mr Wm C Hall, who was quite young. He fell from the mizen topmast head to the qrtr-deck yesterday, & expired instantly. He is from Queen Ann Co, Md; no parents, & an only sister lvg. He will be buried in the church yd at Norfolk this day.

FRI MAR 18, 1814
The Senate yesterday confirmed the nomination of Return J Meigs, of Ohio, to ofc of Postmstr Genr'l of the U S.

SAT MAR 19, 1814
Ezekiel Bacon, Compt of the Treas of the U S, arrived in Wash City on Wed, & has entered on the duties of the ofc to which he has been recently appt'd.

Drowned on Nov 28 last, nr the hse of Lot Dixon, a boy named Jas Van Houten, age ab't 15 yrs, in the Rockaway rvr. On Nov 30th he was decently buried, at the burying ground in Union Village. -Rockaway Neck, N J, Jan 21.

MON MAR 21, 1814
For sale, land warrants for 2,560 acs, [Act of Cong passed on Mar 3, 1807] at the option of the hldr of the warrants, in any of the pblc lands of the U S, lying on the west side of the Miss rvr. -John G Gomegys, 153 1/2 Mkt st, Balt, Md.

TUE MAR 22, 1814
Wash Co, D C. Case of Francis Jenkins, insolvent debtor, confined in Wash Co prison, for debt. -Wm Brent, clk.

WED MAR 23, 1814
Wash Co, D C. Case of Jas White, insolvent debtor, confined in Wash Co prison, for debt. -Wm Brent, clk.

Died: on Mar 12, at Mt Zion, Caroline Co, Va, Col Jas Taylor, a rare relic of the glorious '76.

Died: on Mar 8, of a short but severe illness, in his 67th yr, Maj Burditt Ashton, of Milford, King Geo Co, Va.

THU MAR 24, 1814
$20 reward for runaway, Harry, negro man, about 23 yrs old. -Carroll Hammond, lvg nr Liberty town, Fred'k Co, Md.

John Adams informs his customers that he will move on Apr 1st, into the commodious brick hse in Boonsborough, Wash Co, Md.

FRI MAR 25, 1814
Died: on Mar 21, at the residence of her eldest son, Genr'l Walter Smith, Mrs Esther Smith, relict of Dr Walter Smith, aged 70 yrs; among the oldest & most respectable inhabitants in this town. Gtwn, Mar 21.

Died: on Feb 26, in his 72d yr, at the hse of his son-in-law, Gen Harrison, in Cinc, John Cleves Semmes, the founder of the Miami settlement & long a Judge of the genr'l crt, in the N W Terr.

For sale-lot 1 in sq 731, for taxes due the Corp of Wash City, assessed to John Shute. Also part of lot 12 in sq 700, assessed to Wiseman G Keadle. Also lot 2 in sq 691, assessed to Edw Langley. -Zachary Walker, Coll of 3d Ward.

Info wanted of Geo Rutherford; make application to Wm Tunnicliff, jr, Bladensburg, Md. He will hear of something very much to his advantage, relative to his estates in Roxboroughshire, Scotland.

SAT MAR 26, 1814
Thos Hughes has just rec'd from Balt, & offers for sale, first quality New Orleans sugar. Liquors & groceries, Pa av, Wash.

MON MAR 28, 1814
Pblc auction-at the hse of J E Greene, all his hsehld & kitchen furn, consigned to Geo Moore. -N L Queen, auct.

For sale-lots 4 & 5 in sq 77; brick hse & lot on Pa av; one lot in sq 1043; 3 lots in sq 951 nr the Navy Yd. -Silas Butler, intending to remove to N Y.

TUE MAR 29, 1814
Died: at Jenkins' Farms, Del, on Mar 21, after a short illness of a few days, Miss Julia M Anner, d/o Peter Anner, of Hudson, N Y, aged 18 yrs.

Died: at Long's Htl, on Mar 24, Gerat Pollock, aged about 32 yrs, second s/o Oliver Pollock, of Wash City.

Runaway-Jim, negro, age 27 yrs; says he belongs to Thos Harrod, of PG Co, Md, nr Queen Ann, Md. -C Tippett, for W Boyd, Mrshl.

WED MAR 30, 1814
Mrshl's sale on Apr 30th, at John M'Leod's Htl, Pa av, Wash City; all the right,

title, int & claim of Leonard Harbaugh in & to part of lot 11 in sq 170, with improvements; at the suit of Geo Kleiber. -Wash Boyd, Mrshl, D C.

THU MAR 31, 1814
Died: at his residence in Nanjemoy, Md, on Mar 3, in his 27th yr, Capt John H T S Mitchell, s/o the late Gen John Mitchell. He leaves a disconsolate wife & 3 chldrn. Capt Mitchell died after a painful illness of 12 days.

Notice-intending to leave this country, requests payment of all persons who may be indebted to him. -An Svertchkoff, at the Russian Mnstr's hse.

Decree of the Chancellor of Md; sale of about 250 acs of land, the residence of the late John Beall, nr Bladensburg; bounded by the lands of Wm D Diggs & Capt Leonard M Deakins. The dwlg hse is 24' x 48'. Apply to Chas Spicknell, lvg on the premises. -Thos Bowie, trustee.

Orphans Crt of Wash Co, D C. Pblc sale of the prnsl est of John Cannon, dec'd; furn, farming utensils, negroes, etc. -Sarah Cannon, admx; D Bates, auctr.

FRI APR 1, 1814
Hse o/Reps. Act for relief of Mary Philip Le Duc; sum of $600, additional allowance for *his* svcs as translator to the board of land com'rs at St Louis.

Dr Wm Gardner, late of Balt, has just mv'd to Wash City; he will be at the hse of Jas A Porter, E & 10th sts, nr the P O. Certificates followed: Fred'k Seyller, Balt, Oct 22, 1813, cured of cancer in my arm. Joshua Dryden, Balt, Oct 13, 1813, cured of cancer. Moses Small, Balt, Jan 3, 1814, cured of cancer of the neck; witness-Eppes Ellerey. S Enos, Balt, Jan 5, 1814-my niece was cured of cancer in the palm of her hand. Witnesses to the cure of cancer of a yellow man: Eppes Ellerey, Nathl Kimberly, & John Hughes, Balt, Mar 16, 1814. Others cured of various complaints: Mathias Mahuny, Balt, Dec 15, 1813; John Scott, Balt, Aug 7, 1813; Mgt Redmond, Wash City, Apr 1-witness: Geo Savage, Wash City, Apr 1.

SAT APR 2, 1814
Died: in Wash City, on Mar 31, of a lingering illness, John Dawson, a Rep in Cong from Va, aged about 52 yrs.

Died: at Balt, a day or two ago, Wm Mac Creery, of Balt Co, Md.

Stop the thief-Bay horse stolen from the Capitol in Wash City. -Mr Boots, Gtwn, or Sam'l Turner, jr. [$20 reward.]

Orphans Crt of Wash Co, D C. Prsnl est of Theophilus Roley, late of said co, dec'd. -Ann Roley, admx.

MON APR 4, 1814
For sale or rent-commodious & best hse of the Six Bldgs, now occupied by Dr Thos Sim. Possession on Jun 1 next. -John Tayloe

TUE APR 5, 1814
Garret Minor is elected Mayor of the city of Fredericksburg.

Mary Pool, mullato woman, was committed to my custody as a runaway; says she belongs to Benj Sprigg of Wash City & that she left home in Jun, 1811. She has since said her name is Matilda. Age about 20 yrs; pregnant & far advanced. -Solomon Graves, Shrf of A A Co, Md.

WED APR 6, 1814
For sale or to let-3 story brick hse & lot on sq 78, lately occupied by Govn'r Tiffin. For termns enquire of Wm O'Neall at the Franklin.

Ranaway-negro man, Fred'k, formerly belonged to John Addison of PG. -Jacob Wagner.

THU APR 7, 1814
Mrd: on Feb 8, Mr Thos Gales, of New Orleans, to Mrs Eliza Ray Yates, d/o Dr Hennon, of Altakpas.

Orphans Crt of Wash Co, D C. Prsnl est of Matthew C Hodges, late of said city, dec'd. -Chas Vardon, adm.

FRI APR 8, 1814
In publishing the late ltrs of John O Creighton, Cmder of the U S brig *Rattlesnake*, to the Sec o/the Navy, we announced him as a Lt; the mstr of the *Rattlesnake* holds the rank of Mstr Commandant, & is entitled by courtesy to the address of Captain.

Nashville, Mar 15-fire destroyed the property or residence of the following:

Jos Woods, merchant;	Mr Duncan Robertson, bindery & dwlg hse;
Robt Rentfroe, tavern hses;	John Anderson's hse
Mr Ernest Benoit, baker	Messrs E & G Hewlett, saddlers;
Wm W Cooke, dwlg hse	Mrs S V Stout, hse he occupied;
Messrs Read & Wash, warehse	Jos T Elliston, dwlg hse & silversmith shop
Wm M Wallace, shoemkr	Jos Sumner, hse he occupied
Mr John Young's property	Mr Joshua Pitcher, hatter's shop

W Tannehill, brick store hse he occupied
Mr D C Snow, shop & dwlg hse, tin plate worker. [No lives were lost.]

For sale-by virtue of deed of trust from Thos Davis to subscriber, 2 story brick hse in lot 2 sq 952, Wash City, nr the Navy Yd. -T Winn

SAT APR 9, 1814
<u>Directors elected on Apr 4 for the Union Bank of Gtwn:</u>

Abraham Bradley, jr	Wash Bowie
Ninian Magruder	Robt Beverly
Thos Corcoran	Francis Dodge
Robt F How	Geo Peter

Elisha Riggs   Chas A Burnet
Daniel Renner   Wm S Nichols

Orphans Crt of Chas Co, Md. Pricy Thomas & John Taylor Wall, admx & admr of Caleb Thomas, late of Chas Co, dec'd; ordered to give notice. -H Barnes, rg o/wills [Notice of same followed.]

Wash Co, D C, in Chancery. Bank of Columbia vs Jane Lingan & others. Ratify sale by Walter Smith, trustee. -Wm Brent, clk.

Died: at Vansville, PG Co, Md, on Mar 3, Gabriel G Van Horn, in his 34th yr, after a short but severe & painful illness.

Sale by virtue of sundry Deeds of Trust from Leonard Harbaugh, & power derived under the last will of Francis Deakins, dec'd; lots or parts of lots in Wash City. -John Hoy & Leod M Deakins, Devisees & Excs of Francis Deakins & John Hoy, dec'd.

Ladies with ltrs in the Wash P O as of Apr 1, 1814:

Vivion Ashby	Jane A Alexander	M Polly Brashears
Nancy Bradley	Miss Baugh	Miss Eliz Burgess
Clarissa Baldwin	Mrs Charlotte Cozens	Miss Crawford
Cath Cornwell	Verlinda Carey	Mary B Davis 2
Miss Sally Dulany	Miss Dulany	Louisa Erwin
Louisa Evans	Miss Polly Fox	Mrs Eliz Gross
Miss Harriet Green	Mrs Edw Gray	Mary Henry
Elenor Johnson	Mrs Eliza Knight	Eliz Kelly
Mary Lowry	Miss Rachel Mercer	Sarah Mason
Sarah Mitchell	Mrs Philippe Marshall	Mrs Mary Mitchell
Mrs Sophia Miles	Mrs Eliza Newland	Susan Osbern
Sarah Parker	Charlotte Russell	Ann Richards
Eliz Russell 2	Maria Squire	Mrs Mgt Smith
Miss Sarah Sarah	Sarah Swam	Eliz Smith
Sally Satchell	Miss Mary Trance	Ann Thomas
Elen Whitten		

MON APR 11, 1814

Pblc sale of all right, title, & int of Ezra Varden to part of lot 11 in sq 226, Wash City, at the suit of Wm H Dorsey against said Varden. -Wash Boyd, Mrshl, D C.

Wash Htl-3 story brick bldg, at Caroline & Lewis sts, belonging to Mr Jas Ross, now opened as a Hse of Entertainment by Sam'l Washington, Fredericksburg, Va.

TUE APR 12, 1814

Wash Co, D C, in Chancery. Sale of right, title, & int of Henry Pratt, Thos Willing, Francis John Miller, jr, John Ashley, & Jacob Baker, assignees of Morris, Nicholson & Greenleaf; of prop mortgaged to Thos Law, cmplnt, by indenture, bearing date the 4th Sep 1795. -Overton Carr, trustee.

Jesse Wharton appt'd Sen in Cong from Tenn, vice G W Campbell, rsgnd.

Partnership of Francis Wrigley & Chas Johnson, lampblack & printing ink mfgrs in Phil, is dissolved, by mutual consent; Chas Johnson will attend to orders from any part of the Union. Phil, Mar 29.

WED APR 13, 1814
Elegant furn at auction at the hse of Mrs Bonaparte, at the Seven Bldgs, all her hsehld furn. -D Bates, auct.

For sale-land of the late Dr Jas Edelen, 1,400 acs, adj the town of Piscataway, PG Co, Md; also land in *Cornwallis' Neck*, Chas Co, Md, 500 acs. -Jos Edelen, Nichl Stonestreet, excs of Dr Jas Edelen.

The heirs of the late C Kurtz offer at pblc sale in Gtwn, their rl est, svr'l lots of ground on Bridge st, with frame dwlg hse, tan-yd, currying-shop; title is indisputable. Apply to Thos Kurtz, Gtwn.

Died: on Apr 11, in Wash City, Mrs Isabella Hopkins, consort of Maj David Hopkin, aged 33 yrs.

THU APR 14, 1814
Horse for sale-Jos Huddleton, Pa av, Wash City.

Mrd: on Apr 12, by Rev Mr Matthews, Christopher Andrews, of Wash City, to Miss Henrietta Maria Webb, d/o Mr Thos Webb, of Montg Co, Md.

FRI APR 15, 1814
Benj S Haw & Co has just opened: for sale-hrdware & cutlery: on Pa av, a few doors from the tavern lately occupied by Mr Davis.

SAT APR 16, 1814
$50 reward for negro man, Basil, about 30 yrs old, who left on Apr 13. Also a negro woman, Monica, about 18 yrs old, about 5 mos pregnant. She will probably pass for Basil's wife. -Ralph Boarman, sr, nr Bryan town, Chas Co, Md.

MON APR 18, 1814
Died: on Apr 15, in Wash City, Mr Geo W Lindsay, a clk in the Ofc of the Hse of Reps. He has left behind a helpless family, which was entirely dependent on him for support. His death was from a violent fall from his horse on Tue, after which he never spoke or evinced sensation. He was buried on Sat with masonic honors.

TUE APR 19, 1814
Val property for sale-340 acs in PG Co, Md; also the tract on which I now live, 300 acs, with dwlg hse. -John Smith Magruder.

Orphans Crt of PG Co, Md. Chas H Plummer, exc of John Plummer, late of said co, dec'd, is to give notice required by law. Notice of same followed.

Acts passed at the 2d session of the 13th Cong: Relief of Geo Walkington; of Jas Crawford; of Rich'd Dale; of Dan'l Boone; of Wm Piatt; of Henry Fanning; of Moses Hook; of Joshua Sands, late coll for port of N Y.

WED APR 20, 1814
For sale-the property on which I now reside, crnr of Wash & Olive sts; the hse is of brick, 2 stories in the front & 3 in the back. -Jeremiah Mesher. [Local ad]

THU APR 21, 1814
The Tavern at Harper's Ferry is enlarged & fitted up for the accommodation of Gentlemen & Ladies for the ensuing summer. -B Williamson, Harper's Ferry.

Washington city baths will be ready for use on May 1. -Fred'k Shuck

FRI APR 22, 1814
The celebrated horse Eagle, will stand the ensuing season at my stable, bet Winchester & Stephensburg, Fred'k Co, Va. -Walter Bell

SAT APR 23, 1814
To be placed on pension list of invalid pensioners: [Name, am't, commence date.]

Name	Amount	Commence date
Sam'l C Arickson	$5 per mo	Jun 10, 1813
Alex'r Bart	$1.25 per mo	Jul 29, 1813
Ezra Bellows	$5 per mo	Jun 20, 1812
Daniel Dodd	$2.40 per mo	May 18, 1813
Joel Terrell	$3.33 per mo	Dec 18, 1813
Geo Dugan	$2.50 per mo	Feb 10, 1814
Jos King	$2.50 per mo	Oct 19, 1813
Andrew Green	$1.67 per mo	Oct 14, 1813
Hugh Barns	$5 per mo	Jun 15, 1813
Enoch Ducker	$5 per mo	Feb 2, 1814
Sam'l Hawkins	$3.33 per mo	Feb 4, 1814
Darby Mars	$5 per mo	Dec 25, 1813
Benj Daniels	$25 per mo	Feb 22, 1814
Robt McCulloch	$2.50 per mo	Feb 14, 1814
John Gilbert	$5 per mo	Jun 30, 1813
Henry Brenneman	$5 per mo	Feb 4, 1814
Wm Blanchard	$5 per mo	Jul 30, 1813
John Kersenar	$3.33 per mo	Mar 1, 1814
Robt Neil	$5 per mo	Mar 5, 1814
John Berry	$5 per mo	Mar 31, 1814
Jonathan Willard	$10 per mo	Mar 17, 1814
Levi Bishop of N Y	$5 per mo	Oct 12, 1812
John Fain	$4 per mo	Sep 10, 1813

Already on pension list; said increase to commence at time noted:

Name	Amount	Commence date
Benj Jenkins	$5 per mo	Feb 16, 1814

Abner Rose	$5 per mo	Mar 4, 1814
Richard Fairbrother	$5 per mo	Sep 30, 1813
Jos Cutler	$10 per mo	Feb 28, 1812
Thos Monday	$5 per mo	Jan 30, 1814
Hazekiah Bailey	$10 per mo	Dec 30, 1813
Elisha Reynolds	$3.33 per mo	Apr 6, 1812

Regimental Rendezvous-20th regt Infty, Fredericksburg, Va. -John Stanard, Maj, Comd'g.

Mrd: in Wash City, on Apr 21, by Rev Mr Waugh, Hon Jonathan Roberts, a senator in Cong from Pa, to Miss Eliz Bushby, d/o the late Mr Bushby, of Wash City.

Died: in Wash City, after an illness of 4 or 5 days, Sam'l Otis, late Sec of the Senate, aet 73. Funeral from his late residence on Capitol Hill, this day.

Pblc sale of all the furn of Wm Rhodes, on Captl Hill, Apr 28th. -N S Queen, auct.

Elected for Pres & Dirs of the Bank of Somerset, Princess Ann. Md. E D Teackle, Pres. Dirs: John Stewart, Geo Handy, Tho Robertson, G W Jackson, J C Wilson, jr, R J King, M Dashiell, John Rackliffe, L Ballard, W Jones.

Furn for sale-Mrs Dowson having given up her Brdg hse establishment on Captl Hill, Wash City.

MON APR 25, 1814
Runaway-Chas, aged about 24 yrs, negro man; says he belongs to Mr Benj Bealer, of Jefferson Co, Va. -Henry Sweitzer, shrf, Wash Co, Md.

Pblc sale at Mr Nathan Browning's tavern in Clarksburgh, all the right & title of Wm Price, Nathan Nabours, Levi Phillips & Eonn Belt, in 3 tracts or parcels of land nr same; 174 acs; to satisfy 2 judgments, one at the suit of Md, & the other of Luke Tiernun & Kinedy Owing. -R W Fleming, shrf of Montg Co, Md.

Pblc sale of property on May 31st, to satisfy for taxes due to the Wash City Corp:
Lots 5 & 6 in sq 38, prop of John G Jones for taxes accrued in the name of David Pollock for the yrs 1803 thru 1808.
Lot 9 in sq 38, prop of John G Jones, in the name of Geo Thompson for 1803 & 04.
Part of lot 4 in sq 56, assessed to Robt Mc Coy.
All of sq 64 assessed to John Newton.
Part of lot 5 in sq 84 assessed to Jas Maitland. -Jos Brumley, Coll 1st Ward, Wash.

TUE APR 26, 1814
Notice-Creditors of Marsham Waring, dec'd, to receive their dividends on May 27, at Upper Marlboro, Md. -Marsham Waring, exc of Marsham Waring, dec'd.

Mrd: on Apr 19, at Clifton Lodge, in Fairfax Co, Va, by Rev Mr Neale, Mr Walter H Jenifer, of Chas Co, Md, to Miss Helen S Patton.

Died: in Loudoun Co, Va, on Apr 18, Mrs Eliza Orie Mason, w/o Col Armistead T Mason, & the only child of Gen Thos Parker, at age 25 yrs; devoted to her parents, her hsbnd, & her God.

WED APR 27, 1814
Died: on Feb 15 last, 1st Lt Jos M Wilcox, 3d regt of U S Infty, age about 21 yrs, a ntv of Conn, but latterly a resident of Ohio; shot thru the body by Indians. Interment was Feb 17th at Ft Claiborne. [From a Natchez paper.]

THU APR 28, 1814
Caution-Whereas my wife Mary Niman has eloped from my bed & brd, on Apr 20th, without the smallest provocation, this is to give notice that I will pay no debts of her contracting, after the date hereof. -John F Niman.

FRI APR 29, 1814
$20 reward for Philip T Norris, aged about 19 yrs, apprentice; ranaway from the subscriber, lvg in Fredericktown, Md. -Henry Heichler.

Died: on Apr 28, Mrs Anne Tingey, consort of Cmdor Tingey, of the Navy Yd, Wash. Her remains will be deposited in the family vault on Sat. [Corr of Apr 30- remains will be interred at the city burial ground.]

SAT APR 30, 1814
Runaway for sale at the jail in Wash Co, DC; a yellow woman, Maria Prout, age about 20 yrs. -C Tippett, for W Boyd, Mrshl.

MON MAY 2, 1814
Ranaway-Jesse Cross, indented appr to the painting business; about 18 yrs old; said he may have enlisted in Balt under Capt Martin. -Patrick Kain, Navy Yd, Wash.

Runaway committed to my custody-Walter, a negro man, who says he belongs to *Tomas* Wells of Albemarle Co, Va. -Geo Semmes, Shrf of PG Co, Md.

TUE MAY 3, 1814
Pvt sale of that well known stand for business, with the whole of the premises now occupied by Maj Wm Reily. Apply to subscriber in Gtwn at Isaac Owens, or of Wm Nichols, Bridge st. -Daniel Keyler.

WED MAY 4, 1814
Died: on May 2, Mrs Sarah C Cutting, consort of Dr John B Cutting, of Stafford Co, Va.

Died: on Apr 12, Lt John Jones Edward, U S Navy, in his 22d yr, & on Sunday his body was interred at this place with military honors. He was a ntv of Charleston, S C; entered the svc at age 17.

Pblc sale of land in PG Co, Md, order from PG Co crt; 333 acs. Francis M Hall, Henry Waring, Jacob Brashiers, John H Brown, Jos W Claggett, com'rs for the division & sale of the rl of Nathl Weems, dec'd.

Miss C A Taylor has remv'd from her late residence in G st, to the 3 story brick dwlg hse, belonging to Mr O'Neale, in I st; to open her *Female Acad & Brdg Schl.*

THU MAY 5, 1814
Died: on May 4, Mr Thos Herty, long a resident of Wash City. His funeral will be today from his late residence in F st next dr to Dobbin's Tavern.

St Mary's Co Crt, Mar term, 1814. The petition of Jas Milton & wife on division of rl est of Cornelius Wildman, late of St Mary's Co, dec'd: would not admit of a division. Jos Wildman, who it is represented, resides out of Md. -Jo Harris, clk.

Original appointments made by svr'l Presidents of the U S in the recess of the Senate, shews what has been the practical construction of the constitution from 1792: Jun, 1792-John Paul Jones, mnstr pleni; peace treaty with Algiers.
Jun, 1797-John Q Adams, mnstr pleni; renewal of treaty with Sweden.
Dec 1799-Rufus King, com'r, rg the treaty of 1794.
1801-Jas Wilkinson, Benj Hawkins, Andrew Pickens, com'rs to treat with the Cherokees, Chickasaws, Choctaws & Creeks, concerning a road, with a view to open a communication bet Ga & Tenn, & the Miss Terr.
Jun 1802-Rufus King, com'r; rg boundaries bet the U S & parts of the territories of the king of G Britain.
Apr, 1803-Jas Monroe, com'r to Spain.
1801-Wm R Davie, com'r.
1803- Wm Short, mnstr pleni to crt of St Petersburgh.
1801-Thos Sumpter, sec of leg to France.
1801-John Graham, sec of leg to Spain.
1799-Jas Read, vice cnsl to Canton.
Jun 1801-Edw Jones, commercial agent to Guadaloupe.
Jun 1801-Thos Aborn, ditto to Cayenne.
Jun 1801-John J Murray, ditto to Glasgow.
Jun 1801-Jas Blake, ditto to Antwerp.
Jul 1801-Jos Pulis, ditto to Malta.

FRI MAY 6, 1814
Died: at Phil, on May 1, Nicholas Gilman, a Senator from N H.

Mrd: on Apr 26th, in Berkeley Co, Va, by Rev Mr Price, Mr Camillus Griffith, merchant of Alexandria, to Miss Eleanor Williams, d/o Dr E O Williams, of the former place.

Died: on May 2d, in her 45th yr, Mrs Ann Ford, consort of Mr John G Ford, nr Gtwn, Col. She leaves her hsbnd & chldrn.

SAT MAY 7, 1814

$20 reward for runaway, Philip T Norris, aged 19 yrs, appr to tinmans trade; very much cross-eyed. -Henry Heichler, lvg in Fredericktown, Md.

Mrd: on May 5, by Rev Mr Gibson, Roger Chew Weightman, to Miss Louisa Serena Hanson, d/o Sam'l Hanson of Sam'l, all of Wash City.

MON MAY 9, 1814

Died: in Harrisburg, Pa, Mr Isaac Wells. He was most baroarously murdered in his store where he usually slept, & robbed of about $2,000.

Richmond, Va, May 3; troops who marched by this post to Norfolk, since Mar 31, 1814, supplied by Jos Wheaton.
Capt Henry St John Dixon, riflemen, Wash Co; 47.
Wm Smith, infty, do; 38.
N J Poindexter, artl, Louisa; 53.
A W Woodson, do, P Edw; 83.
W Sale, cvlry, Amherst; 51.
M'Mullen, infty, Rockbridge; 68.
J Dickson, do, do, 79.
John W Bailey, artl, Shenandoah; 61.
J Richardson, infty, Frederick; 58.
Thos Cromer, do, do; 83.
Jas Rowland, do, Botetourt; 96.
Wm Gregory, do, Berkeley; 150.
Lt Davenport, infty, Jefferson; 103.
Wm Cackley, do, Bath; 34. [Total number, 1004]

Died: at Alstead, Va, of the spotted fever, on Mar 20, Geo W Gary, aged 5 yrs, sick 20 hrs; Mon, 21st, Chas S Gary, aged 3 yrs, sick 25 hrs; Tue, 22d, Eunice Gary, aged 11 yrs, sick 17 hrs; Thu, 24th, Otis P Gary, aged 9 mos, sick 13 hrs, same day, Mrs Polly Gary, aged 38 yrs, sick 54 hrs; Fri, 25th, Polly Gary, aged 16, sick 3 days & 18 hrs. The above were the wife & chldrn of Mr Aaron Gary. He had buried 3 chldrn before. -Verm pap.

TUE MAY 10, 1814

New & fashionable paper hangings-John A Stewart, Alexandria.

WED MAY 11, 1814

New Spring Goods-Thos W Pairo, nr the Centre Mkt, Wash City.

From the Clarion-loss of Maj Lemuel P Montgomery, of 39th regt U S infty, in the battle of Tehopiski; first military exploit of our hero; age about 25 yrs.

Died: in Hudson, N Y, on Apr 27, Mrs Lydia Hicks, consort of the late Mr T Hicks, in her 54th yr. Mrs Hicks took a large dose of Heabane for a headache.

THU MAY 12, 1814
Barnard O'Brien, s/o Barnard O'Brien & his wife, Eliz; was born in Groton, Conn on Jan 29, 1785; now on board his Britanic Maj ship *La Hogue*. Request for his release was signed S Decatur, Preston, Apr 5, 1814. Others soliciting release of same: Gerard Galley, Nathl Kimball, Jos Tuttle, Geo A Sylleman, Ro S Avery, Crustus T Smith. Copy certified by Amos A Niles, T Clk. Noyes Barber, Selectman for Groton.

Mrd: on May 10, by Rev Mr M Cormick, Mr Edw DeKrafft, to Miss Maria Evans, both of Wash City.

FRI MAY 13, 1814
Strayed or stolen, from the commons of Wash City, a sorrel mare-reward $5. -Peter Valet.

Died: on Apr 25th, at his house in Scott Co, Ky, Col Wm Johnson, 2d s/o Col Rt Johnson; called into svc of the Union, to protect the post of Ft Meigs from the British. His exposure & unhealthy situation at Ft Meigs, undermined a constitution too frail to undergo such vicissitudes. Ky paper.

Sale of all the right & title, vested in Walter Dulany at time of his decease, of lots in Wash City. -Henry M Ridgely, exc; by Chas Lee, his atty.

Persons owning shares in the Potomac Steam-Boat Co, requested to attend a genr'l meeting at Triplett's Htl, Alexandria, on Mon. -Hazlewood Farish, Sec. Fredericksburg, May 13.

For sale-well built carriage: for hire-a negro srvnt girl. -Thos Tingey, Navy Yd.

Wash Co, D C. Petition of Lewis De Blois, insolvent debtor, confined in Wash Co prison. -Wm Brent, clk.

SAT MAY 14, 1814
Orphans Crt of A A Co, Md. Sale negroes at the old residence of Rich'd Darnall, now the residence of John Weeks, a part of the prsnl est of Henry Darnall & Dorothy Darnall, infant legatees & distributees of Francis Darnall, late of A A Co, dec'd, consisting of men, women & chldrn, 34 in number. These negroes will not be sold to any person out of the state. -John Weeks

St Mary's co Crt, Mar Term, 1814. Petition of Edw Calvert Smith, insolvent debtor, praying benefit of the insolvent laws of Md. -Jo Harris, clk.

For sale-land in Chas Co, Md; 5 to 600 acs. Apply to Wm Hamilton, Chas Co, Md. -Letitia H Hamilton

MON MAY 16, 1814
Wash Co, D C. Mrshl's sale of brick hse & lot on sq 690, at suit of John M'Connell against Henry Tims & others. -W Boyd, Mrshl, D C.

THU MAY 17, 1814
Richmond Enquirer advertised the sale, under a decree of the Hon Chancery Crt for Wmsburg dist, *Cabin Point*, Westmoreland Co, Va, to raise $7,500; 1,500 acs stretching from Machatic to Nomony bay. I would prefer selling by pvt contract. -Th Rowand, Cabin Point, Wetsmd Co, Va.

Peekskill, N Y, May 7. Died: Pierre Van Cortlandt, on May 1, at his seat at Croton Rvr, in the town of Cortlandt, in his 94th yr.

Ltr in the Conn paper rg John Spencer, an enlisted sldr in the 25th Regt U S army, advised to desert the svc by John Sharp & Jos Dresser, of Winsted, Conn. They informed that Solomon Rockwell & Deacon Rockwell, of Winsted, wld keep me from the ofcrs of the army, at any rate; consequently I deserted. -John Spencer, sldr 25th Regt U S Infty, Hartford, May 3.

Wash Co Crct Crt, D C. Mrshl's sale-all right, title, int & claim of Mary Bushby, excx of Wm Bushby, to lot 13 in sq 977; suit of John Smith, adm of Rebecca Greenway, against Mary Bushby, excx of Wm Bushby. -W Boyd, mrshl-D C.

Wash Co, D C. Case of Henry Wertz, insolvent debtor, confined in prison of Wash Co, for debt. -Wm Brent, clk.

WED MAY 18, 1814
Mrd: on May 12, by Rev Mr Muhlenberg, Col Jas Gibson, U S Army, to Miss Matilda Hubley, d/o John Hubley, of Lancaster, Pa.

I will contract for 10,000 bushels of corn & 3,000 of rye, to be delivered in Gtwn, at intervals, during the ensuing summer. -O Rich, Gtwn.

Wash Co, D C. Case of Wm B Cavyico, insolvent debtor, confined in Wash Co prison for debt. -Wm Brent, clk.

THU MAY 19, 1814
Dr Gustine offers his professional svcs to the inhabitants of Gtwn & vicinity. He resides in the hse formerly occupied by Capt J Mitchell, dec'd, oppo the Mkt Sq.

Appt'd com'rs for Wash City: 1st Ward-Jas Hoban, Wm Waters, Jos Brumley.
2d Ward-Andrew Coyle, David Shoemaker, Sam'l Heit.
3d Ward-Daniel Rapine, Geo Blagden, Jas Young.
4th Ward-Jos Cassin, John Davis of Abel, John W Brashears.
Attest, Wm Hewitt, Sec'y.

Com'rs of PG Co, Md, appt'd by the County Crt for the valuation & division of the rl est of the late Alex'r Jackson, of said co: Thos Bowie, Kidd Morrell, Rich'd Ross, John Chew, John Wilson of Henry.

Pblc sale at the late dwlg of John Brashears, dec'd, in PG Co, Md, neighborhood of Vanville; mscl property, including 2 negro boys from 8 to 10 yrs; 2 negro girls from 2 to 4 yrs, furn & stock. -Benedick Brashears, ex'r.

I will sell my farm nr Benedict, Chas Co, Md; dwlg hse & 600 acs. -Chas Somerset Smith.

Orphans Crt of Wash Co, D C. Prsnl est of Thos Herty, late of said city, dec'd. -Geo Andrews, Nicholas Callan, adms.

FRI MAY 20, 1814
$100 reward for Austin *Bryant who eloped from my farm on Aug 27, tolerable blacksmith, dark complexion, about 27 yrs old. He has an uncle-Will *Bryant, lvg in Ohio. The said Will was freed by Mr Ellick Hay, of Shenandoah Co, Va, svr'l wks ago. -Gerard J Banks, Madison, Va, 8 miles above the Crt Hse. *As copied.

Pblc auction on Tue on Pa av, Wash City, all the stock in trade of said Varden & Hodges: a coach, coachees, chariot, anvile, blacksmith tools, etc. -Chas Varden, for himself & as adm of Matthew C Hodges, dec'd. N L Queen, auct.

Wash Co, D C. Petition of Sam'l C Dorman, insolvent debtor, confined in Wash Co prison. -Wm Brent, clk.

SAT MAY 21, 1814
For sale-2 frame & 2 brick hses in Wash City, nr the Navy Yd. -F Wayne

MON MAY 23, 1814
$20 reward for Poll, black woman, runaway. -J F Waters, lvg in PG Co, Md.

Orphans Crt of Wash Co, D C. Prsnl est of Geo W Lindsay, late of said co, dec'd. -Judith Lindsay, admx.

TUE MAY 24, 1814
Fairfax, Va, spring races; entries by: Col Jno Tayloe; Gustavus R A Brown; Jas Allen, jr; Abel Seymour; Abner Robinson; Mark Alexander; Branch Jones; John Drish; Edgar McCarty; Wm Lyles; Jas White; M W Brooke; N Luffborough; Armistead Hoomes.

Died: in Boston, on May 12, the Hon Robt Treat Paine, aged 84.

WED MAY 25, 1814
On Tue last, John Lester, jr, & Daniel Keeney, jr, were committed to prison in New London on suspicion of treason. -Columbian

Lt Thos Weller, of Roxbury, Conn, ofcr in the U S army, stationed at New Milford, was shot & killed by Warner Knap, on Tue last. -N Y, May 21. Com Adv.

$120 reward for 2 horses stolen from my pasture. -Wm H Foote, nr Alexandria.

THU MAY 26, 1814
Died: in Person Co, N C, on Mar 31 last, Mr Robt Davis, a ntv of Wales, Eng, aged, as is supposed, 100 yrs. A sldr in the British svc in 1744; at the battle of Preston Pans in 1745, he was taken prisoner by the Pretender's troops. He srv'd in the American army during the revolutionary struggle.

Bldg lots for sale in Wash City. Apply to John Randal, at Annapolis, Md; or to Peter Hagner, 18th st West, Wash City.

FRI MAY 27, 1814
Bourbon family, from the Boston Daily Advertiser. Louis XVI, late king of France, was beheaded on Jan 21, 1793, & Maria Antoinette, his queen, on Oct 16 1793. They left 1 son & 1 dght-Chas Louis, cld Louis XVII, being 8 yrs old at the time of his fr's death, was entrusted to Simon, a shoemaker. He died soon after from rude treatment or poison as some suppose. Maria Theresa Charlotte was born Dec 19, 1778, was mrd in Austria to the Duke of Angouleme, her cousin; & on Jan 31, 1796 she arrv'd in Vienna. Louis Stanislaus Xavier, Louis XVIII, eldest bro/o Louis XVI, was born Nov 17, 1755; mrd May 14, 1771, to Maria Jos Louisa, d/o Victor Amadeaus, King of Sardinia. He is now a widower without issue.
Chas Philip, Count of Artois, is second bro/o the late King & heir apparent to the crown of France. He was born on Oct 9, 1757; mrd on Nov 15, 1773, to Maria Theresa of Savoy, d/o Victor Amadeus. His chldrn are: Louis Antony, Duke of Angouleme, born Aug 6, 1775, mrd to Maria Theresa Charlotte, d/o Louis XVI. Chas Ferdinand, Duke of Berry, born Jan 24, 1778. Maria Adelaide, w/o Emanuel IV, King of Sardinia.

$100 reward for apprehending & delivering to any ofcr in the army, or in Gtwn, D C, John Waggoner & Geo Hess, pvts in the 36th Regt of U S Infty, deserted from Piscataway, PG Co, Md, on May 14th. Hess is 22 yrs old. -Henry Dunlap, Ensign 36th Regt, U S Infty. Camp, Cool Springs, St Mary's Co, Md.

SAT MAY 28, 1814
Mrd: on May 25, by Rev Mr Paxton, Capt Henry B Breckenridge, U S M C, to Miss Cath Cowan, of this Borough.

MON MAY 30, 1814
Headqrtrs, French Mills, Nov 16, 1813; killed & wounded in the affair of May 11: Killed-Lt Wm W Smith, light artl; Lt David Hunter, 12th regt infty; Lt Edw Olmstead, 16th regt infty. Brig Gen Leonard Covington, wounded, since dead. Wounded: Maj Talbot Chambers, ast adj genl. Maj Darby Noon, aid de-camp to Brig Gen Swortwout, slightly. Col Jas P Preston, 23d reg infty, severely, his right thigh fractured. Maj Wm Cummings, 8th do, severely. Capt Edmund Foster, 9th do, slightly. Capt Davis S Townsend, 9th do, severely. Taken prisoner, Capt Mordecai Myers, 13th do, severely; Capt John Campbell, 13th do, slightly; John B Murdoch, 25th do, slightly. Lt Wm S Heaton, 11th do, slightly; Lt John Williams, 13th do, slightly; Lt John Lynch, 14th do, severely. Lt Peter Pelham, 21st do,

severely. Lt Jas D Brown, 25th do, slightly. Lt Archibald C Crary, 25th do, severely. -J B Walbach, Adg Gen.

TUE MAY 31, 1814
Died: on May 20, at his residence in Salem, N J, Jacob Hufty, a Rep from that District in Congress.

$50 reward for the apprehending & delivering of Wm M'Coy, age 21 yrs, pvt in 36th U S Infty, deserted on Apr 4, 1814. -Henry Dunlap, Ensign 36th Infty, Gtwn rendezvous, May 31.

Notice-subscriber informs the public that he is about to establish a factory for Carding Wood, in Gtwn vicinity, at the place formerly occupied by Mr Westerman. -N P Bixby.

Andrew Jackson, of Tenn, appt'd a Maj Gen in the army of the U S, vice Wm Henry Harrison, resigned.

The undersigned is extremely desirous of selling the following tracts of land in Calvert Co, Md: 200 acs with 2 log dwlg hses; 300 acs with dwlg hse, etc. -Jno Jas Brooke, St Leonards, Md.

Claims against the est of Benj Owens, of B, late of PG Co, Md, dec'd, are hereby warned to present same. -Archd Edmonston, Sen, adm.

Wash Co, D C. Insolvent debtors: Jas Hewitt; & Walter Greenfield. Wm Brent- clk.

WED JUN 1, 1814
Wash Co, D C. Insolvent debtor-Stephen Parry, confined in the Wash Co, prison. -Wm Brent, clk.

THU JUN 2, 1814
Wash Co, D C. Petition of Robt Ober, insolvent debtor, confined in Wash Co prison. -Wm Brent, clk.

FRI JUN 3, 1814
Intending to remove from Wash City, I will sell or rent my hse nr the wind-mill, oppo Mason's Island. -Nathl G Maxwell

SAT JUN 4, 1814
$10 reward for strayed or stolen bay horse; from the subscriber at Camp Cool Springs, Wash City, about Apr 25. -John B Zanona

MON JUN 6, 1814
Plattsburg, May 20. Prisoners who recently arv'd at this place from Quebec: Jas Van Horn, Jos Knowles, Paul Gummow, Elias Mills, Jos Bowan. Nathan Edson, Dyson Dyer, Jas Corbin, & Phelim Corbin, 1st U S infty, who survived the

massacre at Ft Dearborn or Chicago, on Aug 15, 1812. John Neads, formerly of Va, died among the Indians bet Jan 15 & 20, 1813, as a prisoner. Mrs Neads & her child died with hunger & cold. Hugh Logan, Irishman, & August Mott, a German, were tomahawked & put to death; as was Mrs Corbin, w/o Phelim Corbin, in an advanced stage of pregnancy.

Wm M'Gee, gunsmith, will open on Va av, Wash City, in a few days.

TUE JUN 7, 1814
A dinner was given at Charleston on Sat wk, to Langdon Cheves, the Rep of that city, in token of the respect of his constituents for his pblc virtue.

Ranaway-Jas, negro man, about 27 yrs of age; he was raised nr *Coles Point* in Westmoreland Co & was purchased last fall from Mr Wm Doleman, nr Westmoreland Crt Hse. Reward-$50. -Thos Seddon, Falmouth, Stafford Co, Virg.

Ranaway on May 27, at Negrofoot Tavern, Hanover Co, Virg, 2 negro men, John Green, alias Whiteside, Mulatto, about 25 yrs old; also Simon, Mulatto, about 22 yrs old, formerly the prop of Mr Burns of Wash City. Reward-$100. -Jas Sheppard, lvg at McMinnville, Warren Co, West Tenn.

Case of Lewis Deblois, insolvent debtor; Buller Cocke & Edmund Law, trustees. Sale of the residence of said Deblois, all his right, title & int in the 2 story frame hse in which he now resides, in sq 948, with lots 1 & 2 adjoining. A lg brick store occupied by Butler & Co in sq 907. A small frame hse in lot 1 in sq 951, & all his hsehld & kitchen furn. Also the lots subject to a mortgage to Thos Young & Thos Foyles in lot 1 in sq 16, part of lot 2 in sq 707, lot 16 in sq 667, & lot 2 in sq 667.

WED JUN 8, 1814
This is to inform the passengers arriving at Gtwn, that Jeremiah Merrill, residing in Gtwn, High st, oppo Jos Milligan's bkstore, [one of the proprietors of the Richmond & Wash Dispatch,] can furnish them with good hacks, gigs, or horses.

Mrd: on May 31, by Rev Mr Schmucker, Lt Sam'l Bacon, of Marines, to Miss Anna Mary Barnitz, d/o Jacob Barnitz of York, Pa.

St Mary's co Crt, Md, Mar term, 1814. Petition of Jos Harrison & others, reps of Benj Suit, late of said co, dec'd; division of rl est was denied. Wm Scott & Eliz his wife, Jos D Suit, & Alexander Suit, 3 of the reps aforesaid, do not reside in Md. -Jo Harris, clk, St Mary's co Crt.

PG Co Crt, Md. Chas L Gantt, insolvent debtor, confined for debt. -John Read Magruder, clk of PG Co Crt, Md.

Pblc sale at the residence of the late Peter D Moore, 1 gold watch, 1 silver watch, 1 negro man, sundry articles of hsehld & kitchen furn. -Louisa Moore.

Notice. Louisville, Ken, May 4, 1814. The subscriber continues his practice in Land Causes & Cases in Chancery, for the dist of Ky. Wm Little, Frankfort of Louisville.

THU JUN 9, 1814
Ltr to Gen Andrew Jackson regarding the heroes of the late expedition against the Creek Indians, signed: J Childress, Geo M Deaderick, E Pritchett, Alex Robinson, John Sommerville, John Baird, Jas Jackson, Andrew Hynes. Nashville, May 14, 1814.

$50 reward for Edw B Tabbs, a sldr who deserted from Camp, nr Clement's Bay, St Mary's Co, Md, on May 27; belongs to the 36th Regt U S infty; by profession a seaman. $100 reward for 2 sldrs, Thos Howard & Richard Gates, 36th regt U S I, who deserted on May 29th. -Wm N Earle, 1st Lt 36th Regt U S I, Camp nr Clement's Bay.

FRI JUN 10, 1814
To let-2 story brick dwlg hse on 7th st. -Geo Sweeney

$25 reward for stolen bay mare. Wm Penefill, lvg about 6 miles above Montg Crt Hse, Md.

SAT JUN 11, 1814
Mrd: on Jun 5, by Rev Mr Matthews, Mr Jos Johnson to Miss Mgt Ann Mattingly, both of Wash City.

Charleston [B co] Gaz. On Fri last President & John Douglas, the only sons of Francis Douglas, were found drowned in Buffalo creek; the former about 13 yrs, the latter about 11 yrs. They have left an affectionate fr & mthr.

The powder mill of Mr Thos Gregg, nr Connelsville, Fayette Co, Pa, blew up on May 6. Mr Chas Duncan, a young man, died of his wounds about 22 hrs after the explosion. He has left a tender mthr.

MON JUN 13, 1814
Mrd: at Brooklyn, by Rev Dr Feltus, Lt John Templer Shubrick,U S Navy, to Miss Eliz Matilda Ludlow, of N Y.

Deserted from Ft Wash, Potomac, on Jun 5: Geo W Williams, drummer, born in Va, aged 22 yrs. Robt Stewart, age 24 yrs, stone mason by profession. Henry Warrell, pvt in the regt of Light Dragoons, nvt of Pa, farmer. $30 reward.

TUE JUN 14, 1814
Corporation elections of Jun 13, Wash City. Jas H Blake, re-elected Mayor. Alex McCormick is re-elected Pres of the Brd of Aldermen. R C Wcightman, Pres of the Brd of Common Cncl. Wm Hewitt, Sec of Brd of Aldermen. P D Stelle, Sec to the Brd of Common Cncl.

$50 reward for stolen or strayed bay stud colt; out of my pasture on Hartford rd, Blockley twnshp, Pa. -Jacob C Wikoef, at aforesaid, or 35 N side Mkt st, Phil.

Savannah, Jun 4. The U S Sloop *Peacock*, Capt Lewis Warrington, went to sea this morning on a cruise. Success to her.

Portsmouth, Jun 4. Col J B Walbach has arv'd in this town & taken command of the forts in this harbor.

Mgrs of lottery for erecting a Masonic Hall in Balt City; the first lottery of importance in the state of Md:

	Thos Watkins	Abraham Lasrh
Edw J Coale	Geo Winchester	Wm Greetham
Jas Barroll	Wm Stewart	Jacob Small
Geo Keyser	Wm Camp	Jos K Stapleton
Edw G Woodyear	Thos Sweeting	Chas Wirgman
Edw Palmer	Peter Little	

WED JUN 15, 1814
Classical teacher wanted to superintend a rising Seminary. Apply to Capt I W Taylor, nr Buckland, Pr Wm Co, Va.

Norwich, Jun 8. At Groton, last Thu, Capt Robt N Avery, of that town, was digging sand proper for the prep of mortar, when the bank gave way & buried him, also a boy who was assisting him. The unfortunate sufferers died.

Died: in Eng, Alex Cumming, an eminent prof of mechanical science.

Died: in Jamaica, Capt Hazzard Stackpole, late cmder of the British frig *Statira*, murdered in a duel with the first lt of the *Argo 74*.

Died: on Apr 4, in his 74th yr, Mr Berthe Gyrma, merchant; & on the same day-Dr Domingo Fleytas, who was attending him. -New Orleans Paper.

Mrsh'ls sale of all the right, int & claim of Henry Tims to one 2 story brick hse & lot in sq 690; prop seized at the suit of John P Van Ness against Henry Tims, Jas Hickey, & Ambrose White. -W Boyd, Mrshl, D C.

Ten cent reward for runaway. Geo Brooke, appr to the hse carpenter business; bet 18 or 19 yrs of age. -John Myers, Gtwn.

Wash Co, D C. Petitions of Josiah Simpson, insolvent debtor, confined in Wash Co prison, for debt. Case of Randall Cashell, insolvent debtor, confined within the prison bounds of Wash Co, for debt. -Wm Brent, clk.

THU JUN 16, 1814
Pblc sale of tract of land cld *The Resurvey on Honesty*, lying about 6 miles above Gtwn; 226 acs. Land will be shown by Leonard H Johns. -Sarah Peter, excx, Geo Peter, L H Johns, excs of D Peter.

FRI JUN 17, 1814

Jos Johnson, negro, was committed to the goal of Hartford Co, on May 28, as a runaway, age about 33 yr; says he was set free by Wm Bayly, of PG Co, Va, & has lived srv'l mos in Balt City with Dr Stewart. -Benj Guyton, shrf, Harford Co.

For sale-bet 6 & 700 acs of land in Chas Co, [Md] on Mattawoman, formerly the prop of the late John Dent. Apply at Dr E Briscoe's, adjoining the prop, to John Dent.

SAT JUN 18, 1814

$25 reward for strayed or stolen bay horse; from the commons of Wash City. -John A Wilson

Pblc sale, deed of trust from John A Burford to the subscriber; at the tavern kept by John Rabbit, jr, in Montg Co, Md: 5 valuable slaves. -R Wallach, trustee

MON JUN 20, 1814

Buffalo Gaz, Jun 7. John Black, Mahlon Christie, Geo Orcotte, & Isaac H Kent, sldrs of the U S army, were shot in Buffalo, on Sat last, pursuant to the sentence of a crt martial, for the crime of desertion.

Died: in England, Robt Digby, Adm of the Red, & Senior Adm of the British Navy, excepting the Duke of Clarence, who srv'd as midshipman under the Admiral in the Americ war. He was in N Y in 1783.

Died: at Wiscasset, a few days ago, suddenly, Hon Sam'l Sewall, Chf Justice o/Mass.

In Chancery, Jun 11, 1814. Campbell & others vs Ray & Duncanson. Ratify sale by trustee. -W Kilty, Chancr. Jas P Heath, Reg C C.

TUE JUN 21, 1814

Three cents reward for runaway, Michael Garity, appr to the shoemaking business, aged about 17 yrs. -Nicholas Cassady, nr the Navy Yd, Wash.

WED JUN 22, 1814

Mrs Brown's Acad will open on Mon next in the hse formerly occupied by Capt John Mitchell, nr the Mkt. Wash ad.

Died: on Jun 15th, at his country seat, Richard E Lee, an aged & distinguished ctzn of Norfolk, Va.

$50 reward for the following sldrs of the 10th regt, U S infty, who deserted from camp nr Wash City, on Jun 12, viz: John *Lefeon, of Capt Cloud's Co, born in Spartansburg, S C, aged 21 yrs, blacksmith. Bennet Smith, a pvt in Capt Williams' Co, born in Mecklenburg Co, N C, aged 21 yrs, farmer. Hazle Brown, pvt in Capt Clay's Co, born in Gilford Co, N C, aged 23 yrs. Lewis Simpson, pvt in Capt Wood's Co, enlisted by Capt Mitchell in N C. -Duncan L Clinch, Lt Col 10 U S I. [*Corr of Jun 30-*Lefever*.]

THU JUN 23, 1814
Just published, and for sale by Jos Milligan, Gtwn, Volumes one & two of the *Historical Register of the U S*, from the Declaration of War in 1812, to Jan 1, 1814; by Thos H Palmer, Phil, Pa.

FRI JUN 24, 1814
Near Benedict, Md, Wed evening, Jun 22, 1814. Rg-loss of Alexandria trooper, Francis Wise, who was shot with a musket by one of the British.

Committee of arrangements for celebration of Jul 4, Wash City:

Thos Monroe	John Graham	John Davidson
B Homans	Robt Brent	Walter Jones, jr
Moses Young	Andrew Way	Dan'l Carroll of Dud'n
Wm Brent	E B Caldwell	Sam'l N Smallwood
Cmdor Tingey	Col F Wharton	Wm Doughty
Butler Cocke	Jas H Blake, Mayor	

SAT JUN 25, 1814
Runaways committed to Wash Co jail, D C, on Jun 9: Negro, Caleb, age 27 yrs, says he belongs to Miss Abbey Kilgrue, of St Mary's Co, nr Charlotte Hall, Md. Negro, Ben, says he belongs to Mrs Henry Ashton, of King Geo Co, Va, age 30 yrs. Negro George, age 20 yrs, says he belongs to Mr Anderson Scott, of King & Queen Co, nr Todd's Bridge, Va. Negro, Sally, age 18 yrs, a bright mulatto, & says she is free; that she is from King Geo Co, Va & that her mthr lives in Pr Wm Co, nr Dumfries, by the name of Betsey Rimus. Negro, Nancy, about 45 yrs old, says she belongs to Mr Sciler, nr Balt, Md. -C Tippett, for W Boyd, Mrshl.

MON JUN 27, 1814
For sale-the town of Harmony, with all its improvements, 9,000 acs of land adjoining on which are 3 villages, in the tenure of Geo Rapp & associates; on the Conaquenessing, Butler Co, Pa. -Geo Rapp

TUE JUN 28, 1814
Orphans Crt of Wash Co, D C. Ltrs of adm on est of Lt Wm Burrows, late of U S Navy, dec'd. -Jas Thompson, adm.

On Sunday, in the attempt to launch the *Independence,* Mr Wm Champney, mstr joiner, was killed by a stroke of a broken block. He has left a widow & 9 chldrn. -Boston Centinel

WED JUN 29, 1814
Copy of a ltr from Col Decius Wadsworth to the Sec of war, Gen John Armstrong, dt'd, Camp nr St Leonard's, Jun 26. Subj-attack & blunders during the action.

Meeting of the clergy of Wash & Gtwn this evening. -Jas Lawrie

THU JUN 30, 1814
Thos Munroe, Post Mstr, Post Ofc, Wash.

Pblc sale at the late residence of Mr John B Rittenhouse, dec'd, in Cherry st, hsehld & kitchen furn. -Harriet Rittenhouse, excx, Thos Robertson, exc, Gtwn.

FRI JUL 1, 1814
$100 reward for Will Brown, sldr, who deserted on May 31, 1814, from Gtwn, DC; born in Fredericktown, as he says-since understood to have been born in N J; age 23 yrs; farmer or trader by occupation. -Henry Dunlap, Ensign 36th Infty.

Philip P Barbour is elected a Rep to Cong from Fredericksburg dist, to fill the vacancy occasioned by the death of the late Mr Dawson. Thos W Thompson is chosen to rep N H in the Senate of the U S, vice Hon Mr Gilman, dec'd.

Mrd: at Dumfries, on Jun 23, by Rev Mr Sedwick, Col Daniel C Brent, of Richmond, to Mrs E Washington, of Windsor Forest, all of Stafford Co, Va.

Geo K Barge thanks his friends for their past favors; he has remv'd from the *Rising Sun* in Bow st, to the *Sign of the Globe*, on Galaspie st, where he has opened a roomy hse of entertainment. Fayetteville, N C, Jul 1, 1814.

Wash Co, D C. On Jun 29th a stray dark brown horse was brought before me by Jas Wingfield. -Jas M Varnum, J P.

SAT JUL 2, 1814
Error corrected. It has been erroneously reported in this country that the French Mnstr, Monsieur Serurier is mrd to the divorced w/o Jerome Bonaparte. Where the errror originated is not known. The Mons Serurier was lately mrd in N Y to Mademoiselle Pageot. -Com Adv.

MON JUL 4, 1814
Mrd: on Jun 30, at *Woodley*, the seat of Philip B Key, Upton Scott Reid, of Md, to Miss Eliza Forrest, d/o the late Gen Forrest.

Died: on the 3d inst, at his plantation on Sapelo Island, Marquis De Montalet, aged 49 yrs; ntv of St Domingo, he emigrated to this state in 1797. S C Pap.

For sale-tract of land containing 1,120 acs, on the N E side of the Shenandoah Rvr, in the counties of Fred'k & Jefferson. -Thos Parker, Fred'k Co, Va.

WED JUL 6, 1814
To all my creditors-I intend to apply at the PG Co Crt in Sep term, for the benefit of the insolvent laws of this state. -Philip Green

Ltr transmitted by Cmdor Perry to the Sec of the Navy; Warham, Mass, Jun 24, 1814. Rg-the British landing at this place on Jun 13. Signed: David Nye, jr;

Abner Basset; Isaac Perkins; Josiah Everett; Noble Everett; Wm Barrows; Perez Briggs; Wm Tearing.

I will rent the farm whereon I now reside; 140 acs, nr the Centre Mkt in Wash City. -Chas Vinson

Ranaway-on Jul 3d, appr to the boot & shoe-mkg bus, Jos Lookingbeel, aged 17 yrs. -Wm M'Closky

Crct Crt for Wash Co, D C. Exparte-Robt Tolmie heirs. Property in this case will not admit of a division without a loss. -Wm Brent, clk.

PG Co, Md-in Chancery. Ratify sale of the rl est of the late John Beall, in PG Co, Md, as reported by trustee; amount-$1,970.25. -W Kilty, Chr. Jas P Heath, R C C.

$50 reward for John Sivley, age about 22 yrs, negro man, ran away from Mr John T Mason's mill, nr Hagerstown, Wash Co, Md, on the 25th inst. -John Cushwa

THU JUL 7, 1814
Norfolk, Jun 28. This morning the body of ensign John B Butler, from Fairfax Co, Va, was discovered by the watchman, lying nr Mkt Sq, in a Mulitia ofcr uniform.

Dissolution of partnership existing under the firm of Young & Black, Tailors, on Sep 11, 1813, by mutual consent. The business has been carried on since that time by Ezekiel Young, F st, Wash City.

Orphans Crt of Wash Co, D C. Prsnl est of John Sword, formerly of St Mary's Co, Md, & late of Loudon Co, Va, dec'd. -Bernard Wheatly, adm.

Crct Crt of Wash Co, D C, in Chancery. Alice Bird vs John Bird & Ann R Bird. Ratify sale by Chas Glover, trustee, to Alice Bird, for the sum of *$184.84. -Wm Brent, clk. [*or 484.84.]

Crct Crt of Wash Co, D C, in Chancery. Ebenezer Nesmith, vs the heirs & adms of Jasper D Karnap, dec'd. Ratify sale by Chas Glover, trustee, of property in this case, for sum of $500. -Wm Brent, Clk.

FRI JUL 8, 1814
Ladies with ltrs in the Wash P O, Jul 1, 1814:

Miss Nancy Auford	Madam Barlow	Mrs Betterton
Aliza Bendy	Mrs Ann Barber	Mrs Brocks
Miss Ann Baker	Mrs Brooks	Miss Isa E Burton
Miss Brown c/o Mr Hawkins	Miss Letitia Butler	Eliz Calvert
Mrs Clark	Mrs Martha Davis	Mrs Sally Howe
Mrs Dorcas Goodwin	Priscilla Graham	Mrs Hellen Harrod
Miss Helena Fenwick	Mrs Nancy Hambleton	Miss E L Jones
Mrs Maria Lee	Mrs Mary Lemley 4	Mrs Mary Lowry
Miss Rebecca Lowrey	Miss Fanny Matthew	Miss M M'Closky

Miss Ann Minchin
Mrs Olsey Pitman
Mrs Jane Riston
Miss Jane Storms
Mrs Eliz Whiting

Miss E Nowland
Nancy Richards
Mrs Smith
Grace Sutton

Jane Owens
Eliza Riston
Mrs Mgt Smith
Sarah Ann William

SAT JUL 9, 1814
Henry O Middleton has established an extensive medical store in Wash City.

For sale by Ferdinando Fairfax: 600 acs of his *Shannon H_ll* tract, Jefferson Co, Va. Tract in same co of about 205 acs on the Shenandoah rvr. 196 acs nr Harper's Ferry, Jeff Co. Svr'l mill seats & svr'l wood lots upon the Short Hill. Other lands also for sale. Apply to F Fairfax in Alexandria; or to Maj Wm Hickman, nr Charleston, Jeff Co; or to Mr Abiel Jenners, nr Waterford, Loudoun Co, Va.

MON JUL 11, 1814
Ltr rec'd at the War Ofc, dt'd Jun 28, 1814. Rg-loss of that valuable ofcr, Lt Col Forsyth; killed while advancing on a party of the enemy about 200 strong.

Killed, wounded, & missing on board the late U S frig *Essex*, David Poster, commanded, in action of Mar 28, 1814, in Valparaiso Bay, with the British frig *Phoebe*, Jas Hillyar, cmder. Killed: 1st lt Jas P Wilmer; 3d lt John G Cowell-had lost a leg; Henry Kennedy, boatswain's mate; Wm Smith, do; Francis Riland, qrmstr; Reuben Marshal, qr gunner; Thos Baily, boats yeo; John Adams, cooper; Wm Johnson, carp's crew; Henry Vickers, do; Z Mayfield, crew; Wm Christopher, capt forecastle; Nath Jones, capt mast; Jos Thomas, capt main top; John Russell, do; F Green, Geo Hill, R W Cook, Geo Wine, Jos Ferrell, seamen; Sam'l Miller, Thos Johnson, 1st do; Philip Thomas, do; Thos Nordyde, do; Wm White, do; Thos Mitchell, do; Wm Lee, 1st ord'y seaman; Peter Allen, seaman; John Alvason, do; John C Keeling, do; Benj Hazen, do; Peter Johnson, 1st do; Thos Brennock, do; Thos Brown, do; Cornelius Thompson, do; John Linghan, do; Geo Douglas, do; Fred'k Hall, do; Jas Anderson, do; Geo Hallet, o s; Thos Terry, seaman; Chas Norgren, do; John Cowell, do; Thos Davis, do; Jas Seller, do; John Clinton, do; R Brown, do; J Jackson, do; J Rippley, do; J Folger, do; Dan'l F Cassimer, o s; Wm Jennings, do; Mark Hill, do; Wm Lee, 2d do; Geo Beaden, do; Thos Russell, do; Lewis Earle, boy; Henry Ruffe, do; Wm Williamson, do. Severely wounded: Edw Barnewell, sailing mstr; Ed Linscott, boatswain; Wm Kingsbury, boatswain Essex Jr; Geo Kinsingen, mstr at arms; Bennet Fields, armourer; John M'Kinsay; Otis Gale, arm crew; Jasper Reed, do; Isaac Valence, capt's steward; Leonard Green, qr gunner; Enoch M Miley, do; Wm Whitney, capt fore top; Thos Milburn, capt of mast; John Stone, seaman; Ephm' Baker, capt waist; John Lanaro, seaman; Eno Males, capt waste; Wm Wood, seaman; Francis Trepany, do; John Penn, do; Geo Williams, do; Wm Cole, do; Henry Barker, do; John Glasscan, o s; Jas Goldsborough, do; Lawnderwas, do; Peter Anderson, do; John Johnson, do; Peter Ripple, do; Thos Oliver, do; Geo Shields, do; Wm Hamilton, o s; Thos Andrews, do; Wm Nichols, do; Benj Barslett, do; Daniel Gardiner, do; Sam'l M'Isaacs, boy. Missing: Geo Martin, gunners mate; Adam Roach, qr gunner; John Thompson, qr mstr; Francis Davis, Jas Chace, Bartholomew Truhumon, Matthew Lawder, Wm

Holmes, John Bagnell, Thos Hobbs, Robt Harrison, Edw Leford, Thos Parrous, Hugh Gibson, Jas Dormas, Henry Humphries, Wm Taylor, Chas Macarty, Jas M'Crae, Jas Mohonny, John Deacon, Simon Rogers, Elias W Saddus, John Owens, Wm Forsyth, Geo Schlossard, John Ayres, Geo Gable, Thos Carrol, Chas Moore, Wm Holland, seamen. Slightly wounded: David Narano, sail mkr; David G Farragret, midshipman; Geo W Isaacs, do; John Langley, carp; John Wible, capt's mate; John Reicess, carpt crew; Wm Boyd, do; Benj Wadden, carpt yeoman; John Francis, capt coxwain; Levi M'Cabe, qrtr mstr; Geo Stoutenburg, Wm M'Donald, Geo Browne, Shubal Cunningham, Robt Scattudes, Antonio Saller, Geo Love, Wm Matthews, Wm Concord, Dan'l Hyde, Jos Williams, Fred'k Hartwell, Wm Burton, John Sacks, Wm Deacon.

TUE JUL 12, 1814
Ltr from a friend of the late Lt Jos M Wilcox, who lost his life during the recent Creek war, to Gen Jos Wilcox, the f/o the dec'd, dt'd Ft Claiborne, on the Alabama, Jan 19, 1814. Lt Wilcox, s/o Gen Wilcox, a rev ofcr, formerly of Conn, now a ctzn of Marietta, Ohio. At age 17 yrs, appt'd a cadet at West Point. At age 23 yrs, on Jan 15, 1814, he died; universally lamented by the corps to which he was attached.

$100 reward for runaway, John Henry, black man, formerly belonging to Mich'l Flannery of this place; his fr lives here. -Wesley Brown, Alexandria.

$10 reward for yellow girl named Mint; formerly the prop of Rich'd Isaac of PG Co, Md; age about 22 yrs. -Barton Duvall

Orphans Crt of Wash Co, D C. Management of the prsnl est of Theophilus Robey, late of Wash Co, dec'd, placed in the hands of John Bridges & Jos Nevitt.

Elegant coach & a pr of horses, for sale. -John Hayne, nr the Navy Yd, Wash.

WED JUL 13, 1814
Ltr from Capt Porter, to the Sec of the Navy. *Essex Junior*, Jul 3, 1814, at sea. For the time we had kept the sea, I had but one case of the scurvy, & had lost only the following men by death, viz: John S Cowan, lt; Robt Miller, surg; Levi Holmes, o s; Edw Sweeny, do; Sam'l Groce, seaman; Jas Spafford, gunners mate; Benj Geers, qr gunner; John Rodgers, do; Andrew Mahan, Cpl of Marines; Lewis Price, Pvt of Marines.

Marshal's sale on Wed; all the right, title, int & claim of Henry Wertz to part of *Long Meadows*, about 36 acs. Suit of Chas Warfield against said Werts. Wash Boyd, Mrshl, D C.

THU JUL 14, 1814
Pblc sale of property to satisfy the Corp of Wash City for taxes due thereon up to the yr 1813.

John Appleton	Wm Armstrong	Ralph Boarman
John Beckley heirs	Eliza Cox	Dan'l Caffray
Chas Carrol, jr	Dr Jas Davidson	Robt Darnall

Reuben Etting	Jas Fenwick	Thos Fenwick
John Guest	Henry Knowles	Adam King
Wm M Landsdale	Philip Lansdale	Dominick Lynch
John Mason	John F Mercer	Martin & Ward
Benj Oden	Edw Plowden	Abigail Pollock
Jonathan Slater heirs	Presley Thornton heirs	Thos Wand
Cornelius Thomas, jr.	Benj Young & others	Notley Young
Morris & Nicholson assignees	Pratt, Francis & others	Wash Tontine Co

Mrd: in Alexandria, on Jul 11, by Rev Dr Muir, Aaron Jewett, Atty at Law, of Shepherd's Town, Va, to Miss Eliza Mark, late of Fredericksburg.

Crct Crt of Wash Co, D C, in Chancery. Alice Bird vs John J Dermot & Ann R Dermot. Ratify sale of prop by Chas Glover, trustee; for the sum of $484.84. -Wm Brent, clk.

Six cents reward-for runaway, appr boy, Barney Higdon, about 19 yrs of age. -Wm H Hamer

Wash Co, D C. Osborn Hughes, insolvent debtor, confined in Wash Co prison for debt. -Wm Brent, clk.

FRI JUL 15, 1814
Ltr from Lt Bessett to John H Dent, cmndg naval ofcr, Charleston, S C; St Helena Island, Jul 2, 1814. Rg-the loss of the U S schn'r *Alligator* on Jul 1st while at anchor in Port Royal Sound, from a squall that appeared to be a water spout or whirlwind. Drowned: Jos Brailsford, Midshpm; Robt Rogerson, do; Thos T Johson, carp mate; Presley B Hathaway, gunners mate; Oliver Salvadore, qr mstr; Nicholas T Rennie, pursers stwrd; Wm Ishum, seaman; Wm Steel, do; Thos Harvey, do; John Nieson, do; John P Rea, o do; Philip Fraser, cook; John Martinburgh, boy; Jeffery Graves, o s; Jerry Stout, do; Sam'l Johnson, do; Wm Scarlet, do. Not found: Mich Rush, o s; Polydore Thompson, boy; Caesar Howard, s; Dan'l Thompson, do. -Russell Bessett, Lt Comdt.

Wash Co, D C. Case of Robt Ober. Trustee-Leonard H Johns, ordered to sell the prop of the said insolvent by pblc auction. -B Thruston.

Wash Inn. Jannaro S Farre informs the pblc that he has lately commenced kpg a pblc inn, at Montg Crt Hse, half way bet Mr Robb's Tavern & where Henry Lauderdale formerly lived, Mont Co, Md.

Crct Crt, in Chancery. M'Kensie & others vs Chas Minifie. Jas Davidson & Richard Forrest, trustees, reportthat Jas M'Kim, one of the purchasers of the sale, failed to comply with the terms of sale. -Wm Brent, clk.

$40 reward for Saml Carroll, pvt, a deserter from the 42d regt U S army, now stationed at Ft Richmond, Staten Island. He enlisted at Wash City, in Feb last; age

39 yrs; born in Ireland; silverplater by profession. -Edmund B Duval, Capt 42d regt U S I, Ft Richmond.

SAT JUL 16, 1814
Mrd: on Thu wk, in Wash City, by Rev Mr M'Cormick, Mr John Lymbourn to Mrs Mary Haynes, both of Alexandria.

Died: at Boston, on Jul 8, John Foster Williams, Cmder of the Rev Cutter *Mass*, aged 70 yrs.

Wash Co, D C. Case of Esias Traver, insolvent debtor, confined within the bounds of Wash Co for debt. -Wm Brent, clk.

$200 reward-deserted from Ft Wash, Potomac, on Jun 19: Jas Bird & Jas Warring, 2 sldrs enlisted in the 10th regt U S I. Bird born in York Dist, S C, age 38 yrs, shoemkr. Warring was born in Spottsylvania, Va, aged 42 yrs, blacksmith. Also deserted on Jul 3d-John E Stromatt, born in Md, age 21 yrs, blacksmith; dressed in the uniform of the Light Dragoons. Also, John Miller, born in Sussex, Dela, age 45 yrs, seaman by profession.

MON JUL 18, 1814
Died: at Phil, on Jul 4, Clement Biddle, Esq.

$50 reward for negro man, Rans, about 30 yrs old, raised in Fauquier Co, Va; ran away from my farm. -Geo Pannill, Orange Co, Va.

TUE JUL 19, 1814
Chancery Crt of Md; sale of land in lying partly in Montg co & PG Co, Md; all the right, title & claim of the heirs of the late Elisha Hoskinson, dec'd; about 70 acs with dwlg hse. -Robt Edmenston, trustee.

WED JUL 20, 1814
Died: on Jul 1, in Fredericksburg, the Rev'd Fred'k V Melsheimer, in his 64th yr.

One cent reward for runaway, Wm Calhoon, appr to the stone cutting trade. He is 17 yrs of age & apt to be drunk. -Isaac Wilson

THU JUL 21, 1814
$30 reward for negro man, Ambrose Thomas, ran away from me nr Trapstown, Fred'k Co, on Jul 11. He belonged to Thos Plater, who sold him in Aug 1813. -Geo Willyard, Newtown Twsp, Md.

FRI JUL 22, 1814
David Porter, a Capt in the Navy of the U S of America, on the part of the U S, takes possession of the Island, cld by the natvies *Nooaheevah*, generally known by the name of Sir Henry Martin's Island, but now cld Madison's Island. Witnesses present: Jno Downes, Lt U S N; Jas P Wilmer, do; S D M'Knight, do; David P Adams, Chaplain U S N; Jno M Gamble, Lt Ma U S N; Rich'd K Hoffman, ac sur

U S N; Wm Smith, Mstr of the A ship *Albatross*; Wilson P Hunt, Agent for the American North Pac Fur Co; Jno M Maury, Mid U S N; P De Mestu, ctzn of U S; Benj Clapp, do; M N Bostwick, Act Mid U S N; Jno G Cowell, Lt U S N; H H Odenheimer, Ac S M U S N. I have buried in a bottle at the ft of the flag staff, in Ft Madison, a copy of this instrument, together with pieces of money of the coin of the U S. [No date]

SAT JUL 23, 1814
Joel Brown has considerably enlarged his stock of shoes. Gtwn, D C.

Notice-the statement of Jas McKim having failed to comply with the terms of a sale is incorrect. Jas Davidson & Rich'd Forrest, trustees, failed to ratify the sale agreeable to the conditions of it. -John McKim.

Died: on Jul 5, at his farm in Black___township, Indiana Co, Pa, Gen Jas M'Comb, late mbr of the hse of reps of that state; ntv of Ire, but emigrated to America at an early age. Altho only 16 or 17 yrs of age, at the time, he endured with heroic bravery the fatigues of the campaign against Quebec under Gen Montgomery.

MON JUL 25, 1814
Pblc sale at Semmes Tavern in Gtwn, on Jul 25th, part of the prop of Robt Ober, given up for the benefit of his creditors; 37,703 acs of land in Randolph Co, Va, has been deeded under a genr'l warrantee from good men; 10 acs nr Alexandria; segars, bridge share, horses, rum, scales, etc, etc. Leo H Johns, trustee.

TUE JUL 26, 1814
The Mayor of DC has appt'd the following persons a Cmtee of Safety:
Rich'd S Briscoe	Thos Barclay	Peter Lenox
Jas M Varnum	Wm Emack	Geo Blagden
Jos Cassin	Matthew Wright	

The creditors of the late Rich'd Ponsonby, dec'd, are to render thier accounts duly authenticated, to Baily E Clark. -Jas M'Cormick, adr, Bladensburgh, Jul 26.

Exam of the students of Gtwn College on Jul 27. -John Grassy, Pres.

Wants a place. A wet nurse who can come well recommended. Inquire at the hse of John B White, *Greenleaf's Point*.

WED JUL 27, 1814
Died: on Jul 14, after a long & painful illness, John Dickson, Editor & Prop of the Petersburg Intelligencer, aet XXXII.

Sheep for sale on Oct 20th next, at Gorden's, on the stage rd, 5 miles below Dumfries. -Thos Harrison

THU JUL 28, 1814
Mrd: at Norwich, Con, on Jul 12, by Rev Mr Tyler, Lt Benj Waller Booth, U S N, to Miss Louisa Brown, d/o the late Jackson Brown, of N Y.

FRI JUL 29, 1814
To let, a commodious 3 story brick hse, on F st, Wash City. -Eliza Clark.

Died: at N Y, on Thu night, of hydrophobia, Mgt Walker, aged 5 yrs, within 48 hrs after the commencement of this fatal malady; 6 wks since she was bitten by a dog.

Land for Sale. Farm on which I reside, bet 5 & 600 acs. Apply to Capt Thos Brooke or the subscriber to see the land. -Clement Brooke, Perrywood, PG Co, Md.

Died: on Jul 25th, at his seat in PG Co, Md, after an illness of 2 days, Mr Chas Duvall, an old & respectable ctzn of that county.

Nathaniel G Maxwell will sell at auction, on Sat, at his hse nr Capt Davidson's warehse, his furn, small library, liquors, gig horse, etc. -David Bates, auct.

SAT JUL 30, 1814
Students of Gtwn College who have excelled in their classes in 1814:

Robt Durkee, Balt
Aloysius Young, DC
Thos Finigan, N Y
Walter Boarman, Chas Co, Md
Thos Mulladey, Va.
Geo Jameson, Chas Co, Md.
Chas Pise, Gtwn.
Henry Gaugh, St Mary's Co, Md.
Angus Wheelen, Balt, Md.
Jas Ryder, N Y.
Denis Doyle
Rich'd Hall, PG Co, Md.
John Lancaster, Chas Co, Md.
Lewis Joncherez, Gtwn.
Alex'r Butler, Wash City.
Chas Dinnies, N Y.
Baker Brooke, St Mary's, Md.
Alex'r Fernandez, Norfolk, Va.
Wm Wells, Balt, Md.

Jas Harold, Ire
Jos Byrne, Fred'k Co, Md.
Edw Dempsey, N Y
Chas Vincendon, Eastern Shore, Md.
Leonard Smith, St Mary's, Md.
Matthew Deagle, Balt, Md.
Geo Matthews, Chas Co, Md.
Wm M'Sherry, Va.
John Smith, Fred'k Co, Md.
Robt Manning, St Mary's Co, Md.
Thos Adams, Hanover, Pa.
John Pye, Chas Co, Md.
Francis Kennedy, Alexandria
Jas Calaghan, Balt, Md.
Geo Dinnies, N Y.
Ignatius Combs, St Mary's, Md.
Hewey Gaugh, St Mary's, Md.
Stephen Durkee, Balt, Md.
Henry Elwis, Balt, Md.

MON AUG 1, 1814
Died: on Jul 12, nr Queenstown, in Upper Canada, the brave & gallant Brig Gen John Swift, a resident of this county. He was this afternoon [13th] buried with all the honors which an admiring army cld pay him. [From the Ontario Repository.]

Paris May 15. The solemn funeral svc for the late kings, Louis XVI & XVII, the late queen Maria Antoinette, & Mad Eliz De France, tk place yesterday in the Metropolitan Chr.

Pblc schools-persons duly elected & appt'd trustees for the yr ending Jul 31, Wash:

Jas Laury	Jos Mechlin	John Graham
Thos H Gillis	And Way, jr.	Wm Matthews
Moses Young	Geo Blagden	Sam'l N Smallwood
Wm Brent	Alex'r McWilliams	Builer Cocke
Wm Doughty		

TUE AUG 2, 1814
The body of Mr Birchett, who was found on Sun in the Eastern Branch, was interred in Wash City, yesterday.

$10 reward for Wm Mooney, appr to the bricklaying business. -Robt Brown, Bricklayer, F st, Wash City.

Died: on May 28, at his seat, nr Broomley, Kent, Eng, Lord Auckland. His Lordship is succeeded in his titles & est by his eldest son, George.

WED AUG 3, 1814
Wash Co, D C. Thos Tippett, insolvent debtor, confined in Wash Co prison for debt. -Wm Brent, clk.

The Rockville Acad in Montg Co, Md, is now in operation under the c/o Mr John Wade, principal. -J Elgar, sec'y.

Ltr from J B Varnum, jr, to Abraham Bradley, jr. Buffaloe, Jul 27, 1814. Rg-the battle of Jul 25, fought nr Chippewa; slaughter on both sides was dreadful. Gen Brown & Gen Scott were both severely wounded. Maj M'Farland of the 1st was killed. Col Brady, Majs M'Neill, Levenworth, Brooke, Jessup, & many other worthy ofcrs wounded.

THU AUG 4, 1814
Balt, Aug 2. Wm Pinkney has consented to be a candidate at the ensuing Congressional Election, to rep the dist of Balt City & Co.

Wash Theatre. Mr & Mrs Jefferson's Benefit Night, Aug 4. Comedy cld *Kiss*.

$40 reward. Ranaway from the subscriber, Huntsville, Surry Co, N C, on Jul 18; Chas age 20 yrs, & Peter Sanders, age 25 or 30 yrs, two likely negro fellows. -W W Chaffin, Elisha Purdom

$200 reward. Deserted from the camp nr St Leonard's Creek a short time since, 2 sldrs of the Light Artl, Robt Burns & Jas Farmer. Burns was born in Berkly Co, Va, age 21 yrs, farmer. Farmer was born in Culpepper, Vir, age 22 yrs, farmer.

Also deserted from Ft Wash, 2 sldrs, of the 20th regt: Ezekiel Addicks & Dozier Horde. Addicks is a ntv of Va, age 16 yrs; was in blacksmith bus. Horde was born in Richmond, Vir; age 24 yrs; blacksmith by profession. -Ft Wash, Aug 1, 1814.

H C Lewis announces that he has opened a new & genteel tavern, sign of the Press & Eagle, Pa av, Wash City.

FRI AUG 5, 1814

Orphans Crt of PG Co, Md. Ordered by the crt, that Martha Duvall & Dennis Duvall, adms of Truman Duvall, dec'd, to give notice required by law. Trueman Tyler, Reg.

Philip Green to apply at the PG Co Crt, [Md] on Sep 1, for the benefit of the insolvent laws.

SAT AUG 6, 1814

Feb 27, 1814. Encounter bet the *Phoebe* & the *Essex*, Capt Porter. was signed by:

Jno Downs	Wm Odenheimer	Edw Barnwell
Richd K Hoffman	Jno R Shaw	M__w Bartnuc
Alex Montgomery	Geo W Isaacs	Saml I Dusenberry

MON AUG 8, 1814

Ofc & establishment of the Petersburg Intell, will be sold at pblc auction on Aug 26. -Anna Dickson, admx, Petersburg, Va.

For sale-small farm about 78 acs, 7 miles from Wash City. -Wm A Scott, lvg on So N J av, nr the Canal Bridge, Wash City.

$50 reward. Eloped yesterday from my bed & board, my wife Lockey, alias Rachel, aged about 27 yrs. It is supposed she went off with a French Fencing Mstr & Barber, Philip Houssey, aged about 35 yrs. He took money & clothing apparel, not even sparing those belonging to the child, whom my wife has left behind. -Chas M'Carthy, 204 Water st, N Y, Jul 8, 1814.

TUE AUG 9, 1814

For sale-*Swanson's Lot*, 200 acs, with dwlg hse, PG Co, Md. -Benj Plummer

Land for sale, the plantation whereon I live, in PG Co, Md, 243 1/2 acs. I am so old & infirm, that I cannot manage it to any kind of advantage. -Wm Bayley

WED AUG 10, 1814

Mr John Craighton, well know for his superiority in the art of nail cutting, has been put in charge of the *Nail Factory* nr the Navy Yd. -Geo Beall, proprietor.

Obit-on Aug 2, in the discharge of his professional duty at the bar, Jethro D Goodman, of Eliz City, N C, was seized with an apoplectic fit; he dropped & expired instantly. He was in his 30th yr.

$100 reward for Jas Rowe, pvt in the 36th regt U S I, who deserted from this rendezvous on Jul 12; age 29 yrs. When he enlisted said he was born in Va, but I believe he is from New Eng. Also Patrick McHenry, pvt in said regt, who left on Jul 27, born in Ire, age 29 yrs; shoemkr. Also Saml Sewell, pvt in said regt, who deserted on Aug 3; born in A A Co, Md, age 22 yrs. -W C Hobbs, Lt Comdt, Gtwn.

THU AUG 11, 1814
Auction of furn at the hse of John Gardiner, 4th hse west of the Pres' Hse, on Pa av, Wash City. -David Bates, auct.

FRI AUG 12, 1814
Wash Co, D C. Hezekiah Langle, insolvent debtor, confined in Wash Co prison, for debt. -Wm Brent, clk.

Best quality lime for sale, enquire of Benj Burns, Captiol Hill, Wash City.

A History of Va, from the discovery till the yr 1781, with Biographical sketches, by J W Campbell. -Jos Milligan, bkseller, High st, Gtwn.

SAT AUG 13, 1814
Marine corps appointments & promotions by the Pres of the U S:
John Hall, to Major. Anthony Gale & Richard Smith, Capts, Majs by Bvt. Wm Anderson; Thos R Swift; Saml Miller; John Crabb; Henry H Forde; John M Gamble; Chas S Hanna; Alex Sevier; Alfred Grayson; Wm Strong; John Heath; Sam'l Bacon, First Lts, to be Capts. Francis B Bellevue; T Raimond Montegat; Philip B de Grandpre; Benj Hyde; Lyman Kellogg; Saml Watson; Wm L Brownlow; Leonard J Boone; Thos W Legge; John L Kuhne; Wm H Freeman; Henry Olcote; Chas R Browne; Thos W Bacot; Benj Richardson; Francis W White; Wm Niccoll; Wm L Boyd; Chas Lord; Levi Twiggs; Edmund Brooke; John Harris, Second Lts to First Lts. Saml B Johnson appt'd a First Lt of Marines.

The fast sailing Pilot-boat schn'r *Susan* will run as a packet bet Blagden's wharf, Wash City, & Potomac Creek. -Capt Silvanus Smith

MON AUG 15, 1814
Committed to the goal of Fred'k Co, Md, negro woman, runaway, Nancy Jefferson, about 35 yrs of age; says she belongs to Gen Joshua Wallace, Chestnut st, Phil. -Morris Jones, shrf, Fred'k Co, Md.

Deserted from my rendezvous in Alexandria, sldr, Wm S Brown, age 25 yrs; born in Balt, stone cutter. -J M Glassell, Lt 20th Inf.

TUE AUG 16, 1814
$10 reward, for David Grooves, who formerly resided in Wash City; deserted from camp at Bladensburg, on Aug 12, pvt in Capt Duvall's co Drafted Md Militia. It is supposed he has gone towards Dumfries, where he was raised. Also, Wm Chew, deserted from same on Aug 11th. -Saml Duvall, Capt

Wash Co, D C. Chas Gobert, insolvent debtor, confined in Wash Co prison bounds for debt. Also, Saml Speake, for same. -Wm Brent, clk.

WED AUG 17, 1814
$100 reward for yellow fellow, runaway, a slave for life, named Peter, about 23 yrs old; was owned sometime by Col Enos Newbold, from whom he was purchased by Geo W Campbell, some 5 yrs ago. -Thos Sim, Wash City.

Wash Co, D C. Case of Ronald Donaldson, insolvent debtor, confined in Wash Co prison for debt. -Wm Brent, clk.

THU AUG 18, 1814
Collectors of tax now in ofc for Md: Geo Brown; Wm Chambers, Geo W Thomas, Stephen H Moore, Richd Duvall, Francis Newman, Jos Swearingen, Thos B Hall, Aza Beall.

Maj Gen Winfield Scott, Petersburg, Va, Aug 16. This gallant sldr, not yet 30 yrs of age, is a ntv of Dinwiddle Co; & educated at Wm & Mary College.

For sale-part of tract of land cld *Billingsley*, 317 acs, in PG Co, Md. -Wm Weems

$50 reward for a sldr of the 36th infty, Wm Hall, a ntv of Canada, age 22 yrs, who deserted on Aug 11. -C J Queen, Lt 36th Infty.

FRI AUG 19, 1814
Brdg Hse-Mrs Odlin can accommodate a few more boarders. The hse is new & oppo Dr Ott's on Pa av, Wash City.

SAT AUG 20, 1814
Sale at auction-negroes, stock, furn, etc. -Ann Sprigg

Hse & lot for sale, on King & Cornwell sts in town of Leesburg, Va. I would take 2 or 3 young negroes in part. -John Triplett

MON AUG 22, 1814
Groceries, etc, for sale at A B Boone & Co, Gtwn.

John Stubbs of Pa, went on a journey southward a few wks since, without leaving his route; an occurrence in the family renders his presence; he is about 18 yrs of age [apparently much older,] 6' high. Info to his grdn, Isaac Kirk, nr York, Pa; or Vincent Stubbs, Little Britain, Lancaster Co, Pa; or John Hewss, Balt, Md.

Runaway, Chloe, negro girl, about 18 yrs of age; says she belongs to Mr Geo French, nr Gtwn, DC; committed to the Fred'k Co, Md, jail. -Morris Jones, shrf.

TUE AUG 23, 1814
Augusta, Aug 12. On Fri last, Ezekiel Alexander, of Columbia Co, & his wife, were murdered on their plantation by 2 Fla negroes, lately brought from St Mary's.

Died: on Aug 20, at Mr M'Leod's Htl, in Wash City, Mr Saml Richardet, of Phil, a Sailing Mstr in the U S N.

WED AUG 24, 1814
The old family mansion of Mr Digges, at *Washburton*, was visited by a tremendous thunder-bolt on Sat, which took away part of the north stack, setting fire to part of the hse. Mr Digges was entirely alone & had a narrow escape of his life. -Local

$15 reward for runaway, Sam Tilman, negro man, age about 18 yrs. -Jacob Mumma, living one mile from Sharpsburg, Wash Co, Md.

AUG 26, 27, & 29-missing on tape.

TUE AUG 30, 1814
The city of Wash was taken by the enemy on Wed, Aug 24th. On Thu night, the interior & combustible part of the Capitol, & the Pres' hse, was destroyed.
-Wm H Winder, Brig Gen 10th Mil Dist.

WED AUG 31, 1814
No houses were half as much plundered by the enemy as by the knavish wretches about the town who profited of the general distress. Pvt bldg destroyed: the dwlg hse owned & occupied by Mr Robt Sewall.

THU SEP 1, 1814
Died: at Bladensburg, a few days ago, Dr Thos H Kent, a young gentleman of distinguished excellence. He has followed to the realms of immortality a lovely wife, whose loss nrly a yr ago he scarcely survived.

For sale-farm on which I reside nr Dumfries, Pr Wm Co, Va; bet 6 & 700 acs, with dwlg hse. -W A C Dade.

FRI SEP 2, 1814
Copy of a ltr from Cmdor Barney to the Sec of the Navy, Wm Jones, dt'd *Farm*, at Elk Ridge, Aug 29, 1814. Rg-the wound of Capt Miller, of Cmdor Barney. Acting Sailing-mstr Martin killed & Sailing-mstr Warner killed. Signed-Joshua Barney

Killed of the left division of the U S army cmnded by Brig Gen Gaines, in the action of Aug 15, 1814, at Ft Erie, U C: Capt Williams & Lt M'Donough, Artl. Lt Fountain, missing, thrown from the bastion. -Roger Jones, Assist Adj Gen.

$50 reward for Cato, a mulatto fellow, ranaway on Aug 16. Jos Gist, Pinkneyville, Union dist, S C.

SAT SEP 3, 1814
A general Hosp has been established on Capitol Hill, under the direction of Dr Catlett. Order of Jno R Bell, Ass't Insp Gen.

MON SEP 4, 1814
Died: on Aug 24, at his plantation below S Wash, N C, Timothy Bloodworth, aged 78 yrs; more than 30 yrs a mbr of the State leg of N C.

TUE SEP 6, 1814
The pblc are informed that Gtwn College has commenced & will continue as usual. -John Grassi, Pres.

WED SEP 7, 1814
Gen John Armstrong has resigned the ofc of Sec of War.

THU SEP 8, 1814
$5 reward. Strayed on Sep 1, from camp nr Gtwn ferry, a sorrel horse. Chas Thornton, Vielleboro, Va.

FRI SEP 9, 1814
The *Boston Centinel* is in an error in stating that the Maj Pinkney, who was wounded at the battle of Bladensburg, is a s/o Gen Pinkney of S C, & late aid to Gen Dearborn. The Gentleman wounded on the occasion is Wm Pinkney, late American Mnstr to the Crt of St Jas, & since Atty Gen of the U S. He commands a battalion of Riflemen. He was severely wounded in the arm, but not taken prisoner. -Balt Pat.

Vandals destroyed a collection of valuable & scarce bks at the Congressional Library. We are sorry to learn that Elias B Caldwell lost the whole of his valuable Law Library. -Wash Items

$50 reward. Ranaway on Aug 29, from Judge Nicholson's farm, on Elk Ridge, nr Balt, negro man, Perry Hemsley, age 30 yrs. -Jas Jack, mgr.

All persons who have saved, or are in possession of any of the property taken from my hse, in the Navy Yd, on Aug 25th & 26th, are requested to return same without further explanation. -T Tingey

Dr J Brown offers his svcs to the ctzns of Bladensburg & vicinity. He has fixed his ofc & residence in the dwlg of Dr Thos H Kent, dec'd.

SAT SEP 10, 1814
I will sell all or part of my est in Wash Co, Md, nr Hagerstown; nrly 1,500 acs. -Tench Ringgold, Wash.

The Fairfax Crt Hse Jocky Club Races will commence on Sep 22. -John Maddox

Ltr to the editor, dt'd Wash City, Sep 8th, 1814. Signed Jas H Blake. Rg-situation at time of invasion of the city & reference to a ltr by Wm Thornton about Blake.

The Pres has conferred Brevet commissions to the following in the U S Army:
Brig Gen Gaines, Aug 15, Maj Gen.
Capt D Ketchum, 25 Infty, Jul 25, Maj.
2d Lt E B Randolph, 20th Infty, Jul 25, 1st Lt.
Capt T Biddle, jun corps of Art, Aug 15, Maj.
Capt A C W Fanning, corps of Artl, Aug 15, Maj.
Capt B Birdsall, 4th Rifle, Aug 15, Maj.
1st Lt N N Hall, 21st Infty, As Insp Gen, Aug 15, Capt.
Capt R Desha, 24th Infty, Aug 4, Maj.

MON SEP 12, 1814
The Ofc of the Clk of the Crct Crt is opened in the hse of Mr Way, next dr to the Genr'l P O, on Pa av, Wash City. -Wm Brent, clk.

TUE SEP 13, 1814
Thos Bolling Robertson is re-elected the Rep to Cong from La, over J B Prevost, the fed candidate.

WED SEP 14, 1814
Killed on board the late U S brig *Argus*, Wm H Allen, late cmder, in action with H B M sloop *Pelican*, on Aug 14, 1813: Mr Wm W Edwards, Mdshpmn; Mr Richd Delphy, do; Joshua Jones, seaman; Geo Gardiner, do; John Findly, do; Wm Moulton, do. Wm W Allen, Cmder, severely wounded, died Aug 18, 1813. Jas White, carp, died Aug 17, at Mill Prison. Jos Jordan, boatswain's mate, died Aug 16, at sea. Francis Eggert, seaman, died Aug 30, at Mill Prison. Chas Baxter, seaman, died Sep 2, at Mill Prison. -Jas Inderwick, Act'g Surg-Argus.

Pblc sale on the premises of the subscriber, a 2 story dwlg hse, on sq 487. Apply to David Bates. Or to-Wm H P Tuckfield.

Wash Co, D C. Oliver Pollock, insolvent debtor, confined in Wash Co prison, for debt. -Wm Brent, clk.

THU SEP 15, 1814
Ltr from Maj Gen Smith of the Md Militia, to the Sec of War, dt'd Head-qrtrs, Hamstead Hill, Balt, Md, Sep 14. Rg-Enemy appear to be retiring; I have good reason to believe that Gen Ross is mortally wounded. Of our ofcrs, the worthy Wm Lowry Donaldson is the only one known to be killed.

FRI SEP 16, 1814
$20 reward. Valuable Pointer, belonging to the subscriber, came home with a great gash in his snout, done by a sharp butcher's knife. Reward for info to prosecute the offender for such brutal conduct. -Geo Hadfield-Wash Item.

Died: lately in Norfolk, after a long & severe disposition, Lt Glen Drayton, U S N, a ntv of Charleston, S C, a young man respected by all.

Reward for a rifle placed in the watch-hse at Gtwn, on Aug 24, stamped *H Deringer, Phil.* It was carried, I am informed, with the pblc arms to Montgomery, thence to Balt. -John Underwood

Lewis Miller, a mbr of my company, is now under arrest for disobedience of orders, desertion & horse-thef. -Wm Doughty

SAT SEP 17, 1814
Capture of the *Ohio* & the *Somers*, on Aug 12th. Killed-John Fifehill, boatswains mate. Wounded-Reuben Wright, shot thru the arm. Sailing-mstr McCally, shot thru the thigh & bayoneted in the ft. Sgt Eastman, 11 Regt of army, wounded in the neck by a musket ball. ____ Granger, 11th Regt, wounded in the arm. ____ Weath, do, do. ____ Whillers, 21st Regt, wounded, cut in the arm. *Somers.* Saml Taylor, shot in the arm & cut in the head. Chas Ordean, cut in the shoulder. -A M Conkling, Lt.

TUE SEP 20, 1814
Twenty-six Americans to be exchanged as soon as possible for a like number of British left at Bladensburg. Signed, Jas H McCulloh, jr, Garrison Surg U S Army.

Jas H McCulloh	John Pidgeon	Henry Brice
Luther A Norris	Geo Reput	David
Jacob Noyle	Wm Collings	John Robinson
John Lamb	Jas N Mariott	Jas Davidson
Chas Goddard	Wm Keane, jr.	Walter Muskett
Jas Gibson	Bryan Allen	Richd K Cook
Geo Reintzell	Robt Smith	Jacob Hubbard
John Jepson	Geo Bennett	Conrad Euler
Benj Fleetwood	Thos Bringman	

[Corrections per dup listing of Oct 14, 1814.]

Killed & wounded in the action of the White Hse in Capt Humphrey's Company of Vols Riflemen, from Frederick Va. Killed-David Harris. Wounded-Lt Blackburn; 1st Sgt, David Humphreys, bro to the Capt, severely, lost his right arm. Hugh McDonald, pvt, mortally. Thos Pledman, pvt, in the head, slightly. Wm Trulding, pvt, in the thigh, a flesh wound. John Miller, pvt, in the face, slightly.

Died: in Wash City, on Sep 18, after a long illness, Mrs Sarah Carter, relict of the late Edw Carter, of *Blenhelm.*

Boarding, oppo M'Keowin's Htl, Wash City. -John Peltz

Runaway, Sam, negro man, committed to the jail of Alleghany Co; says he belongs to Rezin Pumphrey, nr Wheeling Va; age 25 yrs. -Thos Pollard, Shrf, Al Co, Md.

WED SEP 21, 1814
Strayed or stolen from the Commons of Wash City, a black gelding. -W B Beall, nr the Six Bldgs, Wash City.

Large assortment of wine & liquors for sale, at his Wine Cellar. Also first quality segars. Orders attended to by his son. -And Ross, Gtwn.

The subscriber will accommodate a small family with lodgings or board. -Thady Hogan, North F st, nr St Patrick's Chr, Wash City.

THU SEP 22, 1814
We understand that a loan of $200,000 has been made to the gov't by John P Van Ness, as Chrmn of a cmtee in behalf of the Banks of this Dist, to be applied to the defence of the Dist.

FRI SEP 23, 1814
Mrd: on Sep 20, by Rev Wm Matthews, Mr Walter Clarke, to Miss Rachael Boon, both of Wash City.

Orphans Crt of Wash Co, D C. Pblc sale on Sep 29, at hse of the late Peter Miller, dec'd; all prsnl prop. -David Bates, auct. G Coombe, Jno M'Gowan, adms.

SAT SEP 24, 1814
Geo Allen of PG Co, Md, brought before me a stray Gelding. -Geo Page, J P, Sep 21, 1814. [Nr Bladensburg, Md.

MON SEP 26, 1814
$15 reward for runaway, Sam Tilman, age 18 yrs. Jacob Mumma, lvg nr Sharpsburg & Hagerstown, Wash Co, Md.

Committed to the jail of Fred'k Co, Md, runaway, negro man cld Basil; says he belongs to Mr Eli Sollers, nr the mouth of Patuxent rvr, St Mary's or Calvert Co, Md. -Morris Jones, shrf, Fred'k Co, Md.

We the undersigned were present at the interview bet Dr Thornton & the British Maj of Brig, who came to burn the bldg containing the G P O, Patent Ofc, etc, on Aug 25. O B Brown; Geo Lyon; Geo Hadfield; Thos Nicholson, Wash, Sep 21.

Runaway committed to the goal in St Mary's Co, Md, negro man, Moses; says he belongs to Mrs Ann Cox, a widow lady lvg in Northumberland Co, Va, nr Kinsale. -Enoch Combs, Shrf, St Mary's Co, Md.

Sale at the dwlg hse of Dr Wm Gardner in F st, Wash City; a variety of hsehld & kitchen furn, prop of Josias W King, for arrear rent due Pierce Purcel. -Brooke Edmonston, Constable.

Prisoners taken by the enemy in the engagement at Balt are on board the *Surprize, Severn,* & *Havana,* frigs. They are in good health & well treated. [Fed Gaz]

Surprize:
Jas Gettings
Wm Balson
Geo Boyle
Andrew Kaufman
Severn:
Nicholas Wilson
Havanna:
Rich'd Lawson
Thos G Prettyman
Lewis Baltzell
John G Pogue
Edw Murray
Ephraim Nash
Adam Miller
Talbot Jones
John Fordyce
John Howard

Ezekiel Partlett
Edw H Dorsey
John Griffin
Richd Polkinhorn
Geo T Henry
John Chesley
Jos Chapman
Thos Bailey
Wm Baltzell
Wm Levely
Francis M Wills
Geo Heidelbach
John Kessler
Morgan Carson
Fred'k Seyler
Jos G Whitney
Geo Collins

Peter Abraham
John Lawless
Thos Herring
Thos Norris
Wm B Buchanan
John Baxley
John Dougherty
Andrew Cole
Henry Suter
John Huzza
Peter Stedham
John Redgreave
P B Powell
Andrew Miller
Henry W Gray
Benj Meredith
Daniel Wells

TUE SEP 27, 1814
Died: in Burlington, Vt, on Sep 13, after a lingering illness of some mos, Maj Ebenezer Beebe, of the 6th Regt. His funeral was attended by svr'l thousand.

Killed on board the U S squadron on Lake Champlain, in the engagement with the British fleet on Sep 11, 1814. Ship-Saratoga:
Peter Gamble, lt
Abraham Davis, q m
Peter Johnson, s
Andrew Parmlee, o s
Eben Johnson, s
Randall M'Donald, o s
Thos Malony, o s
Peter Hanson, s
Jerome Williams, o s
Earl Hannemon, s
Brig Eagle:
John Robero, s
Jas Winship, o s
Nace Wilson, o s
Robt Stratton, mrne
Peter Vandermere, mast mate
Schn'r Ticonderoga:
John Stansbury, lt
Henry Johnson, s
Sloop Preble:
Rogers Carter, a s mstr
Gunboat Borer:
Thos Gill, boy

Thos Butler, q g
Wm Wyer, slmkr
John Coleman, s
Peter Post, s
Jos Couch, lndmn
John White, o s
Andrew Nelson, s
Jacob Laraway, s
Jas Carlisle, marine

Jacob Landman, s
Thos Lewis, boy
John Wallace, mrne
Jas M Hale, musician

John Fisher, b m
Deodrick Think, mrne

Jos Rowe, bts mte

Jas Day, marine

Jas Norberry, btsw mate
Wm Brickell, s
Benj Purrill, o s
David Bennet, s
Thos Stephens, s
Sam'l Smith, s
John Sellack, s
Edw Moore, s
John Smart

Perkins Moore, o s
Thos Anwright, o s
Jos Heaton, marine
John Wood, musician

John Atkinson, b m
John Sharp, marine

Arthur W Smith, prs stew

For sale or exchange for prop est of the Allegany Mtns in either Pa, Md, Va, or D C: for a plantation in Ky, nr Louisville; 250 acs; cabins, corn-cribs, smoke hse. -Nathl Frye, jr, Wash City.

Ad-I will rent the whole of my farm in Calvert Co, Md, on Battle Creek; about 1,000 acs. -M Taney

WED SEP 28, 1814
Those killed belonging to the 1st Regt of Artl, Lt Col D Harris, Detachment at Ft M'Henry, Sep 13, 1814. Capt Nicholson's co: killed-Levi Claggett, 3d Lt; John Clemm, 2d Serjeant. Capt Berry's co: killed-Thos V Beeson, Pvt.

Deserted from the Militia Co, now commanded by Capt Stephen Parry:

John Adamson	Henry Carabe	Isaac Henry
John Hunt	John Myers	Noel Perroe
Nathl P Heath	Thos Wartling	Jas Gray
Michl Herrity	Reeson Davis	Nathl Plant
H Merrea	[Wash Camp Hill, Sep 27]	

$5 reward for the following Pvts:

Chas Lenman	Geo Harbin	Thos Tooly
Lewis Frank	John Barnett	Seth Shell

who deserted, since the battle of Bladensburg, from their company cmded by R S Briscoe, Capt. Wm Moore, Capt, 2d regt Columbian Militia, Camp Hill, Wash.
Also deserted:

Jas Wedding	Walter Mitchell	Noah Wheat
John B White	Thos Gaines	Stephen Steward

THU SEP 29, 1814
Brig Gen Thos Flournoy, it is stated in the Savannah papers, has resigned his commission in the army.

Died: at Norfolk, on Wed, after a short illness, Maj Lewis L Taylor, 26 U S I.

For sale-*Middle Brook Mills & Estate*, Montg Co, Md, about 580 acs. -Hiel Peck, on the premises.

$50 reward-for Saml Matthews, pvt, who deserted from this place on Sep 10th; age 30 yrs, cooper by profession, born in Balt, Md. -H Cohen, 1st Lt, U S Rifle Regt. Recruiting Rendezvous, Shepherdstown, Va.

FRI SEP 30, 1814
Hse o/Reps. The petition of Wm H Washington, of Va, praying for indemnification for prop destroyed by the ofcrs of the army of the U S, to prevent its falling into the hands of the enemy; referred to the cmttee of claims.

Died: nr the island of Tristan d'Acuna, in Jan last, Capt Jonathan Lambert; formerly of Salem. Enterprizing adventurer, who had effected a settlement on that island. He was passing to Nightingale Island, in a boat with 4 others, when overset by a sudden squall, all were drowned. Only one man was left on the island.

$75 reward for delivering at Camp Hill, Wash City, the following deserters:
Danl Beall	Jos Balls	Ninian Benson
Alex'r Duggins	Saml Duvall	Zadock Duvall
John Merson	Thos Owings	Robt Rattle
David Shutley	Jas Smith	Wm Barbour
Michl Turney	Stephan Watkins	Gassaway D Lizure

-Robt T Dade, Capt, Comdg a Com M M.

SAT OCT 1, 1814
Bath, Berkley Springs, Va. The subscriber continues as usual to keep a Hse of Entertainmant, in the lge bldg nr the baths. -Wm Abernathy

Died: in Wash City, on Sep 30, after a short illness, Mr Jos Seymour, late of the Phil Theatre.

$5 reward, for Levi Pumphrey, who deserted on Sep 27, from Capt Wm Moore's Co. -Wm Moore, Capt, 1st Brig 2d Reg 2d Bat.

MON OCT 3, 1814
Ltr from Maj Gen Brown to the Sec of War, Hon Jas Monroe, dt'd H Q Ft Erie, Sep 20, 1814. In the battle of Niagara Falls, my Aid-de-camp Capt Ambrose Spencer, being mortally wounded, was left in the hands of the enemy; the corpse of Capt S was sent to the American shore. -Jac Brown

Isaac Wayne, of Chester Co, s/o Gen Anthony Wayne, nominated for Govn'r of Pa, has positively declined to serve.

Runaway, Rachel, negro woman, was committed to my custody; she says she formerly belonged to H Hattan, of PG Co, Md, & that she was sold to a Mr Smith, of Ky, from whom she escaped. -Geo Simmes, shrf of PG Co, Md.

TUE OCT 4, 1814
Genr'l Crt Martial is to assemble in Wash City on Oct 10th, for the trial of Capt Sam'l T Dyson, of the Corps of Artl.

WED OCT 5, 1814
Died: on Oct 1, Gen Jas Robertson, U S agent for the Chickasaw nation & one of the first settlers of West Tenn.

The following have deserted from the company under my command: Wm Mullican & Wm D Belt. -Jno Wailes, Cmndg Co Md Militia.

THU OCT 6, 1814
The Pres of the U S nominated to the Senate, Alex'r J Dallas, of Phil, to be Sec of the Treas, yesterday.

Died: at Charleston, on Sep 3, after an illness of a few days, Lt Russell Bassett, U S N, aged 30 yrs; ntv of New Haven, Conn.

Jas Lowry Donaldson, who was killed in the action nr North Point, on Sep 12, was a ntv of Ire; has resided in this country since he was 11 yrs old; third s/o Col Wm Lowry, of this city. His name having been changed by an act of the Assembly of this State, in compliance with the wishes of a relation. Mr D was about 33 yrs of age; he has left a widow & 5 small chldrn. He acted as Adjut in the 27th Regt; rec'd a musket ball through his head, which put an immediate period to his life. -Fed Gaz.

The copartnership [groc bus] of Henry Herford & Edw Stephens, has been dissolved by mutual consent. Henry Herford will continue the business.

Was left on Aug 24, at Dr Worthington's Farm, in D C, a bay mare, bridle & saddle. Owner is requested to pay charges & take the above away.
-Chas Warren, mgr, for Dr Worthington.

FRI OCT 7, 1814
Came to the farm of the late Anne E Queen, dec'd, 2 steers. Owners are requested to come for them.

SAT OCT 8, 1814
Killed of the Left Division of the Army at Ft Erie, cmded by Maj Gen Brown, on Sep 17, 1814, in the sortie against the enemy's batteries. Killed-Lt Col E D Wood, Capt & brvt Lt Col of Engrs. Capt I Bradford, 21st Infty; Capt H Hale, 11th Infty; Capt L G A Armistead, 1st Riflemen. Ensign O'Fling was mortally wounded, since dead; 23d Infty. Col Jas Gibson was mortally wounded; died on Sep 18, 4th Riflemen. 1st Lt E Childs, 9th Infty, was severely bayoneted thru the thigh. 1st Lt Ballard, Adj, 4th Riflemen, prisoner. Of the Militia killed:
Brig Gen David, Vol Brig; Capt Buel, Lt Col Crosby's Regt; Lt Brown, of Lt Col McBurney's Regt; Lt W Belknap, of Lt Col Fleming's Regt; Ensign Blakesley, of Lt Col McBurney's Regt.

$50 reward-for Jos Wallace, deserted on Oct 6, a pvt sldr in the 38th Regt U S I, age 29 yrs, born in N H; cooper by profession. Said Wallace has twice taken the bounty, first in the 38th & lastly in the 20th infty. Deliver to Jas Cochran, Lt 38th Infty, Camp Snowden nr Wash, or any ofcr attached to the army of the U S.

MON OCT 10, 1814
Extract of a ltr rec'd by the Sec of War, from Col Athanasius Fenwick, dt'd, Leonard Town, Oct 7, 1814. Rg-the whole of the enemy's force that lay in the Potomac rvr, have gone down the bay. -A Fenwick

Ladies with ltrs in the Wash P O, Oct 1, 1814:

Lucy R Anderson	Miss Sinthey Ashford	Mrs Brooks
Eliz Belt	Miss Martha M Brown	Henrietta Branton
Mrs Barlow	Mrs Eliza Burdy	Dolly Barisford
Sarah Boyce	Mrs Ann Beatty	Charlotte Cozens-3
Eleanor Cowan	Ann Maria Davis	Mgt Edglin
Lucia Evans	Miss Mary Earle	Mrs Mary Foulon
Polly Frank	Miss Flora Ford	Mrs Ann Goins
Jane Hutchens	Miss Caroline Harris	Maria Howard
Mrs Maria Jordan	Madam Kantzow	Mrs Maxwell
Mary McDowell	Eliz Minitree	Mrs Sarah Miles-3
Mrs Mary Martin	Mrs Eliz M'Kann	Mrs Cath Nicely
Mrs Eliza Orr	Widow Orford	Miss Susan Poston
Jane Posey	Mrs Mary Rodgers	Mrs Eliz Smith
Mrs Charlotte Russell	Miss K Simmeymon	Miss C Stillings
Mrs Martha Young		

TUE OCT 11, 1814

Wanted immediately-a good rope mkr & twine do. E W Barge, Fayetteville, N C.

TUE OCT 12, 1814

Ft Bowyer, created in 1812, by Lt Bowyer, consists of common logs filled with sand. Maj Lawrence, who commanded Ft Bowyer, ia an ofcr of high promise; a ntv of Calvert Co, Md.

Sale of furn, etc, at the hse of S B Elles, oppo Mr Matthew Wright's store, Wash City. -David Bates, auct.

Philip Huissy, barber & hair dresser; keeps good rezors; shop oppo Centre Mkt.

Runaway committed to my custody on Sep 20th, negro girl, Kitty, otherwise Mary Johnson, age about 16 yrs; said she belonged to Wm Capel, Mgr of Northampton Forge, nr Balt, since says she is free. -Geo Semmes, shrf, PG Co, Md.

Wash Co, D C. Treacy Johnson, insolvent debtor, confined in the prison bounds of Wash Co for debt. -Wm Brent, clk.

THU OCT 13, 1814

For sale-100 barrels of best Balt lime. Enquire of Cornelius M'Lean, Pa av, Wash.

Died: on Fri evening, at Brighton, in his 44th yr, Francis Jas Jackson, late his Majesty's Envoy Extra & Mnstr Pleni to the U S of America; affectionate son, brother, hsbnd & fr.

$10 reward for black man, John Dublin, formerly the prop of Robt Sewall. -Danl M'Keowin.

Jeremiah Perkins, insolvent debtor, confined in Wash Co prison, for debt.

-Wm Brent, clk.

FRI OCT 14, 1814
The following, belonging to the U S svc, having been exchanged by agreement of Oct 7th, are discharged from parole, & free as before they became prisoners: Captured at Bladensburg:

Joshua Barney, Capt U S Flotilla
Sam'l Miller, Capt U S M C
G Von Harten, Lt
Thos Dukchart, Actg Mstr
John M Howland, 5th Regt Balt Vols
David Robinson, Actg Midshpmn, U S Flotilla
John Reagan, Lt Col Militia
Dominick Bader, Capt Militia
Robt M Hamilton, Mstr, U S N
Jesse Huffington, Sailing Mstr
J B Martin, Surg

Pvts:

Robt M'Call
Edw DeKraft
Thos Goswick
Jesse Edwards
Wm Wysham
Jos Bennet
Michl Vanemiller
Jacob Iler
Jos Grizel
Henry Hoffman
Barnard Thompson
Nathl Smith
John De Groot
Danl Rynchart

Isaac Johnson
Wm Gaylor
Jacob Young
Michael Mawe
Lewis Lambert
Christr Johnson
Sam'l Diser
David K Richardson
John Montgomery
Jeremiah Morgan
Brooks Bell
Jas Folks
Danl Bradley
Jos Chase.

Thos Holiday
John Cook
Geo Amick
Walter Tall
Abraham Claude
Jos Fabie
Thos Holbrooks
Partick Dorfe
Chas Smith
John Leith
Henry Zimmerman
Jacob Wise
Wm Goodrick

Wash Co, D C. Bartheson Fox, of Gtwn, brought before me as a stray, found in Wash City, a bay horse. -Thos Corcoran, J P.

For sale-4,300 acs of Potomac Land: *Montalbino*, 2,000 acs, with lg brick mansion. *Bloomsbury*, 1,500 acs, with lg old dwlg hse. *Belvidere*, 500 acs, with lg brick dwlg hse, out of repair. *Cintra*, farm of 300 acs, with new overseer's hse, etc. - Wm C Somerville, H V Somerville, Leonard town, Md.

Wash Co, D C. Ann Casenave brought before me stray horses. -T Fenwick, J P.

Sale at the hse of Mrs Coltmon, a quantity of hsehld furn. -Natl Moore, Pa av.

SAT OCT 15, 1814
Mrd: on Oct 13, in Wash City, by Rev O B Brown, Mr Presley Davis, of Nelson Co, Ky, to Mrs Sarah Ann Davis, of this dist.

Died: at St Louis, Mo Terr, Sep 18, after an illness of 12 days, Brig Gen Benj Howard, U S army, late Govn'r of that territoty.

MON OCT 17, 1814
Trustees of the pblc schools are to meet at M'Keowan's Htl, Wash City, on Wed. -Jas Laurie, Pres.

TUE OCT 18, 1814
Every able bodied man from the age of 18 to 45, who will enlist under me for the oldest army, for 5 yrs, or during the present war with Eng, shall be pd a bounty of $100; after serving the term for which he enlisted, & obtained an honorable discharge, he will be allowed $24 & 160 acs of land; same to his heirs & reps shld he die in svc. -Perrin Willis, Capt, 2d Regt Infty.

Ranaway from the subscriber about Jul last; appr to the Tailor's business, John Sheetz, about 14 yrs of age. -Jas Black, Wash City.

WED OCT 19, 1814
Pblc sale of a frame stable on Capitol Hill, prop of Geo Frank, to satisfy taxes due the Corp of the City of Wash. Sale at Jas Johnson's. -Z Walker, Coll 3d ward.

Pblc sale at Mr Alex M'Cormick's store on Capitol Hill, of beds, furn, glassware, etc. Apply to Alex'r M'Cormick or Wm O'Neal. -N L Queen auct.

TUE OCT 20, 1814
Sale at auction of hsehld & kitchen furn, at the late dwlg of Mr Bryan, Pa av, Wash City. -N L Queen, auct.

FRI OCT 21, 1814
The Tanyard, formerly the prop of Richd Tomlin, dec'd, will be leased to the highest bidder. -John Merchant, adm, w a. Dumfries, Va.

Died: in Richmond, Virg, on Oct 4, Saml Pleasants, jr, Editor of the *Va Argus*.

Pblc sale-all the prsnl est of Wm Lodge, dec'd, of Montg Co, Md. -Johannah Lodge, admx. Wm O Lodge, adm.

Pblc sale, at the late dwlg place of Jos Soper, of Montg Co, Md, dec'd, all prsnl prop. -Barton Soper, Jas P Soper, adms.

SAT OCT 22, 1814
Sale of merino sheep, of John Warner, of Wilmington, Dela, [one of the late firm of Warner, Trimble & Co of Phil city] -Wm Warner, John Wardell, assignees.

Hse & lot for sale in Gtwn; also a likely negro fellow, plasterer. -Jas Kennedy

Election will be held at Jas M Varnum's ofc, on Oct 25, in rm of Mr Saml Holt, rsgnd. -Jas M Varnum, Geo Andrews, T H Gillis, comr's of election.

MON OCT 24, 1814
Teacher wanted in a pvt family. -John T Mason, nr Hager's Town, Wash Co, Md.

Dividend to be pd of the effects of Moses Tabbs, on Jan 1. -Danl Hughes, jr, & Hy Sweitzer, Trustees. Hagerstown, Md.

TUE OCT 25, 1814
If the sldr or ctzn who tk a horse from a clover lot in Tenly-Town, on Aug 24, is satisfied with the use of him, so far; he will oblige the owner by delivering him to Jere Merrell, on High st, Gtwn.

Orphans Crt of Chas Co, Md. Prsnl est of Edw *Boone, late of said co, dec'd. -Charity *Boon, adm. [*2 splgs.]

$15 reward for negro boy, John, age about 12 yrs. -Ann Lee, DC *Society Hill*, nr Gtwn.

Halifax, Sep 30. The bodies of the gallant Maj Gen Ross & Sir Peter Parker, late of H M S *Menelaus*, were brought here in the *Tonnant;* interred with military honors.

Runaways commited to Wash Co jail, DC: negro Michael, says he belongs to Wm Hoomes of Montg Co, Md. Negro Nace, says he belongs to Maxmilian Horvel, of Calvert Co, Md, nr Huntington, Md. -C Tippett, for W Doyd, mrshl.

$20 reward for deserter, Jos Joice, a pvt in the Marine Corps; age 32 yrs, born in Ire, farmer by occupation. -A Sevier, Capt com'g-Marine Barracks, Wash City.

$100 reward for 2 deserters: Chas Smith, musician, ntv of France, about 30 to 40 yrs of age. Also Rich'd B Randolph, pvt in the 35th regt U S I, about 36 yrs of age, an old offender, having deserted 3 times & rec'd the bounty money twice. -Meriwether Taliaferro, Capt 35th U S I; Rendezvous, Fredericksburg, Va.

WED OCT 26, 1814
Mrd: some days ago, by Rev F C Schaeffer, his excellency Simon Snyder, govn'r of Pa, to Mrs Mary Scott, of Harrisburg.

In an advertisement of Sep 28, Nathl P Heath's name appeared among others as a deserter, this was done by mistake; no person by the name of Heath was intended to be advertised. -Stephen Parry, Capt.

Wanted-smart active woman that is a good cook & of a good character. Also a smart active boy is wanted. -Nathl H Heath

Sale of the rl & prsnl prop of Eliz Eversfield, in the village of Piscataway; decree of the Chancery Crt of Md. -Edw Eversfield, trustee

THU OCT 27, 1814
Orphans Crt of Wash Co, D C. Prsnl est of John Jolley, dec'd. -Eliz Jolley, admx.

$30 reward for black mare taken from my plantation, by the British, on Aug 22; also 1 grey mare & 3 mules. -W B Beanes, Upper Marlboro, Md.

Mrd: on Oct 16, by Rev Solomon Sharp, Mr Walter Douglass, of Mordington Mills, Kent Co, Del, to Miss Harriett M Clayton, d/o Mr Jas Clayton, of Milford, Del.

FRI OCT 28, 1814
Died: on Aug 16, at Montrose, Westmoreland Co, Va, after a short but painful illness, Robt F Ralph, s/o R Ralph, a resident of St Mary's Co, Md.

SAT OCT 29, 1814
Strayed away-a young mare. John H Higgenson, lvg in Gtwn, D C.

Leonard Gates, insolvent debtor, confined in the Wash Co [DC] prison, for debt. -Wm Brent, clk.

For sale-75 acs of land 2 miles from the Eastern Branch Bridge. -O Carr

In Chancery, Oct 24, 1814. Creditors of John S Peters, dec'd, to exhibit their claims. -Jas P Heath, Reg C C Md.

MON OCT 31, 1814
Chilicothe, Oct 20. Dr Edw Tiffin is appt'd Srvyr Genr'l of the dist in which Ohio is included, vice Josiah Meigs, rsgn'd.

Mrd: on Oct 22, by Rev O B Brown, Wm H Beard to Miss Harriet Bestor, both of Wash City.

Land for sale-*Magruders Tavern*, formerly Baldwins, with farm attached; 211 acs; in P G Co, Md. -Thos Magruder, of Isaac.

TUE NOV 1, 1814
The Patentee of the mfgr of Woollen Blankets by felting, is willing to dispose of his share of the Blanket factory now in operation in PG Co, Md, about 12 miles from Wash City, at the *Paint Mills*. -Elkanah Cobb, patentee, PG Co, Md.

Proposals will be rec'd for bldg a Magazine on *Greenleaf's Point*, in Wash City, on Nov 2. -F Martsteller, Deputy Q M Genr'l 10th M D, Wash City.

Stray cows came to my farm; 2 miles above Gtwn; owners are requested to prove their property, pay damages, & take them away. -Rebecca Forrest, *Rosedale*.

Sale at the nursery of the late Tho Main, nr Little Falls of Potomac. -Wm Bunyie, nr Gtwn, D C.

Overseer wanted. -Chas A Pye, Cornwallis' Neck, Chas Co, Md.

Fishing landings at Gisborough to be rented. Mr Philip Webster, mgr there. -Jno Thos Shaaff.

WED NOV 2, 1814
100 thousand good seedling thorns for fencing, for sale. Wm Sersey, lvg nr Poolesville, Montg Co, Md.

Mrd: on Oct 26, by Rev Mr Vernes, Jas Brooke, of Chester town, Eastern Shore, Md, to Miss Mary Ann Hill, d/o Henry Hill, of PG Co, Md.

Hezekiah Hall brght before me a stray gelding. Wash City, D C, John B Kirby, J P.

THU NOV 3, 1814
Svr'l fine stray sheep are at my Farm. -John Threlkeld

Allen, negro man, committed to the Harford co goal; age about 26 yrs. Also Betsey, about 23 yrs old, negro woman. Said negroes say they belong to Mrs Mary Fowler, lvg nr Hampton, in Eliz City Co, Va. -Ben Guyton, shrf of Harford Co.

FRI NOV 4, 1814
Town of Harmony for sale; description at the store of Isaac Beall, in Mkt st, Pittsburgh. -Fred'k Rapp, atty in fact for Geo Rapp, & associates. Harmony, 1814.

SAT NOV 5, 1814
The subscriber has opened an Oyster-Hse at the crnr of E & 11th sts west, Wash City. -Jacob Dixon.

MON NOV 7, 1814
Mrd: in Alexandria, on Nov 3, by Rev Mr Wilmer, Mr Jacob Leonard, of Gtwn, to Miss Sophia Eliza Faw, y/d/o Abraham Faw, of the former place.

TUE NOV 8, 1814
Tenants wanted for 2 excellent brick hses in Gtwn, D C. -Saml Turner

Philip Faiussy proposes opening a Fencing schl for the inhabitants of Wash.

Biog of an American Hero, Gen Francis Marion, of S C is now being prepared for publication. [Illluminated this Western Hemisphere during the Rev war.] To be delivered to subscribers for one hundred cents.

For sale or exchange-tracts of land in Ky; 4,000 acs on the Ohio rvr; 500 acs adj Jeffersonville; 5,000 acs on Greene rvr; small tract nr Waynesburg, county town on Ten Mile [apply for this prop to R Whitehill, in Waynesburg, or Jacob Brown, in Brownsville.] 450 acs above Hagerstown, apply to me or Maj Otho H Williams in Hagerstown. Sell or exchange for prop within or nr DC or Montg Co, Md or PG Co, Md. -Elie Williams, Gtwn.

Labourers wanted to work at Ft Wash. -Henry Herford, 2d Ward; Henry Ingle, 3d Ward; John Brashears, 4th Ward.

WED NOV 9, 1814
Hse o/Reps. Petition of John R Plater, of St Mary's Co, Md, praying an abatement of his assessment because of the loss of 49 slaves stolen from him by the enemy; referred to the Cmtee of Ways & Means.

Greensburgh, Pa, Oct 29. A mammoth pumpkin was raised on the farm of Mr John P Clingansmith, in Hempfield twnshp; 7' 8" in circumference, 201 lbs.

Benj King will give a reward of $2 for Wm Ridgeway, one of his apprentices, who has improperly absented himself since the latter end of last month.

Runaway, Leroy, negro man; says he belongs to Mr Ruben Hutcheson, of Loudon Co, Va. -Henry Sweitzer, shrf of Wash Co, Md.

THU NOV 10, 1814
$6 reward for return of 3 strayed cows; deliver to John M'Donald, overseer. -Danl Brent.

Claims against the est of Henry C Pearce, late of Montg Co, Md, dec'd; submit same by Jan 1. -John Pearce, adm

Orphans Crt of Wash Co, D C. Prsnl est of John Collet, late of Wash City, dec'd. -Ann Collet, excx; Mark W Collet, exc.

FRI NOV 11, 1814
Pblc sale, at *Windsor Forest*, the resid of the late Bailey Washington, in Stafford Co, Va; the whole of the prsnl est. -John McRae, adm w a.

Mrd: on Nov 8, by Rev Jas Laurie, Mr John D Barclay to Miss Ann A Woodside, d/o John Woodside.

Richd Wallace appt'd a mbr of the cmtee of 2d ward, vice Wash Boyd, who declines.

Bible Soc to meet at St Paul's Chr, in Alexandria, Mon. E B Caldwell, Rec Sec.

SAT NOV 12, 1814
Robt Goodloe Harper, of fed memory, appt'd by the Govn'r of Md, Maj Gen of the 3d Div of Md Militia, vice Gen Smith, rsgn'd.

For sale-a flock a mixed blood merino sheep. Athan Fenwick, about 30 miles below Alexandria, & about 30 miles at my farm in St Mary's Co, Md. -Leonard Town, Nov 11, 1814.

Died: on Nov 2, at his residence nr Chaptico, St Mary's Co, Md, John Bond, long a respectable ctn of the county. His death will be lamented by 3 dutiful chldrn.

Died: in Wilmington, Dela, on Sunday last, Mr Walter A Corry, Printer, a mbr of the Pa State Guards.

MON NOV 14, 1814
For sale-a Farm of 312 1/2 acs, which is held on lease for lives, adj *Snowhill* & *Carter's Green*, the seats of Edmund Brooke & Carter B Fontaine, of Pr Wm Co, Va; with dwlg hse. I have lived on this farm the last & present yr & will shew it to any person disposed to purchase. Terms may be known from Dr Wm Graham, lease-hldr, who lives 3 1/2 miles from Haymkt. -Wm M Prosser

TUE NOV 15, 1814
Wilson Cary Nicholas is chosen Govn'r of Va for the ensuing yr.

Wash Co, D C. Elisha Perry, insolvent debtor, confined within the prison bounds of Wash Co, for debt. -Wm Brent, clk.

For sale, 90 to 100 acs of land, on the Turnpike Rd from Wash City towards Balt; prefer it be sold together. -Issachar Schofield, *Cool Run*.

WED NOV 16, 1814
A judgment for $547,000 having been finally pronounced, in favor of John Holker, formerly Cnsl Genr'l & Agent Genr'l of the Royal Marine of France, at Phil, in the suit depending for many yrs, bet him & Dan'l Parker, of Watertown, formerly merchant of Boston, & contractor of the U S army in 1783 & 1784, but now residing in Paris, France. Reward for discovery of any property of said Dan'l Parker, in any part of the U S, on which execution may be levied towards satisfying said judgment. John Holker, at the hse of Ephraim Jones, Pearl st, Boston; or at his plantation nr Berryville & Milwood, Fred'k Co, Va. At Boston, Aug 10, 1814. John Holker. [Great injury has been sustained by Mr Holker thru the misconduct of Dan'l Parker; suit originally commenced in 1796. It is meritorious to assist a fellow ctzn in rescuing his property from the fatal grasp of an unlawful & unprincipled hldr of it.] J H

Jas Martin, from Phil, informs the pblc that he has est'd a bk bindery in all its various branches, on Jefferson st, Gtwn.

THU NOV 17, 1814
Orphans Crt of PG Co, Md. Ltrs of test with w a, on prsnl est of Thos H Kent, late of said co, dec'd. -Jos Kent, exc.

FRI NOV 18, 1814
A General Crt Martial, for the trial of Maj Gen Jas Wilkinson, will assemble at some suitable place in the village of Utica, N Y, on Jan 3d next.
<u>Pres</u>-Maj Gen Henry Dearborn.
<u>Mbrs</u>: Maj Gen Morgan Lewis   Maj Gen Geo Izard

Brig Gen J Bloomfield
Brig Gen D Bissell
Col Jonas Simonds-6th Infty
Col P P Schuyler-13th Infty
Col Robt Purdy-4th Infty
Supernumeraries:
Col Denny McCobb-45th Infty
Lt Col W S Talmadge-46th Infty

Brig Gen John P Boyd
Brig Gen E W Ripley
Col J Kingsbury-1st Infty
Col Jas Burn-L D
Col D Brearley-15th Infty

Col Geo McFeely-25th Infty
E A Bancher-Army Judge Advocate
-by order of the Sec of War, John R Bell, Inspec Genr'l.

Wash Co, D C. Ignatius Hall brought before me a stray mare. -Wm Waters, J P.

Mrs M Sweeny, at her old stand in F st, has rec'd a stock of Fancy Goods.

$20 reward for white mare, taken by the British, on Aug 25. -Jos Walker, Wash City.

Sheriff's sale, PG Co, Crt, at suit of Thos G Addison, adm of Thos H Hanson, against Thos Moore. Sale of all the right, title, etc, of said Thos Moore, in & to, part of tract of land cld *Silver Hills*, 45 acs. -Geo Semmes, shrf, PG Co, Md.

SAT NOV 19, 1814
Pblc sale of all the right, title, etc, of Ambrose White, in a frame dwlg hse, on sq 903, in Wash City, to satisfy Eliz Brown. -David Bates, auct.

MON NOV 21, 1814
Genr'l Crt Martial held at Wash City; on Nov 12. The crt decided that Capt Sam'l T Dyson, U S Corps of Artl, cmdng ofcr of the U S Fort, Ft Wash, did on or about Aug 27, 1814, when an enemy was approaching said Fort, misbehave himself before the enemy & shamefully abandon the Ft & Post; also, did cast away & destroy his arms & destroy the Fort. Dyson to be dismissed the svc of the U S.

Fredericksburg, Nov 9. Mr John Hansbrough, of King Geo Co, was murdered on Nov 2, by John Smith, a ntv of Ireland.

TUE NOV 22, 1814
Info wanted of Mr Alex'r Quarrier, who remv'd about 30 yrs since to this country from Scotland, & resided many yrs in Richmond city. Transmit a copy of the advertisement which appeared this yr, to the Hon Jas Caldwell of the Hse o/Reps.

For sale-40 acs of ground about 2 1/2 miles from the Capitol. -Jno G M'Donald, Capitol Hill.

$10 reward for strayed bay mare colt, from the commons of Wash City. Jno Peltz

Wash Co, D C. Jos S Merrick, insolvent debtor, confined in the prison bounds of Wash Co for debt. -Wm Brent, clk.

WED NOV 23, 1814
Killed on board the U S Sloop of War the *Wasp*, Johnston Blakeley, Cmder, in the action with his B M's Sloop of War ____, on Sep 1, 1814. Jos Martin, btswn; Henry Staples, Qr Gnr. Wounded: Jas Snellings, clavicle or collar bone fractured by a wad.

Died: on Oct 15, nr New Orleans, in an action with a band of pirates who infested that qrtr, Mr Archibald G King, s/o Mr Ezekiel King, of Wash City, in his 18th yr. The dec'd was attached to the U S schn'r *Carolina*, Capt Henley. He had volunteered his svcs under Lt Crowley & rec'd his mortal wound in the act of charging upon them. His remains were interred the ensuing day in the Prot burial ground.

Stray cow has frequented nr the Little Falls bridge, some mos. Owner is requested to prove property, pay charges & take her away. Jo Brooke

Sale at auction, at the hse of his Excell Mr Daschkoff, Russian Mnstr; furn, piano, etc; under the superintendence of A L Joncherez. -David Bates, auct.

THU NOV 24, 1814
Died: yesterday, Elbridge Gerry, V P of the U S, in his 70th yr, in Wash City. Funeral today at 3 o'clock.

Orphans Crt of PG Co, Md. Prsnl est of Jas Waring, late of said co, dec'd. -Wm Waring, adm of Jas Waring, dec'd.

$20 reward for Chas, negro man. -Marcus S S Waring, nr Magruder's Ferry, PG Co, Md.

FRI NOV 25, 1814
For sale, in Richmond city, all the printing materials & stock in trade of Sam'l Pleasants, dec'd, late printer of the *Va Argus*. -Deborah W Pleasants, admx.

Daniel Parker, late Chf Clk o/the War Dept, appt'd Adj & Inspec Gen in the Army.

SAT NOV 26, 1814
David Clendenin is appt'd Rep in Cong from Ohio, vice Reasin Beall, rsgn'd.

Died: at Camp Clark, nr Fort Strother, on Oct 27, of a pleuritic complaint, Lt Col John Anderson, U S Army.

Oysters, served up in any way desired, at my hse, crnr of E & 11th sts East, Wash City. -Jacob Dixon.

MON NOV 28, 1814
$60 reward for lg bay horse, taken on Aug 24, after the battle of Bladensburg; also a mare & red waggon, with the mkr's & owner's names, J Kline & C Tood, marked on the hind gate. -Saml Bacon, Capt & Q M of U S M C.

Orphans Crt of Wash Co, D C. Prsnl est of Jas M'Kim, late of said city, dec'd. -John M'Kim, adm.

TUE NOV 29, 1814
One Cent Reward-for runaway, Wm Scags, appr to the baking business. -John C Heise

$8 reward for negro woman, Ara, age about 23 yrs, who ran away. -Thos Claxton

I must sell the plantation on which I now live; 2 miles from Wash City, 243 1/2 acs. I am in debt, old & infirm, & cannot manage it. -Wm Bayly

WED NOV 30, 1814
For sale-sundry furn & glasses. -Saml Burch

Orphans Crt of Wash Co, D C. Distribution of the assets in hand of David Whann, dec'd, on Dec 19. Apply to John Wiley, Gtwn. Wm Maffitt, adm, Gtwn.

Female teacher wanted in the female Acad at Raleigh, N C. Jos Gales, Pres of Brd of Trustees, at Raleigh, N C.

THU DEC 1, 1814
Mrshl's sale on Dec 5, at Wilmington, N C; cargo of the ship *Fortuna*. -Beverly Daniel, mrshl.

Elbridge Berry, dec'd, our late V P, another of our Rev worthies; was born in Marblehead, Mass, in 1746; s/o a respectable merchant with a handsome fortune. Rec'd his B A at Harvard in 1762.

Crt martial of Capt Sam'l T Dyson, U S Corps of Artl; guilty of all charges, including drunk while on duty. Sentence-dismissed from the svc. Signed, W Scott. By command, Francis S Belton, Assist Adj't Gen 10th Mil di.

FRI DEC 2, 1814
Union Bank of Alexandria; election of Dirs on Jan 2. -C T Chapman, Cashier.

Sale by auction of all the hsehld furn etc, of John C Brush, oppo the Indian Queen Htl, Dec 12. -David Bates, auct. [N B-The whole for a brdg hse, with furn, may be contracted for with Mr Brush; who now has 16 boarders.]

SAT DEC 3, 1814
Hse o/Reps. Petition of Sarah Easton & Dorothy Storer, dghts & legal reps of the late Robt H Harrison, of Md; to be allowed the commutation of half pay & the grant of land to which their fr was entitiled as aid-de-camp & first Sec to Gen Washington during the Rev war-referred.

Notice-the subscriber forewarns the pblc not to trust or run up any acc'ts with Letitia Hilleary, the w/o Lewis Hilleary; for I am determined not to pay any of her debts or contracts. -Lewis Hilleary, Wash City, D C.

In Chancery-ratify sale of rl est of Elisha Hoskinson, made & reported by Robt Edmonston, as trustee; sold at $5 per ac. -Jas P Heath, Reg C C.

Wash Co, D C. Wesley Carlin, insolvent debtor, confined in Wash Co prison, for debt. -Wm Brent, clk.

Black mare strayed or stolen from the commons, Wash City. -John Orr, nr the P O.

Pvt pvt sale-200 acs of land in PG Co, Md, with small dwlg hse. -Jas Beck

Wm Norris, jr, has opened a wine & liquor store, 256 Mkt st, Balt, Md.

MON DEC 5, 1814
Hse o/Reps. Petition of Wm Thornton & A S Smoot, of Wash City, praying comp for a vessel belonging to them, which was sunk at the entrance of Balt harbor, to aid in defence of that place against the late attack by the enemy. Referred to the cmtee of claims.

TUE DEC 6, 1814
Hse o/Reps. 1-Petition of Jesse Youngs, of Ontario Co, N Y, praying for a pension, having been wounded in the military svc of the U S. Rfrd to cmtee of pensions & Rev claims. 2-Petition of Lewis H C Schutt, of Charleston, S C, praying that certain judgments against the est of his late fr, by the U S, may be remitted. Rfrd.

WED DEC 7, 1814
The Pres of the U S has conferred Brvt Rank on the following ofcrs of the Army, for gallant & meritorious conduct, during the last campaign:
Benj Forsyth, Maj 1st Rfl Rgt, to Lt Col, Feb 6, 1814.
Andrew H Holmes, Capt, 24th Infty, to Maj, Mar 30, 1814.
Robt H McPherson, Capt, Lght Artl, to Maj, Mar 30, 1814.
Geo E Mitchell, Lt Col Artl, to Col, May 5, 1814.
Daniel Appling, Maj 1st Rfl Rgt, to Lt Col, May 30, 1814.
Turner Crooker, Capt 9th Infty, to Maj, Jul 4, 1814.
Henry Leavenworth, Maj 9th Infty, to Lt Col, Jul 5, 1814.
John McNeal, Maj 11th Infty, to Lt Col, Jul 5, 1814.
Nathan Towson, Capt in Artl, to Maj, Jul 5, 1814.
Thos Harrison, Capt in Artl, to Maj, Jul 5, 1814.
Loring Austin, Capt in 42d Infty, to Maj, Jul 5, 1814.
Wm J Worth, 1st Lt 23d Infty, to Capt, Jul 5, 1814.
Geo Watts, 2d Lt Light Dragoons, to 1st Lt, Jul 5, 1814.
Stephen Rector, 3d Lt of Rangers, to 2d Lt, Jul 13, 1814.
Winfield Scott, Brig Gen, to Maj Gen, Jul 25, 1814.
Jas Miller, Col 21st Infty, to Brig Gen, Jul 25, 1814.
Wm McRee, Maj of Engrs, to Lt Col, Jul 25, 1814.

Eleazer D Wood, Bvt Maj to Lt Col, Jul 25, 1814.
John B Murdoch, Capt, 25th Inrty, to Maj, Jul 25, 1814.
Benj Watson, Capt, 25th Infty, to Maj, Jul 25, 1814.
Daniel Ketcham, Capt, 25th Infty, to Maj, Jul 25, 1814.
Edmund B Randolph, 2d Lt, 20th Infty, to 1st Lt, Jul 25, 1814.
Robt Desha, Capt, 24th Infty, to Maj, Aug 4, 1814.
Edmund P Gaines, Brig Gen, to Maj Gen, Aug 15, 1814.
Jacob Hindman, Maj of Artl, to Lt Col, Aug 15, 1814.
Saml D Harris, Capt of Light Dragoons, to Maj, Aug 15, 1814.
Thos Biddle, Capt of Artl, to Maj, Aug 15, 1814.
John T Chunn, Capt 19th Infty, to Maj, Aug 15, 1814.
Alex'r C W Fanning, Capt, 19th Infty, to Maj, Aug 15, 1814.
Wm S Foster, Capt, 11th Infty, to Maj, Aug 15, 1814.
Morril Marston, Capt, 21st Infty, to Maj, Aug 15, 1814.
Benj Birdsall, Capt, 4th Rfl Rgt, to Maj, Aug 15, 1814.
R A Zantzinger, 1st Lt Artl, to Capt, Aug 15, 1814.
Nathaniel N Hall, 1st Lt, 21st Infty, to Capt, Aug 15, 1814.
Jonathan Kearsley, 1st Lt, 4th Rfl Rgt, to Capt, Aug 15, 1814.
Jos Gleason, 1st Lt, 9th Infty, to Capt, Aug 15, 1814.
Chas Cissna, 3d Lt, 19th Infty, to 2d Lt, Aug 15, 1814.
John Watmaugh, 2d Lt, Artl, to 1st Lt, Aug 15, 1814.
Rich'd H Lee, 3d Lt, 4th Rfl Rgt, to 2d Lt, Aug 15, 1814.
Alex'r Macomb, Brig Gen, to Maj Gen, Sep 11, 1814.
Geo Armitead, Maj in Artl, to Lt Col, Sep 12, 1814.
Wm Lawrence, Maj, 2d Infty, to Lt Col, Sep 15, 1814.
Wm A Trimble, Maj, 19th Infty, to Lt Col, Sep 17, 1814.
-D Parker, Adj & Inspec Genr'l.

$25 reward for Jas Kenner, laborer in the Ord Dept, age 21 yrs; deserted from the Lab, *Greenleaf's Point*, Nov 21, 1814; boxer by profession. -N Baden, Lt U S Ord.

Orphans Crt of PG Co, Md. Ordered that Ann Mudd & Benj N Mudd, excs of Thos Mudd, give notice required by law. -Truman Tyler, reg.

Lost-pillow case containing clothing & papers. -David Ramsay, Ross's Tavern, Bladensburg, Md.

Pblc sale on Jan 5, at Mr Leonard Ferrall's tavern, adj tract of land known as *Green Hill*, 700 acs, in Chas Co, Md. -Saml S Hamilton, Edw H Hamilton.

Orphans Crt of Wash Co, D C. Prsnl est of Wm Duvall, late of Gtwn, dec'd. -Sarah Duvall, admx.

Crct Crt of Wash Co, D C. Joanna Barry, cmplnt, against Jas D Barry, adm & *Patrick Barry, & other heirs & reps of Garrett Barry, dfndts. Rg-a decree for the sale of the rl est of Garrett Barry, dec'd; or sum alleged to be due cmplnt by said Garrett Barry. *Reside out of jurisdiction of this crt beyond sea. -Wm Brent, clk.

THU DEC 8, 1814

Hse o/Reps. 1-Bill for the relief of John C Hurlburt, of Chathan, Conn, was further considered. 2-Pet of Isaac Belknap, Lt Col & other ofcrs of Gen Herman's brig of N Y militia, in svc of U S, in behalf of John P Coxe; Paymstr, 20th Regt of said brig; Coxe may not be held accountable for money stolen from him. Referred.

Wash Co, D C. Wesley Carlin, insolvent debtor, confined in Wash Co prison, for debt. -Wm Brent, clk.

One cent reward-for indebted svt girl, Eliz Jane Brayne, not quite 10 yrs of age; ranaway from the subscriber. -W Cooper

Pblc sale on Dec 10th; a small parcel of furn at the hse of Mr Wm Esby, nr the Navy Yd, who is about moving from the city. -David Bates, auct.

FRI DEC 9, 1814

Horrid murder; ltr from Capt Wm Anderson of Marines, to Col F Wharton, dt'd Marine Barracks, Charlestown, Mass, Nov 28, 1814. Sgt Jas M'Kim & pvt Thos Hasey were shot & killed by a marine, Travers, on Nov 27th. They were cld to quell a riot in the barracks. Sgt M'Kim leaves his wife, & bros & srs.

SAT DEC 10, 1814

B H Tomlinson has opened a Hse of Entertainment on Water st, Gtwn.

For sale-the nursery of the subscriber on Rock Crk, 3 miles from Gtwn. -Isaac Peirce

Mrsh'ls sale-at David Dobbyns' tavern, all the right, right, title, etc, of Sam'l Cloaky, to lot 7 in sq 283, with improvements; at the suit of John P Van Ness against said Cloaky & others. -Wash Boyd, mrshl of D C.

MON DEC 12, 1814

Hse o/Reps. Petition of Jas Blahany, of Balt, Md, who opened a small groc store, in ignorance of the law which required him to take out a license; thrown into prison, where he has remained for 6 mos. Referred to the Ways & Means cmtee.

TUE DEC 13, 1814

An adjourned meeting of the Journeymen printers of D C will be held at the hse of Mr H C Lewis, Pa av, Wash. -Wm Duncan, sec.

Charlestown, Virg, Dec 1. On Nov 23, Reuben Cooper, of Loudoun Co, Va, was committed to the jail of this county, for attempting to circulate counterfeit notes.

Mrd: on Dec 8, by Rev Mr McCormick, Mr Zacariah Walker, of Wash City, to Miss Sarah Toulson, d/o Mr Francis Toulson, of PG Co, Md.

Sale by auction; 60 shares of the Gtwn Potomac Bridge Stock & lots in sq 323, Wash. Sold under the authority of a conveyance & covenant from Benj Stoddart, dec'd, to Henry Foxall.

Wash Co, D C. Rhode Butler, insolvent debtor, confined in the prison of Wash Co, for debt. -Wm Brent, clk.

WED DEC 14, 1814
The subscriber will deliver timber of any description. P Hansbrough, jr, Stevensburg, Culpeper Co, Va.

THU DEC 15, 1814
Mrd: on Mon wk, by Rev Geo Towers, Mr Truman Graves, to Miss Eliz Chapman, d/o Thos Chapman, of Harrison Co, Va.

Mrd: on Nov 14, by John Levingston, of Pa, Mr Gilbert Murphy, of *Bell Air*, to Miss Sarah Green, of *Slate Ridge*, & both of Harford Co, Md.

FRI DEC 16, 1814
Killed under the command of Maj Gen Ross, in action with the enemy, on Aug 24, 1814, on the heights above Bladensburg: Capt D S Hamilton, Lt G P R Codd; 95th Light Infty. Lt Thos Woodward, 4th or King's Own. -H G Smith, D A A G

To be sold at the hse of the subscriber, variety of hsehld furn. -Mary McNamara -N L Queen, auct.

John D Davis appt'd Chimney Sweep for Ward 3, Wash City.

SAT DEC 17, 1814
Wanted-for the Shrewsbury & Jersey Stage & Steam Boat Co; 50 horses bet the ages of 7 & 10 yrs. -John D Delacy, agent; Shrewsbury,Mammouth Co, N J.

Hse o/Reps. 1-Petition of Ephraim Morgan, Wm Neafus, & Paul Pomroy, of N Y state, praying that the duty on stills be remv'd; rfrd. 2-Pet of Spencer Glascock, of Va, praying for payment for a waggon & horses lost in the svc of the U S, & comp for use of said waggon; referred.

$50 reward-a certain Wm Thompson Murtland, alias Wm Thompson, who lived in this town many yrs, & who stated his present residence to be in Columbia, Pa, or bet that place & Lancaster, rec'd for us a load of sugar at Pittsburg on Oct 29 last, & was to deliver same to Mr Robt Munro, Gtwn, Col, in 22 days. He has not complied with his contract; we belive he has absconded with the proceeds of the sugar. -R & J Mandeville, Alexandria, D C.

Pblc sale on Jan 6, of some of the prsnl est of Basil Talbert, dec'd: 1 negro woman & 4 girls, corn, fodder & straw, one horse, 5 head of cattle, & 2 feather beds. Order of the Orphans Crt of PG Co, Md. -Peter Talbert, exc.

MON DEC 19, 1814
Notice to the creditors of John Creaver, now in the jail of Franklin Co, Pa; creditors to appear in the Crt Hse in Chambersburg, in said Co. Rg: Creaver-insolvent debtor. -John Creaver

Hse o/Reps. Petition of Johnson Clarke, of Balt praying comp for a lg garden & other prop destroyed by the troops in U S svc-rfrd to Cmtee of Claims.

Pres of the U S conferred the brvt rank of Maj on Capt Alex Sevier, U S M C, for gallantry displayed by him in the field of battle at Bladensburg, on Aug 24.

Pblc sale-deed of trust from Wm Wilson to Rich'd Wallach, trustee; hack #58, a pr of bay horses, and sundry furn. -Rich'd Wallach, trustee.

Notice-John D Davis appt'd Chimney Sweep for the 3d Ward.

TUE DEC 20, 1814
Hse o/Reps. Bill reported for the relief of Wm H Washington; of Wm Robinson & others, ctzns of Knox Co, Ky; read by Mr Yancey of N C.

Notice to the heirs of Philip Waters; distribution of said est in Upper Marlboro, Md, on first Tue in Jan. -Jos Cross, adm P Cross, PG Co, Md

WED DEC 21, 1814
Orphans Crt of PG Co, Md. Prsnl est of Chas Duvall, late of said co, dec'd. -Chas Duvall, exc.

THU DEC 22, 1814
For sale-carriage & harness; enquire at Mr John Carne's Livery Stable, Capt Hill.

Labourers wanted; apply to Maj F Marsteller, Dep Q M Genr'l, at Ft Wash.

FRI DEC 23, 1814
Mrd: in Alexandria, on Dec 20th, by Rev Dr Muir, Francis Adams, Jr, to Miss Mary R Newton, d/o Wm Newton, all of that place.

Election will be held at capt Stephen Parry's Tavern, nr the Navy Yd, on Tue; to elect a mbr of the Common Cncl, to fill the vacancy occasioned by the resignation of Gustavus Higdon. Judges: John W Brashears, Matthew Wright, Wm Prout.

SAT DEC 24, 1814
Runaway-Toney, black man, committed to Wash Co, D C, jail; says he belongs to Saml Frederick of Ky. -C Tippett, for W Boyd, Mrshl.

MON DEC 26, 1814
Lost-pkt bk on Capt Hill on Dec 23. -Wm Riter, Wash Co, Md.

WED DEC 28, 1814
Mrd: at Norfolk, on Dec 13, by Rev Mr Symes, Lt Benedict Neale, U S N, to Miss Mary Whittle, eldest d/o Conway Whittle, of that place.

Mrd: on Dec 26, at Wash City, by Rev Jas Laurie, Wm Ambrose Loyd, merchant of Fred'ktown, Md, to Mrs S H Young, eldest d/o Gen Bull, of Northumberland, Pa.

Orphans Crt of PG Co, Md. Ltrs of adm on est of Benj Belt, jr, late of said co, dec'd. -Levi Belt, adm.

THU DEC 29, 1814
Francis Locke, a decided Rpblcn & enlightened Patriot, is elected by the Leg of N C to the Senate of the U S, vice David Stone, rsgn'd.

Hatters Attend! Sale of 7,000 racoon skins & 170 lbs of beaver. -Sam'l Swayne, Winchester, Va.

Died: at Alexandria, on Dec 26, after a short illness, Wm Newton, merchant, of that place. Hsbnd, fr, friend & ctzn.

Died: at Alexandria, a few days ago, Burdett Fitzhugh, a resident of this city, 2d s/o Judge Nicholas Fitzhugh, of the former place. He was a young gentleman much respected, & whose loss is deeply lamented by his friends.

Geo Kneller on Pa av, Wash, oppo the Canal, has Dry Goods of all descriptions.

Chs Moxley intending to leave this Dist, has disposed of his stock of goods & requests claims against him for payment to be presented. -Chs Moxley

FRI DEC 30, 1814
Died: at Alexandria, on Dec 26, Lt Walter Berryman, in his 22d yr; a young ofcr of promise in his profession; a ntv of Westmoreland Co, Va.

Died: on Dec 26, Mr John Sullivan, an old inhabitant of Alexandria.

The teacher at Staunton Acad, as prof of languages, in the rm of Mr Wm White, dec'd, is Rev John Boyle. He was educated at Trinity College, Dublin. -Alex St Clair, Pres; Saml Clark, Sec.

Journey saddler wanted-John Peltz, Wash City.

John Hagerty, jr, has rec'd an assortment of beaver hats; manufactory, crnr of Bridge & Jefferson sts, Gtwn.

SAT DEC 31, 1814
Died: in Wash City, on Dec 30, Rich'd Brent, a Senator from Va. He has left behind no mourning wife or chldrn, but a long train of friends.

DAILY NATIONAL INTELLIGENCER
WASHINGTON, D C
1815

MON JAN 2, 1815

Wheat-I will pay the highest price given in Gtwn, delivered at my warehse or at the Columbia Mills. -Geo Johnson

TUE JAN 3, 1815

Wash Co, D C. Jas Gillespie, insolvent debtor, confined in Wash Co prison, for debt. -Wm Brent, clk.

Mrd: on Dec 27, by Rev Mr Reed, Mr Robt Ould, of Gtwn, to Miss Panlina Gaitier, of Montg Co, Md.

Mrd: on Jan 1, by Rev Alex'r M'Cormick, Mr Chas Ashworth, to Miss Lois M'Kim, all of Wash City.

Mrd: on Jan 1, by Rev Alex'r M'Cormick, Mr John M'Kim to Miss Augusta Porter, all of Wash City.

Horse stolen with equipage, nr St Jos' Chr, in St Mary's Co, Md, on Dec 25; $20 reward. -Athan's Ford, Gtwn, D C.

WED JAN 4, 1815

$30 reward for Stanley Watkins, about 28 yrs of age, negro man; absconded from his mtr's svc on Thu. -Thos Claxton

THU JAN 5, 1815

Died: at Bladensburg, on Jan 4, in her 53d yr, after a short illness, Mrs Dorothy Lowndes, relict of Benj Lowndes, dec'd. She leaves a family of affectionate chldrn.

FRI JAN 6, 1815

Hse o/Reps. 1-Petition of Thos Sprigg, of Balt, praying comp for hempen yarns, destroyed by order of an ofcr of the U S army of Balt, upon the late attack of the British forces on Balt; rfrd. 2-Pet of Geo Hite, of Va, praying comp for negroes stolen from his fr by the Cherokee Indians; rfrd.

Family flour for sale. -Jos Dean, Alexandria.

Copartnership dissolved by mutual consent; Coachmkg business; Doe & Bowling. Dearborn Doe requests immediate payment & intends to leave the city in a short time. Robt Bowling will continue the business.

SAT JAN 7, 1815
Six cents reward for appr boy, Benj Sheppard, aged about 16 yrs. -Wm Serrin

Elisha Riggs & Geo Peabody have purchased of E Riggs & Beeding, their entire stock of dry goods; business to commence at the old stand, nr the Union Bank.

Hostages Returned. The following Americ ofcrs have been held for a long time by the British gov't; they arrived at Plattsburgh from Quebec.

John Machesney, maj 6th U S I
Alex'r McEwen, capt 16th infty
Thos Karney, capt 14th infty
John Waring, 1st Lt 14th infty
John W Thompson, 1st Lt 14th infty
Nich N Robinson, 2d Lt 14th infty
Massom Mude, 2d Lt 14th infty
Jas Smith, 3d Lt 25th infty
W Dennison, Ensign
Henry Flemming, capt 14th infty
Isaac Roach, capt 23d infty
Sidney Smith Lt U S N
Thos Randall, 1st Lt 14th infty
Geo Murdock, 2 Lt 14th infty
David P Polk, 2d Lt 12th infty
Saml B Griswold, 3d Lt 23 infty
J Chanson, Lt
[-J B Palmer, Deputy-Waggon-mstr.]

MON JAN 9, 1815
Pblc auction at the store of Thos C Wright; mscl piece goods, etc; Gtwn, D C.

TUE JAN 10, 1815
We hear at second hand, that Richd Bache is appt'd Postmstr of Phil city, vice Michl Leib, rmv'd.

Hse o/Reps. 1-Petition of Joshua Penney, of L I, stating that he was taken from his bed in the night-time by an armed British force & carried on board a British ship of war, confined as a P O W for 9 mos; praying remuneration; rfrd. 2-Pet of John F McGrew, of Miss terr, praying further time to establish his right to a tract of land in said terr; referred.

Ladies with ltrs in the Wash City, P O, Jan 1, 1815:

Lucy Adams	Mrs Cath Ardrey	Alida Armstrong
Prudence Akins	Miss Eliza Albert	Mrs Sally Cheeny
Mrs Champe Carter	Eliz Clubb	Mrs Fatimre Cooners
Mrs Anne Cassanave	Mary Crowley	Miss Eliz Crady
Miss Fanney Dixon	Mrs Mary B Davis	Miss Sarah Estep
Miss Phillis Franklin	Mrs Wm Frost	Miss Anne Fowke
Mrs Jas Hamilton	Mrs Rachel Harris	Mrs Hebron
Mrs Maria Handy	Mrs Mary Hodges	Mrs Jane Hyatt
Mrs Fanny Hampton	Mrs Eliza James	Mrs Mary King
Mrs Sally Kanah	Miss Lee [2]	Mary Lowry
Jane Love	Miss Nelly Lucus	Mrs Mary Mudd
Mrs Mary O'Brien	Letty Perkins	Maria Piercy
Mary Richardson	Mary A Rowland	Mrs Mary Randles
Eleanor Sward	Eliz Speage	Betsey Speak
Eliz Speake	Ann D Stock	Deborah Spooner
Sarah Sherlock	Mary Anne Steward	Mrs Mary Slaye

Mrs B Stelle   Eleanor Talbutt   Mrs Dolly Thorper
Mrs Walton   Cath Ann Wayne   Polly Walker
Miss Anne White   Anne Yonge   Sarah H Young
Mrs Mgt Young
Mrs Harriet Baltimore

Six cents reward for appr boy, Peter Goodyear, aged about 19 yrs. -Barbara Miller

Crct Crt of U S for D C. Pblc sale of the prop lately possessed by Lewis Deblois; brick warehse on sq 907, & a crnr lot on sq 907; land in Camden Co, Ga, one tract of 500 acs, one of 1397 acs, one of 496 acs, & an undivided moiety of a tract of 17,579. -Buller Cocke, Edmund Law, trustees.

WED JAN 7, 1815
Phil, Jan 7. Dr Caspar Wistar, late one of the V P's of the American Phil Soc, was elected to the Chr of the Soc, vice Mr Jefferson, having resigned the Presidency.

$50 reward for runaway, John Bradley, negro man, about 35 yrs of age. -Cartwright Tippett, lvg in Wash City.

Wash Co, D C. Case of John S Newton, insolvent debtor, confined in Wash Co prison for debt. -Wm Brent, clk.

Hse o/Reps. John C Hurlburt, of Chatham, Conn, now confined in prison in Hartford, Conn, to be discharged; provided however, that nothing contained in this act shall exonerate any property which the said Hurlburt now has, or hereafter may acquire. -Langdon Cheves, Spkr of Hse o/Reps, John Gaillard, Pres, pro tem, of Senate, apprv'd Jas Madison.

THU JAN 12, 1815
Died: on Jan 10, Mrs Mary Young, relict of the late Notley Young, of Wash City, in her 72d yr.

FRI JAN 13, 1815
Aquila Webb, of PG Co, Md, insolvent debtor, to be discharged from prison. -Daniel Clarke, Assoc judge; John Read Magruder, clk.

<u>Brevets for gallant & meritorious svcs granted by the Pres of the U S on:</u>
Thos Aspinwall, Lt Col 9th Infty, brvt Col Sep 17.
Jas M'Donald, Lt Col 1st Rifle, brvt Col, Sep 17.
Talbot Chambers, Maj 4th Rifle, brvt Lt Col Sep 17.
Geo M Brook, Maj, 23d Infty, brvt Lt Col Sep 17.
Donald Fraser, 1st Lt 15th Infty, brvt Lt Col Sep 17.
Richd H Lee, brvt 2d Lt 4th Rifle, brvt 1st Lt Sep 17.
Saml Riddle, 3d Lt 15 Infty, brvt 2d Lt Sep 17.
Patrick O'Fling, 3d Lt 9th Infty, brvt 2d Lt Sep 17.
Joshua Brant, 2d Lt 23d Infty, brvt 1st Lt Sep 17.
Geo Bomford, Maj of Engrs, brvt Lt Col Dec 22.

John E Wool, Maj 29th Infty, brvt Lt Col Sep 11.
Danl Appling, brvt Lt Col 1st Rifle, brvt Col Sep 11.
Jos G Totten, brvt Maj Engrs, brvt Lt Col Sep 11.
Alex'r S Brooks, Capt Artl, brvt Maj, Sep 11.
Geo M'Glassin, Capt 15th Infty, brvt Maj Sep 11.
White Youngs, Capt 15th Infty, brvt Maj Sep 11.
Edw De Russy, 1st Lt Engrs, brvt Capt Sep 11.
Geo Trescott, 2d Lt Engrs, brvt 1st Lt Sep 11.
John Mountfort, 1st Lt Artl, brvt Capt Sep 11.
Chester Root, 1st Lt Artl, brvt Capt Sep 11.
Harold Smyth, 1st Lt Artl, brvt Capt Sep 11.
J J Cromwell, 2d Lt Artl, brvt 1st Lt Sep 11.
-D Parker, Adjt & Inspec Genr'l.

Died: on Jan 13, in her 41st yr, Mrs Christiana Marsteller, consort of Mr Philip G Marsteller, of Alexandria.

Ezekiel Hildreth, late of Harvard Un, has opened a pvt Acad for both sexes in the hse contiguous to Mr Wash Boyd's, on F st, Wash City.

Furn sale at the hse occupied by Capt Bacon, on Va av, bet Danl Carroll's & Capt Smallwood, nr the Navy Yd. -David Bates, auct.

SAT JAN 14, 1815
Mrd: on Jan 13, by Rev Mr Shinn, Mr Wm Righter to Miss Charlotte Sutherland, both of Wash City.

Died: at Quantico, on Dec 26, on his way home, after a long absence from his family, Geo Purcey, in his 43d yr; leaving an affectionate wife & chldrn.

Agent for the Fire Ins Co of Alexandra; Wm Reily, Wash City.

$50 reward for negro man, Chas; has a brother belonging to Mr Edmund Turner, Wash Co, Md. -Sam'l Maddox, Chaptico, St Mary's Co, Md.

MON JAN 16, 1815
Contagious distemper; from the Richmond [Va] Enquirer. Extracts of a ltr from a gentleman in Stafford Co, to this city, dt'd Falmouth, Jan 3.
Jas Waller, just from Aquia, was in pursuit of a Dr to attend his bro, Wm; Mr Garnet died at Aquia a few days ago; John Cooke lays at the point of death; Andrew Leach, his wife, son & dght are dead; old Mr Jas Steward has lost his son, Stephen, & his dght Sally, his dght Nancy is now ill at Mr Norman's place. Old Mr Carpenter & his son are also dead. Mr Ball, just below the Crt-hse, has made 13 coffins in the course of 8 or 10 days. The disease is typhus fever, others call it a violent inflammatory sore-throat, the most of them as a putrid sore-throat.

TUE JAN 17, 1815
Strays taken up by Wm Rutherford, *Greenleaf's Point*, apply to same.

Distillery for sale; being called to the Country, by business requiring my personal attention. Sale of the hse & lot I now occupy, So E st; brick hse is 33' x 60' with attached distillery, Wash. -Wm H Hyles

Wash Co, D C. 1-Nahum Warren, insolvent debtor, confined in the prison bound of Wash Co for debt. 2-Peter Vallet, insolvent debtor, confined in Wash Co prison, for debt. -Wm Brent, clk.

WED JAN 18, 1815
Found on a soap tombstone in the Friend's burying-ground in Arch st. Jos Rakestraw, s/o Wm, shot by a negro, 30th day of Sep 1700, in the 19th yr & 4th mos of his age. [Phil pap]

Jas Nabb appt'd Senator of the state of Md, vice Edw Lloyd, rsgn'd.

Casualties at Wysox, Luzerne Co, Pa. 1-Mrs Lydia Strope was thrown from a light wagon & survived the fall but a few seconds. 2-A child of Mr Nathaniel Hicock, jr, died when its clothes took fire. 3-On Dec 28, Miss Lydia Bolton, aged 15 yrs, died on Fri last, from burns.

Died: on Jan 14, Mr Jos Thomas, in his 61st yr; long a ctzn of Alexandria.

Wash Co, D C. Spencer Moxley, insolvent debtor, confined in the prison bounds of Wash Co. -Wm Brent, clk.

THU JAN 19, 1815
Hse o/Reps. 1-Petition of Campbell O White, prop of an extensive distillery in Balt, praying relief from the burthen of a part of his licence-tax-rfrd. 2-Pet of Hannah Lamont, wid/o Saml Lamont, who was killed & rifled by the enemy, whilst bearer of a flag of truce from Gen Harrison's Hd Qrtrs; praying some provision for the loss of her husband.

Orphans Crt of Wash Co, D C. Prsnl est of Adam Ingham, late a pvt in the U S 2d regt of infty, dec'd. -Jno Hewitt, Reg.

FRI JAN 20, 1815
Died: at his seat in Stafford, Va, on Jan 13, the day he completed his 55th birthday, Danl Carroll Brent. In the space of a fortnight, two brothers, Rich & Danl C Brent, died. Danl was the elder bro.

SAT JAN 21, 1815
$100 reward for the thief who stole 3 horses from the subscribers, living in Wmsport, Wash Co, Md. -John Irvin, Pater A Carns.

Hse o/Reps. Petition of Richd Ridgely, Edw Pie, & C W Hanson, of Md, praying comp for damages on their farms by the encampment of a lg number of Va militia in the svc of the U S-rfrd to the cmte of claims.

MON JAN 23, 1815
H T Beatty, Atty At Law, Gtwn; nrly oppo the Medical Shop of Dr B Bohrer.

Patentees of Looms beware! In 1811, Mr Richd Crosbie deposited in the Patent Ofc a specification of his inventions, improving the loom; he obtained a patent in Jan 1812. -Ch W Goldsborough, sole agent of Richd Crosbie.

Wanted-wish to purchase a good woman servant; also a gardner. -R Ross

TUE JAN 24, 1815
Hse o/Reps. Petition of Ann L Moore, of Tenn, wid/o Lt R Moore, who was killed in action; rfrd to the cmtee of Pensions & Revolutionary claims.

Henry Herford thanks his fellow ctzns for their exertions to extinguish the fire which tk place in his Brewery on Sat. Wash Item.

B L Lear offers his svcs as Atty at Law; ofcs on Pa av, Wash City.

Wash Co, D C, in Chancery, Jun, 1814. Bennet Jarboe, cmplnt, vs Rich B Brashears, dfndnt. Rg-obtain a decree for the sale of a part of lot 1 in sq 348, Wash City, formerly sold by the cmplnt to the dfndnt, but on which is due $55 int; cmplnt resides out of D C. -Wm Brent, clk.

Died: on Jan 10, Mrs Louisa Sophia Bomford, of New Paltz, N Y, w/o Col Geo Bomford, most deepy regretted by all who knew her.

Va Land Ofc, Dec 16, 1814. Rg-one acre & a half of land, in Petersburg, of which Robt Heblethweatt, a ntv of Eng, was seized & possessed at the time of his death, has been found, by an inquest, taken before said escheator, on Oct 21, 1814, to have escheated to this commonwealth. -Wm G Pendleton, Reg'r.

WED JAN 25, 1815
Music! Lost in the snow-storm, a most valuable German Flute. -Wm Esenbeck

THU JAN 26, 1815
Runaway, Lewis, negro boy, committed to the Fred'k Co, Md, jail; says he belongs to Mr Jos Harris, nr Leonard's Town, St Mary's Co, Md. -Morris Jones, shrf, Fred'k Co, Md.

FRI JAN 27, 1815
Stop the runaway. Absconded from me in Dec; mulatto boy named Sam, about 16 yrs old. -John Mulloy, Capitol Hill, Wash City.

The subscriber offers for sale 287 acs of land, about 2 miles from Wash City. -Walter T G B Beall, nr the Eastern Branch Upper Bridge.

Ranaway-Phill, negro fellow, about 25 yrs old; brought up to the barber's business in Richmond, Va; reward-$25. -Caleb Clarke, Winnsborough, S C.

For sale in Sharpsburg, Wash Co, Md, an excellent well built stone hse, 40' x 35'. Apply at Col Michl Nourse's nr the city, or to Mrs Eliz Chapline, nr Sharpsburg.

New Liquor Store. Jos Huddleston & Co; Pa av, Wash City.

SAT JAN 28, 1815
Wash Co, D C. Case of John Jeffers, insolvent debtor, confined in Wash Co prison, for debt. -Wm Brent, clk.

Col Isaac A Coles, U S Army, acquitted of all charges at a Genr'l Crt Martial, begun & holden at N Y C on Dec 18th last. -Robt Bogardus, Pres & Col-41st rgt Infty.

Deserters-sldrs of the 3d Regt of Riflemen, Army of the U S.
Late Blounts Company:
Henry Polk, [properly Hugh,] b in Mecklenburgh Co, N C, age 25 yrs; carpenter; deserted from Charlotte, N C, Jun 1814.
John Edwards, b in N Y, aged 24 yrs; laborer; deserted from Cabarrus Co, N C, Jun 11, 1815.
Jos Harper, b in Tenn, aged 21 yrs; laborer; deserted tom Germanton, N C, Jul 21.
Ira W Adkerson, b in Bedford Co, Va, aged 26 yrs; farmer; deserted from Guilford, N C, Aug, 1814.
John Wilson, b in Pasquotank Co, N C, aged 40 yrs; hatter; deserted from Randolph Co, N C, Sep 9, 1814.
Jas Williams, b in Randolph Co, N C; laborer; deserted from Randolph C H, N C, Sep 12, 1814. [Age not given]
Wm Milwee, deserted from Cantonment Greene, nr Charlotte, N C, Oct 30, 1814.
Jas Broom, b in Cumberland Co, N C, aged 25 yrs; hatter; deserted from Randolph Co, N C, Nov 1, 1814.
Richd Furguson, b in Randolph Co, N C; aged 20 yrs; laborer, deserted do.
Michl Summy, b in Lincoln Co, N C; aged 24 yrs; hatter; deserted from cantonement Greene, nr Charlotte, N C, Nov 13, 1814.
Robt Dean, b in Guilford Co, N C; aged 28 yrs; laborer; deserted from Rowan Co, N C, Nov 10, 1814.
Wm Turner, b in Chatham Co, N C; aged 30 yrs; laborer, deserted from Rowan Co, N C, Nov 20, 1814.
Hardy D Davis, cpl, b in Wake Co, N C; aged 23 yrs; saddler; deserted from camp nr Daville, Va, Nov 26, 1814.
Late Robeson's Company:
Wm B Lynn, b in Chatham Co, N C; aged 29 yrs; laborer; deserted from Laurens, S C, Sep 3, 1814.
Anthony Miller, b in Duplin Co, N C; aged 21 yrs; farmer; deserted from Fayetteville, N C, Sep 19, 1814.
Wm Britt, b in Robeson Co, N C; aged 35 yrs; farmer; deserted from Lumberton, N C, Sep 29, 1814.

Wm Musgrove, b in Liverpool, Eng; aged 28 yrs; schoomstr; deserted from Cambridge, S C, Oct 14, 1814.
Jos Jenikins, b in Rowan Co, N C; aged 19 yrs; bricklayer; deserted from Cambridge, S C to Charlotte, N C, Oct 16, 1814.
Jas Crosby, b in Marion Dist, S C; aged 21 yrs; farmer; deserted from Marion, S C, Oct 17, 1814.
Jas Henderson, b in Robeon Co, N C; aged 25 yrs; gun smith; deserted from Fayetteville, N C, Oct 22, 1814.
Wm Edwards, b in Columbus Co, N C; aged 21 yrs; farmer; deserted from cantonment Greene, nr Charlotte, N C, Nov 1, 1814.
Tarleton Renfrow; aged 18 yrs; deserted at cantonment Greene, nr Charlotte, N C, Nov 10, 1814.
Capt Campbell's Company:
John Daughtery, b in Northampton Co, N C; aged 28 yrs; silver-smith; deserted from Rowan Co, N C, Nov 20, 1814.
Jas Thomas, b in S C; aged 23 yrs; looks like an Indian; deserted from Richmond, Va, Dec 21, 1814.
Capt Brandon's Company:
Wm Lane, b in Culpeper Co, Va; aged 30 yrs; farmer; deserted from Wilkesborough, N C, Aug 3, 1814.
Franklin Caldwell, b in Anson Co, N C; aged 21 yrs; laborer; deserted from Morganton, N C, Aug 30, 1814.
Wm Polk, b in Mecklenburg, N C; aged 38 yrs; farmer; deserted from Ashe c h, N C, Aug 20, 1814.
Jas Yearly, b in Rutherford Co, N C; aged 24 yrs; farmer; deserted from Rutherford c h, N C, Sep 21, 1814.
John Yonts, b in Ashe Co, N C; aged 25 yrs; blacksmith; deserted from Wilkesborough, N C, Sep 25, 1814.
Jesse Still, b in Guilford Co, N C; aged 37 yrs; farmer; deserted on march from Charlotte, N C to Richmond, Va, on Nov 21, 1814.
Capt Colhoun's Company:
Robt Crafton, b in Pitt Co, N C; aged 36 yrs; farmer; deserted from Union c h, S C, Sep 10, 1814.
Adam Huffsteller, b in Lincoln Co, N C; aged 33 yrs; farmer; deserted on march from Charlotte, N C, to Richmond, Va, Nov 20, 1814.
Daniel Toler, b in Orangeburg dist, S C; aged 18 yrs; farmer; deserted from Edgefield, S C, Oct 6, 1814.
John Hembree, b in Pendleton dist, S C; aged 27 yrs; carpenter; deserted from Franklin, Geo, not date known.
Ephraim M'Lain, b in York dist, S C; aged 27 yrs; farmer; deserted on Nov 25, 1814.   -W J Gordon, Acting Adj 3d Rifle Regt.

Orphans Crt of Chas Co, Md. Prsnl est of John Chandler Cox; & ltrs of adm d b n on est of Saml Cox & Sarah Cox, all of Chas Co, dec'd. -Walter Cox

Crct Crt of Wash Co, D C, in Chancery. Sarah Cannon, admx of John Cannon, dec'd, John Naylor & Nickolas Wedding, cmplnts, against Benj Mackall, Leonard Mackall, Richd Mackall & John Horrell & Rebecca Weems, chldrn & heirs of

Barbara Horrel, dec'd; late Barbara Mackall, Walter Mackall & Mgt Weems, chldrn & heirs of Levin Mackall, dec'd, & Rebecca Covington, late Rebecca Mackall, who are the heirs at law of Walter Mackall, dec'd; Wm Bayley, Jas S Morsell, trustee of Wm Bayley's est, & Ezekiel Masters, Geo Masters, Enoch Spalding & Eliz his wife, late Eliz Masters, Walter Mitchell & Matilda, his wife, late Matilda Masters, Jas Wedding & Nancy, his wife, late Nancy Masters, John Masters & Benj Masters, [which said John & Benj Masters are under the age of 21 yrs] chldrn & heirs of John Masters, dec'd. Rg-two tracts of land, 86 acs, in Wash Co, D C cld *Discovery,* & *French's Discovery*; exhaustion of prsnl est of John Masters; all except Benj Mackall, Jas S Morsell & Ezekiel Masters, reside without the jurisdiction of this crt. John Cannon,, John L Naylor & Nichodemus Wedding, sureties of bonds of Masters. -Wm Brent, clk.

MON JAN 30, 1815
Extract of a ltr from an ofcr of the frig *Pres*, to his friend in N Y, dt'd on board H B M frig *Pomona*, at sea, Jan 20. News of our capture the night after sailing from Sandy Hook; poor Lts Babbitt, Hamilton, & acting Lt Howell are no more.

TUE JAN 31, 1815
Thos Dougherty, of Ky, appt'd Clk of the Hse of Reps, v P Magruder, rsgn'd.

Died. on Jan 24, Mrs Rachel Shoemaker, w/o Mr David Shoemaker, of the Soc of Friends, in her 54th yr.

Orphans Crt of PG Co, Md. Sale of all hsehld & kitchen furn of John Smith Brookes, dec'd; bet 30 & 40 negroes; stock & utensils. -Benj Brookes, adm of John Smith Brookes, Upper Marlboro, Md.

Wash Co, D C. Jacob Dixon, insolvent debtor, confined in Wash Co prison, for debt. -Wm Brent, clk.

Md-in Chancery, Jan 18, 1815. John Bennet & Saml Cecil, vs John Lewis, Sarah Harvey, John Harvey, Mgt Johnson, Joshua Johnson, Jas Thorpe, Mgt Thorpe, Susanna M'Claskey, John M'Claskey, Thos M'Claskey, Anna M'Claskey, Jos M'Claskey, Chas M'Claskey, Emelina M'Claskey & Arthur M'Claskey. Rg-cnvynce of land in Montg Co, Md, cld *Strats Never,* about 125 acs. Some yrs ago John Lewis sold to Jos Lewis the said tract, for 130 lbs & rec'd payment for same; Jos Lewis lived there until his death; John Lewis also died. Jos L died without a will & left one child, Mgt Lewis, who mrd Jas Thorpe. John L, at the time of his death, left John Lewis, Thos Lewis, Sarah Lewis, who mrd John Harvey, Mgt Lewis, who mrd Joshua Johnson, since which Thos Lewis hath died, the rest being still alive residing in Ohio. Mgt Thorpe & Jas Thorpe, her hsbnd, live in Va; they, on Aug 24, 1805, by power of atty, authorized Chas F Wall to sell & cnvy said land for their emolument; Wall did sell same to cmplnts on May 26, 1814. The heirs of the said John Lewis, or some of them, made a pretended sale to Jos M'Claskey, without any right or authority to do so. -Jas F Heath, Reg C C.

WED FEB 1, 1815
Wanted to rent-a brick bldg in the vicinity of O'Neale's Htl, Wash. -John Frank

Coshocton Co, Ohio, Crt of Common Pleas, Dec term, 1814, in Chancery. Chas Wms vs Hedijah Bailes. Rg-Chas Williams prays to be invested in the title of lots 19 & 20, & 99 acs of lot 33, 1 ac of lot 34, in 3d qrtr, in the 8th twnshp & 6th Range U S Military Land, agreeable to a deed executed by the Coll of non-resident taxes for the 4th dist in Ohio, aforesaid, to the said Chas Williams, which said land the said Hedijah Bailes was seized & possessed. -A Johnston, clk.

THU FEB 2, 1815
Pblc sale of one sorrel mare, prop of John S Newton, insolvent, for the benefit of his creditors. -Saml Speake, trustee; Nichs L Queen, auct.

John Johnson, negro man, age about 25 yrs, committed to the goal of Fred'k Co, Md; says he belongs to Mr Fenley Roy, lvg about 5 miles from Wilkinson, Ga. -Morris Jones, shrf, Fred'k Co, Md.

M A Chantelin informs the ladies of Gtwn & Wash City, that she has rec'd a lg assortment of fashionable winter goods; at the New Store, Bridge st, Gtwn.

FRI FEB 3, 1815
Com'rs to meet on Capt Hill on Feb 7. -Thos Swann, Francis S Key, John Law.

SAT FEB 4, 1815
U S Military Warrants. Wanted a few hundred acs. Apply to Michl Nourse, Wash City.

Mrd: on Jan 31, by Rev Mr Balch, Mr John Gulick, of Princeton, N J, to Miss Mgt Y Wiley, d/o the late Rev David Wiley, of Gtwn.

Died: on Jan 24, in the village of New Balt, Fauquier Co, Va, John Callighan, a ntv of Ire, a boot & shoemkr by profession. His bro, Peter Callighan, is requested to come forward & take charge of the remaining prop, by a friend to the dec'd.

MON FEB 6, 1815
Phil, Feb 3, 1815. We understand that the Govn'r of Mass, has appt'd the Hon Harrison G Otis, Wm Sullivan, & Thos H, Delegates from Mass to the Gov't of the U S, to solicit a redress of grievances.

Elias B Caldwell has a Power of Atty from Mrs Blodget, relict of the late Saml Blodget, with full power to settle her claim of dower in lots in Wash City, & other prop in D C. -Elias B Caldwell

TUE FEB 7, 1815
Phil Wool Warehse, 31 North Front st, Phil, Pa. -Henry Simpson, com merchant.

WED FEB 8, 1815
Hse o/Reps. 1-Act for the relief of Farrington Bakelow, adm of Mary Rappleyea; rg-loan ofc certificates issued to latter from the ofc of N J, both dt'd Jun 8, 1778; one for $600, the other for $500, with int. 2-Relief of Wm Arnold; rg-loan issued from the loan ofc of Mass for $600 on Oct 25, 1777, payable to Christopher Clark. 3-Relief of Jas Brahany, of Balt City, release after long confinement in jail, at the suit of the U S, for selling spirituous liquor w/out license. -Langdon Cheves.

$15 reward for 2 horses who broke away from the srvnt on Feb 5. -Benj G Orr.

Died: on Feb 2, at Gtwn, Mrs Anne Ott, consort of Dr John Ott of that town.

Died: in Wash City, on Feb 4, Mr F Shuck, baker & prop of the City Baths, an upright & industrious ctzn, who has left a wife & svr'l chldrn to regret his loss.

Runaways-Geo, negro, says he belongs to Mr Thos Richards, of Culpepper Co, Va. Andrew, negro, says he belongs to Mr Janet Cussein, of St Mary's Co, Md.
-C Tippett, for W Boyd, mrshl

THU FEB 9, 1815
In the engagement bet the U S ship *Wasp*, & the British brig of war *Reindeer*, 2 ofcrs on the *Wasp* were wounded, viz Henry S Langdon, Jr, & Frank Toscan, Midshipmen of Portsmouth, N H. They have both since died from their wounds.

New invention may be seen at the Patent Ofc, a new & improved machine for weaving cloth by water. -Hezl Healy, Patentee.

Obit-died: Col Jas Henderson, of this country; fell at the siege of Orleans. He leaves an affectionate wife & 8 lovely chldrn.

FRI FEB 10, 1815
Mrd: on Feb 2, by Rev Wm H Wilmer, Alex'r Hunter, of Alexandria, to Miss Louisa Ann Adelaide Chapman, of Alexandria Co.

Died: on Jan 31, Cle_ Moore, aged 66 yrs. He had resided in the town of Alexandria for more than 30 yrs.

SAT FEB 11, 1815
Will be sold; part of the prop of Fred'k Myers, dec'd, consisting of 30 head of sheep, a horse, & some wearing apparel. -Thos Eno, adm.

The partnership of Wms & Carrolls is this day dissolved by mutual consent; exhibit claims to Elie Williams. -Elie Williams, Ch Carroll, of *Belle Vue*, Danl Carroll, of *Dudn*. Gtwn.

Pblc sale of the brick hse in Bladensburg, lately occupied by Benj Stoddert, dec'd. -Richd T Lowndes, Trustee, Bladensburg, Md.

MON FEB 13, 1815
Maj Gen Jacob Brown departed hence on Sat morning, on his return to the frontier.

Hse o/Reps. An act to extend the time of Oliver Evans' patent for his improvement on steam engines; patent issued Feb 14, 1804.

TUE FEB 14, 1815
Notice. The pay due Richd Stewart, as a Messenger of the Hse o/Reps, will be stopped in the hands of Mr Dougherty. The pblc are cautioned against trading for it. -Thos H Herndon

Orphans Crt of Mong Co, Md. Pblc sale at the late dwlg of Henry C Pierce, dec'd; 1 negro woman & 4 chldrn. -John Pierce, adm of Henry C Pierce.

To Rent-3 story brick tavern, lately occupied by Jacob Holtzman, dec'd, on High st, Gtwn, oppo Mr Danl Bussard's store. Apply to Abner Ritchie, Gtwn, or the subscriber, Fredericktown. -Henry M'Cleery

WED FEB 15, 1815
Orphans Crt of Wash Co, D C. Prsnl est of Verlinda Selby, late of said co, dec'd. -Pamela Selby, admx.

Pblc sale of prop in Wash City, of Nicholas Voss; at the suit of Wm Herbert, adm of John Potts, against the said Nicholas Voss & John L Naylor. -Wash Boyd, Mrshl.

THU FEB 16, 1815
Phil, Feb 14. The lady of Albert Gallatin has rec'd a ltr from him, dt'd Ghent, Dec 24, wherein he states-*We have this day signed a Treaty of Peace highly honorable to the U S.*

Mrd: in Providence, R I, on Feb 4, by Rev Mr Edes, Chas Morris, Capt in the U S Navy, to *Mrss Harriet Bowen, y/d/o Dr Wm Bowen. [*as written]

PG Co, Md, Crt, Sep term, 1814. Com'rs appt'd on the petition of Jasper M Jackson for a division or sale of rl est of Alex'r Jackson, state that the est cannot be divided. -John Read Magruder, clk P G C C.

FRI FEB 17, 1815
Hse o/Reps. An act for the relief of Benj Wells, John Wells, Wm Erving, Jas Brice, John Webster, & Jos Junkin, late collectors of internal duties in Pa-audit & settle same.

SAT FEB 18, 1815
The trustees of the pblc schools, are to meet at the hse of Mr Andrew Way on Monday. -Jas Laurie, Pres.

For sale-prop in Wash City, belonging to the est of Robt Underwood, dec'd. Apply to Jno Underwood, Thos Underwood.

MON FEB 20, 1815
Died: at his residence, in Fauquier Co, Va, on Jan 24, Dr Gustavus Horner, in his 54th yr. Entered the Rev war as a pvt; after the war he settled in Va.

Horse for sale at my stable. -Wm A Scott

TUE FEB 21, 1815
Election on Mar 13th for the purpose of choosing 15 dirs. Wm Paton, jr, cashier; Mechanics Bank of Alexandria.

WED FEB 22, 1815
Came as a stray, a black cow. -Cath Mara, Greenleaf's Point. Local Item.

THU FEB 23, 1815
Capt Jonathan Kearsley, of the Rifle Corps, has been appt'd an Assist Adj Gen in the Army of the U S, to rank from Aug 20, 1814, on which day, in a skirmish nr Ft Erie, he rec'd a wound which has disabled him from further active svc.

Died: Feb 14, Gen Jas Singleton, Pres of the Winchester Bank; leaving a wife & 7 chldrn, most of them of tender age.

Died: in Gtwn, on Feb 17, in his 19th yr, Mr Edw S Isaacs, the eldest s/o Col Ralph Isaacs.

Ranaway-Nelson, negro man, aged about 30 yrs; persuaded away with him, my son, King Prather, who will be 13 yrs old next Mar. Deliver my son to me in Laurens Dist, S C. -Josiah Prather.

FRI FEB 24, 1815
John M'Leod informs the pblc that he has opened a Tavern on Capitol Hill.

SAT FEB 25, 1815
Persons engaged with the British tender, on Feb 7, 1815, a the Ice Mound, nr Jas' Island, Dorchester Co, at present ascertained, or recollected. [Easton, Md.]

Jos Stewart	Moses Navy	Wm Geohagan
John Bell	Moses Ceohagan	Robt Travers
Henry Travers	Danl Travers	Matthias Travers

-Jos Stewart, pvt in the militia of Dorchester Co, Md. -Henry Haskins, Dep mrshl for Dorchester Co, Md.

Died: on Feb 23, at Ellicott's Mills, where he had recently removed to, Edw Aisquith, in his 36th yr. [Local Item]

MON FEB 27, 1815
Mrd: on Feb 16, by Rev Mr Gadsden, Maj Alex'r Sevier, U S M C, to Miss Jane Bacot, d/o Thos W Bacot, of Charleston, S C.

Died: at N Y, on Feb 23, of a fever which confined him for svr'l days, Robt Fulton, well known as the Author of many noble inventions.

TUE FEB 28, 1815
Died: after a short illness, at *Mt Air,* his residence, in Chas Co, Md, on Feb 19, Col Luke F Matthews, aged 41 yrs. A bereaved widow, & numerous offspring, survive.

Wash Co, D C. Francis Beveridge, insolvent debtor, confined in the prison bound of Wash City, for debt. -Wm Brent clk.

WED MAR 1, 1815
Mrd: on Feb 22, at Clarksburgh, Md, by Rev B Waugh, Edmund Fitzgerald, of U S Navy, to Miss Mary H Bushby, late of Wash City.

Coach & harness mkg, crnr of Chatham st & M'Clellan's alley, adj the Pblc Fountain Stables, kept by Joel Morgan. Jos R Brooks, his late foreman, taken into partnership under the firm of Everson & Brooks. -Jos Everson, Balt, Md.

THU MAR 2, 1815
For rent-2 story brick hse in Gtwn nr Mr Walter & Clement Smiths, presently occupied by Mr John Haw. -Wm Digges, living in Gtwn.

New Orleans; hd-qrtrs, 7th Military Dist. Adj Genr'l ofc, Jan 31, 1815. Capt M'Mahan & Pace, & Lt Cramford, of Gen Coffee's brig, in the action of Dec 23, fell like freemen worthy of the name; Col Anderson, of Maj Gen Carroll's div, fell in a sortie on the 9th, at the head of his command. -By command, Robt Butler, Adj't General.

PG Co, Md. Commissioners appt'd on petition of Josias Simpson & Ann Brian, for a division of the rl est of John Simpson; number of parties & small quantity of land, the est cannot be divided. -Jos N Burch, grdn.

Ranaway, Donald Chace, negro fellow, age about 23 yr. Nathan Porter, of Chas, living in Annarundle Co, Md, nr Elicott's Mill.

FRI MAR 3, 1815
Hse o/Reps. Daniel Perine, of the Indiana terr is permitted to bec the purchaser at pvt sale of the s e qrtr of section 25, of twnshp 6, in range 1, west, in Cinc dist.

Hero of the Revolution-Gen Francis Marion; history of this sldr; documents furnished by Brig Gen P Horry, of Marion's brig, & by his nphw, the Hon Robt Marion, late of Cong, price $1. M L Weems, Author of *Biography of Wash*, has a few copies left.

Died: on Feb 26, in his 56th yr, Maj Thos Beatty, Rev ofcr, of Gtwn, in this Dist; affectionate hsbnd & fr. -Gtwn, D C, Mar 2.

Anacostia Bridge Co; directors for 1815: Thos Ewell, Jesse Ewell, Thos Murray.

SAT MAR 4, 1815
Banj Pond, a Rep elect to Cong from N Y, has died since his election.

Acts passed by the 13th Cong at their 3d session: acts for the relief of John Chalmers, jr; of John Castile, of New Orleans City; of John C Hurlbert, of Chatham, Conn; of Wm Robinson & others; of Wm Arnold; of Jas Brahany; of Farrington Barkelow, adm of Mary Rappleyea; of Western Jenkins & others; of Benj Wells & others; of Jos Perkins; of Isaac Smith & Bratton Caldwell; of Harry Nimmo-of Warren, in R I; of Uriah Coolidge & Jas Burnham; of Daniel Perine; of Jacob Shinnick & Shultz & Vageler, of Christian Chapman, & legal reps of John Calet, dec'd. Acts for the relief of Joshua Sands-late coll of N Y port; of Edw Hallowell, of Phil; of Solomon Frazer & reps of Chas Eccleston, coll of the Port of Vienna, Md; of heirs of Jas Hynum, of Miss Terr-widow, Mgt Hynum; of Wm H Washington; of Thos Sprigg nr Balt; of Wm P Bennett, of N Y state; of Jas Savage & others.

MON MAR 6, 1815
Died: on Mar 3, after a short illness, Mrs Sarah B M'Kinney, consort of Col John M'Kinney, of Alexandria.

Died: on Mar 1, in his 42d yr, Capt Theodore Skinner, long a respectable inhabitant of Alexandria, & lately one of the firm of Bayne & Skinner.

Appointments made by the Pres, with the consent of the Senate:
Fulwar Skipwith, to be Cnsl for the U S at Paris.
J R Fenwick, late a Col in the Army, to be Cnsl at Alicante.
Wm Drayton, late a Col in the Army, to be Cnsl at L'Orient.
Dan'l Strobel, of S C, to be Cnsl at Nantz.
Wm B Barney, to be Cnsl at Trieste.
Rich M Hall, of Pa, to be Cnsl at Barcelona.
Jas Murray, former Cnsl, to be Cnsl at Liverpool.

TUE MAR 7, 1815
Hse o/Reps. Mrshl to discharge Edw Martin, of Newport, R I, from imprisonment.

All responsibility on the part of Wm Jarvis, in the mercantile hse established in this city under the firm of Wm Jarvis & Co, ceased on Mar 5, 1811; Jas Eames is responsible for all the transactions of the said hse of Wm Jarvis & Co. Signed: Jas Eames, Wm Jarvis. Editors of the Alexandria Gaz please copy.

Wash Co, D C, in Chancery. The Pres, Dirs & Company of the Bank of Columbia, vs Benj Stoddert, Thos Ewell & Eliza his wife, Geo W Campbell & Harriot his wife, Thos Gantt & Ann his wife, Wm Stoddert, Rebecca Stoddert & Christopher

Stoddert. Benj Stoddert in his life time being indebted to the cmplnts for $33,890; a further advance to the sum to the amount in the whole of $50,000 dt'd May 9, 1801. No part of said money was pd or satisfied; Benj Stoddert, the mortgager, has since died, leaving the dfndnts his heirs at law. -Wm Brent, clk.

WED MAR 8, 1815
Lost-on the rd thru High st, Gtwn; a small pktbk. -Peter Colter, Wash City.

To be placed on the pension list of invalid pensioners:

Pensioner:	mo-rate:	commencement date:
Robt Holbert	$5	Mar 13, 1814
Eli Short	$3.75	Mar 13, 1814
Spencer Darnall	$5	Feb 14, 1814
Willis Tandy	$1.25	Apr 17, 1814
Abraham Estes	$3.75	Apr 17, 1814
Saml Sharon	$2.50	Aug 17, 1814
Alex'r Naismith	$2.50	Aug 20, 1814
Isaac Gray	$6.66	Sep 22, 1814
Thos Williams	$2.50	Jul 27, 1814
John R Rappleye	$5	Sep 2, 1814
John Sweeny	$7.50	Mar 17, 1814
Joshua Merrill	$2.50	Aug 4, 1814
Grieve Drummond	$5	Jan 28, 1815
John Ward	$2.50	Nov 30, 1814
Chas Rumsey	$5	Jul 12, 1814
Grant Taylor	$5	Nov 24, 1814
Henry Bateman	$5	Mar 7, 1814
John Norton	$2.50	May 11, 1814
Jesse Young	$5	Aug 6, 1814
John Bell	$10	Sep 9, 1814
Danl Averill	$2.50	Jan 3, 1814
Minny Ryneason	$2.50	Jan 6, 1815
Wm Bond	$5	Dec 8, 1814
Richd Osburn	$2.50	Sep 5, 1814
Julius Turner	$3.75	Aug 18, 1814
Wm Cook	$2.50	Aug 18, 1814
John Frazer	$3.75	Nov 16, 1814
Christopher Sites	$2.50	Feb 17, 1815
Wm Barton	$30	Jan 1, 1815
Wm Barry	$5	Mar 31, 1814
Jas Neal	$5	Sep 13, 1814
Emanuel Kent, jr	$5	Sep 13, 1814
Jeremiah Searcy of S C	$5	Mar 3, 1815

Pensions to be increased: [increased to the sums herein annexed to their names]

Chas Hunton	$2.50	Nov 14, 1814
Thos Williams	$5	Oct 29, 1814
Saml White	$3.75	Dec 28, 1814
Thos Machin	$25	Oct 29, 1814

John M'Clennon	$5	Nov 3, 1814
Richd Gressum	$5	Nov 8, 1814

THU MAR 9, 1815

Hse o/Reps. Audit & settle the claims of: [hses & prop destroyed by order of Maj Gen Alex'r Macomb.]

Jas Savage	Henry Platt	Enoch Chase
John Wells	Dan'l P Clarke	Potash & Cairn
Jos J Green	Levi Platt	Roswell Wait
Edw Wait	Henry Powers	Jonathan Griffin
Chas [as written]	D Backus	Jos S Thomas
Geo Freligh	Mgt Beaumont	Lois Baker
John L Fouquet	Maj A Stone	Noah Broadwell
Nathan Averill, jr		

Patapsco cotton factory in complete operation, nr Ellicott's Mill, Md; warehse-140 Mkt st. Edw Gray, & Co.

Died: at his residence in PG Co, Md, of the prevailing epidemic, on Feb 25, after an illness of 5 hrs, Chas John Carroll, aged 46 yrs. It had only been a few mos since he remv'd from St Mary's Co, Md, where he had suffered greatly from the depredations of the enemy. He has left a lg family who severely feel the loss.

Died: on Feb 24, in his 35th yr, Morris Jones, Shrf of Fred'k Co, Md, after a short but severe illness of a few days.

Died: on Feb 24, after a short illness, at the seat of Jas Patton, of Alexandria, Midshipman Robt Hamersley, in his 19th yr, y/s/o the late Mrs Eliz Brent Hamersley, whose death was announed but a few days ago.

Wash Co, D C, in Chancery. Jacob Hoffman vs Nancy D Hewitt, Jas Hewitt, & Wm D Beale. Obtain bal due [$834.62] with int from the yr 1812, of note given by Thos Hewitt, dec'd, for himself & Jas Hewitt, to the cmplnt with int from May 15, 1804. *Nancy D Hewitt, is widow of the dec'd; Jas Hewitt & *Wm D Beall, securities. *Reside out of D C. [2 splgs of Beale, Beall] -Wm Brent, clk.

FRI MAR 10, 1815

Bank of the Metropolis, Pa av, Wash City. -A Kerr, Cashier.

SAT MAR 11, 1815

Lost-$10 by my appr, Benj McMahon, bet my hse & Gtwn. -Wm H Hamer

Montg Co, Md. Jos Gittings, of said co, brought before me a stray sorrel Gelding. -Thos Gittings, J P

Gtwn Importing & Exporting Co, formed by the following subscribers; subscription bks at Semmes' Tavern, Gtwn, under the following Com'rs:

Geo Peter	Wm Whann	Obadiah Rich

John S Williams	Chas W Goldsborough	Danl Bussard
Wm S Nicholls	Chas King	Romulus Riggs
Nathan Lufborough	John Lee	Thos Hyde
Thos T Gantt	Leonard H Johns	Robt F Howe
At Montg Crt-hse:		
Upton Beall	Honore Martin	Thos P Wilson
At Fredericktown:		
John M'Pherson	Wm Campbell	Dr John Tyler
Geo Baer	John Ritchie	
At Hagerstown:		
Upton Lawrence	Frisby Tilghman	Otho H Williams
John Beall Clagett	John Harry	
At Shepherdstown:		
Col Abraham Shepherd	Jas S Lane	Thos Van Swearengen
At Williamsport:		
Matthew Van Lear	Jacob T Towson	John Irvin
At Cumberland:		
Wm M'Mahon	John Hoye	Roger Perry

Mrd: Mar 7, by Rev Mr M'Cormick, Mr Jas Moore, jr, to Miss Sarah Miller, d/o the late Peter Miller, both of Wash City.

MON MAR 13, 1815
Wanted-a young man from 15 to 18 yrs of age to attend in a Groc Store in Gtwn, nr the Mkt Hse. -Lynde Elliott

Pblc sale of hsehld & kitchen furn, at his hse, nr the Seven Bldgs, Hugh Judge, about to leave Wash City. -David Bates, auct.

TUE MAR 14, 1815
Orphans Crt of Wash Co, D C. Pblc sale at the late dwlg of Josias Ray, late of said co, dec'd, the prsnl est of same. Also, at the same time, the pblc sale of the prsnl est of Ann Ray, dec'd, late of Wash Co. -Saml Hamilton, Agent for Jas Ray, adm.

Orphans Crt of Wash Co, D C. Prsnl est of Patrick C Young, late of said city, dec'd. -Jemima Young, admx.

Deed of trust from Cloe Douglas to me; pblc sale in Piscataway, of 9 negroes. -Thos Mundell

WED MAR 15, 1815
Copy of ltr from Lt Watson, 1st of the late U S Sloop *Argus*, to the Sec of the Navy, dt'd Norfolk, Mar 2, 1815. Killed on board the U S brig *Argus*, Wm H Allen, Cmder, during encounter with the English on Aug 14, 1813:
Richd Delphy, Midshipman, Wm W Edwards, do, Joshua Jones, seaman, Wm Finlay, do, Wm Knowlton, do, Geo Gardner, do. Died of their wounds: Wm H Allen, Capt; Jas White, carpenter; Jos Jordan, btswns mate; Francis Eggert, seaman, Chas Backster. do. Wounded: Wm H Watson, 1st Lt; Colin McLeod,

btswns; John Sniffer, Carp Mate; John Young, Qrtr Mstr; John Nugent, seaman; Jas Hall, do; Jos Allen, do; John Faddon, do; Geo Starbuck, do; Wm Hoventon, do; John Scott, 1st do; John Scott, 2d do.

Died: on Mar 10, after a short but painful illness, Mrs Letitia Colquhoun, of Dumfries, Va; survived by her hsbnd.

Died: on Feb 18, at his seat, nr Wash, Culpeper, Virg, Col Gabriel Smither, in his 39th yr; an affectionate hsbnd & father.

Died: on Tue wk, at Winchester, Virg, Dr Robt Dunbar, of a severe attack of the present prevailing complaint, which terminated his existence in a few days.

THU MAR 16, 1815
Promotions in the , Marine Corps, & Flotilla Svc of the U S.

John Rodgers, Isaac Hull, & David Porter, Capts in the Navy, appt'd Com'rs of the Naval Brd, Feb 28, 1815

Promoted to Capts:
Thos Macdonough, Sep 11, 1814
Wm Crane, Nov 24, 1814
Jas P Leonard, Feb 4, 1815
Chas G Ridgely, Feb 28, 1815
Danl T Patterson, Feb 28, 1815

Lewis Warrington, Nov 22, 1814
Jos Bainbridge, Nov 23, 1814
Johnston Blakely, Nov 25, 1814
Jas Biddle, Feb 28, 1815
Robt T Spence, Feb 28, 1815

Promoted to be Mstrs Commandant:
Robt Henley, Aug 12, 1814
Danl S Dexter, Dec 10, 1814
David Deacon, Dec 10, 1814
Michl B Carroll, Feb 4, 1815
Sidney Smith, Feb 28, 1815
Wm Lewis, Mar 3, 1815

Stephen Cassin, Sep 11, 1814
Jas Renshaw, Dec 10, 1814
Louis Alexis, Dec 10, 1814
John M Gardner, Feb 4, 1815
Thos Brown, Mar 1, 1815

Promoted to be Lts:
Francis H Gregory, Jun 28, 1814
Kervin Waters, Jun 30, 1814
Edw Barnewall, Jul 22, 1814

Chas A Budd, Jun 18, 1814
Wm H Odenheimer, Jul 16. 1814

Promoted to be Lts, Dec 9, 1814:

John M Maury	Fred'k Baury	Benj Cooper
Philip F Voorhees	Wm H Haddaway	Henry Gilliam
John H Clack	Wm Salter	Wm A Spencer
Wm L Gordon	David Geisinger	Richd Winter
John T Wade	John Percival	Jas Ramage
Wm V Taylor	Mervine Mix	Thos M Newell
Edw Haddaway	Chas F M'Cawley	John H Bell
Dulany Forrest	Bladen Dulany	Thos W Magruder
Francis B Gamble	Richd Dashiel	John Taylor
Geo B M'Culloch	Robt Spedden	Geo Senat [dead]
Thos T Webb	Walter G Anderson	Stephen Champlin
Chas T Stallings	Jas M'Gowan	Wm Law
Eli F Vallette	Henry Aulic	Chas T Clarke

Silas Duncan	Thos Cummingham	Isaac M'Keever
Robt F Stockton	Walter N Monteath	Lawrence N Montgomery
A C Stout	Silas H Stringham	Geo Vancleave
Paul Zanzinger	John W Gibbs	John T Drury
Chas E Crowley	Wm Laughton	Nelson Webster
Wm A C Faragut	Rich G Edwards	

Promoted to be Lts, Feb 4, 1815:

Wm K Latimer	Wm Mervine	Gustavus W Spooner
Isaac Mayo	W H Brailsford	Wm Elliot
Thos Crabb		

To Be Surgeons:
Josephus Maria S O'Conway, Jun 27, 1814
Richd K Hoffman, Jul 16, 1814
Richmond Johnson, Mar 1, 1815

Appt'd Surgeon's Mates:
John C Richardson, May 17, 1814   Jno W Pearce, Jun 23, 1814
Archimedes Smith, Jul 5, 1814   Alex'r M Montgomery, Jul 16, 1814

Appt'd Surgeon's Mates, Dec 10, 1814:

Oliver Le Chevalier	Wm Butler	Thos M'Kissoch
John Wise	Thos J H Cushing	Artemas Johnson
John H Steel	S B Whittington	Francis Gerrish
Edw Woodward	Benj A Wells	Enoch Jones [rsgnd]
Wm N Richardson	F P Marleham	Wm D Conway
Jas N Tunstall	Davis D Tuck	Benj S Tyler
Robt C Wardle	Jas Norris	Thos C Gardner
Wm F Bradbury	Benajah Tickner	Wm P Jones
Thos G Peachy	John Mairs	John M'Adam
John S Mughon	Chas Chase	John Manners
Thos V Wiesenthal	Geo B Dean	Amos King
Pliny Morton		

Nathaniel Miller, Jan 6, 1815   Wm Burchmore, Jan 10, 1815

Pursers: Melancton W Bostwick, Jul 16, 1814
John Todd, Mar 1, 1815

Marine Corps. John Hall promoted to be a Maj, Jun 18, 1814.

Promoted to Capts, Jun 18, 1814:

Wm Anderson	Thos R Swift	Saml Miller
John Crabb	Henry H Ford	John M Gamble
Chas S Hanna	Alex'r Sevier	Alfred Grayson
Wm Strong	John Heath	Saml Bacon

Dec 10, 1814:

Henry B Breckenridge	Wm Hall	Francis W Sterne

Marine Corps-to be 1st Lts, Jun 18, 1814:

Francis B D Bellevue	John R Montegut	Philip B D Grandpre
Benj Hyde [dead]	Lyman Kellog	Sam'l E Watson
Wm L Brownlow	Leonard J Boone	Thos W Legge
Wm H Freeman	Jos L Kuhne	Henry Olcott
Chas M Broome	Thos W Bacot	Benj Richardson
Francis B White	Wm Nicoll	Chas Lord

Wm L Boyd	Levi Twigg	Edmund Brooke
John Harris	Saml B Johnston-Jul 16, 1814	

Appt'd to 2d Lts, Feb 28, 1815:

Octavius Crips	Henry Stephens	Richd Auchmuty
Jos Bosque	Thos A Linton	

Appt'd to 2d Lts, Mar 1, 1815:

Richd D Green	Jas Edelin	Geo B English
Jas J Mills	Park G Howell	Francis A Bond
Henry W Kennedy	Wm F Swift	Singleton Duvall
Chas Snowden	Christopher Forde	Jas Martin
John S Machan	Jas T Singletary	

Wm C Garrard, Mar 3, 1815

Note: Capts Anthony Gale, Rich'd Smith, Saml Miller, & Alex'r Sevier, have respecively, rec'd the Bvt rank of Maj.

Flotilla Svc:
Joshua Barney appt'd Capt, Apr 25, 1814. Jacob Lewis, appt'd Apr 26, 1814. Bernard Henry, appt'd Dec 24, 1814. Solomon Rutter, appt'd a Lt, Apr 25, 1814. Solomon Frazier, appt'd a Lt, Apr 26, 1814.

Crct Crt of Wash Co, D C. Pblc sale of lots 148 & 149 on Gay st, Gtwn, late the residence & prop of Benj Patterson, dec'd. -Nathan Lufborough, trustee.

FRI MAR 17, 1815
Edmund I Lee was on Sat chosen Mayor of the town of Alexandria.

Wash Co, D C. John Hart, insolvent debtor, confined in Wash Co prison, for debt.

SAT MAR 18, 1815
Died: on Mar 12, after a lingering complaint, in his 33d yr, Jas Dawes, late Cashier of the Franklin Bank of Balt.

Died: at Copenhagen, Denmark, on Nov 7, 1814, in her 27th yr, Mrs Maria L Pedersen, of Phil, w/o P Pederson, Kt of Dannebrog, Chg des Affaires, & Cnsl Gen from his Danish Maj to the U S of America.

Deserted from the barracks of the 2d regt of Infty, in Wash City, a few days past, 3 sldrs enlisted to serve for 5 yrs, to wit: John Burrish, ntv of N Y C, age 23 yrs, seaman; Walter Golden, born in Chas Co, Md, aged 23 yrs, laborer; accompanied by John Gardner, Irishman by birth, age about 32 yrs, sldr. -Richd Randolph, Lt of the 2d regt of Infty, stationed in Wash City.

MON MAR 20, 1815
City of N Y, Wash Hall, the subscriber informs his friends & pblc, that he has taken the above establishment, & will be happy for their patronage. - P McIntyre, N Y.

Died: at his residence, in Chas Co, Md, on Mar 10, after a short illness, Dr Edw Briscoe, in his 48th yr.

Sawyers-wanted immediately at the Anacosta Bridge. -Thos Murray, mgr.

TUE MAR 21, 1815

Mrd: on Mar 19, by Rev Mr M'Cormick, John Law, of Wash City, to Miss Frances Ann Carter, d/o the late Geo Carter.

Died: on Mar 19, at the Marine Barracks, Sgt Thos M'Can, of Marines, in his 33d yr, after a painful & lingering pulmonary complaint.

Sheriff's sale-part of *Brookfield*, about 127 acs; levied on as the prop of John P Greenfield, & will be sold to satisfy debts due John I Donaldson, adm of Chas S Perrie, for use of Levin Skinner, Geo Rust for use of Peter Hoffman, jr, & Geo Biscoe & Geo W Biscoe. -Geo Semmes, shrf of PG Co, Md.

WED MAR 22, 1815

Killed on board the pvt armed brig *Chasseur*, of Balt, Thos Boyle, cmder, in her action with H B M chr *St Lawrence*, Lt Jas E Gordon, cmder, on Feb 26, 1815: Jacob Burk, carpenter; Alex P White, carp's mate; Hugh Cres, 2d gunner; Sam'l M'Connel, & John Carpenter.

Mrd: on Mar 16, in Md, Thos P Grosvenor, a Rep in Cong from N Y State, to Miss Mary I Hanson.

Phil, Mar 20. Yesterday the Lamberton packet *Traveller*, Capt Lenox, on her passage from Trenton, was struck with a flaw of wind, & upset. Drowned were: Eliza Johnson, w/o John Johnson; Mary Ann & Jas Johnson, chldrn of Eliza Johnson; Mrs Davidson; Mrs Cox, wid/o Genr'l Cox; Sgt Lovett, of Balt; a gr-dght of Mr Jackson.

Crct Crt of Wash Co, D C, in Chancery. Pres, Dirs & Company of the Bank of Columbia, against, Wm Steuart, Vincent King, John Goszler, Eliz Peter, Wm Peter, Jane Peter, Geo H Peter & Jas Peter, Thos Robinson & Sarah his wife, Wm R Thurston & Wm W Robinson, Thos Peter, Geo Peter, Jas Dunlap & Eliza his wife, Mgt Dick, Jas S Lane, David Steuart & Benj S Forrest. Wm Steuart, dfndnt, is indebted unto the cmplnts for $11,919, did on Sep 20, 1810, by deed, cnvy to David Peter, since dec'd, part of lot 48 in Gtwn, DC; also lot 1, cld *Frog-land*; all leasehold int time & term of yr, then to come, on 11 & 12. The legal int in said prop is now in Thos Robertson & Sarah his wife, Wm Richard Thruston & Wm W Robinson, the heir at law of Thos Richardson, formerly of Gtwn. Thos Richardson's heir, & said Jas S Lane are not residents of D C. -Wm Brent, clk.

Wash City, P O-Mr John Bailey will commence the duties of ltr carrier on Mar 21.

THU MAR 23, 1815

Died: at Alexandria, Pa, on Mar 12, the Rev David Bard, mbr of Cong from Pa; dec'd was on his return from Wash, was in apparent good health, on Thu evening. He breathed his last at the hse of Dr Buchanan, his son-in-law.

Died: at *Honeywood*, Berkely Co, Va, on Mar 5, in her 21st yr, Mrs Jane Colston, w/o Edw Colston, & d/o the late Chas Marshall, of Faquier Crt Hse, Va.

Orphans Crt of PG Co, Md. Prsnl est of John Smith Brookes, late of said co, dec'd. -Benj Brookes, adm.

FRI MAR 24, 1815

Val prop for sale-the hse & lot on Cherry st, now occupied by Judge Morsell. Also 23 acs of land, adj the prop of Mr J K Smith, & the lot on which Mr R Parrott formerly lived, less than 3/4s of a mile from Gtwn. -Harriet Rittenhouse, excx; Thos Robertson, exc of John B Rittenhouse, dec'd.

Jas L Hawkins is appt'd Cashier of the Franklin Bank of Balt, vice Jas Dawes, dec'd.

SAT MAR 25, 1815

Ranaway-on Mar 23, an indented mulatto, Betsey Innis, with a child which she calls Ellen. -Alex'r Cochrane, First hse east of the Bank of the Metropolis, Wash.

Died: on Feb 19, Henry Daingerfield, Sec of the Miss Terr, & Reg of the Land Ofc west of Pearl Rvr.

Died: at New Orleans, on Feb 20, Gen Byrd Smith; an early settler in Tenn; mbr of the Legislature; commanded the West Tenn brig of Militia at the day of his death.

MON MAR 27, 1815

Sale of all the right, int, & title, of Henry Tims, in 3 two story brick hses, with back bldgs, on sq 690, Wash City, at the suit of Saml N Smallwood against the said Henry Tims, Thos Dunn, & John T Frost. Wash Boyd, Mrshl.

TUE MAR 28, 1815

Orphans Crt of PG Co, Md. Prsnl est of John Waring, jr, of said co, dec'd. -Eliz Waring, admx.

WED MAR 29, 1815

Wash Library Rm-meeting of brd of dirs held this day, Messrs Moses Young, Geo Way & Christopher Andrews. -T H Gillis, Pres pro tem.

$20 reward for runaway, negro man, Mile; once belonged to Truman Compton, who formerly resided in Wash City. -Stephen S Johns

Doylestown, Pa, Mar 20. On Mar 13th, Geo Wash Stelle, of Northampton twnshp, was injured when his ox-cart overturned; on Mar 14th he expired.

New Orleans, Feb 13, 1815. Died: on Sat evening, Thos Buford, late a mbr of the Hse o/Reps of this state, from the parish of Concordia. He was walking on the levee, at the same moment, a detachment of sldrs were performing a funeral ceremony in front of the church; a ball struck Mr B in the head; he died that night.

Two pvt carriages will leave Wash City, this wk for Phil & N Y. Apply to Robt Fearon, at Mr Pic's, Capitol Hill.

Wilkesbarre, Luzerne Co, Pa, Mar 17th. It is feared that Jabes Ames, aged 17 yrs, & his bro, Jas, aged 9, sons of Mr Wm Ames, have drowned.

THU MAR 30, 1815
Died: on Mar 24, after a severe illness of ten days, Miss Rebecca P Tayloe, 2d d/o Col John Taylor, of Mt Airy, Va. She had scarcely reached her 17th yr. Miss T was buried in the family vault on the Sunday following.

FRI MAR 31, 1815
Maria alias Sally Prout, ran away from my farm on Mar 18; light colored negro woman about 23 yrs of age. -N Ellicott, Occoquan, Va.

SAT APR 1, 1815
Ranaway-Wm M'Near, about 19 or 20 yrs of age, appr to the boot & shoe mkg business. Also, $5 reward for Josias Wade, about 16 yrs of age; it is supposed he has gone to Winchester, Va. -Wm Parsons

MON APR 3, 1815
The wife & child of Col Silas Chapin, of Springfield, Mass, died last month when their hse caught fire.

TUE APR 4, 1815
Ranaway, Milly, negro woman, from the subscriber, nr Wash, in Culpeper, Va. Reward-$25. -Eliz Spiller

Orphans Crt of Chas Co, Md. Pblc sale at the late residence of the dec'd, at Mattawoman, Chas Co, all the prsnl est of Mrs Priscilla H Courts, late of said co, dec'd; consisting of 61 negroes, stock, utelsils, etc. -John T Stoddert, adm

Thos L McKenney has est'd a Commission hse in Gtwn, D C.

WED APR 5, 1815
Info wanted of 2 female chldrn taken prisoners at Ft Niagara by the British; released & sent into the interior of N Y state; their fr is the only parent they have alive, & is stationed in the svc of the U S, stationed at Boston, by the name of Edw Fitzpatrick; together, with their only bro, John, & their sister, Mary. John is now in the corps of artl, at Buffalo; Mary is living in Pittsburg, Pa. Their names are Margarette & Ann, the former bet 4 & 5 yrs of age, the latter bet 13 & 14 yrs of age, supposed to be now in Genessee Co, N Y. Buffalo, N Y, Mar 30.

The subscriber has declined business in the Groc line, requests all who are indebted to him to come forward. -John B Forrest, Navy Yd.

Mrd: on Apr 4, in Alexandria, by Rev Dr Muir, the Rev Jas Laurie, of Wash City, to Mrs Eliz B Hall, d/o the late Andrew Shepherd, of Orange Co, Va.

Elected Dirs of the Metropolis Bank, Wash City, on Monday last:

Alex'r M'Cormick	John M'Gowan	John Graham
Matthew Wright	Jas Thompson	Wm Brent
Jas H Blake	John P Van Ness	Peter Lenox
Jas M Varnum	Walter Jones, jr.	Benj Oden
Moses Young	[John P Van Ness re-elected Pres]	

Conrad Shafer informs the pblc that he continues to keep the Fountain Inn, in Mkt st, [a tvrn] in Fredericktown. He will sell at pvt sale, the above mentioned prop, or barter it for its val in eligible propor hses or both. -Conrad Shafer, Fredericktown.

THU APR 6, 1815

Case of Capt J Nelson, of Phil. We the undersigned, lately p o w's at Melville Island, testify that the treatment we rec'd was inhuman & barbarous: Eben'r A Lewis; Nath'l H Lewis; Hugh Orr; Jed'h Hunt, Capt N Y Vols; Nath'l Case, do; John J Fontaine, Lt U S Art; Jos Clark, Lt N Y Vols; J Gillis, Coronet, do.

P O Ws, ofcrs of the N Y Militia, captured at the sortie from Ft Erie, on Sep 17:

W L Churchill, Lt Col	E Wilson, Maj	O Wilcox, Qr Mstr
Henry Crouch, Capt	Nath'l Case, Capt	Jas Case, Lt
Jesse Church, Lt	Jos Clarke, Lt	Jas Chambers, Ens

Halifax, Mar 4. On Mon, Mr Neil M'Lean, his wife, & Michl Ray were drowned.

Charleston, Mar 22. Mrs Andrew Kerr died from severe kicks from her horse.

Dirs of the Wash Library Co:	Rev O B Brown	Moses Young
Wm Parker	Geo Way	Wm W Seaton
Christopher Andrews	Wm Dupuy	

Runaways committed to Wash Co, D C, jail: negress, Nancy, says she belongs to Stephen Handshaw, of Berkley Co, Va; negro, Chas, says he belongs to Mrs Polly Chesletine, in St Mary's Co, Md. -C Tippett, for W Boyd, mrshl.

FRI APR 7, 1815

Ladies w ltrs in the P O, Wash, Apr 1, 1815:

Eleanor Buchanan	Miss Keath Brown	Mrs Ann M Baine
Miss Nancy Baker	Eliz Burrows	Mrs Carety
Mrs Anne Collett	Verlinda Cary	Mrs Charlotte Cousins
Mrs C Davis	Miss Eliza Finagan	Miss Rosana Finagan-3
Mgt Gallaspy	Mrs Gallasby	Mrs Mgt Hasty
Eliz Hoot	Miss Betsey Hawkins	Mary Hurley
Mary Anne Hurdle	Amelia Howard	Mrs Sally Kanall
Mrs Mgt Kelly	Eliz O Lowera	Mrs Milbourn

Mrs Julia Martin	Miss Ann Maria	Mrs Grace Magruder
Eliz Mc Munn	Miss S McLaughlin	Miss Charity Peake
Miss Hope Scovelle	Mrs Nancy Smith	Miss Sarah A K Smith
Ann Smith	Miss Eliza Smith	Miss Jane Stewart
Mrs Mary Traverse	Mrs Rebecca Tomson	Mrs Caroline Thornton
Henrietta Vermillion	Miss Polly Williams	Alice Wilson
Hannah Witherall		

Mrd: in Wash City, on Apr 4, Alex'r Anderson, of Tenn, to Miss Louisa Maria Hamilton, d/o Sam'l Hamilton, dec'd.

Died: at Gtwn, on Apr 4, Mrs Sarah Mackey, relict of Alex'r Mackey. [See corr of Apr 8.]

Val prop for sale-situated on the crnr of Bridge & Wash sts, formerly occupied by Ross & Getty; enough for 2 stores & dwlg hses over the stores. -Andrew Ross & Stephen Pleasonton.

SAT APR 8, 1815

Jas M'Guire, of Alexandria, has been appt'd Principal Assessor of the Direct Tax for D C.

In announcing the death of Mrs Mackey, it was stated that she was the relict of Mr Alex Mackey, dec'd. Mr A Mackey we are happy to learn, is living & well.

MON APR 10, 1815

Mrd: at Carlisle, Pa, on Mar 31, by Rev Mr Wilson, Col Arthur P Haynes, U S Army, to Miss Frances Duncan, d/o Thos Duncan, of that place.

Died: in Middlebury, Vt, on Sat the ____ ult, Gen John Nixon, aged 90 yrs; commanded a Brig during the Rev, & was wounded at the battle of Bunkerhill.

Died: lately, at an advanced age, Col Andrew Bruce, of Allegany Co, Md; ntv of Scotland, but at a very early period of his life emigrated to this country, while yet in its colonial state. He settled in this country when it was but a wilderness; his pursuits were agricultural, & he lived to rear a large & respectable family.

$50 reward for runaway, Harry Turner, bet black & mulatto, dialect is negro, aged about 30 yrs. Abraham B Hooe, King Geo Co, Va.

Deserted from *Greenleaf's Point*, Wash City, bet Mar 23 & Apr 3, the following sldrs of the 36th regt, U S Infty: 1-Wm Hawkins, aged 21 yrs, farmer, born in N C. 2-Nelson Dozier, aged 33 yrs, laborer, b in London, Eng. 3-John Williams, aged 24 yrs, farmer, b in Matthews Co, Va. 4-John McCue, aged 26 yrs, stone-mason, b in Dublin, Ire. 5-Thornton Garrison, no description, enlisted in Petersburg, Va. - N Baden, Lt, Cmdg at Greenleaf's Point.

TUE APR 11, 1815
Law decision; Salem, Mass, Apr 4. The contest bet the legatees, & the heirs at law of Mrs John Norris, of this town, dec'd, respecting $30,000 to the Foreign Mission Soc, & $30,000 to the Theological Instit in Andover, has been decided by the Sup Crt of Boston in favor of the legatees in both cases. John Norris, hsbnd of this lady, gave $10,000 while he was living.

Mrd: on Sun wk, Col Robt Johnson, late of Scott Co, fr/o Col Rich'd M Johnson, aged 70 yrs, to the amiable Miss Fanny Bledsoe, d/o the Rev Wm Bledsoe, aged about 22 yrs, all of Gallatin Co, Ky.

Died: in Wash City, on Apr 6, in his 37th yr, Mr Jos Anthony Franzoni, sculptor; ntv of Italy, & came to this city a few yrs ago. He has left a widow & 6 chldrn.

Died: on Mar 22, in Frankfort, Mrs Mgt Talbot, consort of Hon Isham Talbot, a Senator in Cong from Ky.

Matthew Wright elected a mbr of the Brd of Aldermen for the 4th Ward, Wash, in place of John Davis of Abel, rsgn'd. -Jas H Blake, Mayor.

WED APR 12, 1815
For sale-3 story dwlg hse on F st, occupied by Seth Pease; also a small 2 story brick hse adj the above, on 12th st, occupied by John Brown. Apply to Overton Carr, Bank of Wash, or to Wm Hebb, PG Co, Md.

Died: on Apr 10, age 76 yrs, Mrs Mariamne Craik, relict of the late Dr Jas Craik, of Fairfax Co, Va.

Orphans Crt of Wash Co, D C. Prsnl est of John M'Cutchen, of said town & dist, dec'd. -Eliz M'Cutchen

N C Maxwell will sell his hse at the West end of the city, nr Capt Davidson's wharf; also 2 excellent black servants.

THU APR 13, 1815
Particulars of the shipweck of the pvt armed schn'r *Surprize*, of Balt. N Y, Apr 3, 1815, bound to Balt, with the following ofcrs & passengers, viz: Col Brook-army, Lts Skinner, Rousseau, Cannon, Bell, & Lattimer; sailing mstr Godfrey; Mdshpmn-Ray, Boarman, Stallings, Wolbert, Stewart, Mosher, Rutter & Sanderson; Mstr's Mates King & Jackson; Marshall, gunner; Davis, btswn; Wells, carp; Ackerman, sail mkr, & 130 seamen. List of those who were lost: Mr Ackerman, sail mkr; Mr Cowan, 2d mate; Mathew Fango, Qr gunner; Thos Boyton, do; Peter Daniels, seaman; Isaac Jeffery, do; John Jackson, do; Solomon Jenkins, John Johnson, Simon Simmons, Wm Chapman, do, Wm Thompson, Jonathan Frazer, Henry Vanlamp & Wm Robbins.

Geo Andrews is appt'd Assist Assessor for the City of Wash, & part of Wash Co.

Runaways committed to Wash Co, D C, jail: Tom Hilliard, negro, age about 30 yrs, says he was set fee by Mary Bushton of Henrico Co, Va. Negress, Eliza, about 21 yrs old, says she was set free by Mrs Nancy Bluster, nr Dumfries, Va. Negro, Jas, age about 20 yrs, says he belongs to Maj Stapleton Crutchfield, of Spottsylvania, Va, nr the Crt Hse. -C Tippett, for W Boyd, mrshl.

SAT APR 15, 1815
Stolen from Francis Corbin, of the Reeds, nr the White Chimnies P O, Caroline Co, Va, in Aug last, Lewis, a mulatto boy, about 14 or 15 yrs old. From all info obtained, he was stolen by one Sam'l Bundy, a wagoner, who is now said to be in jail in Salisbury, N C. -Geo Sale, mgr for Francis Corbin. [Bundy changed his name to Bill, & his own name occasionally to Simon Bently.]

Sale of 2 tracts of land, *Cool Springs* & *Forrest*, lying in PG Co, Md; taken as the prop of Arthur Campbell & Michael Lovejoy, to satisfy suit of Benj Robertson. -John Darnall, late Shrf of P G Co, Md.

MON APR 17, 1815
Bedford Springs. L Price, late of Hagerstown, has taken that lg 3 story brik hse in Bedford, Pa, lately built by Mr Schell, in which he opened a Tavern.

TUE APR 18, 1815
Testimonials to the improved fire place of John C Brush, by the ctzns of Wash City,
Apr 11.
Gen Waterston
John Gardiner
Jno M Moore
Robt King
Nathan Lufborough
Jno Lamb
Benj Harrison
G C Grammer
Wm H B Sewall
Geo A Carroll
Geo Sweeny
Nath'l Frye, jr
Alex Cochrane
Jno Lindsay
Reuben Burdine
A Ramsay
Chas DeKrafft
Return J Meigs
Ezra Gilman
Abraham Landes
David Ott
Separate testimonials:
J Mason

Walter Clarke
Henry Herford
O B Brown
N B Van Zandt
J Meigs
J Knapp
Benj Harrison
John N Lovejoy
Jas Bennett
T Gunton
Geo W May
Rosanna Finagan
Thos L Washington
Christopher Andrews
Valentine Welsh
C T G Worthington
John Bridges
Greenbury Gaither
Abraham Bradley, jr.
Jas B Preston
Seth Hyatt
S Hanson o/Sam'l

Jas N Taylor

Jno Peltz
John M'Leod
Fred D Tschiffely
Jos S Collins
Wm Williamson
Rd S Briscoe
And Ross
Chas Peal Polk
B L Lear
W W Seaton
Jos Gales, jr
Robt Brent
John C Brent
Richd T Queen
Wm Ramsay
Athanasius Ford
John Gaither
A & G Way
W Wood
Jas Gaither
Jno Underwood

Sarah Wilson

Tench Ringgold	Richd Rush	Jas Monroe
T Winn	Phineas Bradley	Andrew Hunter
Pre Varon	T Winn	W Jones, jr
Hanson Catlett	Dan'l M'Keowin	Dan'l Carroll of Dud'n
Sam'l K Jennings	Stephen Belknap, Balt	Silas Hawes, Bennington, Vt
Jas Tilton, Wilmington, Del		

Visitants at Wash City,-testimonials:

Robt Sewall	Calvin Preston	H Newman
Guy Gaylord	Levin W Ballard	W E Horner, M D
Edw Stephens	Wm G Orr	Edw Ross

Experienced same while residents of Wash: [Gentlemen of Congress]

Aylett Hawes	Jas Pleasants, jr	Stephen Ormsby
Wm Alston, jr	John W Taylor	Dudley Chase
Jas Fisk	P P Barbour	John Alexander
Wm C Bradley	Jas Clark	W Creighton, jr
John Culpeper	Robt Wright	Wm P Duvall
Wm Barnett	S Archer	Thos Newton
J R Howell	J Rhea of Ten	J Johnson of Virg
R M Johnson	Thos Bines	W Strong
Obadah German	S D Ingham	Dan'l Avery
E Champion	J O Mosely	T Montgomery
A Hasbrouck	Thos Ward	John Condit
J H Hawkins	J Wharton	Jos Kent
Jonathan Roberts	John Roane	A Cuthbert
Jonathan Fisk	Chas Cutts	T Dougherty

[One flue or chimney will serve for as many fireplaces as you can attach to it.]

Pblc sale at the hse of the late Archibald M Johnson, dec'd, nr to Capt Jos Cassin's, all the prsnl est of said Johnson, consisting of 2 val young negro men; also furn etc. -David Bates, auct.

Died: in Boston, Tue wk, Dr John Warren, Pres of the Mass Med Soc; bro to the celebrated Gen Jos Warren, who was killed at the battler of Bunker Hill.

Intending to remove to the Western country, I offer the plantation on which I now reside, for sale; about 308 acs. Jas Young, on Horsepen Run, lower edge of Loudoun Co, Va; or Jas C Deneale, Alexandria. -Jas Young

$20 reward for my negro woman, Mary, who ran off on Apr 11; formerly the prop of Henry Wanemiller, dec'd, of Fredericktown. She is a handsome negro about 24 yrs of age; has a hsbnd lvg in Balt; her mthr lives on the Md track nr Fredericktown. -John C Thompson, High st, Gtwn.

WED APR 19, 1815
Sidney Wished, Potomac Creek, Belle Plaine, offers to rent his dwlg hse & ware-hse for the purpose of a Tavern & Store hse. -Sidney Wished.

THU APR 20, 1815
Jacob Gitt, Hatter, confined in the jail of Adams Co, Pa; insolvent debtor.

Ranaway-Tom Cooper, negro, age about 26 yrs. -John Bast, nr Fred'k town, Md.

Notice-claims against the est of Col Thos Harris, late of Chas Co, Md, dec'd, to exhibit same. Mr Nathan Harris, residing on the est, will settle the said claims. -Th Harris, exc, Annapolis, Md.

FRI APR 21, 1815
Capt Dan'l Cushing, U S artl, late a resid of Lebanon, Ohio, was drowned crossing the Little Auglaize, on his way to Ft Winchester. Ltr dt'd Liberty Hall, Mar 23.

SAT APR 22, 1815
Sale of Land. Decree of Chancery Crt of Md, wherein Alex'r C Magruder is cmplnt, & Wm Marbury, jr, & the infant heirs of Jane Marbury are dfndnts. Sale of land cld *Three Bros*, part of the resurvey of the north part of the *White Marshes*, & part of *Silver Hills*; about 250 acs, 3 miles from Wash City, nr the rd leading from that place to Philip Spalding's Tavern, & adj his land. Wm Marbury, Jr; John Read Magruder.

Ohio Eagle. Beware of Jane Smith, of Greenfield twnshp, Fairfield Co, as she is a liar & I can prove her such. -John Short

$50 reward for runaway, Ralph, negro; almost beat his overseer to death. -P Hansborough, jr, Stevensburg, Culpeper Co, Va.

$10 reward for strayed or stolen horse. -Thos Sutherland, E st, Wash City.

$25 reward for runaway, appr boy named Wm Simpson Williams, in his 19th yr. -Danl Campbell, tailor.

MON APR 24, 1815
Died: at Norfolk, on Sat last, after a long indisposition, Dr Garret Barry, in his 32d yr, late surg's mate to the 38th regt U S Infty; ntv of county Cork, Ireland.

TUE APR 25, 1815
Elected Dirs of the Bank of Columbia:

Gen John Mason	Jas Dunlop	John Threlkeld
P B Key	Henry Foxall	John Ott
John Cox	Walter Smith	Dr Chas Worthington
J S Williams	Thos L M'Kenney	Chas Carroll, of Belle Vue

[Gen John Mason, Pres, & Thos Peter to fill the vacancy.] Gtwn, Mar 20.

Valuable lots at auction, on Pa av; part of lot 1 in sq 291, now occupied by W Dupuy; 3 vacant lots 10, 11, 12, in back of above prop; also lot 4 in sq 292, adj the Coach Mkrs shop of C H Varden; also lot 7 in sq 349. Plans may be examined at the Apothecary Shop of Dr David Ott. -P Mauro

WED APR 26, 1815
The Com'rs of the Navy met yesterday & appt'd Lyttleton W Tazewell Sec to the Board, & Messrs Chas W Goldsborough & C G De Witt, clks.

Negro, Phill, hired for the present yr to Mr Sam'l Henkle, of Jefferson Co, Va, eloped on Easter Sun; formerly belonged to the est of Mr Mottrom Ball, of Northumberland Co, Va, who was the f/o Mr Henry Ball. -Bacon Burwell, Jefferson Co, Md.

Maj Gen Jas Wilkinson is released from arrest, & his sword restored.

Committee appt'd to superintend the repairs of the brick chr in Queen Anne parish, nr Upper Marlboro, PG Co, Md: Dennis Magruder, Francis Magruder, Sam'l Sprigg, Clement Brooke.

THU APR 27, 1815
Biog sketch of the late Gen John Nixon; b in Framingham, Mass, on Mar 4, 1725; enlisted as a sldr about age 17 yrs; continued in the svc, sometimes in the army, & sometimes in the navy; mbr of the Congregational Chr; remv'd to Middlebury, Vt, & lived with his chldrn; died on Mar 24, 1815.

Wilkesbarre, Apr 14. 1-Died: at Cazenovia, Apr 8, Theophilus Wilson, M D, aged 30 yrs. 2-Geo Brack guilty for the murder of Robt Dixon, in Aug last; verdict was murder in the 2d degree; sentence-12 yrs in the pen; 11 at hard labor, & 1 in solitary cells.

Mrd: on Thu evening, by Rev Dr Inglis, Edw Patterson to Miss Sidney Smith, d/o Gen Sam'l Smith, all of Balt, Md.

Orphans Crt of Wash Co, D C. Ltrs of adm on the est of Electius Middleton, late of said co, dec'd. -Wm Doughty, adm.

FRI APR 28, 1815
Va election returns-Dan'l Sheffey, having no opposition, is re-elected from the Abingdon dist.

Died: at Boston, Mr P Jenkins, whose death was occasioned by eating Woodcocks. Those birds feed at this season on dogwood berries, & other poisonous things.

Public baths will be open on May 25. -Eliz Shuck

Mr Jas Wheatley, of Fauquier Co, Va, tk out a patent for an oblong still, on Nov 13, 1813; he having seen my model, dt'd Apr 2, 1810. We have agreed to unite our plans. -Robt Gillespie. Teste, John Strother, jr; Thos Brown, jr. Held at the Culpeper co crt, Mar 20, 1815. Wm Broadus, jr, clk.

SAT APR 29, 1815
Mrd: at Elderslie, on Apr 27, by Rev Dr Addison, Lt John L Elbert, of the U S Army, to Miss Martha Banning Watts.

Isaac Clark, nr the Centre Mkt, Pa av, has just rec'd a very handsome assortment of hats, boots & shoes.

New Books: Jrnl of a cruise made to the Pacific Ocean, by Capt David Porter, in the U S frig, *Essex*, in 1812-1814. Also, the life of Gen Wm Eaton.

MON MAY 1, 1815
Mrd: on Apr 27, by Rev Mr Matthews, Geo Brown, of Md, to Miss Mary Burch, d/o Capt Benj Burch, of Wash City.

I have returned to Wash City, to my old stand in 10th st, on Pa av; to carry on my business as usual in dying all colours, silk, cotton, etc. -J Woodworth

Robt Bailey thanks the pblc for their patronage at Berkeley Springs; he has rented out his retirement, remv'd to Hagerstown, & taken the Stage-hse, lately occupied by Mr L Price. -Robt Bailey [I will sell 440 acs of land in Hampshire Co, Va.]

TUE MAY 2, 1815
Lt Timothy P Andrews has been appt'd Adj of the 3d Regt of the 1st brig M D C & will be obeyed & respected accordingly. -Michl Nourse, Lt Col Comdg.

John Laub to decline business; stock consists of boots, shoe, brushes, etc. The stand he now occupies in Gtwn is for sale.

Pblc sale of lot 1 in sq 731, taken as the prop of John Shute, of Exeter, Eng, to satisfy taxes due the corp of Wash City. Also to be sold: 5000 sq ft of ground in sq 695, with improvements, assessed to Hugh Densley. Lot 9 in sq 758, with improve, assessed to Mrs Jane Burch; & part of lot 11 in sq 690, with improve, assessed to Robt Campbell's heirs. -Zach Walker, coll of taxes-3d ward.

Orphans Crt of Wash Co, D C. Prsnl est of Jos Franzoni, late of said city, dec'd. -Camilla Franzoni, admx; Geo Blagden, adm.

Romulus Riggs has commenced business on Bridge st, Gtwn; genr'l goods.

WED MAY 3, 1815
Mrd: in Gtwn, on Apr 27, by Rev Mr Brown, Mr Wm Peckham to Miss Sophia Ladille.

<u>Academic Ofcrs of the Military Acad at West Point, N Y:</u>
Brig Gen Jos G Swift, Inspec.
Capt Alden Partridge, Prof of engr, Superintendant.
Lt Wm S Eveleth, Assist, do.
Jared Mansfield, Prof of Natural & Experimental Philosophy.

Lt David B Douglas, Assist, do.
Andrew Ellicott, Prof of Mathematics.
Lt John Wright, Assist, do.
Rev Adam Empie, Chaplain, Prof of History, Geography & Ethics.
Christian E Zoeller, Teacher of Drawing & Practical Geometry.
Claudius Berard, Teacher of French Language.
Sam'l A Walsh, Surgeon.
Pierre Thomas, Sword Mstr.

Died: at Fredericktown, Md, on Apr 25, Dr Philip Thomas, Pres of the Medical Soc of Md; aged 68 yrs.

An island & a lime stone quarry, for sale; nrly oppo Leesburgh, Va, 280 acs. For terms apply to Wm Stewart, on Cherry st, Gtwn.

Brickmkr wanted: apply to Wm Dudley Digges or Mr Sheckles, his mgr.

THU MAY 4, 1815
Mrd: on May 1, by Rt Rev Bishop Kemp, Jos White to Miss Isabella Pinkney, d/o Wm Pinkney, all of Balt, Md.

The subscriber having taken his bro Isaac into partnership, the business will be under the firm of Wm S Nicholls & Co; Dry Goods. -W S Nichols, Gtwn.

New shoe store opened on F st, Wash, by subscriber. -T Wannall

FRI MAY 5, 1815
Died: at Fredericktown, Md, on May 2, John Hanson Thomas, of that place.

Lost-pktbk bet Gtwn & Tenly town. -Michael Brady, reward-$5.

Pblc sale of lot 14 in sq 290, with frame hse thereon, on F st, Wash. Apply to Julia Kean at Mr Docker's, Capitol Hill. -Julia Kean

Porter Cellar remv'd from the Navy Yd to Capitol Hill, Wash. -Ralph Charlton

SAT MAY 6, 1815
Orphans Crt of PG Co, Md. Pblc sale at the dwlg hse of Thos C Duvall, in Bladensburg, the prop of John Tilley, dec'd; furn, billiard table, & 2 negroes. -Thos C Duvall, adm.

Orphans Crt of PG Co, Md. Pblc sale in Bladensburg, all prsnl prop of John Berry, dec'd; negroes, stock, furn, coopers tools, fishing boat, etc. -Thos Ferral, adm.

MON MAY 8, 1815
For sale-the land on which I reside, nr Orange Crt Hse, Va; 700 acs of first rate tobacco land; with dwlg hse. I also wish to sell 500 acs in Amherst Co, Va, within 5 miles of Lynchburg. Robt H Rose, Orange Crt Hse, Va.

Died: at his residence in Stokes Co, N C, on Apr 21, Col Jos Winston, in his 69th yr; ctzn of N C; Rev hero; began his career in 1755, at Braddock's defeat, under the command of Col Washington, where he rec'd a ball in his body, which was never dislodged. He was an indulgent fr, kind mstr, Rpblcn, & honest man.

Died: at his seat in PG Co, Md, on May 4th, after a short illness, in his 76th yr, Peter Savary, a ntv of France, & upwards of 36 yrs an inhabitant of this country.

Ohio, Va & Ky lands for sale; per last will of Francis Muir, dec'd. 3,150 acs in Ohio; the half of 300 acs in Dela Co; 1,000 acs in Ky; also, 2,000 acs in Va in Harrison [supposed to be Randolph] on the Gauly rvr. Title papers relative to the lands in Ohio, Ky, & Va, are in the hands of Mr Chas Jas Mac Murdo of Richmond. -B P Yates, adm with w a of F Muir, dec'd. Dinwiddie, Va.

Val prop for sale, in consequence of a severe illness two yrs ago, which incapacitates me; about 300 acs, with dwlg hse. Enquire of Wm Lorman, of Balt; John Yates, nr Chas Town, Jefferson Co, Virg; John Love, Buckland, Pr Wm Co, Virg, or Josiah Watson, Postmstr in Alexandria. Also, 1,113 acs nr Ely's Ford with farm hse. -Chas Urquhart, Germanna, Orange Co, Va.

TUE MAY 9, 1815
For sale or rent; Tavern Stand in Cumberland, Md. Also, about 300 acs of land 8 miles from Cumberland. -Henry M'Kinley, of said town.

WED MAY 10, 1815
Adam Lindsay, nr the Navy yd, of Wash Co, D C, brought before me a stray mare. -Saml'l N Smallwood, J P.

$30 reward for runaway, Sam, negro man, about 21 yrs old. -W H Rochester, living nr Battletown, Fred'k Co, Va. [Or info to Mr John Dorsey, living on Bullskin, Jefferson Co, Va.]

Trustee's sale, deed of trust undersigned by Ferdinando *Fairfair, dt'd Nov 3, 1813, of record in the ofc of Crt in Jefferson, Va. Sale of *Shannon Hill*, about 1,000 acs. Said land cnvyd to the undersigned in trust for the indemnity of Chas Gibbs. -Thos Griggs, trustee. [*as written]

$10 reward for black man, Joe, runaway. Deliver to Mr Jas Brindige, Balt, Md, or Geo Sweeny, living on Cedar Run, Pr Wm Co, Va. -Geo Sweeny, Pr Wm Co, Va.

THU MAY 11, 1815
To let-the residence of the late Peter Miller, dec'd; in Wash, D C. Apply to Griffith Coombe or John M'Gowan.

J Sterett is the cashier of the City Bank of Balt. [Md]

For sale-the farm cld *Hope Park*, formerly the residence of Dr David Stuart, dec'd, lying in Fairfax Co, Va; nrly 2,000 acs, with dwlg hse & grist mill, etc. Also, I will sell 300 acs on Allegany Mntn, adj the land of Thos B Martin & Alex'r King-510 acs adj the land of King, Michl Miller, & Benj Beeler; 480 acs on the *Great Cacapionl;* 405 acs adj the lands of Danie Royce; 300 acs nr *Dove's Mill.* Also, 500 acs nr the prop of Geo Lane. -Wm Robinson, Howard, Apr 22.

Balt, May 9. No. 6739, which came out a prize of $10,000 yesterday, in the Liberty Engine Hse Lottery, was sold at Cohen's, 110 Mkt st, to Mr John Andrews, vender of lottery tickets, who had the number remaining in his ofc unsold.

Thos Herty, about 14 yrs of age, eloped from his grdns. -Nicholas Callan, Geo Andrews, Grdns, Wash, May 11.

FRI MAY 12, 1815
Orphans Crt of Wash Co, D C. Sale of the prsnl prop of Wm Hamden, dec'd; or as much as will raise about $320. Pvt sale of lot 1 in sq 762 & lot 4 in sq 725, with some improvements, all on Capitol Hill. -David Bates, auct.

SAT MAY 13, 1815
St Mary's Co, Md, Mar term, 1815. Application of Jas Goddard, of said co, insolvent debtor, for release from his imprisonment. Jo Harris, clk.

Orphans Crt of PG Co, Md. Sale at the dwlg of Jacob Green, late of said co, dec'd; a part of his prsnl est; stock, furn, utensils, etc. -Thos Magruder, adm

MON MAY 15, 1815
Died: on May 5, at his seat in Pr Wm Co, Va, Chas Tyler, Sen'r, age 64 yrs. Hsbnd, fr, mstr, & sldr of the revolution.

TUE MAY 16, 1815
Died: at Charleston, on May 8, in his 66th yr, Dr David Ramsay, the historian of S C; deprived of life by the hands of Wm Linen, who shot & killed him. Some yrs ago, when Linen was put to the bar for wounding Mr Henry Bailey, the Dr had given testimony, that he believed the said Linen was not in his right mind.

Six cents reward for runaway, Decius Edmonson, appr to the baking business; on Mar 26. -Jacob Wineberger, Gtwn.

Land for sale in Montg Co, Md; petition of Francis Dodge vs Eliz, Louisia & Maria O'Reily; at the hse of Chs Stewart, tenant on the premises. About 208 acs, being part of *Good Will, Hard Struggle, & Friendship,* sold by Upton Beall to the late Henry O'Reily, dec'd, adj the est of the late Col Gaither, in Montg Co, Md. Mrs O'Reily, the widow of the dec'd Henry O'Reily, has agreed to relinquish her dower. -Clement Sewall, trustee appt'd by the Chancellor.

Non-residents. I solicit persons at a distance, who wish money collected or taxes pd on land in this country, to confide their business to my agency. -John H Morton, Lexington, Ky.

Geo Kneller has opened a well est'd Confectionary, on Pa av; Mr Anth Kohl, has associated with him.

Contract will be made for repairing the Blacksmith's Shop in the Navy Yd; proposals by Apr 20. -John Rodgers, Pres.

WED MAY 17, 1815
The Lyceum, a seminary for young ladies, is opened in Congress st, Gtwn. -John Lathrop

Notice-the assocition of H O Middleton & I K Hanson, is this day dissolved by mutual consent.

The subscribers have transferred their bks to Mr Thos C Wright, & given him full powers to collect all their debts. -W G Gerard, Thos Greeves, Gtwn.

$50 reward. Black horse stolen from Abraham Landes' stable, in High st, Gtwn. He was stolen by Jos Minor, age about 20 yrs. -Abraham Landes, Gtwn.

Bay mare strayed from my stable nr the Captiol Hill; $5 reward. -John Cairns

Grey horse strayed off the commons of Wash City; $5 reward. Robt Tweedy, F st.

$70 reward. Ranaway for the U S Ship *Alert*, lying at the Navy Yd in Wash City, the following hands:
Wm Thompson, American born, deserted Apr 23, 1815.
John Hamson, Englishman born, deserted Apr 25, 1815.
Wm Leonard, American, deserted May 2, 1815.
Jas Quinn, Irishman, deserted May 2, 1815.
Thos Looal, American, deserted May 6, 1815.
Jas Madison, American, deserted May 12, 1815.
John Roberts, Irishman, no date.   -N Haraden, Navy Yd.

FRI MAY 19, 1815
Mrd: in Alexandria, on May 6, by Rev Oliver Norris, Thos Wilson, Merchant, of Balt, to Miss Mary H Cruse, d/o Mr Thos Cruse, Merchant, of Alexandria.

Killed on board the U S frig, *Constitution*, on Feb 20, 1815, in action with his B M ships *Cyane* & *Levant:* John Fullington, ord seaman; Antonio Farrow, Marine; Wm Harral, Marine. Wounded & since dead: Tobias Fernald, seaman; John Lancy, ord seaman; Thos Fessenden, ditto.

Crct Crt of Wash Co, D C, in Chancery, Dec term, 1814. Luderwell Lee, exc of Thos Lee, senr, vs Henry Moscrop. Bill is to obtain the foreclosure of a mortgage from Lee of sundry lots in Wash City. -Wm Brent, clk.

SAT MAY 20, 1815
Died: nr Phil, on Tue last, at his country seat on the banks of the Schuylkill, Gen Jonathan Williams, a mbr of the Fourteenth Cong from that city.

Saml Chester, shoe store, Bridge st, Gtwn.

For sale: *Glebe Land*; per decree of the U S Crct Crt of DC for Alexandria Co; 520 acs. -Geo Deneale, & John Muncaster, Chr Wardens of the Episc Chr in Alexandria.

MON MAY 22, 1815
Army Register; Genr'l Staff.
Jacob Brown, Maj Gen, Div of the north
Andrew Jackson, Maj Gen, Div of the south.
Alex'r Macomb, Brig Gen, Jan 24, 1814; Sep 11, 1814, Maj Gen brvt.
Edmund P Gaines, Brig Gen, Mar 9, 1814; Aug 15, 1814, Maj Gen brvt.
Winfield Scott, Brig Gen, Mar 9, 1814; Jul 25, 1814, Maj Gen brvt.
Eleazer W Ripley, Brig Gen, Apr 15, 1814; Jul 25, 1814, Maj Gen brvt.
[Followed by a page & a half listing; ord dept, med dept; pay dept, etc.]

TUE MAY 23, 1815
Neighbors & fellow ctzns-thank you for removing our furn, etc, when our hses were expected to be enveloped in flames. -Mord Booth, Saml N Smallwood

Notice-I intend to move to Gtwn on or about Jun 12th; the hse I now live in is for sale or rent. -Wm O'Brien

Soap & candle utensils, for sale; all the tools in the factory lately carried on by Z Farrell & J Hancock. Pa av, Wash City.

Cash will be given for 20 or 30 young negroes by the subscribers in Wash City, at Mr Geo Miller's, in F st. -Jas Childress, Geo A Phifer.

Ground plaister on hand-for sale, at the mill on King st. -A P Gover, Alexandria.

Sale of furn, at the hse of Mr John Norvell, who is about to remove to Balt, Md.

Mrshl's sale-all the right, title, etc, of Wm M'kee, in part of sq 797 with improvements; at the suit of John P Van Ness. -Wash Boyd, mrshl, D C.

WED MAY 24, 1815
Election in the first Ward of Wash City, will be held at Mrs Kortwright's on Jun 5; for Alderman & cnclmen. -W Waters, J Brumley, J Thompson, committee.

Election in the 4th Ward of Wash City, will be held at H B Joy's tavern on Jun 4; for Alderman & cnclmen. -Wm Prout, John W Brashears, Jas Friend, committee.

$50 reward for negro, Dennis Jenkins, about 21 yrs of age, eloped on May 16th. -Valentine Reintzel, Gtwn.

Shoe store, Bridge st, Gtwn. -Sam'l Chester

The heirs & reps of the late C Kurtz offer at pblc sale in Gtwn, their rl est, consisting of svr'l lots of ground, fronting on Bridge st & running back to Green st. -Thos Kurtz, Gtwn.

Val lands & mills for sale. Deed of trust by Isaac Webster & Ann S his wife, & confirmed by Christopher Tompkins & Mary his wife, by their deed of record-prop of the late Ralph Wormley, dec'd, in King Wm Co, Va; 409 acs with dwlg hse, etc. Also, by deed of trust of Isaac Webster & Ann S his wife, 250 acs in Buckingham Co, Va. -Thos Taylor, Wm Nekervis, Wm Marshall [Sam'l Shelton, John Staples]

Desirous of moving to the upper country, I offer tracts of land in King Geo Co, Va, 600 acs; also tract of nrly 600 acs; also 800 acs owned & occupied by the late Maj Burde_ Ashton, dec'd, cld *Millford*. -Y Johnson, King Geo C H, Va.

THU MAY 25, 1815
Chosen Dirs of the new Merchants Bank of Alexandria:

Dan'l M'Phersons	Danl Annin	Peter Saunders
Wm Tyler	Ferd Marsteller	Danl Somers
John Jackson	Camillus Griffith	Jos Mandeville
Nimrod Farrow	Peter Heiskell	Jas Anderson
		Edmund Brooke

$300 reward. Robbery. At my warehse in South st, 7 cases of Turkey opium stolen therefrom. -Geo Williams, Balt, Md.

Dr Wm Gardner continues his svcs at his residence on F st, Wash City.

FRI MAY 26, 1815
Cmdor Joshua Barney was presented a sword by the City of Wash on Aug 24, 1814.

Carlisle, Pa, May 12. On May 2, Mr Elijah Wright, of Rutland, Gailia Co, was killed by the falling of a tree.

Mrshl's sale on Jun 21, at Wilmington, N C, for negotiable paper in the banks of Wilmington, at 60 & 90 days, the barque of *Amiable Isabella* & cargo; captured by pvt armed schn'r *Roger*, of Norfolk, Roger Quarles mstr. Beverly Daniel-mrshl.

Chas co Crt, Md, Mar term, 1815. Petiton of Chas Chunn, of said co, for act of insolvent debtor. -John Barnes, clk.

Mrshl's sale, at Thos W Pairo's store on Pa av, all the right, title, int, of Nicholas Whelan in part of lot 3 in sq 408, with 2 small frame hses, Wash; at suit of Griffith Combe & Jas D Barney. -Wash Boyd, Mrshl D C.

$10 reward for negro woman, Dinah; ran away on May 22 from the subscriber, living nr Piscataway, PG Co, Md. -Ann Dyer

SAT MAY 27, 1815

Election for Alderman & cnclmen to rep the Second Ward of Wash City, to be held on Jun 5. -Geo Andrews, Andrew Coyle, T H Gilliss, comrs.

All persons having flour on storage with the late firm of Butts & Cawood, are to come forward; pay storage & remove same. -Mark Butts, Crafton Cawood.

$20 reward for runaway, negro boy, John Pool, age about 14 yrs. Mathew Robinson, Alexandria.

Mrd: on May 25, by Rev Mr Addison, Mr Dawson P Burgess, of Culpeper Co, Va, to Mrs Henrietta Craig, of Gtwn.

MON MAY 29, 1815

Mrd: on May 25, by Rev Mr Waugh, in Alexandria, Rev Geo S Bull, of Balt, to Miss Rebecca A Jordan, of St Mary's, Md.

Opium stolen from Mr Geo Williams has been found in Balt City & a part in Phil; except for 30 lbs. The villains have been taken & secured.

Died: at N Orleans, on Apr 11, of wounds rec'd on Dec 14 last, in the action of the gun boats, midshipman, Wm P Canby, of the U S Navy.

Died: at Plymouth, on Apr 21, Hon Wm Watson, aged 85; 1751 grad of Harvard college. Of 35, the original number of his class, not one now survives. Mr Watson was the first naval ofcr of Plymouth, appt'd under the state gov'r.

Info wanted of the owner of a sloop named *Experiment*; found on May 17th. On board was a lg hair trunk with ltrs belonging to Jos Kitchen, of Savannah, & ltrs from his wife in Phil, & a family bible with the names Jos & Ann Kitchen, presented by Matthew James, of Phil. Lying loose were some saddler's tools. Info rec'd at the P O, Marnaroneck, Westchester Co, N Y. May 29, 1815.

Died: on Oct 17 last, in the parish of Derrivollann, Enniskillen, Andrew Stewart, late shepherd of Earl Belmore, & his wife Bell Stewart, after 57 yrs of matrimonial tranquility, departed this life both at one moment, both interred on the 19th-their united ages formed 160 yrs.

Mrshl's sale-all right, title, int, etc, of Leonard Harbaugh in lot 11 in sq 170, with small 2 story brick bldg, Wash; to satisfy a judgement in favor of Geo Kleiber.

2-All right, title, int, etc, of Henry Tims in 3 two story brick hses & lots in sq 690 on So B st, Wash; at suit of Edmund Law. -Wash Boyd, mrshl, D C.

TUE MAY 30, 1815
$200 reward for Elijah Dotson, proper name is thought to be Wm Craddock; says he was born in Surry Co, N C, age about 20 yrs; hatter by trade, at other places a silversmith. He stole numerous things from me. John McKee, Chester C H, S C. N B-since writing the above, I have seen a man who says his name is Elijah Dotson, & that he enlisted in the 43d regt, U S I, 6th Military Dist at Columbia, S C, under the name of John Evans, & deserted; $50 was advertised for him.

Runaways committed to the jail of Wash Co, DC: negro, Mary Adams, age about 25 yrs; says she is free & srvd her time with a Mr Powel at Gtwn, & has a gr-fr lvg nr Mr Isaac Peircy, by the name of Joe Adams. Negro, Jess, 14 yrs old, says he belongs to Sam Jack nr Port Tobacco, Md. -C Tippett, for W Boyd, Mrshl

Died: in Wash City, at the hse of Mr David Dobbin, on May 27, Mr Wm M'Caula, of Orange Co, N C.

Orphans Crt of Montg Co, Md. Ltrs of adm on est of Lawrence O'Neale, of said co, dec'd. -Henry O'Neale, adm.

In Chancery, May 25, 1815. John Benson vs Mary Coolidge, John, Sally, & Patricius Hepburn. Rg: decree for tract of land in Montg Co, Md, cld *Resurvey on Hanover*, 398 1/4 acs, in pursuance of a brd of cnvync executed by Sam'l Hepburn to the cmplnt on Dec 27, 1799. Plntfs reside outside of Md. -Jas P Heath, Reg C C

Ranaway-negro man, Emanuel. Eloped in Apr last, negro woman, Winney. She is w/o the above negro man. -Fred'k A Chapman, Fauquier C H, Va.

WED MAY 31, 1815
$20 reward for runaway, Cloe, negro woman, age about 23 yrs, & her child about 8 yrs of age. -Eliz Neal, lvg on Oxen Run, PG Co, Md.

THU JUN 1, 1815
Mrd: on May 30, Mr Adam Lindsay to Miss Maria Rose, both of Wash City.

For sale or exchange-for prop in Phil city; sale of 3 story brick hse & lot on Pa av, Wash City; at present occupied by Hon Jas Monroe, Sec of State. Apply to Mr Andrew Ross, nr the Union Tvrn, or to the subscriber. -Timothy Caldwell, 214 Race st, Phil, Pa.

$250 reward-for pktbk containing $2,250; lost on May 29 bet Semmes' tavrn in Gtwn & F st, Wash. -Wm M Loftin, 3d Lt 3d R R.

FRI JUN 2, 1815
Mrd: on May 27, at *Belle Field*, nr Annapolis by Rev Mr Dashiell, Henry E Ballard, Lt Cmndnt in the Navy, to Miss Julliana Macubbin, of A A Co, Md.

SAT JUN 3, 1815
E Burk, upholsterer & paper hanger, High st, Gtwn, nrly oppo the Union Library; and Gustavus Beall is cabinet mkr.

$50 reward for runaway, a Mulatto man slave, Stephen Gray, about 22 yrs of age. Deliver to Francis Keene, of Wood Co, Va. -Wm Barker, Fairfax Co, Va. Aaron Barker & Wm Barker, jr, of Fairfax Co, Va, came before me, Rich'd Ratcliffe, J P; & certified that Stephen is a slave for life & the bona fide prop of Wm Barker.

Mrd: on May 1, by Rev Mr M'Cormick, Mr Jas Larned of the Treas Dept, & s/o Col Larned, U S Army, to Miss Ann Jane Herford, of Wash City.

Died: at Albany, N Y, on May 10, Wm Geo & John Richards, twin bros, chldrn of Randall & Eliz M'Collum, aged 23 mos & 6 days; born on one day, died on one day; placed in one coffin, & interred in one grave.

Died: in Scotland, John Davis, aged 108. He used to walk 6 miles every Sat.

40 shillings reward for appr boy, Michl Low, jr, age 20 yrs on Feb 8 last; ranaway on Oct 20 last. As per indenture from his fr, bound to me to learn the cabinet business. -Wm Worthington, jr.

MON JUN 5, 1815
Alexandria, Jun 3. Fire yesterday in a shed belonging to Mr Isaac Entwisle on his new wharf; consumed the shed, but no further damage was done.

A continuation of Burk's History of Va, by L H Girardin, is now under press in Petersburg, Virg.

Mrd: at Alexandria, on Jun 1, by Rev Mr Wilmer, Mr Horatio Scott to Miss Caroline Koones, d/o Mr Fred'k Koones of this town.

Dirs of the Wash Library Co are to meet on Tue. -John Sessford, librarian.

Small farm of about 70 acs for sale; part of tract cld *Long Meadows*, in D C. -John Dobbyn, Navy Yd.

Lots in Wash for sale; aggreeably to the will of Mr Jos Carleton, late of this town. -John Laird, exc, Gtwn.

TUE JUN 6, 1815
St Louis, Apr 29. Traitors; residents within this & neighboring territories previous to the war, & always claimed to the rights of ctzns of the U S, but as soon as the war was declared, they tk part against us, & were active agents in the British interest in parts of the Indian Country: Robt Dickson, Jas Aird, Duncan Graham, Francois Boutilher, Ed La Gouthrie, Brishois of Prairie du Chein,

Jacob Franks, the bros Grigneaus of Greenbay, Jos La Croix & Lassailer of Milwakee, Jos Bailly & his cousin Barrott of St Jos', Mitchel La Croix, Louis Buisson, Louis Benett, formerly of Peoria.

Teacher wanted. Francis Hawks, Pres o/the Brd o/Trustees, of Newbern Acad, N C.

Orphans Crt of Chas Co, Md. Ltrs of adm on estates of Henry Dent & Richd Owen, & ltrs of adm d b n on the estates of Ann M'Donald & Zachariah M'Donald, all of Chas Co, dec'd. Hugh Cox-authorised to settle all business. - Charity Dent, admx.

Crct Crt Wash Co, D C, Dec term, 1814. Luderwell Lee, exc of Thos Lee, senr, cmplnt, vs Henry Moscrop, dfndnt. Rg-foreclosure of a mortgage from Lee, senr, of sundry lots in Wash City, etc. Moscrop resides w/out D C. -Wm Brent, clk.

WED JUN 7, 1815
Died: at his seat in PG Co, Md, about the middle of last month, Osborn Sprigg, a gentleman venerable for his yrs.

Died: at Phil, on Jun 2, Thos Willing Francis, an eminent & wealthy ctzn of that place, to whose prosperity he had actively contributed.

THU JUN 8, 1815
To non-residents. My situation in pblc life enables me to transact business for non-residents with convenience. -John H Morton, Lexington, Ky.

FRI JUN 9, 1815
Ltr to the editors: rg impression made of Michl Lowe, s/o Henry H Lowe, as my appr who absconded. Indentures dt'd Apr 13, 1812, stating that he is bound until he be of age of 21 yrs, being now 17 yrs old the 8th of Feb last. -Wm Worthington Ltr from Henry H Lowe regarding same.

SAT JUN 10, 1815
Died: at New Brunswick, on Jun 2, in his 71st yr, the Hon Robt Morris, Dist Judge of the N J Dist.

Mrd: at Gtwn, on Jun 6, Gustavus Harrison, to Miss Eliz T Magruder, d/o Col G Magruder.

Orphans Crt of Chas Co, Md. Prsnl est of Maj Luke F Matthews, dec'd. -Rose Matthews, excx, Port Tobacco, Md.

I will sell *Bushfield*, 800 acs, in Westmoreland Co, Va. Apply to Maj John Turberville, of same, for info. -Saml Lewis, Westmoreland Co, Md.

MON JUN 12, 1815
Val prop for sale. In consequence of a severe illness 2 yrs ago, which incapacites me from active pursuits, I am disposed to part with my establishment at this place on the Rappahanock rvr; mills; the hse is lg & commodious; saw mill; farm contains 800 acs; tract of 400 acs on oppo side of the rvr, etc. Enquire of Wm Lorman, of Balt; John Yates, nr Chas Town, Jeff Co, Virg; John Love, Buckland, Pr Wm Co, Virg; or Josiah Watson, Postmstr in Alexandria. -Chas Urquhart, Germanna, Orange Co, Va.

TUE JUN 13, 1815
$10 reward for runaway, negro David. Anthony Hardey, nr Piscataway.

Massacre at Dartmoor; insurrection by the prisoners. Persons killed & wounded in Dartmoor prison, on Apr 6, with their abodes, agreeably to their protections, & the vessels that belonged to etc, rec'd by the cartel ship which arrv'd at Boston, from Plymouth: John Washington, Copstown, Md, *Rolla* of Balt, shot thru the brain. Jos Johnson, Hartford, Con, *Paul Jones*, N Y, shot thru the heart. Jas Man, Boston, *Siro*, of N Y, do. Jas Campbell, N Y, dismissed from the *Volunteer* man of war, in the brain. John Haywood, Centervill, Md, do, *Scypion*, do, right side. Thos Jackson, boy, aged 13, N Y, ship *Orbit*, N Y, in the belly. Wm Liturage, N Y, *Saratoga*, do, in the heart. [Followed by a listing of those wounded.]

Wash Co, D C. Case of Benj Beall, insolvent debtor, confined in the prison of Wash Co for debt. -Wm Brent, clk.

Woodfort Farm. The subscriber will sell at pvt sale that val farm, in A A Co, Md, 900 acs. Land within a mile of Col John E Howard's farm; 6 miles from Ellicott's Mills. -Wm H Marriott

WED JUN 14, 1815
Biog of Maj Gen Wm Carroll, of Tenn; born nr Pittsburg, Pa; in 1810 he emigrated to Tenn & settled in Nashville; upwards of 26 yrs old; a large athletic form. [Two & a half columns followed regarding his battles, etc.]

Wm Floyd & Jesse Smith have formed a connection with Smith & Nicoll of N Y, having opened a groc store in Gtwn, D C.

Thos Hardin alias Jos Minor, who was late committed to the jail of Pr Wm Co, Va, on suspicion of being a dangerous & felonious person, escaped on May 31, 1815. Oath of Saml Johnson; given under my hand & seal, Wm Smith.

Died: on May 27, at Halifax C H, Va, Matthew Clay, a Rep Elect from Campbell dist, in that state, to the Congress.

Died: on May 7, at Fredericktown, Gen Roger Nelson, a Rev hero, & long a distinguished mbr of Cong.

Died: on Apr 30th, nr New Holland, Pa, Elijah Sparks, presiding Judge of the 3d crct of the Indiana Terr.

Deserted from Carlisle, on Jun 1; Fred'k E Hedges, 2d lt of the 7th infty, late of the 5th; age 24 yrs. -W J Gordon, Lt & Adj, Carlisle Barracks, Pa.

THU JUN 15, 1815
Capt T G Shorthand was kpr of the Dartmoor Prison on Apr 6th; day of the massacre of American prisoners.

Runaways committed to the PG Co, Md, jail; negro bros, John White & Wm White; John is 23 & a cooper; Wm is 22 & a shoemkr. Their mthr was Sarah White, manumitted by John Prittle, a Quaker, of Rolin Co, where they were born & raised-says their mthr bound them to 2 bros, John to John Hare; Wm to Wm Hare. John High, appr to Wm Hare, says Jas Warren & John Cox of Rolin Co, knows all they have stated to be correct. -Philip Spalding, for Geo Semmes, Shrf, PG Co, Md.

Wash Co, D C. Case of John Gordon, insolvent debtor, confined in Wash Co prison, for debt. -Wm Brent, clk.

Land for sale; *Archer's Purchase*; about 289 + acs; nr Nottingham. -Thos Eversfield.

FRI JUN 16, 1815
Biog notice of Maj Gen Jacob Brown; about 45 yrs of age; born in Bucks Co, Pa, a few miles below Trenton; his fr was a farmer of the soc of Quakers. He remv'd to Cinc, Ohio, at age 21 yrs, for 2 yrs; after some yrs as a teacher in a Quaker schl in N J. From Ohio he migrated & fixed his residence in N Y C. In 1799 he purchased a lg tract of land nr the shores of Lake Ontario & est'd a settlement there. [Note-Military record followed]

$100 reward for dark mulatto slave, Aleck Francis. -Richd Bland Lee, Wash City.

SAT JUN 17, 1815
Mrd: at Bellmont, Loudon Co, Va, on Jun 12, by Rev Oliver Norris, Robt Campbell of S C, to Miss Mary Ann Lee, d/o Ludwell Lee.

Dartmoor Prison, Apr 7, 1815. Report of the Cmtee on the massacre of Apr 6. Undersigned & sworn by: Wm B Orne, Wm Hobart, Jas Boggs, Jas Adams, Francis Joseph, J F Trobridge, John Rust, Henry Allen, Walter Colton, Thos B Mott.

In addition to the ofcrs in svc for the Military Peace Establishment, the following ofcrs will be retained: Col Wm Linnard, Dep Q M Gen, Apr 12, 1813.
Col Tobias Watkins, Hosp Surg, Mar 30, 1814.
Col Geo W Maupin, Garrison Surg Mate, Nov 5, 1802.
Col Jos Goodhue, do do do, Feb 8, 1803.

Col Abraham Stewart, do do do, Mar 6, 1806.
Col Jas H Sargent, do do do, Mar 6, 1806.
Col Cornelius Cunningham, do do do, Oct 15, 1810.
Col Wm Ballard, do do do, Mar 24, 1812.
Col John H Sackett, do do do, Mar 22, 1813.
Col Chas Taylor, do do do, Apr 3, 1813.
Col John Travett, do do do, Apr 8, 1814.
Col Macauley, do do do, Apr 8, 1814.
Col Solomon Wolcott, do do do, Apr 8, 1814.
-by order of the Sec of War, D Parker, Adj & Ins Gen.

To be sold at pblc sale for cash; 60 shares of Gtwn Potomac Bridge Stock; lots 3, 4, & 14 in sq 323, & lot 7 in sq 120, Wash City. Under the cnvync & covenant from Benj Stoddard, dec'd, to Henry Foxall.

MON JUN 19, 1815

Savannah, Jun 8. On Jun 3, John Bessent, s/o the late Coll of the port of St Mary's, was robbed & murdered about 8 miles from this place.

New store, seasonable dry goods. Horatio & Sabrett Scott, Gtwn.

Middleburg, Vt. On Jun 5, at Waltham in this vicinity, Isaac Hobbs, aged 73 yrs, was murdered by his son-in-law Mr Selah Heacock of that place.

Pblc sale-deed of trust to the subscriber from Mackall S Cox, of PG Co, Md, dt'd Apr 16, 1812; about 125 acs nr Nottingham, cld part of *Mansfield & Collins Comfort*. Also a negro woman, Nell, abou 28 yrs old, with her chldrn, Nancy 11 yrs, Mary 8 yrs, & Maria 5 yrs, with 2 younger ones. -Notley Maddox, John Darnall.

Died: in Wash City, on Jun 11, Mr Wm Henry Washington, of Alexandria Co, after a long & tedious illness, in his 26th yr.

Died: at Nashville, Tenn, Mr Jas Conden, jr; wounded by a 6 pounder, in firing a salute to Gen Jackson on his return, which wound, we are sorry to say, proved mortal. He was a young man, beloved by all who knew him. [No date-recent]

State of N C, Warren Co, in Equity, Apr term, 1815. Fred'k Talley vs Richd Russell, adm of Jas White, dec'd, Betsy White, wid/o Jas White, Matthew White, Thos White, Wm White, Levi White, Chas White, Edw Denton & Eleanor his wife, Henry White, Peter White, Jas White, Matthew Ellis, s/o Stephen Ellis & Fanny his wife, now dec'd. Rg-Levi, Jas, Wm, Matthew, & Henry White are non-residents, or without the limits of this state. -Geo Anderson, C M E.

M Dupont, the pblc spirited prop of the Powder Mills on Brandywine, [Del] at which svr'l persons were killed in an explosion on Jun 8; has settled a yrly pension of $100 on the family of ea of the svr'l persons who were killed on that occasion.

TUE JUN 20, 1815
Lost-pktbk bet Gtwn & Tenlytown, $10 reward. -John Bridges, Gtwn.

Died: some time last month, after a short & painful illness, Capt John Prosser, of *Contest Farm*, Pr Wm Co, Va, in his 65th yr; ofcr of the revolution & a disciple of Jesus Christ. He has left a wife & chldrn. -By a friend. Middleburg, Va, Jun 14..

$5 reward for a young girl, Mgt Adams, who was bound to me, & was taken from my hse on Sun, while I was absent, by her mthr, Charlotte Adams. -Sarah Mathers, Captiol Hill.

Wash Co, D C..Jos Woodworth, insolvent debtor, confined in the prison of Wash Co for debt. -Wm Brent, clk.

WED JUN 21, 1815
Wanted, 6 carpenters at *Greenleaf's Point*. -Andrew Fagan

Wash Co, D C. Case of Ignatius Howe, insolvent debtor, confined in the prison bounds of Wash Co for debt. -Wm Brent, clk.

THU JUN 22, 1815
Gold watch key was lost bet the Treas Dept & Navy Yd on Jun 19th. -Jos Cassin

Wash Co, D C. Case of Thos G Slye, an insolvent debtor, confined in Wash Co prison, for debt. -Wm Brent, clk.

FRI JUN 23, 1815
Orphans Crt of PG Co, Md. Geo Richards, exc of Jonathan T Sasser, ordered to give the notice required by law, to the decd's creditors. -Trueman Tyler, Reg.

SAT JUN 24, 1815
Orphans Crt of Chas Co, Md. Ltrs of adm on est of Rev John Ashton, late of said co, dec'd. -Notley Young, exc.

For sale-350 acs of land in Alexandria Co. Capt Wm Minor or Mr Jas Birch, at the Cross Rds, will shew them. For info apply to Mr Wm Crawford, of Gtwn, or to J Swift, of Alexandria.

Land for sale, 200 acs lying on the Eastern branch of the Potomac; inquire of Mr Mau Young, nr the Anacosta Bridge. -Amelia T Donsett

Pblc sale of all the prsnl est of Jas Shaw, dec'd, late of PG Co, Md; stock, furn, utensils, etc. -Evan Shaw, exc.

Notice: Geo Noud, formerly of N Y C, & lately a sldr in the U S army, died suddenly Jun 23, of an apoplectic fit; relations may apply for his effects. -Robt Leckie

MON JUN 26, 1815
Pblc sale of 6 horses & carts, the prop of D Bashaw, nr the Centre Mkt, Jul 1.

$200 reward for runaway, mulatto man named Billy, who calls himself Wm Whitington, aged 30 yrs. At the same time, & in company, negro, Clem Hill, about 20 yrs old. -Sam'l Sprigg, Northampton Farm, PG Co, Md.

Pblc sale at the late residence of Kidd Morsell, nr Vansville, PG Co, Md, dec'd; 3 negroes, stock furn, etc, being part of the prsnl est of the said dec'd. -John Morsell, adm.

For sale-*Buzzard Island*, lately the prop of Richd Wms Harwood, dec'd; about 750 acs in Calvert Co; dwlg hse is 20 by 30'. View same by applying to Dr Thos Gantt; Dr Wm Weems; Gen Wilkinson; Gustavus Weems, Isaac Wood & Thos Billingsly, who reside within a few miles of the above farm. Judge Ridgely, residing on Elk Ridge, A A Co, can give a good description of this farm. -Thos Harwood

TUE JUN 27, 1815
At a late trial, Col Plumber, plntf, & the Earl of Derby & Sir T Stanley, Bart, dfndnts, the plntf's title to a manor in question, was traced from the era of Alfred the Great! -London paper.

Died: at her fr's residence, in Md, PG Co, Md, on Jun 22, Mrs Dorothy *Glen, d/o Mr Philip Spalding & w/o Noble *Glenn, Mrshl of Savannah, Ga, after a long & painful illness. She has left her hsbnd & 3 chldrn. [-*2 splgs]

Died: in Salem, Mass, on Jun 17, Capt Geo Crowninshield, aged 81. He was grson of John C R Crowninshield, Physician, who was of the first generation of settlers in Salem, & from Germany. He was s/o Capt John Crowninshield, & f/o Jacob Crowninshield, late mbr of Cong, & the present Sec of the Navy, by Mary, d/o the late Rich Derby.

PG Co, Md. Sale of negro woman, Mary, about 27 yrs old, & 1 Roan Mare; prop of Robt Clarke, to satisfy 2 judgments at suit of Francis I Michell, & sundry ofcrs fees due. -Geo Semmes, Shrf of PG Co, Md.

To let-the store & dwlg hse now occupied by Mr John Laub, at Bridge & Wash sts, adj the stores of Rich Anderson & Co, & Clagett & Riggs, Gtwn. Also the dwlg hse of the store of the latter gentlemen. -And Ross or Stephen Pleasonton.

WED JUN 28, 1815
It appears, by a certificate of the Escheator of Spottsylvania Co, that a lot in the town of Fredericksburg & co aforesaid, Va, bounded by Zachariah Lucas' crnr, along the main st 29 ft, cld Roystons's one hundred feet, of which Robt Gallaway died, in the yr 1794, seized & possessed, in fee simple, has been found, in an inquest taken before said Escheator, on Dec 1, 1813, to have escheated to this

commonwealth, for want of heir, of him, the said Gallaway; capable of holding the same. -Wm G Pendleton, Reg.

Wm A Rind & Co have remv'd their printing ofc from Jeff st to the hse in High st lately occupied by Mr J Milligan as his Bk-store & Library, Gtwn.

Orphans Crt of PG Co, Md. Ltrs test on prsnl est of Wm H Wilson, late of PG Co, dec'd. -Amelia Wilson, Jos H Wilson, adms.

Died: at the residence of her hsbnd, in PG Co, Md, Mrs Cynthia Machen, w/o Lewis H Machen, late of Wash City, in her 24th yr.

THU JUN 29, 1815
Died: at his seat in Fauquier Co, Va, on Jun 24, Chas Lee, of Alexandria, aged about 58 yrs.

For sale-all the rl est of Martin Fisher, late of Montg Co, Md, dec'd, lying in said co, about 440 acs lying on the waters of Watt's Branch; with good dwlg hse, etc. -Benj Higgins, atty.

Memoir-Maj Gen Eleazer Wheelock Ripley was born at Hanover, N H, Apr 15, 1782; gr-son of Dr Eleazer Wheelock, the founder of Dartmouth College; & nphw of the present Pres, Hon John Wheelock. His fr, Rev Sylvanus Ripley, a grad of the first class, died in 1787. The subj of this sketch was the 2d son of 6 chldrn, & age 5 yrs when his fr died. [Note-Gen Ripley has been honored with a brvt appointment of Maj Gen, bearing date Jul 25th, the day of the battle of Niagara.]

FRI JUN 30, 1815
Orphans Crt of PG Co, Md. Ltrs test on prsnl est of Wm Morton, late of PG Co, dec'd. -Saml Morton, exc.

Appt'd by the Mayor & Alderman, Wash, for the ensuing yr:
Comrs: Wm Waters, Henry Herford, Henry Ingle, J W Brashears.
Constables: Nathan Moore, Brooke Edmonston, N Griffin, Geo Adams.

Pktbk found on May 16th; apply to Mr John Gaither in Wash City, or to Mary Gaither, nr Snell's Bridge, A A Co, Md.

To Let-tavern stand on High st, Gtwn; lately occupied by Capt Holtzman. -Abner Ritchie.

SAT JUL 1, 1815
For sale-groceries, soap, etc, at my warehse in Gtwn. -Thos Thorpe

Cinc, Jun 16. Drowned on Tue on return to his residence from Brookville, Mr Wm Cooms, age about 66 yrs; Anna Rose, d/o Uriah Rose, & his niece, Phoebe Rose.

Notice. Mortgage made by Edw Boothe to the undersigned, dt'd Jul 14, 1813, recorded in the land records of Wash Co, D C, in sum of $661.41, in which default has been made, will be for pblc sale on Wed at my dwlg hse nr Booth's wharf; for ready cash, the following prop: negro woman, Henney, & her 3 chldrn, Lewis, Alex'r, & Verlender, to satisfy said mortgage. -Jos Johnson. David Bates, auct.

MON JUL 3, 1815
In Chancery, Jun 9, 1815. Ratify sale made by Richd T Lowndes, trustee, for the sale of prop in the cause of Benj Stoddert & others, cmplnts, & Wm Stoddert, & others, dfndnts. Amount to be $5,125. -Jas P Heath, Reg.

Gardener wanted-John Green, *Rosedale*, nr Gtwn.

For sale-500 acs, prop of the late John Dillard, in Culpeper Co, Va, with dwlg hse. Adjs the lands of Gen Moses Green, Mr John Stewart, & the late Philip Latham. Will be shewn by Mr Wm Coones. -Chs Duncan, Exc.

TUE JUL 4, 1815
Ohio land for sale or will exchange for land in Wash City, or vicinity. Land in Ohio, nr the Hockhocking rvr, in Athens Co; 640 ac tract & a 262 ac tract. -John Hines, Wash City.

For sale-new fire engine. -John Achman, Coppersmith & Fire engine mkr, Pa av.

Mr E Oliver, Sen, remv'd from Gtwn to Wash City; fine assortment of dry goods.

Runaways committed to Wash Co jail: negro, Moses, aged 25 yrs; says he belongs to Nat Jentching, of Nansemond Co, on Chickatuck creek, Va. Negro, John, age 22 yrs; says he belongs to Robt Johnson, of Greenville Co, S C. -C Tippet, for W Boyd, mrshl.

THU JUL 6, 1815
Died: in Wash City, on Jul 5, Mrs Eliz Forrest, consort of Mr Jos Forrest. Funeral today from her late residence, at 10 o'clock.

G Watterston, Librarian of Congress.

Horse strayed or stolen from the common of Wash City; $15 reward. -Wm Doughty.

Washington Hotel, Pa av, now ready to accomodate the pblc in general. -Pendleton Heronimus.

New commission hse. -Francis Dodge, Gtwn; J Kettell, Alexandria.

Fresh druge & medicine; Wm F Thornton & Co, Alexandria.

FRI JUL 7, 1815
General assortment of hrdware. -Richd Libby, Alexandria.

St Louis, Jun 10. Last Sun, Mr Alex'r Spencer was shot, stabbed & scalped within 3 miles of the town of St Chas, on the rd to Cuivre. Indians were seen daily in Portage & other villages beyond the Mo.

Ladies with ltrs in the Wash P O, Jul 1, 1815:

Charity Austin	Miss Jane Betts	Eliz Balderston
Miss Bayley	Harriet Baltimore	Mrs Cloe Butler
Mrs M Burns	Miss F Compton	Mary Corles
Mrs H DeKrafft	Mrs E Doughlass	Ellen Enniss
Nelly Ellis	Mrs Fleury	Nancy Gray
Mrs Ann Hill	Miss Ann Hamilton	Rebecca Hyames
Mrs Mary Johnson	Ann M'Williams	Mrs Eliz M'Cann
Miss H Mahoney	Mrs Chas Nevitt	Miss Betsey Rodolph
Mrs Charlotte Russell	Mary Ann Stewart	Ann Smith
Eleanor Stillings	Susannah Saunders	Miss Rachael Smith
Mrs Mary Stewart	Miss Cath Smith	Cath Thomson
Sarah Watson	Sarah Willman	Mrs E Weisenfells

Crct Crt of Wash Co, D C, Jun term, 1815, in Equity. Jas Moore vs John P Van Ness & wife, & Blunt's heirs. Rg-setting aside certain articles of agreement entered into bet John P Van Ness & Marcia his wife, with Geo Blunt, dec'd, for cnvynce to Robt Blunt & Geo Blunt, chldrn of said Geo Blunt, of half of lot 14 in sq 226, Wash City, on 14th st, & to have the same cnvyd to the cmplnt, Jas Moore, on certain terms. Robt & Geo Blunt reside beyond sea. -Wm Brent, clk.

Crt of Chancery of Md. Pblc sale in Port Tobacco, Chas Co, Md, of tract cld *West Hatton*, 500 acs, on Wycomico rvr. Also, part of tract cld *Hard Bargain*, otherwise cld *Wicomico Fields*, 42 1/2 acs. -Th Harris, Trustee, Annapolis.

Orphans Crt of Chas Co, Md. Ltrs of adm on prsnl est of John Brent, late of said co, dec'd. -Wilfred Manning, Adm

State of Md, in Chancery, Jun 23, 1815. Ratify sale of rl est of the late Henry O'Reilly, made & reported by Clement Sewell, as trustee; 37 1/2 acs at $10 per ac. -Jas P Heath, Reg.

SAT JUL 8, 1815
Died: on Jun 24, in his 58th yr, at his residence in Fauquier Co, Va, Chas Lee, long a resident of this town, an eminent cnslr & practitioner of law.

Mrd: on Jul 6, at *Ellerslie*, the residence of Richd Parrot, by Rev Mr Addison, Dr Saml Horsley, a surg in the U S Navy, to Miss Mary Ann Denny.

Wash Co, D C. In Chancery. Pres & Dirs of the Bank of Wash, against Mary Miller & others. Ratify sale by Zachariah Walker, trustee, of lots 16, 17, 18, & the int of Peter Miller in lot 19 in sq 728, with improvements, in Wash City, to Dan'l Carroll, of Dud'n, for $8,071; & part of lot 5 in sq 771, with improvements, to John Chalmers, jr, for $2,000. -Wm Brent, clk.

Lots in Wash City, for sale; Crct Crt of D C, in Chancery; sale at Heronimus' Htl, late John M'Leod's, the prop of the late Col Henry Gaither, lots in sq 127, 22 & 23, occupied by John Knap, as a garden; lots 2 & 3 in sq 104. -Benj Gaither, Danl Gaither, trustees.

Sale at auction-all the right & est of Fred'k Mayer, dec'd, in lot 7 in sq 576 in Wash City; by deed in trust from Fred'k Mayer, dec'd, made to secure th payment of a sum of money due to Andrew Scholfield. -John Hewitt, Jos Scholfield, trust.

MON JUL 10, 1815
Died: on Jul 2, in Loudoun Co, Va, Brig Gen Hugh Douglas, in his 55th yr; hsbnd, fr, & bro.

Land for sale-200 acs about 2 miles from Wash. Info from Mr Mau Young, nr the Anacosta Bridge, Eastern Branch. -Amelia T Dorsett. [Dorsett was spelled Donsett in previous notices.]

Notice-to the heirs & grdns of the minors, that I have, at last Mar term of St Mary's Co Crt, [Md] obtained a commission on the rl est of Thos Brown, late of said co, & returns will be made to Aug crt. -Jas Brown

TUE JUL 11, 1815
Orphans Crt of PG Co, Md. Pblc auction of the hse of the late Gen Covington, in said co, the present residence of the subscriber, a part of the prsnl est of the late Rinaldo Johnson, dec'd; horses, furn, utensils, blacksmith tools, etc, for sale. -Ann E Johnson, admx. [Mrs.]

WED JUL 12, 1815
Died: at New Brunswick, N J, on Jun 24, Mr Henry Guest, in his 80th yr. In the revolution he ranked among the foremost advocates of his country's freedom, etc.

Mrd: in N Y, on Jul 5, by Rev Dr Bowen, Geo W Rodgers, mstr cmdnt in the U S N, to Miss Ann M Perry, d/o Christopher R Perry, of R I.

One cent reward-for John Dickinson, age about 20 yrs, appr to the taylor business. -Jos Ward.

THU JUL 13, 1815
Firewood for sale. Shadrach Davis, clk o/the works at the Capitol.

Died: in Petersboro, N H, on Jun 8, venerable & aged Lt Wm Robbe, long known for healing powers in the disorder cld King's Evil.

Mrd: in Wash City, by Rev Mr M'Cormick, on Jul 12, Mr Jas Entwisle to Mrs Mary Ann Mason, both of the Theatre.

Crt held for Culpeper Co, Va, Mar 20. Rg-agreement bet Jas Wheatley & Robt Gillespie, settlement of *still rights*. Testimonial from Geo Crump, Fauquier Co, Va. Others named: Benj Roberts; Mr Arthur Sharpe, Zachariah Crimm; Mr Jas Stringfellow, Leonard Courtney, Philagathus Roberts, [bro o/Benj Roberts] Wm Broadus, jr, C C C, Wm Thompson, Minor Winn, Wm Wheatley, [bro o/Jas Wheatley,] Eliz Brown, Geo Martin, Wm Brooke o/Falmouth. In 1799, Francis Martin was agent for his fr, Chas Martin; sold corn, bacon, & whiskey belonging to his fr, to Mr Jas Allen, of Fauq, & tk in payment a bond on Col Wm Green & Saml Green, of Culpeper. Eliz Brown writes that during her widowhood, nr 7 yrs, she resided in the hse of her fr, Chas Martin, o/Fauq Co; Jas Wheatley is her bro-in-law; Francis Martin is her bro. Also named-Nimrod Farrow, Robt Green, Moses Gibson, Zach Shurly, Caleb Tait o/Lynchburg, Armistead Morehead o/Ky.

FRI JUL 14, 1815
Pblc sale of lots 132 thru 136 in Gtwn, on Fayette st; in the case of Jas & Wm Calder, John Cox & John Peabody against the heirs & reps of Mary Mitchell, dec'd. -Chas Glover, trustee.

Pblc sale-deed of trust executed by the late Geo Baltzer, to secure a debt due Thos Cramphin; yellow man cld Sam Dorsey, age about 20 yrs, butcher. -John Ott, Tr.

SAT JUL 15, 1815
We understand that brvt rank in the line has been conferred by the Pres of the U S on the following ofcrs, attached to Maj Gen Jackson's div of the army, for svcs during the siege of New Orleans, & general good conduct in said army:
Robt Butler, brvt Lt Col-Adjt Gen; Alex'r A White, do; Henry D Piere, do; Wm Platt, do,-Q M Gen; Walter H Overton, do; Arthur P Hayne, brvt Maj-Inspec Gen; Henry Chotard, do-A Adj Gen; John M Davis, do-A Insp Gen; John Reid, do; Wm O Butler, do; Isac L Baker, do; Wm Lavall, do; Thos L Butler, do; Sam'l Vail, do; Geo C Allen, do; Elijah Montgomery, do; Enoch Humphreys, do; Sam'l Spotts brvt Capt; Wm Gibbs, do; Jos :Leach, brvt 2d Lt.

For sale: prop at Port Sligo, 2 rvr lots, 5 & 6, that front on Caroline st. Can be seen with Mr Anthony Buck. -John Mortimer, Fredericksburg, Va.

Central Bank of Gtwn & Wash; Commissioners:		
John Rodgers	Burton Whetcroft	John Tayloe
John S Haw	Obadiah Rich	Jacob Wagner
Thos C Hodges	Thos Hyde	Christ Carlisle
John Macdaniel, Jr	Wm Grayson	Thos T Gant
		Geo Clarke

Orphans Crt of Wash Co, D C. Application of Jehu Stockwell for ltrs of adm on prsnl est of John O'Donnell, late a pvt in the U S 25th regt of infty, dec'd. -Jno Hewitt, reg.

Orphans Crt of PG Co, Md. Prsnl est of Geo Hilleary, late of said co, dec'd. -Lloyd Hilleary, exc.

All claims against the late firm of Electius & Jas Middleton: present same to Jas Middleton, surviving partner.

For sale-lot 1 in sq 700, with 2 story brick hse, occupied by Wm Radcliffe; lot 4 in sq 796; lot 15 in sq 762. -Jas Middleton

MON JUL 17, 1815
Orphans Crt of PG Co, Md. Ltrs of adm on est of Zephaniah Cissel, late of said co, dec'd. -Rachel Cissel, Saml Cissel, adms.

Died: at Richmond, on Jul 16th, after a lingering illness, Maj Archibald Denholm, an ofcr of the Rev war.

Orphans Crt of Wash Co, D C. Ltrs test on the will & prsnl est of Wm H Washington, late of Alexandria Co, dec'd. -Geo A Washington, exc.

Crct Crt for Wash Co, D C, in Chancery. Wm Bryden vs Jas Bryden. Rg: foreclosure of a mort from dfndnt to Wm Bryden, of ground in Wash City, sq 862; Jas Bryden resides without the Dist of Col. -Wm Brent, clk.

Valuation of lands, lots, dwlg hses, & slaves, subj to U S Direct Tax, may be seen at the hse of Mr Chas M'Knight, of Alexandria; & at Danl Reintzel's in Gtwn. -Jas M'Guire, Principal assessor of D C.

TUE JUL 18, 1815
For sale-a good bargain in the stills, apparatus & materials of a small distillery erected on my farm last yr. -Will Hebb, St Osyth, PG Co, Md.

WED JUL 19, 1815
Elijah Dotson, who robbed Mr John M'Kee of 5 watches, & stole his horse, on Jul 11, in Chesterville, has been apprehended. He was taken to the goal of Salisbury, where he is now confined. -Columbia, [S C] State Gaz.

For sale or rent-valuable tan yd in Wash City. -Seth Hyatt

THU JUL 20, 1815
Balt, Jun 5, 1815. Inclosed you will find $1,000, in the name of the *First Balt Hussars,* to erect a monument to the memory of ctzns who fell on Sep 12 & 13, in the battle at No Point, & at the bombardment of Ft M'Henry. -J Smith Hollins, S M'Clellan, S Hollingsworth, Eli Simkins.

For sale-annuity for my life, of $400 per yr, *Woodville,* etc. -Sarah White, nr Winchester, Va.

Died: on Jul 5, Hon John Bradley, of Concord, N H, aged 71, a patriot, philanthropist & christian. In 1747, when John was 3 yrs of age, his fr, Saml Bradley, together with Jonathan, his uncle, & 3 others, wer ambuscaded & killed about 1 mile west from Concord st, by a party of Indians from Canada. His mthr, who will be 97 in Aug, is the oldest person lvg in town.

Dirs of the Salisbury Branch Bank:
David Howard
Wm Handy, Sen
Eben Christopher
Francis W James
Jas Herron
John Rider
Handy H Irving
Thos Hooper
Henry Parsons

FRI JUL 21, 1815
Fire at Petersburg, overwhelming calamity; seen to issue from a stable in the rear of the dwlg hse occupied by Mr John Walker, on Bolling-brook st; svr'l lives lost-among which was Saml Myers, a ntv of Balt, who was in the employ of Mr Thos Wallace. Over 400 hses were devoured on Jul 16th.

Info is wanted of Jas Linwell, who, in 1796, lived nr the Gap Tvrn, Salisbury twnshp, Pa, is supposed, he remv'd to N Y. Info of said Linwell, direct to Dan Eaton, Missquitoe Creek P O, Trumbull Co, Ohio; will confer a favor on the widow M'Curdy, formerly of Salisbury twnshp, who at this time is in a pitiful situation.

Mrshl's sale-all title, right, int, etc of Fred'k A Plate, in lot 3 sq 376, on F st; at suit of John Fritchie against the said Plate. -Wash Boyd, Mrshl, D C.

Gtwn College. Examination of the students, Jul 25. -John Grassi, Pres.

SAT JUL 22, 1815
To Printers-sale of founts of type. -Chas De Krafft, Wash City.

The vestry of the upper part of St John's Parish, in PG Co, Md, will meet at Addison's Chapel on Jul 31. -Geo Calvert, Richd T Lowndes, Bladensburg, Md.

Runaway, Joe Tyrer, negro, age about 35 yrs, committed to Wash Co, D C, jail; says he belongs to Maj John Miller, nr Port Royal, Va. -C Tippett, for W Boyd, mrshl.

Farm to lease; formerly the residence of Evan Thomas; 460 acs, in Montg Co, Md; with brick dwlg hse, etc. -Edw Connelly, residing in Gtwn.

Pblc sale in Port Tobacco, all the rl est of Saml Hamilton, dec'd, lying in Chas Co, Md, & adjoining ea other, to wit: *Herefordshire, Green's Forest, Slater's Benefit, Poverty, Coomes' Park, Uncle & Nphw, Smith's Chance,* addition to *Green's Forest, Hanson's Trifle,* addition to *Herefordshire, & Ferrell's Neglect*; the whole about 677 + acs. -Jos Green, Wm P Ford, Henry M'Pherson of Henry, Gerard Greenwell, Comr's for the sale of the rl est of Sam'l Hamilton, dec'd.

MON JUL 24, 1815
Sale of Wash City lots for taxes:
Delius, Frederick
Hemmersley, Wm
M'Mahon, Robt
-Zach Walker, Coll of Third Ward.

Appleton, John
Graham, Richard
Langley, Edw
Tilghman, Richd

Appleton, Henry
Hooe, Robt T
Leeke, Ann
Thomas, Richd

Committees on the fire at Petersburg, Va: [Jul 16, 1815]
Geo H Jones
Thos Shore
Robt Bolling
Robt Birchett
Saml Chrisman
E Powell
Edw Pescud
Wm Moore
Thos E Gary
Robt Ritchie
Chas Kent
Abraham S Lochhead

Wm Haxall
John Allison
Geo K Taylor
Wm Clarke
Jas Durell
John Osborne
Patrick Durkin
Francis Lynch
Alex'r Taylor
Christopher T Jones
John V Willcox
Geo H Jones, Chrmn

Donald McKenzie
John F May
Wm Prentis
Dr Richd Field
John Grammar
Nathl Friend
Jos Caldwell
Joel Hamilton
Jabez Smith
Johnson Henderson
Timothy R Ryan
J F May, Sec'y

For sale-prop on Pa Av, with good frame hse. -Geo Creager

TUE JUL 25, 1815
Died: on Jul 22, after a lingering illness of nrly 6 mos, Mr Thos Baker, former merchant of Gtwn. He has left an affectionate wife & one small child.

Sale of Wash City, lots for taxes:
John Allen
John Beall
Benj Bacon
Saml Clark
Henry Hilliary, jr
David Kemp
Thos Ketland
Saml Miller
Christian Orandor_
Henry Robinson
Chris'n Shell heirs
John Weem heirs
Porter & Sterrett
-Jos Brumley, Col 1st ward.

Jacob Boyer
Thos Beall &
Walter S Chandler
Hezekiah Claggett
John Hadrick
Danl Kesler
Thos S Lee
John Marshall & J Hopkins, & Jas Marshall
Nathl Orme
Andrew Scolfield
Thos L Shippin
R Wignell heirs
Stoddert & Templeman

Matthias Buckey
Leo M Deakens
Danl Carmack
Henry Goil
Thos Johns
Peter Kemp
Philip H Myers

Matrthias Rednover
John Shepherd
Jas Strange
Marsham Waring

Hse for sale, lot 18 in sq 457, Wash. -Gilson Noell

WED JUL 26, 1815
Died: in Belgium, the celebrated Duke of Beluno, Marshal Victor.

THU JUL 27, 1815
Died: in Wash City, on Jul 26, very suddenly, Nicholas Lefevre, of Huntingdon, Pa, aged about 70 yrs. He emigrated from Ireland about 15 yrs ago.

State of Md, in Chancery, Jul 18, 1815. Thos Price vs John C Jones, Maria H Jones, Robt C Jones & Susanna Jones, heirs of John C Jones. Rg-sale of rl est which descended from John C Jones, dec'd, for the payment of his debts. -W Kilty, Ch.

Carpetings & rugs. Thos W Pairo has just opened his store on Pa av, Wash.

FRI JUL 28, 1815
Pblc auction at the hse of Mr Jos Tiffin, on Aug 1; all his hsehld & kitchen furn. -David Bates, auct.

Orphans Crt of PG Co, Md. Prsnl est of Geo Stevenson, late of said co, dec'd. -Mgt Stevenson, admx.

SAT JUL 29, 1815
Partnership of Truman Beck & Joel Brown, was dissolved on Jul 10, 1815, by mutual consent. Accounts will be settled by Truman Beck.

Sale of Wash City, lots for taxes:

Ann Brodeau	David Crawford heirs	Tunis Craven
Wm Cowper	Bernard Hart	Nathl Ingraham
Edw Parry	John Race	Jas Reed
Jos Slater	David Slater	Thos Slater
Mark Stockwell heirs	Ann Slater	Henry Slater
Sarah Slater	Jona Slater heirs	Henry Shroeder
Francis Sands	Richd Thomas	Jas Thompson
Geo Walker heirs	Walker & Wheeler	Eliz Wheeler
Jas Walker	Wm Wilson	Willink & Wilham
John Ward	Jas Waugh	Benj Young heirs
Bernard Elliott heirs	Thos Brown	

-Geo Adams, Coll 4th Ward.

MON JUL 31, 1815
Land agency, in Ohio. Info wanted respecting land in Ohio can be obtained by ltrs to Chas Lofland, Chillicothe.

Died: lately at N Y, in his 22d yr, Jas M Baldwin, midshipman in the U S Navy, in a fit, which was occasioned by a wound he rec'd on Lake Champlain on Sep 18.

TUE AUG 1, 1815
$20 reward for runaway, negro man named Robin, age about 36 yrs. -Jas Ferguson, lvg in Fred'k Co, Va, nr the Rock's Ferry.

$20 reward for runaway, black man named Moses, age 34 yrs. -John Payne, lvg in Orange Co, Va.

WED AUG 2, 1815
Lt Col Thos Spindle o/the 34th regt Culpeper, Va militia, chg'd with disobedience o/orders & neglect of duty, acquitted & his sword restored. -Wm Madison, Pres.

John Smith, Senior, of Spottsylvania Co, Va, obtained a patent on Apr 28, 1815, for a machine for gathering clover seed. -Jos Y Smith, Fredericksburg, Va, sole agent.

THU AUG 3, 1815
John G McDonald is authorized to dispose of any lots in Wash City, under my care. -Jas Greenleaf

Bank of Metropolis, A Kerr, cashier. Patriotic Bank of Wash, Overton Carr, do.

Strayed or stolen; sorrel horse off the common nr Mr Miller's brick yd on G st, Wash City. Secure same & bring him to Capt John R Dyer, lvg on G st, nr Mr Clephan's, Wash City; $5 reward. -Giles Dyer, nr Broad Crk, PG Co, Md.

FRI AUG 4, 1815
For sale, prop where I now live, on Wash st. I wish to remove. -J Mosher, Gtwn

SAT AUG 5, 1815
Comrs appt'd for making a Turnpike Rd from Gtwn towards Leesburg; subscriptions under the direction of:

		Wash Bowie
John Eliason	Wm Whann	Edgar Patterson
John Hoye	John W Bronaugh	Wm Marbury
Wm Steuart	Geo Johnson	

Trustees of the Institution for the education of youth in Wash City.:
Josiah Meigs	Dr Wm Matthews	Benj Homans
Moses Young	Saml N Smallwood	Geo Blagdon
Wm Prout		

Died: on Aug 2, in Wash City, Richd Freeman, many yrs a clk in the Treas Dept, & formerly of the Srvyr Gen Ofc of the state of Pa.

New Auction & Commission Hse, Bridge st, Gtwn. Danl Mallory & Richd Key Watts, jr.

The copartnership of Richards & Mallory is this day dissolved by mutual consent. The bkselling & stationer's business will be carried on by Geo Richards, at the old stand, in Bridge st.

MON AUG 7, 1815

$20 reward-ranaway from me in Staunton, Va, on Jul 14, negro man, Henry; purchased of Dr Trent, of Richmond. -John G Wright, Staunton, Va.

Sale at auction, by deed of trust to subscribers from Fred'k Mayer, dec'd, to secure money due to Andrew Scholfield; all the right, etc of said Mayer in lot 7 in sq 576 in Wash City, with tenement hse. -John Hewitt, Jos Scholfied, trustees.

TUE AUG 8, 1815

Pblc sale; order of the Orphans Crt of PG Co, Md, on Aug 19th, at Mr Henry Boswell's tvrn in the town of Nottingham, all the prsnl prop of Chas S Perry, dec'd; furn, etc. -John Carter, auct

WED AUG 9, 1815

Died: on Jul 28, at his seat nr Gtwn, Philip Barton Key. As a politician he was eminent; as a lwyr, he stood in the first rank of his profession; as a genteman, he was greatly respected.

THU AUG 10, 1815

Jas A Bayard is no more! He died on the evening of the 7th, in consequence of the bursting o/the abscess in his breast, having with calm resignation expected his fate.

Died: at Phil on Aug 6, after a lingering illness, John Smith, Post Capt-U S N.

$30 reward for appr boy to the carpenter's business, Stanislaus Mudd, age bet 19 & 20 yrs. -Cornelius M'Lean, Wash City.

Burke's Garden Grave. John Daly Burke, a ntv of Ire, but an American by adoption, fell, in duel, on the banks of the Appomatto; he lies buried in the garden of Gen Jones. -From the *Union*.

FRI AUG 11, 1815

Assessors-Wash City. Alex McIntire, Jas Hewitt, Henry Herford, Lloyd M Low, Henry Ingle, John T Frost, John W Brashears, David Bates.

SAT AUG 12, 1815

Wash Co, D C. Lewin Talbert of said co, nr the Eastern Branch Bridge, brought before me a stray mule. Sam'l N Smallwood, J P.

$50 reward for mulatto woman, Jane, who absconded on Jul 9. -Lewis H Machen, Wash City.

For sale-per last will of Saml Robertson, 3d, all the prsnl est of same, of Montg Co, Md, dec'd; 10 negroes, stock, waggon with geers, etc. Also, *Goshen* mills & lands; 300 acs; also another tract of 53 acs, with improvements. -Wm Robertson, & Aaron Offutt, excs.

Orphans Crt of Montg Co, Md. Prsnl est of Benj Nichols, late of Montg Co, dec'd.

-Wm Culver, adm.

Orphans Crt of Wash Co, D C. Prsnl est of Richd Freeman, late of said city, dec'd. -Jos Stretch, John Gardiner, adms.

MON AUG 14, 1815
Mrd: on Aug 11, in Wash City, by Rev Mr M'Cormick, Mr Jos F W Harris to Miss Sophia Douglass Abercrombie, both of the Theatre.

Mrd: on Aug 13, by Rev Mr Balch, Mr Wm Anderson to Miss Euphemia Jefferson, d/o Mr Jos Jefferson, all of the Theatre.

Died: on the last of Jul, 1815, at his country seat in Fred'k Co, Va, after a short but severe illness, Capt Saml B Green, in his 54th yr; in the death of whom society has sustained a severe loss. He leaves his wife & chldrn.

Biog sketch of the hero of Thames; Col R M Johnson, s/o Robt Johnson, a farmer & one of the first settlers of Ky. He killed Tecumseh in fair prsnl combat; the fame of his exploits preceded him as he resumed his seat in Congress.

John C Drodly pleaded guilty to an indictment against him at the last Fayette Crct Crt, for passing counterfeit bank notes. -From the Western Monitor.

Students who excelled at an examination held on Jul 25, 1815, Gtwn College:
Aloysius Young, DC
Geo Dinnies, N Y
Chas Pise, Gtwn
Henry Gough, St Mary's, Md
Jas Ryder, N Y
Fred'k Barber, N Y
Victor Dugoure, W Indies
Robt Beale, Wash City,
Thos Jameson, Chas Co, Md
John Lancaster, Chas Co, Md
Jos Schneller, Phil
Isaac Inskeep, Romney, Va
Patrick Byrne, Balt, Md
Jas Almeda, Balt
Robt Neale, St Mary's Co, Md
Chas Vincendon, Estrn shore, Md.
Chas Dinnies, N Y
Geo Mathews, Chas Co, Md
Angus Wheeler, Balt
Geo Fenwick, Gtwn
John Smith, Fred'k Co, Md.
Dennis Doyle, N Y
Lewis Joncherez, Gtwn
Michl Murray, N Y
Robt Digges, Chas Co, Md
Jas Calagan, Balt
Waldron Godwin, N Y
Francis Bowling, Chas Co, Md
Thos Lee, nr Balt
Pearl Durkee, Balt
Wm Christie, Phil
[-John Grassi, Pres, Gtwn, D C.]

Orphans Crt of Chas Co, Md. Prsnl est of Dr Edw Briscoe, late of said co, dec'd. -Sarah M Briscoe, admx.

Pblc sale of *Groomslot*, 300 acs in PG Co, Md; with dwlg hse. Also a tract about 340 1/2 acs. -John S Magruder, Captiol Hill, Wash.

TUE AUG 15, 1815

For Liverpool, ship *Superior*, John Hamilton, mstr; will sail from Phil. Apply to John Trimble, Balt, or Jos A Longstreet, or Saml Spackman, 24 Church st, Phil.

Orphans Crt of Wash Co, D C. Prsnl est of Thos Baker, late of said co, dec'd. -Catherine Baker, Admx.

Elegant farm for sale, the subscriber having lost nrly all his negroes, 21 in number, taken from him on Jul 21, 1814, by the British squad, then up the Patuxent, under the command of Jos Nourse; crop taken; stock plundered, etc. 1,000 acs in Calvert Co, Md, with lg 2 story dwlg hse, 52' x 36'. Nothing could induce him to part with this farm, for centuries in his family, but for the great, unmerited & cruel losses he has sustained by the late fatal war. -M Taney, Calvert Co, Md.

WED AUG 16, 1815

Died: on Jul 26, Capt Francis Pearl, of Woodford Co, Ky. He died without any child, & has left an est bet $60,000 & $100,000, which he devised to be vested in a Free School to bear his name, superintended by the County Crt of Woodford.

THU AUG 17, 1815

Proposals for publishing, in Wash City, a wkly jrnl-*The Nat'l Register*; forming a complete Annual Reg of all Pblc Documents & State papers. -Joel K Mead

Tobacco lost; inspected in Dugan & O'Donnell's Warehse, Balt, Md. -J Laidler, Chas Co, Md.

FRI AUG 18, 1815

Fred'k land for sale, at the late dwlg hse of Thos Fawcett, dec'd, 304 acs, in Fred'k Co, Va. -I Fawcett, E Fawcett, excs.

SAT AUG 19, 1815

Shrf's sale-*The Forest*, & part of *The Forest of Sherwood*; 143 acs, levied on as the prop of Arthur Campbell, & will be sold to satisfy debts due Chas S Pierce, use of Peter Hoffman, Jas & Thos Contee Worthington, exc of Thos Contee, use of Eliz Sadler, excx of Thos Sadler. -Geo Semmes, shrf, PG Co, Md.

Pvt sale of *Bellassise*, a beautiful farm in Montg Co, Md; 252 acs; adjs the land of the late Jas Lockland. -Mallory & Watts, aucts

Shrf's sale-2 negro boys & land cld *Digbeth*, about 100 acs; prop of Levin Clarke, wlll be sold to satisfy a debt due Henry T Compton, survivor of Walter T Greenfield, use of the reps of Geo W Gibbons. -Geo Semmes, shrf of PG Co, Md.

Shrf's sale-suit of John Hodges of Thos, use of Richd Snowden, against Fielder Dorsett, exc of Wm N Dorsett, at the residence of the late Fielder Dorsett, in PG Co, Md: 4 negroes. -Geo Semmes, Shrf PG Co, Md.

MON AUG 21, 1815
For sale-brick warehse & the wharf oppo, on West Landing or Water st, Gtwn. -Jane Lowndes, Fras Lowndes, Gtwn.

Died: in Bavaria, Alex'r Berthier, Prince of Neufchatel, aged 62, by a fall from a window, while looking at some troops passing by. He was mrd to the niece of the King of Bavaria, at whose crt he resided.

TUE AUG 22, 1815
$5 reward for a sorrel mare that strayed from the Paymstr's ofc in Wash City, on Fri. Deliver to me, or to Mr Heronimus in Wash City. -Matthew D Reardon, Sign of the Eagle, Alexandria.

Pblc sale at the late residence of Wm N Dorsett, late of PG Co, Md, dec'd, nr Mr Fielder Bowie's, all the prsnl prop of the dec'd, including 14 negroes. -Gerard T Greenfield, Henry Boswell, adms.

Notice is hereby given to the ctzns of the U S & the inhabitants of Wash Co, D C, that my wife Catharine Wilson has eloped from my bed & board without provocation, etc. -Thos Wilson, Aug 21, 1815

C L Weisskopff-Confectinary Store, Bridge st, Gtwn.

WED AUG 23, 1815
Sales of rl est. The mansion hse & lot of Geo Johnson, 150' on Fred'k st, & 50' on Prospect st. Also, the prop of W G Maxwell, on the bank of the Potomac rvr. -Mallory & Watts, aucts.

For sale-farm on *Slago Branch*, in Montg Co, Md, 400 acs; nr Mr Thos Simpson's farm, with 2 story dwlg hse. Mr Thos Gettings, or Mr Thos Simpson, who live adjoining will shew the land. For terms, apply to Robt B Beall, lvg in Gtwn.

Wash Co, D C. Edw Randell, mgr of Maj Geo Peter's farm, in said Co, brought to my view, a stray gelding. -Danl Reintzell, J P, Wash Co, D C.

For sale-the hse I now occupy. Also, the lg stone warehse at the mouth of the Tiber. -John P Van Ness

THU AUG 24, 1815
$30 reward for runaways, 2 apprs to the Printing Bus; Peter Keen, aged bet 19 & 20 yrs; Saml Weir, aged bet 18 & 19 yrs. -Jas Peacock, Harriburg, Pa.

Partnership bet David Ott & John Ott, dissolved by mutual consent. The stock in trade purchased by David Ott. The subscribers have formed a connection in the Apothecary & Drugg bus cld David Ott & Co; store at Pa av, lately occupied by David Ott. -David Ott, Philip Mauro

For sale, prop advertised by Geo Creager; crnr lot so of Pa av, with good frame hse, Wash. -Jonathan Appler

Pblc sale, about 760 acs in Upper Marlbro, PG Co, Md, with dwlg hse. -Wm Gover

Copartnership of Queen, Belt & Co, lumber bus, is dissolved by mutual consent. The bus will carry on as Queen & Moore. Nicholas L Queen, Geo Moore.

FRI AUG 25, 1815
Mrd: in Knoxville, Ten, on Aug 7, by Rev Thos Nelson, Maj Gen Edmund Pendleton Gaines to Miss Barbara G Blount, d/o Wm Blount, dec'd.

Died: on Aug 18, after a lingering illness, Chauncey Goodrich, Lt Gov of Conn.

Hsekpr wanted-Wm H Hamer. Wash Item.

SAT AUG 26, 1815
Mrd: on Aug 22, in Gtwn, by Rev Mr Norris, Mr Isaac K Hanson, of Wash, to Miss Maria Harrison Jones, of the former place.

Shot & Glass ware-oppo the Marine barracks, Navy Yd. -Garston Powell

For sale-*Strawberry Hill*, 180 acs, within 2 miles of Upper Marlbro. -W B Beanes

MON AUG 28, 1815
Providence, R I Patriot. Man-stealing; Mr Saml Hopkins, of Foster, & Mr Henry Stone, of Scituate, R I, have recently returned home, the first absent 17 yrs, the latter 13 yrs. They were impressed into the naval svc of Gr Britain, from American vessels; they have been immured in the dungeons of Dartmoor. Mr Hopkins has a grown son; his family long since thought him dead. Mr Stone wrote to his fr repeatedly while in slavery, documents were sent, but in vain.

Land for sale-bet 350 to 400 acs of land in Montg Co, Md, lying nr the head of Seneca Crk. -Wm Grayson, Gtwn.

Bell's London Messenger. Dead, Mr Saml Whitbread, by suicide, at his hse on Thu, in Dover st. He mrd the sister of Earl Grey, & has left 2 sons & 2 dghts; the eldest dght was mrd a short time since to the bro of the Earl of Waldegrave. Mr Whitbread was 57 yrs of age, the only s/o the 3d d/o Earl Cornwallis. Lady Eliz, & her unmrd dght; John Weir, who had lived with the dec'd as a butler for 27 yrs, were in the hse. Coroner's jury returned a verdict of *Insanity*.

Stray cow taken up on Aug 26th. -Judson Richardson, Navy Yd, Wash, D C.

Crt of Inquiry for the 60th regt Va Militia, at Fairfax Crt-hse, on Sep 22, for the assessment of fines against the following persons, to wit: Wm Jenkins
John Perry   David Allen   Jas Williams

Giles Fitzhugh	Jesse Bladen	Wm Hughes
Francis Graves	Jas Thompson	John Lacy
John Farmer	Geo Lawson	John Campbell

[Above for refusing to obey the call under orders of Dec 1813.]

John Harrison	Horatio Moreland	Thos Ball
Wm Spencer	John Lacy	

Same for May 13, 1814. -John Reid, Adj 60th Reg Va Mil.

TUE AUG 29, 1815
Partnership of D Rapine & Jonathan Elliot is dissoved by mutual consent.

Ranaway-appr to hair dressing business, Jos Plumber, has about 17 mos to serve. -Peter Vallet

Drowned-on Aug 27, while stepping from the Potomac Bridge, on board the Steam Boat, Mr John Hines, printer, of Winchester, Va.

WED AUG 30, 1815
Wash Co, D C, in Chancery. Geo King, John Davidson & John B Evans, vs Ann Young, the widow of Saml W Young, Eliz Young, Susanna Young, Richd Young, John Young, & Chas Young, the chldrn & heirs of Abraham Young, dec'd, & Wm King & Adam King of D C, & *Jos Ball, *Henry Pratt, *John Ashley, *Thos Willing Francis, *John Miller, jr, & *Jacob Baker. Bill states that Abraham Young, dec'd, late of Wash, did on Sep 16, 1792, sell to Wm King & Wm Prout, land in Wash cld *Chance, Hogpen Enlarged, & Knock*. Wm King, on Jul 20, 1794, sold his moiety to John Nicholson, late of Phil, now dec'd, etc. *All resided in Phil. -Wm Brent, clk.

THU AUG 31, 1815
Pblc sale as excx of the last will & test of Saml Norwood, late of Balt Co, dec'd; 500 acs, dwlg plantation, about 6 miles from Balt City; stock etc. -Mary Norwood, excx.

FRI SEP 1, 1815
Ossian Hall, for sale. The land on which I now reside, 830 acs, 9 miles from Alexandria; with frame dwlg hse, etc. -Wm S Stuart, Fairfax Co, Va.

Geo Pitts requests all who stand indebted to him, to pay their acct's. Gtwn, Sep 1.

SAT SEP 2, 1815
Obit-Chactaw Agency, Jul 8, 1815. About the 1st, Col Richd Sparks, late of the 2d infty, was relieved from duty, & put in snug qrtrs, till the grand reveillie shall awaken the armies of the universe.

Orphans Crt of Chas Co, Md. Ltrs of adm on est of John T Wood, late of said co, dec'd. -Ann W Wood, admx.

MON SEP 4, 1815
Died: at York, Pa, on Aug 28, Mrs Anna Mary Bacon, consort of Capt Saml Bacon of the Marine Corps, & for some time a resident of Wash City.

Wash Co, D C. 1-Chas L Nevitt, insolvent debtor, confined in the prison of Wash Co for debt. 2-Geo Rowland, insolvent debtor, same. -Wm Brent, clk.

TUE SEP 5, 1815
Wanted-a journeyman currier. Apply to Jos Huber, Dumfries, Va.

WED SEP 6, 1815
For sale-10 cases Irish Linens. Geo S Hough, Alexandria.

Died: a few days ago, after a lingering & painful illness, at his seat in Kent Co, Md, Dr Benson Bond Blake.

Died: on Sep 3, in her 28th yr, Mrs Sarah D Semmes, consort of Mr Jos Semmes, of Gtwn. She was afflicted with a long & lingering sickness. Her loss is severely felt by her surviving affectionate hsbnd & friends.

Ohio bottom land for sale; 2 tracts of land in Mason Co, Va; 1304 acs & 1411 acs. -Jas M Garner, Loretto, Essex Co, Va.

THU SEP 7, 1815
Land for sale-270 acs in PG Co, Md. Also a tract of 74 acs, about 1 mile from the former. Also, negroes, stock, utensils. -Benoe Soper

Messrs Benj Henry Latrobe & Robt King have been appt'd Srvyrs of Wash City, & Superintendants of bldgs. -Thos Munroe, super'dt.

FRI SEP 8, 1815
The subscriber is willing to dispose of the copyright of a work entitled *The History of Virginia*, by Edmund Randolph. -Peyton Randolph, Richmond, Aug 19.

For rent-store & front cellar on Pa av, Wash. -H O Middleton, Gtwn.

Ingle, Sweeny & Lindsley, have opened their hrdwre store on Pa av, Wash.

From the Boston Daily Advertiser. Ferdinand IV, King of Sicily, is the s/o Chas III, King of Spain, & born Jan 12, *1751; ascended the throne on Oct 5, 1769, on his fr's becoming king of Spain. He mrd Apr 7, *1761, Princess Mary Caroline, d/o the empress Maria Theresa o/Austria, & aunt o/the present emperor. His nose immoderately long like that of his fr & bro Chas III & Chas IV, Kings of Spain His older bro is Chas IV; Philip Duke of Calabria, the oldest bro. The late Queen died on Oct 8, 1814. [*Born in '51 & mrd in '61-as copied.]

SAT SEP 9, 1815
Mrd: on Sep 5, by Rev Obadiah B Brown, Mr Alexander M'Intire to Miss Eliz E Moore, d/o the late Joshua J Moore, all of Wash City.

Mrd: on Sep 7, in Wash City, by Rev O B Brown, Mr John Potter, of Alexandria, to Miss Ann Campbell.

Subscribers will sell prop in Culpeper Co, Va; one tract of 828 acs, with dwlg hse; tract of 2,300 acs, with dwlg hse. Also another tract of 570 acs. Apply to John W Green, Fredericksburg, or to the subscribers, Jeremiah Strother, & Co. John Strother, jr, & Co. Lewellen Mills, Culpeper, Va.

Negro girl, Kitty, committed to St Mary's Co, Md, jail; prop of Josias Samuel, of N C. -Enoch Combs, shrf.

Ad by Geo Blagden, Mstr of the Stone Cutters, for boatmen to transport tons of Freestone from a quarry on the Potomac rvr.

MON SEP 11, 1815
Died: at Doden, in A A Co, Md, on Aug 29 last, after a short illness, Mstr Cmdnt John McPherson Gardner, U S N, formerly a resident of Phil.

TUE SEP 12, 1815
Mrd: in Hagerstown, Md, on Sep 5, Mr Thos Mustin, of the War Dept, to Miss Sophia Western Helm, d/o the late Thos Helm, of that place.

Notice-ltrs of adm on est of Clement Kennedy, late of Chas Co, Md, dec'd. - Daniel Kennedy, Sandy Point, Chas Co, Md.

WED SEP 13, 1815
Dissolution of partnership, by mutual consent, bet Daniel Deveny & Chas Deveny, Gtwn.

Orphans Crt of Chas Co, Md. Sale of late dwlg of Caleb Thomas, dec'd; also stock, furn, etc. -Pricey Thomas, Grdn, Chas Co, Md.

Thespian Benevolent Soc, of Wash & Gtwn, meeting at Heronimus Htl, Wash. -Enoch M Lowe, Sec.

Lots for sale in the borough of Pittsburgh, Pa, prop of the U S; part of the scite of Ft Fayette-lots 91 thru 94. -A Tennehill, A R Woolley, Comrs, Pittsburg, Pa.

Balt, Md, oil floor cloth mfgr. Chas Sprague

THU SEP 14, 1815
Henry Blaney, an Irishman by birth, but 14 yrs a ctzn of the U S, has lately returned to N Y; was taken prisoner at Queenston & one of 25 men transported to Eng. Also Abraham Fulsen a ntv of the U S. -Columb.

Land for sale in Fairfax Co, Va; 100 acs, with good dwlg hse. -Sabrett Scott, Gtwn.

Pblc sale of 400 acs, belonging to the heirs of the late John M Gantt; land on the west of the rd bet Nottingham to Brown's Ferry. Terms of the sale at Mr Hugh Perry's, on day of sale. Also the land now under rent to Mr Peregrine Stallings. -Mary S Gantt, Fielder Gantt, excs of J M Gantt.

Orphans Crt of PG Co, Md. Ltrs of adm on prsnl est of Chas John Carroll, late of PG Co, Md, dec'd. -John Henry Carroll, adm.

FRI SEP 15, 1815

Geo Watterston, Librarian of Congress; a request for bks, graphics, etc, after the loss suffered at the hands of the enemy..

Died: on Sep 10, Mr Pierce Purcell, long a respectable inhabitant of Wash City.

Died: at Dumfries, Va, on Sep 5, Mr Jas W Colquhoun, in his 49th yr, an old & respectable inhabitant of that place.

Mrd: in N C, on Sun wk, Lt Jesse Wilkinson, U S N, to Miss Frances Coleman, d/o the late Saml Coleman, of this place.

SAT SEP 16, 1815

For sale-*Little Worth*, 122 acs, in Chas Co, Md; with dwlg hse. -Stephen Latimer, trustee.

Claims against the est of Wm Cottrell, dec'd; exhibit same; Chas co Crt, Md. -S Latimer, trustee.

MON SEP 18, 1815

Orphans Crt of Wash Co, D C. Ltrs of test on the will & prsnl est of Pierce Purcell, late of said co, dec'd. -W Matthews, Jas Hoban, excs.

TUE SEP 19, 1815

Pvt sale of small farm on the NW branch, with dwlg hse; 3 miles from Bladensburg, Md. Wm A Scott, at his hse on the hill, & at the Tyber Mill, keeps the best family flour, cornmeal & horse feed. -W A Scott

Mrd: at St Louis, on Aug 19, G C Sibley, to Miss Mary Smith, d/o Rufus Easton, the delegate from Mo Terr.

Died: at Shawnee Town, Ill Terr, on Aug 21, the Hon Stanley Griswold, one of the Judges of that Terr, & a ntv of Conn.

Watch found at my htl, at Rockville, Md. -Iver Campbell

Drowned-on his passage from N Y to Newport, on Aug 26, in the L I Sound, John C Gardner, merchant of Charleston, S C, & s/o the late John Gardner, of Newport, aged 34 ys. Mr G had resided in Charleston for 10 yrs.

WED SEP 20, 1815
PG Co, Md-Jos Jones, of said co brought before me a stray gelding. -John B Bowie

The Pres of the U S has appt'd, under genr'l orders of May 17, 1815, viz:
Saml Shaw, hosp surg, Apr 6, 1813.
Wm H Buckner, surg of late regt of dragoons, Jul 6, 1812, to hosp surg mate, v J B Whiteridge, declined.
Alex'r Blair, surg o/late 5th infty, Mar 30, 1814, to hsp s m, v Wm Jones, dcln'd.
Tobias P Cambridge, hosp surg mate, Sep 12, 1814, v Donaldson Yeates, dcln'd.
C G Garrard, S M of late 44th infty, Mar 11, 1814, to srg mte of 1st infty, v Henry Field, do.
S H Littlejohn, S M of late dragoons, Apr 3, 1813, to surg mate of 2d infty, v Wm Southall, dcln'd.
Josiah Everett, S M of late 21st infty, to s m 2d infty, v Carter Edmunds, dcln'd.
John Gale, S M of late 23d infty, Jul 9, 1812, to s m 3d infty, v R F Hall, dcln'd.
Jacob De Lamotta, R S May 1, 1812, to s m, 4th infty, v W J Cocke, dcln'd.
Robt C Lane, S M late 3d rifle, Mar 11, 1814, to s m 4th infty, v Jas Bates, dcln'd.
S M Ingersoll, S M of late 37 infty, Sep 16, 1814, v Ashel Hall, do.
Wm Thomas, hosp surg, Feb 18, 1814, to surg of rifle regt, v L L Near, do.
Saml C Muir, S M late 1st infty, Apr 7, 1813, to s m 8th infty, v Wm Beaumont, do. By order, D Parker, Adj & Insp Gen.

THU SEP 21, 1815
Died: on Sep 6, at Ft Lewis, in the 28th yr of his age, Bvt Maj John B Murdock, of the 6th Reg U S I, formerly of Bozrah, in Conn.

Notice-I forwarn all persons from harboring or trusting my wife Susannah Bryan on my account, as I will pay no debts of her contracting from this date, Sep 21. -Thos Bryan

FRI SEP 22, 1815
Bricklayers wanted-$2.50 per day; at the Treasury ofc & Episc Chr. -Peter Morte

Wash City, & Gtwn stages; admitting only 6 passengers; fare $4; allowance of 25 lbs of baggage. Balt: Jacob G Smith, John Gadsby, Stockton & Clarke. Hy M'Coy, Elk Ridge. John Davis, Rossburg; Wm Crawford, Gtwn; Danl M'Keowin & Wm O'Neal, Wash.

SAT SEP 23, 1815
J & A Holmead have just opened their Dry Goods store; east of the Centre Mkt.

Orphans Crt of PG Co, Md. Prsnl est of Jonathan H Burch, late of said co, dec'd. -Thos N Burch, Wm L Weems, adms.

For rent-store now occupied by Maj Reily, Pa av, Wash. -Alex'r Estep

$5 reward for Jas H Bidgood, appr to the painting & glazing bus, about 16 yrs old. -Isaac Randolph, Wash City.

Large assortment of boots at Benj Mayfield's manufactory, Bridge st, Gtwn.

MON SEP 25, 1815
Republican nominations in Md:
Balt city-Thos Kell, Christ Hughes, jr, & Wm Steuart.
Alleghany Co-Upton Bruce & Benj Tomlinson.
Wash Co-Jacob Schnebly, John Bowels, Ed G Williams, Martin Kershner
PG Co-Robt Bowie, Jos Kent, Wm Lyles, Jos Cross.
Cecil Co-Wm C Miller, David Cummings, John Wroth, David Mackey.
Kent Co-Cuthbert Hall, Fred Wilson, Benj Massey, Richd Brice.
Balt Co-Tobs E Stansbury, Peter Little, Geo Harryman, B Randall
A A Co-Thos Sellman, Roderic Dorsey, C Stuart of David, Maj T H Dorsey.
Caroline co-Wm Hardcastle, Peter Willis, Monty Denney, Thos Styll.
Queen Ann's Co-Saml Burgess, Robt Stevens, Wm E Meconikin, Kensey Harrison.
Talbot Co-Edw Lloyd, Danl Martin, Solomon Dickinson, Jos Kemp.
Calvert Co-Richd Ireland, B H Mackall, Danl Kent, Stephen S Johns.

Nath'l P Bixby is opening his Dry Goods store in Bridge st, oppo Gen John Peabody's.

For sale-*Cedar Grove*, Chas Co, Md, 8 to 900 acs, with dwlg hse. -B Fendall, Cedar Grove, Chas Co, Md.

G Beall, cabinet mkr; warehse on High st, Gtwn.

TUE SEP 26, 1815
Pblc sale-Chancery Crt of Md, at the late dwlg of Henry Mgt Ogle, in Annapolis city, the whole of the rl est of same, dec'd; commodious brick dwlg in that city.
Also, *Talley's Point*, farm on the Chesapeake Bay, 470 1/2 acs, with dwlg hse.
Also, *Horn Point*, or the *President*, 809 3/4 acs, oppo the city. -Benj Ogle, trustee.

Died: at Richmond, on Sep 21, Saml Shephard, late Auditor of State.

Sup Crt of Chancery for Winchester Dist, Va; case of Wm Byrd Page's adms vs Ferinando Fairfax, hearing dt'd Jul 14, 1814. Sale of land of said Fairfax in Loudoun & Jefferson counties as unsold as of this date. -Thos Parker, Robt I Taylor, Rich H Henderson, Comrs.

Bank of Winchester, Va. Cashier-Lewis Hoff.

For sale-475 acs in Pr Wm, Va. For terms, apply to Mr Chas Tyler, Alexandria, John Gibson, Dumfries, or the subscribers lvg on the premises. -Ann Hancock, Mgt Hancock, & Cath Hancock. Possession at commencement of ensuing yr.

Land for sale-935 acs in Fairfax Co, Va; with dwlg hse. Also, 670 acs in Loudoun Co, Va. Mr Mathias, of Leesburg, or Mr Ludwell Lee, of Belmont, will shew the land. -Richd H Love, Rokeby.

WED SEP 27, 1815
Died: on Sep 6, in Powhatan Co, Col Wm Skipwith, an ofcr of the Revolution; distinguished himself at the seige of York Town.

Died: on Sat wk, in his 86th yr, John Whitehill, of Lancaster Co, Pa; active Patriot during the Rev; in the Leg of Pa.

Wash Co, D C. Thos Johnson brought before me a stray gelding. Wm Waters, one of the J P's in said co. -Wm Brent, clk.

Union Bank of Gtwn-D English, Cashier.

THU SEP 28, 1815
Runaways for sale-negro, John Batemen, 22 yrs old, says he belongs to Robt Johnston, of Greenville Co, S C. Also, negro, Joe Tyrie, age about 35 yrs, says he belongs to Maj John Miller, nr Port Royal, Virg. -C Tippett, for W Boyd, mrshl

FRI SEP 29, 1815
Balt races will be run on Oct 2; purse of $1,000 the 4 mile heat. Mr John Wooden, of Govanne's Town, is authorised to rent out ground for booths.

SAT SEP 30, 1815
Orphans Crt of St Mary's Co, Md. Ltrs test on prsnl est of Mary Abell, late of said co, dec'd. -Philip Greenwell, exc.

Orphans Crt of Chas Co, Md; sale at the hse of the subscriber, the prsnl est of Priscilla Waters, late of said co, dec'd. -Zepheniah W Harbin, Adm.

MON OCT 2, 1815
Boston, Sep 25-violent hurricane on Sep 23. In Middleton, Mr J Irish, Isaac Brownell, & Bedford Hazard, were drowned. At So Kingston, Wm Knowles, his son, & 4 workmen were drowned. Mr David Butler & Mr Reuben Winslow drowned at India Point.

$45 reward for apprehending Tom Lucas, negro man, who eloped from my empoyment about Sep 1. He was hired from Dr J B Cutting, nr Falmouth. -Wm Dent, lvg at the quarries of Cooke & Brent, on Acquia Crk, Va.

TUE OCT 3, 1815
For sale-Robt Bailey offers his prop in Middletown, Fred'k Co, Va, known as Bailey's Retirement.

WED OCT 4, 1815
Mechanic's Bank of Alexandria. -Wm Paton, jr, Cashier.

Warren, Ohio. On Wed, Chas A Austin, s/o Calvin Austin, was killed by the falling of a tree.

David Marble, s/o Isaiah Marble, was killed at Mr Brinckerhoff's Nail Manufactory, Troy, N Y, on Tue, when his clothes got entangled in a machine; he was aged 12 yrs.

Mercer, Pa, Sep 13. On Sep 13, the Powder-mill of Mr Levi Arnold was accidentally blown up; a s/o Mr Arnold, age 18 yrs, was injured & died on Sunday.

Buffalo, Sep 15. On Sep 30, Wm Green, s/o Luther Green, of Pembroke, was killed when his horse fell on him & crushed him to death.

PG Co Crt, Md, Sep term, 1815. Case of Wm Brashears & others, for division or sale of rl est of which Philip Waters died possessed, which descended to the reps of Saml Brashears; present claims by Mar 1. -John Read Magruder, clk, PG Co, Md.

THU OCT 5, 1815
Mrd: on Oct 3, by Rev Mr Matthews, Mr Thos Hughes to Miss Ann M'Cardell, both of Wash City.

College of N J, holden at Princeton, Sep 27, 1815, admitted to first degree in the Arts:

Edw Allen	Danl Baker	Lawrence Battaile
Thos I Biggs	Wm Boyd	Saml C Brinckle
Thos Cadwalader	John P Carter	Robt I Clark
Christopher Cox	Elijah R Craven	Wm Darrick
Philip R Fendall	David M Forrest	Levin I Gillip
John Goldsmith	Jas V Henry	Symmes C Henry
Chas Hodge	John Jones	Enos W Johnson
G L Kirkpatrick	Hugh Kirkpatrick	John R Ludlow
B R M'Connell	Jas R Murray	Chas Oliver
Isaac W Platt	Asbel G Ralston	B W Richards
Ravaud K Rodgers	Geo Ross	Chas S Stewart
Persifor F Smith	Stephen N Strong	Henry Ten Brook
Geo Wikoff	Geo N Woodruff	Ezra Young
F W Jenkins		

Alumni-admitted to the second degree in the arts:

Alem Marr	Jas Birney	Chas H Ogden
John Wiley	Shepard K Kollock	Asa Hillyer, jr.
Jas Boyd	Peter Gansevoort	Saml Hepburn
N W Worthington	John S Haines	Richd M Green
David Bishop	Kensey Johns	Chas Thomas
Wm T Read	N Vandyke, jr	John M Sherrerd

Mstrs of Arts in other colleges, were admitted ad eundem:

Thos F Herbert   Leveritt L F Huntington   Fred'k H Vethake
John Witherspoon   Jacob Green
B A conferred on Jacob M Douglass, of Phil, Pa.
Dr of Laws conferrred on: Hon Saml Johnson, late Govn'r of N C, & Saml Bard, M D, of N Y.
Dr of Divinity conferred on Rev Jas Blythe, of Lexington, Ky.
Mstr of Arts conferred on Rev Philip M Whelpley, of N Y.

Dickinson College exercises on Sep 28, 1815.
Salutatory oration by Julius Forrest, of Wash, D C. Orations by: Francis Whiting Brooke, of Fauquier Co, Va; Peter Ibric, of Easton, Pa; David Nelson Mahon, of Carlisle; Geo Thos Martin, of Easton, Md; Chas Nisbet M'Coskry, of Carlisle; Geo Wash Nabb, of Easton, Md; Alder Piper, of Newville, Pa; Wm M'Dowell Sharp, of Newville, Pa; Geo Sweney, of Adams Co, Pa; Wm Henry Thomas, of Easton, Md; David Wills, of Cumberland Co, Pa; David Watts Huling, of Carlisle, Pa.

Died: in Portland, Me, Lt Kirvin Waters, U S N, aged 18 yrs; Midshipman on the *Enterprize* at the time of her capturing the *Boxer*; rec'd a wound & lingered until Sep 26. Portland Argus [Lt Waters was a ntv of Wash City, & s/o Wm Waters.]

Died: at Gonrock, Scotland, on Dec 1 last, Gillis M'Kechnie, aged 104 yrs, supposed to be the last of the warriors that fought with Prince Chas in 1745.

$30 reward for the following who deserted from Ft Wash; pvts in the artl:
Jas M'Intire, b in Bucks Co, N J, age 28 yrs; carpenter.
Martin Leary, b in Ireland, age 24 yrs; sldr.
Abraham Davis, b in Waterford, Va, age 23 yrs; farmer.
-Felix Anscut, Lt Cmdg Ft Wash, Oct 5.

FRI OCT 6, 1815
Orphans Crt of PG Co, Md. Prsnl est of Gabriel P Van Horn, late of said co, dec'd. Sale at *Vansville*, Nov 6, the greater part of the prsnl prop of said dec'd.
-Archibald Van Horn, adm.

Orphans Crt of PG Co, Md. Prsnl est of Wm Warman Berry, late of said co, dec'd.
-Ann Berry, Ach Van Horn, adms.

English teacher wanted, Rockville Acad. -Jos Elgar, Sec, Rockv, Montg Co, Md.

Copy of the last ltr of Gen Pike; My Dear Clara; included was-remember me with a fr's love, a fr's care, to our dear dght. Your, Montgomery.

Runaway committed to the jail of Wash Co, D C, Negro Tom, 34 yrs old; says he belongs to Mrs Nancy Tricc, of Falmouth, Va. -C Tippett, for W Boyd, mrshl.

SAT OCT 7, 1815
Mrd: at Alexandria, on Oct 3, by Rght Rev Priest Neale, Wm Henry DeCourcey, of the Eastern Shore of Md, to Miss Eliza Bond Rozier, of that town.

Nat'l Advocate-Monument erected by Mr Matthew L Davis, in N Y C, to the memory of Wm Burrows, late Cmder of the U S brig *Enterprize*, mortally wounded on Sep 5, 1813, in an action with the Britannic Maj's brig *Boxer*, after a severe contest of 45 mins. For 2 yrs the remains have been interred without a record.

MON OCT 9, 1815
Fred'k Co, Md. Md elections; Jas Johnson, Joshua Howard, Jos Taney, sen, John Thomas, all Feds, chosen delegates. No Rpblcns ran.

Desirous of mvg to one of the Western States; I have the tract of land on which I now reside, about 600 acs, for sale; with dwlg hse, in Chas Co, Md. -Robt Taylor

Ladies with ltrs in the Wash P O, Oct 1, 1815:

Mrs Eliza Armistead-3	Miss Cath Boughman	Miss Susanna Barry
Miss Margaretta Baker	Mrs Brown	Mrs Sarah Doill
Miss Eliza Davis	Mrs Harriot Davis	Mrs Edwards-2
Harriott Feedin	Eleanor Green	Mrs Cath Holbert
Priscilla Johnson	Miss Mary Johnston	Miss Eliza Kerr
Mrs Ann Lewis	Madame Lorandere	Miss Anne Lee
Mrs Anne Lee	Mrs A S Middieton	Miss Nancy Merran
Cath M'Donald	Mrs J S A Middleton	Mrs Mitchell
Nancy M'Dermott	Mrs Susan Mosher	Mrs N Penn
Miss Anny Right	Charlotte Russell	Mrs Ann Stewart
Miss Matilda Stamp	Mrs Mgt Salmon	Mary Anne Stewart
Mrs Mary W Stewart	Mrs Stewart	Miss Julian Taulburd
Mrs Sarah Washington	Miss Ann White	
Mrs Elizh Weissenfels		

THU OCT 10, 1815
Mrd: on Oct 6, by Rev Mr Breckenridge, Wm P Zantinger, of U S N, to Miss Louisa F Heyer.

Died: on Oct 8, after a long & painful indisposition, Mrs Eliz Hamer, consort of Mr Wm H Hamer, of Wash City; in her 23d yr. She leaves her hsbnd & an infant child. In the duties of wife, dght, & mthr, the dec'd was truly exemplary.

$30 reward for Nace, negro man, age about 22 yrs. -Ann Key, nr Gtwn, D C.

Notice-to all persons whom I am indebted to, to come forward. -Andrew Bartle.
N B-I wish to hire about 100 able laborers.

For sale-prop advertised by Geo Creager, dec'd; crnr lot so of Pa av, Wash City. -Jonathan Appler

WED OCT 11, 1815
Dissolution of partnership bet Jos King & John Crow, by mutual consent. Claims to John Crow, Gtwn.

THU OCT 12, 1815
Tayloring business, on Royal st, Alexandria. -Olaus Lofberg

Mrd: on Oct 10, in Gtwn, by Rev Mr Balch, Mr Wallard Drake to Miss Mgt Wilson, both of Wash City.

Mrd: at Alexandria, on Oct 10, by Rev Dr Muir, Mr Isaac Clarke, of Wash City, to Miss Mary Smith, d/o Mr John Smith, of Alexandria.

Mrd: on Oct 12, by Rev Mr Onderdonk, John R Shaw, of U S N, to Mrs Mgt E Riker, d/o Dr Thos W Montgomery, of N Y.

Mrd: on Oct 7, by Rev Philip F Myers, Mr John M'Laughlin, of Alexandria, to Miss Juliana Way, d/o Mr Andrew Way, of Phil.

FRI OCT 13, 1815
Orphans Crt of Chas Co, Md. Sale at the hse of Priscilla Waters, late of said co, dec'd; all the prsnl est. -Zepheniah W Harbin, admx.

SAT OCT 14, 1815
St John's College revived under the superintendance of Dr John M'Dowell, formerly princ of this seminary, & late Provost of Pa Un. -Saml Ridout, sec, Annapolis.

Chas co Crt-Md. Petition of Smallwood Cawood, of Chas Co; insolvent debtor. -John Barnes, clk.

MON OCT 16, 1815
For Rent-Fishery cld *Spring Landing*, on Md shore & oppo Crane Island. -Chas A Pye, Cornwallis' Neck, C C, Md.

TUE OCT 17, 1815
Died: on board the ship *Indian Chief* on her passage from London bound to City Point, Mrs Mac Rae, consort of Colin Mac Rae, of Manchester.

Died: on Oct 16, in the 30th yr of his age, Richd Henry Lee, Atty at Law, of Norfolk Borough.

Just opened-Dry Goods store, in hse lately occupied by R C Weightman, as a bk store. -Perrin Willis

WED OCT 18, 1815
Auction sale at the dwlg hse of Mrs Prevote, nr the Navy Yd; beds, quilts, wearing apparel, etc. -David Bates, auct.

Farm for sale in PG Co, Md; 330 acs, formerly the prop of Mr Basil Warren; adjs the farms of Dr J Kent, & Mr D Slater; with dwlg hse. -Geo Williams, on prem.

Wash Co, D C. Bazil Ragan, insolvent debtor, confined in Wash Co prison, for debt. -Wm Brent, clk.

THU OCT 19, 1815
Wash Co, D C. John D Davis, insolvent debtor, confined in Wash Co prison, for debt. -Wm Brent, clk.

Mr John Delaborde to open a night school to teach the French language. -Wash.

FRI OCT 20, 1815
Mrd: on Oct 5, Daniel Bryan, of Harrisonburg, Va to Miss Rebecca Davenport, d/o Maj Davenport, of Jefferson Co, Va.

Mrd: on Oct 12, by Rev Mr Hemphill, Mr Saml Dove to Miss Ann M'Closkey, both of Wash City.

Died: on Oct 18, Mrs Maria De Krafft, consort of Mr Edw B De Krafft, of Wash City, after a few days illness; in her 25th yr. An infant babe has been deprived of the care of an affectionate mthr.

Died: at Wilmington, N C, on Oct 6, Wm S Hasell, Editor of the *Wilmington Gaz*.

Died: on Oct 10, in Savannah, Geo, Mrs Ann Dunn, aged 56 yrs, a ntv of Eng, but for 15 yrs past, resided chiefly with her chldrn in the U S.

SAT OCT 21, 1815
Mrd: on Oct 19, by Rev Mr M'Cormick, Mr Hiram Caver, merchant of Chambersburg, Pa, to Miss Hannah Zenobia Myer, of Wash City.

$20 reward for runaway, Negro Lewis; from Simon Sommers, nr the little falls chr, in Alexandria Co.

Orphans Crt of Wash Co, D C. Ltrs of adm on est of Josiah Gale, late of said co, dec'd. -Wm Doughty, adm.

New invented patent gas light; rights may be had at Lewis Entris, Phil, or of Wm Zeigler, in Gtwn, D C.

MON OCT 23, 1815
Lady Harriet Ackland, aged 66, died in Eng, Jul 21. Her hsbnd, Maj Ackland died from an argument with a fellow British ofcr, in England.

Died: at the residence of her fr, at Attakapas, in La, Mrs Eliza R Gales, consort of Col Thos Gales. Her hsbnd & infant dght have suffered an irreparable loss.

TUE OCT 24, 1815
Died: Gen John Sevier, of Tenn, a Com'r appt'd to run the boundary line bet the U S & the Creek nation of Indians, at Ft Decatur, nr Tookabatchee, under a lingering indisposition. [Recent] Notice also on Oct 27 paper.

I have just opened a Dry Goods store on Pa av, Perrin Willis.

WED OCT 25, 1815
Orphans Crt of Wash Co, D C. John Kreemer, insolvent debtor, confined in Wash Co prison for debt. -Wm Brent, clk.

THU OCT 26, 1815
Orphans Crt of PG Co, Md. Prsnl est of Col Fielder Dorsett, late of said co, dec'd; sale at late dwlg on Nov 15, all prsnl est. -Amelia Dorsett, admx.

To be rented-dwlg hse & garden. -Jos Scholfield, nr the P O, Wash City.

Mrsh'l sale of all the right, title, int, etc of Jos Wheaton, of Wash City, to lot 17 in sq 254 with improvements; lot 15 & part of lot 13 in sq 253, with brick hse. Prop seized at the suit of Francis Sexton & Wm D Williamson against the said Jos Wheaton. -Wash Boyd, mrshl D C.

Orphans Crt of PG Co, Md. Pblc sale of prsnl prop of Jas Crawford, dec'd; furn, stock, negroes, etc. -Priscilla Crawford, admx

For sale-my hse now in my occupancy, fronting on I st, Wash. -Chas Vinson

FRI OCT 27, 1815
Leather for cash. -John C Thompson, currier, Hight st, Gtwn.

Died: in Lexington, Ky, on Oct 13, Gen Geo Trotter, aged 37 yrs.

For sale-tract of land in Montg C H, Md, 145 acs, with good dwlg hse. -Eleanor West

SAT OCT 28, 1815
Mrd: on Oct 24, by Rev A T M'Cormick, Mr Richd Young, merchant of Wash City, to Miss Matilda Berry, of Holy Spr, PG Co, Md.

MON OCT 30, 1815
Geo W Campbell, late Sec of Treas, & John Williams, late a Col in the Army, are chosen Senators from Tenn, vie, Mr Anderson & Mr Wharton, who resigned.

For sale-land in Fairfax Co, Va; 700 acs. Mr Jos Crouch, lvg at Mr Jenney's Mills, nr the land, will shew it. For terms apply to Wm M M'Carty, residing in Loudon Co, nr Leesburg, Va.

TUE OCT 31, 1815

New shoe store now opening on Pa av, Wash. -S Dunham Walker

Died: a few days since, at his residence in Gallatin Co, Ky, Col Robt Johnson, the f/o Col R M Johnson, one of the oldest inhabitants of Ky.

WED NOV 1, 1815

Died: on Oct 25, at his seat on Elk Ridge, Balt Co, Md, Col Edw Norwood, at an advanced age; patriot & defender during the Revolutionary contest.

Mahlon Dickerson is elected Govn'r of N J; a sterling Rpblcn.

THU NOV 2, 1815

Wash Co, D C. Wm M'Gee, an insolvent debtor, confined in Wash Co prison, for debt. -Wm Brent, alk.

Auction-at Mrs Helen Brown's, F st, all her Groc & Spirit business utensils, & some hsehld & kitchen furn.

FRI NOV 3, 1815

Henry Bird remv'd in 1797 from Fred'k Co, Va, where he was born in 1767, to Sandusky, Ohio; accompanied by his neighbours, John Peters & Thos Philips. Bird lived there til 1811 & was f/o 5 chldrn. Oct 17, 1811, Indians attacked, killing Peters & Philips; a total of 19, 3 men & 3 women & 13 chldrn. Bird survived; eventually was aided by Randall M'Donald, a Scotchman. Bird came to Vt, thence to Wash, arriving on Jul 6, 1815. From the *Analectic Magazine*.

Died: on Oct 30, after a lingering illness, Walter Hellen, aged _9 yrs; for many yrs a highly respected inhabitant of Wash City. [Cld be 49 yrs.]

SAT NOV 4, 1815

Died: at Colrain, Mass, on the 3d inst, Mr Thos Bell, s/o Mr Walter & Mrs Sally Bell, in his 28th yr; shot by an unknown assailant.

MON NOV 6, 1815

Died: on Nov 2, after a short but severe illness, Mrs Martha Farrell, consort of Mr Zephaniah Farrell, of Wash City, in her 45th yr. Her hsbnd & chldrn survive.

Orphans Crt of PG Co, Md. Ltrs of adm on est of Kidd Morsell, dec'd. -John Morsell, adm.

$50 reward for negro girl, Lydia Piles, age 18 yrs, originally came from Pr Wm Co, Va. -Mgt Compton, Williamsport, Md.

Mrshl's sale at David Dobbyn's Tvrn, in F st, Wash; right, title, int, etc of Zachariah Hazle to lot 24 in sq 378; prop seized at suit of John M Wight & Geo Moore, at the suit of the U S, two at the suit of John N Taylor, for sundry ofcrs fees & militia fines. -Wash Boyd, mrshl, D C.

Land for sale in PG Co, Md, cld *Wood's Joy*, 600 acs, was the residence of the late Peter Wood, jr. The heirs are selling the land. -Thos Wood, Robt A Crain, Acquasco Mills, PG Co, Md. [Both residing on the premises.]

TUE NOV 7, 1815
Died: on Oct 22, at the hse of Jos Dougherty of Wash City, Lewis Busharie, a ntv of France, but for the last 8 yrs, a ctzn of this country.

Deposition of John Dagnet, on the British 74, the Dragon, about 2 yrs since saw a young man, Jas Guedron, who had been impressed into British svc some yrs since; he being an Americ ctzn & whose parents reside in N Y. -Sam Trumbull, Ast Justice-Oct 17, 1815.

Died: on Oct 15, in Laurens dist, S C, Mr Solomon Niblet, aged *143 yrs; born in Eng, where he lived until he was 19 yrs; emigrated to this country & resided in Md until about 55 yrs ago when he remv'd to S C. *Copied as written.

WED NOV 8, 1815
Teacher wanted-nr Hay Mkt P O, Va; pvt school of 10 or 12 pupils. -Thos Turner

Teacher wanted in pvt family, 8 to 15 scholars. Enquire of Mr Andrew Ramsay, Wash, D C, or subscriber nr Dumfries, Va. -Thos Harrison, Thos Chapman, Chappawansie.

Land for sale; 150 or 60 acs; nr Centreville, PG Co, Md. -Ann Berry

Sale of furn at Mr Benj Burn's hse, on Capt Hill, Wash. -David Bates, auct.

Runaways committed to Wash Co, D C, jail: Stephen, negro, age about 20 yrs; says he belongs to Hanson Posey, nr the Hill Top, Chas Co, Md. Also, Nace, negro, age about 19 yrs; says he belongs to Mr John Warder, nr Thompson Simms store, Chas Co, Md. -C Tippett, for W Boyd, mrshl.

Dissolution of partnership by mutual agreement; drugs & medicines, paints, etc. -Alex'r M'Williams, Edw W Clarke. Clarke will continue the business.

For sale-lots & lands, at Adam Lindsay's, Navy Yd, a parcel of lots in Wash City, lying bet the Capt & the Navy Yd. Also, 220 acs in *Bradford's Rest*, Montg Co, Md. Apply to Lloyd Adamson, nr the prem. -Henry Slater, David H Slater, attys in fact for the heirs of Jos Slater, dec'd.

Wash Co, D C. Sarah Cannon brght before me a stray mare. Jas W Varnum, J P.

THU NOV 9, 1815
Ezekicl Hildreth has remv'd his acad to his new bldg, in 10th st, Wash.

Mrd: on Nov 7, at Alexandria, by Rev Wm H Wilmer, Lt Col Robt Hector Macpherson, late of the Army, to Miss Julia Anna Chapin, of that place.

Mrd: at Coton, Loudoun Co, Va, on Oct 31, Tench Ringgold, of Wash City, to Miss Mary A Lee, 3d d/o Thos L Lee, dec'd, of said co.

Partnership of E Reynolds & Co was dissolved by mutual consent; Wm M Chick & Co will continue. Wash. [Groceries]

H R Burden & Jos Cassin from Phil, have est'd a Fancy & Windsor Chair Factory on Pa av, next door to Mrs Dinsmore's Brdg Hse.

FRI NOV 10, 1815
Died: a short time since, in Cambridge, N Y, Mr Solomon Cronge; he had mrd 2 sisters & lived with ea alternate wks & ea had 13 chldrn. -Ver Report

Died: on Oct 12, at his residence in N J, Sir Jas Jay, Knt of Md.

Died: at Phil, on Nov 1, Edw Tilghman, Cnslr of Law, in his 65th yr; ntv of Md, but long a resident of Phil.

SAT NOV 11, 1815
Pktbk found in Clarksburg, Montg Co, Md. -*Abraham Webster, Thorton's Gap P O, Culpeper Co, Va. [*Found by me.]

For sale-frame hse on lot 3 in sq 825, Wash City, prop of Ronold Donaldson, to satisfy ground rent due to Alex'r Kerr. -Geo Adams, Cnstbl.

Negroes for sale at the late dwlg of Wm Jones, on Dec 18. -Ann Jones, admx.

Oysters, etc; quantity of Cove Oysters; .25 per pint for stewed oysters, & pickles & butter. One pt of raw-12 1/2. -Jacob Dixon's, E & 11th sts.

Pblc sale of dwlg hse, nr the Navy Yd; furn etc. About to leave the city, Abigail Hebron.

MON NOV 13, 1815
Deed of trust dt'd Dec 9, 1809, by Richd Cole, dec'd, for debt due to Nathl Greaves; sale of prop of said Cole-merchant mill, & about 90 acs in Stafford Co, etc. -Richd H Gaines, Trustee, Fauquier Co, Va.

Drowned: on Oct 9, in the St Lawrence rvr, at Ogdensburgh, slg-mstr Henry Davis, of N J, cmder of the U S schn'r *Lady on the Lake*, together with acting Lt ----- Bowton, 2d in command, Mr Walsh, pilot, & 3 seamen. -*Lansingburgh Gaz*

$20 reward for mulatto boy, Gabriel, about 17 yrs old. -Robt Gaw, lvg in Woodstock, Shenandoah Co, Va.

Make haste-lay up your winter's supply of wood. -Varral Gibbs, toll hse of the Turnpike Co, leading to Bladensburg, constantly found on the premises.

TUE NOV 14, 1815
Died: on Oct 30, David Slater, of PG Co, Md, in his 49th yr.

Died: nr Chapico, St Mary's Co, Md, on Nov 3, after an illness of 6 wks, Mrs Rebecca White Briscoe, consort of Mr Henry Briscoe, aged 26 yrs.

$60 reward for negro man, Davey, age 26 yrs; formerly the prop of Abraham Haff. -Matthew Galt, lvg within 2 miles of Taney Town, Fred'k Co, Md.

WED NOV 15, 1815
Wash City Wkly Gaz will resume on the first Sat in Dec. -Jonathan Elliot, Pa av

Warning! I forewarn all persons from taking a note said to be given by me to Peter Cavenaugh, for 7 hogsheads of Tobacco. -John Hill, PG Co, Md.

I wish to hire 20 or 30 negroes to work in my brick yd; liberal wages, good clothing, & humane treatment. -Val Reintzel, Gtwn.

THU NOV 16, 1815
Ct Martial held on the U S ketch *Vesuvius*, for Robt Cranston, Midshp of U S ship *Java*, chg of abusive language to Midshp Handy; etc. To be dismissed from the Navy. -Jos Bainbridge, Pres. Saml R Marshall, Actg Judge Adv, Navy Dept, Nov 10, 1815. Approved B W Crowinshield.

$100 reward for an old white man, John Valentine, a Polander by birth, who robbed me & ran away from my employment. May have changed his name to Van Hoffen; known to have a family in Fred'k city, Md. -Edgar Patterson, Gtwn.

Philip Lansdale against Thos Woodward & Cassandra Woodward-In Chancery. Rg-sale of the rl est of Thos Woodward, late of PG Co, Md, dec'd, for payment of debts due to Walter Clagett, surviving partner of Lansdale & Clagett. Woodward at his death left 2 chldrn, Thos & Cassandra Woodward; Thos lives in D C. The rl est is: *Ample Grange, Frye's Choice & Sway's Rsrvy*, 247 + acs in PG Co, Md. -Jas P Heath, Reg C C.

For sale-*Gunston Hall*, Fairfax Co, Va; about 3,000 acs, with lge brick dwlg hse, etc. Geo Mason, residing on the premises, Fairfax Co, Va.

FRI NOV 17, 1815
Mrd: on Nov 14, at Locust Grove, Pr Wm Co, Virg, by Rev Mr Mathews, Mr Geo Sweeny, of Wash City, to Miss Mary S C Hooe, d/o the late Bernard Hooe, jr, of the former place.

Mrd: on Nov 14, at Hackwood, nr Winchester, Va, Geo W Murdoch, of

Fredericktown, Md, to Miss Jacquelina Smith, d/o Gen John Smith, of the former place.

Died: on Nov 14, Mrs Maria Davison, consort of Maj Wm Davison, Pstmstr of Winchester, & d/o Gen John Smith. The day preceding her death, she rode to her fr's, for marriage preparations for her sister, [see above] when on her return she was severely injured from a fall & kick from her horse.

Died: on Nov 4, at her residence in Chas Co, Md, Mrs Mary McPherson, in her 73d yr, after a tedious illness.

Died: at Petersburg, on Nov 10, G R Taylor, an eminent Lwyr of that place.

Died: at Petersburg, on Nov 16, Capt W G Russel, late of the U S Corps of Artl.

Died: at Phil, on Sun last, Lt Wm H Odenheimer, late of the U S Navy.

Furs for sale-raccoon skins from the lakes. Trueman Beck, Gtwn.

SAT NOV 18, 1815
Mrd: on Nov 16, by Rev Mr Hemphill, Dr Chas B Hamilton, Surg in the U S Navy, to Miss Eliza Shanly, of Wash City.

Mrd: at Alexandria, on Nov 13, by Rev Mr Wilmer, Mr Enoch M Lowe, of Wash City, to Miss Juliana Faw, d/o Abraham Faw, of Alexandria.

Six cents reward for appr to the baking business, Lewis Low, aged about 16 yrs; ran away in Sept. -Jacob Wineberger, lvg in Gtwn.

For sale-waggon & 2 horses. -Francis Burke, nr Petty's Tvrn, Navy Yd Hill.

$50 reward for negro, Bill, about 24 yrs old. -Wm Early, Madison Co, Va.

MON NOV 20, 1815
Pblc sale of lot 6 in sq 667; lot 13 in sq 120; & undivided sundry lots cnvyd by Wash Boyd, late Coll of the co chgs, to Catharine Connel. N L Queen, Auct.

John Gill, Notary Pblc, lvg in Balt, attests that Richd Moon, mstr of the schn'r *Patapsco*, of Balt, named the following who were impressed at Gibraltar by ofcrs of the British frig, *Meander*, viz-John Davisson, Geo Bradshaw, & John Dixon. -Notarial Seal the 11th day of Nov, 1815.

Died: on Nov 17, after a lingering illness, Mr Alex'r S Smoot, in his 48th yr; for a number of yrs a Clk in the Treas Dept.

For sale-small farm in PG Co, Md; 287 acs, with dwlg hse, etc. Apply to Mr Saml Philips, adj the prem, or to Thos Sanford, lvg in Alexandria. -Thos Sanford

TUE NOV 21, 1815
$100 reward for negro boy, Geo Diggs. His fr belongs to Mr Davidson, of Gtwn. He was formerly the prop of Domingo Gambra, of Chas Co, Md. Ranaway from the subscriber, lvg in Wash City, on board his schn'r the *Rambler*. -Wm R Maddox.

$40 reward for Cato Claiborne, negro man, age about 25 yrs. Ranaway from the subscriber, lvg in Petersburg, Va. -David Maben, jr.

Whereas, Abraham Hargreaves, late of Heirs Hse, nr Colne, co of Lancaster, who died in Mar 1814, by his will gave premises in trust for the eldest son, or only one of his bro, Christopher Hargreaves, if lvg. High Crt of Chancery, in Eng; Tillotson vs Hargreaves, dt'd Jun 16, 1812. The said C Hargreaves left Eng prior to 1785 & went to S C; is supposed to have mrd Priscilla Ward, in 1794, by whom he had Abraham, John, & Thos; all lvg in 1804, with their fr, in Pendleton Dist, S C, & afterward left their fr & went Westward. Said persons-lawful chldrn of said C Hargreaves, to come before Francis Paul Stratford, Chambers, Southampton Bldgs, London. -Carr & Hargreaves, solicitors, Blackburn, Lancashire, Sep 11, 1815.

WED NOV 22, 1815
Died: on Nov 17, in her 22d yr, Mrs Anna M Davis, consort of Mr Gideon Davis, of this place.

Died: on Nov 5, at Savannah, Geo, Maj John Berrien, aged 55 yrs; remains were interred on Tue with military honors. He was a ntv of N J; at 15 yrs he was app't a lt in the 1st Ga regt & was promoted to captaincy during the ensuing yr; as brig maj he joined the grand army at Valley Forge, actively engaged in the battle of Monmouth; srvd till the close of the Rev war.

Wash Co, D C. Geo Evans, insolvent debtor, confined in the Wash Co prison. -Wm Brent, clk.

THU NOV 23, 1815
All ofcrs lately attached to the U S Flotilla, *St Mary's*, state of Geo, commanded by Hugh G Campbell, are to claim their prize money. N W Rothwell, prize agent, will be in Gtwn on or before Dec 25.

Died: in Wash City, on Nov 21, after a lingering indisposition, Wm Dupuy, Teller of the Bank of Wash, & for many yrs a resident of Wash City. His widowed consort mourns his loss. Funeral from his late dwlg on Pa av, this day.

Pblc sale of part of the est of the late Peter Miller, dec'd; 40 shares of Canal Co of Wash & 136 shares of the Comerc Co of Wash. -Griffith Coombs, John M'Gowan, adms of Peter Miller, dec'd. -David Bates, auct.

FRI NOV 24, 1815
Chas co Crt, Aug Term, 1815. Henry Clements, & Eliz Clements, vs Christiana Hamilton, Saml Hamilton, Mary C Hamilton, Edw Hamilton, Alex'r O Anderson,

& Louisa his wife, Letitia Hamilton & her dght, Harriet S Hamilton. Rg-cnvycn of land in Chas Co, which Saml Hamilton, in his life time, sold to Mary Clements, mthr of the cmplnts. Land has been pd for; Saml Hamilton has died; dfndnts reside out of Md; Harriet S Hamilton, is an infant. -John Barnes, clk.

Died: suddenly, on Nov 18, at the hse of Burr Harrison, Mrs Ann Lithgow, late of Dumfries, Va, in her 73d yr.

Died: a few days ago, at his seat in Westmoreland, Va, Maj John Turberville.

Info wanted of Jos Alston, who left Wilmington, Del, for Charleston, S C, in 1784, is lvg, his dght, whom he left in the care of Mr Jas Knowles, wld be glad to hear from him. Address Mrs Polly Jones, nr London, Madison Co, Ohio.

SAT NOV 25, 1815
Died: lately, the Rev Timothy Priestley, bro/o the celebrated Dr Priestly, & formerly mnstr of the dissenting chapel in Cannon st, Manchester.

Mrd: on Nov 23, by Rev Mr Balch, Mr Saml Meigs to Mrs Jane Clarke, all of Wash City.

Negroes for sale-residue of the prsnl est of Mrs Helen G Hull, dec'd, late of Dumfries, Va. -John King, exc.

Application of Richd Byon, of St Mary's Co, Md; insolvent debtor. -Jo Harris, clk.

MON NOV 27, 1815
Appt'd mgrs of Wash City Assemblies: Jas H Blake   Jas Eakin
Thos Tingey   Jas Thompson   Richd B Lee   Edw W Duval
Henry Huntt   Saml Miller   John P Todd   Henry Carroll
John Law   Tench Ringgold

$100 reward for Augustus Lavake; former lt in the U S army; supposed to be with his wife & sister, with a lg quantitiy of Dry Goods. -Jos P Le Clerc, 49 2d st, Phil.

Died: in Wash City, on Nov 25, Jos Tarbell, a Post Capt in the U S Navy; leaving a family to mourn his decease.

TUE NOV 28, 1815
Wish to take as apprentices, 2 youths, to learn painting, etc. -Edw Henry.

Died: on Nov 22, after a short illness, at Dumfries, Va, Alex'r Henderson, in his 79th yr; resident of Va for nrly 60 yrs. His loss will be regretted by his numerous family.

WED NOV 29, 1815
Orphans Crt of PG Co, Md. Ltrs of adm on the est of Wm Tunnicliff, late of said co, dec'd. -Jos Huddleston, adm.

THU NOV 30, 1815

$20 reward for runaway, Harriet, negro girl; was seen at Col Wm Lyles' plantation, nr Piscataway, some time past. She was purchased from the est of Col Beans; do expect she is in the neighborhood of Miss Stonestreet, in Chas Co, Md. -Benj Ray.

Orphans Crt of Montg Co, Md. Sale at the late residence of Lawrence O'Neale, of said co, dec'd. -Henry O'Neale, adm.

Died: on Nov 27, Mr Jos Maguire, Printer, formerly of Balt, Md.

Died: a Raspbury Plain, in Loudon Co, Va, on Nov 17, Stephen Thompson Mason, the y/s/o the late Gen Stephen T Mason.

Died: on Nov 26, at Alexandria, Mr John Mandeville, in his 64th yr; ntv of Cumberland Co, Eng, but for nrly 30 yrs a resident of Alexandria.

Union Bank, Alexandria-C T Chapman, Cashier.

$50 reward for negro, Len Johnson, age 22 yrs; raised by the late Mrs Lizbeth Ford, & by her heirs, sold to me in 1812. -John Ford, Chas Co, Md.

FRI DEC 1, 1815

$100 reward for negro man, Jarrod, age 35 yrs. -Abram Hargate, lvg on *Carroll's Manor*, Fred'k Town, Md.

Sale at the farm occupied by the dec'd, Thos Main, nr the Little Falls of Potomac; crop, utensils, furn, etc. -Joncherez & Davis, aucts. Also-plants. -Wm Bunyie

To Rent-the prop lately occupied by Thos Eno, in Wash City, belonging to the late Walter Hellen, on 14th st, in sq 247; frame dwlg hse. -Thos Cook, Gtwn.

Pblc sale at the Navy Yd, Wash, 3 gun boats. -Thos Tingey

Died: in Wilbraham, Mr Rowland Crocker, in his 80th yr. His own mthr who lived with him, still survives him in her 101st yr; she is still able to walk & see.

Died: in Dover N H, Mehetable Jenkins, aged 84, of the Soc of Friends, among whom she had been a preacher in Runnin, Ireland, & the U S. In Eliot, Sarah Jenkins, aged 93, also of the Friends, & a companion of Eliz J.

Died: in Newton L I, Mrs Bolton; burnt to death by her clothes taking fire.

Died: in Eng, J S Copley, an eminent painter, a ntv of Boston.

Died: in Paris, M Anguie, fr-in-l to Marshal Ney. The 4 sons of the Marshal attended the funeral.

Fred'k Cana has recommenced the Confectionary business on Pa av, Wash.

SAT DEC 2, 1815
Orphans Crt of PG Co, Md. It is stated that Wm Hurley, who intermrd with Sarah Taylor, one of the reps of Sarah Taylor, late of PG Co, Md, dec'd, remv'd from this state some yrs ago to Tenn, & Thos Taylor, adm of said Sarah Taylor, dec'd, is ready to make distibution of the est of said Sarah Taylor. -Trueman Tyler, reg

Died: on Nov 28, suddenly, Abiel Smith, aged 68; formerly a merchant & a Rep of Boston in the Genr'l Crt. -Chron.

MON DEC 4, 1815
New winter arrangement to passengers for the steam-boat, *Wash*. -Hazlewood Farish, sec to the P S B C, Fredericksburg.

TUE DEC 5, 1815
Died: at Balt, on Dec 3, the most Rev Dr John Carroll, Archbishop of Balt, Md, of the Cath Chr, in the 80th yr of his life.

Fall & Winter Goods. Mr Wm O'Brien has remv'd from Wash City, to Bridge st & High st, Gtwn.

Mrd: on Nov 30, by Rev Mr Wilmer, Mr W C Lipscomb, of Gtwn, to Miss Phebe Adgate, of Alexandria.

Died: at La Fourche, Lou, on Nov 21, Gen Stephen A Hopkins, of Donaldsonville; shot by Pierre Valet, who had employed him as an atty.

Orphans Crt of PG Co, Md. Sale at late resid of Eleanor Mullikin, all her prsnl est. -Jas Mullikin, exc, PG Co, Md.

WED DEC 6, 1815
S & J Matlock, merchant taylors, have commenced business on Capitol Hill, Wash.

John Hill, of PG Co, Md, cnvyd his rl & prsnl est to the subscribers, for payment of his debts. -Eleanor Hill, Wm Hill, Chas Hill, Francis M Hall, John Graham.

Mrd: on Dec 3, by Rev Mr Addison, Mr Lewis Johnson to Mrs Anna Reinagle, d/o Mr P I Duport, all of Gtwn.

Francis Locke of N C, had to resign as Senator in the Cong of the U S, because of ill health.

THU DEC 7, 1815
Ready Made Cloathing -Geo Sprung, oppo Crawford's Union Htl, Gtwn.

FRI DEC 8, 1815
Mrd: on Dec 3, by Rev Mr M'Cormick, Mr Edw Simmons Lewis, to Miss Susan Jean Washington, both of Wash City.

Died: on Dec 4, at the seat of her bro, A C Hanson, Mary Jane Grosvenor, w/o Thos P Grosvenor, Rep in Cong from N Y. She died from a pulmonary complaint.

Runaway, negro Jas; prop of Mrs Clary Williams, of St Mary's Co, Md, lately employed by Mr Geo Moore, of Wash Co, Md. -Basil Bowling, shrf-PG Co, Md.

SAT DEC 9, 1815
Excs of the will & test of Alex'r Henderson, late of Dumfries, Va. -Richd H Henderson, lives in Leesburg, Loudoun Co, Va; Thos Henderson, at Warrenton, do.

MON DEC 11, 1815
The new mbr from Dela is Thos Clayton, not Chas, as published in our Cong list.

Wm Findley is indisposed from attending in Cong, & feared he may not be able to attend at all this session. -Greensburgh paper.

For sale-the plantation on which I reside; 200 acs, with framed dwlg hse, etc. John Digges, nr the P O, at Allen's Fresh, Chas Co, Md.

TUE DEC 12, 1815
Wilson Cary Nicholas is re-elected Govn'r of Va.

Saml J Potts & Hezekiah Miller have formed a co-partnership; fancy goods,etc; in store lately occupied by Thos L M'Kenney, Bridge st, Gtwn.

Wanted-a young man acquainted with the Dry Good Business & book-kpg. -Perrin Willis, Pa Av, Wash.

Mrd: on Dec 10, by Rev Mr Brown, Mr Thos Given to Miss Eliz B Edmonston, all of Wash City.

Orphans Crt of Wash Co, D C. Ltrs of test of prsnl est of Robt Brown, late of said city, bricklayer, dec'd. -Mgt Brown, admx.

Notice-all indebted to the est of John Gibson, late of Pr Wm Co, Va, are given notice to make payment. -John Spence, Jas Reid, excs of John Gibson.

Jas D Gaither is now opening a *Fancy Store*, in the hse lately occupied by Mr Leonard, nr Union Tvrn, in Bridge st.

Orphans Crt of PG Co, Md. Ltrs of adm on est of Wm Tunnicliff, late of said co, dec'd. -Jos Huddleston, adm.

WED DEC 13, 1815
Lots for sale, 203 thru 206 on Wash st; lot 240 on West st; 120' on Green st, Gtwn; prop of Thos Lee, of Balt. -John Travers, auct.

Wash Co, D C. Petition of John J Will, insolvent debtor, confined in Wash Co prison, for debt. -Wm Brent, clk.

Order from PG Co Crt-land for sale, all the prop of the late Jos Smith, dec'd; 264 acs cld *Croom* with wooden dwlg hse, etc; *Farehill & Addition*, with small dwlg hse, etc. -Robt Bowie, Benj Oden, Henry Boswel, Frs Hamilton, John H Brown, comrs.

THU DEC 14, 1815
Hse o/Reps. 1-Petition of Menassch Miner for reimbursement of expences attending wounds rec'd by his son at Stonington. 2-Pet of J B Fribeau for payment of a Rev claim. 3-Pet of Caleb Earl & John Keen, to be indemnified for loss of vessel & cargo, which fell into the hands of the enemy at Alexandria, having been detained there by the embargo. 4-Pet of John T David, late paymstr-army, settle his acc'ts destroyed by fire. 5-Pet of Saml Black-Rev claim. 6-Pet of Geo Gale, to be pd for wagon & team lost in svc of the U S. 7-Pet of John Armstrong, late Coll of Inter Rev, for commissions withheld. 8-Pet of Tabitha Wiley, relief since her hsbnd was killed whilst a vol at Pittsburg. 9-Pet of Saml Truby, Jos Foster, Jos Gillet, Bethuel Goodrich, Jas Hutton, Thos Goodrum, Robt Elliot, John Q Talbott, Jas Campbell; all praying for pensions. 10-Pet of John Ingles, payment of claim arising out of the Rev war. 11-Pet of Jacob Shoemaker, merchant of Phil, for drawback on exportation of merchandize in 1805; & Francis David, relief in same case. 12-Pet of Danl T Patterson, Capt in the Navy, & Col Geo T Ross, Army, for portion of prize money. 13-Pet of Jacob Ritter & John Greiner, of Phil. 14-Pet of Robt Porterfield contesting the election of Wm M'Coy, mbr of the Hse from Va. 15-Pet of Saml Deck, Wm Bruce, & Asa Kitchell, by Mr M'Lean of Ohio. 16-Pet of John W Winn, to locate a land warrant given to Chas Lloyd, dec'd, on Pblc land in La. 17-Pet of Fred'k Smith for donation of land in Miss Terr. 18-Pet of Wm Crawford, comp for svcs as Land Com'r West of Pearl Rvr.

Died: on Nov 23, at his residence in Chas Co, Md, the Rev Dr Benj Contee, in his 61st yr; ofcr in the Rev army.

Sale of city lots & hses for taxes to satisfy the Corp of Wash City; including 1814:

Wm Fletcher	Wm Fitzgerald	Lancelot Griffin
Wm Givison	Levi Green	Patrick Healey-heirs
Zacharish Hazle	Corns M'Dermot Roe-heirs	John Minitree
Lewis Morin, senr	Edw M'Dermot Roe-heirs	Varden & Hodges
Nicholas Whalen	Whalen & Crowley	[-Geo Allen, Coll-2d ward.]

Dividend to be pd to creditors of the late Theophilus Robey, of Tenley Town, dec'd. -John Bridges or Jos Nevitt, adms, Gtwn.

FRI DEC 15, 1815
Prop for sale to satisfy the Corp of Wash City, for taxes due:
Thos Triplett, sq 254, brick hse, lot 12-$6.20.
John Stockwell, sq 347, frame hse, lot 5-$19.20.
-Geo Andrews, Coll of 2d Ward.

Hse o/Reps. 1-Petition of Susan Smith, wid/o John Smith, that the copy right of bks by Smith, be renewed & extended. 2-Pet of John Cook, of Albany, prop of a library, reduce postage on bks, etc. 3-Pets for Rev claims: John Polhemus, Capt in Rev army; Thos Baldwin; John Armstrong; Geo S Wise. John Ansley-reimbursement for transporting Americ prisoners from the isl of Barbadoes, during the war. 4-Jos Sims, of Phil, of like nature. 5-Pet of John T Wirt, late A D QM Gen-settle his acc't. 6-Pet of Jos Harrison & Fred'k Cross, pay for waggons & teams lost in svc of the U S army. 7-Pet of Wm Morrissett, refund a forfeiture pd by him to the Rev Ofcrs at Norfolk, for unintentional violation of the Rev Laws. 8-Pet of Jas Innerarity & Isabell Narbonne Campbell, of Geo Brewer, of Jos Bates, claims in regard to the pblc lands. 9-Pet of Jacob Greer, comp for coll of Direct Tax in Orange Co, N C. 10-Pet of Isaac Lambert & John Dixon, & sundry inhabitants of territories of Ind & Ill.

SAT DEC 16, 1815
Info wanted of Mr John M Charlton; by his friends in Gtwn, Dec 16.

Orphans Crt of P G Co, Md; sale at former dwlg of Humphrey Pope, late of said co, dec'd; furn, stock, etc. -Nathl Pope, adm.

$50 reward for runaway, Jupiter, negro, age 31 yrs; pretends to have a wife at Mr John Gibson's in this county; tolerable shoemkr. -Thos Grasty, Orange Co, Va.

Millinery & Fancy Goods, Pa av, Wash City. -Ann Johnson

MON DEC 18, 1815
Mrd: on Dec 14, at Alexandria, by Rev Dr Muir, Mr Robt Brocket, jr, to Miss Betsey Longden, all of that town.

TUE DEC 19, 1815
The trial, acquittal & vindication of Capt Jos Treat, late of the 21st regt U S I, against the unfounded chg comprehended in Maj Gen Brown's official report of the battle of Chippeway; price 25 cents. -R C Weightman.

Land for sale; decree of Sup Crt of Chancery for Fredericksburg Dist, Va; case of Bernard exc vs the heirs of Thos Lomax, dec'd; sale of *Port Tobago*, late the prop of the same; 606 acs, with 2 story brick hse. -John Tayloe Lomax, Com'r & adm.

$150 reward for runaway, mulatto boy, Joshua, formerly the prop of Wm Hodgson; age 21 yrs; $25 if taken in Alexandria. -Louis Beeler

Died: at New Orleans, the last of Oct, in his 23d yr, midshpm Geo Parker, U S N.

Wash Co, D C. Osborn Vermillion, insolvent debtor, confined in Wash Co prison, for debt. -Wm Brent, clk.

WED DEC 20, 1815
Gtwn Dancing Assembly mgrs:
John Cox	Geo Peter	Wash Bowie
Geo C Washington	Robt F Howe	John S Williams
Richd Burgess	John Marbury	John Lee
		John Peter

Hse o/Reps. 1-Petition of Thos I Allen, bro & administrator of Wm H Allen, late cmder of U S brig *Argus*. 2-Pet of John Frothingham & Arthur Tappan, relief from penalties. 3-Pet of John Redman Coxe, prof of Chem in Pa U; remission of duties on certain philosophical apparatus imported at his individual expence.

THU DEC 21, 1815
I certify that Ignatius F Young, of Wash Co, D C, brought before me a stray horse. -John B Kerry, J P.

Orphans Crt of PG Co, Md. 1-Ltrs of adm, d b n, on prsnl est of Benj Young, late of said co, dec'd. 2-Ltrs of adm on prsnl est of Martha Young, late of said co, dec'd. -Notley Young, adm

Orphans Crt of Wash Co, D C. Sale of all the prsnl est of Fred'k Shuck, dec'd. -Eliz Shuck, admx. -N L Queen, auct.

Pblc sale of the rl est of the late Col Henry Gaither, 827 acs in Montg Co, Md; with mansion hse of brick, etc. Also-*Labyrinth*, 37 acs, adjs the farm of Mr Thos Simpson. -Henj Gaither, truster.

FRI DEC 22, 1815
Hse o/Reps. 1-Petition of Richd G Morriss, payment of 2 loan ofc certificates found among his late fr's papers. 2-Pet of Alex H Sanders, comp for svcs as sldr in the army of the U S prior to 1802. 3-Pet of Jas Horne & Joshua Horne, for lands in Lyle Co, Tenn, may be leased to them. 4-Pet of Mr John King, of Northern Neck, Va; his hse destroyed by the enemy; at the same time he was kidnapped & taken to Halifax.

Mrd: on Dec 12, by Rev Mr Weems, in Chas Co, Md, Mr Geo Forbes, of PG Co, Md, to Miss Mary Craig Jennifer.

Died: at Winchester, on Dec 20, Mr Chas Grim, one of the few surviving vets, who, with the gallant Morgan, was made prisoner, attempting to scale the walls of Quebec. -Gaz.

SAT DEC 23, 1815
Wm Blount is elected a Rep to Cong, from Tenn, vie John Sevier, dec'd.

Wash Co, D C. Isaac Tenny, insolvent debtor, confined in Wash Co prison for debt. -Wm Brent, clk.

MON DEC 25, 1815
Orphans Crt of A A Co, Md; sale of part of the prsnl prop of John Bell, of said co, lately dec'd; at his residence nr Richd Owing's Mills; stock, fodder, furn, etc. -Thos Waters, of Plummer; Benj Carr, jr, adms.

Mrd: in Dumfries, Dec 20, by Rev Mr Norris, John P Duval to Miss Ann F Tebbs, y/d/o the late Col Tebbs, of that place.

Died: in Phil, on Dec 19, in his 49th yr, Dr Benj Smith Barton, Prof-Pa Un.

Died: at Richmond, on Dec 11, John Douglas, stone cutter, of Wash City, one of the partners employed in erecting the Monumental Chr in Richmond. He has left an affectionate wife & 5 chldrn to lament his loss.

WED DEC 27, 1815
Died: on Dec 13, in Centreville, after a painful illness, John Browne, clk of Queen Ann's Co, Md; ntv of this country.

Died: on Dec 20, in Caroline, Md, Thos Richardson, clk of that co.

THU DEC 28, 1815
Hse o/Reps. 1-Petition of Thos Murray, late head cooper of the Navy Yd, Wash; comp for svcs rendered. 2-Pet of Walter Sims, for time to release to the U S of his title to land in the Miss Terr. 3-Pet of Wm Farris, sen, for renewal of his patent right for propelling vessels & land carriages.

Orphans Crt of PG Co, Md. Sale at the residence of Wm K Clagett, dec'd, nr Piscataway, PG Co, Md, all the prsnl est of the dec'd; negroes, hsehld furn, stock, etc. -Thos Mundell, adm.

Orphans Crt of PG Co, Md. Ltrs of adm, d b n, on prsnl est of Gaven Hamilton, late of said co, dec'd. -Thos Mundell, adm, d b n.

Mrd: on Dec 14, by Rev Mr Glass, Capt John P Smith, of Fauquier Co, Vir, to Miss Mary G Barton, y/d/o the late Mr Undril Barton, of Fred'k Co.

FRI DEC 29, 1815
Died: at his seat in PG Co, on Dec 27, Col Wm Lyles, aged about 62 yrs, ill 2 days.

SAT DEC 30, 1815
Died: at Attakapas, La, on Nov 18, Col Thos Gales, 2d s/o Jos Gales, of N C, in his 26th yr. His complaint was a violent fever, of long duration, produced by violent grief on the death of his wife, who led the way to the tomb about 2 mos before him. His loss will be felt by his fond parents, bros & sisters.

DAILY NATIONAL INTELLIGENCER
WASHINGTON, D C

1816

MON JAN 1, 1816

Died: in Salem, N H, on Dec 11, 1815, widow Sarah Morse, age 100 yrs & 3 mos; her remains were remv'd to Newbury, her ntv place, & interred with her ancestors, at the bridge lane burying place, Dec 15. She was the gr grandchild to Mary Brown, the first white child born in the ancient town of Newbury. Her living descendants are 2 chldrn, 6 gr-chldrn, 15 gr gr-chldrn & 20 gr gr gr-chldrn. She lived a widow upwards of 66 yrs.

Died: on Oct 30, Maj Stephen Minor, Pres of the Bank of Mississippi.

Montg co Crt, Md; in Chancery. Wm Scott & wife vs Benj Dulany, Jos Forrest, Timothy Winn & Rebecca his wife, & Elias B Caldwell. Rg-lease by Benj Dulany dt'd Jun 25, 1808, for 273 acs; same was defectively executed. -Upton Beall, clk.

TUE JAN 2, 1816

Crct Crt of D C, crt of Equity, for Wash Co. Sale of all right, title & int of Wm Roberts & wife, & Abner Cloud's heirs, in land in Wash Co. *Amsterdam, Arrel's Folly, Whitehaven*; & their re-surveys. -Abraham Wingard, trustee; John Travers, auct.

WED JAN 3, 1816

Died: on Jan 1, in Wash City, Miss Jane Easton, in her 18th yr. Funeral will take place from the dwlg of her fr, North G st, Wash, Jan 3d.

In Chancery, Montg co crt, Md. Thos Gittings vs Saml B Beall, Walter B Beall, Robt B Beall, Isaac Beall, Thos Beall, Gustavus Beall, Sarah B Bennett, Mary Beall & John Aldridge, & Harriet, his wife. Cnvynce of 80 acs of land, part of land cld *Labyrinth*, sold to Gittings, in his life time; bond of cnvynce issued on Feb 26, 1792. Saml, Walter, Robt-living; Thos & Sarah have died. -Upton Beall, Clk.

Ladies with ltrs in the Wash P O, Jan 1, 1816:

Miss Eliza Brown-2	Susan M Burch	Miss Susan Abell
Mrs Elenor Butler	Mrs Eliza P Custis	Verlinda Beall
Miss Cath Dinsmore	Miss Eliza Finnigan	Mrs Eliz Cain
Miss Cordelia Forrest	Alice Hepburn	Miss Eliza Glenn
Miss Mary Hampleton-2	Mrs Mary Ann Hill	Clementine Howard
Miss Mgt Jacobs	Madame Larandar	Mrs Ann Hodges
Madamosell Le Moine	Miss Eliza Magruder	Miss Ann Lee
Miss Amelia Parry	Miss Charity Peake	Mrs Budget O'Boyle
Miss J Richardson	Mrs Mary A Rowland	Miss Eliz Roberts
Mrs Polly Schorus	Mrs Peggy Salmon	Mrs Ann Rich
Miss Eliza Tench	Mrs Mgt Techam	Cath Thompson
Mrs Alice Wilson-2	Mrs Dorothy Wailes	Miss Eliz Varden
		Mrs Ann Wade-2

THU JAN 4, 1816
Hse o/Reps. 1-Petition of Eliz Morgan, wid/o Capt Jacquelle Morgan, who died while in the U S army; to be placed on the pension list.

Notice-Gamaliel Taylor has obtained from the Orphans Crt of PG Co, Md, ltrs of adm on prsnl est of Jos Taylor, of said co, dec'd. -Thos H Hanson, agent for adm.

FRI JAN 5, 1816
Mrd: on Dec 31, by Rev Mr Breckenridge, Mr David Shoemaker, jr, to Miss Abigail Pierce, both of Wash City.

Died: at Pittsburg, on Dec 13, Col Stephen Bayard, in his 67th yr; sldr of the Rev; resided in Pittsburg since 1783.

Died: in London, Nov 1, Dr Lettsom, aged 70 yrs.

SAT JAN 6, 1816
Ranaway-Jas, negro man, about 49 yrs of age. -John Graves, in Madison Co, Va.

MON JAN 8, 1816
Died: in Eng, T Evans & W Middlemore, bankers, at Nottingham, partners thru life-the former, while at a game of chess with one of his dghts, & the latter, who was previously indisposed, & never spoke after he rec'd the account of his partner's death.

Died: in Dover, N H, Mehitable Jenkins, of Berwick, aged 84; & at Eliot, Sarah Jenkins, aged 93. Both of the dec'd were mbrs of the Soc of Friends, the former having long preached in Gr Britain, & the latter being her companion.

Notice-stray cow came to my farm. -Benj Burgess, nr the Eastern Branch Bridge.

Sam'l M'Kenney has opened a China, Glass & Queen's Ware store, on Bridge st, west of Jeff st, Gtwn.

TUE JAN 9, 1816
Hse o/Reps 1-Petition of Phebe Baldwin, wid/o Capt Danl Baldwin, dec'd; extension of his pension to her. 2-Pet of Dan'l McCrimmin, for a pension. 3-Pet of Jonathan Rogers, jr, to be dischg'd from prison. 4-Pet of Elisha T Hall, paymstr to 7th Regt Infy of U S Army, settlement of his accounts, the sum of $641 of which he was robbed.

Mrd: on Dec 24, 1815, by Rev Mr Brown, Mr Alex'r Graham, of Phil, to Miss Sarah Clementson, of Gtwn, D C.

Mrd: in Dumfries, by Rev Mr Lemmon, on Dec 31, Inman Horner to Miss Mary Henderson, y/d/o Alex'r Henderson, dec'd.

Died: in Gtwn, on Jan 4, Mr C Fox, & on Jan 5, Mr B Fox, his bro. Both were afflicted with a long lingering sickness. Their 2 coffins were placed side by side in the same grave, next to 2 sisters, the dghts of Mr B Fox. The distress of the 2 widows, & their helpless chldrn, cannot be described.

Orphans Crt of PG Co, Md. Prsnl est of Ignatius Boone of Nicholas, late of said co, dec'd. -Levin Boone, Isidore Sunsberie, adms.

WED JAN 10, 1816
PG Co Crt, Sep term, 1815. Application of Dennis Mitchell, of said co, benefit as insolvent debtor. -John Read Magruder, clk.

THU JAN 11, 1816
Mrd: on Jan 3, by Rev Mr Broadhead, Mr Geo Marquert, of Wash City, to Miss Eliz Peltz, eldest d/o Philip Peltz, of Phil.

Died: on Dec 31, at Kennet, 10 miles from Wilmington, Dela, Christian Webb, in her 94th yr. She was the last of the 17 chldrn of Daniel & Jane Hoopes. Her fr & gr-fr came from Eng with Wm Penn, in 1682. Of those 17 chldrn, 11 averaged upwards of 80 yrs. All of them had their dwlgs, died & lie interred within 20 miles of the last residence & burial place of their said ancestors.

Orphans Crt of PG Co, Md. Sale at the late residence of Edw Willett, dec'd, nr upper Marlboro, PG Co, Md, all the prsnl est of said dec'd; negroes, furn, stock, etc. -John Hodges of Thos, exc. John Caster, auct.

FRI JAN 12, 1816
Died: suddenly, at his seat nr Dumfries, Va, on Jan 6, Thos Harrison, leaving his wife & chldrn.

Orphans Crt of PG Co, Md. Ltrs of adm on prsnl est of John Bing, dec'd; persons with claims to exhibit same by Mar 25. -Thos Ferral, adm

SAT JAN 13, 1816
Nicholas R Moore has rsgn'd his seat as mbr of Hse o/Reps of U S from Md, in consequence of ill health.

Dr Thos R Hodges, intending to leave Upper Marlboro, Md, offers his hse & lot for sale.

MON JAN 15, 1816
Pblc sale at the store lately occupied by Jas Cassin, all the goods & stock in trade, late the prop of the said Cassin, cnvyd by him to trustee, dt'd Jan 10, for the benefit of his creditors; horse, cart, gig, tobacco, lead, whiskey, etc. -Gustavus Harrison, trustee, Gtwn.

TUE JAN 16, 1816
For sale-prop nr New Brunswick, N J, hse now occupied by the subscriber, formerly the residence of Gen Anthony Walton White. Also a Farm, nr the residence of Miles Smith; 130 acs. Isaac Lawrence, New Brunswick, N J.

$30 reward for negro man, Tuliver, ranaway on Sep 26. Lewis Waller, Fauquier Co, Va, nr Elk Run Chr.

$30 reward for negro man, Kellis, ranaway in Sept, age 30 yrs. -John Fox, Oak Hill, Dumfries, Va.

WED JAN 17, 1816
Hse o/Reps. 1-Petition of Jane A Blakely, of Boston, Mass, stating her fears for the loss of her hsbnd, capt Johnston Blakely, U S ship of war *Wasp*; support of herself & the dght of the said capt. 2-Pet of Jacob Davy, of Vt, that duties due to the U S on nails & tax on his establishment, may be remitted; lost same by fire.

Montg co Crt, Md, in Chancery, Jan term. Henry Schnoeder vs Wm Belt & Eliz his wife, Ann S Waters, Nancy Waters, Rachel Waters, Richd R Waters, & Somerset Waters. Sale of the rl est of Richd Waters, late of Montg Co, dec'd; which was devised to him by his fr, Richd Waters; his dwlg plantation, 400 acs. Dfndnts are the heirs of said Richd Waters, his will having been so defectively executed as to be void as to the rl est. 5 dfndnts reside in Md & 2 in D C. -Upton Beall, clk of Montg co Crt.

THU JAN 18, 1816
Hse o/Reps. Petition of Wm O'Neale & J Taylor, of Wash City, comp for a vessel destroyed by the enemy whilst in the employ of the gov't.

Mrd: on Jan 15, at Balt, by Rght Rev Bshp Kemp, Cumberland D Williams, to Eliz, eldest d/o the Hon Wm Pinkney.

FRI JAN 19, 1816
Geo W P Custis is appt'd to be Justice of the Peace for Alexandria Co, D C.
Nathan Lufborough, Walter S Chandler, & John Heugh, appt'd J Ps for Wash Co, D C.
Andrew Steuart, of Md, appt'd Cnsl for the Island of Manilla. Thos Johnston, of Md, to be Cnsl at Calais, France.

SAT JAN 20, 1816
For sale or rent-Mississippi plantations. Wm Dewees, now residing in Wash City.

MON JAN 22, 1816
Frank, mulatto man, committed to Harford co jail, on Sat; aged about 21 yrs; says he belongs to Dr Moore Falls of Balt Co, Md. Also, John Reed, negro, about 19 yrs; says he belongs to John S Horn, of Balt Co, Md. -Jason Moore, Shrf.

TUE JAN 23, 1816
Loudon land [Va] for sale; 660 acs, where I now reside; with 2 story brick hse. Apply in my absence to Michl Keogly. -Edgar M'Carty

WED JAN 24, 1816
Sale of hse & lot in Port Tobacco, Chas Co, Md, now in occupation of Mr John Meredith, known as lot 1 in said town. -Benj C Ridgate

THU JAN 25, 1816
Andrew Coyle has remv'd his Boot & Shoe Store to his new bldg bet the groc store of Mr Thos Hughes, & the millinery store of Mrs Doyne. -Local ad.

FRI JAN 26, 1816
Ohio lands for sale; 1,600 acs nr Champaign Co; 1,200 acs s e of Urbanna, on Buck Creek; 600 acs nr Madison Co. -Th S Hinde, Chillicothe, Dec 25.

SAT JAN 27, 1816
Wm Schultz, of N Y, has just obtained a patent for an improvement in the *Boilers of Steam Engines,* from the Pres of the U S.

Geo Travers, Atty at Law, High st, Gtwn.

MON JAN 29, 1816
Dr Darrah, surg dentist, has taken a rm in Mr Rutherford's hse, Bridge st, where he will wait on them, or in their hses, in the line of his profession.

To Be Rented-for one yr; *Rose Hall,* & The Ferry commonly cld *Laidler's Ferry,* in Chas Co, Md. -Eliz B Laidler

TUE JAN 30, 1816
Notice-claims against the est of Richd Edelin, of Thos, late of PG Co, dec'd; bring same by Mar 8. -Edw C Edelin, Francis Edelin, excs, PG Co, Md.

Farm for sale on which I now reside; 1,200 acs in Culpepper Co, Va; dwlg hse, etc. Apply to the Hon Aylett Hawes, to Geo Hamilton, nr Fredericksburg, John M'Neale, nr the land, or the subscriber. -Philip R Thompson, Culpepper, Virg.

Partnership bet Henry Ault & Walter Gody; tin ware business, was dissolved by mutual consent. Ault will continue the business.

WED JAN 31, 1816
Died: on Jan 18, at his fr's seat, in Bedford, Va, Maj John Reid, U S army, an aid of Genr'l Jackson, in his actions against the Creeks & the British. Fell a victim to a fever on Jan 18, 1816. This is the 2d loss to his family this yr; the day after the Maj arv'd from Wash, whither he had accompainied his beloved Genr'l, he saw his sister, Maria, a blooming young girl of 18, expire. His aged fr, his mthr, & his bereaved consort, mourn his loss.

Henry Mayer intends to remove to the country, & will lease his hse on High st, where he now resides. -Henry Mayer, Gtwn

THU FEB 1, 1816
Owner can recover his horse found on the commons of Wash City, nr the Navy Yd, on Jan 26, in distress. -Moses Stickney

FRI FEB 2, 1816
Wanted-8 to 10 axemen to cut wood. -John W Bronaugh

Hse o/Reps. Petition of Abigail O'Fling, on acc't of her hsbdn & 3 sons, all in the svc of the U S, praying pensions for their military svc.

Copy of ltr rg death of Capt Abraham F Hull, s/o Genr'l Hull, of Newton. Capt Hull fell on Jul 25 last, at the battle of Lundy's Lane & was buried in the chr yd at Lundy's Lane, under an oak tree. -Maylon Burwel, Lt Col 1st reg Middlesex Militia, U Canada. [Capt H Hickman, 17th reg. U S I Chilicothe, Oct 7, 1814]

Mrd: on Jan 30, by Rev A T M'Cormick, Mr Brook M Berry, of Wash City, to Miss Emma C Magruder, of PG Co, Md.

SAT FEB 3, 1816
$20 reward for runaway, negro named Frank, age 55 yrs. -Mathias Weaver, Madison Co, nr the Crt Hse, Va.

Mrd: on Feb 1, by Rev Mr Hemphill, Mr Chas Venable, of Wash City, to Miss Eliza Shropshire, of Alexandria.

Mrd: on Feb 1, Mr John Robertson, of the Marine Corps, to Miss Jane Bostick, of Wash City.

Died: on Feb 2, David Dobbin, an old & respected inhabitant of Wash City. The masonic mbrs of Union Lodge are to meet this day for his funeral at 2.

MON FEB 5, 1816
Wash Co, D C. Wm Prentiss, insolvent debtor, confined in the prison of Wash Co, for debt. -Wm Brent, clk.

Pblc sale-by a mortgage given Jos Soper by John A Burford, in Nov 1813, sale of negroes for payment of money to Robt Edmonston, exc of John Selby, dec'd; John A Burford has left these parts. Sale at Jas P Soper's farm, Montg Co, Md. -Barton Soper, Jas P Soper, adms of Jos Soper, dec'd.

Land for sale or exchange; 1,350 acs lying in Randolph Co, Va, for lots in or adj Wash City, or Gtwn. -John M Hepburn

TUE FEB 6, 1816
Cmtee for distribution to the poor of the 1st Ward, Wash, are: Rev Dr Laurie, Maj John Davidson, Mr Jos Mechlin, & Mr Thos Barclay.

Died: at his seat in Montville, Con, on Jan 12, in his 88th yr, the Hon Wm Hillhouse; for more than 50 yrs he was in the Leg as a mbr of the Hse or the Cncl.

Died: lately, in the West Indies, Thos W Hooper, of Mass, some time since an ofcr in the marine corps.

Orphans Crt of Montg Co, Md. Ltrs of adm on prsnl est of Geo Riley, late of said co, dec'd. -Isaac Riley, adm.

$25 reward for appr boy named Leonard A King, age about 20 yrs; ranaway on Jun 22, 1815; Boot & Shoemkg business. -Wm Parsons, lvg in Gtwn.

WED FEB 7, 1816
Died: in Bedford Co, Pa, a few days ago, Gen John Piper, in his 87th yr; bore his share in the revolution with great credit as an ofcr.

Thos B Gloster, leased the premises known as *Johnson's Tvrn*, Warrenton, N C.

New bacon for sale. -Israel Little, nr the Navy Yd.

THU FEB 8, 1816
$40 reward for runaway, negro, Davy, about 22 yrs old; from nr Been-town, PG Co, Md. -Wm Fletcher, lvg in PG Co, Md.

FRI FEB 9, 1816
Died: at his seat in Northumberland Co, Va, on Jan 31, Walter Jones, aged 70 yrs; physician; better known for serving for many yrs, as Rep in the Cong of the U S.

SAT FEB 10, 1816
Mrd: on Feb 8, by Rev O B Brown, Mr Henry Rich, to Miss Ann Eliza Oliver, all of Wash City.

Fresh Garden seeds, etc. -John Ott, Gtwn.

Mrd: on Feb 8, by Rev Mr Breckenridge, Mr Wm M'Murray to Miss Mgt Talbert, both of this district.

Died: on Feb 8, in her 35th yr, at her fr's residence in this town, Mrs Mary George, consort of Rev Enoch George, an elder in the Meth Chr.

Orphans Crt of PG Co, Md. Prsnl est of Danl Clarke, late of said co, dec'd. -Richd Duckett

Chas co Crt, Aug Term; [Md.] Ignatius Middleton vs Jas Canter, Senr. Case in Chancery: bill brought to foreclose a mortgage from the dfndnt to the cmplnt, given in 1810, to secure a debt in tobacco due from said Canter, Senr, to said Middleton. -John Barnes, clk.

For sale-Good Groceries. -Thos Thorpe, Gtwn.

MON FEB 12, 1816
Passed-1-An act for the relief of John G Camp; to settle his accounts; assist dep q m genr'l, as may be equitable & just. 2-An act for the relief of Jonathan White; to renew military land warrant #875, which heretofore is issued to Jas Gunn, & to issue same in the name of Jona White, to whom it was assigned by said Gunn. -H Clay, Spkr o/ Hse o/Reps. John Gaillard, Pres o/Senate pro temp. Feb 6, 1816

TUE FEB 13, 1816
I wish to sell the hse & lot on which I now live, on Water st, bet Mkt st & Duck Lane, Gtwn. -Jane Eastburn

Died: on Jan 12, after a long & severe illness, at his residence in Springfield, Tenn, Dr Levi Noyes, in his 49th yr; a ntv of Worcester, Mass, & formerly of a resident of Wash City. He has left a wife & 6 chldrn to deplore their loss.

WED FEB 14, 1816
Died: on Feb 10, in her 57th yr, Mrs Mgt Foxall, consort of Rev Henry Foxall. For 20 yrs & upwards, death was engaged in undermining the life of our dead departed friend. -Gtwn, Feb 12, 1816.

Hse o/Reps. 1-Act for relief of Martin Cole, John Pollock, Geo Westner, & Abraham Welty; to withdraw their erroneous entries made in Madison, Canton, Vincennes & Zanesville, respectively; & monies pd be to their credit on purchase of pblc land in same districts. 2-Act for relief of Chas Markin; permitted to withdraw his entries made on Feb 23, of $1,815, at the Land Ofc at Chilicothe; money to be placed to his credit for purchase of land in same dist. -H Clay, Spkr.

THU FEB 15, 1816
For sale-land in Calvert Co, Md, on the bay side; 3 miles above St Leonard's Crk town; 384 acs with dwlg hse for a small family. View same with Mr Gid Turner. Immediate possession can be had. -B Tabbs, St Mary's Co, Md.

FRI FEB 16, 1816
Pblc sale of hse & lot in Bladensburg, now occupied by Dr Fitzgerald; in PG Co, Md. -Jos Kent, exc of T H Kent.

Pblc sale at Isaac Clarke's Shoe Store, Pa av, Wash City; sideboard, bureau, beds, etc. -N L Queen, auct.

SAT FEB 17, 1816
E Oliver, sen, informs her friends, that she has remv'd her store to the new brick hse nrly oppo the Union Tvrn; fancy goods, etc.

Who is to be the next Pres? If the people of Tenn were to be consulted, there wld be no difficulty in determining, Jas Monroe.

Mrd: on Feb 13, by Rev Mr Hemphill, Mr Geo Adams to Miss Jemima Collard, both of Wash City.

Orphans Crt of PG Co, Md. Pblc sale of all the prsnl est of Wm Hall of Wm, late of said co, dec'd; stock, negroes, furn, etc. -Richd D Hall, adm.

Orphans Crt of Wash Co, D C. Sale at auction rm of David Bates, Pa av, the prsnl prop of Jane Baker, dec'd; hsehld furn, etc. -Hezekiah Simtson, adm.

MON FEB 19, 1816
The Leg of Va have chosen the following ctzns to compose the Brd of Pblc Works: Alex'r Smyth; Lewis Summers; John Stokely; Andrew Alexander; Jas M Marshall; Thos Jefferson; Chas F Mercer; Wm J Lewis; John Mercer, Littleton W Tazewell.

Obit notice. On Sunday was interred, at Ft Columbus, Govn'rs Island, Maj Jas H Boyle, U S corps of artl.

Sale of prop that I now own in Front Royal; 20 acs of land with 2 elegant dwlg hses, merchant mill, etc, on main rd to Richmond, Va. -Hezekiah Conn

TUE FEB 20, 1816
Pblc sale-per deed of trust from Patrick White; all right & title in lot 1 in sq 256. -Richd Wallach, trustee; P Mauro, auct

Mrd: on Feb 19, by Rev Mr M'Cormick, Mr Jas C M'Callion to Miss Sarah Walker, d/o Mr Geo Walker, of Wash City.

Mrd: on Feb 15, by Rev Mr M'Cormick, Mr Jas Townley to Miss Sarah Knowles, d/o Mr Henry Knowles, of Gtwn.

Died: on Feb 17, after a long & severe illness, Mrs Sibyl Stretch, w/o Mr Jos Stretch. Funeral from her late dwlg on 19th st, this morning.

WED FEB 21, 1816
Died: at his seat in Henry Co, Va, a few wks ago, Dr Wm Hereford, Sen, in his 52d yr; from a severe attack of croup, a rare disease at that age. As a hsbdn & fr, few ranked higher.

Died: on Feb 8, in his 91st yr, Capt Jas Overton, an old & very respected inhabitant of Louisa Co, Va.

Died: on Feb 24, at his farm in Isle of Wight Co, Va, Col Richd Cocke, aged 67; took an active part in defence of his ntv state during our revolutionary struggle.

Workmen wanted [150] to work on a bridge to be built at Mr R Lewis' ferry, across the Rappahannock rvr. Write to me in Alexandria or in Fredericksburg, to the care of Mr Jas Young. -Andrew Bartle

Orphans Crt of PG Co, Md. Ordered that Wm Dixon, adm of Wm Wall, give notice required by law. -Trueman Tyler, reg.

THU FEB 22, 1816
The Public Jrnl of the U S, to be printed at Wash City, in a few wks. -A Lucas

FRI FEB 23, 1816
Robt Taylor vs Jos Maddox, Isaac Brawner, Polly Taylor & Betsey Brawner, Molly & Geo Maddox. Rg-sale of lands in Chas Co, Md, to wit: *Difficult Darnhse, Level's Blue Plains, John's Trouble, Brawner's Amendment, The Grove, Hopewell, Tanner's Hole, Brawner's park, Buck Range, & Hard Bargain*, late the prop of John Maddox, dec'd. Dfndnts Polly Brawner, Taylor Brawner, Betsey Brawner, Molly Maddox & Geo Maddox, reside out of Md. -Thos H Bowie, Reg.

SAT FEB 24, 1816
Died: at his lodgings in Wash City, on Feb 23, the Hon Elijah Brigham, a Rep in Cong from Mass; after a short illness. He was interred yesterday.

Pblic sale at the late dwlg of John C Thompson, in Gtwn; all the prsnl prop of the dec'd; [curriers & shoemkrs attend;] leather, kipskins, calf-skins, etc. -Mgt Thompson, Edw Dawes, adms.

Mrd: on Feb 22, by Rev Mr Cone, Mr Thos Warfield to Miss Mgt Foster, both of Wash City.

MON FEB 26, 1816
Nominations as electors of Pres & V P; democ mbrs of Va Leg, Richmond city, Feb 14: 1st dist, Miles King, jr, Norfolk
The 2d Chas H Graves, Surry
The 3d Gen John Pegram, Dinwiddie
4th-Mark Alexander, Mechlenburg
5th-Thos Read, sen, Charlotte
6th-Branch T Archer, Powhatan
7-Jos C Cabell, Nelson
8-John Dabney, Campbell
9-Geo Penn, Patrick
10-Wm G Poindexter, Louisa
11-Spencer Roane, Hanover
12-Shreshley Reynolds, Essex
13-Robt Taylor, Orange
14-Isaac Foster, Fauquier
15-Brazure W Pryor, Eliz City
16-Wm Jones, Gloucester
17-Wm Lee Ball, Lancaster
18-John T Brooke, Stafford
19-Hugh Holmes, Frederick
20-John Dixon, Jefferson
21-Archibald Rutherford, Rockingham
22-Archibald Stuart, Augusta
23-Andrew Russel, Wash
24-Chas Taylor, Montgomery
25-John Webster, Harrison

Mrd: on Feb 22, by Rev Mr M'Cormick, Mr Jonathan B Benson to Mary Ann Talbert, d/o Lewin Talbert, of D C.

Mrd: on Feb 22, Thos Conner, aged 81 yrs to Miss Susanna Jones, aged 16, both of PG Co, Md.

Orphans Crt of PG Co, Md. Ordered that Wm H Lyles, exc of Wm Lyles, dec'd, give notice required by law. -Trueman Tyler, Reg. Said notice follows signed by Wm H Lyles, Exc.

Wash Co, D C. Fred'k Goulding, insolvent debtor, confined in Wash Co prison for debt. -Wm Brent, clk.

Lottery to build a fulling mill with a carding & spinning mach in Chas Co, Md; mgrs: Clem Dorsey   Chas S Smith   Theodore Mudd
Nicholas Miles   Zephaniah Waters

TUE FEB 27, 1816
Died: on Feb 18, Dr Wm Somerville, of Balt, in his 54th yr, after a lingering illness of svr'l mos; leaving a widow & lg family of chldrn. The dec'd had recently remv'd from Calvert to Balt, Md.

$50 reward for mulatto boy, Wm Felps, who broke from the Alexandria jail on Jan 30th; I purchased him of Mr Wm Brewer, of Annapolis, about 12 mos since; who had hired him to Maj S Clark, of Wash, & Dr Hall, of the army. -Horo M'Elderry

PG Co Crt, Md. Case of Jasper M Jackson, for division or sale of the rl est of Alex'r Jackson; reps to appear on first Mon in Apr. -John Read Magruder, clk.

WED FEB 28, 1816
The co-partnership of Mandeville & Carlisle has expired; Christopher Carlisle will pay the demands upon it. -Jos Mandeville, C Carlisle, Gtwn, Feb 26, 1816. Christopher Carlisle has formed a connection in the groc business with his fr, under the firm of Christopher Carlisle & Co. -Jas Carlisle, Christopher Carlisle

Orphans Crt of PG Co, Md. Ordered that Isabella A Oneale, admx of Wm Oneale, dec'd, give notice required by law.

THU FEB 29, 1816
Land for sale-160 acs in PG Co, Md. -Jas Beck

FRI MAR 1, 1816
Died: on Feb 19, Mr Wm Reese, of Dublin District, in Harford Co, Md, after having breathed this sublunary air for the space of 108 yrs & 17 days. He was a ntv of Caecil Co, Md.

Pblc sale at the late dwlg of Peter Kemp, dec'd, the prsnl prop of same; by order from the Orphans Crt of Montg Co, Md. -Henry Culver, exc.

Jesse Garner informs his customers that he has a fresh supply of oysters; N & G sts, Wash City.

SAT MAR 2, 1816
In Chancery, Feb 15, 1816. Rich Duvall & Nathan Soper, vs Hannah West, exc of Stephen West, John S Belt, Edw Wash Belt, Parmelia Belt, Wm Belt, John Sprigg Belt, Jas Belt, & Mary Belt, heirs at law of Tobias Belt, *Mary Hodges, **Richd Belt & Beall Duvall. Rg-return of money pd by Alex'r Duvall, f/o the cmplnt, Richd, & cmplnt Nathan Soper, to Stephen West, late of PG Co, Md, dec'd, for land cld *Recovery*, in PG Co, Md. [More details followed] *Resides in Ky. **S/o Edw Belt, resides in Ky. -Thos H Bowie, Reg C C.

Orphans Crt of PG Co, Md. Ltrs of adm on est of John Tilley & Martha Tilley, late of said co, both dec'd. -Thos C Duvall, adm.

MON MAR 4, 1816
For sale or rent-plantation where I lately lived on the Miss, nr Baton Rouge, adj the plantation of Fulwar Skipwith; 700 acs. -Wm Dewees, now residing in Wash City.

Hse o/Reps. An act for the relief of Jonathan Rogers, jr, of Waterford, Conn; be discharged from imprisonment, for debt due from him to the U S. -H Clay, Spkr.

Hse o/Reps. An act to increase the pensions of Robt White, of Reading, Vt, who lost both his arms at Ft Erie-$40 a mo. To Jacob Wrighter, of Trenton, N J, who lost his right arm & right leg, at the capture of Little York, Upper Canada; $30 per mo. To John Young, of Boston, Mass, who lost both arms at French Crk; $40 per mo. To John Crampersey, of Beverly, Mass, who lost both arms in the late war with Gr Britain; $40 per mo. -H Clay, Spkr.

TUE MAR 5, 1816
Died: on Feb 27, at his residence at Greenwich, in his 68th yr, Rt Rev Nenjamin Moore, D D Bishop of the Prot Episc Chr in N Y, & Rector of the Trinity Chr in N Y C.

Died: on Feb 1, in Ross Co, Ohio, Armistead Carden, aged 24 yrs; a tolerable mechanic in wood; died after a short illness. His relations are to come or send for his small property. His jrnl commences at Stokes, N C, on Oct 30, 1815. -A Gustine

WED MAR 6, 1816
Mrd: at New Orleans, on Jan 27, Dr Robt Morrell, U S Navy, to Miss Laurette de Tousard, d/o the Chevalier de Tousard, French Cnsl in that city.

Wood for sale. Augustine J Smith, one mile below Alexandria.

Mill Prop for sale-deed of trust from the late capt Geo North; mill seat on Holmes' Run, Fairfax Co, Va; 42 acs; with dwlg hse. -John M'Kinney, N S Wise, trustees.

Spring Goods & Merino Shawls. Richd Anderson & Co, Bridge st, Gtwn.

Orphans Crt of Montg Co, Md. Ltrs of test on goods, chattels & credits of Baley E Clark, late of Montg Co, dec'd. -Eliza Clark, admx w a.

For sale-the Tavern, late the prop & residence of Gabriel P Van Horn, dec'd; at Vansville, PG Co, Md; 160 acs. -Archibald Van Horn

THU MAR 7, 1816
The subscriber wishes to dispose of his prop on Pa av, Wash City, at present occupied by Mrs Myers, as a brdg hse. -Jas Moore, sen.

FRI MAR 8, 1816
Lumber-yard, on Tyber Creek; notice to the ctzns of Wash & Gtwn. -Thos Carbery

Dissolution of partnership bet A I Hyatt & David H Wilson, by mutual consent. Claims to be presented to A I Hyatt on the wharf, or John Okely, Bridge st.

SAT MAR 9, 1816
Ranaway-in PG Co, Md, negro, Chas; 19 yrs old; $40 reward. -Ignatius Lot Hardy

Geniune Old Wines. John H Crease, Alexandria.

MON MAR 11, 1816
Hse o/Reps. An act for the relief of Lt Col Wm Lawrence, U S army, & those composing the garrison of Ft Boyer, on Sep 15, 1814; allowance of prize money.

TUE MAR 12, 1816
Saddle found on Feb 27th, on Pa av. -Thos Magrath, on Pres' sq, Wash.

WED MAR 13, 1816
For sale-all the rl est of Gabriel P Van Horn, dec'd; hse & lot in Vansville, PG Co, Md. Prop will be shewn by Mr Jos R Willett, lvg at same. -Richd Snowden, trust.

THU MAR 14, 1816
Obadiah Rich, of Boston, appt'd by the Pres to be Cnsl at the Port of Valencia, Spain.

For sale-by last will & test of Thos Smith, dec'd; *Goodwill*-100 acs; *Timothy's lot enlarged*-74 acs; *Jackar Strinactim*-90 acs; all in PG Co, Md. -Thos Smith; Eliz Smith, adms.

Orphans Crt of Wash Co, D C. Ltrs of adm on prsnl est of David Dobbin, late of said city, dec'd. -Rachel Dobbin, admx, cum testo anno. [w a]

FRI MAR 15, 1816
Died: on Mar 10, at Richmond, after a short illness, Mrs Judith Randolph, 3d d/o the late Thos Mann Randolph, of Tuckahoe, & relict of the late Richd Randolph, of Bizarre, Cumberlan Co.

Mrd: on Mar 12, by Rev O B Brown, Mr David Stewart to Miss Eliza Byrne, all of Wash City.

In Chancery, Mar 5, 1816. Philip Mains vs Elie Williams & others. Rg-compel the payment of a debt due by Denton Jacques to the cmplnt. Lancelot Jacques is also named; Elie Williams has remv'd out of Md. -Jas P Heath, Reg C C.

SAT MAR 16, 1816
Leg of Pa-electoral tkt:
1st Dist-John Geyer, John Conard, Danl Bussier, Wm Brooks.
2-Isaac Anderson, Mathew Roberts.' 3-John Molar, John Harrison.
4-Jacob Hestetter 5-John Rea, Wm Gilliland.
6-Michl Fackenthall, Jas Wilson 7-Gabriel Hester
8-Jas Maloy 9-Jas Banks
10-Robt Clark, Abiel Fellows 11-David Merchand
12-Thos Patterson. 13-Jos Husson
14-Saml Scott 15-Jas Alexander
[Paul Cox, David Mitchell]

Died: at his seat in Gtwn, Thos Turner, accountant of the navy dept. Funeral from his late residence in Gtwn, this afternoon.

Died: in London, on Dec 29, Phineas Bond, for many yrs Cnsl Genr'l of H B M for the Middle & Southern states of America. Mr Bond was a ntv of Phil.

For sale- the prop of the late John Dunlap, dec'd, on High st, on the crnr where Prospect st is directed to be opened. Also, 8 lots, adj the above. For terms apply to John Barnes, or to the subscriber in N Y. -Alex'r Dunlap

MON MAR 18, 1816
Orphans Crt of PG Co, Md. Prsnl est of Wm Berry, late of said co, dec'd. -Martha Berry, Benj Berry.

TUE MAR 19, 1816
$90 reward for deserters from Ft Wash, the following pvts in the corps of artl, viz:
John Millen, b in Vt, aged 26 yrs, cabinet mkr; deserted Mar 3, 1816.
Isaac Marble, b in Mass, aged 31 yrs, seaman; deserted Mar 6, 1816.
John Middleton, b in Phil, aged 20 yrs, seaman; deserted Mar 6, 1816.
David Hannah, b in Phil, aged 24 yrs, mariner; deserted Mar 8, 1816.
Eleazer Bishop, b in Sussex Co, N J, aged 26 yrs, farmer, deserted Mar 8, 1816.
Geo Collins, b in Va, aged 27 yrs, blacksmith; deserted Mar 11, 1816.
Leonard Cutler, b in Shaftsbury, Vt, aged 15 yrs, farmer; deserted Mar 11, 1816.
Moses Williams, b in N C, aged 14 yrs, farmer, deserted Mar 11, 1816.

Chas Bartly, b in Poughkeepsie, N Y, aged 23 yrs, farmer, deserted Mar 11, 1816. -Felix Ansart, Lt Com, Ft Wash.

Died: on Mar 16, Mrs Mary Ann Campbell, in her 24th yr, consort of Mr John Campbell, nr the Seven Bldgs, in Wash City.

Died: on Mar 17, after an illness of nine mos, Mrs Lucy Polk, consort of Mr Chas P Polk, in her 34th yr.

Chewing tobacco, Spanish Segars, at his store. -Lewis Labille, Gtwn.

WED MAR 20, 1816

Shrf's sale; PG Co, Md; tract cld *The Forest,* also *The Forrest of Sherwood,* nr the Brick Chr, in said co, about 140 acs; prop of Arthur Campbell, to satisfy debts due the excx of Thos Soolee & Peter Hoffman, jr. -Geo Semmes, Shrf

Auction on Wed of the entire stock of Mrs Mary An Chatelin; jewelry, laces, silks, etc. -Joncherez & Davis, aucts.

FRI MAR 22, 1816

To close the concerns of the late firm of Williams & Carrolls, their rl prop is for sale; 400 acs nr Wash & Gtwn; brick distillery, & grist mill adj, worked by the Sligo brook; brick dwlg, etc. Also, a paper mill, with 2 vats on Oaks' plan, on Rock crk, adj Gtwn, about 12 acs. Apply to Mr Danl Carroll of Dudn, in Wash City, or in Gtwn to Elie Williams.

SAT MAR 23, 1816

Constant Freeman, late a Col in the U S army, appt'd to be Acc't of the Navy Dept, vice Thos Turner, dec'd. Wm Wirt is appt'd to be Atty of the U S for the dist of Va, vice Geo Hay, rsgnd. Miles King is appt'd to be Navy Agent at Norfolk.

Died: on Mar 22, in her 41st yr, Mrs Mary Fell Stuart, consort of Gen Philip Stuart, a Rep in Cong from Md. She has left her hsbnd & 8 chldrn. Funeral this morning from her late dwlg in Wash City.

Died: on Mar 21, Mrs Mgt Fennel, relict of Edw Fennel, in her 62d yr.

THU MAR 24, 1816

Mrd: on Mar 22, by Rev Mr M'Cormick, Mr Thos Billmyer to Miss Cecilia Dixon, both of Wash City.

Wash Co, D C. Aaron Greeley, insolvent debtor, confined in Wash Co prison for debt. -Wm Brent, clk.

Orphans Crt of PG Co, Md. Ordered that Sarah Slater, excx of David Slater, give notice. -Truman Tyler, reg. [Said notice followed; claims to be presented to Dr Jos Kent, of PG Co, Md. -Sarah Slater, excx.]

Stone masons wanted-at Ft Wash, on the Potomac. Belitha Laws, John Cohagan.

MON MAR 25, 1816
Nathl P Bixby has remv'd to the no side of Bridge st, into the store lately occupied by Col John Cox, & a few drs below Gen John Peabody's; he has a genr'l assortment of Dry Goods.

Dissolution of the partnership bet Peter W Cook, & Geo J Henderson, by mutual consent. P W Cook will continue at the old stand on Pa av, Wash.

TUE MAR 26, 1816
For sale-lots 2, 3, & 4 in sq 380, on Pa av; deed of trust from Henry Herford.
-John M'Gowan, David Ott, R C Weightman, Andrew Way, trustees.

Pblc sale of hsehld furn, crockreyware, etc; on Pa av, Wash. -Eliz Braden

WED MAR 27, 1816
Land at pblc sale-part of the rl est o/the late Gen Crabb, 807 acs, Montg Co, Md. Apply to Mr Chas H Crabb, residing nr the prop. -Thos Linstid, Robt P Magruder, trustees.

THU MAR 28, 1816
Sale at the hse of Jos Stretch, 19th & G sts, Wash; sundry hsehld articles.

Pblc sale at my residence in E st; furn, etc. -Horace H Edwards. P Mauro, auct.

Taxes due for the yr 1815 to the Wash City Corp & payable Apr 1, 1816; notice to non-residents.

John Allen	J B Arridah	Benj Armitage
Wm M Beall	Jacob Boyer	Matthia Buckey
Jas Beall o/Jas	Jacob Backman	John Baker
Thos Beall & Leod M Deakins	J Strange	John Beall
Benj Bacon	J Barclay & John Simpson	
John Cunningham	Hugh Campbell	Danl Carmack
Thos Buchanan	Walter S Chandler	Wm Conrad
Saml Clark & John Wilson	David Caldwell	Hezekiah Claggett
Jos N Chiswell	Levin H Campbell	Jas Campbell
Wm Carmack	Chas Carter	Mary Chapman
Geo W P Custis	Everard Delius	John Doll
Jas Duer	Geo Doll	Elias Davidson
Jos Doll	Isaac Dewes	Andrew Fleck
Wm M Duncanson-heirs	Shinah Etting	Abraham Faw
Rev Mr Goulding	Michl Groff	Saml Griffin
Arnold Gouges	Henry Gaither	Anthony Holmead
Wm Hindman	Robt Hendlcy	John Hooff
Henry Hilliary, jr	John Husses-devisees	John Hacket
John Hoffman	John Hadrick	Wm Henderson
Peter Ham	Maurice Jones	Chas C Jones

Philip Barton Key-assignees	Jas Kirk	Henry Koontz
David Kemp	Lodowick Kruger	Peter Kemp
Christian & David Kemp	Mary Kemp	Ann Kerr
Andrew Kesler	Peter & Fred'k Kurtz	Henry Klinger
Danl Kesler	Thos Kitlan	John Singerfilter
Nathn Loughborough	Thos Sim Lee	Nathl G Maxwell
Casper Mantz	Jas M'Cormick	John Matthews
Phiip H Myers	Geo Murdoch	Henry Moscrop
Honore Martin	Benj Morris	Henry M'Clarey
Eleanor Murdoch	John Minor	John Mantz
Jacob Middart & Saml Liddy	Robt Moore	Wm M'Creery
Jas M'Henry	Jas Marshall & John Hopkins & John Marshall	
Morris & Nicholson assignees	Peter & John Mantz	Luther Martin
Moses Myer	Jacob Moyer	Michl Nicholls
Saml Mould-trust of Nicholas Sluby		John Newton
Christian Orandorf	Lawrence Oneale	Henry Pawling
Thos Pierce	Wm Pierce	Cuthbert Powell
Mary Patterson	Aaron Reclanier	G W Riggs
Matthias Rednover	John & Andrew Rench	Michl Raymer
Danl Ragan	Thos S Ridgeway	Henry Robinson
Jacob Rench & Lodowick Young	Sarah Ratcliff	Geo Reeder
Wm Raborg & Wm Taylor	John Shepherd	Chas Shell
M Shaffear	Isaac Smith	Thos Swann
John Stephens	Henry Schnebley	Saml Smith
John Stewart	Wm Sidebothom-heirs	Amos Smith
Andrew Scholfield	Isachar & Mahalon Scolfield	
Geo Swingle	John Shellman	Jacob Stivers, jr
Walter Stewart-heirs	Christian Shell-heirs	Dr Wm Shippin
J Strange	Henry Hall	John Swann
Caleb Swann-heirs	Saml H Harrison	John Southgale
Saml Sterritt	Stoddert & Templeman	Thornton Jacob
Smith, Calhoun & Co	Philip Thomas	Barton Tabbs
Richd Thomas	John Templeman	Jos Taylor-heirs
Nicholas Voss	Abraham Vanbidder	Richd Veitch
Marsham Waring	John Walgamot	Fred'k Witsall
Chas Wadsworth-heirs	Applemonia Whitchair	Richd Wilson
Eliz & Jos W Wilson	Thos O Williams	John A Wilson
Geo Winters	John Winters	Wilson & Dennis
Henry Walker	Chas Wayman-heirs	Thos Wallack
Levin Winder	Jas Williams	Alex'r Wilson
Richd Young	Henry Yost	Jacob Zeller
-Jos Brumley, coll 1st ward		

Mrd: in Wash City, on Mar 26, by Rev Dr Laurie, Chas Larned, Atty Gen o/Mich terr, s/o Col Simon Larned, late of the U S army, to Miss Sylvia E Colt, of Pittsfield, Mass.

Mrd: at Albany, N Y, on Mar 14, by Rev Mr Chester, George B Larned, of Detroit, s/o Col S Larned, late of the army, to Miss Emily Morisceau Watson, d/o Eikarnah Watson.

$50 reward for runaway, negro man, Davy, about 36 yrs old; owned by Mr Geo Chapman, nr Fauquier Crt Hse, Va, where he had a wife, but she has lately died. -Zephaniah Franklin, lvg about 8 miles from Port Tobacco, Chas Co, Md.

SAT MAR 30, 1816
Taxes due for the yr 1815 to the Wash City Corp & payable Apr 1, 1816; notice to non-residents. Geo Andrews, coll of 2d ward:

John Appleton	Chas Albridge	Saml Blodget-heirs
Thos Buchannon	Stewart Brown, jr	Ball & Ford
John Beckley-heirs	Jacob Cist	Jas Crawford, jr
Jos Covachichi	Wm Campbell	Chas Carroll, jr
Wm Deakin-heirs	Dr Jas Davidson	Robt Darnall
Henry Edwards	Richd Fenwick	Arnaud Gouges
Wm Givison	Wm Heyle	Lambert Hylan
John Heathcoate	John Hoy	Robt Kidd
Chas Lowndes	Danl Ludlow	Wm Lansdale, jr
Violetta Lansdale	Philip Lansdale	Dominick Lynch
Wm Lorman	Jas M'Cormick, jr	Wm Mackey
John F Mercer	Stepehen Moylan	John A Oswald
Edw Plowden	Isaac Pollock	Pratt, Francis, & others
Sarah Porter	Richd Powell	Abigail Pollock
Jos & Isaac Perkins	David Pollock	John B Rattree
Israel & John P Pleasants		Jos Riddle
Chris Richards-heirs	Saml Sterrett	Shrieve & Unthank
Comfort Sands	Hugh Thompson	Presley Thornton-heirs
Cornelia Thomas, jr	Rudolph Vogeler	Anthony Van Manick

Chs G Paleskie & John Gardner, jr
B G Minturn & I T Champlain
Morris & Nicholson-assignees
Lynch & Sands, & Saml Blodget-heirs & Wm Deakin-heirs
Luke Wheeler & others

Taxes due for the yr 1815 to the Wash City Corp & payable Apr 1, 1816; notice to non-residents. Zachariah Walker, coll of 3d ward:

Thos Addison	Polkinhorn & Andrews	Clement Biddle
Rudgate & Barnes	Thos C Bowie-heirs	John B Boardley
Henry Bradford	Wm Bean	Jas Brown
Matthew L Bevan	Morgan Curran	Mary Carroll
Levin H Campbell	Judson Cooledge	John Campbell
Richd Conway	Saml Chase-heirs	Jas Craig
Chas Carroll o/Crltn	John Craig	Robt Campbell-heirs
Mason & Clagett	Saml Coolidge	Jacob Chandler
Alex'r Cochrane, jr	Jas Campbell	Walter Delany
Gen John Davidson-hrs	Fred'k Delius	Stewart & Dick

Wm Diggs	Jas Earle	Jas Fisher
Lynde & Richd Elliot	Ignatius Fenwick-heirs	Job Fowler
Saml Galloway	Fred'k Gramma	Richd Graham
Arnaud Gouges-heirs	Henry Hill	John Hoye
Jonathan Hall	Wm Hemmersly	Danl Jennifer, jr
Jas Johnson, jr	Arthur Jones	Francis Kirby
Eliza Beidler	Francis Leeke	A Leitch
Darby Lux	Wm Lux	Adam Lynn
Moses Myers	Benj Mills	Griffith & Nicklin
Jas Neale o/Bennett	Philip Nicklin	Benj Oden
Edw Parkinson	Jas Penrose	Jas Paton
Andrew Parke	Nathl Phillips	Davin Ross
Wm Russell	Thos Rutter	Matthew Ridley
Isaac Reed	Robt Sands	John Stephens
Jos Spears	Wm Sidebottom	Upton Scott
Jas S Stephenson	Mahlon Scholfield	Chas Steuart
David Slater-heirs	Robt Sewall	Richd Thomas
Evan Thomas	Richd Tilghman	Wm H Tilghman
Matthew Tilghman	Peregrine Tilghman	Jas Tilghman
Edw Tilghman	Wm Veitch	Thos Willock
Bazil Waring	Geo S Washington	Notley Young-heirs

Taxes due for the yr 1815 to the Wash City Corp & payable Apr 1, 1816; notice to non-residents. Geo Adams, coll of 4th ward.

G Blagg & Laigh	Abraham Vanbibber	Zachariah Barry
David Carcud	John Crowley	Tunis Craven
Wm Cranch	Gabriel Duvall	Bridget Denmore
John Dobbyn	Bernard Elliot-heirs	Josiah Fox
Ferdinando Fairfax	Lewis Farrington-heirs	Thos T Gantt
Benj Hitchburn	Bernard Hart	Henry Howard
Isaac H Jackson	Nathl Ingraham	John King
J Lard & J Mayson	Aaron Lambert	Chas Minifie
Richd Parrott	Jas B Potts	John Randall, jr
Jas Read	Jos Slater-heirs	David Slater-heirs
Jas S Stephenson	Mark Stockwell-heirs	Benj Stoddert-heirs
Henry Slater	John Smith	Ann Slater
Sarah Slater	Jona Slater-heirs	Philip Spalding
Wm Stewart	John Steel	Lewis Somers
Wm Sandford	Richd Thomas	Geo Templeman
Nicholas Voss	Thos C Wright	Geo Walker-heirs
David Wilson	Jas D Westcot	Jas Ward
Jas Walker, jr	John Ward	Walker & Wheeler
Wm Wilson	Chas Wayman	Benj Young-heirs
Notley Maddox	Wm Yeaton	E Young
Abraham Young-heirs	Susan Young	John Minitree
Saml A Otis		

Ltr from Govn'r of Va, W C Nicholas, to Judge Washington, dt'd Richmond, Feb 21, 1816. Requesting that the remains of Gen Washington & his wife be remv'd to Richmond, to be interred nr the Capitol, etc. Reply of Hon Bushrod Washington, Wash City, Mar 18, 1816; I decline to comply with the request-no small degree of pain I inflict on myself in not yielding to that request, etc.

Hse o/Reps. Act for relief of Erastus Loomis, pay of 2d lt of marines, from Aug 1, 1814, to Dec 28, 1815, also expences incurred from wound rec'd on board the brig *Eagle*, in action on Lake Champlain, Sep 11, 1814. -H Clay, spkr.

Wash Co, D C. Richd T Spalding, insolvent debtor, confined in Wash Co prison, for debt. -Wm Brent, clk.

Isaac Johnson of Gtwn, D C, has chng'd his Pblc Tvrn to a Brdg Hse; sign of the Red Lion, Bridge-st.

MON APR 1, 1816
Pblc sale by deed of John H Fawn, surviving partner of Theo Armistead; sale of Tannery. -Albert Allmand, Wm A Armistead, Francis S Taylor, trustees.

Pblc auction of *Oakland*, in St Mary's Co, Md, 410 acs. I lived there for 3 yrs. Also 2 other tracts; 120 acs & 100 acs. -Richd B Mason

TUE APR 2, 1816
Died: in Wash City, on Mar 31, Mrs Martha Magruder, consort of Parick Magruder, & d/o Hon P Goodwyn, a Rep in Cong from Va. A loss to her chldrn.

For sale-tract of land in DC; 206 acs; adjs Mr John Veach & Marsham Jemmison; particulars apply to W Hebb, in PG Co, Md. -Aquila Johns.

$50 reward for runaway, negro, Richd, age 30. -Henley Boggess, Fauquier Co, Va.

WED APR 3, 1816
W S Radcliff, Atty & Cnslr at Law; ofc remv'd to bldg lately occupied by the Adj Gen, Wash City.

THU APR 4, 1816
Mrd: in Berkley Co, Va, on Mar 27, Maj Sam Miller, U S M C, to Miss Maria Bedinger, d/o Henry Bedinger, of that co.

Ladies with ltrs in the Wash City, P O, Apr 1, 1816:

Sarah Alburts	Ann Adams	Nancy Askins
Juliet Anderson	Sarah J Anderson	Eliz H Beall
Joanna Berry	Ann Baker	Polly Beatman
Ann Beatty	Eliz Braden-3	Mrs A Breckinridge
Miss L C Belman	Eliz Brown	Mgt Connelly
Hannah Cohart	Mary Commus	Maria Corson
Miss Cubbon	Miss Ann Crawford	Mrs July R Compton

Mary B Davis	Miss Martha Davis	Eliz Dick
Mrs Doyne	Miss Dick	Eliz P Davis
Mary Davis	Eliz Dwarigen-2	Sarah Duval
Mary Jane Davis	Jane Esteubueu	Maria Elieson
Miss Maria Gibbon	Miss Gibbs	Mgt Gibbs
Sarah Ann Graves	Mary Gilliss	Mrs Ann Gardiner
Mrs Eliz Griffin	Mrs Ann D Halkar	Martha Hall
Eliz Harpelieth	Sarah Harrison	Mrs Adel Hellen-6
Mgt R Hollingshead	Dorcas Henderson	Miss Kitty Johnson
Miss E L Jones	Mrs Eliz Kelly	Miss Mgt Kelly
Mrs Lucy Kincaid	Eliza Kolp	Miss Key
Eliz Kendle	Mrs Jane Lewis	Ann Lee
Eliza Lane	Mrs Linding	Ann Ligan
Abigail Landsale	Eliz Middleton	Mrs Pricilla Maddox
Ellen Moale	Eliz Morris	Editha G M'Kenny
Isabella Morton	Mrs Charlotte Morton	Miss Susan Meade
Miss Mary M'Ray	Isabella M'Cantus	Hannah Middleton
Martha Nachy	Ann Norris	Mrs Martha A Piatt
Mrs Hannah Reiley	Charlotte N Rind	Mrs Minta Rivers
Miss C Russell	Betsey Russel	Maria W Rhodes
Mary M Ringold	Miss J Richardson	Nancy Sims
Mary Sinart	Mgt C Smith	Maria Sewal
Nancy Sotum	Miss M W Stuart	Mrs M Stewart
Mrs Ann Shaw	Susan Smith	Nancy Tanner
Miss Eliza Tench	Mrs Mary Travers	Mrs Jane Wallert
Dorothy Wailes	Mgt Weaver	Cath K William-2
Sarah B Williams	Miss Young	Celia Young
Mrs Sarah Young	Mrs I F Young-2	-Thos Munroe, P M.

FRI APR 5, 1816
Mrd: at Havre de Grace, on Mar 31, by Rev Mr Stevens, Capt John D Henley, of the Navy, to Miss Eliza Denison, of that place.

Decree of Montg co Crt, Crt of Chancery, Md. Sale of the whole rl est of Wm Holland, of Capel, late of Montg Co, dec'd; 200 acs nr Clarksburg, with dwlg hse; Mr Nathan Holland living on same. -Augs Taney, trustee.

SAT APR 6, 1816
Orphans Crt of PG Co, Md. Ltrs of adm on prsnl est of Elisha Williams Harwood, late of said co, dec'd. -Thos Harwood, adm.

Orphans Crt of PG Co, Md. Ltrs of adm on prsnl est of Jacob Wells Brashears, late of said co, dec'd. -Wm Wells, adm.

MON APR 8, 1816
Mrd: in Balt, Md, on Apr 3, by Rt Rev Bishop Kemp, John Travers, jr, of Lisbon, to Susan Rebecca, y/d/o Saml Moale, of that city.

TUE APR 9, 1816
Died: at N Y, on Mar 26, after a short & severe illness, John H Plummer, formerly from Tenn, & late Commissary Gen of Purchases, 9th U S Military Dist.

Appt'd by the Pres: Henry Wilson, o/Md, to Cnsl at L'Orient, in France. Thos L M'Kenney, of D C, to be Super of Indian Affairs, v John Mason, rsgn'd.

Orphans Crt of Wash Co, D C. Ltrs test on will & prsnl est of Mgt Fennell, late of Wash City, dec'd. -A L Joncherez, exc.

WED APR 10, 1816
Died: at his lodgings in Gtwn, yesterday, Hon Richd Stanford, a Rep in Cong from N C, aged about 47 yrs. Erysipelas was his complaint. Funeral is today.

Died: on Mar 31, nr Fredericksburg, Va, in the 72d yr of his age, Francis Asbury, Bishop of the Meth Episc Chr.

Died: in Balt, on Apr 8, Nathan W Munroe, merchant, of that city.

THU APR 11, 1816
The partnership bet Chas Moxly & H Cassmann, has been dissolved by mutual consent. -Local Item.

Land for sale, nr Brookville, Montg Co, Md; all the rl est of Wm Holland, late of said co, dec'd; *Holland's Addition*-80 acs; part of *Chas & Benj*-40 acs; *Friendship*-20 acs; *Richard & Nathan*-10 acs; *Charlotte*-10 + acs. Will be shewn by Mr Rezin Holland, who resides on the premises. -John Adamson, Jonathan Duley, Walter C Williams, Com'rs.

FRI APR 12, 1816
Directors elected for the Union Bank of Gtwn, on Apr 1:

Abrah Bradley, jr	Robt Beverly	Wash Bowie
Chas A Burnett	Thos Cochran	Francis Dodge
Robt F How	Ninian Magruder	Wm S Nichols
Geo Peter	Danl Renner	Elisha Riggs

Pblc sale of 600 acs, late the prop of John Smith Brookes, dec'd, nr Upper Marlborough, PG Co, Md; also warehse & ground in said town, prop of said Brookes. -Benj Brookes, trustee

Orphans Crt of PG Co, Md. Dorothy Edmonston, of PG Co, Md, & Brook Edmonston, of Wash City, have obtained from Orphans Crt of PG Co, Md, ltrs of adm on est of Ninian Edmonston, dec'd. -Brook Edmonston, Dorothy Edmonston, adms. [Notice followed of sale of prsnl est at the late dwlg hse of the dec'd.]

SAT APR 13, 1816
Died: in N Y, on Mar 20, Dr Thos Bruff, about 44 yrs of age; long a respectable inhabitant of Wash City. He has left a wife & 5 chldrn to lament their loss.

Died: in Wash City, on Apr 12, after a short illness, Mrs Cath Frost, the respected consort of Mr J T Frost.

Mrd: in Alexandria, on Apr 11, by Rev M Hass_n, Mr Wm M *Chick, of Wash City, to Miss Anne Smith, d/o Jos Smith, of Va. [*_hick, clear/1st ltr a possible]

MON APR 15, 1816
Land for sale cld *Lynn & Little Lynn*, in Nanjemoy, Chas Co, Md, formerly the est of Capt John Jordan; 300 acs. -Edmund Key

TUE APR 16, 1816
Lots in Wash for sale: John Murdoch of Gtwn, will give info. -Wm H Dorsey

WED APR 17, 1816
Wash City:-John M'Lelland appt'd Com'r of ward 2 vice Henry Herford. John M'Gowan, appt'd Trustees of the Poor. Brd consists of Wm Waters, Peter Lenox, Henry Ingle, Thos Holliday, & John M'Gowan.

Died: suddenly at Piscataway, PG Co, Md, on Apr 9, Mrs Mary M Duckett, consort of Jacob Duckett, of that place; affectionate wife & fond mthr.

Died: at Gtwn, on Apr 15, aged 19 yrs, Gerardus W Wiley, 2d s/o the late Rev David Wiley, of that place.

Died: on Apr 13, in Tenn, of wounds rec'd in a rencontre with Col Simpson, Gen Thos K Harris, lately a Mbr of Cong from Tenn.

THU APR 18, 1816
Highest price will be given for 20 likley young negroes; apply at Mr Geo Miller's, F st, Wash City, or to Thos Tarrant.

FRI APR 19, 1816
Mrd: on Apr 14, by Rev Mr M'Cormick, Mr Jas Thomson to Mrs Julia Kean, all of Wash City.

Crct Crt of U S for Wash Co, D C. Henry Knowles vs Eliz Mountz, wid/o John Mountz, Senior, John Mountz, Jacob Mountz & Geo Unsler & wife Eliz Walker & Cath Knowles wife to cmplnt, heirs of John Mountz, Senior. [Total copy of said bill is required.] *Excerpts only*-Judgements rendered against Jacob Mountz & Geo Reintzel, at suits of Hodgson & Thompson, of Balt, Md, Dec term, 1805; Mountz & cmplnt committed to Wash Co prison-1806; Securities-Nicholas Hedges & Andrew Hoover. John Mountz, Sr, fraudulently transferred to Geo Mountz, now dec'd, a hse & lot in Gtwn, val of $1500 to $1800. Geo Mountz has died w/out issue, leaving his bros John Mountz, Jacob Mountz, Jos Mountz, & his sister Cath Knowles, w/o cmplnt, Mgt Unsler, w/o Geo Unsler, & Eliz Walker, wid/o Elijah Walker, dec'd, his heirs at law. -Wm Brent, clk.

Died: on Apr 16, Mrs Eliz Peltz, consort of Mr John Peltz, aged 29 yrs, after an illness of more than 2 yrs.

Crct Crt of Wash Co, D C, in Chancery. John Barnes vs Wm Brown. On Jul 11, 1803, Barnes bght of Brown part of lot 9 in sq 347, Wash City, with improvements, & pd for same; deed never recorded; Brown is not a resident of D C, & believes him to be a resident of La. -Wm Brent, clk.

Ratify sale by Ethelbert Cecil, trustee for the sale o/rl est of Peter Carbery, dec'd. Rl est sold for $4,249.17-00 current money. -Jos Harris, clk, St Mary's Co, Md.

SAT APR 20, 1816
Hse o/Reps. Act to increase the pension of Wm Munday, of Balt City, Md, who lost both his arms in an attack on the enemy at St Leonard's Crk, on Jun 28, 1814.

Mrd: on Apr 18, by Rev Mr Matthews, Mr David Kurtz, of Gtwn, to Miss Eliz Burch, of Wash City.

Thos Woodward & Geo Cooke have dissolved partnership, by mutual consent: Groceries, China & Glass. -Local Item

Tenant wanted for a brick hse in Cherry st, Gtwn, lately occupied by Mr Cathcart's family. -Saml Turner, jr.

MON APR 22, 1816
Appt'd: Maj Danl Hughes, late of the U S Army, Factor for the U S, at Ft Hawkins.

Mrd: on Apr 20, at *Kalorama*, the seat of the late Joel Barlow, by Rev Dr Laurie, Lt Col Geo Bomford, of the Ord Dept, to Mrs Clara Baldwin, all of Wash City.

TUE APR 23, 1816
One cent reward for runaway, Wm King, appr to the painting business; age about 19 yrs. -Patrick Kain

WED APR 24, 1816
Died: in Gtwn, D C, on Apr 21, Mr Alexander Mackey, aged about 75 yrs; formerly of Phil city, but for the last 15 yrs been an inhabitant of Gtwn.

Died: in St Mary's Co, Md, a few days since, Mr Francis Neale, late a 1st Lt in the U S Army; a geneours & industrious young man.

Wm Pinkney, of Md, appt'd by the Pres, to be Mnstr Extra to the Crt of Naples, in addition to his Embassy to Russia.

Stolen from my stable, on Apr 14, a light bay mare; $15 reward. -Mathew Carpenter, lvg at a place cld the *Trap*, in Loudon Co, Va, nr the Blue Ridge.

Wash Co, D C. Jos Tucker, insolvent debtor, confined in Wash Co prison for debt.

-Wm Brent, clk.

In consequence of the increase of comp of the Mbrs of the Senate & Hse o/Reps, I am induced to raise the price of shaving & dressing to them 50%. The Clks in the different depts will be shaved as usual, as no extra comp has been given them.
-Peter Valett, ofc nr the Wash Htl, Wash City.

Orphans Crt of Wash Co, D C. Sale of all the prsnl prop of Chas French, late of said co, dec'd; at his residence nr Gtwn: hsehld articles & 2 negroes, etc.
-Mariamne C French, admx.

New Spring & Summer Goods. Horatio & Sabrett Scott, Bridge st, Gtwn.

THU APR 25, 1816
Timothy Upham appt'd to be coll of Portsmouth, N H, vie Jos Whipple, dec'd.

John F Parrott appt'd to be Naval Ofcr for Portsmouth.

Mrd: on Apr 23, by Rev Mr Francis Neale, Mr Geo H Garrad to Miss Eliza Ann Travers, all of this district.

FRI APR 26, 1816
In Chancery, by Fred'k co Crt, Crt of Equity, Mar Term, 1816.
Jacob Sharp, vs Henry Hitechew, Philip Hitechew, Jacob Hitechew & Barbara his wife, Mary Hitechew, Jacob Hilderedle & Eliz his wife, Jacob Hitechew, jr, Wm Hitechew, John Hitechew, Abraham Henner & Hannah his wife, Abraham Crouse & Eliz his wife, David Hitechew, Gideon Hitechew, Eliz Hitechew, Bernard Hitechew, Izrael Hitechew, Susanna Hitechew & Elias Hitechew. Rg-Wm Hitechew, dec'd, in his life time executed to the cmplnt 2 notes with sureties, on payment of $550, on Apr 1, 1817; the other $550, on Apr 1, 1818. Wm Hitechew died intestate about Jan 17, 1815, seized of part of a tract of land in Fred'k Co, Md, cld *Bedford*, 78 1/2 acs, & part of *Buck Lodge* in same co. Dfndnst are heirs at law of said Wm Hitechew, dec'd: prsnl est insufficient to pay his debts. Henry Hitechew, one of the dfndnts, resides out of Md. -John Schley, clk, Fred'k C C, Md.

Irish Linen, direct from Ire. Mrs M Stewart, Gay st, Gtwn.

SAT APR 27, 1816
Persons of color were brought into Charleston, S C, in the ship *Lord Somers*, from London, as distress American Seamen-they are supposed to be Fugitive Slaves: 1-Adam Adams, b in Md, aged 29 yrs; sailed in the employment of Capt Byers, & of Mr Sims, in the Schn'r *Grace*, of Port Tobacco. 2-London Nicholson, b at Norfolk, Va, prop of Mr Robt Boush in 1806; about 43 yrs of age. 3-John Williams, b in Savannah, Ga, aged 19 yrs, his mthr lives in the family of Mr Means in that city. 4-Levin Spencer, b at Snow Hill, Md, about 41 yrs; says he belongs to Capt Martin, of Balt, Md. 5-John Tilman, b in Talbot Co, Md, aged 30 yrs; belongs to Wm Whetcroft of Annapolis. Othniel J Giles, City Mrshl, Charleston, S C.

Notice-The invidious distinction made by Mr Peter Valett, may be to his chagrin at learning, the the barbers of the Dist refused to accept comp for shaving the Mbrs of Cong, but actually pd them at the rate of 8 to 9%, for permission to perform the operation. -Anthony Pasquin

MON APR 29, 1816
Teacher wanted. Apply to Mr John Jack, Romney, Hampshire Co, Va.

Groceries, china, glass, etc. -John Okely, crnr of Bridge & Wash st. -Local ad.

Orphans Crt of Montg Co, Md. Ltrs of adm on est of John Newgent, late of said co, dec'd. -Ephraim Gaither, of Wm, exc.

TUE APR 30, 1816
New Cash Store-crnr of 12th st & Pa av; dry goods, grocs, etc. -Thos Drane

Roger C Weightman & Wm S Ratcliff appt'd J P's for Wash Co, D C.

WED MAY 1, 1816
New Lumber Yd in Wash City; nr Capt Davidson's Stone Warehse. -H Goldsbrorough, Rezin Orme, Agent.

THU MAY 2, 1816
Mrd: on Apr 22, by Rev Mr Verner, Mr Henry V Hill, of Wash City, to Miss Maria Ann Hamilton, d/o Francis Hamilton, of PG Co, Md.

Runaway-Mack, negro man, about 25 yrs of age; raised in Orange Co, Va, by people of the name of Corbett. -Edw Currie, Robeson Co, Lumber Bridge, N C.

Lost-small red morocco pkt bk nr Gtwn bridge. Leave at printers; $5 reward. -P G Washington

FRI MAY 3, 1816
St Mary's co Crt, Mar Term, 1816. [Md] Petition of Lewis Fenwick, one of the reps of Edw Fenwick, late of said co, dec'd; if rl est of said Fenwick wld admit of division. It wld not admit to division. Benj Fenwick, one of the reps, does not reside in Md. -Jo Harris, clk, St Mary's C C.

Hse o/Reps. 1-An Act for the relief of Patrick O'Fling, & Obigail O'Flyng, & Edmund O'Flyng. Patrick & Abigail granted a land warrant for 480 acs of land; Edmund granted a military land warrant for 160 acs of land. Patrick & Abigail O'Flyng, to rec half pay for 5 yrs for ea of their sons, Lt Patrick O'Flyng, & ensign Temple E O'Flyng, who died while in the svc of the U S. -H Clay, Spkr.
2-John T Courtnay & Saml Harrison, ctzns of Va, if dead-their leg reps, the sum of $375 bet them, for their exertions in saving the gun boat schn'r *Asp*, U S, when set on fire, in Jul 1813, in the Potomac Rvr. -H Clay, Spkr.

St Mary's Co Crt; petition in writing of Wm Hayden, of Wm & Michl Raley, of said co, for benefit of insolvent debtors. -Jo Harris, clk, St Mary's C C, Md.

Deserted from Ft Wash: 1-Thaddeus Granger, b in Mass, aged 21 yrs; farmer, deserted Mar 14, 1816. 2-Thos B Swift, b in R I, aged 21 yrs, farmer; deserted Apr 21, 1816. 3-Wm Cretcher, b in Va, aged 22 yrs, farmer; deserted Apr 21, 1816. -Felix Ansart, Lt Com'g Ft Wash.

SAT MAY 4, 1816
I will either sell my Rope-Walk & the Stock in Alexandria, or take a partner in the rope making business. -Nathl H Heath

Mrd: on May 2, by Rev Mr Breckenridge, Mr Daniel Smith, of Balt, Md, to Miss Ann Harvey, of Wash City.

MON MAY 6, 1816
Died: suddenly, on May 3, at the Franklin Htl, in Wash City, Mr Saml Thwing, aged 20, a Midshipman in the U S Navy. He had taken his passage in the stage to proceed to N Y on Fri morning.

Died: on May 4, after a lingering illness of 3 mos, Mrs Mgt Powell, consort of Mr Garston Powell, aged 26 yrs.

Reward of $15-for lg black horse stolen on May 1 from a waggon on King st, Alexandria. Deliver to Butts & Cawood in Alexandria, or Enos Williams, nr Waterford, Loudon Co, Va.

100,000 acs of land in Ky to be disposed of. Enquire of Chas G Wilcos, Phil; Chas R Caldwell, Balt, or Jos Watson, Wash.

$10 reward for lost watch with hair chain, etc. Deliver to the bar of the Wash Htl; receive $10 reward. -Jeremiah Campbell

$50 reward for Geo Kesterson, appr to the cabinet mkg business, who ran away on Mar 1. Wm King, jr.

TUE MAY 7, 1816
$60 reward for runaway, Geo, negro. Leonard Shafer, lvg in A A Co, Md, nr Poplar Springs.

John S Skinner is appt'd Postmstr of Balt City, vice Chas Burrall. [Md.]

Notice-intending to decline business & close my bks, requests those indebted to make payment by Jun 1. -C L Weiskopff

WED MAY 8, 1816
<u>Persons promoted & appt'd in the Second Regt of the First Brig of the Militia of DC; promoted:</u>

Wm Moore, to Maj, Oct 6, 1815.
Zachariah Mattingly, to Capt o/Infty, from Mar 31, 1815.
John W Brashears, to Capt of Infty, from Apr 1, 1815.
Appt'd: Saml Cox to Capt of Riflemen, from Jun 8, 1815.
Marsham Jamieson, to Lt of Infty, from Apr 1, 1815.
Andrew Forrest, to Lt of Riflemen, from Jun 8, 1815.
Thos Wheat, to Lt of Infty, from Aug 12, 1815.
Jas Carlon, to 3d Lt of Riflemen, from Jun 8, 1815.
John Bean, to Ensign of Infty, from Aug 12, 1815.
-T P Andrews, Adjt 2d Regt, 1s Brig, M D C.

An act: list of invalid pensioners of the U S entitled to rec pensions:

John Huie	$20 per mo	commence Dec 27, 1815
Erastus Desbrow	$6 per mo	Nov 18, 1815
John B Williams	$6 per mo	Sep 12, 1815
Ptolemy Sheldon	$8 per mo	Jun 9, 1815
Humphrey Webster	$17 per mo	Jun 1, 1815
Asa Glazier	$24 per mo	Jan 26, 1816
Jos Westcott	$6.67 per mo	Jan 6, 1816
Alston Fort	$8 per mo	Sep 16, 1814
Luther Gregory	$4 per mo	Feb 22, 1816
Henry Parks	$8 per mo	Feb 22, 1816
Lemuel Hewlit	$4 per mo	Jan 12, 1816
Peter Mills	$8 per mo	Jan 5, 1813
Bethuel Goodrich, jr	$4 per mo	Nov 18, 1815
Wm Vineyard	$4 per mo	Nov 2, 1815
Aaron Stewart	$4 per mo	Oct 4, 1815
Michl M'Dermott	$8 per mo	Mar 25, 1814
Wm Bowyer	$8 per mo	Oct 10, 1815
Saml Jacaway	$4 per mo	Jan 9, 1815
Jos S Van Dreeson	$8 per mo	Mar 4, 1813
Jacob Kendelsperyer	$4 per mo	Nov 17, 1814
Thos Fugate	$8 per mo	May 31, 1814
Cornelius Williams	$4 per mo	Dec 18, 1815
John B Fuller	$8 per mo	Nov 28, 1815
Michl Chapu	$4 per mo	Feb 5, 1816
Jos Henderson	$8.50 per mo	Dec 24, 1814
John Pidgeon	$4 per mo	Feb 8, 1815
Geo Fitzsimmons	$4 per mo	Jun 1, 1815
Jesse Beach	$20 per mo	Jan 3, 1816
Danl Stagg	$8 per mo	Feb 26, 1816
Daniel Bailey	$4 per mo	Dec 18, 1815
Calvin Barnes	$4 per mo	Dec 18, 1815
Calvin Barnes	$4 per mo	Feb 14, 1816
Noble Morse	$8 per mo	Oct 31, 1815
David M'Cracken, jr	$8 per mo	Feb 9, 1816
John Patterson	$4 per mo	Dec 29, 1815
Thos Baldwin	$8 per mo	Jun 6, 1815

Zenas Hastings	$8 per mo	Nov 29, 1815
Jas Nowell	$8 per mo	Apr 5, 1811
Chas Hagin	$8 per mo	Nov 8, 1815
Jos Foster	$8 per mo	Oct 10, 1815
Levie Frisbie	$8 per mo	Nov 9, 1815
Jos Gillett	$17 per mo	Apr 18, 1815
Saml Truby	$8 per mo	Sep 9, 1815
David Hawkins	$8 per mo	Nov 17, 1815
Philip Ulmer	$15 per mo	Jan 22, 1816
John Hamilton	$10 per mo	Feb 5, 1815
Nathaniel Thompson	$4 per mo	Jun 16, 1815
John Downs	$4 per mo	Mar 22, 1816
John Fenton	$4 per mo	Feb 6, 1816
Wm Collins	$4 per mo	Jan 18, 1816
Jas Allen	$4 per mo	May 3, 1815
Wm Richardson	$4 per mo	Apr 12, 1815
Jas Devourix	$8 per mo	Jul 8, 1815
Jas Guthrie	$4 per mo	Sep 27, 1815
Nathaniel Clark	$6 per mo	Feb 20, 1815
John Haskell	$8 per mo	Dec 11, 1815
Jas Nourse	$4 per mo	Nov 17, 1815
John M'Nulty	$8 per mo	Jun 12, 1815
Jos Kerr	$4 per mo	Oct 23, 1815
Stephen M Conger	$4 per mo	Oct 17, 1815
Socrates Swift	$8 per mo	Mar 18, 1815
Nathan Lockwood	$4 per mo	Dec 1, 1815
Saml Gurnee	$8 per mo	Mar 6, 1816
Emory Lowman	$8 per mo	Jun 16, 1815
John M'Millan	$15 per mo	Aug 23, 1815
Reuben Goolsby	$4 per mo	Apr 1, 1816
Wm Rhodes	$4 per mo	Nov 3, 1814
Daniel Ruminer	$6 per mo	Jul 4, 1815
Beverly Williams	$20 per mo	Sep 24, 1815
Jas Shaw	$8 per mo	Sep 5, 1815
Edmund Borum	$8 per mo	Aug 21, 1815
Matthew Williams	$6 per mo	Jul 11, 1815
Wm L Sypert	$4 per mo	Aug 24, 1815
Saml Scott	$8 per mo	May 27, 1815
David Hubbard	$4 per mo	Jun 17, 1815
Hugh Hays	$4 per mo	Jul 4, 1815
Wm Dennie	$6 per mo	Sep 16, 1815
John Bruce	$6 per mo	Sep 16, 1815
Geo Sleeker	$6 per mo	Aug 23, 1815
Robt C Davis	$6 per mo	Sep 15, 1815
Bracket Davison	$6 per mo	Dec 17, 1815
W I Shumate	$14 per mo	Jul 27, 1815
Alexander M Gray	$8 per mo	Jul 27, 1815
John Patterson	$4 per mo	Sep 18, 1815

Paul Bonnel	$4 per mo	Jan 29, 1816
Daniel Hannah	$4 per mo	Feb 28, 1816
Joshua Mercer	$4 per mo	Mar 27, 1816
Saml Schoonover	$8 per mo	Mar 18, 1816
Alston Cook	$8 per mo	Oct 26, 1814
John Chittim	$6 per mo	Jan 1, 1815
Abraham Johnson	$5.33 1/3d	Feb 11, 1816
Thos Gadd	$4 per mo	Jul 11, 1814
Wm Oneale	$4 per mo	Feb 15, 1816
Thos Edmondson	$4 per mo	May 27, 1815
Josiah B Pachard	$8 per mo	Jan 22, 1816
John I Talbotts	$4 per mo	Apr 5, 1815
Jas Jackson	$4 per mo	Aug 21, 1815
Jean Du Peron	$8 per mo	Dec 28, 1814
John Lamb	$8 per mo	Apr 1, 1816

Pensions of the following already on the pension list to be increased by sums annexed to their names; increase to commence at the times herein mentioned, & to be in lieu of the pensions they at present receive, that is to say:

Nero Hawley	$8 per mo	commence Oct 30, 1815
Nathan Hawley	$8 per mo	Oct 30, 1815
Jas Porter	$4 per mo	Jan 22, 1816
John Durell	$8 per mo	Jun 29, 1815
Jas White	$8 per mo	May 27, 1815
David Scott	$20 per mo	May 18, 1814
Hugh Barnes	$20 per mo	Mar 4, 1816
Edmund Stevenson	$8 per mo	Apr 1, 1816

Peter Hagner is appt'd Additional Accountant of the Dept of War.

Died: on May 7, after an illness of a few days, Mrs Eliza Brent, w/o Daniel Brent. She has left an inconsolable hsbnd, & an infant son, a few days old. Obit-May 14.

Wash Co, D C. Wm Paine, insolvent debtor, confined in Wash Co prison for debt.

THU MAY 9, 1816
An Act for the relief of Eliz Hamilton, widow & rep of Alex'r Hamilton, dec'd; to allow her 5 yrs full pay for the svcs of her dec'd hsbnd as a lt Col in the Rev war, which 5 yrs full pay is the commutation of his half pay for life.

Died: at Athens, N Y, on his way home from this city with his family, the Hon Saml Dexter, of Mass; after a very short illness.

For sale-land in Middlesex, Va, with grist mill; about 1,277 acs. Apply to John Tayloe, of Wash City, or John Chew, of Richmond city, or to the subscriber, Francis Corbin, *The Reeds*, Caroline Co, Va.

Wash Co, D C. Henry Norris, insolvent debtor, confined in Wash Co prison, for debt. -Wm Brent, clk.

FRI MAY 10, 1816
Died: at his residence in Wash City, on May 6, Capt Eversfield Bowie, late of PG Co, Md. His amiable wife has lost a husband, who during 13 yrs never used towards her one harsh expression; 3 promising childrn have lost an affectionate fr.

SAT MAY 11, 1816
Pblc auction of the hse & lot lately the residence of Mr Hezekiah Wood; 25 acs, 1 1/2 miles from the Capitol. -John Breckenridge, Phineas Bradley.

MON MAY 13, 1816
Robt Kirby & Co-Wines, grocs, bacon, etc. Gtwn.

Orphans Crt of A A Co, Md. Sale of all the prsnl est of Henry Deavor, dec'd, consisting of 5 negroes, & many other articles. -Thos Waters, of Plumer, adm.

TUE MAY 14, 1816
Hse o/Reps. An act for the relief of Saml Manac, a friendly Creek Indian of the half blood, for his prop which was destroyed by the hostile Creek Indians, in the late war.

Lands for sale; power of atty from Maj Josias T Beall, of PG Co, Md; *Layhill & Beall's Reserve*, lying on the NW Branch, & *Cowper* on the Paint Branch, all in Montg Co, Md; also land in PG Co, Md, adjs the lands of Maj Thos Williams & Messrs Berry's, about 2,000 acs. -Jas A Beall, Robt A Beall.

Obit-died at Wash, May 7, after a very short illness, Mrs Eliza Brent, w/o Danl Brent, of that city, & d/o Robt Walsh, of Balt, Md. [Copied from a Balt paper.]

WED MAY 15, 1816
Mrd: on May 12, by Rev Mr Glendy, Capt Alfred Grayson, U S M C, to Miss Eliza Coulter, d/o Dr Coulter, of Balt, Md.

Died: on May 4, at his residence in Hagerstown, Md, in his 36th yr, Col John Ragan; appt'd a Capt in the U S Army in 1808; srvd at N Orleans & Camp Terre au Boeuf about 18 mos; in 1810 he returned to his ntv place, & mrd & resgn'd his commission. He was appt'd by the Exec of Md, Lt Col of the 24th Regt Md Militia; distinguished himself at the battle of Bladensburg, Md.

THU MAY 16, 1816
Hse o/Reps. 1-Act for the relief of Thos Farrer, Wm Young, Wm Moseley & Wm Leach-assistant mrshls, appt'd to take the census, etc, in S C, in 1810; comp. 2-Relief of John Crosby & John Crosby, jr; settlement for the loss by fire of their store, hse, goods & wharf in Hambden, Mass. 3-Relief of the widow & chldrn of Chas Dolph, dec'd, late of Saybrook, Conn, $500; Dolph was killed during the late war with Gr Britain, in an engagement bet vols, & the crew of a British privateer, cld the *Rover*.

Died: on Wed wk, in his 64th yr, Wm Pennock, Pres o/the Union Ins Co o/Norfolk.

Died: in Wash City, on May 13, Mrs Matilda Hendley, w/o Mr R Hendley. Mrs H left an infant child just a few days old & her sorrowing hsbnd.

Ranaway-Lloyd Harper, appr boy, aged about 17 yrs; bound to the farming business. -Robt Briggs, Montg Co, Md. [Lvg nr the mouth of Big Seneca.]

Pblc sale of the rl est of Wm Segwick, late of Montg Co, Md, dec'd; 230 1/2 acs with dwlg hse, in Mont Co. Thos Segwick will shew the prop; or-John Darby, Edw Burgess, Saml Darby.

FRI MAY 17, 1816

Died: Saml Dexter, age 54 yrs, the rpblcn candidate for the chf magistracy of Mass; 2d s/o the Hon Saml Dexter, a merchant of Boston, where the son he was visiting was born. The grfr was a clergyman. [Recent-no date.]

SAT MAY 18, 1816

Va Ohio bottom land for sale; 200 acs in Cabell Co, cld *Wm Cearn's* tract, being part of 28,627 acs granted to John Savage, Robt Langdon, & other patentees, [for military svcs] together with Wm Cearns, who cnvyd to Danl Leet, & Leet to Benj Hixson, late of Harrison Co. Apply to Jas Campbell, Morgantown, or Mr Thos Knotts, of Harrison Co. Ltrs to: John H Dye, Atty for the heirs of Benj Hixson, dec'd, nr Centreville, Fairfax Co, Va.

MON MAY 20, 1816

Will sell at pblc auction, on May 22, all my hsehld furn, etc; also the hse where I now live; also lot 10 in sq 996, Wash. Gaston Powell. Geo Adams, auct.

Sale at auction; hse on High st cld Globe Tvrn, with 22 rms. Abraham Landes. -John Travers, auct.

Mrshl's sale-all the est, right, title, etc of Ambrose Moriarty, of & in lot 7 in sq 432, Wash City; suit of Jas Martin, & the suit of Chas Varden, against said Moriarty. Wash Boyd, Mrshl.

TUE MAY 21, 1816

Liberal wages will be given to good Stone Cutters, Bricklayers & Masons, at the Pblc Bldgs U S. Apply at the Capitol or at the Pres' Hse. -Saml Lane, Com'r.

In Chancery, Fred'k co Crt, Mar Term, 1816. Wm M Beale & Adam Schisler, vs Jas F Huston & Agnes Huston his wife, Cecilius Head & Eliz his wife, & Tobias Butler. Rg-sale of rl est of Tobias Butler, late of Fred'k Co, Md, dec'd; Agnes Huston, Eliz Head & Tobias Butler, are the heirs at law of the said Tobias Butler. Cecilius Head & Eliz Head his wife, resid in Ohio; Tobias Butler resides in Ohio. -John Schley, clk.

I take leave to tender my professional svcs to the pblc; ltrs directed to St Leonard's, Calvert Co, Md, will be duly attended to. -John J Brooke, [practice of the Law.]

WED MAY 22, 1816
Died: on May 20, after an illness of 3 days, Mrs Sarah Belt, consort of Benj M Belt; & on the same night her infant child.

Died: on May 16, Mrs Sarah W Kent, consort of Danl Kent, of Calvert Co, Md.

Died: on May 10, at Blandfield, Va, Mrs Jane Beverly, in her 43d yr.

THU MAY 22, 1816
Mrd: on May 15, at Chilicothe, by Rev John McFarland, Edw King, s/o Hon Rufus King, of N Y, to Miss Sara Ann Worthington, d/o Govn'r Worthington, of Ohio.

Mrd: on May 16, by Rev Jas Muir, Mr Wm C Gardner, merchant of New Port, R I, to Miss Eliza F Cazenove, d/o Anthony C Cazenove, of Alexandria.

In Chancery, PG Co Crt, Apr Term, 1816. Wilham Messenger, Jos Huddleston & John Law, against the State of Md & Wm Tunnicliff, jr. Rg-sale of the rl est of Wm Tunnicliff, dec'd. Wm Tunnicliff, jr is his only son & resides out of state. -John Read Magruder, clk.

FRI MAY 24, 1816
Died: on Thu last, Mr Geo Moore, carpenter, an old inhabitant of Wash City.

Mrd: on May 21, by Rev Mr Addison, Wm Beverly Randolph, of Va, to Miss Sarah Lingan, eldest d/o the late Gen Lingan, of Md.

I will sell my residence nr the mouth of Muddy Branch; 182 acs, Montg Co, Md. -Alexander Campbell

Orphans Crt of Wash Co, D C. Ltrs of adm on prsnl est of Alex'r Mackey, late of said co, dec'd. -Wm Mackey, adm.

SAT MAY 25, 1816
Died: on May 18, at Boston, after a severe illness of but a few days, Abijah Adams, aged 62 yrs, senior editor of the *Independent Chronicle*.

Wash Co, D C. Richd Crosbie, insolvent debtor, confined in prison for debt. -Wm Brent, clk.

MON MAY 27, 1816
Wash Co, D C. 1-Elie P Perry, insolvent debtor, confined in Wash Co prison, for debt. 2-Same for Thos Kurtz, insolvent debtor. 3-Same for Christopher Byrne, insolvent debtor. -Wm Brent, clk.

TUE MAY 28, 1816
Mr O Rich, being about to depart for Europe, will offer for sale, at his dwlg hse in Gtwn, a part of his furn; a few bottles wine of Val de Christ, 130 yrs old; bks, maps & prints, etc. -Mallory & Watts, aucts.

WED MAY 29, 1816
The death of Maj John Reid has long since been announced; he was late aid to Gen Jackson, was the s/o Maj Nathan Reid, nr New London, in Campbell Co, Va. He mrd Miss Eliz Maury, d/o Maj Abm Maury, of Franklin; & by whom he has left the posterity of honor in the persons of a little son & dght.

Orphans Crt of Wash Co, D C. Sale of all the goods & chattels of the late Geo Pitt, dec'd: furn, utensils, etc. Also, one negro man. Sale to take place at the late residence of the dec'd, *The Golden Anchor Tvrn*. -Thos Simpson, John Ott, excs.

Mrs Mary Ann Clements having lately become a resident of Wash City, nr the lower bridge, leading to Gtwn, offers her svcs as a Midwife. Rd S Briscoe has been acquainted with her character for nrly 20 yrs; Md is his ntv state.

Pblc sale of all the prsnl prop of Brice S Gassaway, dec'd, viz: 2 negro men, 4 cows & 1 horse; furn, etc. -Geo Gassaway, adm, Brookville, Montg Co, Md.

THU MAY 30, 1816
Mrd: on May 26, at Broad Creek, Md, by Rev Mr Young, Mr John Weightman, merchant of Wash City, to Miss Sidney Lyles, d/o the late Col Wm Lyles.

Fayette Co, Pa. Jas Wilson vs Edw Green & others claiming under said Green. Rg-purchase of 150 acs on Oct 18, 1814, at Shrf's sale; land in German twnshp; sold as the prop of Henry Hithrington, who is a resident of Md. The original title from Pa, in the premises, was purchased by a certian Edmund Green, of Eng, who in 1801 cnvyd the same to said Henry Hithrington, who lost all the papers while descending the Potomac rvr. -Richd Wm Lane, Pro.

FRI MAY 31, 1816
Died: on May 19, at N Y, Mrs Mary E Sanford, w/o Hon Nathan Sanford, Senator in Congress from N Y.

Promotions in the U S Navy, Apr 27, 1816; to be *Capts*:
Saml Angus	Melancthon T Woolsey	John Orde Creighton

To be *Mstrs Commandant*:
Nathl Haraden	Saml Woodhouse	Chas C B Thompson
Alex'r S Wadsworth	Geo W Rodgers	Geo C Read
Henry E Ballard	Thos Gamble	Wm Carter, jr.

To be *Lts*:
John Hill, jr	Jas Armstrong	Jos Smoot
Robt B Randolph	Wm Berry	Saml L Breese
John Evans	Richd Heath	Benj Page
John T Ritchie	John A Wish	John Gwinn

Wm A Weaver	Thos W Wyman	Jas L Morris
John A Belsches	Jas Mork	Andrew Fitzhugh
Wm M Caldwell	John K Carter	Jos Cross
Abraham S Ten Eick	Thos Hamersley	John White
Wm M Robins	Robt Field	Hiram Paulding
Enoch Lowe	Jonathan D Williamson	Chas L Springer
Wm A Lee		
To be *Surgeons*:		
Wm Barnwell	Wm C Whittelsey	Peter Christie
John Young	Chas M Reese	
To be *Surgeons' Mate*:		
Jas R Boyce		

Died: Maria, the Queen of Portugal, on Mar 20; b on Dec 17, 1734; disabled by infirmity her son, John Maria Jos Lewis was appt'd Regent. He succeeds to the Crown of Portugal; age 39 yrs; his son the heir apparent is about 18.

Dr Geo A Carroll has remv'd to 8th st north of Pa av, nr the Centre Mkt, Wash.

SAT JUN 1, 1816
Died: on May 27, at Richmond, after a lingering indisposition, Wm Marshall, the Clk of the Fed Crt of the dist, & the State's atty for that city.

Orphans Crt of Montg Co, Md. Sale in Rockville, in said co, all the prsnl prop of the late Thos Linsted. -Anna M Linsted, admx.

MON JUN 3, 1816
Monument now erecting in Trinity Chr, N Y in memory of Capt Jas Lawrence, U S Navy, who fell on Jun 1, 1813, in his 32d yr, in the action bet the frigs *Chesapeake* & *Shannon*; distinguished himself when he commanded the sloop of war *Hornet*, by capturing & sinking H B M sloop of war *Peacock*, after action of 14 mins, etc.

Pblc baths on C st, nr McKeowin's Htl, will be opened on Jun 1; single bath-.50; for the season-$10. -B H Tomlinson

Died: on May 31, at the hse of his bro, in Wash City, Dr John D Orr, of Fred'k Co, Va, aged 44 yrs. Having perfected in Scotland the education of which the foundation was laid in this his ntv country, he practised medicine for svr'l yrs in Alexandria; relinquished it after his removal over the Ridge, devoted himself to his chldrn & farm.

TUE JUN 4, 1816
Mrd: on Jun 2, by Rev Mr M'Cormick, Mr Gillies Thompson, merchant, to Miss Mary L Carter, d/o the late Geo Carter, of Stafford Co, Va.

Died: at Bennington, Vt, Anthony Haswell, one of the earliest printers in Vt.

WED JUN 5, 1816
To let-lg & convenient brick hse in Bridge st, at present occupied by Mr Truman Beck. For terms apply to Wm Worthington, jr, Wash City, or to Benj F Mackall, Gtwn. Possession on May 1 next. -W Worthnington, jr.

THU JUN 6, 1816
Sketch of Jas Monroe; now about 56 yrs of age, b in 1759 in Westmoreland Co, Va, on the land of which his ancestor, who first migrated to America, 150 yrs ago, was the original grantee. He was educated at Wm & Mary College; in 1776 he entered as a cadet in the 3d Va regt.

Mrd: on May 28, by Rev Mr Ryland, Mr Chaven K Beeding, merchant of Gtwn, D C, to Miss Rosetta L Lackland, d/o the late Jas Lackland, of Montg Co, Md.

Died: on Mon wk, at his residence in Dorchester Co, E S, Md, Mr John Mitchell, at the advanced age of 105 yrs & 9 mos.

Died: Lately at Ft Johnson, S C, Capt Andrew Lewis Madison, 4th rgt U S I; ntv of Va.

Orphans Crt of Wash Co, D C. Ltrs of adm on prsnl est of John Shaw, late of said co, dec'd. -Mary Shaw, admx.

The trustees of Cambridge Acad, E S, Md, are anxious to supply the vacancy in the choice of Princ, occasioned by the death of Rev Mr Laird. -Jos E Muse, Pres.

FRI JUN 7, 1816
Biog of Danl D Tompkins. John Tompkins, gr grfr of our subj, together with his bro Nathl, emigrated with their families from the north of Eng to Plymouth, then the province of Mass; remained but a short time, having joint patentees in land in East Chester, N Y; John died at an advanced age leaving 2 sons & a dght; his eldest son Joshua, from whom the govn'r is descended, lived to an advanced age. He had 12 chldrn; of whom Jonathan Griffin T, the Govnr's fr was the sixth. He was born on Jun 8, 1736, & at age 4 was adopted by the Jonathan Griffin family, who was his uncle by marriage. In 1758 he mrd Sarah, d/o Caleb Hyatt, of White Plains. She bore him 12 chldrn & died in Apr, 1810, age 70 yrs. The subject of this memoir is the 7th s/o Jonathan G & was born on Jun 21, 1774, at Scarsdale [Fox Meadows,] West Chester Co.

Mrd: at Newark, Dela, on May 28, by Rev Andrew K Russell, Col Geo E Mitchell, U S Army, to Miss Mary Hooper, of Dorchester Co, Md.

SAT JUN 8, 1816
Mrd: on Jun 2, in Gtwn, by Rev Mr Balch, Thos Orme to Miss Sarah Kurtz.

Mrd: on Jun 4, at Gtwn, by Rev Mr Neal, Lt Erastus Loomis, of U S M C, to Miss Celia M Thompson, d/o Mr Thompson, of that place.

Mrd: on Jun 4, by Rev Mr Waters, Mr Lewis Barrett to Miss Ann Carr, both of PG Co, Md.

Mrd: on Jun 6, in Gtwn, by Rev Mr Balch, Garret Heyer, of N Y, to Miss Harriot Siffert, of Balt, Md.

Notice-Claims against the est of Wm Marlowe, late of PG Co, dec'd; present by Dec 20, 1816. -Robt Baden, adm.

MON JUN 10, 1816
St Mary's co Crt, Mar Term, 1816. [Md] Rg-division of rl est of John Mills, Sr, late of St Mary's Co, dec'd; same wld not admit of div. Petition by Wm Mills, one of the reps. Chas N Mills, John Edwards & Ann T Edwards his wife, & Wm G Mills, 3 of the reps, do not reside in Md. -Jo Harris, clk.

TUE JUN 11, 1816
Mrd: on May 25, at Brooklyn, N Y, by Rev Mr Henshaw, Mr Geo W Fairfax, of Va, to Miss Isabella Kingsley, of the former place. [Jun 13-the N Y Evening Post says that on May 25, the gentleman mrd Miss Kingsley; the Evening Post tells us he was the very next day mrd to Miss McNeill. Answer-We can assure you that he was not blessed with taking 2 wives; Mr Geo Wm Fairfax is actually mrd to Miss Isabella Kingsly M'Neill; we copied same from the Alexandria paper.]

Died: in Prussia, Field Mrshl Mallendorff, aged 92 yrs; the oldest Gen in Europe.

Died: on May 20, at Capt P N O'Bannon's, Russellville, Kent, Mrs Abigail Morgan, aged 73; wid/o the celebrated Gen Morgan, a hero of '76.

W S Radcliff, of Wash City, has declined the military appointment recently conferred upon him.

WED JUN 12, 1816
Pblc auction, on the premises, a commodious brick hse on Mkt Space, Gtwn; now occupied by Mr Richd Shekells as a Tvrn. -John Travers, auct.

Died: on Jun 8, nr Orange crt-hse, Va, Dr Francis Dade.

THU JUN 13, 1816
Died: at Piscataway, Md, on Jun 4, Mr Jacob Duckett, an old inhabitant of that place, in the 68th yr of his age.

Orphans Crt of Wash Co, D C. Prsnl est of Geo Moore, late of said city, joiner, dec'd. Benj M Belt, of Wash City, atty. -Verlinda Moore, admx.

Mont co Crt, Mar term, 1816, in Chancery. Robt Smith vs Kinsey Beall & others. Bill to record a deed from the dfndnts, Kinsey Basil, Benj Middleton, Axy & Zadock Beall, John Dent & Verlinda his wife, Alex'r Adams & Sarah his wife, & Zepheniah Offutt, as grdn of Rezin B Offutt, to the other dfndnts, Lloyd & Cephas

Beall, dt'd on Nov 10, 1791; land cnvyd by Lloyd & Cephas Beall on Aug 18, 1795. -Upton Beall, clk.

Rome, N Y. On Mon last, Thos Tilliston Lynch, only surviving s/o Jas Lynch, of this village, aged 4 yrs & 5 mos, drowned.

Wash Co, D C. Geo W Howard, insolvent debtor, confined in Wash Co prison for debt. -Wm Brent, clk.

FRI JUN 14, 1816

Pblc sale of groceries; King & Columbus sts. -P G Martsteller. [Local ad]

Mrd: on Jun 11, by Rev Mr Matthews, Mr John Allen, printer, of Phil, to Mrs Bridget Deary, of this place.

Died: at Richmond, on Jun 8, after a short illness, Gen John Minor, in his 56th yr; ctzn of Fredericksburg; hsbnd, parent & mstr. Funeral svc was in the Episc Chr on Monday, & interred in the family burying ground at Sligo. -Va Herald.

SAT JUN 15, 1816

Partnership bet C T G Worthington & R Osbourn is this day dissolved by mutual consent; payments to Worthington, Gtwn.

Died: on Jun 4, Mrs Cath Dupuy, relict of the late Mr Wm Dupuy, late of Wash City. Funeral from the dwlg of Mr Jas Davidson, F & 13th sts, today.

Died: on Wed, Jun 5, after a long & painful illness, at her residence in Chaptico, Md, in her 48th yr, Mrs Eliz Attaway Briscoe, relict of the late Dr John Hanson Briscoe, of St Mary's Co, Md. [Affectionate mthr.]

MON JUN 17, 1816

For sale-part of *Cool Stream Farm*, 35 acs, 1 mile from the Capitol; with frame hse. -John McLeod

TUE JUN 18, 1816

$10 reward for runaway negro woman, Fanny, age about 45 yrs; she was harbored by a fellow of Dr Blake's, in Wash City, who owned her as his wife. -Richd Lyles, lvg in Montg Co, nr Poolesville, Md.

Jesse Garner informs that he has opened the Boot & Shoe Blacking Business, in the cellar, one dr west of the Wash Htl, Wash City.

Notice-Chas Blare, formerly of Loudon Co, Va, remv'd about 20 yrs ago to Ky or some part of the western country. He is notified that his relation, John Blare, of Loudon Co, Va, has died & left him, his sole heir agreeable to his last will & test. Chas Blare, if lvg, or his lawful reps, are to come forward. -Jas White, Saml Clendining, adms of Jane Blare, dec'd. Lexington Reporter & Ohio Fredonian will copy same, & send accounts to S Clendining, Hillsboro P O, Va.

$30 reward for runaway negro man, Dick Scott, age 25 yrs, formerly the prop of Henry Dent, dec'd. -Alexander Dent, Chas Co, Md.

Act of Assembly of Md; sale of tract of land cld *Alexandria*, 300 acs, lying 4 miles from Upper Marlboro, P G Co, Md. -Thos R Hodges, trustee.

WED JUN 19, 1816
Died: at Phil, on Jun 14, Jas Fennell, Tragedian & Prof of Elocution.

Orphans Crt of Montg Co, Md. Prsnl est of Solomon Spunaugle, late of said co, dec'd. -Jesse Leach, adm.

THU JUN 20, 1816
At Pisa, in Tuscany, Mar 19, in his 86th yr, died Philip Mazzei, formerly a ctzn of the U S; author of political & historical work on North America; descended of parentage in Tuscany.

Army Info. Promotions to fill vacancies, May 17 last. First Regt o/Infty: 2d Lt Jas Smith to 1st lt, Jun 10, 1816, vice N Smith, rsgn'd.
2d Regt o/Infty: 1st Lt Jas Bailey to Capt, Jun 17, 1816, vice Spencer rsgn'd.
2d Lt John G Munn to 1st Lt, Jun 17, 1816, vice Bailey promoted.
7th Regt of Infty: Capt John Nicks of 8th infty to be maj, Jun 1, 1816, vice Appling, rsgn'd.
8th Regt of Infty; 1st Lt Lewis B Willis to be capt, Jun 1, 1816, v Nicks promoted.
2d Lt Luther Hand to be 1st lt, Jun 1, 1816, vice Willis promoted.
Ord Dept: 2d lt Jas Hall to be 1st lt, May 1, 1816, vice Radcliff dcln'd.
3d lt Wm F Rigal to 2d lt, May 17, 1816, vice Hall. -D Parker, Adj & Ins Gen.

Great Marriage-on May 2, Princess Charlotte, d/o the Prince Regent, with his Serene Highness Leopold Geo Frederick, Duke of Saxe, Margrave of Meissen, Landgrave of Thuringen, Prince of Cobourg, of Saalfeld.

Mrd: in Wash City, by Rev Mr Balch, John B Timberlake, Purser, U S Navy, to Miss Mgt O'Neal, d/o Mr Wm O'Neal, of Wash City.

Died: in Feb last, at St Bartholomews, Lloyd Hilleary, late a resident of PG Co, Md.
Excellent & intelligent young man [says his friend who informs us of his death.]

Wash Co, D C, in Chancery, Jun Term, 1816. Peter Godefroy & others vs Thos Munroe, *Jas Greenleaf, *Henry Pratt, *John Miller, jr, *John Ashley & *Jacob Baker. Rg- lots & sqs in Wash City, from Jas Greenleaf to cmplnt, dt'd Jul 28, 1794-said deed recorded. *Do not reside in this dist. -Wm Brent, clk.

Crct Crt of DC; case of Jas Middleton & Thos Foyles, vs Wm Doughty, adm of Electius Middleton, Ann Middleton, widow & others, infant heirs. Sale of rl est of said Electius Middleton, dec'd. -Zachariah Walker, trustee.

$5 reward for Minny, negro, runaway. -Alfred H Powell, Winchester, Jun 15.

For sale-negro woman & her child. Apply to John Goszler, Gtwn.

Amon Bowman brght before me a stray bay horse on Jun 12. Thos Ferrall, J P, PG Co, Md.

FRI JUN 21, 1816
Teacher wanted-to teach the languages to 3 chldrn only. Richd Stuart, King Geo Co, Va.

Pblc sale, all the rl est of the late Alex'r Jackson, dec'd, about 350 acs; *Jackson's Necessity, Jackson's Mount,* etc; nr Mr Davis' Tvrn & Adelphi Mills, P G Co, Md. Apply to Mr Jasper M Jackson, sr lvg on the premises. -Thos Bowie, John Wilson, of Henry, comrs.

Orphans Crt of PG Co, Md. Ltrs test on the prsnl est of Eliz Lamar, late of PG Co, Md. -Thos Bowie, exc.

Partnership bet John Frank & Jas Tuttle is dissolved by mutual consent; Tuttle will continue the Boot & Shoe Mkg, oppo McKeowin's Htl, Wash.

In Chancery, Jun 1, 1816. His Creditors vs the Est of John Beall. Ordered that Thos Bowie, trustee, give notice to the creditors. -Thos H Bowie, Reg Cur Can.

SAT JUN 22, 1816
Mrd: on Jun 20, by Rev Bishop Neale, Mr John Holtzman, of Gtwn, to Miss Mary Newton, of the same place.

Died: on Jun 20, in Wash, after a short illness of 5 days, Richd Davis, aged 30 yrs; y/s/o Mr Richd Davis, of Fred'k Co, Md. Mr Davis had been a resident of Fred'k Co, but had recently remv'd to Wash City, to aid the Com'r of the Pblc Bldgs.

Died: on Jun 10, at Lebanon, Madison Co, N Y, Col Wm S Smith, aged 68; son-in-law of Pres Adams, formerly Srvyr of the port of N Y & late mbr of the 13th Cong.

Howard Duvall, a boy about 11 yrs of age, went away from his mthr on Jun 11th. If anybody will bring the said boy to me, bet Wash & Green sts, Gtwn, shall be satisfied for their trouble. -Lowrina Duvall

MON JUN 24, 1816
Md nominations: John Bennett, as rpblcn candidate for elector of Pres & V P of the U S, for Caroline & Talbot Cos, & upper part of Dorchester; & will vote for Jas Monroe & Danl D Tompkins. [Patriot] Thos Culbreth, of Caroline, rpblcn cndte for Cong in Talbot, Queen Anne & Caroline Cos. Lawrence Brenile will be supported as an elector of Pres & V P, in conjunction with John Buchanan, of Wash Co. Both gentlemen will vote for Monroe & Tompkins, if elected. -Fred Ex.

Died: on Jun 13, at his residence in Chas Co, Md, after a few days severe illness, Maj Alex'r Johnson; leaving a disconsolate wife & 8 chldrn to mourn their loss.

Wm Barroll, Richd Ringgold, Eze F Chambers, commitee of Wash College, Chestertown, Md.

Wash Co, D C, in Chancery. Geo Grundy sr, Geo Grundy jr, & Byrom Grundy vs John Hossack, John Hoye, & Jacob Mountz. Bill filed to procure foreclosure & sale of ground in Wash Co. Hossack is not a resident of D C. -Wm Brent, clk.

TUE JUN 25, 1816
Mrd: on Jun 23, by Rev Mr Brown, Mr Washington Drane, of Wash City, to Miss Anne M S Dade, of Alexandria.

Died: at the Creek Agency on Jun 6, Col Benj Hawkins, Agent for the Indian Affairs, at an advanced age.

WED JUN 26, 1816
Md Rpblcn nominations-Electors of the Senate:
Wm Kilty-Annapolis   Jos H Nicholson-Balt City
Geo Harryman & Geo P Stevenson-Balt Co
Thos B Dorsey & Thos Sellman-A A Co
Thos Hawkins & Joshua Cockey-Fred'k Co
John Thompson Mason & Frisby Tilghman-Wash Co
Robt Bowie & Jos Cross-P G Co
John Forwood & Jacob Michael-Harford Co
Edw H Veazy & Jos Harlan-Cecil Co
Benj Massey & Thos Carvell-Kent Co
Solomon Dickinson & John Bennett-Talbot Co
Fred'k Holbrook & Jas Kean-Caroline Co
Solomon Frazier & Wm W Eccleston-Dorchester Co
Jos Wilkinson & Lewis Sutton-Calvert Co

Mrd: in London, on May 2, after making a deal of fuss about it, Mr Geo L Coburg to Miss Charlotte A Guelph, d/o Mr Geo F Guelph, commonly cld the Prince Regent of Eng.

Notice-persons having claims against the est of Henry Smoot, late of Chas Co, Md, dec'd; to exhibit same. -Cath Smoot, admx.

Mrshl's sale of the right, title, etc of Henry B Joy, in part of lot 1 in sq 882, with 2 story brick hse; suit of Ignatius Waters against said Joy. -Wash Boyd, Mrshl-DC.

Mrd: in Gtwn, on Jun 20, by Rev Mr Addison, John Wiley to Miss Sarah Ann Clagett, all of Gtwn.

THU JUN 27, 1816
Dissolution of partnership bet Andrew Ross & Templin W Ross, trading as Andrew Ross & Son. Andrew will settle the business. He has added to his old stock of wines. -Andrew Ross, Templin W Ross, Gtwn.

Appointments for Wash City:
Wm Hewitt, Reg
Jos Elgar, Srvyr
Geo Andrews, Coll-Ward 2
Geo Adams, Coll-Ward 4
John M'Clelland, Com'r-Ward 2
John W Brashears, Com'r -Ward 4
Brooke Edmondson, Cnstbl-Ward-2
Geo Adams, Cnstbl-Ward 4
Henry Whetcroft, Treas
Jos Brumley, Coll-Ward 1
Zachariah Walker, Coll-Ward-3
Wm Waters, Com'r-Ward 1
Henry Ingle, Com'r-Ward 3
Nathan Moore, Cnstbl-Ward 1
Lancelot Griffin, Cnstbl-Ward 3

Persons indebted to the est of Wm J Greer, late of PG Co, Md, dec'd; to make payment by Aug 1. -Matilda Greer, admx.

For sale-Tract of land nr Dumfries Town; 750 acs, w dwlg hse, etc. Will take payment in slaves, bank stock of D C, or Chartered Bank of Va. Philip Harrison, Dumfries, Va.

$80 reward for negroes, Tom Moody, age ab't 23 yrs; Geo, age ab't 19 yrs. -John Harry, Hagerstown, Md.

Mr Francis Chase, jr, died at Newtown, N H, on Sat last, in the 32d yr of his age, from Hydrophobia. He leaves a wife & 2 young chldrn.

FRI JUN 28, 1816
Final dividend to creditors of the late Geo W Lindsay, late of Wash Co, dec'd; to be pd Jul 19. -Judith Lindsay, admx.

Mrd: on Jun 25, by Rev Mr M'Cormick, Henry Stephen, of Tenn, to Miss Isabella M'Kim, of Wash City.

SAT JUN 29, 1816
Died: on Jun 28, after a long & painful illness, Capt Robt Greenleaf, of the Marine Corps. His remains were interred with military honors, yesterday afternoon.

MON JUL 1, 1816
New Drug Store-oppo McKeowin's Tvrn. -John A Brereton [Local ad]

TUE JUL 2, 1816
Orphans Crt of PG Co, Md. Ltrs of adm, with w a, on prsnl est of Ann E Johnson, late of said co, dec'd. -Jos Kent.

Died: at Mastic, L I, on Jun 25, in his 81st yr, Gen John Smith, Mrshl for the dist of N Y; faithful hsbnd & affectionate parent. -Mer Adv.

Died: in Meredith, N H, on Jun 18, Hon John A Harper, formerly a Rpblcn Rep in Cong from N H.

Died: on Jun 25, after a tediou illness, at Carlisle, Pa, the honourable Henry Hugh Brackenridge, one of the Judges of the Sup Crt of Pa, for nrly 17 yrs. Affectionate hsbnd & a kind & attentive parent. He died at age 67 yrs.

Died: at N Y, on Jun 28, Mr Lazarus Beach, formerly a printer in this dist.

Bath Establishment; on the water lot he purchased of the heirs of Fred'k Haas. -John Brown, Winchester, Va. Subscribers declare the Bath Hses are clean, etc:

C Baldwin	Chas Magill	Lemuel Bent
Alfred H Powell	H St Tucker	John Bell
Jos Tidball	Edw Conrad	Robt White
Edw M'Guire	H Holmes	Wm Hill
Dabney Carr	Danl Lee-Winchester, Jun 20	

WED JUL 3, 1816

Boston, Jun 17. Sat last a quarrel arose bet Geo Coomes, a sailor, a ntv of Md, & Tama Ham, a ntv of Portsmouth, N H, with whom he had co-habited, though they were not mrd. Coomes struck the woman & stamped on her, that a little past midnight she died. Coomes was arrested & is in the goal.

Hartford, Conn, Jun 24. Peter Lung was executed at Middletown on Thu last, for the murder of his wife.

Hudson, Jun 25. On Tue last, Maj John Huyck, late of the U S army, attempted suicide, by shooting himself in the head; on the grave of his fr, in a small family burying ground, nr the city. Little prospect of his recovery.

Wash Co, D C. 1-Petition of Jesse Nevitt, insolvent debtor, confined in Wash Co prison for debt. 2-Ditto for Erasmus Carter. -Wm Brent, clk.

$15 reward for runaway, Francis Brown, negro man, aged 23 or 24 yrs. Expences pd by Mrs R Miles, lvg in A A Co, 5 miles from Queen Ann, or Baruch D Wheeler.

$30 reward for Chas Coffee, negro, runaway. -Geo Jacobs, Nelson Crt-Hse, Va.

THU JUL 4, 1816

Died: on Jun 30, Mr Patrick Callan, a ntv of Ire. Gardener by Profession & for 10 yrs past a resident of Wash City, & its vicinity; aged 50 yrs.

Died: at Boston, Thos O Selfridge, Cnslr at Law, aged 40 yrs.

Hdw & Cutlery Store, Bridge st, Gtwn. David English, jr.

SAT JUL 6, 1816
Mrd: on Jul 3, by Rev Mr Brown, Rodger Galvin, Stone Cutter, to Mrs Hicks, both of Wash City.

Dissolution of the partnership bet Hezekiah Miller & Saml J Potts, by mutual consent. Miller will carry on the business. -H Miller, Gtwn.

Notice-ordered that Enoch Combs, Coll of the tax for St Mary's Co, Md, advertise the the tracts of land with persons chargeable for same. *Persons* only extracted:

Allston James	Wm Baker	Brown Richd-heirs
Boarman Benedict	Burch Cath & Jane	Clarke Benj-heirs
Chesley Hena-heirs	Contee Leod-heirs	Horrell John-heirs
Campbell John & John Ritchie	Elmore John-heirs	Johnston Jas-heirs
Greenfield Wm T-heirs	Heard Jas of Wm	Lock Jesse
Johnston Jas-heirs/Chas Co	Johns Thomas-heirs	Ralph Robt
Lancaster Jerea	Mason Richd-heirs	Reeder Hy-heirs
Sothoron Saml	Suit Benj-heirs	Thompson Igns
-E I Millard, clk		

$50 reward for runaways, Mulatto man, Cyrus Thomas, age about 32 yrs, & his negro woman, Margery. -Jacob Huyett, lvg nr Cave Town, 7 miles from Hagerstown, Wash Co, Md.

MON JUL 8, 1816
Potomac Acad-Brd of Trustees: Richd Stuart, John Stith, Townshend S Dade. [Hampstead, King Geo Co, Va.]

Mrd: on Jul 2, by Rev Mr M'Cormick, Mr Christopher Byrne, printer, to Miss Maria Farrell.

TUE JUL 9, 1816
In Chancery, Jul 3, 1816. Richd Duvall & Nathan Soper vs Stephen West, Richd W West, Harriet Oden, Benj Oden, Maria Mullikin, Benj Oden, jr, Ellen Oden, Sophia Oden, Eliza Oden & Christiana Oden. Bill to revive a suit by cmplnts against Hannah West, excx of Stephen West, late of PG Co, dec'd, abated by the death of Hannah West. Extracts-Jeremiah Belt was indebted to said Stephen West for land cld *Recovery*; said land was bght by Alex'r Duvall, f/o cmplnt, Richd Duvall, for himself & Nathan Soper; cmplnts were evicted by John Belt, who had the better title. Sup bill filed-John S Belt, Tobias Belt-now dec'd, Mary Hodges, Beall Duvall & Richd Belt, s/o Edw Belt. The est of Stephen West has been divided among the following persons, his heirs & legal reps: Stephen West, Richd W West, Harriet Oden, formerly Harriot West w/o Benj Oden, Maria Mullikin, d/o Sophia Oden, formerly West, Benj Oden, jr, Ellen Oden, Sophia Oden, Eliza Oden & Christiana Oden, which said Benj, Ellen, Sophia, Eliza & Christiana are minors, except Benj, reside in Pa, together with Maria Mullikin are the chldrn of Sophia Oden, one of the chldrn of said Stephen West, dec'd. -Thos H Bowie, Reg C C.

WED JUL 10, 1816
Died: at Maj Wm Gholson's in Brunswick Co, Va, on Jul 4, after a lingering disease, Hon Thos Gholson, Rep in Cong from Va.

New school, on Wash st, above the Union Tvrn. -John Hagerty, jr, Gtwn.

Ladies with ltrs in the Wash P O, Jul 1, 1816.

Campbell, Eliz	Carrell, Lucy	Dexter, Miss C G
Doyle, Miss E	Dorsett, Mrs Amelia	Dennison, Mrs J
Dennison, Louisa	Darnall, Miss Eliz	Evelyth, Mrs Mary
French, Lucinda	Henson, Milly	Howard, Mrs Mary Ann
Hill, Harriet	Hampton, Fanny	Johnson, Cath
Kindell, Mrs Sarah	Lyon, Mrs Eliz	Matthews, Rachel
Martin, Eliz	M'Quinn, Miss Ann	Mitchell, Miss Eliza
Parsons, Mrs Eliza	Peters, Mrs Harriet	Patton, Miss Ann
Queen, Mary	Reed, Nancy	Robertson, Mrs Mary-2
Sayrs, Mrs Sophia	Stuart, Miss Mary A	Stillings, Miss Elenor
Sewart, Mrs Mgt	Thomas, Lydia	Williams, Susan
Waltham, Mgt	Washington, Susan H	

One cent reward for runaway, appr boy, Thos Higden, about 16 yrs old; eloped without cause. -Alex Carmichael, Plaisterer, Gtwn.

$10 reward for strayed black horse. -Clement Mayhew, lvg on Jersey av, Wash.

THU JUL 11, 1816
Walter Todd informs the inhabitants of Gtwn, that he commences his school in Congress st, nr the Engine Hse, on this day. Gtwn.

Orphans Crt of PG Co, Md. 1-Ltrs of adm on prsnl est of Wm Perkens, sr, late of said co, dec'd. -John Perkens, Wm Perkens, jr, excs. 2-Ltrs of adm on prsnl est of Paoli Lloyd, late of PG Co, Md, dec'd. -Nich Snowden, adm. 3-Ordered that John Turton, adm, d b n, of John Fairall, give notice required by law to the decd's creditors. -Truman Tyler, Reg.

Asbestos-the editor of this paper [V P] well recollects in 1794, seeing svr'l pieces of asbestos on an island in Parker's rvr, cld *Kent Island.* In 1800, about 15 miles from Balt, asbestos was found; cloth made of it was used by the ancients for a shroud to the ashes of the dead; a 24" napkin in China costs $170. A Newburyport paper states, that Mr Bole has found nr Parker's rvr, in Newbury, mineral substance which appears to be asbestos. -Virg Pat.
Asbestos, a sort of ntv fossil stone, which may be split into threads from 1 to 10 inches long, very fine, silky, & of grayish color; is endowed with the property of being unconsumable by fire.

Died: at Beaufort, S C, on Jun 30, Hon Paul Hamilton, late Sec of the U S N.

Orphans Crt of Montg Co, Md. Prnsl est of Peter Kemp, late of said co, dec'd.

-Henry Culver, exc.

FRI JUL 12, 1816
Mrd: on Jul 2, by Rev Mr Matthews, Mr Chas Warthen to Miss Henrietta Collins.

Killed: on Jun 21, Maj Matthew Anderson, only s/o Geo Anderson, of Chartiers twnshp, Wash Co, Pa; killed by a log striking his breast.

Pblc sale, in the case of John L Naylor, cmplnt, vs Saml Hanson of Saml, Amariah Frost & Saml Treat, dfndnts; of lot 3 in sq 947 in Wash City. -Zach Walker, Tr.

SAT JUL 13, 1816
For sale-my farm, *Petworth*, about 2 1/2 miles from Wash; with dwlg hse; 300 acs. Mr Greerson, the mgr, will shew the place. -John Tayloe

MON JUL 15, 1816
John Hurley, lvg at Anacosta Bridge, brght before me 2 stray horses. -Danl Rapine

TUE JUL 16, 1816
Notice-creditors of Nathl H Heath are to meet at the Wash Htl in Wash City, this day, where he will meet them.

$50 reward for Robt Francis, jr, formerly of Aylsham, Norfolk Co, Eng; came to America about 1800; for sometime was in partnership with Dr Dinmore, of Gtwn; afterwards he remv'd to Balt, Md, & connected with Messrs Casenave & Walker; about 1806 he tk up residence in Va or Md. Reward will be pd to any persons who shall produce evidence of his death. -B Henry Latrobe, Wash City.

WED JUL 17, 1816
Runaway negro man, Jas Hall Brooks, was committed to Fred'k Co, Md, jail; says he belongs to Mr Francis Reid, of Alleganey Co, Md; age about 23 yrs.
-J M Cromwell, Shrf of Fred'k Co, Md.

Died: in Middletown, Conn, on Jul 5, Jonathan Griswold, jr, s/o Capt Jonathan Griswold, of that place, in his 21st yr. He was a Cpl in the Militia Co, & was killed while crossing the street, by some one who was careless & struck him in the head with the deadly contents of a musket.

THU JUL 18, 1816
Promotions in the first regt, second brig of Militia, DC: Adam Lynn, to Col; Wm Minor, to Lt Col; Lewis Hipkins, to Maj.

Orphans Crt of Alexandria. Sale of the hse & part of lot in sq 878, late the prop of Azariah Gatton, dec'd; prop is subj to $20 ground rent annuity. -Clement Mayhew & Mary Mayhew, adm & admx.

FRI JUL 19, 1816
Grand Jury of Wilkes Co, Ga: John B Lennard, foreman
John Hendley   Joshua Jackson   Abner Wellborn
Levi H Echols   Isaiah T Irwin   Jos Callaway
John Favour, jr   John W Cooper   Henry B Gibson

Died: on Jul 13, Mr Wm Jones, y/s/o the late Mr Chas Jones. The dec'd kept a groc store & carelessly flung the stump of a segar that caused a keg of loose powder to explode. -Fredericksburg, Va, Jul 17.

Died: on Jul 4, Mr Ezra Boyer, of Lexington, Ky, from a stab in the side, in attempting to quell a riot; volunteer of the late war, & among the heroes of Raisin: son & hsbnd.

Died: on Jul 18, after a painful illness of a few days, Mrs Ann Hughes, w/o Mr Thos Hughes, of Wash City. She leaves her widowed hsbnd & a 7 day old infant. Funeral from her late residence on Pa av, this morning.

Gustavus Beall has remv'd his Cabinet & Upholstering Warehse to the west side of High st.

Wash Co, D C. Alex'r Proctor, insolvent debtor, confined in Wash Co prison, for debt. -Wm Brent, clk.

SAT JUL 20, 1816
Elected Vestrymen of St John's Chr, [Prot Episc.] in Wash City, to serve until Easter Monday, 1817:
Thos H Gilliss   John Tayloe   Peter Hagner
John Graham   Roger C Weightman   Jas Thompson
John P Van Ness   Jas H Blake

$50 reward for prisoner, John Bryan, age 25 to 30 yrs; broke open on Jul 19 from the Wash Co jail; gambler by occupation. -Wash Boyd

MON JUL 22, 1816
Runaway slaves-negro men, Jerry Lewis, age ab't 28 yrs, & his bro, Aaron Lewis, about 24 or 25 yrs old. They belong to Mrs Fox, of Mott's, Fredericksburg, Va.

$20 reward for strayed or stolen horse. -Michl Lyddane, Montg Crt Hse, Md.

TUE JUL 23, 1816
Jos Dougherty will sell his flock of part blooded Merinos; view same at his residence on 14th st west, bet F & G sts, Wash.

The relatives of Pierre Forget, a ntv of Lyons, France, who emigrated to the U S from St Domingo, because of the Rev in that Island, ab't 1794, & who died in this country, are anxious to obtain info ab't his prop. Transmit same to Dept of State.

WED JUL 24, 1816
Tvrn Kprs attend. For sale or rent, 4 story htl, at present occupied by Mr Jos Semmes in Gtwn; possession on Oct 1. -Geo King, Gtwn.

Orphans Crt of Chas Co, Md. Ltrs test on est of John Smith, of Gtwn, D C, dec'd. -Jas Hamilton, exc of John Smith, dec'd.

THU JUL 25, 1816
Attention. Richd Anderson & Co have an assortment of seasonable Dry Goods; foreign notes of every kind will be rec'd at par; notes of Merchants Bank of Alexandria, will be rec'd at a reasonable discount. -Gtwn.

FRI JUL 26, 1816
Land to be sold-tracts in Montg Co, Md; 700 acs. John Yates, lvg on the premises, will shew the land. -Wm Blanchard

For sale-150 acs of land in Chas Co, Md; deeded to the subscriber by Horatio Clagett, for the use of J Calhoun, jr. -Clement Dorsey

SAT JUL 27, 1816
Ogdensburgh, Jul 16. Louis Croteau was hung at this place on Fri for the murder of Mrs Scarborough; Croteau was a Frenchman, formerly from Lower Canada, but resided sometime in the lower part of this county; he was about 25 yrs old. [Copy of his confession followed; he was a Roman Catholic.]

PG Co, [Md] Crt, Apr Term, 1816. Commission: Josias Simpson & Ann Brean, for division or sale of rl est of John Simpson, under the act of Direct Descents. Reps to appear on first Mon in Sept. -John Read Magruder, clk.

MON JUL 29, 1816
Subscribers to the Metropolitan Assoc are to meet on Jul 27, at McKeowin's Htl, to form a constitution for the gov't of the Soc. -E Cutbush, Sec pro temp.

The town of Alexandria was laid out by act of assembly in 1749; census in 1791-2,676; in 1800-5,443; in 1810-7,143; now-8,527, with 500 beyond the corp limits; town incorporated in 1779, charter amended in 1804; first settlers were most part Europeans, particularly from White Haven & Glasgow, with a proportion of Pennsylvanians.

Died: on Apr 16, 1816, at his residence in Downing st, the Rt Hon Patrick Duigenan. Although violently hostile to Roman Catholics, he mrd a lady of that persuasion.

Eloped from the subscriber on Jul 17, Philemon Clagett, an appr boy to the shoemkg bus; 17 yrs old. -Barton Harriss, Rockville, Montg Co, Md.

TUE JUL 30, 1816
Died: on Jul 18, at Bryantown, Chas Co, Md, after a few days illness, Dr Jesse Jamieson.

Orphans Crt of PG Co, Md. Sale in Piscataway, of the prsnl est of Jacob Duckett, dec'd. -Horatio C M'Elderry, exc.

WED JUL 31, 1816
Mr Adolphus W Campbell, of parents of Hackensack, N J, went to sea in the brig *Jason*, Van Beuren, from Balt; was impressed at Havana on the Spanish frig *La Atocha*, & released after much difficulty. -N Y Nat Adv

Capt Saml Twycross, of Charlestown, aged 38, was drowned on Sat last, while bathing in the Chas rvr. -Boston, Jul 25.

One cent reward for appr girl, Jane Wardlen. -David Walker, at the Columbian Foundry.

Students of Gtwn College who excelled:
Chas Dinnies, N Y
Geo Dinnies, N Y
G Matthews, Md
John Delary, Pittsb, Pa
Robt Diggs, Md.
Dennis Donlevy, Trenton, N J
Jas Lynch, Pa
Francis Bowling, Md
Elcon Jones, Gtwn, Ca
Jas Patton, Alexandria
Richd Wright, Gtwn, Ca
Jas Faulkner, Va
Dan'l O'Brien, Gtwn, Ca
Fred'k Barber, N Y
A Melvin, Gtwn, Ca
Thos W Gough, Md
John Janney, Alexandria, Ca
Angus Wheeler, Balt
Thos Duffy, N Y
Benj H Meakings, N Y
Wm Waite, N Y
Benj Latrobe, Wash City,
Philip Smith, Phil
Henry Gough, Md
Edw Bergh, N Y
Edwin Bergh, N Y
Jas Callaghan, Balt
Lewis Joncherez, Gtwn, Ca
Thos Jameson, Md
Jos Johnson, Md
Jas Dixon, Balt
Jos Jameson, Md
Wm Gwynn, Md
Henry Elwes, Balt
Henry Riley, N Y
Robt Tate, Md
Wm Gwynn, Md
Jervais Roebuck, W Indies
Wm Deane, Alexandria, Ca
Edmond M'Cabe, Md
Thos Sim Lee, Md
John Fenwick, Md
Jas Brent, Md

THU AUG 1, 1816
PG Co Crt, Md. Sale of the right, title, etc of Richd Taylor in land cld *Gowen's Adventure;* at suit of Culver & Hall, to satisfy ofcrs fees. -Bazil Bowling, shrf.

Died: at Bladensburg, on Jul 25, Mrs Jane Lee, consort of Francis L Lee, of Sully, Fairfax Co, Va.

FRI AUG 2, 1816
Pvt sale of frame hse on 12th st, Wash City. -Saml Hoot

$30 reward for the following pvts who deserted from Ft Wash:
Abraham Miller, aged 18, b in N J; farmer.
Thos Scars, aged 26, b in Berkshire Co, Town of Sheffield, Mass; armourer.
Wm Glenn, aged 24 yrs, b in Balt, Md; shoemkr.
-Felix Ansart, 1st Lt. Corps Artl Com'g. Ft Wash, Aug 2.

SAT AUG 3, 1816
Pblc sale of part of #11 in sq 690, Wash City, prop of Arthur Jones, to satisfy the sum of $66.70 due the Wash City Corp for taxes. -Zach Walker, Coll of 3d Ward.

Mrd: on Aug 1, by Rev Mr Matthews, Mr Wm Duncan, Printer, to Miss Sarah McEvoy.

Died: in PG Co, Md, on Aug 2, Rt Rev Dr Thos John Clagett, Bshp of the Prot Episc Chr of Md.

MON AUG 5, 1816
Promotions to fill vacancies in the Military Peace Est of the U S.
Corps of Artl:
1st Lt Milo Mason, to be capt, May 17, 1816, v Herriot, dcln'd.
2d Lt John W Kincaid, 1st lt, May 17, 1816, v Mason promoted.
2d Lt Robt Goode, 1st lt, Jul 15, 1816, v Morgan, rsgn'd.
3d Lt Richd H Lee, 2d lt May 17, 1816, v Kincaid, promoted.
3d Lt Jesse M'Ilvain, 2d lt, Jul 15, 1816, v Goode, promoted.
3d Lt Wm L Boothe, 2d lt, Jul 16, 1816, v Whetmore, rsgn'd.
5th Regt of Infty:
2d Lt Subael Butterfield, to 1st lt, Jun 30, 1816, v Cilly, rsgn'd.
7th Regt of Infty:
2d Lt Jacob Tipton, to 1st lt, Jul 5, 1816, v Hays.
8th Regt of Infty:
2d Lt Russell B Hyde, to 1st lt, Jul 1, 1816, v King, rsgn'd.
-D Parker, Adj & Ins Gen.

For sale-*Bushfield*, Westmoreland Co, Va; apply to John Campbell, of said co, who will shew the land; 800 acs. -Saml Lewis, Westmoreland, Va.

Hse painting & glazing-Danl Fagan; business on Pa av, Wash City.

TUE AUG 6, 1816
From the Carolina Observer. Copy of authentic paper, now in my possession, written by the late Col Robt Rowan, of this town; *The Assoc of Cumberland Co;* a death warrant as it was termed; for the defence of their country; 7 who signed are lvg, & among the oldest inhabitants of the state. Present were the Ashes, Moores,

& Lillingtons of New Hanover Co; the Howes & Moores of Brunswick; Archibald Mac Lain, of Wilmington; Jun 20, 1775. -Ctzn of Fayetteville. Signed by:

Robt Rowan	Lewis Barge	Maurice Nowlan
Lewis Bowell	Martin Lennard	*Theophilus Evans
Thos Moody	Jos Delespine	Arthur Council
John Oveler	*David Shepherd	Micajah Terrell
Peter Messer	John Wilson	Thos Cabeen
Thos Rea	Danl Douse	Jas Emmet
Jas Dick	Aaron Vardey	John Stephenson
Onerius West	Wm Bathgate	Geo Fletcher
Chas Stephens	Jas Pearl	John Parker
*Walter Murray	John Carway	Wm Gillespie
Wm Herin	Philip Herin	David Evans
Robt Varner	Jas Gee	*John Elwell
*Benj Elwell	David Dunn	Wm White
Simon Banday	Jos Greer	Robt Greer
Thos White	Joshua Hadley	John Jones
Wm Blocker	Robt Council	Saml Hollingsworth
Jas Giles	John Clendenen	Robt Carver
Saml Carver	*Wm Carver	Geo Barns
Jas Edmunds		

*Those lvg. Col Rowan was in the continental svc-at the defence of Charleston in 1776, when attacked by Sir Peter Parker. Arthur Council died early in the Rev. Jas Emmet was a continental ofcr, Col of Cumberland Co. Jas Pearl & Robt Varner, ofcrs in the cntl svc, till the close of the war. Robt Greer, though a Quaker, was an ofcr, at the battle of Brandywine, etc. Thos White was Capt in cntl line & died in svc. Joshua Hadley, Capt during the whole war, now lives in Tenn. David Evans, ofcr in the state troops. Details of the action at Cape Fear rvr, was under the command of Browne, Owen & Robeson.

Died: at St Louis, Mo Terr, on Jul 13, Col Jonas Simonds, late of the 6th infty.

Six Cents reward for appr boy, Jas Garner, age bet 19 & 20 yrs, very fond of drink; deserted the svc of his benefactor & mstr. -Thos Wannell, Bootmkr.

Fire at Fredericksburg, Va, on Jul 31, 1816; persons deprived of their homes were- Mr Ed Shaw, dry good & groc; Mr Walter Gregory, taylor; Messrs H & E Raymond & Co, hat factory; Dr Chas L Carter, shop & dwlg hse; Mr Peter Spilman, taylor, shop & dwlg hse; Dr Carmichael & Browne, shops; Mr Harris Walker, taylor, shop & dwlg hse; Mr Jas Heath, dwlg.

WED AUG 7, 1816
Vt Baptist Assoc, 1812. Joshua Young, late Pastor of the Chr in Brandon, has been convicted before an Ecclesiastical Cncl of unlawful connection with another man's wife, & of attempts to seduce another woman; he has since left his family for parts unknown. Churches are to beware of him. -Sylvanus Haynes, Moderator; Clark Kendrick, clk. -From the Nat'l Standard.

Benj Tallmadge & John Davenport, jr, of Conn, have dcln'd re-elec to Congress.

Died: on Jul 31, at *Long Meadows*, their seat in Wash Co, Md, Mrs Eliz Lawson Belt, consort of Thos Belt.

PG Co Crt, [Md]-Notice to the reps of the late John Jackson, of said co; meeting for the val & div of the rl est of the dec'd, Aug 29. -Thos Bowie, Robt F Chew, John Crown, Thos Patterson, John Willson, of H'ry. Comrs.

THU AUG 8, 1816
Small Cow strayed from my residence on Thu. -Thos Robertson, Bridge st, Gtwn.

Orphans Crt of PG Co, Md. Ordered that Eliz Bacon, admx of Benj Bacon, dec'd, give the notice required by law. -Truman Tyler, reg.

FRI AUG 9, 1816
Mrd: on Aug 6, by Rev Wm Matthews, Mr Jas Spratt to Miss Sarah Bryson, both of Wash City.

Obit-died on Jul 17, in his 65th yr, Gen Jacob Read; render his memory dear to Carolina, a favorite son; tender hsbnd & indulgent parent.

On Aug 3, Erastus W Ingals, of Middlefield, Otsego Co, N Y, committed suicide by cutting his throat with a razor.

Litchfield, Conn, Jul 25. On Tue, Benj Peck, age 17 ys, s/o Mr Eliada Peck, of same, & Isaac Jackson, age 39, a man of color, were drowned in the East Rvr.

SAT AUG 10, 1816
Wash Co, D C. John Lathrop, insolvent debtor, confined in Wash Co prison, for debt. -Wm Brent, clk.

For sale-nail manufactory, Union st. -Horace Field, Alexandria.

MON AUG 12, 1816
Pblc sale at Stephen Parry's Tvrn, nr the Navy Yd, on Sep 2, val lots in Wash City. -Sarah Slater, admx of David Slater, dec'd.

Partnership uner the firm of Floyd, Smith & Co of Gtwn, is this day dissoved by mutual consent. -Wm Floyd, Jesse Smith, Edmund Smith, Edw H Nicolle.

TUE AUG 13, 1816
Orphans Crt of Wash Co, D C. Ltrs of adm on prsnl est of Patrick Callan, late of said co, dec'd. -Nicholas Callan, adm. Notice was followed by: sale of sundry articles of the dec'd, at the dwlg hse of same on F st. Also the lease of a frame hse on Capitol Hill, sq 729, occupied at present by Jilson Noel, as grocery.

Wash Livery Stable; built by Mr Evan Evans; open for business. -Isaac Allen

I certify that Jos Brooke, of Wash Co, D C, brght before me a stray Bay Horse. -Jas H Blake, J P. [-Jos Brooke, lvg at Little Falls Bridge.]

WED AUG 14, 1816
Mrd: on Aug 11, by Rev Mr Lynch, Mr Thos Broxton to Mrs Mary Seymour, of the Theatre.

THU AUG 15, 1816
Notice-pblc sale at Queen's Tvrn, Capt Hill, on Dec 24; part of lot 11 in sq 690, Wash, taken as prop of Arthur Jones, to satisfy sum of $66.70 due the Wash City Corp for taxes. -Zach Walker, Coll of 3d Ward

Wash Co, D C. 1-Petition of Nathl H Heath, insolvent debtor, confined in Wash Co prison for debt. 2-Same for Jos Sutherland. -Wm Brent, clk.

FRI AUG 16, 1816
London, Jun 10. Mrs Jane Lewson died lately at her hse in Cold Bath sw, aged 116 yrs; mrd early and became a widow at age 26 yrs with an only child, her dght.

Obit-died at Croom, his seat in PG Co, Md, on Aug 2, Rt Rev Thos John Claggett, Bshp of the Prot Espic Chr in Md; age 73 yrs; ordained upwards of 40 yrs.

SAT AUG 17, 1816
Phil, Aug 14. Died: Mr Francis Cope, 2d s/o Thos P Cope, of Wash City. The dec'd was on a visit to the sea side for his health, but when bathing, was swept away by the surf, & lost; he was a young man.

Died: at Balt, on Aug 14, Jas Calhoun, aged 73 yrs.

Notice-Ltrs of adm on the prsnl est of Jos Parsons, of St Mary's Co, Md, dec'd. -Zachariah Spalding, adm d b n.

MON AUG 19, 1816
Crct Crt, M_ Dist, Jun 22, 1816. Case of Robt Treadwell, b at Ipswich, on Aug 2, 1795; enlisted into the navy of the U S in May 1815; deserted soon after; apprehended on Jun 19 past. He has a fr at sea who is still lvg. Robt Treadwell was to be in the custody of his cmndg ofcr. -Boston Patriot.

Died: on Aug 18, after an illness of more than 2 mos, Maj Geo Andrews, an old & valuable inhabitant of Wash City. Funeral from his late dwlg this morning.

TUE AUG 20, 1816
Orphans Crt of Wash Co, D C. Prsnl est of John Brady, late of U S M C, dec'd. -John B Forrest

Died: at Onondaga, N Y, on Jul 18, Benj Ketchum, aged 101 yrs on Feb 19 last. His wife, with whom he had lived nrly 80 yrs, died 4 yrs ago on Apr 3, wanting but 3 days of 102 yrs of age. They had lived to see their 5th generation.

Died: in Phil, on Aug 7, John Barclay, a ntv of Ireland.

For sale-my prop in Pr Wm Co, Va; 700 acs. Apply to Dr Humphrey Peake or Mr John Henning, at Centreville, Fairfax Co, Va. -H Peake.

Wash Co, D C. John Myers, insolvent debtor, confined in Wash Co prison for debt. -Wm Brent, clk.

WED AUG 21, 1816
New Hat & Shoe Store, under the firm of Chas Hunt & Co, on Bridge st.
-Wm Noyes, Chas Hunt, Gtwn.

Notice-will be sold by order of the Orphan's Crt, on Sep 4, at Geo Adams' auct rm, a small black girl almost 11 yrs old; part of the prsnl est of Josias Gale, dec'd.
-Wm Doughty, adm; Geo Adams, auct.

THU AUG 22, 1816
The Pres of the U S has recognized Wm Dawson as Cnsl of his Brit Maj for Md.

Indiana Election-warm contest in the new state for the ofc of Govn'r; Thos Posey & Jonathan Jennings are the candidates.

FRI AUG 23, 1816
$20 reward. Deserted from Ft Wash, pvts of the corps of artl:
Jesse Green, aged 30 yrs, b in Fairfax Co, Va; cooper; deserted Aug 17, 1816.
John Little, aged 27 yrs, b in Hardy Co, Va; farmer; deserted Aug 17, 1816.
-Felix Ansart, Lt Comd'g.

Mrd: on Aug 22, by Rev Mr Matthews, Mr Wm M Sawyer to Mrs _nn Johnson, both of Wash City.

Obit-died a few days ago, in N Y, Rev Gershom Mandes Seixas, late mnstr of the Hebrew congregation in that city, in his 71st yr, & 50th yr of ministry.

MON AUG 26, 1816
For sale-Botanical collection, known by the name of Botanical Garden of St Mary's College. -Alex De La Tullaye, 257 Mkt st, Balt, Md.

Mr Jeptha A Wilkinson, the inventor, though a New Englander by birth, resides in Otsego Co, N Y.

Mont co Crt, Md, in Chancery, Jul Term, 1816. Danl Lee vs Saml B Beall, Robt B Beall, Walter B Beall, Aza Beall, Isaac Beall, Thos Beall, Gustavus Beall, Mary Beall & Sarah B Bennett. Rg-obtain a decree for the cnvynce in fee simple, of land in a bond given by Thos B Beall to Danl Lee, dt'd May 21, 1794; parcel of land used by Richd, Jas & Benj Gittings for pasture; being all the land then unsold of the land allotted to the said Thos B Beall in division bet him & his bros; part of the land left by Richd Beall, of Saml, to be divided among his chldrn; all the chldrn of Richd Beall, of Saml who are living, & heirs of those who are dead are made dfndnts in this bill. -R H Harwood, Assoc Judge; Upton Beall, clk-Montg co crt.

TUE AUG 27, 1816
$100 reward for runaway, Pharoah Evans, negro man, aged 33 yrs, waggon-mkr. -Conrad Crebs, Sen, Winchester, Va.

$20 reward for negro, Jacob, about 45 yrs old; formerly the prop of Wm K Cleggett, dec'd. His wife who now lives at Mr Gwynn's shop, PG Co, Md, by name of Patty Butler, with a small child, her dght. -Theo Wall, Nottingham, PG Co, Md.

Land for sale-late the rl est of Thos & Henrietta Chesley, of Calvert Co, Md; 200 acs nr St Clements' Bay, St Mary's Co, Md. Also, in Calvert Co, 266 acs; tract of 444 acs; tract of 205 acs. Mr Benj Card resides on the first tract of Calvert lands & will shew same. -Peter Eimerson, trustee, Calv Co, Md.

WED AUG 28, 1816
Wash Co, D C. Wm M Chesney, insolvent debtor, confined in Wash Co prison, for debt. -Wm Brent, clk.

For sale- my farm on Md Point, 900 to 1,000 acs. Danl Jenifer, at Port Tobacco, or Allen's Fresh, Md.

Orphans Crt of PG Co, Md. Sale at the late residence of Richd Marshall, all the prsnl est of the dec'd. -Mgt Marshall, excx.

THU AUG 29, 1816
Crct Crt, Jun Term, 1816, Wash Co, D C. Ann Garey vs Wm Roberts, Susannah Roberts, Artimezia, Emza Naomi, Susannah & Trammel H Cloud. Ratify sale made by Abraham Wingard, trustee in this case. -Wm Brent clk.

Orphans Crt of Wash Co, D C. Prsnl est of Geo Andrews, late of said city, dec'd. -Chr Andrews, T P Andrews, adm.

FRI AUG 30, 1816
Notice-Miss Mary Matthews, late of Grantsfield, King Geo Co, Va, dec'd, by her last will did bequeath to her 1st & 2d cousins, money arising from her est; same to forward their names. -Townsend S Dade, exc, Hamstead P O, King Geo Co, Va.

SAT AUG 31, 1816
For sale-Brewery & Dwlg hse, in Fredericktown, formerly occupied by Fred'k Diehl. -John Baker

Richmond, Va, Aug 2, 1816. Persons recommended as Electors, & will vote for Jas Monroe as Pres, & Danl D Tompkins as VP:

Wm Brockenbrough
John Coalter
Andrew Stevenson
John Campbell

Francis T Brooke
Thos Ritchie
John Preston
Chas Everett

John Robertson
Wm Wirt
Alex'r McRea
[Cntrl Corr cmtee]

Rpblcn Electoral Tkt:
Geo Newton-Norfolk Borough
John Pegram-Dinwiddie
John Purnail-Pr Edw
Jos C Cabel-Nelson
Geo Penn-Patrick
Spencer Roane-Hanover
Robt Taylor-Orange
Brazure W Pryor-Eliz City
Wm Lee Ball-Lancaster
Hugh Holmes-Fred'k
Archibald Rutherford-Rockingham
Andrew Russell-Wash
John Webster-Harrison

Chas H Graves-Surry
Mark Alexander-Mecklenburg
Branch T Archer-Powhatan
Chas Yancey-Buckingham
Wm G Poindexter-Goochland
Sthreshley Reynolds-Essex
Isaac Foster-Fauquier
Wm Jones-Gloucester
John T Brooke-Stafford
John Dixon-Jefferson
Archibald Stuart-Augusta
Chas Taylor-Montg

Vacancies since Feb last: Miles King, of Norfolk, by the acceptance of an ofc of trust & profit from the Pres of the U S; Thos Read, sr, of Charlotte, delicate health; Judge Dabney, dec'd.

Dr Saml Horsely has taken a hse on Capitol Hill, Pa av, to svc the ctzns of Wash.

Funeral svc of the late Rt Rev Dr Thos John Clagett, will be at the Chapel of St Paul's Parish, nr his dwlg hse, in PG Co, Md, on Sep 5.

MON SEP 2, 1816
For sale-lot 11 in sq 79, on 22d st. Apply to Mr Saml M'Intire.

TUE SEP 3, 1816
Smith's Mount for sale; in the town of Leeds, Westmoreland Co, Va; 1,600 acs; now occupied by Daniel Payne. -Battaile Ftizhugh, Flintshire, Caroline Co, Va.

PG Co, Md. I certify that Richd Cissel brought before me a stray black mare. -Jos I Jones, J P.

WED SEP 4, 1816
Phil, Jun 18, 1816. Democ cmtee for Pa; electors, Paul Cox, John Geyer, John Conrad, Danl Bussier & Wm Brooks. Fellow ctzns-Thos Sergeant, John Binns, Jos M'Coy, Jacob Sommer, John M'Leod, Wm Runkel.

Claims against the est of John Brent, late of Chas Co, Md, dec'd, to appear in Port Tobacco first Mon in Nov. -Wilfred Manning, adm.

Wash Co, D C. Turman Burns, insolvent debtor, confined in Wash Co prison, for debt. -Wm Brent, clk.

$60 reward for 3 negro men slaves, Yellica, Phil, John. -Allison F Beall, mgr at Piscataway farm, PG Co, Md.

Orphans Crt of Wash Co, D C. Ltrs of adm on prsnl est of Capt Thos Beatty, late of said co, dec'd. -John Wiley, adm.

THU SEP 5, 1816
Mrd: on Sep 3, at Gtwn, D C, by Rev Mr Grassi, the Hon Wm Gaston, a Rep in Cong from N C, to Miss Eliza Worthington, of that town.

Mrd: by Rev Mr Addison, Mr Richd H Fitzhugh, to Miss Mary Ann Marbury, both of Gtwn. [No date-but recent]

Mr Jas M Elford, of Charleston, S C, has invented a universal & perpetual circular Tide Table.

Notice-Eloped from my bed & brd, my wife,Rosanna Walker. I will pay no debts of her contracting. -Jas Walker

FRI SEP 6, 1816
Died: on Sep 4, Mrs Martha Webster, w/o Toppan Webster, of Wash City. Funeral this afternoon.

SAT SEP 7, 1816
Ins Co of North America; John Inskeep, Pres, Phil, Pa. Aug 30, 1816.

MON SEP 9, 1816
Wash Co, D C, in Chancery, Jun Term, 1816. Thos C Wright vs Margaretta King, wid/o & admx, & Mary King, Susan & Saml D King, heris at law of Nicholas King, dec'd. Ratify sale by trustee for sum of $1,800. -Wm Brent, clk.

Promotions & appointments to fill vacancies in the U S army, which occurred since Aug 1, 1816:
2d Lt Francis O Byrd, to 1st Lt, Aug 30, 1816, v Vandeventer, appt'd Maj in staff.
2d Lt Geo D Snyder, to 1st Lt, Aug 30, 1816, v Robeson appt'd Capt in staff.
3d Lt Thos I Baird, to 2d Lt, Aug 1, 1816, v Mitchell, dcln'd.
3d Lt Jabez Parkhurst, to 2d Lt, Aug 30, 1816, v Byrd, promoted.
2d Lt Robt L Armstrong, to 2d Lt, Aug 30, 1816, v Snyder, promoted.
Capt Wm L Robeson, appt'd Assist Dep Q M Gen, Aug 30, 1816.
Post Surg Walter V Wheaton appt'd Surg o/2d Infty, Sep 4, 1816, v Bache, rsgn'd.
Hosp Surg Mate Wm H Buckner, appt'd surg 4th Infty, Sep 4, 1816, v Buck, do.
Chas Davies appt'd 2d Lt corps of Engs, Aug 31, 1816.
Britton Evans appt'd 2d Lt 2d regt of Infty, Aug 30, 1816.
Wm Downey appt'd 2d Lt 5th regt of Infty, Sep 3, 1816.
Wm Elgin appt'd 2d Lt 8th regt of Infty, Sep 3, 1816.

1st Lt Sackett & 2d Lt Strother, of 4th Infty, never having reported & joined their regt, since the consolidation of the army, are considered out of the svc. By order of the Sec of War, D Parker, Adj & Ins Gen.

TUE SEP 10, 1816
Died: at his residence in Richmond Co, N C, on Aug 27, Duncan M'Farland, formerly a rep in Cong from N C.

Billiard rm on F st, newly opened, Wash City. -H F Doyhar

Wash Co, D C. Benj Thomas, insolvent debtor, confined in Wash Co prison, for debt.

Ltr from Passey, Mar 17, 1783; from Benj Franklin, notes the intended marriage of Miss Anna Maria. The Bishop to whom Franklin alludes, was the Bishop of Asaph, whose dght Sir Wm Jones mrd.

WED SEP 11, 1816
$500 reward for Jas Essex alias Jas Essex Crosby Sterling, age 30 yrs; escaped from Chilicothe prison, Ohio. -John Hamm, mrshl of Ohio Dist. Zanesville, O, Jul 25

THU SEP 12, 1816
Orphans Crt of PG Co, Md. Ltrs of adm on prsnl est of Wm Wallis, late of said co, dec'd. -Wm Wallis, adm. [Sale in town of Bladensburg, Md, of prsnl est of Wm Wallis dec'd.]

FRI SEP 13, 1816
New stationary, from London. Geo Richards, Bridge st, Gtwn.

SAT SEP 14, 1816
$50 reward for negro, Geo, & woman, Celia, with her child, Mary. Latter 2 belong to E Ridgeway. -Alex Soper, Eleanor Ridgeway, nr Spaldings' Tvrn, PG Co, Md.

For sale, Bryan Town, in Chas Co, Md; bet 6 & 7 acs; with dwlg hse. -Enos Schell, on the premises.

Mrd: on Sep 10, by Rev Mr Anger, Augustus Taney, of Montg Co, Md, to Miss Mary Young, d/o Nicholas Young, of this Dist.

For sale-*Bloomfield*, 820 acs, on the South rvr in A A Co, Md, with 2 story brick hse in which the mgr lives. -John Contee

MON SEP 16, 1816
Land for sale-cld *Alexandria*, about 4 miles from Upper Malborough, PG Co, Md; upwards of 300 acs. -Thos R Hodges, trustee.

TUE SEP 17, 1816
Teacher wanted; apply to Zachariah M'Caney, Robt Carr, Philip Pindell, John T Richardson, Geo Gardner; lvg on West rvr, A A Co, Md, 12 miles from Annapolis.

Died: at his residence in Va, on Sep 11, the Hon John Clopton, for more than 20 yrs a Rep in Cong from Va.

WED SEP 18, 1816
Caution. Whereas my wife Ann Martin has eloped from my bed & board without any provocation, I am determined not to pay any dbts of her contracting from this date. -John Martin, his x mark. Geo Adams, Sep 18.

$20 reward; deserted from Ft Wash, pvts of the corps of Artl, viz:
Thos Richardson, 19, born Sussex Co, Dela; laborer, deserted Sep 14, 1816.
Wm Kelly, 19, born Halifax, Nova Scotia; sldr, deserted Sep 14, 1816.
-Felix Ansart, Lt Com'g, Ft Wash.

Wash Co, D C. H T Beatty, insolvent debtor, confined in Wash Co prison, for debt. -Wm Brent, clk.

Norfolk, Sep 5. Obit notice-on Aug 20, 1815, John Granbery, Merchant & Pres of the Marine Ins Co, sailed from this place in the schnr *Martha & Ann*, bound for Bermuda; passengers were his son, Mr Geo Granbery, & Willis R Stowe, of Bermuda, the only bro/o Mrs Granbery. No tidings at this period have been gained; conclusion is that the vessel & all on board have been lost.

From Franklin's history of his own life, we gather the fact that before 1720 there was one nwspaper printed in America, the *Boston News-ltr*. In that yr the *New Eng Courant* commenced. In 1771 there were no less than 25.

THU SEP 19, 1816
Mrd: on Sep 17, by Rev Mr McCormick, Mr Henry H McPherson, merchant, to Miss Eliz Stelle, d/o Mr P D Stelle, all of Wash City.

FRI SEP 20, 1816
Land for sale, my residence, about 340 acs, in Newport, Chas Co, with dwlg hse. Also a small hse nr Newport. -W Corry, Newport, Chas City, Va.

PG Co, Md. Application in writing of Walter W Harwood, of said co, insolvent debtor. -John Read Magruder, clk.

Died: on Sep 15, Mrs Eliz Dowson, in her 56th yr. She knew the widow's heart & supported herself & family, by keeping a brdg hse in Wash City, for 9 yrs. Mbr of the Presb Chr.

Died: on Sep 10, in S C, Gen Jos Alston, late Govn'r of S C.

SAT SEP 21, 1816
Committed to the jail of Talbot Co, Md, on Jul 21, runaway negro woman, Harriot; says she was sold by Mrs Fraize, of Balt to a Mr Stapleton, of S C. -Jas Clayland, shff, of Talbot Co, Md.

MON SEP 22, 1816
Died: on Sep 12, at Hillsborough, on Easter Shore of Md, in his 59th yr, Rev Jesse Lee, late Chaplain to Cong, & for 33 yrs a preacher among the Methodists.

Died: on Sep 14, at his Botanical Garden, cld *Upsal,* nr Phil, Mr Bernard M'Mahon; came to that city from Ire about 20 yrs since.

Mrd: on Sep 19, by Rev Mr Waters, Mr Robt O Edmonston to Miss Eliz Waters, both of PG Co, Md.

Mrd: on Sep 3, Mr Thos Gantt of A A Co, Md, to Miss Mary Hall, d/o Dr Richd Hall, of PG Co, Md.

Mrd: on Sep 16, Mr Henry Lyles to Miss Barbara Dorsey, d/o Mr Philip Dorsey, all of Calvert Co, Md.

TUE SEP 24, 1816
Mrd: on Sep 14, in Phil, Mr Wm G Orr, of Va, to Miss Sarah P Moore, d/o Mr John Moore, of Phil.

WED SEP 25, 1816
Died: in Albany, on Sep 9, Gen K Van Rensselaer, a sldr of the rev. In Jul 1777, at Ft Ann, he was attacked & rec'd a musket shot to his thigh, the ball was never extracted until since his death, when it was taken out by Dr Wm Bay, of Albany, after having been carried by the dec'd upwards of 39 yrs.

Died: in Eng, in Dec last, Mr Horatio Clagett, a ntv of Md; Ofcr in the Americ Army during the entire Rev war; since 1783 a Merchant & underwriter in London.

THU SEP 26, 1816
Creditors of John B Turner, late of Chas Co, Md, dec'd; to present their claims. -John Ferguson, Nathl P Causin, adms.

For sale-the hse I now occupy in Wash City. -Chas Vinson

FRI SEP 27, 1816
Val prop for sale-21 acs of land on the N W Branch, nr Bladensburg; title indisputable. -John Peerce, in Bladensburg; Igns Peerce, PG Co, Md.

SAT SEP 28, 1816
Butchers attend; sale of young cattle, on my farm, nr Port Tobacco, Chas Co, Md. -Jas Blair

MON SEP 30, 1816
Pblc sale by excs of the late Jos Covachiah, of Cadiz; numerous lots in Wash City, belonging to the est of the said dec'd. -Wm Brent

TUE OCT 1, 1816
$200 reward for detecting Aaron Wright; he absconded this morning from the Wash Htl, where he is employed as Bar-kpr; he tk a pkt bk belonging to a gentleman lodger in the hse, containing about $1,300. Wright is about 25 yrs of age. -Philemon Towson, Balt, Md.

Land for sale-part of the rl est of the late Dr Thos Bourne, cld the *Manor Land*; 1,000 acs, with dwlg hse; St Leonard's Crk Town, Calvert Co, Md. -T H Wilkinson, trustee.

WED OCT 2, 1816
Bldg materials at the Factory of the Steam Co of Princess Anne, [Md]. -Geo M Willing, Sec.

Notice-My son, about 29 yrs of age, Benj Howard, has been for some yrs past in a state of insanity, he left me in Mar last & told me he was going to a bro's in Hagerstown, Md; I have not heard from him since that period. -Mary Ann Stewart, on Navy Yd Hill, Wash City.

THU OCT 3, 1816
Robt Smether, Dentist; took up his residence in Wash City, at Mr Brush's Brdg Hse, on Pa av.

Wash Co, D C. Henry Forrest, insolvent debtor, confined in Wash Co prison, for debt. -Wm Brent, clk.

FRI OCT 4, 1816
Ten cents reward for delivering to me my apprentice, Thos Leatch. -B M Belt

For sale-Hardware & Ironmongery, King st, Alexandria; also the stock of the late Richd Slade & Co. -Richd Slade

Died: suddenly at Frankfort, on Sep 20, Harry Innis, Judge of the U S Crt for the dist of Ky.

Died: on Oct 3, Mr Geo Jarrad, of Wash City. Funeral this afternoon from the hse of Mr Thos Foyles.

Ladies with ltrs in the Wash City, P O, Oct 1, 1816:

Austin, Mrs Martha	Armstrong, Mgt	Ball Mrs Cath W
Brown Mrs Cath	Collins Susan	Cagely Miss Sarah
Connelly Bridget	Connino Mrs M	Crawford Mrs Eliz
Dend Miss Fanny	Davis Mrs	Guillard Mrs Henry
Glenn Mrs Eliza	Gross Miss Eliz	Hardy Mrs Louisa

Henson Milly	Jones Sarah	Kirkwood Eliz
Johns or Miss Minty Ann	Mod Miss Mary	Morris Miss
Johnston Miss Susannah	Martin Susannah	Merren Miss Nancy
O'Connell Mrs Ann	Posey Mrs Jane	Quinn Mrs Ann
Redmond Miss Cath	Roberts Mrs Ann	Robison Mrs Mary
Skidmore Mrs Sophia	Snow Mrs	Steuart Mrs Ann-2
Shorter Mrs Jane	Stephens Mrs Elenor	Sutherland Mrs Danl
Stapeler Deborah	Smoot Mrs Eliz-2	Shaw Mrs Eliz
Thomas Miss Eliza	Tench Miss Eliza	Toulbat Miss Eliza
Turner Mrs N	Williams Miss Charl	Wells Mrs Ann
-Thos Munroe, P M		

Wash Co, D C. Nicholas Ledan, insolvent debtor, confined in Wash Co prison, for debt. -Wm Brent, clk.

SAT OCT 5, 1816
$50 reward for Gasper Bowman, who came to this place last Jun & set in as a Silversmith; he left here Tue, Aug 27, with watches, jewelry, etc; speaks Eng & German; wears a band round him in consequence of a rupture. -Jos S Spangler, John S Ball, Isaac Reese, Andrew Huffman, Jos Snapp, Jacob Reager, Saml Gardner, Jona Bowman. Strasburg, Shenandoah City, Va.

Notice-sale of prop, *Fortepiano*, of Richd Elliot, to satisfy taxes due the Wash City Corp. 2-Sale of sofa & pr of mahogany card tables, prop of Jas Thompson, for taxes due. 3-Sale of furn taken as prop of John Lowrey to satisfy taxes due. 4-Sale of lot 19 in sq 16, prop of Jas Dunlap to satisfy taxes due. 5-Sale of lot 19 in sq 16, with improve, prop of Thos Peter to satisfy taxes due. -Jos Brumley, Col 1st Ward.

MON OCT 7, 1816
John Davis of Abel rsgn'd; Danl Kealy was elected in his place as a mbr of Cncl in the 4th Ward Wash, on Oct 2. -Jas H Blake, Mayor.

TUE OCT 8, 1816
Wash Co, D C. Nicholas B Vanzandt, of said co, brought before me a stray gelding. -Jos Cassin, J P.

WED OCT 9, 1816
Balt Fender Manufactory. -Thos Everett & Geo D Ebsworth, 224 Mkt st, Balt, Md.

Died: on Oct 7, at Balt, in his 62d yr, Col Nicholas Ruxton Moore, late a mbr of Cong & Cmdant of a Cvlry Regt attached to the 3d Div M M. He has left a wife & 4 chldrn to mourn his loss.

For sale-*Sully*, 750 acs, in Fairfax Co, Va. Apply to Francis Lightfoot Lee, next the P O at Pleasant Valley, in Fairfax.

THU OCT 10, 1816
Died: on Jun 19, at Stralhendey Bleachfield, Scotland, from a fall, Mr Peter Kilgour, in the 102d yr of his age.

Mrd: on Oct 8, by Rev Mr M'Cormick, Wm S Radcliff to Miss Rebecca A W Burns, of Wash City.

Died: on Oct 6, Mr John Hines, of Wash City, aged 72 yrs; an affectionate hsbnd, & f/o 9 sons grown to manhood, who were all present on the occasion of his death.

Wash Co, D C. Edwin T Satterwhite, insolvent debtor, confined to Wash Co prison for debt. -Wm Brent, clk.

Notice of dividend, Fred'k Myers estate; at the hse of Jas Moore, jr, on Oct 17. -Thos Eno, adm.

Nashville, Tenn, Sep 11. Died, on Mon, Caleb Hewett, high shrf of this county, from a blow by Jas Maxwell, carpenter; when Hewett told him he had a writ for him.

FRI OCT 11, 1816
For sale-Lumber. Josiah Hewes Davis, Alexandria.

SAT OCT 12, 1816
Chambersburgh, Sep 24. In Hamilton twnshp, yesterday wk, Mr Wm Worrick accidentally shot & killed his bro-in-law, Mr Geo Weaver, in pursuit of a squirrel. He has left a wife & one child.

Mr Henry G Heth drowned on Sep 30th; s/o Col Wm Heth-col at Burmuda Hundred.

Mrd: at Gtwn, on Oct 8, by Rev Dr Balch, Dr John Ott to Miss Ann Cruirshane.

Died: in Wash City, on Oct 11, Col Tobias Lear, Accountant of the Dept of War.

MON OCT 14, 1816
Petersburg Acad-[Va;] Cmtee-Richd Field, Thos Robinson, J F May.

TUE OCT 15, 1816
Portrait Painting-J Wood has taken a rm at the Union Tvrn, Gtwn, & will remain one month.

Died: in the city of St Domingo, West Indies, after a few days severe illness, Robt Walter Dyer, in his 27th yr, s/o Mr Giles Dyer, of PG Co, Md.

WED OCT 16, 1816
For sale-the 1/3d part of the steam boat, *Camden* of Gtwn. She runs from Alexandria to Gtwn daily. Enquire-John Gird, Alexandria; Robt Munroe, Gtwn.

THU OCT 17, 1816
Dr Darrah, surg dentist, has returned to his old stand in Bridge st. -Local ad.

FRI OCT 18, 1816
King Geo Co, Oct 14. On Oct 13, Robt B Massey was accidentally shot & killed by Wm Went; Massey leaves a wife & 4 chldrn.

Mrd: on Oct 10, at Leesburg, Va, Mr Geo Richards, of Gtwn, D C, to Mrs Ann B Saunders, eldest d/o John Rose, of Leesburg.

SAT OCT 19, 1816
Robt Wharton is re-elected Mayor of Phil City, Pa.

Mrd: on Oct 17, by Rev Mr Cormick, Mr Thos R Walter, to Miss Mary Winters, all of Wash City.

Died: on Oct 16, in his 25th yr, Mr Jos Harris, of Balt & Phil Theatres.

Wash Co, D C, in Chancery. Geo Grundy, Sen & Geo Crosdale, vs John Hossack. Bill is secure a foreclosure & sale of lot 114 in D C, prop mortgaged by Hossack, with int from Oct 25, 1797. Hossack is not a resident of D C. -Wm Brent, clk.

MON OCT 21, 1816
Jos Arny has purchased the entire stock of Confectionary of C L Weiskoppff; will sell same at the usual prices. He has worked in London, Bordeaux, & other lg cities in Europe. -Gtwn.

Leather for sale & hides wanted. Tanyd in Bladensburg, late the prop of Thos T Gantt. Currying shop is in Wash on 26th st. -Tench Ringgold

TUE OCT 22, 1816
Orphans Crt of PG Co, Md. Pblc sale of all the prsnl prop of Wm Wall, dec'd. -Wm Dixon, Eliz Wall, adms.

Notice. Exhibit claims against the est of Dr Jos Mudd, late of Chas Co, Md, dec'd. -Theodore Mudd

WED OCT 23, 1816
To let-the brick hse at present occupied by Richd Hendly, nr the P O; from Nov 5, 1816, to Jan 1, 1818. Pblc auction of all goods. -N Queen, auct.

THU OCT 24, 1816
Obit-died on Mon last, at Paris, Bourbon Co, Ky, after svr'l wks confined by a painful illness, his excell Geo Madison, govn'r of this state. Gabriel Slaughter, Lt Govn'r, will administer for 4 yrs; Constitution does not provide for a new election.

Ohio Rpblcn tkt for electors of Pres & V P:

Othniel Looker	Abraham Shepard	Benj Hough
John Patterson	Jas Curry	Aaron Wheeler
Wm Skinner	John G Young	

St Mary's co Crt, Md. Sale of all the rl est of Jos Ford, late of said co, dec'd, that lies in Md, to wit: store hse & lot in said town; lot adj; also a tract of land cld *Britton's outlet*, 198 acs. -E I Millard, trustee.

Mrd: on Oct 22, by Rev Mr M'Cormick, Mr John Brannan to Miss Sarah Salome Meyers, all of Wash City.

Orphans Crt of Wash Co, D C. Prsnl est of Thos Hunter, late of said co, dec'd. -Wm Prout, adm. [Sale of frame hse in sq 977, Wash City, late the prop of Thos Hunter, dec'd.]

FRI OCT 25, 1816

Mrd: on Oct 22, by Rev Mr McCormick, Mr Saml O Smith, of N Y, to Miss Ann W Bowling, of Wash City.

In Chancery, Oct 10, 1816. Wm Raborg & John Hearn vs Jas Barry's heirs & others. Ratify sales in this case by the trustees. -Wm Brent, clk.

In Chancery, Jun Term, 1816. Beale Gaither vs Henry Gaither's heirs. Ratify sale of lots 22 & 23 in sq 127, & lots 2 & 3 in sq 104, in Wash City. -Wm Brent, clk.

SAT OCT 26, 1816

Justices of the Sup Crt at Amherst, Hillsborough Co, N H, Oct, 1816; shew that Nabby E Starrett, of Mt Vernon, in said co, mrd David Starrett on Sep 12, 1802, he a resident of said co. David has absented himself from her & their chldrn for more than 3 yrs & unheard of; Nabby prays for a divorce. -Nabby E Starrett, by her Attys, John Burnam & Levi Woodbury.

MON OCT 28, 1816

E & S Handy-Military & Fancy Hatters, F st, Wash. -Local ad.

Longevity-died, in Wash Co, Md, a few days since, Mammy Lucy, a woman of colour, aged at least 130 yrs, having been the mthr of 19 chldrn. She belonged to the est of Mr Thos Henry Hall, dec'd.

TUE OCT 29, 1816

Died: on Oct 22, after a long & painful illness, Anderson McWilliams, late Srvyr of the port of Fredericksburg, leaving a widow & 2 dghts.

Ann Sawyer [late Ann Johnson] has remv'd her millenary stand to the stand formerly occupied by Mrs M Sweeney, on F st, Wash.

WED OCT 30, 1816
Md-those in the present Cong:

Alex C Hanson*	Philip Stuart*	John C Herbert*
Geo Baer*	Saml Smith	Peter Little
Stevenson Archer	Robt Wright	C Goldsborough*

Next Congess:

Geo Peter*	Philip Stuart*	John C Herbert*
Saml Ringgold	Saml Smith	Peter Little
Philip Reed	Thos Culbreth	Thos Bayly*

*Federal, rest are rpblcn.

Mrd: on Oct 24, at Belmont, Loudon Co, Va, by Rev Mr Dina, Jas L M'Kenna, of Alexandria, to Miss Cecilia Lee, d/o Ludwell Lee.

Died: in Canton Mass, on Oct 10, Danl Johnson, aged 12 yrs, s/o Nathan Johnson, of the East Parish of Bridgewater; accident in the Cotton Factory of that place.

THU OCT 31, 1816
For sale-*Mill Mont*, 998 1/2 acs, lower end of Calvert Co, Md. Apply to J R Plater, at Sotterley, St Mary's Co, Md.

FRI NOV 1, 1816
Mrd: on Oct 30, by Rev Mr McCormick, Lewis Edward, of Wash City, to Miss Sarah Perry, of Nantucket.

SAT NOV 2, 1816
For sale-val farm where Maj Adlum lives, within 5 miles of this place & adj the farm of Jas Dunlop; 300 acs. -John Heugh, Gtwn.

For rent-a lg & commodious store at present occupied by Mr Benj Hodges, of Thos, on Bridge st; possession on Oct 23. -J Abbot, Gtwn.

Otho M Linthicum & Co, drug & medicine store on High st, Gtwn, formerly occupied by Dr Magruder.

In Chancery, Oct 26, 1816. Ratify sale of rl est of John Chambers, late of Montg Co, Md, made by Zachariah Gatton, trustee; sale to be $1,941.68 3/4. -Thos H Bowie, rg c c

MON NOV 4, 1816
Wash, Pa, Oct 21. Jas M Munn escaped out of the goal of this co on Oct 20.

Orphans Crt of A A Co, Md. Prsnl est of Chas Moxley, late of Gtwn, in said Dist, dec'd. Wm M Worthington, agent & atty. -John Moxley, admx.

Orphans Crt of Montg Co, Md. Pblc sale at the late residence of Jas Ray, dec'd; all the prsnl est of dec'd. -Elisha Brown, of Saml & Saml Hamilton, adms.

Notice-There is now, as agent for Jas Ray, dec'd, late adm of Anne Ray, late of Wash Co, D C, dec'd, a bal of prsnl est, subj to distribution. -Saml Hamilton

TUE NOV 5, 1816
Wash Co, D C. Benj Murphey, insolvent debtor, confined in Wash Co prison, for debt. -W Brent, clk.

Mrs Clementson has just opened her store, next dr below John Peabody's, Bridge st, Gtwn. Fall & winter bonnets, caps, turbans, etc.

Sale of lot 19 in sq 1, with improvements; prop of David Walker, to satisfy taxes due the Wash City Corp. -Jos Brumley, Col 1st ward.

$50 reward for negro man, Baucher, about 21; has an uncle lvg with Mr Jas Hawkins; his mthr Kate lives nr Broad Crk, probably on Col Lyles' land. -Nathl Washington, St Mary's Co, Trent Neck.

Notice-my wife Betsy Kenedy, lawfully mrd to me, has left my hse without any just cause; I am determined to pay no debts of her contracting. -Lewis Jas Kenedy.

WED NOV 6, 1816
Notice-I forwarn persons from receiving notes drawn by me in favor of Danl Bussard, as I am determined not to pay them. -Dawson P Burgess

Died: Mr John Speyer, ctzn of the U S, & formerly cnsl at Stockholm: died at Paris on Sep 14. Mr I Cox Barnet, American cnsl arranged the funeral of Sep 18.

THU NOV 7, 1816
Berkeley Co, Va. This day came Nicholas Orrick before me & made oath that Mr Jas Rumsey informed him, in 1784, that he was projecting a boat to work with steam. Given under my hand, Nov 24, 1787. -Wm Little

Wash Co, D C. John L Naylor vs Saml Hanson of Saml, Amariah Frost & Saml Treat. Ratify sale by Zachariah Walker, trustee, of lot 3 in sq 949, to Nathl Haraden, for $350, this 9th day of Oct, 1816. -Wm Brent, clk.

Geo Stiles is elected Mayor of Balt, Md.

Christopher Hughes, jr, & family, sailed from Balt on Nov 5; he leaves as Sec of the American leg at the Crt of Sweden; Mr Russell being desirous to return to America.

Pblc sale at the late residence of Henry Harvey, nr Upper Marlboro, Md; all the prsnl est of Saml Marlowe, dec'd. -Eliza Marlowe, admx of Saml Marlowe.

Six cents reward for runaway, Ignatius Lucas, appr to the Morocco finishing business. -John Laurence

Wash Co, D C, in Chancery. Jas Middleton & Thos Foyles vs Electius Middleton's heirs. Ratify sale by Zachariah Walker, trustee, of part of lot 4 & 3 in sq 826 to Saml N Smallwood, for $2,400; & lot 3 in sq 796, with improvements, to Henry J Allen, for $2,275. -Wm Brent, clk.

Wash Co, D C, in Chancery. Pres & Dirs of Bank of Wash vs Mary Miller & others. Ratify sale by Zachariah Walker, trustee, of lots 3 & 6 in sq 771, with improvements, to Elias B Caldwell, for $7,200. -Wm Brent, clk.

FRI NOV 8, 1816
Mrd: on Nov 5, by Rev Francis Neale, Mr Richd T Queen, of Wash City, to Miss Mary E King, of Gtwn.

For sale- part of *Chew's Folly*, 100 acs; also tract of 26 acs on Paint Branch; also 200 acs adjacent. All in PG Co, Md. John Wilson, lvg on the premises, will shew the land. -Stephen Wilson, Peter Moran

Wm A Davis has his printing est for sale; the purchaser will be entitled to the contract for the printing for the 14th Congress. -John Brannan, Wash City.

SAT NOV 9, 1816
For sale-sq 528, Wash City, on which Mr Saml Burch's hse is. -John Peltz. -N L Queen, auct.

Wash Co, D C. John Foley, insolvent debtor, confined in Wash Co prison, for debt. -W Brent, clk.

MON NOV 11, 1816
Mrd: at Raspberry Plain, Va, on Oct 24, by Rev Mr Dunn, Wm Mason McCarty to Miss Emily R Mason, y/d/o the late Gen Stephens Thompson Mason.

Died: at his seat nr N Y, on Nov 5, Gouverneur Morris, in his 65th yr.

Died: at New Orleans on Oct 3, C Lavaux Trudeau, an old & much respected inhabitant of La.

Teacher wanted. -Rich Snowden & John C Herbert, lvg nr Vansville, PG Co, Md.

Orphans Crt of Wash Co, D C. Ordered that Mrs Jemima Young, admx of Patrick Young, dec'd, give notice to creditors. Followed: I shall distribute the prsnl est of the late Patrick Young, dec'd, on Dec 2, at my hse in Gtwn, D C. -Jemima Young.

To Let-brick hse on High st, Gtwn, known for the groc bus. -Tobias Nixdorff, lvg in High st, nr the crnr of 2d st, Gtwn.

Land for sale-at the *Hill Top*, Chas Co, Md, 679 acs; nr Port Tobacco, Nanjemoy dist. -H H M'Pherson, Wash City.

Beware of swindler! $2,000 reward for Chas T Billings, b in Dublin, Ire; age about 35 yrs; has sold counterfeit bills. -Saml C Vance, Cashier M C Co. -John W Tilford, E Pearson & Co. Cincinnati.

For rent or lease-Middlebrook Mills, Tvrn & est, of late Gen Lingan; bet Gtwn & Fredericktown. -John Tayloe, residing in Wash.

For sale-land in Chas Co, Md, nr Matawoman Crk & Checkamuxon; 2 parcels cld *St John's* & *St John's Addition*, 244 1/4 acs. Also will be sold the hsehld furn of Geo Robt Leiper, dec'd, & a quantitiy of corn & corn fodder. -Andrew L Moore, Thos Moore.

TUE NOV 12, 1816

Mrd: on Nov 10, by Rev Mr M'Cormick, Mr Saml Magill, of Cumberland, Md, to Miss Christiana Miacha Myer, of Wash City.

Mrd: at Wmstown, Mass, Saml R Betts, of Newburgh, N Y, mbr of Cong, to Miss Caroline A Dewey, d/o the late Judge Dewey, of that place.

Mrd: on Nov 5, by Rev Mr Burch, Mr Thos B Dashiell, of Wash City, to Miss Mary B Beall, of PG Co, Md.

Bell Tvrn will be opened on Nov 18, by Robt Bailey, [from Berkley Springs, Va,] on Capitol Hill, in Wash City; at the Sign of the Bell.

WED NOV 13, 1816

Died: at Ft Montgomery, Miss Terr, on Aug 31 last, Capt Jeoffrey Robertson, of the 7th regt U S Infty.

Died: on Sep 18, at Ft Jackson, on the Alabama, Maj John Machesney, 7 rgt U S I.

THU NOV 14, 1816

Genr'l Crt Martial, of which Maj Gen Winfield Scott is Pres, convened at N Y on Sep 2, 1816; Maj Gen Edmund P Gaines was tried on 4 specific charges; the Crt acquitted him of the same.

Adam Cooke is appt'd Srvyr & Inspec of Fredericksburg port, v Anderson McWilliams, dec'd.

Died: at Milton, N H, Mr Barnabas Palmer, aged 96; an ofcr in the British svc at the battle of La; a hero of the American Indep, & many yrs a mbr of the Leg of Mass.

Potsdam, N Y, Oct 25, 1816. On Wed last, Mr Edmund Chase, of Stockholm, was drowned while crossing the St Regis Rvr, when his canoe upset.

Died: on Nov 11, Mathew M'Connel, long a well known ctzn of Phil; a surviving ofcr who served in the revolution with honour.

Sale of land-Chancery Crt of Md; Alex'r Magruder vs Wm Marbury jr, & the infant heirs of Jane C Marbury; land cld *Three Bros*, 250 acs-part of *White Marshes* & part of *Silver Hills*. -Wm Marbury, jr; John Read Magruder

FRI NOV 15, 1816
Survey of Jas Rvr by Mr John Wood; Norfolk, Va, Nov 6. [Details of his srvy.]

Timbered lands for sale, per will of the late Col Wm Ball, pblc auction at the Northumberland Crt Hse, Va, Dec 9; 395 acs whereon said Ball lately resided, with a nrly new small frame dwlg hse. Also *Coan Mill*, now out of repair. -Thos Towles, adm with the will annexed of Wm Ball, dec'd.

Partnership of Thos R Walter & Horace Duvall is dissolved by mutual consent; Walter will continue the business in the future.

Gun & White Smith Business, High & Gay sts, Gtwn, adj Leonard Cokendorfer. -Ernestus Putman, Gtwn

Farm for sale in Montg Co, Md; 700 acs, with log dwlg hse, etc. Mr Joshua Wright lives on the premises & will show same. -Chas Warfield

SAT NOV 16, 1816
Lost- Morocco pktbk, bet mkt hse in Wash City, & Capitol Hill, on Nov 8. - Michael Kananagh. [Deliver same to Mr Mortee or Mr Callan, at the Pres' Bldg.]

Mrd: on Nov 13, by Rev Wm Wilmer, Lt Felix Ansart, of the corps U S Artl, to Miss Martha Livinia Brown, of Pr Wm Co, Va.

MON NOV 18, 1816
Pblc sale-deed of trust from John Campbell, of Chas Co, Md, farm cld *Glasscoe*, on which Campbell resides, 600 acs, with dwlg hse. Also a tract cld *Chas Town* or *Digges' Settlement*, upwrds of 600 acs, Chas Co, Md. Also, 13 or 14 val slaves & crop & stock. -Wm Cooke, John B Morris, trustees.

Notice-a young gentleman would engage to teach in a pvt family. A line addressed to E B Caldwell, Wash, wld be attended to.

Trustee's sale of the whole stock in trade of the late firm of Ratcliffe Richards & Co-dry goods; at the store over Mr John C Richards, 205 Mkt st, Balt, Md.

TUE NOV 19, 1816
Mrd: at Boston, by Rev Dr Freeman, Maj David S Townsend, U S Army, to Miss Eliza Gerry, d/o the late V P. Maj T lost a leg at the battle of Christler's field, on the St Lawrence. [No date-recent]

WED NOV 20, 1816
Sale at auction on Dec 3, at the Blanket & Woollen Fctry, PG Co, Md; entire stock to close the concern. -Daniel Bussard, Jacob Getzendaner, John Hildt

Orphans Crt of PG Co, Md. Prsnl est of Greenberry Barnes, late of said co, dec'd. -Joannah Barnes, excx.

THU NOV 21, 1816
Mrd: on Nov 18, by Rev Mr Addison, John Nelson, of Frederickstown, to Miss Frances Harriett Burrows, of Wash City.

Mrd: at Balt, on Nov 12, by Rev Mr Glendy, Barnaby Barnes, of Phil, to Miss Christiana Pechin, eldest d/o Maj Wm Peckin, of Balt.

Mrd: in Amelia Co, Virg, on Nov 6, by Rev Mr Logan, Dr Jas H Conway, to Miss Augusta Giles, eldest d/o Wm B Giles.

Died: on Oct 28, at his residence in Walton, N Y, D Platt Townsend, the sage, the patriot, the founder of his vicinity; aged 83 yrs.

Died: on Nov 8, ;after a short but painful illness, at her country seat, *Mt Pleasant*, Phil Co, in her 56th yr, Mrs Marianne Williams, wid/o Gen Jonathan Williams.

Mrs J Thorton has opened a brdg hse on Pa av, Wash; nr Davis' Htl.

For sale-at *Sotterley*, nr Leonard Town, Md, Nov 27: stock, sheep, ploughs, waggon, hsehld furn, etc. -John R Plater

FRI NOV 22, 1816
Notice-I forwarn all Negro traders from purchasing a negro boy, Bill, belonging to me, who is now in the possession & living with Gustavus Beall, Gtwn. -David Westerfield

SAT NOV 23, 1816
Pblc sale at the late residence of Henry Harvey, nr Upper Marlboro, Md; all the prsnl est of Saml Marlowe, dec'd. -Eliza Marlowe, admx.

MON NOV 25, 1816
Alexandria meeting on Nov 21, at the City Tvrn; Edmund I Lee, Mayor o/Alex, chrmn, Alex'r Moore, sec. Cmtee: Geo Deneale, Thos Swann, Jacob Hoffman, Anthony C Cazenove,& John Longden.

Gtwn meeting on Nov 22, at Semmes' Tvrn; John Peter, Mayor, chrmn, John Lee, sec. Cmtee: Thos L M'Kenney, Thos T Gantt & Leonard H Johns.

Mrs Tabitha Burnam has petitioned for a divorce from her hsbnd, because he has become insane. A cmtee reported in favor of the petition, but the hse rejected it 141 to 30. -Verm pap.

Govn'r of Va has proclaimed the following to be Electors of Pres & V P for Va:

Geo Newton	Chas H Graves	John Pegram
Mark Alexander	John Purnal	Branch T Archer
Jos C Cabel	Chas Yancey	Geo Penn
Wm G Poindexter	Spencer Roane	Sthreshley Reynolds
Robt Taylor	Isaac Foster	Brazure W Pryor
Wm Jones	Wm Lee Ball	John T Brooke
Hugh Holmes	John Dixon	Archibald Rutherford
Archibald Stuart	Andrew Russell	Chas Taylor
John Webster		

Orphans Crt of PG Co, Md. Ltrs of adm on prsnl est of Allen Taylor, late of said co, dec'd. -Francis Mulliken, adm; Cassandra Mullikin, admx.

TUE NOV 26, 1816
Fred'k Cana, with deference, has remv'd his Confectioner Store oppo Dr D Ott's, Pa av, Wash.

WED NOV 27, 1816
Appt'd Electors of Pres & VP, for Georgia:

John McIntosh	Chas Harris	H Mitchell
Jared Irwin	John Rutherford	Gen Meriwether
John Clark	David Adams	

On Oct 23, on Lake Geo, 4 persons drowned: Thos Burdick, Ira Rhodes, Jas Degrushe & Wm Comstock. Rhodes & Comstock left lg families. -Warren Pat.

Wash Co, D C. Francis Aukerd, insolvent debtor, confined in Wash Co prison, for debt. -Wm Brent, clk.

Thespian Benevolent Soc, meeting on Nov 27. -John H Reily, sec.

Jas W Johnston will recommence kpg his Livery Stable in 9th st, Wash.

THU NOV 28, 1816
Mrd: in Gtwn, on Nov 26, by Rev Francis Neal, Mr Geo King, of Chas, to Miss Susanna Maria Ford, d/o John G Ford, all of that place.

Died: on Nov 26, in his 45th yr, after a long & painful illness, Mr Wm Crawford, the prop of the Union Tvrn of Gtwn. He leaves his wife & chldrn. His remains will be deposited in the Chr burying ground, on this day.

Died: on Nov 24, in Gtwn, Mr John Cruikshank, after a short illness; a young gentleman.

Orphans Crt of PG Co, Md. Ltrs of adm on prsnl est of Verlinda R Williams, late of said co, dec'd. -Colmore Williams, adm. [Followed by-sale of all prsnl est of same, at her former dwlg, about 7 miles from Bladensburg, Md, & 2 miles from Thos McGruder's Tvrn; 28 negroes, stock, hsehld & kitchen furn, etc.]

FRI NOV 29, 1816
Pblc sale, on the premises, lot 25 in sq 882, with 2 story dwlg hse, it being the life time est of Mrs Mayhew, late wid/o Azariah Gatton, dec'd. -D Bates, auct.

SAT NOV 30, 1816
Mrd: in Alexandria, on Nov 28, by Rev Mr Henson, Mr Robt Bowling, of Wash City, to Miss Jane C Neal, of Alexandria.

Died: in M'Intosh Co, Geo, on Nov 12, Col Ferdinand Oneale, in his 60th yr; ntv of Pa; commenced his military svcs with the Rev war.

MON DEC 2, 1816
$20 reward for lost or stolen pktbk, nr Middletown, containing $225 in paper, & one doubloon. -Chas Wills, Charles Co, Md.

For sale-corn at my Westphalia Farm, adj Mr Dennis Magruder's, in PG Co, Md. -Henry V Somervell

TUE DEC 3, 1816
Died: on Dec 2, at the hse of Mr Alex'r McCormick, Capitol Hill, Mr Wm Walker, Merchant of Wash City. Funeral this day at 12 o'clock.

Wash Co, D C. Petition of Meschack Campbell, insolvent debtor, confined in Wash Co prison, for debt. -Wm Brent, clk.

Pblc sale of lot 19 in sq 1, prop of David Walker, to satisfy taxes due the Wash City Corp. -Jos Brumley, Col 1st ward.

WED DEC 4, 1816
Crt of Chancery of the dist of Fredericksburg, Va. For sale-*Merchant Mill*, 150 acs adjoining it, late the prop of Richd Cole, dec'd; within 6 miles of Dumfries, Va. -Thos Chapman, Com'r, Dumfries.

Jas Melvin & Co, Merchant Tailors, Bridge st, Gtwn. Local ad.

TUE DEC 5, 1816
For sale-Madeira Wine, grocs, etc. -John H Crease, Alexandria.

Land for sale-desirous of mvg Westward; sale of 300 acs, in Montg Co, Md, 2 miles from Patrick Magruder's Mill. -John Wallace, Montg Co, Md.

Died: on Nov 5, at New Orleans, after a severe illness of four wks, Maj Danl Carmick, U S M C; born in Pa; in the Corps since its formation. He has left an amiable wife with her infant child to mourn his loss. He was buried the next day.

Mrd: on Nov 26, by Rev Mr Balch, Mr Lewis H Machen to Miss Caroline Webster, d/o Toppan Webster, all of Wash City.

Orphans Crt of Wash Co, D C. Ltrs of adm on prsnl est of Tobias Lear, late of said city, dec'd. -B L Lear, adm.

Notice to the creditors of Jas H Drane, dec'd; dividend will be pd at the hse of Geo Kleiber, on the 3d Mon of this mo. -Jas White

S W Handy & Trueman Beck have an assortment of hats at their Hat Factory, oppo Jefferson st, in Gtwn.

FRI DEC 6, 1816
Journey tailors wanted. -John Gustavus Hoge, Upper Marlborough, PG Co, Md.

Jas A Buchanan was unanimously elected Pres of the Branch Bank of the U S in Balt, Md, on Dec 3.

Dissolution of Co-partnership; firm of Stout & Merrill. Payments to Geo Travers. -Jacob Stout, Jeremiah Merrill, Gtwn.

SAT DEC 7, 1816
To lease for term of yrs, lot 2 on Pa av, Capitol Hill. -Patrick Rogers, Pa av, Wash.

MON DEC 9, 1816
Mrd: on Dec 3, by Rev Wm Waters, Dr David English, jr, of Gtwn, to Miss Mary C Slade, of Alexandria.

Mrd: on Nov 19, by Rev P Davidson, Maj Alexander M'Ilhenny, late of the U S Army, to Mis Eliz Reid, of Runny Meade, Fred'k Co, Md.

Died: on Dec 8, John Campbell. Funeral from his late dwlg, nr the Centre Mkt, today.

Orphans Crt of Wash Co, D C. Ltrs of adm on prsnl est of Dr Thos Bruff, late of said city, dec'd. -Mary Bruff, adm.

Wm A Collins has opened an Oyster Hse at the crnr of Water & High sts, at the sign of the Ship, Gtwn.

Orphans Crt of Wash Co, D C. Ltrs of adm on prsnl est of Wm Crawford, late of Gtwn, in said Co, inn kpr, dec'd. Mr Richd Burgess, of Gtwn, is appt'd agent & atty in fact. -Sarah Crawford, admx of Wm Crawford.

TUE DEC 10, 1816
Electors of Pres & VP for the state of Ky:

Robt Ewing	Saml Caldwell	Saml Murrell
Alex'r Adair	Willis A Lee	Wm Logan

Richd Taylor   Wm Irvine   Duvall Payne
Robt Trimble   Thos Bodley   Hubbard Taylor

In Ohio, lately, Mgt Logan, recovered $1,000 of Robt Gray, for a breach of promise of marriage, by a due course of law.

Wanted, a young man to assist in a Groc Store. -Lynde Elliott, nr the mkt hse, Gtwn.

Thos Crawford informs his friends that he now occupies the well known Union Tvrn of Gtwn, D C, lately in the occupancy of his bro Wm Crawford, dec'd.

Orphans Crt of PG Co, Md. Pblc sale at the farm of Josias Fendall Beall, dec'd, in Montg Co, Md, on Dec 31; prsnl prop of the dec'd. -Jas A Beall, exc.

WED DEC 11, 1816
Hse o/Reps. 1-Petition of Eliza Tarbell, wid/o Jos Tarbell, dec'd, late a capt in the navy, praying provision for support of herself & 2 chldrn. 2-Pet from Thos I Allen, bro & adm of the late Capt Allen of the U S N, praying comp for svcs by Capt Allen, during the late war. 3-Pet from Wm H Rose for an honorable discharge from the 38th Regt of Infty. 4-Pet of Jas Ware to be placed on the navy pension list. 5-Pet of Jos Storer, coll of Kennebunk, comp for his svcs.

THU DEC 12, 1816
Died: on Dec 10, at Alexandria, Mr Jerome Plummer, of the hse of J & G Plummer, of that town.

FRI DEC 13, 1816
Died: in Kent Co, state of Dela, Mr John Irvin Walies. [No date-recent]

Notice-Sale at Wm Wert's Tvrn, Bladensburgh, on Jan 1, 1817, following land, to wit: part of *Basil Warring's Lot Enlarged*, 286 1/4 acs; part of do-170 acs; part of *Beall's Pleasure*, 57 acs; second addition to *Warring's lot*, 874 acs; addition to do, 36 acs; *Warring's Discovery & Second Thought*, 7 3/4 acs; taken as prop of Jas Wert, at suit of John Darnall. -Basil Bowling, Shrf.

Wash Co-I certify that Jos Nally brght before me a stray mare. -Danl Rapine, J P.

SAT DEC 14, 1816
Died: at Norfolk, on Sat last, Lt Jas Saunders, of the U S Navy, in his 24th yr; his complaint was pulmonary, expedited by a blow he rec'd on the breast from a brick, thrown at him while endeavoring to keep the spectators out of danger at the launch of the Franklin, 74.

Mrd: on Dec 12, by Rev Mr Montgomery, Mr Jacob Smull, of Phil, to Miss Nancy Fry, of Wash City.

For sale-hse with lot of 9 to 10 acs, known in Gtwn as the late residence of Robt Beverley; title is perfect. -J B Beverley, Gtwn.

MON DEC 16, 1816
Wine & Liquor Store, Pa av, Wash City. -John Graeff, jr.

Wash Co, D C. Petition of Stanislaus P Miles, insolvent debtor, confined in Wash Co prison, for debt. -Wm Brent, clk.

TUE DEC 17, 1816
List of taxes now due the Corp on real prop in Wash City, for 1816, by Non Residents, to be pd on or before Jan 1 next:

Avidesh A B	Armitage Benj	Beall Wm M
Bayer Jacob	Beall Jas of Jas	Matthias Buckey
Breckenridge John Revd	Backman Jacob	Baker John
Barksdale Wm	Chandler Walter S	Conningham John
Barclay Jas & John Simson		Carmark Danl
Clarke Saml & John Wilson		Caldwell David
Clagett Hezekiah	Cheswell Jos N	Campbell Levin H
Campbell Jas	Carter Chas	Chapman Mary
Crawford Jas, jr.	Doll John	Duer Jas
Doll Geo	Davidson Elias	Doll Jos
Dewes Isaac	Dunham Lewis	Faw Abraham
Freeman John		Rev Mr Goulding
Floyd Wm T & Edw H Nichols		Groff Michl
Gilpen Bernard	Holmead Anthony	Holmead John
Hindman Wm	Hoof John	Hilleary Henry jr
Hass John-devisees	Hacket John	Hamm Peter
Hughes Christopher	Hoge John	Johnson Thos
Johns Thos	Johns Maurice	Jones Chas C
Key Philip B-heirs	Kirk Jas	Koontz Henry
Kim David	Kemp Peter	Kerr Ann
Kemp Christian & David		Kesler Andrew
Kurtz P & F	Kesler Danl	Ketland Thos
Lingan Jas Mrs-heirs	Luffborough Nathan	Lee Thos Sim
Maxwell Nathl G	Mantz Casper	McCormick Jas
Matthews John	McGrath Wm	Myers Philip H
Murdoch Geo	Moscrop Henry	Murdock Eleanor
Mantz John	Meddart Jacob	Moore Robt
McCreery Wm-heirs	McHenry Jas	Marshall Hopksui & Marshall
Mason Geo-heirs	Mantz Peter & John	Martin Lusher
Mayer Jacob	Mackell Wm	Miller Fred'k
Miley Fred'k	Nicholls Michl	Newton John
Orandorf Christian	Orme Nathan	Ohara Jas
Pauling Henry	Pierce Thos	Plowden Edw
Pierce Wm	Powell Cuthbert	Patterson Mary
Porter Edw	Reclenear Aaron	Riggs Geo W
Rednover Matthias	Rench John & Andrew	Raymer Michl

Ragan Danl	Robinson Henry	Ratcliff Sarah
Rench Jacob & Ludowick Young		Reeder Geo
Raborg Wm & W Taylor		Shepherd John
Shell Chas	Shaffer M	Smith Jas
Swann Thos	Shaff Arthur	Stevens John
Schnebley Henry	Smith Saml	Steward John
Scolfield Isachar & Mahalon		Smith Amos
Swingle Geo	Schelman John	Steiner Jacob jr
Stewart Walters-heirs	Shippen Wm Dr	Stall Henry
Swann John	Southgate John	Smith Isaac
Stoddert & Templeman		Smith, Calhoun & Co
Skyren Jacob	Thornton Jacob	Thompson Geo
Thomas Philip	Templemon John	Vanbibber Abrams-heirs
Veitch Richd	Ward Jas	Warring Marsham
Walgamot John	Wetsell Fred'k	Whitehair Appelonia
Wilson Richd	Wilson Eliz & Jos W	Williams Thos O
Winters Geo	Winters John	Wilson & Dennis
Walker Henry	Wayman Chas-heirs	Winder Levin
Wilson Alex'r	Yost Henry	Zeller Jacob
-Jos Brumley-Coll 1st Ward		

Mrd: on Dec 15, by Rev Mr Breckenridge, Mr Chas Lyon to Miss Cath Jeffers, both of Wash City.

Mrd: on Dec 16, Mr Benedict White to Miss Cath Osburn, both of Wash City.

Orphans Crt of St Mary's Co, Md. Ltrs of adm on prsnl est of Walter Lyon, late of said co, dec'd. -Wm Lyon, adm.

Died: Dec 15, in Wash City, Mrs Burwell, consort of Wm A Burwell, a Rep in Cong from Va. Her remains were yesterday cnvyd to Balt for interment in the family burying ground.

WED DEC 18, 1816
Mgrs of the Gtwn Dancing Assembly for the season:

John Mason	John Peter	John Cox
Wash Bowie	Wm Whann	Robt F How
John Marbury	John Lockerman	Robt French
W M Worthington		

THU DEC 19, 1816
Mrd: on Dec 15, by Rev Mr Collins, Mr John Grierson to Miss Mary Osbourne, d/o Mr Archibald Osbourne, both of this dist.

Mrd: on Dec 17, by Rev Mr Mathews, Mr John Larkum, of Phil, to Miss Eliz Tench, of Wash City.

Mrd: in Gtwn, on Dec 17, by Rev Mr Balch, Mr A L Mills to Miss Matilda A Holtzman, both of Gtwn.

FRI DEC 20, 1816
Consignment of Writing, Printing & Wrapping paper, for sale at factory prices. -S B Goddard [New store lately occupied by R C Weightman.]

For sale-*Bradford's Rest*, 2,000 acs of land in Montg Co, Md, the prop of the late Mr Key. -Thos Plater, Gtwn.

SAT DEC 21, 1816
Notice to Non Residents; taxes due for 1816 to the Wash City, Corp, payable Jan 1, 1817; Geo Adams, Coll 4th Ward:

Blodgett Saml-heirs	Brady Nathl	Blagg Geo & Laigh
Bary Zachariah	Bryden Jas	Ball Jos
Bucis-heirs	Craven Tunis	Cranch Wm
Carson Geo	Duvall Gabriel	Dye Reuben
Dobbyn John	Elliott Bernard-heirs	Fry John London
Fox Josiah	Farrington Lewis-heirs	Hunter John
Hebb Wm	Hitchburn Benj	Hebron Abigail
Hart Bernard	Howard Henry	Hunter Thos-heirs
Jackson Isaac H & Robt Ober	Ingerham Nathl	King John
Lard John & John Mason	Lewis Jos-in trust	Mattox Notly
Minifie Chas	O'Brien Wm	Parrot Richd
Potts Jas B	Randle John Senr	Roach Mahlon
Read Jas	Slater David-heirs	Stevenson Jas S
Simms Henry	Stoddard Benj-heirs	Spalding-heirs
Slater Jonathan-heirs	St Clare Arthur	Spalding Philip
Smith Wm	Slater Sarah	Sands Francis
Steel John	Somers Lewis	Sandford Wm
Thomas Richd	Teakle Littleton D	Voss Nicholas
Vint John	Walker Geo-heirs	Wilson David
Westcoat Jas D	Ward Jas	Walker Jas jr
Ward John	Walker & Wheeler	Wilson Wm
Wheeler Eliz	Young Thos	Young Susan
Young Abraham-heirs	Young Wm	Young Morduit
Young Mary	Young Ann	

Zanesville, O, Dec 12. On Fri last, Jacob Lewis, of Jefferson twnshp, was committed to jail of this co, on chg of murdering his neighbor, Mr Saml Jones; dischgd 2 ball thru his heart. Altercation over a saddle.

Crct Crt of U S for Wash Co, DC; in Chancery. Jas Barry & John Barry vs Jas D Barry, Robt Barry, David D Barry, John D Barry, heirs & reps of Jas Barry, formerly of Wash, D C, dec'd; Garret Gould, Geo Gould, Christiana Gould, Mrs Donavan, Hannah Gould & Mary Gould, heirs of Johanna Barry, dec'd, & the other heirs of the said Jas Barry, dec'd, of Johanna Barry, dec'd, & of Ann Gould Barry, dec'd. In 1799 the said Jas Barry purchased land cld *Trinidad*, of Notley

Young, in Wash Co, D C, 99+ acs; purchased at the request of Dr Edw Barry, formerly residing in the Island of Trinidad, W India Islands; before he took possession, he died without having pd for the land; at the request of the said Jas Barry, f/o the cmplnts, Jas Barry, then an inhabitant of the Island of Teneriffe, & bro of said Edw Barry, took upon himself the purchase of said land, & pd the full amount to said Jas Barry, of Wash, thereby becoming entitled to a cnvynce of same to himself; but prior to that, the said Jas Barry, of Wash, died, leaving the said Ann Gould Barry, his only surviving child, who died unmrd, intestate, & without issue, & the said Johanna Barry, his widow, has died leaving no issue. Garret, Geo Christianna, Hannah & Mary Gould, & Mrs Donavan are her bros & srs & heirs at law, & the said Jas D, Robt, David D, & John D Barry, are nphws & only heirs of the said Jas Barry, of Wash, dec'd, known to the cmplnts. After payment of the purchase money, Jas Barry, of Teneriffe, died, lvg the cmplnts & their sister, Ann, his chldrn & heirs at law & residuary Legatees, & the said Ann Barry having renounced all claim to said land in favor of cmplnts. Dfndnts, except Jas D Barry, do not reside within D C. All to appear in Crct Crt, on or before the first Mon in Jun next. -Wm Brent.

MON DEC 23, 1816

Died: on Sat wk, in his 55th yr, Capt Geo Hite, of Charlestown, Va; entered into the army as an Ensign at age 16; srvd under Gen Green, in the Southern army.

Orphans Crt of PG Co, Md. Ltrs test on prsnl est of Mary Belt, late of said co, dec'd. -Levi Belt, adm.

Pblc sale of the Fountain Inn, in Fredericktown. Apply to Conrad Chafer.

TUE DEC 24, 1816

Hse o/Reps. 1-Petition of Elihu Lester, sldr of the Rev army, praying for a pension. 2-Pet of Susannah Machin, wid/o the late Capt Thos Machin, arrearages of pension. 3-Pet of Humphrey Webster, for inc of pension granted. 4-Pet of Abraham Davis, do. 5-Pet of Matha Owen, wid/o the late Col Abraham Owen, killed at battle of Tippecanoe, praying for provision for support of herself & 7 chldrn. 6-Pet of John Thompson, & Sarah Thompson his wife, late the wid/o Edw Spear, a lt in the military svc of the U S, killed in battle, praying support to the chldrn of the said Edw Spear. 7-Pet of Benj Hale, praying for a pension. 8-Pet of Robt Sewall, comp for his hse & furn destroyed by the British forces in Aug 1814, at their entrance into Wash City.

Direct Tax of the U S on D C, for 1815; prop in Wash Co, D C, unpd for 1 yr; will be sold on Feb 24 next, until taxes are satisfied:

Robt Allison	Thos Armstead	Adam Aults-heirs
Theodorick Armstead	Mgt Adams	Andrews & Polkinhorn
Thos Addison	Henry Appleton	John Appleton
Jas Ambush	Thos Allen	Wm Adams
Henry Addison	Wm Armstrong	Walter Adams
Gerard Boarman	Robt L Beall	Matthew L Bever
Wm Bailey	Saml Blodgett-heirs	Geo Blount-heirs

Jas Barclay & Geo Simpson		John Bassett
John B Beall	Richd Boyd	Jos Bently
Wm T Beall-heirs	Saml Beall	Wm Bushell
Wm Barksdale	Jas Brown	Clement Biddle
John Boytt	Alex'r Bateman	Jas Bryden
Jos Ball	Quintin Bean	Robt Barry
John Barnett-heirs	John Brice	Abraham Vanbibber
C Blagg & W C Laight		Matthew Browne
Thos C Bowie	Benj Bean	Wm Bean
Ralph Boarman	Robt Brown-heirs	Clement Biddle
Edw Burrows	John Barnes	Michl Brady
Paul Bustic	John Beckley-heirs	John Beall
Wm Bartleman	Benj Brookes	Dr John Bussard
John Burchan-heirs	Walter Barron	Jacob Boyer
Wm Bailey	Rachel Bartlett	Matthew Brown
Edw Bland & Geo Grant		Henry Bradford
Jane Burch	Francis Boone	Robt Campbell-heirs
Maj Danl Carmick	Hugh Campbell	Cath Claney
Saml Clarl	Wm Campbell	Saml Chase-heirs
Judson Cooledge	Chas Carroll, jr	Jas Craig
David Caldwell	Wm Crown	Chas B Calwell
Jacob Cist	Danl Caffray-heirs	Josh N Chiswell
Crookshank & Thomson-heirs		Cath Connell
Martin Casner	A Carmichael	Hugh Campbell
John Callahan-heirs	Jas Corrie	Robt Craig
Hezekiah Clagett	Danl Carmichael	David Caucaud
John Cunningham	Wm & Eleanor Dowson	
Wm Davidson	Wm Diggs	Wm Deakin-heirs
Francis Deakin-heirs	Jasper D Carnap-heirs	Robt Dennison
Eliza Davidson	Everard Delius	Cath Dalton
Lewis Deblois	Fred'k Deblois	Dick & Stewart
Chas Dent-heirs	Dr Jas Davidson	Henry Dearborne
Thos Dick-heirs	Robt Darnell	Trinian & Alex Edmonson
Henry Edwards	Geo Ehrenzeller	Bernard Elliott-heirs
Richd Eno-heirs	Wm Eustis	Jas Earle
John Eden	A Fisher-heirs	Nicholas Franklin
Thos Fry	Ferdinando Fairfax	Levin Farrington
Joh Fry	Jas Fisher	Arriana French
Betsy Fletcher	Jas Fenwick	Wm Fletcher
Christiana Flaut	Thos Fitzgerald	Geo French-heirs
Job Fowler	John Fowler	Amariah Frost
Andrew Flick	Ignatius Fenwick-heirs	Amond George-heirs
John Granberry	John Guess	Jas Green
Thos T Gantt	Thos F Gantt	Saml Griffin
Richd Graham	Jas Graham	Saml Galloway
Thos Gilham	Henry Goil	Michl Groff
Rev Mr Goulding	Michl Gangeware	Grundy & Crossdale
John Gibson	Bernard Gilpin	Saml Goldthwaite

Christopher Gore	Wm Ginison	Fred'k Goulding
Geo Gerrard	Lancelot Griffith	Gilliss, Greenvelott & others
Ester Gardner	Roderick Hampton	Geo Hume
Richd Henderson-heirs	Mgt Hawker	John Hepburne
Wm Howard	Henry Howard	Jos Howard
John Hunter	Wm Harrison	Mary Hurley
Richd Henderson	R T Hooe	Jonathan Hall
John Hembler	Arnold Hurley	Peter Hamm
Wm Hindman	John Hadrick	Geo Holstein
Maxinilian Hugster	Jos Hodgson-heirs	Bernard Hart
Wm Hemersley	Wm Hill	Thos Hunter
John Hebron	Benj Hitchburne	Jas Holliday
Alban Howe	John Hall	John Homer
Lambert Hyland	Ignatius Howe	Saml Hepburn-heirs
John Hackett	Thos Johnston-heirs	Jasper Jackson
Isaac H Jackson	Jas Johnston	Jas Johnson
Capt Chas Johnson	Francis Jenkins	Nathl Ingraham
Danl Jennifer	Raphael Jones	John Johnson
Jas Johnson, jr	Saml Jones	Walter Johnson
Loenard H Johns	Thos Johns-heirs	Thos Jennings
Morris Jones	Geo Johnson	Walter Jamieson
Thos Jones	Ludowick Kruger	Jas Kirk
Andrew Keisler	David Kemp	Peter Kemp
Nicholas King of Va	Christian & David Kemp	Henry Klinger
Thos Kelland	Henry Kramer	John Kale
Thos Kitchley	Patrick King	Francis Kirby
Christian Kemp	Wm H Lyles	Jas M Lingham-heirs
[to be cont'd]		

WED DEC 25, 1816

Mrs J Gouges, just arv'd from Balt, will open a Fancy Goods store, on Bridge st, Gtwn; at dwlg hse of Mr A L Joncherez.

Calvert Co, Md, in Chancery, Aug Term, 1816. Henry Gardiner vs Walter Smith, *Jos Smith, *Richd Smith, *Saml Chew & Ann his wife, *Thos Chew & Eliz his wife, *Zachariah Taylor & Mgt his wife, *Sarah Ann Chesley, Ann S Hellen, Jos Wilkinson, Jas Heighe, Jas Morsell & John Dare. Reimbursement of money pd for land in Calv Co, rl est of Capt Walter Smith, late of said co, dec'd, purchased 700 acs that he pd the heirs of the late Capt Walter Smith, for $16 per ac; resrvy of same finds it deficient of 53+ acs. *Reside out of Md. -Wm S Morsell, clk.

Tax list cont'd-see Dec 24.

Geo Lake	Wm Lorman	Lawrence Lewis
Adam Lynn	Lynch & Sands	Darby Lux
Andrew Lynch	Dominick Lynch	Chas Lowndes
Francis Leeke	Ann Leeke	Edw Langley
Wm Lamble	John Lingerfetter	Wm Lowry
John Leyland	----- Lowderwick	Philip H Myers

John F Mercer	Moses Myers	Wm Muckle
Henry Maclary	J Marshall & J S Hopkins	
Robt M'Mahon	Philip Mara-heirs	John Meckle
John Minor	John Moore Miller	Barbara Marshall
Morris, Nicholson & Prout		Jesse M'Coy
B G Mintum & J T Champlain		Geo M'Farland
Robt M'Coy	Chas Minifee	Henry Moscrop
Thos M'Lean	Stephen Moilan	Martin & Eastburn
John Mercer	Reuben Meriweather	Jas M'Cormick, jr
Peter Miller-heirs	Ebenezer Mackay	Thos M'Intosh
Jas Mewburn	Thos C Wright	Wm Macbreery
Morrison & Nicholson-assignees		Wm Mackay
Robt McClan	Jennett McDonald	Philip H Myers
Jacob Moyer	Wm McQuackin	Peter & John Mantz
Jas McHenry	Morris & Mordat	John McDade
Alex'r Moore	Benj Morris	John Matthias
Luther Martin	John Mantz	Wm McGrath
John McPhial	Stean Mattree	Michl Nicholas
John B Neale	Jos H Nicholson	Jas Neale o/BennetM
John S Newton	Philip Nicklin	Henry Nicholds
Jas O'Harra	Dennis O'Conner	Lawrence Oneile
Nathl Orme	Christian Orandorf	John A Oswald Pratt
Francis & others	John Pickrill	Sarah Porter
Isaac Pollock	Philips, Grant & West	Jos B Parsons
Andrew Parks	Jos Parson-heirs	Wm Pierce
Henry Paulding	Cath Powell	Fielder Parker
Ann Peter	Jas B Pitts	Edw Perry
S Sterrett & S Potter	Eliza Perry	Thos Pierce
Robt Pollard	Jas Patton	Peter B Pervost
Edw Plowden	Nathl Philips	Richd Powell
Jas B Parsons	Israel & John Pleasants	Edw Parkinson
David Pollock	Abigail Pollock	Jas Penrose
Josias Rhea-heirs	Wm Rider	Matthew Riddle
Wm Read & Co	Isaac Read	Jos Riddle
Wm Russell	Henry Rozier	Thos Rutter
John B Rattree	Ringold & Hillary	Dr Wm Rodgers
John Rousling	Danl Ragan	Geo Reeder
Wm Raborg & Wm Taylor		Isaac or John Race
Jacob & Ludowick Young Rench		John & Andrew Rench
Aaron Relaimer	David Rawin-heirs	Matthew Rednover
Jos Slater	Capt John Shaw	Edw Stone
John Stricker	Jas S Stephenson	Stoddert & Templeman
Comfort Sands	Wm Sisterson	Ann Shaw
Hannah Smith	Saml Smallwood	Wm Sandford
Henry Slater	John Steel	Ann Slater
John Swank	Francis Sands	Thos Slater
Chas Slater	Jas Smith	Henry Schroeder
Jonathan Slater-heirs	David Slater	Chas Stewart

Jas Scott	John Stewart-heirs	Noble H Spooner
Jane Shorter		
[Dec 27 paper]		
Ben Stoddert & D Burn-heirs		Smallwood & Smith
John Skam	Rachel Shoemaker	Andrew Smith
Robt Sutton	Christian Shell-heirs	Dr Upton Scott
John Sears	Walter Stewart-heirs	Jacob Skinner, jr
Edw Skinner	Jas Stranger	Levin H Campbell
Geo Slye	Benj Sharp	Saml Snowden [Md]
Caleb Swan-heirs	John Shrub	Saml Sterrett
John Southgate	Wm Sidebotham	Geo Swingly
Arthur Shaff	Seybert Scott	John Shellman
E & M Scholfield	John Swann	Thos L Shippen
Henry Schnebley	Saml Snowden	Michl Shafer
John Shepherd	John Steward	Saml Speake
Henry Stall	Mrs Soper	Richd Shuckle
Wm Stewart	Henry Selby	Presley Thornton-heirs
Jas Thorburn	Rich Thomas-heirs	Thom Tunnell-heirs
Christopher S Thorn	Henry Thompson	Tompkins & Minor
John Templeman	Louis Tousard	Patrick Tewell
Eliza L Thompson	Thos Truxton	Edw Tilghman
Jas Tilghman	Matthew Tilghman	Wm H Tilghman
Jos Thomas	Taylor & Toland	Richd Tilghman
Ezra Thompson & J Smith		Thompson & Veitch
John C Thomas	Philip Thomas	Jacob Tornton
Jos Taylor-heirs	Henry Umholt	Jas Vaughn
Jas Ward	Archibald Walker	Mary White
Jas White	Jas Ward & others	John Ward
Jas Walker	John C Wilson	Benj Wright-heirs
Thos Wharton	Levi White	Sarah Walker
Chas Wayman-heirs	Chas Wayman	Jane Wilson
Thos Wand	Bazil Warring	Eliza L Washington
Jas Wickham	Geo Walker	Dr Whitehead
Levin Winder	Jas D Wescott	David Wilson
Thos Williams	Thos L Washington	Wm Wilson
Jas Wormley	Jane Wharton	Luke Wheeler
Wm & Jas Willink	Augustus B Woodward	Benson White
Henry Walker	Henry Waring	Appleton White-heirs
John Weems-heirs	Marsham Waring	B Wignell
Thos Willock	Fred'k Whitesall	Geo Winter
Eliza & Josiah W Wilson-heirs o/Jos		John C Wilson
Jos Wilson	John Walljamotte	Wilson & Dennis
Chas Wadsworth-heirs	Thos O Williams	Gen Geo Washington-heirs
Thos Wheat	Benj Young	E Young
B Young-heirs	Mary Young	E Young
Walker, Young & Prout		Wm Young
[R Young, Nice Young, Ann Chapan, Thos Fenwick & E & Robt Brent]		
Saml Young	Jos Young	Mary Yates

Ann Young   Alex'r Young   Jacob Zeller
-Jas H Blake, coll

FRI DEC 27, 1816
Mrd: on Dec 24, by Rev Mr M'Cormick, Capt Geo Bender, U S Army, to Miss Mary Briscoe, of Wash City.

Taxes due on rl prop to the City of Wash Corp, for 1816, by non-residents: Wm Ingle, Coll for 3d Ward:

Appleton Henry	Addison Thos	Andrews & Polkinhorn
Anderson Alex'r	Barnes & Rudgate	Biddle Clement
Bowie Thos C-heirs	Bradford Henry	Bean Wm
Barry Robt	Brown Jas	Brent Danl C-heirs
Beall Wm T-heirs	Brown Robt	Bacon Benj-heirs
Bassell John	Bevan Mathew L	Carroll Chas jr
Carroll Mary	Carroll Henry-heirs	Carroll & Oden
Cooledge Judson	Campbell John	Conway Richd-heirs
Chase Saml-heirs	Craig Jas M D	Campbell Robt-heirs
Carroll Chas o/Crlton	Craig John-heirs	Clagett & Mason
Coolege Saml-heirs	Chandler Jacob	Crown Wm
Cook David	Cochran Alex	Carlton Jos-heirs
Dulany Walter	Dulany Benj	Dunlop & Carlton
Dalton Cath	Duvall Horace	Dearnborn Henry
Douglass John-heirs	Dick & Stewart	Dick Thomas-heirs
Diggs Wm	Earle Jas	Ewell Thos
Fisher Jas	Fenwick Ignatius-heirs	Fowler Job
Galloway Saml	Geouges Arnand-heirs	Graham Richd
Herty Thos & Wm Fletcher		Holliday Jas
Hill Henry	Hooe Robt T	Hall Jonathan
Hemmersly Wm	Hepburn Saml-heirs	Henderson Rich-heirs
Henning Geo	Jenifer Danl	Johnson Jas, jr
Jones Arthur	Kirby Francis	Kurtz Henry
Lee Eliza	Leidler Eliza	Leek Francis
Leitch A	Lewis Lawrence	Lux Darby
Lux Wm	Lyles Wm H	Lynn Adam
Merryweather Nichl	Mackey Ebenezer	Minor John
McMahon Robt	Maddox Wm R	McKenny Benson
Neal Jas o/Bennet	North Richd	Nevett Mary
Nicholson Jos H	Oden Benj & Notley Young-heirs	
Parkinson Edw	Penrose Jas	Patton Jas
Park Andrew	Pennock & Ash	Philips Nathl
Rutter Thos	Ross David	Ringold Mary C
Ridley Matthew	Rozier Henry	Russell Wm
Stevens John	Spears Jos	Sidebotham Wm-heirs
Scott Dr Upton	Sayer Daniel	Shaw Alex'r-heirs
Schoolfield Mahlon	Stewart Chas	Sewell Robt
Shute John	Suttle Henry	Sutton Robt
Strange Jas	Stewart Philip	Schoolfield Andrew

Tilghman Richd	Tilghman Wm H	Tilghman Matthew
Tilghman Peregrine	Tilghman Jas	Tilghman Edw
Thruston Buckner	Traverse John	Thomas Evan
Veitch Wm	Waring Basil	Waring Henry
Washington Geo S	Young Notley-heirs	Young Jos
Young Mary & Eliz Carroll		

SAT DEC 28, 1816
Died: on Nov 30, Mr John Hallum, of Pendleton, S C, aged about 27 ys, from a fall from his horse.

MON DEC 30, 1816
Hse o/Reps. 1-Petition of Sarah Dewees, on behalf of herself & heirs of Wm Dewees, dec'd, late of Pa, comp for hses & prop destroyed during the Rev war. 2-Pet of Christie Cameron, wid/o John Cameron, who was taken sick in military svc of the U S, died after his return home, provision for support of herself & 7 infant chldrn of said Cameron. 3-Pet of Eliz Albert, wid/o Christian Albert, who died while in military svc of the U S, praying to be put on the pension list.

Phil, Dec 27. Wm D Robinson, eldest s/o the late Capt Jas Robinson, of this city, was slain in attack of Ft Guazalcos, So America, in Oct last.

Taxes due on rl prop to the City of Wash Corp, for 1816, by non-residents; Harvey Bestor, Coll for 2d Ward:

Allen Wm	Atkinson Francis	Atkinson John
Armistead Theo	Albright Chas	Appleton John
Burke John	Brown Stewart	Barlow Joel-heirs
Basti Paul	Benson John	Ball & Ford
Beck Trueman	Brady Michael	Burrows Edw
Baltzer John-heirs	Beckley John-heirs	Brevett John
Boarman Ralph	Barrie Gasper	Cooper Isaac
Calder Jas	Campbell Wm	Cochran Wm & David
Clarke Edw	Cox John	Cist Jacob
Covachichi Jos	Corlass Mathias	Cox Eliza
Cope Israel & Jasper	Cammach Wm	Davidson John-heirs
Dobbin David-heirs	Dorsey Wm H	Dupuy Wm-heirs
Dale Richd	Dent Chas	Davidson, Dr Jas
Darnall Robt	Edwards Henry	Foxhall Henry
Fennel Edw-heirs	Fletcher Wm	Fenwick Jas
Fenwick Thos	Gillis, Groenveldt & others	
Gowan John	Guest John	Gannan Jas
Grammer Fred'k	Gallaher Robt	Godefroy Peter & others
Givison Wm-heirs	Granbury John	Heyle Wm
Hillard Thos	Hellrigles Christian-heirs	Heath Nathl H
Hume Geo	Heathcote John	Haley Patrick
Johnson Chas	Knowles Henry	Kirk Thos M
Kidd Robt	Kidd Wm	King Adam
Laird John	Lowndes Chas	Ludlow Danl

Lansdale Wm M   Lynch Dominick
[Lynch & Sands, Saml Blodget, & Wm Deakin-heirs]
Landsdale Violetta Logan Geo W   Landsdale Philip
Lorman Wm   McCormick Jas jr Myers Moses
Mason John   Mayer Henry   Moylan Stephen
Mintrum B G & I T Champlain   Morris & Mordall
Muson Jacobus   Mudd Jas I   Martin & Ward
[Mason John Thompson] Mereer John   Massey Henry
Morris & Nicholson-assignees   Morin Lewis, sen
Mara Philip-heirs McDermothroe Cornelius-heirs
McPhail John   McDermot Roe Edw-heirs
Maguire John   McDermothroe Owen-heirs
Neale Rev Francis Nichlin Philip   Nichlin & Griffith
Oswald John A   Oliver Benj   Oden Benj
Plowden Edw   Plater John R   Porter Sarah
Pollock Isaac   Powell Richd   Pratt, Francis & others
Paleskie, Chas G & John Gardiner jr   Pickett Geo
Pollard Robt   Pollock Abigal   Pres of Gtwn Coll
Patterson Edgar   Pollock David   Pleasants Israel & John
Rogers Wm   Ratree Wm B   Perkins Jos & Isaac-heirs
Randall John   Ross Richd   Ross Jas
Riddle Jos   Roy John H   Richmond Chris heirs
Shreve & Unthank Smith Walter   Sands Robt
Sands Comfort   Sharp Benj   Sprigg Wm O
Solomon Merto   Stewart Saml   Sprigg Mgt
Sterrett Saml   Steuart John-heirs Sly Geo
Thompson Hugh   Triplett Dr Thos Travers Nicholas
Thornton Presley-heirs Thompson Henry Thompson Wm
Thomas Cornelia jr Tool Patrick   Talbert Chas
Vaughan John   Vageler Rudolph Van Mannick Anthony
Whitehead Dr   Willock Thos   Wheeler Luke
Webb Thos   Walker David   Waud Thos
Williams Jas   Wightt John M   William David
Willis John-heirs Wightt Benj-heirs Warder Jeremiah & John H
Wright Stephen   Whalen Nicholas-heirs Young Benj-heirs
Young Nicholas Young Rev Notley
[Young Benj-heirs, Nicholas Young, Ann Cassanave, Thos Fenwick, & Robt Y & Eleanor Brent]

TUE DEC 31, 1816

Mrd: on Dec 25, by Rev Mr Ryland, Mr Henry Gaither to Miss Abie Ann Heughes, both of Gtwn.

| DAILY NATIONAL INTELLIGENCER |
| WASHINGTON, D C |

1817

WED JAN 1, 1817
Notice-John Steward, of Wash Dist, stone cutter, has petitioned for benefit of the Insolvent Law; not me, John Steuart, the hse carpenter.

THU JAN 2, 1817
Died: at the Navy Yd, Sgt Anthy F Shaub, of the Marine Corps. Friends & Masonic brethern to attend the funeral this day at 2 o'clock.

One hundred & fifty hams for sale. Owen McCue, nr the Navy Yd, Wash.

Orphans Crt of PG Co, Md. Sale of 5 negroes, prop of the late Agnes Hoge, dec'd. -John G Hoge, adm

FRI JAN 3, 1817
Hse o/Reps. 1-Petition of Eliz Matilda Shubrick, wid/o the late Capt John T Shubrick, U S N, cmded the brig *Epervier*, & was lost with same on passage from Mediterranean to the U S; provision for support of herself & infant son of said Capt Shubrick. 2-Pet of Paul D Luke, kpr of the light hse at Old Point Comfort, praying for incr of his salary.

$20 reward for Red Morocco pktbk lost about Dec 25, with certificate of 50 acs of land at Ft Cumberland, lot 1504, endorsed Jas Devereux, etc. Return to Richd Fenwick, Bank o/Metropolis, or Benedict J Fenwick, Port Tobacco, Chas Co, Md.

Orphans Crt of PG Co, Md. Ltrs d b n on prsnl est of Geo Hilleary, late of said co, dec'd. -Benj Belt, adm

Notice-Messrs Robt Beverly, Carter Beverly, Byrd Beverly, Peter R Beverly, McKenzia Beverly & Munford Beverly, on the 5th day of the next Sup Crt of Chancery for Fredericksburg Dist, I shall move that Crt to award a writ of Certiorari to remove a suit depending in Culpeper Co Crt, in Chancery, in which you are plntfs & I am dfndnt, for unreasonable delay in the trial. -Thos Hickman

Died: at the residence of Mr Wm Wilkinson, in Brunswick Co, Va, Gen John Woods, of Pittsburg, Pa, a mbr from that state in Cong of the U S. [no date-recent]

PG Co Crt, Sep Term, 1816. Application of Abraham Turner, of said co, for insolvent debtor. -John Read Magruder, clk

John Goulding, Notary Public, Cong & Bridge sts, Gtwn. -Local notice.

SAT JAN 4, 1817
Orphans Crt of Wash Co, D C. Ltrs of adm on prsnl est of Col Fielder Dorsett, late of said co, dec'd. -Amelia T Dorsett, admx.

Died: at Lempster, N H, on Dec 17, Mr Joshua Booth, aged about 55, of hydrophobia.

Died: of Yellow Fever, at St Pierres Martinique, on Nov 19 last, on board the brig *Commerce*, of which he was Supercargo, Col Nathan Frick, aged 27 yrs, s/o Mr Isaac Frink, of Waterford. At the time of his sailing, he was from New London, a Lt Col in the Horse Artl of Conn.

MON JAN 6, 1817
Wash Co, D C. Chas Gibson, insolvent debtor, confined in Wash Co prison for debt. -Wm Brent, clk.

For sale-superior champagne wine. Apply to Wm P Zantzinger, Capitol Hill

TUE JAN 7, 1817
Jos Ward & John Griffiths drowned in the Seneca Lake on Sat morning, while unloading wood from off a schooner into a smaller vessel. -Geneva, N Y, Dec 25.

Died: on Dec 24, at his seat, Mantapike, King & Queen Co, Va, Mr Richd Brooke, f/o Col Geo M Brooke, of the U S Army, who is left exc. His presence in Va is in consequence of this event.

For sale-farm in PG Co, adj Adelphia Mills, 70 acs with good brick hse, barn, etc. Enquire of Stephen Long, the owner, upon the farm, or of Messrs Key & Dunlap, Attys, Gtwn. [The owner is going to remove to a Mill in Pa.]

Unsettled accounts with Jos Wheaton, bet Aug 1809 & Mar 1, 1812, are to present same to Sarah Wheaton, at her hse, in F st, Wash City. -Sarah Wheaton, duly authorised by Jos Wheaton.

WED JAN 8, 1817
John C Faber is elected Pres of the Ofc of Discount & Deposit, est'd in Charleston.

Wanted to hire-one or two negro men, by the yr, from the country will be preferred. -Jas Cassin, Gtwn, nr the Roman Chapel.

Country seat at auction-the mansion hse, late the residence of Robt *Beverly, with the lot, 10 acs, on the confines of the town, just without the limit of the Corp, on the heights of Gtwn. -J B *Beverley. Mallory & Watts, auct. [*2 splgs]

THU JAN 9, 1817
Wanted to purchase-Rev land warrants. -Wm Mechlin, Exchange bkr, Wash.

Pblc sale, by the heirs of Martin Fisher, late of Montg Co, Md, dec'd; all the rl est of said dec'd, in Montg Co; 440 acs on Watts' Branch, cld the *Plaister of Paris*; with framed dwlg hse, etc. Thos Fisher lives on it & will shew it. -Thos Fisher, Aquila Fisher, Attys.

Died: at Alexandria, yesterday wk, Mr Eliza Vowell.

Mrd: on Jan 7, by Rev Mr Burch, Mr Peter Cook to Miss Jane S Bowling, both of Wash City.

Hse o/Reps. An act for the relief of Nathl Williams, of Rockingham, N C; to be dischg'd from imprisonment at Rockingham Crt Hse, N C; Treas Dept to credit $429 to said Williams. -H Clay, Spkr.

$50 reward for 2 negroes, Jacob & Stephen; ranaway on Apr 17 last. -Zenas Alexander & Geo Alexander, lvg in Mecklenburg Co, N C, nr Charlotte.

FRI JAN 10, 1817
$50 reward for mulatto boy, John, ranaway on Dec 27. -Matthew Ranson, lvg in Charlestown, Jefferson Co, Va.

Orphans Crt of PG Co, Md. Prsnl est of Lewis T Gibson, late of said co, dec'd. -Josias Gibson, adm.

SAT JAN 11, 1817
Ladies with ltrs in the Wash P O, Jan 1, 1817:

Archer Mrs Eliza	Ball Mrs Cath	Barry Miss Sifley
Black Mrs Nancy	Braiden Miss Eliz	Bryan Mrs Mary
Brown Miss Ann	Broughton Mrs C B	Boaring Miss Eliz
Cluff Miss Mary	Cooper Miss Mary	Clements Mrs Sarah
Clements Mrs Mary Ann	Crain Miss Eliz	Carr Miss Eliza
Clabourn Miss Jane	Digges Mrs Eliz	Eagling Mrs Mgt
Ferris Mrs Mgt	Goodrich Mrs S	Glenn Miss Eliza A
Hilborn Mary-2	Hamilton Mrs Cath	Hawkins Mrs Eliz
Hardy Mrs Louisa	Johnston Susanna	Jones Charlotte
King Miss Lucy	Lukeus Miss Abby	Long Miss Eliz
Mackall Miss Harriet	Palmon Lydia	Russell Miss C-2
Richmond Miss	Robertson Mrs Sarah	Reid Mrs Ann
Steward Mrs Mary A	Smith Mrs Mary	Stagton Miss Eleanor
Shaw Mrs Eleanor	Stansbury Mrs Ellen	Trasel Mrs Eliz
Soper Alex or Eleanor Ridgeway		White Miss Mary A
Williams Miss	Ward Miss Matilda	Williams Susan
Webb Milly	Williams Mary	

For sale-his landed est on Rhode Rvr in A A Co, Md, cld *Haylands*; bet 12 & 1,500 acs; adj those of Col Mercer, lg 2 story brick hse, etc. If desired, all the stock, except the negroes, will be sold with the farm. -Jas Carroll, Balt, Md.

MON JAN 13, 1817
Hse o/Reps. 1-Petition of Mary Bruff, wid/o Thos Bruff, dec'd; comp for invention of her late hsbnd during the late war, & set at work within the navy yd, Wash City, a machine for manufacturing leaden bullets, buck shot, etc; same destroyed at the burning of that yd in Aug 1814. 2-Pet of Jas Wood, adm & heir of capt Edw Wood, Rev army, commutation of half pay, to which the said Edw Wood was entitled. 3-Pet of Francis J Dallum, comp for his svcs as assist brig q m to a brig of Md militia in the svc of the U S, in 1814. 4-Pet of Mgt Houtchens, wid/o Bennett Houtchens, dec'd, who died in the military svc, leaving her, with 7 small chldrn.

Drudging Machine-patentee, John Eveleth, Gtwn.

TUE JAN 14, 1817
Mrd: in King Geo Co, Va, on Dec 25, by Rev Mr Davis, Capt John McGonegal, of Ohio, to Miss Jane R Yates, of the former place.

Mr J Moore was taken into partnership with Vincent King, lumber business; under the firm of Vincent King & Co. -Local Item

Elsworth Bayne, o/PG Co, Md, brght before me a stray mare. -Notley Maddox, J P.

WED JAN 15, 1817
Mr J S Williams, of Gtwn, patentee of a machine for kpg the channel of navigation free from ice during the winter season.

Albany, Jan 2. Died: on Sat last, at his residence at Hamiton College, in this state, after a short but severe attack of fever, the Rev Dr Backus, Pres of that Institution; ntv of Conn; rec'd his education at Yale College; B A degree in 1787.

Mrd: in N Y, on Tue last, by Rev Dr Romeyn, Maj John Marshall Gamble, U S M C, to Miss Hannah Letitia Lang, eldest d/o Mr John Lang.

Mrd: on Dec 18, in Buncombe Co, N D, by a Magistrate, Mr Lewis Sawyers, sen, aged 80 yrs, to Mrs Hannah Poston, aged 90, both of Green Co, Tenn. The lady who waited on the bride was 100 yrs old.

Died: at New Haven, Conn, on Jan 11, the Rev Dr Timothy Dwight, in his 65th yr, Pres of Yale College.

THU JAN 16, 1817
Chas co Crt, Md, Mar term, 1816. John L Hawkins vs Walter Cox, Saml Cox, Charity Dent, Robt Guest & Ann his wife, Hugh Cox & Mgt his wife, Sarah Cox, John Walter Gody, Jas Johnson & Jane Johnson. Cnvy part of 2 tracts cld *Fortune's Retreat* & *Fortune Enlarged*, in Chas Co; that John Chandler Cox, in his life time, sold same to Smith Hawkins. Smith Hawkins died having devised the said land to the cmplnt; Cox died intestate, without having cnvyd the said land to the said Smith Hawkins or to cmplnt, leaving Walter Cox, Saml Cox, Charity

Dent, Ann Guest, mrd w Robt Guest, Mgt Cox, mrd with Hugh Cox, Sarah Cox, John Walter Gody, s/o a dec'd sister, Rebecca, who had mrd Walter Gody, & Cecilia Johnson, mrd w Jas Johnson, which said sister Cecilia is since died, lvg a dght named Jane, entitled to the legal inheritance of said lands. Walter Cox, Saml Cox & John Walter Gody, reside in D C. -John Barnes, clk.

Orphans Crt of Chas Co, Md. Ltrs of adm, with will annexed, on prsnl est of Rev Dr Benj Contee, late of said co, dec'd. -Philip A L Contee, adm.

Chas Co Crt, Md, Aug term, 1816. Chas Moran, petition to divide land. John Moran, late of said co, dec'd, died seised of land in Chas Co, Md; left same to Henry Moran, then of Halifax Co, N C, Chas Moran, the petitioner, Elijah Moran, John Moran, Ann Davis, Rebecca Moran, who mrd Andrew Moran, Mary Carter, who mrd a certain Carter, who emigrated, but where the peitioner knew not, Henry Lyon, John Lyon, Elijah Lyon, Chapman Lyon & Delilah Lyon, infants, & chldrn of Eliz Lyon, dec'd, who was the d/o the said John Moran, dec'd, & Eliza Moran, d/o Jane Moran, who was also a d/o said dec'd. -John Barnes, clk.

FRI JAN 17, 1817
Wash Co, D C. Wm Burdine, confined in the prison bounds of Wash Co, for debt. -Wm Brent, clk.

SAT JAN 18, 1817
Peyton S Symmes has been appt'd Reg of the Land Ofc for the Dist of Cinc, vice Daniel Symmes, resigned.

Land for sale-cld *Clean Shaven*, about 103 acs, Montg Co, Md. This land was sold by Danl Lee to Francis Power, in his life time, bu not cnvyd to Power by deed. -Augus Taney, Trustee.

MON JAN 20, 1817
Alex'r Jas Dallas, late Sec of the Treas, died on Thu last, of a sudden attack of a disease to which he was subject.

Died: on Dec 31, at his residence on *Sand-hill*, in the 55th yr of his age, Maj Jas Peare, a ntv of Md, but for 32 yrs an inhabitant of Augusta, Ga.

TUE JAN 21, 1817
New Orleans, Nov 24. We are informed that the famous Chas T Billings, for whom a reward of $2,000 is advertised in this gaz, was apprended at the Balize by a sldr. It is said that $30,000 was found in his possession.

WED JAN 22, 1817
Orphans Crt of Wash Co, D C. Prsnl est of John Campbell, of Gtwn, late of Wash City, dec'd. -John Abbot, adm.

Died: at Ft Warren, in the harbor of Boston, on Jan 15, Capt Armstrong Irvine, of the light artl, a ntv of Carlisle, Pa. He was distinguished for his gallant svcs in the Niagara campaign of 1814.

Wash Co, D C. Jos Gatton, insolvent debtor, confined in Wash Co prison, for debt. -Wm Brent, clk.

THU JAN 23, 1817
Valuable Bridge st prop for sale; the hse & lot which I now occupy. -John Hagerty, jr, Gtwn.

FRI JAN 24, 1817
Wanted-a convenient hse, suitable for a small family, on one of the back sts nr the Ave. Apply to Isaac Clark.

Notice-a new line of waggons will run from Gtwn & Wash to Balt once in every wk. -John Stinchcomb, Gtwn.

SAT JAN 25, 1817
For sale-shad & herrings. -Gustavus Harrison, Gtwn.

Phil, Jan 20. On Sat last, the remains of Alex'r Jas Dallas were cnvyd from his residence in 4th st, to St Peter's burial ground in 3d st. Mr Dallas died on Jan 16 in the 58th yr of his age.

Wash Co, D C, in Chancery, Dec Term, 1816. Thornton Washington & others vs Bushrod Washington. Ratify sale by Geo C Washington, trustee, of prop of the late Gen Geo Washington, in Wash City, to wit: lot 16 & part of lots 6 & 7 in sq 634, to David English; lots 12, 13 & 14 in sq 667, & also lots 4, 5 & 6 in sq 667, to Chas Glover, & lot 5 in sq 667, to John G McDonald. -Wm Brent, clk.

Crct Crt of the U S for Wash Co, D C. Petition of Jas Goldsborough for division of the rl est of John M Goldsborough; same cannot be divided. -Wm Brent, clk.

MON JAN 27, 1817
Mahlon Dickerson is appt'd a Sen in Cong, from N J, after Mar 4 next, vie Mr Condit, whose term then expires.

TUE JAN 28, 1817
Partnership of John Clark & Chas De Krafft was dissolved on Jan 14, by mutual consent. Persons indebted are to pay John Clark. Wm H Barron & Edw De Kraft, have entered into partnership under the firm of Wm H Barron & Co-[Dry Goods.]

WED JAN 29, 1817
Prize Money, Georgia sta. To be distributed, with the consent of the Hon Wm Stephens, Judge o/the Dist of Ga; to the forces under the command of Cmdor H G Campbell, made during the late war. -Wm Sinclair, U S N, Charleston, S C.

Wm Lee is appt'd Accountant of the War Dept, in place of the late Col Lear. [Lee is late Cnsl at Bordeaux.]

Wash Co, D C. Geo St Clare, of said co, brought before me a stray horse. -Thos Fenwick, J P.

THU JAN 30, 1817
Persons appt'd on Mon last, to be Dirs & Cashiers of the Branch Banks of the U S, in Wash, Cinc, Ohio, & Lexington, Ky:
Wash
Richd Cutts	Thos Munroe	B Thruston
R C Weightman	G Bomford	G Graham
Wm Brent	Thos Tudor Tucker	J Deane, Alexandria
Thos Swann, Alex	W Smith, Gtwn	W S Chandler, Gtwn
Richd Parrott, Gtwn	Richd Smith-cshr	

Cinc:
Martin Baum	Jacob Burnett	Jas Findlay
Danl Drake	Jas Riddle	John H Piatt
David K Estee	Geo P Torrence	W Sterritt-Chllcth
John Sutherland	John S Gano	Hugh Glenn
Jas Keys	Garsham Worth, of Albany, cshr	

Lexington:
Jas Morrison	John W Hunt	Jas Prentis
Jas Taylor	John H Hana	Wm T Barry
John Tilford	John H Morton	John T Mason
Cuthbert Bullett	Wm Morton	A S Barton
Alex Parker		

J H Morton Salomon, of Phil, cshr.

Mrd: on Jan 28, by Rev Mr Balch, Mr Saml J Potts to Miss Mary Ann Ross, d/o Andrew Ross, of Gtwn, D C.

Orphans Crt of Wash Co, D C. Ltrs of adm on prsnl est of John King, late of said city, laborer, dec'd. -Bridget King, Admx.

FRI JAN 31, 1817
Mrd: on Jan 30, by Rev O B Brown, Mr Saml McIntire to Mrs Ruth Lord, both of Wash City.

For sale-I offer for sale my dwlg hse & land in the village of Pittsfield; also farm of 160 acs; also 156 acs. -Tho B Strong, Pittsfield, Berkshire Co, Mass.

SAT FEB 1, 1817
Mrd: on Jan 28, in Gtwn, Mr Richd M'Sherry, of Jefferson Co, to Miss Ann King, d/o Mr Geo King, of Gtwn.

Va Land Ofc, Jan 1817. Subj-rl est of John McLoud, an alien, died seized & possessed of; 4 1/2 acs in Chesterfield Co, cnvyd to McLoud, by Robt Anderson,

Oct 20, 1814; 2 half ac lots in Manchester, with 7 hses thereon; adj the lots of Kennon Jiles & others, cnvyd by John Archer [srvg trustee of Geo Robertson & John Archer] to said McLoud on May 30; adj the lot of Robt Grayham & others, cnvyd to said McL from Branch T Archer, May 1, 1811. -Wm G Pendleton, reg.

MON FEB 3, 1817
For sale-*Bassenheim Est*, on the Conaquenassing crk, partly in Butler & partly in Beaver cos, Pa; 6,000 acs; mansion hse is about 70' x 30'. Info from Mr Hekenwalder, at Bethlehem, Andrews & Elliott, 61 Chestnut st, Phil, or the Prop. -Dettmar Basse, at Bassenheim. [Acquainted with same: Henry Baldwin, Sutton & M'Nickle, Wm B Foster, A Beelen, Jos Patterson, Morgan Neville, Wm Wilkins.]

TUE FEB 4, 1817
Pblc sale: order of Orphans Crt of PG Co, Md; about 50 slaves, at the plantation now occupied by Dr Richd T Hall, 6 miles below Nottingham, adj the late residence of Mr Rinaldo Johnson. -Jos Kent, adm d b n of Rinaldo Johnson.

WED FEB 5, 1817
Hse o/Reps. 1-Petition of Cath Young, m/o Dr John Young, jr, dec'd, lately surg of U S ship *Peacock*, praying for a pension. 2-Pet of Christiana Ulmer, wid/o Philip Ulmer, dec'd, praying for a pension. 3-Pet of Montjoy Bayly, an ofcr in Rev army, praying for a grant of land. 4-Pet of Sarah Atkinson, wid/o Wm Atkinson, a sldr in Rev army, praying for a pension.

Six cents reward for runaway, appr girl, Ailcey McCormick, about 13 yrs of age. -Thos Murray, Wash City.

Carpenters tools & hrdware for sale. Henry Hazel, Bridge & High sts, Gtwn.

THU FEB 6, 1817
The Reading Room in Wash City is closed. -Wm Prentiss

$20 reward. Ranaway from the subscriber, lvg nr Queen Ann, PG Co, Md, on Jan 25, negro, Jim; about 33 yrs of age. He was raised by Mr Leonard Soper, [now dec'd,] nr the Eastern Branch Bridge, where he has a fr & other relations. -John Jinkins

Fresh Groceries. -C Carlilse & Co, Gtwn.

For sale-Jordan's Htl. -Dillon Jordan, Fayetteville, N C.

FRI FEB 7, 1817
New Eng potatoes, groceries, etc, for sale. -Joel Cruttenden, Gtwn.

SAT FEB 8, 1817
Mrd: on Feb 4, in PG Co, Md, by Rev Mr Vergennes, Lt Edmund Brooke, U S M C, to Miss Ellen M Young, only d/o Benj Young, dec'd, of PG Co, Md.

Mrd: in Alexandria, on Feb 6, by Rev Mr Breckenridge, Mr Jas W Johnson, of Wash City, to Mrs Rachel Dobbins, of Alexandria.

MON FEB 10, 1817
Mrd: on Feb 6, by Rev Mr Montgomery, Walter McDaniel to Sarah Cannon, both of Wash City.

Mrd: by Rev Wm Clingan, Dr Joshua Hickman to Miss Eliz Perry, d/o Erasmus Perry, all of Montg Co, Md. [no date-recent]

Died: in Marietta, Ohio, on Jan 18, in his 61st yr, Gen Jos Wilcox, a ntv of Killingsworth, Conn; ofcr in the army of the Rev.

TUE FEB 11, 1817
John C Heise & Co, wholesale & retail confectioners & distillers; so crnr of Green & Bridge sts, Gtwn.

WED FEB 12, 1817
To Col Gabriel Slaughter & Wm Hord, of Ky. Take notice that on Mar 3, 1817, we shall have the nuncupative will of Hawkins Hord, dec'd, recorded in the Pr Wm Co, Va, crt. -Thos Hord, Robt Hord.

THU FEB 13, 1817
Detroit, Jan 4, 1817. Died: Mrs Emily M Larned, w/o Geo B Larned, & d/o Elkanah Watson, of Albany, N Y; a resident here but a few months.

FRI FEB 14, 1817
For sale-the *Farm*, on which I lately resided; nr Baton Rouge, Miss; adj the plantation of Fulwar Skipwith; 700 acs; with ferry-profits $500 per annum. Terms apply to Skipwith; or Gen David H Morgan, at Madisonville, at Cheponeta, or the undersigned, at Wash. -Wm Dewees.

Hse o/Reps. 1-Act directing the discharge of Oliver Spellman from imprisonment in a goal in R I. 2-Act directing the discharge of John Ricaus from imprisonment, in the jail at Balt; late pay-mstr of 36th regt of Infty.

Mrd: on Feb 12, by Rev Mr Balch, of Gtwn, Columbia, Mr Chas Cruikshank to Miss Martha Brown, of the same place.

Mrd: on Thu evening last, by Rev Mr McCormick, Mr Stuart G Thornton, of Va, to Miss Mary F A Stuart, of Chas Co, Md.

Died: in Charleston, S C, on Feb 4, Mr John Peltz, late a respectable inhabitant of Wash City.

SAT FEB 15, 1817
Lots for sale on Pa av, in sq 226, Wash. -John Murdoch, Gtwn.

Died: at Balt, on Feb 11, Mrs Eliza Brent, w/o Robt Young Brent, of Wash City; after a long & severe illness.

MON FEB 17, 1817

Fancy Hardward Store on King st, Alexandria, Va. -Thos Mount

Info wanted of a widow. Hector Holcomb, of N Y, who srvd on board Cmdor Perry's fleet, was lost in 1813 or 14, leaving a widow & child, who are now in distress. She needs to know the cause of her hsbnd's death. Communicate same to Mr Michl Nourse, of Wash.

Wash Co, D C, in Chancery. Wm Bryden vs Jas Bryden. Ratify trustee sale of prop to Andrew Way, jr, for $3,301. -Wm Brent, clk.

TUE FEB 18, 1817

Mrd: on Feb 16, by Rev Mr McCormick, Mr Levi Tarman to Miss Leona Turton, both of PG Co, Md.

Absconded on Thu, negro girl, Betty, age 12 yrs. -I K Hanson, F st, Wash City.

$50 reward for runaway, black woman named Phillis, formerly the prop of the late Capt Richd Stonestreet. She has a free hsbnd, Wm Adams. -Jos N Stonestreet, lvg in Cornwallis Neck, Chas Co, Md.

WED FEB 19, 1817

Died: on Feb 13, at Alexandria, Mr Ferdinand Marsteler.

Tuition. $400, board, washing & lodging will be given to a gentleman to take charge of a private School. -Wm Chiswell, nr Poolesville, Montg Co, Md.

THU FEB 20, 1817

Mrd: on Feb 18, in Wash City, by Rev Mr Matthews, Mr Overton P Lipssomb, of Richmond, to Miss Mary Ann Dillon, of Wash City.

Mrd: on Feb 18, by Rev Mr Hyatt, Lt Jos Cross, of the Navy, to Miss Cecilia Duval, d/o the late Chas Duval, of PG Co, Md.

For sale-my land in Allegany Co, Md; 17,000 acs; a small part is in Pa; some nr Mr Jesse Tomlinson's. -Thos Johnson, nr Fredericktown.

Copartnership bet Henry Taylor & Z C Chesley [Henry Taylor & Co] is dissolved by mutual consent. In the future the firm will be John Dix & Co, at the late store of Henry Taylor & Co. -John Dix, Z C Chesley.

The subscriber has obtained ltrs of adm on the prsnl est of Wm Orme, late of Berkley Co, Va, dec'd. -Jas Orme, Berkley Co, Va.

For sale-3 black women, with 7 chldrn. -B B Beall, So of the Seven Bldgs, Wash.

Orphans Crt of Calvert Co, Md. Ltrs test on the prsnl est of Wm Weems, late of said co, dec'd. -Elijah Weems

FRI FEB 21, 1817
Mrd: in Wash City, on Feb 18, by Rev Mr Matthews, Mr Fred'k Miller, Printer, of N Y, to Miss Mary Ann Johnson, of Wash City.

For sale-*Benfield*, Chas Co, Md, about 1,000 acs. Also, tracts *Grange* & the *Mill Farm*, together about 1,000 acs. *Grange Farm* has a lg & elegant mansion; in residence of 22 yrs, no mbr o/the family o/the present prop has ever been attacked by an intermittent or fall fever of any kind. -H Newman, Grange, Port Tobacco, Md.

For sale-the est in Benedict, Md, late the prop of John Forbes, dec'd, comprising the town, [with the exception of 3 lots,] & 80 or 100 acs attached thereto. -Horatio C McEldery

For sale-part of the rl est of the late David Slater, dec'd-200 acs; adjoins the land of Dr Jos Kent, who will show same. -Sarah Slater, admx, PG Co, Md.

For sale-about 35 acs of land, bordering on the Corp line of Gtwn, & adj Mr John Threlkeld's, fronting on Fredericktown rd. Apply to Mr Francis Fenwick, Gtwn, or to Jos West, Gtwn College. -Jos West

SAT FEB 22, 1817
Hse o/Reps. 1-Resolution to employ John Trumbull, of Conn, to compose & execute 4 paintings commemorative of the Americ Rev, to be placed in the Capitol of the U S. 2-Act for relief of Henry Malcolm, Coll of the customs for Dist of Hudson, N Y, the sum of $1,000; money lost in its transmission from Hudson to N Y C, in the mail.

Mrd: on Feb 20, by Rev Mr Addison, Josias Wilson King to Miss Cath Whetcroft, both of Wash City.

Died: at Pomfret, Conn, a few days ago, Hon Sylvanus Backus, a Rep elect to Cong from Conn.

For sale-*Rosedale*, the residence of the subscriber, about 126 + acs of land on the Fred'k Rd, above Gtwn; lg dwlg hse, etc. -Rebecca Forest

MON FEB 24, 1817
We, the subscribers, inhabitants of Westchester Co, certify that during the Rev war we were well acquainted with Isaac Van Wart, David Williams & John Paulding, who arrested Maj Andre. [Van Wart is of Mt Pleasant, Westchester Co.]
Jonathan G Tompkins, aged 81   Jacob Purdy, aged 77
John Odell, aged 60   John Boyce, aged 72
J Requa, aged 57   Wm Paulding, aged 81

John Requa, aged 54
Geo Comb, aged 72
Jonathan Odell-age 87
Thos Boyce, aged 71
Jacobus Dyckman, aged 68
John Romer

Archer Read, aged 64
Gilbert Dean, age 70
Cornelius Vant Tassel, aged 71
Tunis Lint, aged 71
Wm Hammond
-N Y Courier

For sale-about 300 acs, adj Hatton's land & Wm Dudley Digges' land; bet Piscataway & Ft Waburton, etc. -Thos A Digges, Warburton, Md.

$50 reward for negro fellow, Joe, who broke Stafford jail on Jan 5. -Hugh Adie, nr Dumfries, Va.

TUE FEB 25, 1817
Died: at *Belmont*, his seat in Wayne Co, Pa, on Feb 10, in the bosom of his family, after a painful illness, Saml Meredith, aged 76 yrs, formerly Treas of the U S.

Dissolution of copartnership under firm of Warten & Smith, carpenters. -Chas Warten

WED FEB 26, 1817
Calvert Co, Md, in Chancery. Sale of plantation whereon Frances Hance, dec'd, formerly lived; immediate possession given, 420 acs; 2 frame dwlg hses, etc. Will be shewn by Mr John Hance, residing thereon. -Benj H Mackall, trustee.

THU FEB 27, 1817
Charleston, Feb. On Feb 3, a sailing boat, on board were Messrs Jas T Coit, Edw Drayton, [of Barbadoes] & Capt Wm Hall, with 3 black men; upset in St Mary's rvr, by a sudden flaw of wind; Mr Hall alone survived. Mr Drayton has left a widow & 2 infant chldrn.

$50 reward for negro man named Sandy, who eloped from the plantation of John Osburn, in Loudoun Co, Va, nr Hillsboro, on Oct 15; formerly the prop of Abraham Young, dec'd, of Wash City; has a mthr, bros & srs in that neighborhood. -Balaam Osburn, lvg in Loudon Co, Va, nr Hillsboro.

For sale-carriages, etc, at the shop formerly occupied by John C Baum, Wash st, Gtwn. -Henry Buddick

$25 reward for negro slave, Ben, age 19. -Eden Edmonston, lvg in Montg Co, Md.

Wash Co, D C. Robt Clarke, insolvent debtor, confined in Wash Co prison, for debt. -Wm Brent, clk.

FRI FEB 28, 1817
Hse o/Reps. 1-Petition of Ann Feran, for wages due her son, John Feran, sailor in the U S N, lost in the brig *Epervier*. 2-Pet of Jas Donaher, praying for a pension, for svcs as sldr in Rev army. 3-Pet of Elias Ware, sldr in Rev army, praying for a

pension. 4-An act that money to be pd to Saml Jennison, of St Mary's Co, Md, or to his legal reps, shall be pd to Saml Tennison, his legal rep o/said Co. 5-An act for the relief of Jacint Laval, late of the U S army. 6-An act for the relief of Geo T Ross & Danl T Patterson, & ofcrs & men lately under their command.

I will sell 46 acs of *Cool Stream Farm*, joining the Eastern border of Wash City. -John McLeod, teacher.

SAT MAR 1, 1817

My prop for sale-3 frame hses in sq 908 on 8th st, Wash. -P Kain

Hse o/Reps. 1-Petition of Park Holland, confined in prison at Castine, Maine, praying to be released. 2-Pet of Fred'k P Stevenson, to be placed on the pension list. 3-Pet of Henry Weist, comp for carrying the mail from Balt, Md, to Carlisle, Pa, during one yr ending on Sep 30, 1804. 5-Pet of Jos Mims & Hannah Mims, adms of est of Saml Mims, dec'd; to be pd for prop of their intestate, destroyed by the Indians during the late war. 6-Pet of Saml Hughes, prop of a cannon foundery in Hartford Co, Md, praying to be pd for damages done to said foundery by the British during the late war. 7-Pet of Francis Henderson, for himself & heirs of John Lawrens, dec'd, a lt Col in the Rev army; comp for svcs.

Died: in PG Co, Md, on Feb 28, Archibald Van Horn, formerly a Rep in Cong from that dist.

Orphans Crt of Wash Co, D C. Ltrs of adm on prsnl est of Haulder N Spooner, late of said city, dec'd. -Mary Spooner, admx.

MON MAR 3, 1817

Wm D Robinson, reported to have been killed in So Americ, was not killed, but taken prisoner.

One cent & a calf's head reward-for runaway, Dicker Folson, appr to the butcher business. -John Dunning, Capitol Hill, Pa av, Wash.

TUE MAR 4, 1817

$50 reward for runaway, negro man named Sam, age about 25 yrs, blacksmith. -Bushrod Washington, Mt Vernon, nr Alexandria.

For sale-120+ acs in Westmoreland Co, Va, adj the land of Mr Danl Payne. Apply to Capt Robt S Hipkins, at *Bleak Hall*, nr the premises. Mr Lankin who lives nrby will shew it. -Bushrod Washington.

For sale-the farm whereon Maj Wm Woodland lately resided; 243 acs in Kent Co, Md; with dwlg hse, etc. Apply to Maj Wm Woodland, Fell's Point, Mr Thos Macilroy, Smith's wharf, or to Wm Grynn, trustee, at the Fed Gaz ofc.

Jos Walker, hrdware store & black smith shop on 13th st, Wash.

WED MAR 5, 1817
Prop for sale-*Clifton*, 530 acs, about 3 miles east of the Blue Ridge Mtns; with dwlg hse; est upon which I reside; Loudon Co, Va; intending to leave the U S next summer, absent 2 to 3 yrs. Also, 2 farms in Piedmont Manor; also land cld *Wakefield*, Culpeper Co, Va, 4,128 acs with 28 tenants, whose leases expire on Dec 7, 1818; tract adj *Wakefield*, about 3,500 acs; land in Madison Co, Va, 450 acs; land in Green Briar Co, Va, 4,104 acs; 2 hses in Charlestown, Jefferson Co, Va; svr'l tracts of land in Ky, totaling about 36,000acs. Apply to the subscriber, during the present session of Cong, at Wash City, afterwards at his residence in Loudoun Co, Va. -Jos Lewis, jr

$50 reward for runaway, Isaac Thomas, a mulatto man; age about 21 yrs. -Ruth Williams, lvg nr Vansville, PG Co, Md.

THU MAR 6, 1817
Wm Wirt is engaged in writing the life of Patrick Henry.

Sir Harry, the celebrated Eng race horse, will stand at *Oaklands*, the farm of Col Ridgeley, 13 miles from Balt, Md. -B B Crawford, mgr, *Oaklands*.

Some of the Acts passed at the 2d session of the 14th Cong-just closed;-relief of:

Nathl Williams	Nathl Taft	Wm Haslett
John Ricaud	Oliver Spellman	Jos Stewart
Henry Malcolm	Jacint Laval	Geo T Ross &
Danl Patterson	Lewis Olmsted	Alec'r Holmes & Benj Hough
Peter Kendall	John De Castanado	Mary Wells
Jas H Boisgervais	Wm Oliver	Francis Cazeau
Wm Smith	Peter Hagrer	Henry Lee
Robt Burnside	Journonville de Villiers	Jos Summers & John Allen
Chas Williams	Geo Buckmaster	Wid & chld of Abr'm Owen
Caleb Nicholls	Peyton Short	Madame Montrieul
Jos I Green	Jas Villere	Isaac Lawrence
Anthony Buck	Asa Wells	Teacle Savage
Wid & chld of Arnold H Dohrman		Wm Chism

FRI MAR 7, 1817
Notice-I forewarn all persons against receiving an assignment of my note drawn in favor of Wm O Howsar, dt'd Mar 3, 1817, for $100, as said note was obtained by fraud & imposture. -Harriot Brooke, PG Co, Md.

Died: on Mar 4, after a short illness, Hon Jos Hopper Nicholson, aged 47, Chf Judge of the 6th Judicial Dist, Md; leaving an affectionate wife & frless chldrn. -Patriot

$50 reward for runaway, Dangerfield, negro fellow about 30 yrs of age. Deliver to my overseer at Hilly Town Culpepper, Va. -John T Barbour, Culpepper Co, Va.

Appointments by the Pres:

Stephenson Archer, of Md, to be Additional Judge in the Miss Terr.
Jos Philips, late U S army, to be Sec of Ill Terr.
Reuben G Beasley, of Va, to be Cnsl at Havre de Grace.
Robt Trimble, of Ky, to be Judge of U S for Ky.
Henry Wilson, of Md, to be Cnsl at Nantz.
Edw Church, of Ky, to be Cnsl at L'Orient.

SAT MAR 8, 1817
John Melish, Geographer & Map Publisher, Phil, Pa. -Ad

MON MAR 10, 1817
Appointments by the Pres:
Bathurst Dangerfield, of Alexandria, to be srvyr & inspec of rev for Alexandria.
Chas Pelham, of Ky, to be srvyr of port of Limestone, Ky.

Promotions in the Navy confirmed by the Senate since Mar 4.
Mstr Cmdant to be Capts:

Edw Trenchard	John Downes	John D Henley

Lts to be Mstr Cmndnt:

Jos J Nicholson	Walter Stewart	John H Elton
Edmund P Kennedy	Alex'r J Dallas	John B Nicolson
Beekman V Hoffman		

Sailing Mstrs to be Lts:

Jas Trant	Uriah P Levy

Mdshpmen to be Lts:

Enoch H Johns	Chas Lacey	Wm Arthur Lee
Clement W Stevens	Chas Boarman	French Forrest
Edgar Freeman	Thos A Tippett	Wm E McKenney
Edw Greenwell	Wm J Belt	Chas H Caldwell
Wm Jameson	Jas W H Ray	Wm Boerum
Ch L Williamson	Wm R Ramsay	Chas Gaunt
Ralph Voorhees	Jas B Taylor	Robt E Searcy
Thos A Conover	Jas Nicholson	Archd S Campbell
Wm Taylor	Thos H Bowyer	Alex'r Eskridge
Ebenezer Ridgeway	Geo W Isaacs	John D Fischer
Henry R Warner	John H Graham	John C Long
Nathl Carter, jr	Henry Ward	

Info wanted of Signor Valaperta, employed as a sculptor for the yr past at the Capitol, absented himself from his lodgings on Tue last, & has not been heard of since. He left in his apartment a will, & it is feared, by his friends, that he has destroyed himself. Communicate to the ofc of the Ntl Intell.

Drowned: in the Miss, Maj Horace Stark, U S army, & 4 others, in crossing the rvr in a skiff, nr St Louis.

Died: in London, on Dec 12 last, at a very advanced age, Col John Hamilton, formerly Cnsl of his Brit maj to Va, where he resided during the period of his cnslr duties in Norfolk.

Wash Co, D C. Wm H Smith, insolvent debtor, confined in Wash Co prison, for debt. -Wm Brent, clk.

TUE MAR 11, 1817
Sale at auction-the prop which Mr John Hagerty now occupies, on Bridge st. -John Travers, auct.

Promotions in the army by the Pres. since Jan 1 last:
Light Artl: 1st Lt Wm F Hobart, to Capt, Jan 1, 1817.
1st Lt Geo N Morris, to Capt, Jan 15, 1817.
2d Lt Elijah Lyon, to 1st Lt, Jan 1, 1817.
2d Lt Saml Washburn, to 1st Lt, Jan 15, 1817.
Bvt 2d Lt Thos I Gardner, to 2d Lt, Jan 1, 1817.
Bvt 2d Lt B L E Bonneville, to 2d Lt Jan 15, 1817.
1st Regt of Infty: 2d Lt Thos Rogers, to 1st Lt, Oct 31, 1816.
3d Regt of Infty: 1st Lt Jas Hackley, to Capt, May 17, 1816.
2d Lt Asher Philips, to 1st Lt, May 17, 1816.
4th Regt of Infty: 1st Lt Wm Neilson, to Capt, Dec 1, 1816.
2d Lt Philip Wager, to 1st Lt, Dec 1, 1816.
2d Lt Jos Shommo, to 1st Lt Dec 31, 1816.
2d Lt Henry Wilson, to 1st Lt, Dec 31, 1816.
2d Lt Geo B M'Claskey, to 1st Lt, Dec 31, 1816.
5th Regt of Infty: 1st Lt Henry Whiting, to Capt, Mar 3, 1817.
2d Lt Nathan Clark, to 1st Lt, Mar 3, 1817.
7th Regt of Infty:2d Lt Jos W Allston, to 1st Lt, Dec 20, 1816.
2d Lt Robt H Goodwyn, to 1st Lt, Feb 1, 1817.
8th Regt of Infty: 1st Lt David Riddle, to Capt, Dec 3, 1816.
2d Lt Chas Stevens, to 1st Lt, Dec 3, 1816.
Appointments: Claude Crozet to be Prof of Engr at Military Acad, Mar 6, 1817.
Capt Wm Tell Pousin to be Assist Topo Engr, Mar 6, 1817.
Abraham Wendell to be 2d Lt in 3d Infty, Mar 5, 1817.
Henry R Dulany to be 2d Lt in 4th Infty, Mar 5, 1817.
Martin Thomas to be 3d Lt of Ord, Mar 5, 1817.
-By order, D Parker, Adj & Ins Gen.

Wash Co, D C. Case of Mgt Mackey, insolvent debtor, confined in Wash Co prison, for debt. -Wm Brent, clk.

Wanted-a youth about 14 yrs old as an appr to the paper hanging business. Apply to Stephen Franklin, at A Coyles.

For sale, by deed of trust from Wm Hebb, assignment in trust from Wm Small; land in St Mary's Co, Md, cld *Chilton's Outlet*, on which Small resides; adjs the lands of Jos Booth & Wm Cocking; about 215 acs. -John Murdoch, Gtwn.

THU MAR 13, 1817
Hse o/Reps. 1-Act for the relief of the Rachel Dohrman, widow, & chldrn of Arnold Henry Dohrman, dec'd, late of Steubensville, Ohio; $300 annually during her life, from Dec 31, 1816. Also, $100 for minor chldrn, payable quarterly. 2-Act for relief of Asa Wells, $488, 95; his costs as ofcr of the U S. 3-Act for relief of Caleb Nicholls, for damages to his hse & store, under orders of Gen McComb, in Sep, 1814, at Plattsburgh, N Y.

St Mary's co Crt, [Md] Mar Term, 1817. Pet of Robt Cole & Ann Cole, his wife, 2 of the reps of Eleanor Cooper, late of said co, dec'd; division of said rl est wld not admit to division. Henry Knott & Cath, his wife, & Robt Fenwick, 3 of the reps, do not reside in Md. -Jo Harris, clk.

FRI MAR 14, 1817
Sketch of Alex'r Jas Dallas; b on Jun 21, 1759, in island of Jamaica; s/o Robt Dallas, a ntv of Scotland, wealthy physician in said island. In 1780 he mrd a lady of Devonshire, Eng. In 1781, after the death of his fr, he left Eng, for Jamaica, with his wife; he found that Dr Dallas' widow had mrd again, & no part of the prop ever came to the rest of the family. He left Jamaica in Apr, 1783, arriving in Phil in the same yr. He died at Trenton, of gout in his stomach, on Jan 16, 1817. Geo M Dallas, o/Phil, s/o Alex'r Jas Dallas, intends to write the biog of his fr.

Notice-stray steer came to my premises last Oct. Giles Hill, lvg nr the Anacosta bridge, Wash.

For sale-parcel of land adjs the lands of Col Geo Minor & Wm Minor, 6 miles from Gtwn. -G W Lane, Centreville, Va.

SAT MAR 15, 1817
PG Co Crt, [Md] Sep Term, 1816. Pet of Jasper M Jackson, for division of rl est of John Jackson; cannot be divided; some reps reside out o/Md. J R Magruder, clk.

MON MAR 17, 1817
Hse o/Reps. 1-Act granting a pension to Cmdor Richd Taylor; $300 per annum; total disability from a wound rec'd in the Rev war. 2-Act for legal reps of John J Yarnall, dec'd, late a lt in the U S N.

Mrd: on Mar 13, Mr Saml Hanson to Miss Eleanor Bayly, d/o Gen Mountjoy Bayly, all of Wash City.

Mrd: on Mar 16, in Gtwn, by Rev Mr M'Cormick, Wm Gamble, Cnsl of the U S at St Eustatia, to Miss Ann Lee, of Blenheim, Chas Co, Md.

TUE MAR 18, 1817
Mrd: on Mar 11, at *Bellville*, the seat of Col John Mayo, by Rev John Buchannan, Gen Winfield Scott, U S army, to Miss Maria D Mayo, the eldest d/o Col Mayo.

$10 reward for runaway, Michl Herrity, aged 20 yrs, appr to shoe mkg business. -Nicholas Cassady, nr the Navy Yd.

WED MAR 19, 1817
Invalid pensioners of the U S, rates & commencing at times stated:

Johnson Cook	$4 per mo	Nov 27, 1816
Jos Wilkinson	$8 per mo	Dec 23, 1816
Wm Maxwell	$4 per mo	Oct 8, 1816
Elisha Lester	$8 per mo	Nov 5, 1816
Danl Collomy	$4 per mo	Aug 1, 1816
Benj Haile	$4 per mo	Dec 5, 1815
John Haney	$4 per mo	Oct 15, 1816
Uriah Warren	$4 per mo	Dec 5, 1816
Jonathan D Carrier	$4 per mo	Feb 28, 1816
John Myers	$5.33 1/3 per mo	Nov 15, 1816
Jas Newberry	$4 per mo	Apr 19, 1816
Wm Arnold	$4 per mo	Oct 23, 1816
R J Lowry	$8.50 per mo	Feb 11, 1816
Jesse M'Annally	$8 per mo	Jul 18, 1814
Apheus Hill	$8 per mo	Jan 1, 1816
Leroy Jones	$5.32 per mo	Nov 5, 1816
Wm Wilson	$4 per mo	Nov 5, 1816
John M'Clure	$4 per mo	Sep 10, 1816
Robt Warrel	$8 per mo	Sep 9, 1816
Wm Carter	$5.33 per mo	Oct 7, 1816
Wm English	$8 per mo	Sep 9, 1816
Henry Doherty	$4 per mo	Oct 7, 1816
Geo Hendrick	$4 per mo	Oct 7, 1816
John Hinkson	$4 per mo	Sep 20, 1816
Jeptha Brown	$4 per mo	Dec 14, 1816
John Miller	$8 per mo	Jan 2, 1817
Aaron Stafford	$5.33 per mo	Jan 8, 1817
Elias Ware	$4 per mo	Jan 16, 1817
Daniel Moffett	$4 per mo	Aug 25, 1815
Fred'k P Stevenson	$8.50 per mo	Jan 6, 1817
Sion Holly	$5.33 per mo	Feb 28, 1816
Robt Lyon	$4 per mo	Nov 8, 1815
Henry Turner	$5.33 per mo	Dec 7, 1816
Mark Miller	$4 per mo	Dec 16, 1815
Geo G Grettin	$2.66 per mo	Feb 1, 1817
Glover Baker	$2 per mo	Feb 1, 1817
Nathan Crosby	$4 per mo	Feb 14, 1817
Jas Heard	$8.50 per mo	Feb 20, 1817
Joshua Penny	$6 per mo	Feb 20, 1817
Enoch Barnum	$8 per mo	Jan 1, 1817
Malye Baker	$4 per mo	Jan 1, 1817
Reuben Thacker	$4 per mo	Jan 1, 1817

Pensioners-to be increased in lieu of present pension:

Nicholas Welsh $25 per mo   Jun 13, 1815
Geo Shannon $12 per mo   Sep 11, 1816

Mrd: at Norfolk, on Mar 13, by Rev Mr Low, Capt Lewis Warrington, U S N, to Miss Carey King, d/o the late Miles King, of Norfolk.

Hse o/Reps. 1-Act for the settlement of the accounts of Lt Flavil Sabin, dec'd, with his adm, Jos Holland. 2-Act for the relief of Park Holland, to be dischg'd from prison at Castine. 3-An act freeing from postage all ltrs & packets to & from Jas Madison, now Pres of the U S.

THU MAR 20, 1817

Lost-Treas note dt'd Nov 11, 1814, for $100; endorsed to Henry M Cooke, Coll of the Port of Beaufort, N C, & by him endorsed to the subscriber. The note was lost at sea by Capt John Rumley, in Sep 1815. -Jas Manney, Beaufort, N C.

Died: on Mar 14, at Lancaster, at an advanced age, Hon Jasper Yeates, one of the Judges to the Sup Crt of Pa.

FRI MAR 21, 1817

Hse o/Reps. 1-Act for relief of the legal reps of Ignace Chalmet Delino, dec'd, & of Anthony Cruzat & L P Deverges; for destruction of prop nr New Orleans. 2-Relief of Mary Wells, excx of Wm Wells, for corn taken by order of Gen Wm H Harrison, for use of the U S army. 3-Act for Geo Buckmaster, for whale boats furnished the U S at N Y, by order of Gen Geo Izard; settlement of val of said boats.

SAT MAR 22, 1817

Petition of 14 Americans, now confined in the prison of St Jago de Cuba, to the Pres of the U S; beg for the mercies of a free country, for which we fought & valiantly conquered our enemies.

John H Buckley, Nantucket	Denard Townsand, Norfolk
Thos Reed, N Y	Benj Brown, N Y
John Daviss, Newport	Wm Handey, N C
Geo Wilson, N Y	Jas Morress, Boston
John Bennett, Phil	John Jackson, Phil
John Anderson, N Orleans	John Dunkin, N Y
John Charles, N Orleans	Francis Barber, N Orleans

Mrd: in Wash City, on Mar 20, by Rev Mr Brown, Mr Jas Druett to Miss Susan Maul.

In Chancery. The Atty Genr'l of the State of Md at the ralation of John W Harris & Sarah his wife, against, Hanson & John Gassaway. Bill to vacate 2 patents improperly obtained by the dfndnts on *Deer Park & Walnut Ridge*, in Alleghany Co, Md, & to direct the same to the relator Sarah Harris. Nicholas Gassaway, May 9, 1792, obtained a warrant for 50 acs in said Co; executed on Oct 5, 1793-*Deer Park*, 107 acs; caution money pd on Apr 27, 1793; certificate assigned by Nicholas to his sister, Sarah Gassaway, now Sarah Harris. *Walnut Ridgeway* was srvyd for Thos Gassaway on Apr 23, 1792, for 80 acs; granted to him on Apr 4, 1792. [Assignments followed] Sarah was mrd to John W Harris-by the date Mar 22, 1810; Sarah assigned to Wm McMahon, in trust; McMahon assigned to Jeremiah Berry 3d, on Jul 4, 1815, etc. -Wm Kilty Chancellor; Thos H Bowie, Reg Cur Can.

$150 reward for runaway, Commodore, age 36 yrs, negro; has a wife & chldrn belonging to Mr Jas Sterling, nr Balt, Md. -Jacob Franklin, West Rvr, A A Co, Md.

MON MAR 24, 1817
Tannery for sale on Duke st, Alexandria; 4 acs with dwlg hse. -John McPherson & Son, Alexandria.

Sale by auction; the farm in Balt Co, Md, belonging to the est of the late Mr Hill Dorsey, cld *Dorsey's Manor*, 500 acs; & unfinished frame dwlg hse. Further info apply to John I Donaldson, 26 Chatham st. -Ridgely & Neilson, aucts, Balt, Md.

Orphans Crt of Montg Co, Md. Prsnl est of Geo Upton, late of said co, dec'd.
-Elley Reynolds

For sale-farm in Montg Co, Md, 500 acs with frame dwlg hse. -Benj Berry, PG Co, or to Robt B Beall, Wash City.

TUE MAR 25, 1817
Hse o/Reps. 1-Act for the relief of Alex'r Holmes & Benj Hough, for expences incurred in srvy in Mich terr; prevented by Indian hostility. 2-Act for relief of the widow & chldrn of Abraham Owen, late a vol aid de camp of Gen Wm H Harrison.

For sale; land in A A Co, Md; 400 acs; with frame dwlg hse, etc. Apply to H & I Gassaway, Wash City, or on the premises. -Amelia Gassaway.

Wash Hat Manufactory-nr the Navy yd, Wash City; in hse formerly occupied by Mr Wm O'Brien. -Merrit Tarlton

WED MAR 26, 1817
For sale-part of lot 6 in sq 491, being nrly 20 ft on Pa av, Wash; adjs the new brick hse of Mr Patrick Rogers. -Thos I Mudd, Gtwn.

Sealed proposals will be rec'd until Apr 10, for supplying the Marine Corps, at this place, with rations. -Franklin Wharton, Lt Col Comt of Marines. Hdq, Wash.

Thank you for the patronage I have rec'd at Bell Tvrn during my absence; Mrs Ann Bailey superintended with the aid of her young men during my absence at my residence in Va. Having a lease of Berkley Springs for the 2 yrs to come, I am compelled to attend in person at that place. -Robt Bailey

THU MAR 27, 1817
Chosen dirs of the Bank of Columbia for the ensuing yr:

John Mason	Jas Dunlop	Chas Worthington
John Threlkeld	Henry Foxall	John Cox
T L M'Kenney	John Ott	Thos Peter
John Rodgers	Danl Bussard	Thos Plater

Richd King, of Gtwn, recently fired his gun at 2 small boys; one is mortally wounded. King was committed to jail to await his trial. -Local Item

Wash City affairs, acts passed at the 3d session of the 14th Cncl: Money to Cornelius F De Krafft, for svcs. Acts to-Nicholas Queen; Chas S Ashworth; Jas Middleton. Resolution to license Geo Miller, Sr, & Wm Digges to make bricks.

Notice-the old establishment of John May, dec'd, tobacconist, on Prince st, is now carried on as Jonathan C May & Co. -Alexandria

Minister wanted at Wm & Mary parish, Chas Co, Md. [Prot Epis preferred.] - John B Hungerford, Reg; Allen's Fresh.

FRI MAR 28, 1817

Died: on Mar 22, in the 21st yr of her age, after a short but painful illness, Mrs Mgt Hill, consort of Chas Hill, of PG Co, Md; dght, wife & friend.

I will rent the hse on No C st, Wash City, in which I live. -Danl Brent.

John Peabody has commenced the auction & commission business, at his store, head of Bridge st, Gtwn. [Dry Goods]

Pblc sale-decree of Montg co crt, in chancery; land cld *Addition to Brook Grove*, part of *Fairhill*, or the R*srvy on Brook Park*, & part of *Brook Piney Grove*, late the prop of John Howse, dec'd, 391 acs. Also 95 acs of *Ray's Adventure*; also 2 acs nrby, all the prop of the dec'd. -Edw Howse, trustee, Montg Co, Md.

SAT MAR 29, 1817

Mrd: in Wash City, on Mar 27, by Rev Mr Matthews, Hon Isham Talbot, a Senator of the U S from Ky, to Miss Adelaide Thomason.

Died: in Wilmington, N C, on Wed wk, Mr Saml Hardinge, Comedian, formerly of the Phil & Charleston Theatres.

For sale-46 acs of *Cool Stream Farm*, adj the Eastern border of Wash City, one mile from the Capitol. -John McLeod, teacher.

For sale or exchange-for property in an eligible part of Wash City, 350 acs of land in Alleghany Co, Md, cld *Rsrvy on St Geo*. Also a tract cld *Mill Seat*, 50 acs. Mr Amos Robinett, residing on Murley's Branch, Alleg Co, will show the latter. -H & I Gassaway, Wash City.

MON MAR 31, 1817
Died: at N Y, on Mar 26, Maj Gen Peter Curtenius, aged 55 yrs.

Fishermen attend! Sale at the Commercial Wharf, 1 sail boat, decked; one keel barge, open; rigging, etc. -Mary Spooner, admx of Holder N Spooner, dec'd.

TUE APR 1, 1817
Patent Water Wheel: Benj Thomas, Wash City.

Distressed seamen sent from London by the Americ Cnsl; no papers to prove their freedom; lost black & persons of color; arv'd on Feb 24 last, in the brig *Samoset*. John Little, alias Jas Brown, age 33, b at Duck Creek Cross Rds, Dela. Jos Stoddert, 31, b at Norfolk, Va; known to Capt Pennock, Mr Myers, & Mr Thos Willup, all of that city. Adam Campbell, 25, b at N Y, lvd in Annapolis, Md with Mr Boardman. John Dolboy, alias Sam Crump, 20, b at St Bartholemews, W Indies. Moses Coe, 21, b at Rye, N Y; well know to Mr Drake Seymour, of that place. Titus Delancy, 28, b in Stanford, Conn. John Thomas, 25, b at L I, N Y, is known to Mr Abraham Croll, Water st. John Williams, b in Chas Co, Va; his mthr is Betty Carter; he was apprenticed to Chas Wilson, wheelright, & he has a bro, Chas Carter, known as race rider. Chas Primus, 28, left the U S about 8 yrs ago when he was apprenticed to Mr Jonathan Tresby. Austin Hendricks, 28, b at Alexandria, D C, s/o Amy Sarcke; known by Mr Dagons Baker, King st, Alexandria. Henry Raymond, 26, b at N Y. Danl Ashby, 30, b in N Y. Wm Arlis, 33, b at Petersburg, Va. Jos Brown, 29, b at Marblehead, Mass. John Blake, b at Albany, N Y, of Indian breed. Thos Carter, has sailed from N Y & New Haven. Ben Dolman, alias Jas Smith, 22, b nr Northumberland crt hse, Va. Vincent Fowler, 30, b nr Amboy, in Jersey. John Hensley, alias Ansley, 29, b at N Y, appr to Benj Taylor, Providence, R I. Lemuel Patterson, 27, b in Balt Co, Md, srvd his time with Mr John Merryman. Geo Sims, 25, b nr Cinc, Ohio. Paul Thomas, 40, b at Portsmouth, Va. Henry Williams, 19, b free, in St Mary's Co, Md; Capt Jas Gardner, or his bro, Thos Gardner, can prove his freedom, & that they live nr Wicomico rvr, St Mary's Co, Md. -Othniel J Giles, city mrshl, Charleston, S C, Mar 5, 1817.

WED APR 2, 1817
For sale-fine farm on which Com Barney resided, Elk Ridge, A A Co, Md; with dwlg hse etc; 300 acs. -Nathl Williams, atty-at-law, Balt, Md.

Mrd: at Balt, on Mar 27, by Rev Dr Inglis, Mr Israel Peyton Thompson, of Alexandria, to Miss Angelica Robinson, 2d d/o Alex'r Robinson, of Balt, Md.

Wanted immediately at the marble quarry, on the Potomac, Montg Co, Md, 100 strong laboring men, by order of the Pres of the U S. Saml Lane, Com'r of the P B U S. Apply to: John Nelson, Fredericktown, Md. John Littlejohn, Leesburg, Va. Joshua Shelton, nr Conrad's Ferry, Loudon Co, Va; Maj Noland, at Aldie; Saml Clapham; John Hartnett, at the quarry.

To rent-lg establishment formerly occupied by Mr Jos Huddleston, at present occupied by Mrs Brush as a brdg hse; Pa av, Wash City. -W H Hamer

THU APR 3, 1817
Mrd: on Mar 19, at Ainwell, N J, by Rev Mr Kirkpatrick, Cmdor Thos Tingey, of the Navy, to Miss Anne Evelina Craven.

Orphans Crt of Chas Co, Md. Prsnl est of Mrs Sarah Russell Contee, late of said co, dec'd. -Philip Ashton Lee Contee, adm.

Wash Co, D C. 1-Case of Chas Warthen, insolvent debtor, confined in Wash Co prison, for debt. 2-Case of Henry Daws, do. -Wm Brent, clk.

FRI APR 4, 1817
Albany seed oats for sale at my store on High st, Gtwn. -Jas Beddo

Mrd: on Apr 3, by Rev Mr Ryland, Mr Robt M Harrison to Miss Susan A Harkness, all of Wash City.

Died: on Mar 19, Mrs Sarah Gardner, consort of Saml Gardner, of Strasburgh, Shenandoah Co, Va, in her 42d yr.

Sale of Wash City lots, for taxes, up to the yr 1816: [Jos Brumley-1st ward.]

John Allen	Benj Armitage
Jacob Boyer	Jas Beall o/Jas
Mathias Burkey	Jas Barcley & Jno Simpson
John Cunningham	Jno Callahan-heirs
Jas Crawford, jr	John Doll
Elias Davidson	Isaac Dewis
Geo French	John Freeman
Rev Mr Goulding	John Gannon
Michl Groff	John Hackott
Thos Johns	Philip B Keys-heirs
Jas Kirk	David Kemp
Lodwick Kruger	Henry Klinger
Nathan Luffborough	Thos Sim Lee
Wm M'Grath	Geo Murdoch
Eleanor Murdoch	Robt Moore
Wm M'Creery-heirs	Jas M'Henry
Luther Martin	Jacob Moyer
Lawrence O'Neale	Thos Pierce
Geo W Riggs	John & Andrew Rench
Danl Ragan	Sarah Ratcliffe
Geo Reeder	Chas Shell
Henry Shnebley	Geo Swingle
Walter Stewart	Henry Stall
John Southgate	Stoddert & Templeman
Jacob Thornton	Geo Thompson

Philip Thomas
John Templeman
Fred'k Wetsell
Jos W & Elisha Wilson
Cha's Weyman-heirs
Jacob Zeller

John Threlkeld
Abram Vanbibba
Applelonia Whitehair
Henry Walker or Walter
Levin Winder
Walter S Chandler

Germanic customs, from the Boston Daily Adv; from a file of the Hamburg Correspondenten. Births, deaths, marriages are uniformly done by an advertisement. 1-Marriage yesterday of F von Doring, of Badow, F von Doring-late von Doring. Kiel, Oct 11, 1816. 2-Mrd on Oct 30: H C Hander & Caroline Hander, late Caroline Prosch. 3-Mrd on the 3d: Hamburg, Nov 6, 1816; Anthony Christian Fred'k Orth, Margaretta Orth, late wid/o F W Sachse, formerly Schlichting. The wine selling business of the late F W Sachse, will be carried on by me, 35 Horse Mkt. Anthony Christian Fred'k Orth. 4-After a long & severe illness, our good fr, Geo Philip Seippel, expired on Oct 29, aged nrly 70 yrs. Hamburg, 1816. Geo Philip Seippel, son; John Philip Seippel, son; T E Seippel, late Kruckerberg, & D M Seippel, late Holm, daur's in law. 5-Died: Col Ulric Augustus von Randorff, royal Danish Chamberlain, suddenly, on the 27th. Ida Sophia Von Randorff, late I S Lepsten. Kiel, Oct 29, 1816. 6-Born: On the 12th inst, a healthy boy, dearly purchased by the death of my beloved wife, Anna Joanna Agatha, formerly Richards, which followed in a few hrs, age 25 yrs, nud one yr. Chas Wesselhooft, Royal Vice Cnsl of Gr Britain.

Wash Botanical Soc. Geo Watterston, Sec. [Local notice]

N Y Mar 29. Gen Curtenius was interred in the new Dutch chr yd, Nassau st, with military honors, yesterday. Among the pall bearers was Danl D Tompkins, V P.

SAT APR 5, 1817
Ladies with ltrs in the Wash P O, Apr 1, 1817:

Agonst Mrs	Brown Miss Polly	Bradley Mrs Nancy
Barry Miss Sealey	Billmier Mrs	Crago Miss Eliza
Downs Miss Jane	Ferris Mrs Ann	Forrest Mrs Jane
Fowler Miss Elenor	Grayham Mrs Priscilla	Gwynne Elie W
Hawley Miss Eliz	Izard Miss Patty	Jones Molly
Lynch Miss Jemimy	Marshall Mgt	Morris Miss Louisa
Moore Mrs Mgt	Mahonna Elenor	Preston Mrs Sarah B
Poel Miss Julien	Richison Miss Nancy	Simmons Mrs Ann
Redmond Mrs Teresa	Redmand Miss M B-3	Stewart Ann
Sanderford Miss Ann	Shaw Mrs Mary	Wadsworth Mrs E-4
Thornton Miss Martha	-Thos Munroe, Post Mstr	

$50 reward for Geo Carter, negro, absconded from Balt, Md. Apply to Felix Jenkins, So st, Balt, or John H Lancaster, lvg in Chas Co, Md.

MON APR 7, 1817
Persons indebted to the est of Bailey E Clark, late of Montg Co, Md, dec'd, to make payment to Abraham Clark. -Eliza Clark, excx of Baley E Clark, with w a.

Mrd: on Apr 5, by Rev Mr M'Cormick, Lloyd N Rogers, of Balt, to Miss Eliza Law, d/o Thos Law, of Wash City.

Mrd: in Wash City, on Mon last, by Rev Mr M'Cormick, Mr Jas Searl, of Phil, to Miss Eliza Ann Parry, of Wash City.

TUE APR 8, 1817
Wm H Fitzwhylsonn is elected Mayor of Richmond city, Va.

Col Appling, who greatly distinguished himself during the late war, died lately, at Ft Montg, Miss Terr.

Mrd: at Pope's Crk, in Westmoreland Co, Va, on Apr 1, by Rev Mr Norris, Maj Henry Lee, late of the U S army, to Miss Ann R McCarty, d/o the late Daniel McCarty, all of the same co.

Mrd: on Apr 3, at the residence of Thos Strachan, by Rev Mr Wilson, Lt John M Maury, U S N, to Miss Eliza Maury, d/o Fontaine Maury, of Fredericksburg.

Died: at his residence in Nottingham, PG Co, Md, on Apr 1, Geo Biscoe, aged 67 yrs; coll for the port of Nottingham, which station he has filled ever since the Rev war. For the last 12 yrs Mr B has been a constant invalid, laboring under excruciating pain. He has left a family & many friends.

WED APR 9, 1817
Mrd: on Apr 2, at Boston, Hon Jonathan Russell, Mnstr to Sweden, to Miss Lydia Smith, d/o Barney Smith.

Died: lately at Burch-hse, nr Bolton, Lancashire, Eng, aged 77, Rev Thos Taylor, the oldest preacher in the Wesleyan Meth connexion.

THU APR 10, 1817
Sale of Wash City lots, for taxes due. Wm Ingle, coll of 3d ward.

Thos Addison	Andrews & Polkinhorn
Richd Andrews, Emmory's heirs, & Adam Lynn	Alex'r Anderson
Henry Appleton	Bird & Co.
Abiel Blackney	Alex'r Buchan
Francis Boone	Clement Biddle
Wm Barkesdale	Benj Bacon-heirs
Thos C Bowie-heirs	Barnes & Rudgate
Wm Bean	Henry Bradford
John B Boardley	John Bassett
Miss Eliz Carrol	John Campbell
Jas Craig, M D	Overton Carr-heirs

Sam Coolidge-heirs
Chas Carroll, jr
Cyrus Cooper
Jacob Chandler
Mary Carroll
Judson Coolidge-heirs
Cath Connell
Wm Diggs
Cath Dalton
John Eden
Jas Earle
Job Fowler
Richd Fraham
Peter Hall
Robt T Hooe
Jonathan Hall
Jas Holliday
Thos Herty & Wm Fletcher
Jas Johnson, jr
Edw Langley
Francis Leake
Eliza Leidler
Wm Martin
Henry Nicholls
Jas Piercy
Jas Penrose
Nathl Philips
Alex'r Reed
David Ross
Mathew Ridley
Wm Semmes
Jonathan Swift
Chas Stewart
Mahlon Scholfield
Mathew Tilghman
Richd Tighman
John Travers
Thos Watkins
Henry Waring
Notley Young-heirs
Mary Young & E Carroll

Nathl Crawford-heirs
John Craig-heirs
Clagett & Mason
Saml Chases-heirs
Jos Carlton-heirs
Carroll, Young, & Oden
Dick & Stewart
Dunlop & Carlton
Henry Dearborn
Thos Ewell
Ign Fenwick-heirs
Thos Fenwick
Richd Henderson-heirs
Saml Hepburn-heirs
Maximilian Husler
Wm Harrison
Henry Hill
Danl Janifer
Francis Kirby
Andrew Leitch
Adam Lynn
Wm Lux
Jas Neill o/Bennett
Odien & Notley Young-heirs
Edw Parkinson
Jas Patton
Andrew Parke
Mary Rose
Wm Russell
Mary C Ringgold
John Story
John Smith
Jas Tilghman
Wm H Tilghman
Edw Tilghman
Peregrine Tilghman
Wm Veitch
Basil Waring
Geo S Washington
Jos Young
Miss Eliz Young

FRI APR 11, 1817
Mr A Huet has rented the frame hse belonging to Mr Varnum, next dr to his brick hse, where he intendes to keep a French School -Local ad.

SAT APR 12, 1817
Died: on Mar 23, at his residence on Savannah rvr, Barnwell Dist, S C, Aaron Smith, in his 59th yr; bore the toils of the Rev war. While lvg on the frontier of S C, his fr & mthr, a bro & sr were killed by the Indians; 3 bros, 1 sr, & himself escaped.

MON APR 14, 1817
$30 reward for a German Redemptioner, who arrived here in Nov last, Maurice Schumacher, age about 30 yrs; absconded on Apr 6; cabinet mkr, & a good German scholar, a Catholic Prof. -Jos K Stapleton, Brush mkr, 139 Balt st, Balt, Md.

TUE APR 15, 1817
Mrd: on Apr 10, by Rev Dr Muir, Geo Wise to Miss Mgt Greer, both o/Alexandria.

Sale of Wash City lots, for taxes. Harvey Bestor, coll 2d ward.

Theod Armstead	Wm Armstrong	John Appleton
Edw Burrows	Ralph Boarman	John Benson
Michl Brady	Wm Campbell	Dan Caffray-heirs
Wm Cammack	Barney Dulan	Dr Jas Davidson
John Davidson-heirs	Reuben Etting	Richd Graham
John Granbury	Lambert Hyland	John Heathcote
John E Housman	Chas Johnson	John King
Robt Kidd	Chas Loundes	Dominick Lynch

[Lynch & Sands, Saml Blodgett & Wm Deakin-heirs]

Danl or Gulian Ludlow	Jas McCormick, jr	Stephen Moylan
B G Minturn & I T Champlain		John McPhail
Morris & Nicholson-assignees		Wm P Mathews
John H Oswald	Oden & Burns-heirs	Benj Oden
Edw Plowden	Richd Powell	Isaac Pollock
Lawson Pierson	Pratt, Francis & others	Robt Pollard
Abigal Pollock	David Pollock	Walter Smith
Chas G Paliski & I Gardiner, jr		Robt Sands
Confort Sands	Benj Sharpe	Saml Sterrett
Geo Slye	Saml Snowden	John Stewart-heirs
Prestley Thornton	Henry Thompson	Wm Thompson
Dr Whitehead	Thos Willock	Thos Wand
Patrick Warren	Benj Young-heirs	Rev Notley Young
Benj Young-heirs	Nich Young, A Cassanove, R Y & E Brent	

Having sold my establishment to my bro, Walter Clarke, all persons indebted to me are to settle their accounts. -Isaac Clarke

WED APR 16, 1817
For sale or exchange-my farm, bet 4 & 500 acs, on the Patuxent rvr, bet Battle & Island Creeks, Calvert Co, Md; with commodious bldgs. -J J Brooke.
[Will exchange for small farm in any of the upper counties, or western shore.]

$50 reward for Daniel, negro, who ran away on Oct 8. -John Wade, lvg nr Antietam iron works, Wash Co, Md.

I will practice medicine & surgery in the neighborhood. -Jas D Barrette, Mt Wilby, PG Co, Md. [Residence of the late Dr Saml Debutts.]

Montg Co, Md. I certify that Henry Lansdale, of said co, brght before me a stray horse. -Brice Selby, J P.

THU APR 17, 1817
Mrd: on Apr 15, by Rt Rev Leonard Neale, Arch Bishop of Balt, Mr Robt Boone, of Fred'k Co, to Miss Cath Frances Queen, of D C.

Sale of Wash City lots for taxes. Geo Adams, coll 4th ward.

Saml Blodget-heirs	Zachariah Berry	Alex'r Bateman
Jasper Cope	John Cox	Bernard Elliot-heirs
Lewis Farington-hrs	Thos T Gantt	Benj Hitchburn
Bernard Hart	Henry Howard	Isaac H Jackson
Henry Kreamer-heirs	Jas King	Jas B Parsons
Jas Reed	Benj Stoddert	Spalding-heirs
Sarah Slater	Jona Salter-heirs	Francis Sands
Andrew Smith	John Steel	Lewis Summers
Wm Sandford	Richd Thomas	Mahlan Roach
Littleton D Teakle	Jas Ward	John Ward
Wm & J Willink	Walker & Wheeler	Wm Wilson
Nicholas Young	Mary Yeates	Susan Young
Abraham Young-hrs		

For sale or exchange, for merchandize or prop in Wash City: I offer a farm in Fairfax Co, Va; 40 acs is cleared. -Thos Drane

Wash Co, D C. John J Stull, insolvent debtor, confined in Wash Co prison, for debt. -Wm Brent, clk.

Pblc sale of land, on the premises, all the rl est of Ignatius Thompson, dec'd, which was devised by him to Aloegeous Thompson & Jas Alex'r Thompson; 150 acs bet St Clements & Briton Bays; with good dwlg hse. -Henry C Neale, trustee, Leonardtown, St Mary's Co, Md.

FRI APR 18, 1817
Wash Co, D C. John S Williams, insolvent debtor, confined in Wash Co prison, for debt. -Wm Brent, clk.

Univ o/Md; Apr 3, admitted to the degree of Dr of Med:
Va-Wm H Patillo   Va-Epaphroditus L Waring
Va-Henry F Thornton   Va-Edw H Carmichael
Va-Geo N Steptoe   DC-Richd Weightman
DC-Jas Harper   Pa: John M'Dowell

Pa-Wm H Magill
Md-John P Cockey
Md-John Fitzhugh
Md-Jacob A Preston
Md-Lennox Birckhead
Md-Horace W Waters
Md-Thos Parran

Pa-Jas A Denny
Md-Saml P Smith
Md-Henry Bond
Md-Geo W Dashiell
Md-Wm Howard
Md-John C Snyder, jr
Md-Saml Davis

St Mary's Co, Md, Crt: in Chancery, Mar term, 1817. Ratify sale by Enoch J Millard, trustee, of rl est of Jos Ford, dec'd: sold for $2,320. -Jos Harris, clk.

Mrd: on Apr 13, by Rev Mr Brown, Mr Jas Shields to Miss Sarah Varden, both of Wash City.

Notice-forwarn all persons from receiving my 2 notes given to Cornelius Wells, dt'd Feb 3 last-$400 ea. He has not complied with his agreement. -Josias Simpson, Wash

Died: on Mar 31, at Lancaster, Upper Canada, on Mar 16, Capt J Southerland, of the Glengary Militia, together with his wife, were drowned on Lake St Francois.

Richmond, Apr 14. On Sat, Mr Danl P Organ, formerly of this city, was accidentally shot & killed.

SAT APR 19, 1817

Montg Co, Md Crt, Mar term, 1817. Thos Sedwick petition to divide lands. Ratify sale of all the rl est of Wm Sedwick, dec'd, lying in Montg Co, Md. -Upton Beall, clk of Montg co Crt.

Wanted-at the Capitol, a number of sawyers. Apply to Shadrack Davis, clk of the works, Wash.

Being low in bodily health, I offer for sale-$3,000 of Wash & Balt Road Stock. -Jos Huddleston

MON APR 21, 1817

Pblc sale on the premises, sq 432, Wash, brick dwlg hse, fronting on 8th st; also all my funr. Ambrose Moriarty -D Bates, Auct.

Mrd: in Balt, on Apr 16, at Friend's Meeting Hse, Abijah Janney, of Alexandria to Mary J Ellicott, of Balt, Md.

Died: on Apr 16, Mrs Alice Riggs, w/o Mr Elisha Riggs, merchant of Gtwn.

TUE APR 22, 1817

Died: on Apr 12, after a long & distressing illness, John Wheelock, L L D Pres of Dartmouth Univ, aged 63 yrs.

WED APR 23, 1817
Committed to the goal of Harford Co, Md, a mulatto lad, about 19 yrs of age; says he belongs to Thos Sims, nr Piscataway. -Jason Moore, shrf.

THU APR 24, 1817
Mrd: on Apr 22, by Rev Mr M'Cormick, Mr Jas Bridges, of Gtwn, to Miss Mary M'Kim, of Wash City.

A lost son! Geo Latimer Cathcart, just turned 14 yrs, left his gr-fr's hse on Oct 19 last, & to avoid his elopement being made known to his parents at Cadiz, where his fr is Cnsl of the U S, I hoped for his return. Six mos have elapsed & ltrs from Cadiz dt'd Feb last, find he has not gone to them. -John Woodside, Wash City.

Orphans Crt of Wash Co, D C. Ltrs test on last will & test & prsnl est of Wm Walker, late of said city, dec'd. -Alex M'Cormick, Wm Emack, Jas Young, excs.

FRI APR 25, 1817
Mrs N King having declined kpg a brdg hse, offers same for rent, in G st, Wash.

SAT APR 26, 1817
The Common Cncl o/N Y, Mar 24th, directed that sts, in the Bowery, be known as: 1st st to be Chrystie st, in honor of Lt Col John Chrystie, ctzn of N Y, who died on the Niagara frontier during the late war, in svc o/U S, Jul 22, 1813.
2d st to be Forsyth st, honor of Lt Col Forsyth, U S rifle corps, who died of a wound rec'd in Lower Canada on Jun 28, 1813. 3d st to be Eldredge st, in honor of Lt Eldredge, of N Y, who was arrested by the tomahawk of the savage, in Upper Canada, Jul 7, 1813. 4th st to be Allen st, in honor of Wm H Allen, of U S N, who died of a wound rec'd on the sloop of war *Argus*, engaged with the Brit sloop of war *Pelican*, Aug 14, 1813. 6th st to be Ludlow st, in honor of Lt Ludlow, U S N, who rec'd his death wound on the U S frig *Chesapeake*, when engaged with the Brit frig *Shannon*, Sep 16, 1813.

<u>Ofcrs retained in the U S M C; An act to fix the Peace Establishment of the Marine Corps; Franklin Wharton, Lt Col Cmdnt.</u>

Capts: Anthony Gale — Archibald Henderson
Richd Smith — R D Wainwrght
Wm Anderson — Saml Miller
John M Gamble — Alfred Grayson
Wm Strong

<u>First Lts:</u>
F B Bellevue — Lyman Kellogg
Saml E Watson — Wm L Brownlow
Thos W Legge — W H Freeman
Jos L Kuhn — Henry Olcott
Chas R Broom — Benj Richardson
Francis B White — Wm Nicoll
Chas Lord — Levi Twiggs
John Harris — Saml B Johnston

2d lts promoted to 1st Lts:
Thos A Linton
Jas Edelin
Christopher Ford
Geo B English
2d Lts:
Edw S Nowell
John S Page
Aug A Nicholson
Wm Brown
Shubael Butterfield
Robt Lyman
Augustus De Rumford

Richd Auchmuty
Jas I Mills
Park G Howle
Richd D Green

Robt M Desha
Henry E Dix
Edwin B Newton
Elijah J Weed
Thos G Chase
John H Duncan

In Chancery-ratify sale by Clement Dorsey, trustee, for the sale of the rl est of Josiah B Grendall; 500 acs sold for $7 per ac; 255 3/4 acs sold for $4 per ac. -Thos H Bowie, Reg Cur Can

Property to be sold on Oct 28, for taxes due the Wash Corp: John Shute [$13.64;] Thos Law [$108.92] -Wm Ingle, coll ward 3.

MON APR 28, 1817
Died: Thos P Grosvenor, lately a rep in Cong from N Y; at the seat of Judge Hanson, in Md, on Fri last, in his 38th yr.

Mrd: on Apr 15, Toppan Webster, of Wash City, to Miss Mary Chauncy, of Harford, Md.

Wash Co, D C. Jonathan Pell, insolvent debtor, confined in Wash Co prison, for debt. -Wm Brent, clk.

Dry goods for sale; wishing to close my business at my store on Bridge st. -N P Bixby -John Peabody, auct.

Sale of city lots for taxes; Geo Adams, coll 4th ward.
Saml Blodget-heirs
Alex'r Bateman
John Cox
Bernard Elliot-heirs
Benj Hitchburn
Henry Howard
Henry Kreamer-heirs
Jas B Parsons
Benj Stoddert
Sarah Slater
Francis Sands
John Steel
Wm Sandford

Zachariah Berry
Jasper Cope
Thos T Gantt
Lewis Farrington-hrs
Bernard Hart
Isaac H Jackson
Jas King
Jas Reed
Spalding-heirs
Jona Slater-heirs
Andrew Smith
Lewis Summers
Richd Thomas

Mahlan Roach
Littleton D Teakle
Wm & J Willink
Wm Wilson
Mary Yeates
Abraham Young-hrs

Jas Ward
John Ward
Walker & Wheeler
Nicholas Young
Susan Young

TUE APR 29, 1817
Mrd: in Boston, Saml M Mackay, Aid to Maj Gen Brown, to Miss Cath G Dexter, d/o the late Hon Saml Dexter. [no date-recent]

In Chancery. St Mary's co Crt, Crt of Equity, Mar Term 1817. Basil Bowling vs Henderson S Boteler & Susanna his wife, John Hawkins, John Truman Washington, Susanna Truman Washington, Olivia Washington, Patsey Washington, Amelia Washington, Mellicent Washington, Wm Washington, & Danl Washington. Geo T Hawkins, late of PG Co, Md is dead; he was indebted to the cmplnt & his prsnl est is exhausted, leaving debts unsatisfied. Dfndnts are his heirs at law, & one of them, John Trueman Washington, resides out of Md. Object is to obtain a sale for the rl est of Geo T Hawkins. Jo Harris, clk St Mary's co Crt.

Wash Co, D C. Henry Gearvis, insolvent debtor, confined in Wash Co prison, for debt. -Wm Brent, clk.

Dry Goods for sale-Wm Ward, Pa av, Wash.

Ran-away, Jos Bartly, appr, on Apr 27. Thos Crown, bricklayer, Wash City. [He has parents in Pittsburgh, & may have gone there.]

WED APR 30, 1817
$50 reward will be given by the banks of this place, for Ronald Francis Murray, chgd with forging a ck on the Bank of Cape Fear; age bet 25 & 30 yrs; he came lately from Liverpool. -Hanson Kelly, Pres of Wilmington Branch of bank of N C. Richd Bradley, Pres of said bank.

Wash Co, D C. Case of Barbara Suter, insolvent debtor, confined in Wash Co prison, for debt. -Wm Brent

Declining kpg boarders, & having rented her hse, the subscriber will sell at pblc auction, hse furn, etc. -Margaretta King   David Bates, auct.

Orphans Crt of Chas Co, Md. Ltrs test on prsnl est of John Laidler, late of said co, dec'd. -Eliz B Laidler

THU MAY 1, 1817
Paris. Feb 14-on Mon last, Madame Robt Patterson, & her 2 sisters, Miss Caton & Miss Louisa Caton, were presented to the king. Their grfr, Mr Carroll of Carrolton, is known for his hospitality, to all strangers who travel in the U S.

Orphans Crt of PG Co, Md. Prsnl est of Walter Edelen, late of said co, dec'd. -Richd L Jenkins

Wash Co, D C. John Mace, insolvent debtor, confined in Wash Co prison, for debt. -Wm Brent, clk.

FRI MAY 2, 1817
Steam bost Camden will commence runnning twice a day from Alexandria to Gtwn. -John Gird

SAT MAY 3, 1817
The Wash Htl in the future will be under the firm of J Tennison & Co, Wash. -Jos Tennison

Orphans Crt of PG Co, Md. Sale at the late residence of John Fairall, dec'd, the prsnl prop of Robt Fairall, late of PG Co, dec'd. -John Turton, adm d b n of Robt Fairall. Also, a negro girl, prop of Eleanor Fairall, late of said co, dec'd.

MON MAY 5, 1817
Levi & Laban Kenniston were acquitted in Massachusetts for the robbery of Maj Elijah P Goodrich in Dec last.

Mrd: on Apr 24, Mr Jas D Cobb, late of the U S Army, to Miss Rachel J Cecil, both of PG Co, Md.

Died: at Saco, Dist of Maine, on Apr 25, after a confinement of only 5 days, Maj Gen Cyrus King, aged 44, late a mbr of Congress.

Orphans Crt of Wash Co, D C. Ltrs test on prsnl est of Philip Evans, late of said co, dec'd. -Mary Evans, John Evans, excs.

TUE MAY 6, 1817
Mrd: on Apr 29, at the Navy Yd, Gosport, Lt Henry Henry, of the U S N, to Miss Mary Ann Cassin, niece of Cmdor Cassin, commandant of that station.

WED MAY 7, 1817
Orphans Crt of PG Co, Md. Ltrs test on prsnl est of Archibald Van Horn, late of said co, dec'd. -Alethia E Van Horn, excx. [The tvrn formerly the prop & residence of Gabriel P Van Horn, dec'd, will be at pblc sale on Jun 7; 160 acs. Sale at the tvrn now occupied by Mr Jos Willet. -Alethia E Van Horn, excx.]

Orphans Crt of Wash Co, D C. Ltrs of adm on prsnl est of Leonard Howard, late of said city, decd. -Eleanor Howard, admx.

THU MAY 8, 1817
John Gardiner, upholsterer, from Dublin: on Pa av, Wash City. -Local ad.

Wash stocking knit factory. Inquire of Jonas Keller, at the old mansion hse of the Young family, nr the Potomac Bridge.

Died: on Apr 14, at his residence on Little Rvr, Abbeville Dist, S C, of a tedious & painful illness, Col Jos Calhoun, in his 67th yr; one of the Rev patriots; former rep in Cong in 1807, from which he withdrew.

Orphans Crt of PG Co, Md. Pblc sale at the residence of Henry Swaine, 3 miles below Nottingham, P G Co, Md; all prsnl est of John Swaine, late of said co, dec'd. -Levin Skinner, agent for the adm.

Pblc sale of 160 acs of land, within 3 miles of the Capitol; Mr Benj Owens, at the Anacosta bridge, will shew the premises. -Amelia T Dorsett

Copartnership bet Thos Murray & Owen McGlue is dissolved, by mutual agreement. Thos Murray will settle accounts. [Local]

FRI MAY 9, 1817
N Y May 6. Arrv'd at this port on May 5, from Liverpool, Mr Wm Cobbett & his 2 sons, Wm & John; board the ship *Importer*, Capt Ogden; in 38 days.

For sale-*Westover*, by direction of the will of the late Col Byrd; 593 acs, with commodious dwlg hse; within 25 miles of Richmond, Va. Also 60 acs contiguous to the *Westover* est. -Wm B Page, exc of Col Wm Byrd.

Mrd: on May 1, at Dr Chas Cocke's, in Albemarle, Va, by Rev Mr Dunn, of Loudon, Gen Armistead T Mason, to Miss Charlotte Eliza Taylor, the y/d/o the late John Taylor, of Southampton.

Died: at Richmond, on May 4, after a long indisposition, David Ross, more than 80 yrs of age, & long a resident of that city. -Enquirer.

SAT MAY 10, 1817
One cent reward & no thanks. Ranaway on May 5, appr boy, John Hayne, about 18 yrs old; appr at the coopering business, nr Barry's wharf, Wash City. -Saml Stevens

MON MAY 12, 1817
Died: on Jan 29, in the 31st yr of his age, Capt John Augustine Thornton, of Culpepper Co, Va, after a lingering & painful illness. -Va Herald.

New comb factory; Fairfax st, Alexandria. -Benj Wood

Newbern, S C, Mar 19. Sup Crt of law for this county passed death sentence on Benj Sparrow & Saml Sparrow, convicted for negro stealing. May 16th is appointed for their execution.

TUE MAY 13, 1817

$30 reward for Bob Smith, negro lad, who absconded on Apr 30; his mthr lives at Mr Henry Warren's, nr Middle Brook Mills, & his sister lives with Mrs Brooke, in the neighborhood. -Edw Digges, nr Clarksburg, Montg Co, Md.

Died: in Balt, Md, on May 9, after a lingering illness, Miss Ann Smith, d/o Gen S Smith, of that city; scarcely reached her 18th birthday.

Isaac Eveleth offers his svcs as Scrivener & Copyist, at his rms in Wash st, Gtwn; the former residence of the late Mr Flores.

Committed to PG Co, Md goal, on Apr 16, mulatto man, Wm Winstern, about 30 yrs of age; says he belongs to Col Wm Meakin, New Kent Co, nr N Kent C H, Va. -Basil Bowling, shrf.

Wanted-5 or 6 hse carpenters. Apply to Handley Price, nr the Centre Mkt, Wash.

Wash Co, D C. 1-John Okely, insolvent debtor, confined in Wash Co prison, for debt. 2-Wm Esenbeck, same. -Wm Brent, clk.

WED MAY 14, 1817

Va land for sale, Augusta Co, Va, 534 acs, with good dwlg hse, etc. -Henry V Bingham, lvg on the premises.

Died: in Wash Co, D C, on Apr 20, Mr Philip Evans, an old & respectable farmer of this dist.

Mrd: on May 11, on *Analostan Island*, by Rev Mr McCormick, Mr Wm H Barron, merchant, of Wash City, to Miss Leeanah Mason, of Pr Wm Co, Va.

Mrd: on May 7, by Rev Mr Riland, Mr Wm Cook, of Gtwn, to Miss Mary Beall.

Ltr from a gentleman in Savannah, to his mthr in this city. Jan 23d, left Norfolk for Charleston, in sloop *Columbia*, Capt I Hatch, with passengers: Mr Henry Thorpe, lady & child; Mr Robt Thorpe, his bro; Mr Peter Stone, bro of Mrs Thorpe, all of Petersburg, Va; Mrs E Vaughan & dght of Charleston; Miss Francis Toney, of do; Mr Robt Slater, of Liverpool; Mr B G Hipkins, of Port Royal, Va. The crew consisting of Capt I Hatch, Lucius Hatch, mate, Wm Bloodgood, John Chalks, & Robt Syms. Jan 26th departed from capes of Va; passed Cape Hatteras; moderate gale until Feb 2; we took on water. Mrs Vaughan & 14 yr old dght, & Capt Syms all drowned; Mr Henry Thorpe froze to death; Mr Robt Thorpe, bro of Henry Thorpe, expired; also Mrs E Thorpe & Master Wm Thorpe. On the 8th day we were taken from the wreck, Capt Hatch, myself & Miss Francis Toney, & put on a brig bound for Balt. The 3d day Miss Toney died.

700 sheep for sale-Wm C Somerville, nr Leonard Town, Md.

For sale-land in Chas Co, Md, formerly the residence of Rev Hatch Dent, about a mile west of Charlotte Hall school, with brick dwlg hse. -Wm H Dent, Bryan town, Chas Co, Md.

THU MAY 15, 1817
For sale-bldg lots in Wash; lot 1 in sq 86; lot 22 in sq 86. -Jos Stretch, Treas Dept.

Wash Co, D C. John Henry, insolvent debtor, confined in the prison bounds of Wash Co, for debt. -Wm Brent, clk.

New Grocery store; Pa av, Wash. -Robt Burnside

For sale-my hse now occupied by the Central Bank of Gtwn & Wash, on Bridge st. Also the one in which I now reside, on First st. -Joel Brown, Gtwn.

FRI MAY 16, 1817
Lands for sale in A A Co, Md; part of the rl est of Belt Mullikin, dec'd, viz *Simpson's Choice*, 337 acs; with framed dwlg hse. Also *Worthington's Beginning*, 300 acs, with dwlg hse now under construction. -Basil D Mullikin, trustee.

$5 reward for runaway, Ann Blackstone, mulatto woman, raised in St Mary's Co, Md; formerly belonging to Henry Hill. -Ilford Van Rissick, nr the Navy Yd, Wash.

SAT MAY 17, 1817
$50 reward for runaway, Christy Brooks, mulatto woman; about 20 yrs old. -J Calder, Gtwn.

Montg Co, Md, Crt, Jan Term, 1817; in Chancery. Joshua Stewart vs Jas B Pleasants, Deborah Stabler, Wm Stabler, Eliz Stabler, Anna Stabler, Robinson Stabler, Wm H Pleasants, & Eliz A Pleasants. Subj-land in bond of conveyance given by Henrietta Marie Pleasants, to said Joshua Stewart, Oct 24, 1809, lying in Montg Co; part of the *Addition to Brooke Grove*, & part of *Brooke Piney Grove*, & part of *Fairhill*, 400 acs more or less. The said Obligor afterwards mrd Benj Bates; Henrietta Maria Bates & Benj Bates have both died without making any cnvynce of said premises, altho Henrietta Maria Pleasants has rec'd a valuable consideration. -Upton Beall, clk of Montg co Crt.

Died: in Gtwn, on May 15, of a protracted pulmonary disease, Arthur Shaaf, of Fred'k Co, Md, in his 49th yr; had srv'd in the Leg & Exec Cncl of his ntv state.

Mrd: on May 13, by Rev Dr Laurie, Mr Saml Anderson, of Hanover Co, Va, to Miss Susan Dayton Wheaton, d/o Maj Jos Wheaton, of Wash City.

Mrd: on May 13, by Rev Mr Breckenridge, Mr Jos Alex'r Burch to Miss Eliz Bell, all of Wash City.

$100 reward for runaway, negro Wm Violet, age 26 yrs, an indented servant, who has about 8 yrs to serve. We purchased him last fall of Mr Arthur Latimore, of Chas Co, Md. -John Lyons & Co, Gtwn.

MON MAY 19, 1817
Wood land for sale-121+ acs, in Westmoreland Co, Va, adjs the land of Mr Daniel Payne, nr the Mattox bridge. Apply to Capt Robt S Hipkins, at Bleak hall, nr the premises. Mr Lamkin, who also lives nrby, will shew the land. -Bush Washington

TUE MAY 20, 1817
Mrd: on May 18, at Ft Wash, by Rev Dr Elliott, chaplain U S army, Mr John Rice to Miss Betsey Weysell.

Mrd: on May 18, by Rev Mr McCormick, Mr Benj Berry, jr, of PG Co, Md, to Mrs Eleanor Brooke Eversfield Forbes, of Wash City.

State of Tenn, 1st Cr t, Sullivan Co, Mar term, 1817. Isaac Robbins vs Peter Mayo & the reps of John Punch, dec'd. Ordered that Thos D Greer, be appt'd grdn pendente lite of the minor chldrn of John Punch, dec'd, to wit, John S Punch, Wm L Punch, Eliza Punch, Rebecca Punch, Emily Punch, Moriah Punch, & Nicholas Punch.; further order that Rebecca Punch, the wid/o John Punch, dec'd, do appear at the next term of this crt. -Wm Anderson, D clk. [Bill is to foreclose on ground that John Punch, dec'd, claimed in Blountville, Sullivan Co, Tenn.]

Wash Co, D C, Crct crt for Dec Term, 1816; in Chancery. Robt S Bickley vs Saml Blodget. Ratify sale by Wash Boyd, trustee, of prop for $4,467. -Wm Brent, clk.

Crct Crt of Wash Co, DC; in Chancery. Petition of Notley Young for a commission to divide lands, which have descended to the heirs of Benj Young, dec'd. It is ordered that the proceedings be ratified. -Wm Brent, clk.

WED MAY 21, 1817
Drowned in Pemigewassett rvr, in Salisbury, on Apr 19, Mr Stephen Clark, of Sanbornton, in his 26th yr; leaving a widow & one child to lament his death.

Hartford, Conn, May 13. On Apr 25, the body of Chas Lee, jr, s/o Mr Isaac Lee, of Berlin, was found at the bottom of a well. He was supposed to be with his gr-parents.

Wash Co, D C. Jos Riffle, insolvent debtor, confined in Wash Co prison, for debt. -Wm Brent, clk.

THU MAY 22, 1817
Orphans Crt of PG Co, Md. Prsnl est of Geo Biscoe, late of said co, dec'd. -Araminta Biscoe, admx.

Mrd: on May 20, at Annalostan, the seat of Gen John Mason, by Rev Mr Hawley, C C Jamison, of Balt, to Miss Ann E M Johnson.

John D Hill has commenced his Cabinet & Chair maker business on 6th st, Wash.

FRI MAY 23, 1817
Bennett's Creek prop for sale; desirous of mvg westwardly; mills, lands, negroes, horses, distillery, every thing; 40 miles from Balt & 32 miles from Wash.
-John Cook, Bennett's Crk.

SAT MAY 24, 1817
John Brown & Thos Davis, mariners, belonging to Balt, Md, shipwrecked in 1815 or 1816 on the coast of Africa, have been released from slavery from the hands of the Arabs of Lower Suze, by the exertions of Mr Simpson, our Cnsl at Tangier. Archibald Robbins, of the brig Commerce, Capt Riley, wrecked on the same coast, is released from the slavery of the Arabs of the Desert of Sahara, by same means.

For sale-a healthy farm, 208 acs, on Muddy Branch, Montg Co, Md. -Geo Graff

Paper & stationery store; Wm A Davis & John Brannan, Pa av, Wash.

Died: in Wash City, on May 21, Madame Dona Federica de Merkleiny Onis, consort to Chevalier de Onis, H C M Envoy Extra & Mnstr Pleni to the U S. She suffered a severe ilness for the last 10 mos.

Died: at Belle Fontaine, Mo Terr, on Apr 22, Capt Edmund Shipp, of the Rifle Regt; distinguished during the late war.

For sale-lg supply of hrdware. Henry Hazel, crnr of Bridge & High sts, Gtwn.

MON MAY 26, 1817
PG Co, Md. Petition in writing of Aquila Wilson, of same, an insolvent debtor. -John Read Magruder, clk.

Mrshl's sale-all right, title, etc of Wm S Radcliffe, to lot 10 in sq 428, Wash City, at suit of John Cooper, against said Radcliffe, to satisfy same. -Wash Boyd, Mrshl.

Land for sale or will exchange for prop in the upper country; land in Chas Co, Md, 1,200 acs; bet the mouths of the Chiccamuxin & Mattawoman Crks; with small dwlg hse. -Wm Mason, jr.

Mrd: on May 22, by Rev Mr Grassie, Mr Bernard Spalding to Miss Ann Ford, d/o Mr John G Ford, all of Gtwn.

TUE MAY 27, 1817
For sale in Upper Marlboro, Md, land cld *More Fields Enlarged*, about 600 acs; belonged to the late John Smith Brookes, dec'd; with dwlg hse. -Benj Brookes, trustee, Upper Marlborough.

Died: on May 15, at his residence in Balt, Md, Eli Simkins.

WED MAY 28, 1817
$100 will be pd for arresting & securing Wm Weaver, a resident of Gtwn, D C, & a Lt in the U S N. Weaver came to Balt with his sister, a few days ago. He stabbed my son [age 19 yrs] four times with a very sharp sword, by which he is dangerously wounded. -Jas Power, Balt, Md.

Stray cow came to my hse, nr the President's sq. -Wm Simmons

THU MAY 29, 1817
Died: in Salisbury, Conn, on May 6, Mr Hezekiah C Lee, aged 33, s/o Deacon Milo Lee. He left a widow & 4 small chldrn. [He was found lying nr his horses, dead.]

FRI MAY 30, 1817
For sale or exchange, prop in Alexandria or stock in any of the banks in the dist; bet 4 & 500 acs of land in Westmoreland Co, Va. -Elliott Muse, lvg in Alexandria.

PG Co Crt, Apr Term, 1817. Petition of Elkanah Cobb, an insolvent debtor. -J R Magruder, clk.

SAT MAY 31, 1817
Election at Mrs Kortwright's tvrn, Ward 1, Wash City, on Jun 2, for one Alderman & 3 Common Cnclmen. -Jos Brumley, Jos Mechlin, Wm Waters, comrs. Election at Davis' Htl, 2d Ward for same. -R C Weightman, Noah Fletcher, John M'Clelland, comrs. Election at Queen's Htl, Ward 3, Capt Hill, for same. -Benj Burch, Saml N Smallwood, Danl Rapine, comrs. Election at J B Forest hse, crnr of 8th & K sts, fourth Ward, for same. -Wm Prout, Adam Lindsay, Jas Friend, comrs.

$100 reward for negro, Jas Duffin, aged about 35 yrs, ranaway on May 24. -Eleanor Gatt, lvg in Montg Co, Md.

MON JUN 2, 1817
Natchez, May 7. On Sat last, nr Point Coupee, the boiler of the steam boat *Constitution* bursted, & destroyed the following passengers: Elephel Frazer, merchant, of Gibsonport, M T. Wm Steel, merchant, Warrenton, M T. John Larkin, silversmith, of same. Wm Yewell, of Wash, Ky. Thos Brown, from Scotland. Mr M'Farland, Wash Co, Ky. Geo D Wilson, do. Alex'r Philpot, Henry Co, Va. Peter Hubert, New Orleans. R Robertson, age 18 yrs.

For Sale-*Westbury*, my est on West Rvr, A A Co, Md; 718 1/2 acs; with frame dwlg hse. -John F Mercer, lvg in the vicinity.

TUE JUN 3, 1817
Died: at Salem, N J, on May 15, Thos Sinnickson, in his 72d yr; mbr of the first Provincial Cong, convened in 1775.

WED JUN 4, 1817
Steam veneering mill; orders from any part of the Union. -Geo Hill, Adam Stewart, Balt, Md.

THU JUN 5, 1817
Aldermen & Brd of Common Cncl elected in Wash City:
Aldermen: Jos Forrest, Thos H Gilliss, John G McDonald, Jos Cassin.

Cmn Cncl: Christian Hines	John N Moulder	Wm O'Neale
Chas Glover	Geo Sweeny	Jas M Varnum
Thos Dunn	Jas Young	Saml Burch
Israel Little	Thos Haliday	John Crabb

Mr Rodolph Schaer, of Zurich, Switz, proposes to open a school in Wash City.

Organ for sale; it plays with a crank. -Contact John Sholl, in High st, Gtwn.

Wash Co, D C. Pblc sale at the dwlg of John Boone, all the prsnl est of Nicholas Boone, dec'd. -Levin Boone, adm.

FRI JUN 6, 1817
Mrd: on Jun 3, by Rev Mr Burch, Mr Geo W Dashiel to Miss Deborah B Beall, all of Wash City.

Danl Hauptman, tin plate, planished ware & sheet iron manufacturer; Pa av, Wash City. [Oppo Walter Jones]

Howard for sale-subscriber wishing to to remove to his farm in Loudoun Co, Va; anxious to sell or rent the place where he now resides, 150 acs 3 miles from Alexandria. -Wm Robinson

SAT JUN 7, 1817
Wash Co, D C. Henry J Rigden, insolvent debtor, confined in Wash Co prison, for debt. -Wm Brent, clk.

Return J Meigs, jr, is post mstr genr'l, Wash, D C.

MON JUN 9, 1817
King Hiram, the capital imported horse, is standing at Nathl Crawford's, Greenwood, PG Co, Md, this season.

Died: at Boston, on May 30, Hon Tristram Dalton, aged 79, formerly of Newburyport; 1755 grad at Harvard Univ.

For sale-farm of 162 acs on Paint branch, nr Vansville. Inquire of Thos Benson, on the premises, or John Benson, nr the mouth of the Monocacy, Montg Co, Md.

TUE JUN 10, 1817
Benj G Orr has been elected Mayor of Wash City; took his oath accordingly.

Iron & Steel warehse, Water st, Gtwn. Orders to Robt French, Gtwn, or to Geo French, nr Gtwn.

Mrd: on Thu last, at the hse of his Grace the Duke of Wellington, Col Harvey, Aidde-Camp to the Duke of Wellington, to Louisa Cath, 3d d/o Richd Caton, of Md, in the U S A. After the ceremony the couple set off for Englefield Green, nr Windsor. -London, Apr 27.

WED JUN 11, 1817
Mrd: on Jun 5, at *Rich-Hill*, Chas Co, Md, by Rev Mr Weems, Thos Swann, jr, merchant of Alexandria, to Miss Sarah Cox, of the former place.

Mrd: on Jun 8, by Rev Mr Matthews, Mr Felix Brady to Miss Susan Dougherty, all of Wash City.

Orphans Crt of Wash Co, D C. Pblc sale at the late residence of Jos Sprigg Belt, dec'd; a part of his prsnl prop. -Chas R Belt, exc.

THU JUN 12, 1817
Died: in Sutton, Mass, on May 5, Ensign John H Bartlett, aged 38 yrs; killed when the wheel of a cart passed over his head.

Died: at Sutton, Mass, on May 8, Lt Jonathan Burden, aged 56 yrs; bro-in-law to Mr Bartlett, [see above] early on Jun 6, from a fall in attempting to get over a fence.

To be sold for whatever it will bring-*Bailey's Retirement*; subscriber offers at great sacrifice; made to pay his debts & move to Wash City. Also *Bear garden, Brush creek, & Sleepy crk*, places clear of all imcumbrances. Also 440 acs in Hampshire Co, encumbered with a deed of trust of $2,000, & a lease of 10 yrs. -Robt Bailey, Berkeley Springs, Va.

For sale-land & mills in Loudon, nr Leesburg, Va; 103 acs; on the premises is a store hse occupied by Lewis M Smith & Co; & a dwlg hse, etc. Also 100 acs in Wash Co, one mile of Hancock. Apply to Fleet Smith, atty, at Leesburg, Va. Or to-Benj Owens or Edw Owens.

FRI JUN 13, 1817
Antiquity Persons employed by Hon Mark L Hill, to make improvements on his farm at Phipsburg, at the remains of the ancient fort built by Sir Geo Popham in 1607, found, in May last, an axe which has lain there 210 yrs. -Bost Cent.

$50 reward for negro man, Joe Mason, who absconded on May 27. I purchased him 2 yrs ago of the adms of Ann Ray, who formerly kept him hired out in Wash City & Gtwn. -Offa Wilson, PG Co, Md.

Died: on May 28, in his 23d yr, Capt Thos Little, of the schnr *Free Mason*, of this city; of bilious fever. He leaves a widow & an infant babe.

SAT JUN 14, 1817
John Heath, late Capt in the Marine Corps, is appt'd by the Pres to be Cnsl of the U S for the Island of Teneriffe.

Died: on Jun 8, in Marlborough, N H, a child of Justus Rhodes, while crossing the rvr. His mthr plunged into the stream to save him but came nr sharing his fate.

Drowned-in Hartland, Vt, Mr Ezekial Sleeper, of Wash, Vt, & Mr Jason Cole, of Plainfield, attempting to pass the rvr in a boat; drawn to the brink of the falls.

Notice-anxious to settle the est of Jacob Duckett, late of Piscataway, I again call on those indebted to make settlement. -Hor C M'Elderry

To rent-the blacksmith shop lately occupied by Wm Whitmore, fronting on Pa av, Wash. Apply at the glass hse. -Jacob Felius

MON JUN 16, 1817
Brig *Mentor*, H Williams, mstr, for Marseilles & return to Alexandria. Apply to John Gird, or Isaac Entwisle, Alexandria.

Mrd: at N Y, some days ago, by Rt Rev Bshp Hobart, Col Geo Croghan, of Locust Grove, Ky, to Miss Serena Livingston, d/o John R Livingston, of Wash City.

TUE JUN 17, 1817
For rent-Orange Htl; anxious to retire from pblc business. -Paul Verdier & Son, Orange Crt Hse, Va.

Notice-to the legatees of Jas Hardage Lane, dec'd, residing in Ky or elsewhere; settlement of the est on Aug 21, at the hse of John Matthias, Mstr in Chancery, in Leesburg, Loudon Co, Va. -Geo Lane, exc of J H Lane, dec'd.

Wash Co, D C. Eliza Wadsworth, insolvent debtor, confined in Wash Co prison, for debt. -Wm Brent, clk.

Pvt sale of brick hse on F st; lowest price is .92 per sq ft. -Lewis Clephane

Died: at Phil, on Jun 13, in his 73d yr, Ebenezer Hazard, formerly Mstr Gen of the U S; a ntv & long an inhabitant of Phil.

Something wrong [if not villainous] in the P O. In Mar I put notes into the p o at Luray, Shenandoah Co, Va, & same have been detained by some villain. -Gabriel Jordan

WED JUN 18, 1817
Died: on board the schnr *Regulator*, Capt Norton, on her passage from Boston to Phil, a passenger, who from his papers, appears to have been Godfrey Danl Lehmann, aged 35 yrs, & to have been in the French military svc; a ntv of Cothens, nr the Rhine. He expected to find a bro in Phil, who emigrated 10 yrs since from Europe. He lost his life by poison; others in the cabin almost shared the same fate. The cook has been committed to prison on suspicion.

Notice-the prsnl prop of Ambrose Baldwin, late of Conn, dec'd, who died in this county last summer, by order of the crt, has been placed in my hands to be sold. -John M'Culloch, shrf of Mason Co, Va.

The Govnr of Canada has issued a proclamation, offering a reward of $1,600, for the apprehension of Chas De Reenhart, Archibald M'Lellan, Cuthbert Grant & Jos Cadot, who had bills of indictment against them for the murder of Owen Keveny.

Wash Co, D C, in Chancery. Alex'r Estep & Barbara Estep late Barbara Morin grdns of the chldrn of *Lewis Morin dec'd. Chldrn of *Louis Morin: Washington, Matilda, Harriet, Adeline & Barbara Morin. Subj-sale of part of lot 1, in sq 292, Wash. -Wm Brent, clk. [*2 splgs.]

THU JUN 19, 1817
Died: on Jun 18, the Most Rev Leonard Neale, in his 71st yr, Archbshp of Balt, & sucessor, in the Archiepiscopal See to the late Most Rev Dr John Carroll, after a short & painful illness of only 36 hrs. His remains will be cnvyd this morning from Trinity Chr to the Cem of the Convent.

Ltr by W A Weaver, Lt U S N. Subj-the death of Jas F Power: dated-U S ship *Franklin,* Phil, Jun 16, 1817. [In same paper-article by Jas Power, the fr. Certified by Benj F Wheeler, student in Gtwn college Apr 1809-Apr 1814. {Balt Jun 6, 1817.} H Bond, M D, saw Jas F Power on May 22. {Balt, Jun 5, 1817.} W W Handy cld to consult with Dr Bond on May 23, 1817. {May 24, 1817.} W Gibson, surg, examined the wounds. {Balt, Jun 6, 1817} Jas Hayden visited Powers at his fr's hse. {Balt, Jun 4, 1817.} Jos McKeldin, assisted Dr Bond, May 22. {Balt Jun 5, 1817}

French bunting for sale. Jas & Thos W Belt, ship chandlers, Balt, Md.

To rent-rms & cellar in brick hse adj the store of Mr Joel Crutenden. -Francis Dodge [Local Item]

Chas co Crt, Md, in Chancery, Jun Term, 1817. Chas Sotheron vs the heirs of John Brooke. Bill to procure from the heirs of John Brooke, dec'd, formerly of Chas Co, Md, & latterly of Ga, a cnvyance of *Westwood Manor, Chas Borough,* & *Inlet,* 325 acs in Chas Co, Md, sold by said Brooke to Jos Thompson, more than 40 yrs ago. Thompson sold to Philip Key & Hanson Briscoe, who sold to Henry Greenfield Sotheron, f/o the cmplnt. -John Barnes, clk of Chas Co, Md.

For sale-*Goshen*, Montg Co, Md, rl est of Sam Robertson, 3d, late of Montg Co, dec'd. Framed dwlg hse & 300 acs, etc. -Thos Davis, Wm Robertson, John H Riggs, Trustees of said est.

Wash Co, D C, in Chancery. Geo Grundy & Geo Crossdale vs John Hossack. Ratify sale by Chas Glover, trustee, of lot 114, in Beatty & Hawkin add to Gtwn, to Geo Grundy, for $1,260. -Wm Brent, clk.

For sale-*Scotland*, 125 acs; as it is generally known my late fr expended double the first cost in its improvement. Just 4 miles from Wash City. -W Tunnicliff

FRI JUN 20, 1817
Hagerstown, Md, Jun 17. On Jun 9, the shop of Mr Blershing, silver-smith, was robbed. Now lodged in jail for trial at the next Nov term is Alex'r Crane, age about 34 yrs; Wm Killinger, about 20; & John Baker, about 20. -Torch Light

$100 reward for runaway, Jas, negro man. -Uriel Glasscock, Fauquier Co, Va, nr Paris.

For sale-the plantation whereon Mr Frances Hance, dec'd, formerly lived, in Calvert Co, Md; 420 acs; with frame dwlg hse. -Benj H Mackall, Calv Co, Md.

Montg Co, Md, Crt, Mar Term, 1817, in Chancery. Eden Beall vs Thos Plater, Anne Key, Eliz R Key, Mary H Key, Philip B Key, Rebecca Ann Key, Louisa Key, Emily Key, Anne Arnold Key, Elijah Beall, Ely Beall, Enoch Beall & Edw Beall. Bill is for cnvyance of 220 acs, *Bradford's Rest*, in Montg Co, Md; purchased of Geo Plater, of St Mary's Co, Md, by Edw Beall, on Oct 9, 1784. Edw Beall, f/o the cmplnt, pd Geo Plater the whole of the purchase money, & that Geo Plater died without cnvyg to the said Edw Beall; it was agreed bet the heirs of the said Edw Beall to sell the whole rl est of the said Edw Beall, & make distribution of the proceeds among the said heirs; that long after this agreement the said heirs, save Elijah Beall, who was absent, & indebted to the est, as exc thereof, assigned & transferred for a val consideration, to the cmplnt, their entire right to any part of the said 220 acs of land; Geo Plater died about 1792 & devised by will all his est in Montg co to his son Thos Plater, who cnvyd *Bradford's Rest* to Philip B Key, who has died, lvg a widow & chldrn, the dfndnts in this bill. -U Beall, clk.

Pblc Summons. St Bartholomews. Mr John Bernhard Elbers, of this Island, petitions he may be permitted to resign the affairs of the late firm of Elbers & Krafft, & those of his own; claims to be presented by Nov 26, 1817. Gustavia, on the Island of St Bartholomews, May 23, 1817. By the resolve of the tribunal. -C L Plagemann, Reg.

SAT JUN 21, 1817
Arthur Polhemus, s/o Benj Polhemus, dec'd, was accidentally killed at Cook's Mill, Hanover twnshp, Burlington Co, N J, on Jun 8; crushed by a water wheel. -Trenton, N J, Jun 16, 1817.

Wash Co, D C. Mary Beeding, insolvent debtor, confined in Wash Co prison, for debt. -Wm Brent, clk.

MON JUN 23, 1817
Jas Beck, of PG Co, Md, brought before me a stray horse. -Saml Franklin, J P.

TUE JUN 24, 1817
Capt Edmund Shipp, ntv of Ky, fought by the side of Gen Harrison at Tippecanoe. [recording of the death of a young ofcr so distinguished for svcs in the late war.] -Ky Argus]

Comrs to the Piscataway & Hynson Turnpike Co, Md: Edw H Calvert, Robt Sewall, Bej Oden, Rd W West, Robt Bowie, Wm Hebb & Edmund Key.

Died: on Jun 15, at St Michaels, E S, Md, of pulmonary complaint, Lt Edw Haddaway, of U S Navy.

Orphans Crt of Balt Co, Md. Present, Owen Dorsey & Jas Carroll, jr. Application of Nicholas Brice, trustee for the sale of rl est of Thos McCreery, late of Dublin, Ire, dec'd; distribution in Feb next, per his will. -Wm Buchanan, reg, Balt Co, Md.

Fancy Goods store, Pa av, Wash. -R D Perdreauville

Mr John Norvell, late editor of the *Balt Patriot*, has formed a partnership with Mr Bradford, in the *Ky Gaz*, printed at Lexington, of which he is to be the editor.

WED JUN 25, 1817
Livery stable, attached to Tennison's, Wash. -Thos Shivers

Mrd: on Jun 19, by Rev Mr Read, Mr Wm B Williams, of Gtwn, D C, to Miss Ann Dorsey, d/o Henry W Dorsey, of Montg Co, Md.

THU JUN 26, 1817
Wellsburg, Va, Jun 6. On Thu last Thos Johnston, for a short time a resident of this county, was tried on chg of committing rape on his dght. He has been sentenced to 21 yrs confinement in the Pen. -Gaz.

New Gig for sale, with plated harness. -Thos Cookendorfer, Gtwn.

FRI JUN 27, 1817
Died: at Phil, on Jun 24, Thos M'Kean, L L D; ntv of Pa, of an old Irish stock.

Died: at Middletown, Ky, on Jun 7, Gen Saml Dirickson, aged 53 yrs, a Rev whig. He had lived in Ky but a few yrs, having remv'd from his ntv state, Delaware.

Died: on Jun 1, after a severe illness of 5 days, Sally Becton Dillahunty, aged 9 yrs & 2 mos, d/o Thos Dillahunty, of Davidson Co, Tenn. She was struck by a shot which passed thru her body when her fr shot at a squirrel a distance off.

Wash Co, D C. Martin King, insolvent debtor, confined in the prison bounds of Wash Co, for debt. -Wm Brent, clk.

Sidney Wishart advertises that he lives at *Belle Plain*, & has a vessel for transporting goods, etc; & has large brick warehse at *Belle Plain*. -Local ad.

SAT JUN 28, 1817
Pvt sale-my farm of about 270 acs of land, in PG Co, Md. Intending mvg to the western country. -Benoni Soper

Died: in Greenfield, Mass, Mrs Harriot, w/o Dr A T Stone, aged 36.

MON JUN 30, 1817
For sale-the whole or part of my farm, 800 acs. It is the late residence of Col Jas B Brookes. -Apply to Isaac Funk.

$100 reward for apprehending the following, deserters from the Marine Barracks, viz: John Bruner, pvt, b in Md nr Frederick, age 27 yrs, tin-worker; deserted on Dec 18. Arther McHenry, pvt, b in Ire, age 26, laborer, deserted Dec 27. Jos McDevitt, pvt, b in Md, age 27, taylor, deserted Jun 27. Eli Lobbett, pvt b in France, about 30, sldr, deserted on Jun 28, was pardoned on Jun 12 by the Pres, of the U S, for the crime of desertion. -Saml Miller, Maj Comdg, Wash, D C.

Bricklayers & stone masons wanted at Ft Wash. -Bolitha Laws, John Cohagan

TUE JUL 1, 1817
Fresh seeds, etc. John Claxton, at his Seed & Toy Store, nr the Mkt Hse, Gtwn.

Wash Co, D C. 1-Thos Hillard, insolvent debtor, confined in the prison bounds of Wash Co, for debt. 2-Henry H Redmond, same. -Wm Brent, clk.

Mrd: on Jun 26, at Alexandria, by Rev Mr Norris, Lt Wm Lowe, of the navy, to Miss Eliz M Korn, of Alexandria.

Just published-a sketch of the life, last sickness & death of Mrs Mary Jane Grosvenor, left among the papers of the late Hon Thos P Grosvenor: price .50.

Orphans Crt of Wash Co, D C. Prsnl est of Henry Halsey, late of Wash Co, dec'd. Payments to Walter Stewart, or to the subscriber. -John P Stewart

Orphans Crt of Wash Co, D C. Ltrs test on prsnl est of Wm Fields, late of Wash Co, dec'd. -John Mountz

WED JUL 2, 1817
Orphans Crt of Wash Co, D C. 1-Wm Miller, insolvent debtor, confined in the prison bounds of Wash Co, for debt. 2-Walter Mudd, same. -Wm Brent, clk.

THU JUL 3, 1817
In Chancery. Chas Co Crt, Md, Crt of Equity, Jun Term, 1817. Peter Gouch & Co, vs Jas Swann, Fred'k Haymaker & Mary his wife, John Elder & Sarah his wife, Rebecca Swann, Justiniah Swann, David Stem & Eliz his wife. Bill-to obtain a decree for the sale of land of Wm Swann, late of Chas Co, dec'd, died seized. Wm Morriss, trustee; prsnl est not sufficient to pay debts. Swann left the following legal heirs & reps entitled to said land, viz. Jas Swann, Mary, mrd with Fred'k Haymaker, Sarah mrd with Jas Elder, Rebecca Swann, Justinian Swann, & Eliz who mrd David Stem, all of whom reside in Pa, excep Jas Swann, a resident of St Mary's Co, Md. -John Barnes, clk, Chas co Crt, Md.

Ladies with ltrs in the Wash P O, Jul 1, 1817:

Adams Mgt	Bowie Mrs Eliz	Boarman Miss C M
Bur Eliz	Chub Louisa	Drury Mrs Winifred
Dyer Mrs Jane	Duncler Mrs Ann	Fleming Miss Mgt
Gamble Mrs-2	Gallagher Miss Ann	Griyn Eliza W
Helen Mrs Susan	Hawley Miss Betsey	Harrison Mrs Susan
Jupee Mrs Lofter	Jones Miss Williamina	Jones Miss Rebecca
Lucas Mrs Nelly	Lowry Miss Mary	Lands Mrs Susan
Morris Mrs	M'Donal Mrs Mgt	Miller Rosena
Miller Mrs Louisa	Morarty Miss Mary	Ninsene Mrs Mary
Powell Mrs Juler	Perry Miss Sarah D	Parsons Mrs Ann
Parsons Mrs Thomas	Parry Mrs Sidney	Redman Miss M J D
Reed Mary	Suter Mrs Sarah	Shorter Miss Ann
Scott Mrs Ann	Saml Jane	Stanton Mrs Mgt
Stuart Miss Eliza	Thompson Miss Cecilia	Thompson Miss Sophia
White Mary Ann	Wonts Mary	Wincett Miss Eliz
Wethwell Mary A	Womesly Mrs Mary	Webb Miss Betsey
Wilson Mrs Sarah-3	Young Mrs Jemimy	-Thos Munore, P M.

Died: on Jun 19, in his 67th yr, John Chalmers, late shrf of Balt Co, Md.

Take pity on a mthr. Went away from his mthr's hse on Jun 11, a boy named Wm Travener, generally cld Wm Ball, about 9 yrs old. Apply to Ellen Ball, Lancaster st, Balt, Md.

FRI JUL 4, 1817
Wash Co, D C. I certify that Alex'r Carmicle [nr Rock Crk Chr] brght before me a stray horse. -Danl Rapine, J P.

Died: suddenly, on Jun 25, Mr Jas Livens, age about 35 yrs; branch pilot of our harbor. -Charleston, Jun 27.

MON JUL 7, 1817
Teacher wanted-single man. Apply to Benj Belt or Walter Smith, nr Queen Anne, PG Co, Md.

Vinegar for sale at my vinegar yd, Fairfax st, oppo the Presby chr. -John T Brooks, Alexandria.

Saddle sale. F Fairfax, Capitol Hill, Wash.

Mrd: on Jul 3, at the residence of Geo Boyd, by Rev Mr Hawley, Nathl Frye, jr, to Mrs Caroline Buchanan, late of Balt, Md.

Mrd: on Jul 3, at Phil, by Rev Dr Holcombe, E W Du Val, of Wash City, to Miss Ellen Jones, d/o Lloyd Jones, of Phil.

Died: on Jul 1, after a lingering & painful illness, Mrs Jane Markward, aged 54 yrs, w/o Mr Wm Markward, of Wash City.

$100 reward for runaway, negro man named Sam. -Chas P Goodall, Hanover, Va.

For sale-farm of Absalom Beddo, late of Montg Co, Md; 101 acs more or less, in PG Co, nr Bussard's blanket factory; with good frame dwlg Inquire of Jas Beddo, exc, in Gtwn, or Mr Thos Rays on the premises.

Jacob Stout has remv'd his blacksmith & wheelwright est to the stand lately occupied by Mr McChesny, as a coach shop, adj the Lancaster school, on Dunbarton st, Gtwn.

TUE JUL 8, 1817
On Fri last, Henry Simpson, who had resided in the village of Catskill a few mos, was accidentally killed by a musket in the hands of Mr Wm Wynkoop. Mr S was in the act of stealing, on the 27th, when he was shot. -Catskill Recorder.

Wash City affairs-appointments:
Wm Hewitt, Reg
Jos Elger, Srvyr
John Sessford, Comr-ward 2
John W Brashears, Comr-ward 4
Brooke Edmonson, Cnstbl for ward 2
Geo Adams, Cnstbl for ward 4
Henry Whetcroft, Treas
Wm Waters, Comr-ward 1
Henry Ingle, Comr-ward 3
Nathan Moore, Cnstbl for ward 1
Lancelot Griffin, Cnstbl for ward 3

Mrd: on Jul 2, at Bedford, King Geo Co, Va, Maj John Gibbons Stuart to Miss Eliza Stith Fitzhugh, d/o Henry Fitzhugh.

Died: at his country seat nr Natchez, on Jul 5, after a long & painful illness, Jas M'Intosh, in the 50th yr of his age.

WED JUL 9, 1817
Sale of prop for taxes, Aug 2, Wash City Corp. Harvey Bestor, col-ward 2.

Jas Bennet
Wm Fletcher
Lancelot Griffin
John Lowrey
Ambrose Moriatta
Isaac Read
David Tweedy
Patrick White

Saml Cloakey
Jas Gannon
Rachael or Raphael Jones
Wm Lowrey
Israel & John Pleasants
Patrick Tool
Chas Varden

Obit-died: in Balt, on Jun 30, Henry Jackson, [age appears to be 75th yr] in the midst of his chldrn & gr-chldrn; a distinguished Irish patriot; ntv of Ire; fr-in-law of Oliver Bond, a martyr to the Irish liberty. He was a hsbnd, fr, & friend.

Millford for sale, lately the prop of Maj Burdett Ashton, dec'd; 838 acs; with dwlg hse, etc. -Y Johnson, King Geo C H, Va.

THU JUL 10, 1817
Died: at Bladensburg, on Jul 9, Wm Arthur Lee, in his 21st yr, s/o the late Chas Lee, of Va, & a Lt in the U S N. He fell victim to the practice of duelling. He was not the challenger to the meeting on Jun 14, which has resulted in his death.

Water lots in Wash City for sale; per last will of Wm Hemsley, late of Queen Anne Co, Md, dec'd; lot 10 in sq 657; lot 10 in sq 667; lot 28 in sq east of 667. Apply to Thos Munroe. -Thos C Earle, Thos Hemsley, excx of the dec'd.

FRI JUL 11, 1817
Died: at Painesville, Geauga Co, Ohio, on Jun 7, Saml Huntington, aged 49, a ntv of Conn; in the summer of 1801 he remv'd to that county; ex-Govnr.

Died: on Jul 6, at Richmond, Va, Wm Rose, after a long & lingering indisposition, in an advanced stage of life; long a pblc jailor of the city. -Enquirer.

Wash Co, D C. John Butler, insolvent debtor, confined in the prison bounds of Wash City, for debt. -Wm Brent, clk.

Sale of Wash City lots, for taxes. Wm Ingle, coll of ward 3.

Thos Addison
Richd Andrews, Emory's heirs, & Adam Lynn
Henry Appleton
Alex'r Buchan
Wm Barkesdale
Barnes & Rudgate
John Basset
Jas Craig, M D
Nathl Crawford-heirs
Clagett & Mason

Bird & Co
Francis Boone
Benj Bacon-heirs
Wm Bean
Miss Eliz Carrol
Overton Carr-heirs
Chas Carroll, jr
Jacob Chandler

Alex'r Anderson
Abiel Blackney
Clement Biddle
Thos C Bowie-heirs
Henry Bradford
John Campbell
Saml Coolidge-heirs
John Craig-heirs
Saml Chases-heirs

Mary Carroll	Jos Carlton-heirs	Dick & Stewart
Caroll, Young & Oden	Cath Connell	Wm Diggs
Dunlop & Carlton	Cath Dalton	Henry Dearborn
Thos Ewell	Jas Earle	Ign Fenwick-heirs
Job Fowler	Thos Fenwick	John Fowler
Peter Hall	Saml Hepburn, heirs	Robt T Hooe
Jonathan Hall	Wm Harrison	Jas Holliday
Henry Hill	Thos Herty & Wm Fletcher	Danl Janifer
Jas Johnson, jr	Edw Langley	Andrew Leitch
Francis Leake	Adam Lynn	Eliza Leidler
Wm Lux	Wm Martin	Jas Neill o/Bennett
Henry Nicholls	Odien & Notley Young-heirs	Jas Piercy
Edw Parkinson	Jas Penrose	Jas Patton
Nathl Philips	Andrew Parker	Alex'r Reed
Mary Rose	David Ross	Mathew Ridley
Wm Russell	Mary C Ringgold	Wm Semmes
John Story	Jonathan Swift	John Smith
Chas Stewart	Mahlon Scholfield	Jas Tilghman
Wm H Tilghmen	Mathew Tilghman	Edw Tilghman
Richd Tilghman	Peregrine Tilghman	John Travers
Thos Watkins	Basil Waring	Notley Young-heirs
Jos Young	Miss Eliz Young	
Mary Young & E Carroll		

For sale or exchange, for merchandize or prop in Gtwn or Wash; 2 farms in Montg Co, Md, nr Goshen; one of 194 acs, formerly owned by Jesse Cromwell. The other tract, 150 acs, formerly occupied by Mr Bates. Apply to Mr John Ricketts, who lives on the premises. Also 570 acs nr Eddyville, Ky. -Thos C Wright, Gtwn.

SAT JUL 12, 1817
Stolen, from King Wm C H, Va, Jul 8, pr of black horses; $50 reward. Wm Burke

Comrs of the Fairfax Turnpike Co:

Wm Moss	Wm H Fitzhugh	B G Thornton
Richd Ratcliff	D Carroll o/Dud	Fred'k May
Wm Thornton	Robt Brent	Geo W P Curtis
Carlile F Whiting	Francis Peyton	Thos Dane

MON JUL 14, 1817
Died: at the hosp in N Y, on Jul 7, Capt Thos S Seymour, of Hartford, Con, formerly of the 25th regt U S Infty.

Died: at Newport, after a long illness, Lt Edw S Nowell, U S M C, s/o the late Edw B Nowell, of Charleston, in his 21st yr.

Commited to the goal of Allegany Co, on Jun 24, a negro man, Joe, about 30 yrs of age; says he belongs to Robt Haushberger, of Augusta Co, Va, nr Staunton.
-W H Dawson, Shrf of Allegany Co.

$50 reward for runaway, negro man Will, about 36 yrs of age. -Azel Beall, nr Bladensburg, PG Co, Md.

Stray cow came to the subscriber. -Cornelius Callaghan, U S Magazine, Little Falls, Jul 14.

TUE JUL 15, 1817
Military & Genr'l Agency, at Wash City; military land warrants, patents, etc. -A T Crane

For sale-decree from St Mary's co crt, Crt of Chancery, pblc sale at Clifton Factory, in said Co, of: tract cld *Good Luck*, 100 acs more or less, adj the Factory. One tract cld *Number Six*, 159 acs; one cld *Nowell's Fancy*, 102 acs. Also, tract cld *Race Ground*, 207 acs. Mr Peter Gough, at the factory, will shew same. -Wm Hebb, trustee.

Stolen-an excellent milch cow; $10 reward. Jonas Keller, at the Young mansion hse, nr the Potomac bridge.

Wicomico land for sale, 250 acs. Jas G Bateman will shew same. -W Courts, Milton Hill, Chas Co.

Launville for sale; 5 to 600 acs in Pr Wm, Va. -G R A Brown, Launville.

WED JUL 16, 1817
Mrd: at the residence of Mrs Pyne, at Charleston, S C, on Jun 25, by Rev Mr Muller, Col Jas Bankhead, U S army, to Miss Ann S Pyne.

Mrd: at Plattsburg, Capt Clark, U S Infty, to Miss Betsey Durand. [No date-recent.]

$50 reward for runaway negro man, John Posey, pump maker. He was raised in Chas Co, nr Beentown, Md, by Mr Miles. I purchased him about 4 yrs ago. His fr & mthr live nr Beentown, at the widow Boon's. -Lewis Smith, Gtwn.

Bedford, Pa, Jul 10. On Sat, in this borough, Mr John Sheetz, about 30 yrs, was killed by John Mackey, who dischg'd a gun with a blank cartridge. Mr Sheetz leaves a widow & 3 small chldrn.

THU JUL 17, 1817
Pblc sale of gound in Nottingham, PG Co, Md, having a store hse & granary; prop of John Duval, taken to satisfy a judgment obtained by John Spicer against said Duvall, surviving obligor of Chas S Perrie, dec'd. -Basil Bowling, shrf-PG Co, Md.

Estate for sale-300 acs, with dwlg hse. -A Dickins, Wash.

FRI JUL 18, 1817
Died: in Phil, on Jul 6, Dr Adam Kuhn, in his 76th yr; lately elected Pres of the College of Physicians.

$100 reward for mulatto woman, Monnaca, about 25 yrs of age, ranaway from the subscriber, on Jun 28. -Jane Thornton

$50 reward for runaway, a German redemptioner, Godfried Pfund, age 24 yrs, miller by profession; ntv of Wirtemburg. -John B Bayles, Selbymills, A A Co, Md.

SAT JUL 19, 1817
Sale of Wash City lots for taxes. Geo Adams, coll 4th ward.

Saml Blodget-heirs	Zachariah Berry
Alex'r Bateman	Jasper Cope
John Cox	Bernard Elliot-heirs
Lewis Farrington-heirs	Thos T Gantt
Benj Hitchburn	Bernard Hart
Henry Howard	Isaac H Jackson
Henry Kreamer-heirs	Jas King
Jas B Parsons	Jas Reed
Benj Stoddert	Spalding heirs
Sarah Slater	Jona Slater-heirs
Francis Sands	Andrew Smith
John Steel	Lewis Summers
Wm Sandford	Richd Thomas
Mahlan Roach	Littleton D Teakle
Jas Ward	John Ward
Wm & J Willink	Walker & Wheeler
Wm Wilson	Nicholas Young
Mary Yeates	Susan Young
Abraham Young-heirs	

Died: on Thu wk, at Petersburg, Va, Griffin Stith, Judge of the Norfolk Dist Crt.

Wash Co, D C. Jas Shorter, alias Legens, insolvent debtor, confined in the prison bounds of Wash Co, for debt. -Wm Brent, clk.

PG Co Crt, Md. Comrs apt'd on the petition of John Stone & Nathl Pope, jr, for division of rl est of Nathl Pope; estate cannot be divided. -John R Magruder, clk.

Wash City ordinance. Relief of Thos Williams for blacksmith work furnished Henry Herford, late Comr of ward 2; $14.66.

MON JUL 21, 1817
Mrd: on Jul 17, by Rev Mr Waugh, Mr Jas Fry to Miss Ann R White, eldest d/o Mr Ambrose White, all of Wash City.

Lumber yard, Wash. Rezin Orme, agent for H Goldsborough.

For sale-land in Orange Co, Va, on the Rapidan rvr, 1,785 acs. For terms apply to Mr Thos Taylor, of Richmond, or to the subscriber. -Thos Macon

TUE JUL 22, 1817
Mrd: on Jul 15, by Rev Mr Epinette, Mr Abner Ritchie, jr, of Gtwn, D C, to Miss Harriot Semms, d/o Benj Semms, of Chas Co, Md.

Wash Co, D C. Pendleton Heronimus, insolvent debtor, confined in the prison bounds of Wash Co, for debt. -Wm Brent, clk.

WED JUL 23, 1817
Mrd: in Alexandria, on Jul 17, by Rev Mr Wilmer, Mr Sabrett E Scott, merchant of Gtwn, to Miss Maria Mandeville, d/o the late Mr Jonathan Mandeville, of Alexandria.

Mrshl's sale-sundry hsehld furn; at suit of Wm Chick, against Wm G Thompson, & sold on account of the same. -Wash Boyd, Mrshl-DC.

THU JUL 24, 1817
Saml Anderson, Atty & Cnslr, has established his ofc in Wash City, on Pa av.

Caspar Henry, at the Perpetual Lime Kiln, on the Schuylkill, below the High st premanent bridge, Phil, will contract for any quantity of stone lime. -Phil, Pa

A Troop of Cvlry is organized at Alexandria, at which Wm F Thornton is appt'd Capt; Wm D Sims, 1st Lt; Saml Thompson, 2d Lt; Richd C Mason, Cornet.

FRI JUL 25, 1817
Balt, Jul 23. A hse in Franklin st was struck by lightning yesterday & Capt John M'Kenley, late of the U S army, was instantly killed. He was formerly a merchant of N Y.

Mrd: at Cragfont, Tenn, on Jun 17, by Rev Mr Hodges, Capt Wm Robeson, U S army, to Miss Selima Winchester, d/o Gen Jas Winchester.

For sale-lot 1 in sq 104, on 20th st, all the right, title & int of Henry Suttle; adjs the prop of Jos Forrest. Deed of trust dt'd Oct 17, 1812, from said Henry Suttle to Nathan Luffborough, to secure a debt due Wm Crawford, dec'd, late of Gtwn. -Nathan Luffborough, trustee. P Mauro, auct.

SAT JUL 26, 1817
Land for sale-*Douglas Hill*, about 700 acs, nr Dumfries, Va. -P Harrison, Dumfries, Va.

Died: on Jul 24, at Balt, Wm Cooke, aged 71 yrs.

Died: on Jul 22, at Balt, Mr David Foreman, in her 73d yr; leaving a number of relatives to lament their loss.

$100 reward for runaway male slave, Robin, mulatto, about 27 yrs of age. -Richd H Love, Kinsley, Fauquier Co, Va.

Farm for sale, on which the subscriber now resides; nr Greenwich, Pr Wm Co, Va, 350 acs. -Aminta E Moxley

MON JUL 28, 1817
PG Co, Md. Sale of the following tracts of land: *Peache's Meadows, Peache's Balance, Peache's Triangle,* & part of *Strife,* 186 acs; taken as the prop of Thos Shorte, to satisfy a judgment at suit of Henry Culver & Edw Hall. -Jos Isaac, for Basil Bowling, shrf of PG Co, Md.

TUE JUL 29, 1817
Notice-persons having claims against the est of Jas Wallace, late of Montg Co, Md, dec'd, are to present the same. -Daniel Lee

WED JUL 30, 1817
Wash Co, D C. Felix Dean, insolvent debtor, confined in Wash Co prison, for debt -Wm Brent, clk.

THU JUL 31, 1817
For sale-farm in the neighborhood of Wash lateley occupied by Robt Brooke Beall. Deed of trust from Benj Berry, sen, of PG Co, Md, & Robt Brooke Beall, of Wash; land in Montg Co, Md-436 1/2 acs. H Cozens, atty. -Benj Berry, jr.

Wash Co, D C. Clarke Burnett, insolvent debtor, confined in Wash Co prison, for debt. -Wm Brent.

Mrd: on Jul 17, by Rev John Dunn, at *Belmont,* the seat of Ludwell Lee, Dr Wilson C Selden to Mrs Mary Alexander, of Alexandria, D C.

Died: at Poughkeepsie, N Y, on Jul 20, Jas Hamilton, of Woodlands, nr Phil, aged 42 yrs.

FRI AUG 1, 1817
Wash Co, D C. 1-Mark Shaw, insolvent debtor, confined in the prison bounds of Wash Co, for debt. 2-Wm C Simmons, stone cutter, insolvent debtor, confined in the prison bounds of Wash Co, for debt. 3-Peter Hoover, insolvent debtor, confined in Wash Co prison, for debt. -Wm Brent, clk.

For sale-land in Albemarle Co, Virg; 1,000 acs; with dwlg hse. Will be shewn by the owner, nr the premises. -Dabney Minor

Notice-I have commenced the blacksmith business. -Leonard Piles, on Beall st, oppo Mrs Holtzman's tvrn. Gtwn.

Gtwn College, D C. Bach of Arts was conferred on Chas Dinnies & Geo Dinnies, both from N Y. Students who distinguished themselves:

Henry Gough, Md
Jas Calaghan, Balt
Edwin Bergh, N Y
Thos Jameson, Md
Edw McCabe, Pa
Thos Lee, Md
Mark Jenkins, Balt
Benoni Neale, Md
Jas Homans, Wash
Peter Menard, Kaskaskia, Ill Ter
Richd McPherson, Md
Wm Lee, Wash
Wm Hardy, Md
Wm Hopkins, Md
Edwin Bergh, N Y
Jas Patton, Alexandria
John Warring, Md
Jos Jameson, Md
Wm Jenkins, Balt
Danl Obrien, Gtwn
Alex Melvin, Gtwn
Jomes Roebuck, N Y
Henry Riley, N Y
Wm Carroll, Md
Francis Trubat, Phil
Elcon Jones, Gtwn
Richd A Wright, Gtwn
Dennis Donlevy, Trenton
Wm Gwynn, Md
Jas Walsh, Balt
Geo W Hopkins, Balt co
Edmund McCabe, Md
Alex Gaston, N C
Wm Wells, Balt
Wm Mauro, Wash
Paul Mooney, N Y
Jas Lynch, Pa
John Gray, Gtwn
John Cremer, Wash
Thos S Lee, Md
Jas Almeida, Balt
Robt Meade, Wash
Andrew Byrne, Porto Rico
Richd Wright

SAT AUG 2, 1817
Land for sale-plantation formerly the prop of Wm Hall, of Wm, late of PG Co, dec'd; 235 acs, with small dwlg hse. Can be shown by Edw Hall, or Richd D Hall.

MON AUG 4, 1817
Notice-persons indebted to the firm of Childs & Robb, & to John N Robb, are to make payment by Aug 6. -John N Robb, Gtwn.

Land for sale in the young but flourishing town of Fort Royal, Fred'k Co, Va; 600 acs with commodious brick dwlg hse. -Thos Buck, Winchester, Va.
[Other acreages in same area are listed.]

We learn that Geo Hall, ntv of Balt, & to have been on board a Spanish Vessel which was wrecked some time ago on the coast of Africa, where he fell into the hands of the Arabs of Lower Suze, has been released from slavery, thru Mr Willshire, British Cnsl at Mogadore, Morocco.

Mrd: on Jul 30, by Rev Mr Matthews, Mr Saml Barkley, of Alexandria, to Miss Teresia C Jameson, of Chas Co, Md.

TUE AUG 5, 1817
Died: on Aug 4, in Gtwn, Lynde Elliott. His remains will be interred today.

WED AUG 6, 1817
Notice. My wife Nancy Burroughs, on Apr 8 last, absented herself from my bed & board, without any provocation from me. I am determined not to pay any of her debts. On the day of her absenting herself, she was with Russell Hill, her fr, & Isaac Murphy, her bro-in-law, who were going to Ky. Great distress of mind to me & my poor chldrn. -John Burroughs, Aquia.

Lexington, Ky, Jul 22. On Sun last, Mrs Eleanor M'Cullough & Mrs Jane Lucket, were killed by lightning in the Presby meeting hse in this town.

THU AUG 7, 1817
Wash Co, D C. Henry T Doyar, insolvent debtor, confined in the prison bounds of Wash Co, for debt. -Wm Brent, clk.

Andrew Oehler, of Leonardtown, Md, has invented a boat that goes by paddles & a machine underneath the deck that creates wind sufficient for 2 small sails. He has obtained a patent from the U S.

Strayed or stolen from the garden of the late Mr Thos Robertson, on Sat evening, a bay horse. -Thos Newell, Bridge st, Gtwn. [Handsome reward.]

Copartnership formed bet John G Hapiner & John McDuell; having taken part of Mr Waigand's hse, next dr to Mr Burk, the upholsterer, High st, where they carry on the Hse, Sign & Ornamental Painting Business.

Orphans Crt of PG Co, Md. Ltrs of adm on prsnl est of Walter S Parker, late of said co, dec'd. -Jos N Burch, adm.

FRI AUG 8, 1817
Sale at auction-the prsnl est of Thos Turner, late of Gtwn, D C, dec'd; furn, wine, etc. -John Tyler, Trueman Tyler, excs. John Travers, auct.

For sale-new & elegant piano fortes; made in Phil; to be seen at Mr Duffey's bk & stationary store, High st, Gtwn. -Saml Dyer, teacher of vocal music.

To the good people of the U S. My fr, an aged man, left this country about 9 yrs ago, intending to go to Tenn, since which I have not head of him. I wld like to discover where he is, where is his family, or his fate. John Ackey, Camden, S C.

SAT AUG 9, 1817
Utica, N Y, Jul 25. A short time since, Capt Jonathan Whitaker, his wife, & grchld, all of Stafford, Conn, were all killed in horse waggon accident.

The subscriber wishes to employ sundry persons on the new establishment of Karthaus & Geissenheiners, on the mouth of the Little Mushannon, Clearfield Co, late Lawrence, at present New Covington twnshp; teacher, shoemkr, music teacher, carter, etc. Adjoins counties-Clearfield, Jefferson, & Warren, Va. -Peter Arn Karthaus

Mrd: on Aug 6, by Rev Mr Williston, at Upper Marlborough, Md, Capt Gamaliel Pease to Miss *Francis F Oliver, of that place. *Copied as written.

Orphans Crt of PG Co, Md. Pblc sale-all the prsnl prop of Jonathan T Sasser, dec'd; furn, carpenter's tools, negroes, etc. Prop sold to make distribution among his heirs. Geo Richards, exc.

Info wanted of John Hunt, a ntv of Edinburgh, came to the U S in the fall of 1815, & was doing business in the nursery & seed line at a place cld New-Corpse, nr Wash, as late as Oct, 1815. Address his bro, Wm Hunt, now in Charleston, S C; or Mr John Kennedy, merchant, Wash City.

MON AUG 11, 1817
Died: at Augusta, Ga, on Jul 30, Mr Henry Herford, of Wash City; while on a tour thru the southern states for his health; death was from a fever of a few days.

TUE AUG 12, 1817
Orphans Crt of Wash Co, D C. Ltrs of adm on prsnl est of Thos Smith, late of said city, waterman, dec'd. -Leah Smith, admx.

Mrd: on Aug 5, by Rev Mr Fenwick, Mr Bennett Clements, jr, to Miss Eliza Hyde, all of Gtwn.

Montg co land for sale; the farm on which I reside; 200 acs; with frame dwlg hse, etc. Enquire of John Hughes, Wash City, Edw Hughes, Damascus, Montg Co, Md, or of the subscriber, on the premises. -Eliz Hughes, Montg Co, Md.

WED AUG 13, 1817
Orphans Crt of Montg Co, Md. At the dwlg place of the late Saml Middleton, sale of all the prsnl prop of the dec'd; negroes, stock, furn, etc. -Wm Culver, adm.

THU AUG 14, 1817
$20 reward for German Redemptioner, Chas Ferdinand Kretschman, aged about 19 yrs, who absconded yesterday. -Edw Burk, Gtwn, Aug 14.

Partnership formed bet C P Beeding & Thos J Barnes; dry goods, Gtwn.

$100 reward for negro man, Clem Dausy, with Celia his wife, & infant boy 6 mos old, the prop of Chas Cutts; absconded from Wash City on Mon. -N B Van Zandt

Lawler wheat for sale at my farm. Humphrey Peake, Centreville, Fairfax Co, Va.

For sale-all Chas J Lancaster's right, title & int in Cobb Neck, Chas Co, Md, cld *Gill's Land*, residence of his dec'd fr, John Lancaster, 126 acs +. -John B Morris

FRI AUG 15, 1817
Died: on Aug 6, at the Eleutherian Mills, on the Brandywine, in Wilmington, Dela, Peter Saml Du Pont de Nemours, aged 78 yrs.

SAT AUG 16, 1817
For sale-the elegant Mansion Hse & Lots, improved & lately occupied by Mr John S Williams, on Gay st. -Clement Smith, Gtwn.

MON AUG 18, 1817
Mrd: on Aug 3, by Rev Mr Burch, Mr Wm Wallis, of Wash City, to Miss Sarah C Harcum, of Alexandria.

Died: on Jul 11 last, in Guadaloupe, after a severe illness of 3 days, Capt Wm Daingerfield, of the ship *Thomas*, of Alexandria.

Lands for sale: *Resurvey on Thos & Mary, & the Meadows*, in PG Co, Md, 407 3/4 acs. Tract cld *Jackson's Improvement & Hard Struggle*, Montg Co, Md, 246 acs; adjs the land of Mr Jasper Jackson. Thos Cecil, the tenant on this land, will shew it. Also 200 acs in Fairfax Co, Va; Janus Falconer, the tenant on this land, will shew it. -John Laird, Gtwn.

TUE AUG 19, 1817
Co-partnership under the firm of Hill & Boteler, expired by limitation, is this day dissolved; Boteler will settle same. -Chas Hill, Alex'r H Boteler.

$100 reward for negro man Clem & his wife Nanny. -Saml Sprigg, Northampton Farm, nr Bladensburg, Md.

Mrd: on Aug 17, by Rev Mr Matthews, Mr Daniel Fagan to Miss Ann Murphy, both of Wash City.

Notice-application will be made to the Sec for the War Dept for the renewal of Land Warrant 499, dt'd Sep 28, 1815, granted to me for svcs as a sldr in the U S army. -John Hinkle, Sgt late 38th infty.

WED AUG 20, 1817
Died: at Charleston, S C, on Aug 6, after a wk's illness, the Rt Rev Theodore Dehon, Bishop of the diocese of Charleston.

$10 reward for runaway negro man, Harry. -Jas Hollis, Pomonky, Chas Co, Md.

THU AUG 21, 1817
Wm Temple Franklin, grson of Dr Franklin, has lately published pvt correspondence, etc, from '53 to '90.

St Mary's co Crt, [Md] Crt of Equity, Aug Term, 1817. Bennet Gough vs Janet Thompson, adm of Jas Thompson & Barzillai Thompson, John W Thompson, Wm Thompson, Henry Thompson, Maria Thompson, Jane Thompson, John Thompson

& Richd Thompson, heirs of Jas Thompson. Rg-Jas Thompson, late of St M Co, was indebted to the cmplnt; the said Jas is dead & his prsnl est not sufficient to pay his debts; the dfndnts are his admx & heirs, & Wm & Jas, reside out of Md. -Jo Harris, clk.

St Mary's co Crt, [Md] Crt of Equity, Aug Term, 1817. Zachariah Mattingly vs Jos Ford. On Apr 22, 1813, Jos Ford executed a deed to Zachariah Mattingly for part of *St Giles*, & part of *Pomfet Fields*, lying in St M Co; same was not recorded agreeably to law. Jos Ford resides out of Md. -Jos Harris, clk.

Died: on Aug 16, at Rockville, Montg Co, Md, Mrs Mary Taney, w/o Augustus Taney, in her 29th yr; & on the same day died their infant & only child, aged 7 wks & 3 days.

Orphans Crt of PG Co, Md. Ltrs of adm d b n on the est of Gabriel Peterson Van Horn, late of said co, dec'd. -Alethia E Van Horn, excx.

St Mary's co Crt, [Md] Crt of Equity, Aug Term, 1817. Robt Bean vs Barton Lynch, John Lynch devisees & Thos Lynch adm with w a of Stephen Lynch. Stephen Lynch, late of St M Co, was indebted to the cmplnt; Stephen is dead & his prsnl est is insufficient for payment of his debts; one of the devisees, John, resides out of Md. Bill is obtain a sale of rl est of the said Stephen. -Jo Harris, clk.

St Mary's co Crt, [Md] Crt of Equity, Aug Term, 1817. Jas Hebb vs the heirs of Willoughby Nugent, Mary Ennis & Nancy Ennis, heirs of Mary Nugent. Eliz Baxter, late of St M Co, died intestate, seized of rl est; Robt Nugent, one of the heirs, has cnvyd all his right, etc, to Jas Hebb, cmplnt; dfndnts reside out of Md. -Jo Harris, clk.

For sale-plantation which John Farrall, of PG Co, Md, late dec'd, was possessed; supposed to be 100 acs. -Jas Macgill, Rich Isaac, Dennis Boyd, comrs.

FRI AUG 22, 1817
Committed to the goal of Fred'k Co, Md; negro man John, alias Tom; says he belongs to a Mr Geo Ash, nr Winchester, Va. -Jos M Cromwell, Shrf o/Fred'k Co.

Persons indebted to Philip B Greenwell & Co, or to Philip B Greenwell or Saml Greenwell, are to make immediate payment thereof to Wm T Maddox, trustee, St Mary's co Crt, Md.

SAT AUG 23, 1817
To be let-hse & lot at present occupied by Walter S Chandler; possession on Sep 1. It is at the crnr of Fred'k & 2d sts. -John Gozler, Gtwn.

MON AUG 25, 1817
Died: on Aug 22, in his 51st yr, Mr Gilbert Docker, a ntv of Eng, & long an inhabitant of Wash City.

Balt, Aug 13. On Aug 9, the d/o Jos Cowman & wife lost her life during a storm which desolated almost every bldg on their farm, in A A Co, Md, nr Snowden's Iron Works. She was about 18 yrs of age. Two or three of the remaining chldrn were injured; the parents were attending a pblc meeting of the Soc of Friends.

On Jul 26th last, a fire destroyed the hse of Mr Wm Jackson, Shanandoah Co, Va. His wife & 8 chldrn, 5 sons & 3 dghts had retired to bed. Mr Jackson & 2 of his dghts fell victims to the flames.

TUE AUG 26, 1817
Mgrs of the lottery, St Paul's Lane & Mkt st, Balt, Md.

Wm Gibson, M D
Ashton Alexander, M D
Geo Winchester
Jas L Hawkins
D A Smith
Nathl Williams
Solomon Etting
Geo S Baker
Jacob Lindenberger
John Stump
Jesse Eichelberger
Michl Tienan

John Owen, M D
Saml Hollingsworth
Henry Thompson
Lemuel Taylor
Henry Didier, jr
Lyde Goodwin
Peter Hoffman
Robt Purviance
Wm Schroeder
Leonard Matthews
Wm Ballard
Jeremiah Sullivan

Marble mantels; manufactory in Phil. -Thos Traquair & Co, N W crnr of 10th & Filbert sts.

WED AUG 27, 1817
Pblc sale-Comr's to divide the rl est of Thos West, late of Montg Co, Md, dec'd, viz: part of the *Two Bros*, *The Race Ground*, *John's Last Sh_f_*, part of *Rocky Point Fortified* & *Long Discovered*, 266 acs. -Wm Darnes, John Adamson, Wm Wilson, comrs.

THU AUG 28, 1817
Land for sale-order of co crt of Fairfax, Va, at the hse of Mrs Balmain, in said co; 250 acs. -Wm H Terrett, John C Hunter, Wm Moss, Thos Moss, F Peyton, comrs.

FRI AUG 29, 1817
Died: at Rockaway, nr N Y, on Aug 21, Mr Holman, tragedian, mgr of the Charleston Theatre.

Stray cow came to my plantation. -John Gettings, nr Rock Crk Chr.

SAT AUG 30, 1817
Norfolk & Balt Line-steam boat & packets; new steam boat *Virginia*, Capt John Ferguson, leave Thu & return Mon. -Benj Ferguson, Bowly's wharf, Balt.

$30 reward for runaway, negro Elleck, age about 35 yrs. -Jesse Conn, lvg in Fairfax Co, Va.

MON SEP 1, 1817
Mrd: on Aug 20, at Hope, Bertie Co, N C, by Rev Moses Gillam, David Stone, of Wake Co, N C, to Miss Sarah Dashiell, of Wash City.

Died: on Aug 23, at the residence of Maj Hugh Cox, in Chas city, Md, Mr Horatio Koones, in his 24th yr, s/o Mr F Koones, of Alexandria.

Ala & Talapoosa lands for sale. -Jas S Walker, Augusta, Geo.

Pblc notice is given that the town of Alabama is established at the site cld Ten Mile Bluff, east side of Ala rvr. Proprietors of the town:

John Scott, Milledgeville, Geo	Jas Manning, Madison Co, M T
Waddy Tate, Madison Co, M T	Thos Bibb, Madison Co, M T
A P Hayne, Nashville, Tenn	Z Lamar, Milledgeville, Geo
Chs Williamson, Milledgeville, Geo	Wm D Stone, Milledgeville, Geo
John Donelson, jr, Nashville, Tenn	Wm E Butler, Nashville, Tenn
Jas Jackson, Nashville, Tenn	

TUE SEP 2, 1817
Died: on Aug 29, after a short but severe indisposition, Wm Paton, jr, late cashier of the Mechanics' Bank of Alexandria.

For sale or exchange for prop in Gtwn, my farm of about 300 acs, in Fairfax Co, Va; adjoins the seat of Danl Dulancy. Apply to Col Wm Minor, of Alexandria city, or at Big Falls of Potomac, Lewis Sewall.

$50 for negro, Jesse Payne, age about 40 yrs; ranaway on Aug 24th from the subscriber, lvg in Fairfax Co, Va. Saml Ager, Little Falls of Potomac.

WED SEP 3, 1817
Crt of Chancery, Wash Co, D C. Sale of brick hse & lot on sq 825, to pay debts of Mr Jos Costigan, dec'd. -Robt Brent, David Bates, trustees.

To Rent-genteel hse, not 10 mins from the capitol. -Wm Holtzman, Pa av, Wash.

THU SEP 4, 1817
To Rent-store & cellar on 9th st. -S Meade, crnr of 9th & D sts, Wash.

Died: Rev patriot, Gen Pickens, on Aug 11, at Tumassee, in Pendleton dist, S C.

The late Mr Jos Geo Holman was a ntv of Eng, & a descendant of Sir John Holman, of Warkeworth Castle, Banbury. His first appearance on a pblc stage was as Romeo at Covent Grdn Theatre, in 1784.

The heirs of Stephen Lanham, late of Montg Co, Md, dec'd, will offer all the real prop of same, cash only, of 112 acs, in Montg Co, on Paint Branch. -Joshua Dyal

Orphans Crt of Chas Co, Md. Prsnl est of Saml A Berry, late of said co, dec'd. -Mary Berry, admx.

Died: Mr John Rodney, eldest s/o Caesar A Rodney, of Dela, in his 19th yr. He died of a malignant fever while a midshipman in the U S Navy, first attacked while on the ship *Ontario*, then remv'd to lodgings in N Y C; expired on Aug 14. He was followed to the tomb, in St Paul's chr, by his parents & friends. -Del Watch.

FRI SEP 5, 1817
Balt, Mar 26. I have relinquished the practice o/law due to my late appointment to the bench, I have committed my business to David Hoffman. -N Brice

SAT SEP 6, 1817
For sale or rent-brick dwlg hse, at present occupied by Mr Jas L Edwards, F & 12th sts; possession on Oct 1 next. -Wm A Bradley, Bank of Wash.

Modern Holland. Wm Frederick the 6th, Sovereign of the Netherlands, Prince of Orange Nassau, was born Aug 24, 1772, & mrd the Princess Sophia Frederica, sr/o Fred'k William, of Prussia, & has issue Wm Fred'k Geo Ludwig, hereditary prince, & Genr'l in the British army, born Dec 6, 1792, & Wilhelmina Frederica Louisa Paulina Charlotta, born Mar 1, 1810.

Mrd: on Sep 4, by Rev Mr McCormick, Mr Kinsey Griffith to Miss Eliz McLeod, d/o Mr Danl McLeod, of Alexandria.

Val farm for sale; prop of the reps of the late Col Norwood, 470 to 500 acs in PG Co, Md, adjoining the farms of Mr Isaac Duckett & Mr Wm Bowie [of Walter.] Apply to Mr John Bassford, resident thereon. -Thos Wm Hall, agent for the reps.

MON SEP 8, 1817
Rare longevity-Herkimer, N Y, Jul 24. Mr Henry S Whiting, of this village, has in his possession the record of Thos Taylor, one of his ancestors, who was descended from Bshp Jeremy Taylor, of Eng. Mr Thos Taylor, a first settler in Daubury 1676, died Jan 1736, aged 92 yrs; had 10 chldrn by one wife, Thos, aged 90; Jos, aged 90; John, aged 70; Daniel, aged 94; Timothy, aged 56; Nathl, aged 100; Theophilus, aged 90; Deborah, aged 80, Rebecca, aged 99; Eunice, aged 90.

Milledgeville, Aug 26. Peter Early is no more! On Aug 15th at his seat in Greene Co, Ga, died, in the prime of his life; patriot, ctzn, statesman.

Philip H Minor was elected Cashier of the Mechanics Bank of Alexandria, on Wed, vice Wm Paton, jr, dec'd.

Mont Co Crt, [Md] Mar Term, 1817; in Chancery. Jannaro S Farre vs Thos W Howard & Edw O Williams. Rg-cnvynce in fee simple of land in Montg Co, about 1 1/2 acs, which Farre purchased of Howard on Jul 22, 1812. Wms resides in Va. -U Beall, clk of Montg co crt.

TUE SEP 9, 1817
Mrd: on Sep 2, at the seat of Dr H Barton, Pr Wm Co, Va, by Rev M Steele, Mr Hanson Gassaway, merchant of that place, to Miss Kitty E A Barron, of the former.

Mrd: on Sep 4, by Rev Mr Anger, Mr Lloyd Pumfrey, of Wash City, to Miss Eliza Spalding, of PG Co, Md.

Pblc sale of all the stock of leather, about $6,000 worth, at the late residence of E Jos Huber, dec'd, in Dumfries, Va. -Geo F Huber, adm.

WED SEP 10, 1817
Rev Wm Lithgow proposes to open an academy for ladies in Gtwn.

Mrd: on Sep 7, by Rev Mr Matthews, Mr John S Galaher, printer, to Miss Cath Shannon, all of Wash City.

Farm for sale-part o/the lands of the late Richd Brent, *Kettle Run*, Pr Wm, Va; ab't 600 acs. Apply to Geo L Brent, Stafford Co, Va; or John D Simms, Alexandria.

THU SEP 11, 1817
For sale-*Benfield*, Port Tobacco, Chas Co, Md; 811 acs. -F Newman, at the Grange, nr Port Tobacco, Md.

Mansion hse for sale; long the residenceof the late Mrs Mary Young; lg 2 story brick bldg; in the vicinity of the Potomac bridge. -Notley Young, jr.

Mrd: on Sep 4, at the seat of Mr Benj Berry, PG Co, Md, by Rev Mr McCormick, Geo Beall, of Wash City, to Mrs Eliza Bowie, of PG Co, Md.

Mrd: on Sep 9, by Rev Mr Matthews, at the residence of Wm Roberts, Wash Co, D C, Mr Lewis Carbery, of Wash City, to Miss Artemesia Cloud, of former place.

Mrd: on Sep 9, by Rev Mr Breckenridge, Mr Jas Gaither to Miss Ann Espey, both of Wash City.

Mrd: on Sep 9, by Rev Mr McCormick, Mr Benj M Belt to Miss Elton S Drane, both of Wash City.

FRI SEP 12, 1817
Bolting cloths for sale at the store of Messrs Butts & Cawood, King st, Alexandria. -Amos Alexander, Alexandria.

Mrsh'l sale, Oct 25, at Nicholas L Queen's htl, Capitol Hill-Wash. All the right, title, int, etc of Geo Burnes to part of lots 3 & 4 in sq 731, with improvements. The hse at present is occupied by Dr Horsley. Prop seized at suit of Israel Little, against the said Burnes, & sold to satisfy same. -Wash Boyd, Mrshl.

Shoes & hats for sale. -John Peabody, Gtwn. [Ad]

Orphans Crt of Wash Co, D C. David Peabody, insolvent debtor, confined in Wash Co prison, for debt. -Wm Brent, clk.

Val small farm for sale; 75 to 100 acs, nr the eastern branch bridge; with new frame bldg. Apply to Ann Berry, lvg in PG Co, Md.

Died: a few wks ago, at St Louis, Mo ter, after an illness of 11 hrs only, Edw Hempstead, formerly Delegate in Cong from that terr; ntv of Conn.

Died: on Aug 25, in the 30th yr of his age, of a consumption, after a painful illness of srvl wks, Lt Thos W Legge, of the U S M C.

SAT SEP 13, 1817
Died: at Charleston, a few days ago, Mr Richd B Brashears, of the U S Navy, & formerly of Wash City.

Orphans Crt of Wash Co, D C. 1-John Rawlings, insolvent debtor, confined in Wash Co prison, for debt. 2-Timothy Bean, same. -Wm Brent, clk.

My est, advertised in the Ntl Intel, is still for sale; I am desirous of mvg to the western country. -Wm P Bayly, Aquia, Stafford Co, Va.

In Chancery, Sep 6, 1817. Ratify sale by John Morris, trustee, in cause of Jas Stone, jr, against Chas J Lancaster; amount of sale-$1,500. Thos H Bowie, reg.

MON SEP 15, 1817
$10 reward for lost pktbk, with dollar notes. Deliver them to the hse of John Lavender, nr the Navy Yd, Wash.

$20 reward for Ramal, negro man, ranaway from Wash City on Jul 9.
-Sarah Love

Orphans Crt of Wash Co, D C. Pblc sale at the dwlg of John Boone, all the prsnl est of Nicholas Boone, dec'd; negroes, horses, hses, furn, etc. -Levin Boone, adm.

TUE SEP 16, 1817
$50 reward for runaway, negro man named Bill, aged about 26 yrs. -Francis Fenwick, Gtwn.

WED SEP 17, 1817
Died: in Rome, in May last, His Eminence Siffrecin Maury, aged 71. His riches are left to his bro, who is in the church, resident in France.

Died: At Brancepeth Castle, Eng, Wm Russell, aged 83, one of the richest of the realm. His son is a mbr of Parliament for Saltash. Lt Gen Sir Gordon Drummond, who srv'd in Canada during the late war, mrd one of his dghts.

Prospectus of a new paper cld the *Virginian*; to be published in Richmond twice a wk, by Wm F Pendleton.

To be sold to satisfy taxes due the corp of Wash City; prop of John Shute-$13.64 due; & Thos Law-$156.98 due. -Wm Ingle, Col 3d ward.

THU SEP 18, 1817
Genr'l Andrew Pickens, who died in S C, on Aug 11, was of French descent; his ancestors were driven from France by the revocation of the edict of Nantz; they first settled in Scotland, & then in the north of Ire. His fr emigrated to Pa. The dec'd was born in Bucks Co, Pa, on Sep 13, 1739; the family remv'd to Augusta Co, Va, & soon after to the Washaws, in this state. He mrd early in life, has left numerous offspring, & his consort, the sister of John E Calhoun, formerly a senator in congress, died but a few yrs before him -Pendleton Mess.

Mrd: on Sep 16, by Rev Dr Hunter, Mr Wm Y Wetsel to Miss Mary Holtzman, both of Gtwn.

Mrd: on Aug 27, in Nashville, Tenn, Alfred Balch, a ntv of Gtwn, to Miss Ann Newman, y/d/o Dr Newman, late of Salisbury, N C.

Died: in Gtwn, on Sep 13, Mr Anthony Reintzel, an old & respectable inhabitant.

Died: on Sep 4, in PG Co, Md, Mr John Evans, sen, an old & respectable inhabitant of that co.

Wm Beastall, *Chemical Manufactory*, crnr of Gough & Bond sts, Fell's Point, Balt, Md. -[Ad]

FRI SEP 19, 1817
Jas M Wayne is elected Mayor of Savannah city for the current yr.

N Y Sep 15. Wm W Jenner, a school mstr, convicted of assault & battery & gross indecency to svr'l female scholars, was on Sat, sentenced to 3 yrs hard labor in the Pen & a $500 fine. -Adv.

Mrd: on Sep 2, by Rev Mr Reed, Mr Horatio Wilcoxen to Miss Ann R Gaither, all of Montg Co, Md.

Richd Ballard, merchant tailor, oppo the Centre Mkt, Pa av, Wash. -Ad.

For sale-Mill Seat with 125 acs, on the waters of Difficult Run, in Fairfax Co, Va, cld *Towlston*. It belongs to Mr Geo W Fairfax. -H Gunnell, agent.

SAT SEP 20, 1817
Died: on Sep 17, after a short illness, at Mt Vernon, Richd Henry Lee Washington, of Fairfax Co, Va, nphw of Hon Bushrod Washington, & grand nphw of the illustrious ctzn of that same name.

Wash Co, D C. 1-John C Shindle, insolvent debtor, confined in Wash Co prison, for debt. 2-Josias Simpson, jr, same. -Wm Brent, clk.

$10 reward for runaway negro man, Jack Proctor, aged 23 yrs; hired last yr to Henry Burford nr the navy yd. He has relations in Wash City & Gtwn. -John A Sommers, Falls Chr, Fairfax Co, Va.

MON SEP 22, 1817
Branch Bank of the U S at Providence, R I; Seth Wheaton appt'd Pres; Nathan Waterman, jr Cashier.

TUE SEP 23, 1817
Wholesale Dry Good Store; Waller Clagett & Co, Wash st, Gtwn.

Land for sale-farm on Chappauamsic Crk, whereon the late Thos Harrison resided; about 1,200 acs; 3 miles from Dumfries, Va. -Ger'd Alexander, jr; & S G Alexander, excs.

WED SEP 24, 1817
For sale-lot 12 in sq 79, Wash. Apply to Thos Dunn, nr the Sugar Hse, Eastern Branch. -Local ad.

Died: at Westport, Mass, on Sep 7, Paul Cuffee, a man of color, in his 59th yr; a descendant of Africa.

Orphans Crt of Wash Co, D C. Ltrs of adm on prsnl est of Mary Pelin, late of said city, dec'd. -John Carnes

THU SEP 25, 1817
Mrd: on Sep 23, by Rev Mr McCormick, Mr Danl Turner to Miss Mary Ann Stewart, all of Wash City.

FRI SEP 26, 1817
Kidnapper punished. State of Md vs John Lacy [Balt Co Crt] In July last John Lacy tk Aaron Hulbert, a mulatto boy, about 9 or 10 yrs of age, from Balt Co to Alexandria, & sold him as a slave for life. The boy was born free-that he had been put to live with Lacy by his grmthr, his parents being dead; agreement bet Lacy & the grmthr, was, that the boy shld be bound an appr; indentures had not been executed. Verdict-Guilty-5 yrs hard labor in the Pen.

Richmond, Sep 12. Robt Gibson, alias Robt Carlton, was convicted on Wed last, of the murder of John N Peatross. Trial was before the Sup Crt of Law for Henrico Co, Va; his cnsl was Andrew Stevenson; verdict set aside & a new trial has been awarded. -Enquirer.

Died: on Sep 21, Mrs Eleanor Brackenridge, w/o Rev John Brackenridge, in her 52d yr, & 22d yr of her marriage. Mrs B left a hsbnd, 3 sons & a dght.

For rent-hse now occupied by Thos Burch, at the Wash Steam Boat Landing; possession given Oct 1, 1817. -A Cheshire, Wash Bridge.

Notice: the relatives of John De Bell, late of Pr Wm Co, Va, are informed he departed this life on Mar 15, last, without having made any will. -Jeremiah De Bell, adm, Paris, Fauquier Co, Va.

$100 reward for negro boy, Jim, about 19 yrs of age, ran away on Aug 30th. -Augustus Werninger, Morganton, Va.

SAT SEP 27, 1817
Orphans Crt of St Mary's Co, Md, Aug Term, 1817. Petition of Henry Ashton, adm of Jos Burroughs, late of St M Co, dec'd, give notice required by law. -Jas Forrest, reg o/wills. [Said notice followed-Henry Ashton, adm.]

Ezekiel Young, merchant tailor; F st, Wash. -Local ad.

MON SEP 29, 1817
$20 reward for runaway, appr boy named John A Judy, aged 19 yrs. -Saml Thompson, Gun smith, High st, Gtwn.

Died: on Sep 12, in his 68th yr, Maj Hanson Briscoe, Clk o/the Co Crt of Cumberland, Md; ntv o/St Mary's Co, Md; had a commission in militia during the Rev war.

Died: on Aug 22, in New Orleans, Mr Jas Hall, distinguished agriculturist.

Died: On Sep 26, in Wash City, Capt Jos Greenwell, of St Mary's Co, Md, formerly mstr of one of the Norfolk packets; after an absence of srvr'l mos. He was returning home to his mthr's fireside, when the hand of death seized him; by the bursting of a blood vessel.

Enquirer of Fri. Thornton Posey, late Col of U S Army, & recently a Col in the Patriot Army under Gen M'Gregor, breathed his last at Wilmington, N C, on Wed wk. He reached that harbour in a vessel from Amelia Island; died of billious fever.

TUE SEP 30, 1817
Farm for sale in Montg Co, Md, 138 1/2 acs; will exchange for prop in Gtwn or Wash City. -Thos Patterson

Orphans Crt of Wash Co, D C. Ltrs of adm on prsnl est of Thos Robertson, late of said co, dec'd. -Jane B Robertson, Michl Nourse, adms.

Mrd: on Sep 23, by Rev Thos C Searle, at Rockville, Montg C H, Md, Brice Selby to Miss Caroline Saunders, all of the above place.

Mrd: on Sep 23, by Rev Mr Matthews, Mr Artemas Bowen to Miss Gracie Plant, all of Wash City.

Died: at N Y, on Sep 20, in his 95th yr, Robt Steel, a ntv of Gloucestershire, Eng; emigrated to this country early in life.

Wash Co, D C. J B Bennett, insolvent debtor, confined in the prison bounds of Wash Co, for debt. -Wm Brent, clk.

WED OCT 1, 1817
Died: at New Orleans, of the prevailing fever, after an illness of only 5 days, Mr Henry Selon Boneval Latrobe, eldest s/o B Henry Latrobe, of Wash City. He was age 24 yrs on Jul 19 last. [No date-recent.]

THU OCT 2, 1817
Died: at Quebec, Peter Sambre, founder of the Roustigouche Soc, celebrated for the agility of its mbrs.

Isabella McDonald has just rec'd a case of straw bonnets. -Local ad.

Thos W F Blagge, Bridge st, Gtwn: assortment of crockery & glass ware, etc.

$20 reward for negro Chas, prop of Mr Thos Seemes, of PG Co, Md. -T Hyar & Son, High st, Gtwn.

One cent reward for appr boy, Caleb Barnhouse, who ran away on Sep 8. He is well grown & rough spoken. -Thos I Hall, St Mary's Co, Md.

Notice-the J B Bennett, insolvent debtor, is Jos B Bennett. This is to give notice of the name of the man. -Jas Bennett, bricklayer.

Intending to move southward: for sale-tract cld *Buckley's Tract*, 77+ acs, with dwlg hse. Also *Patchart's Tract*-56 acs. Also, I will lease for a term of yrs, tract of land on which I reside, 332 1/2 acs. These lands lie nr Centreville, Va. All persons to whom I am indebted will please present their claims. -Wm B Melvin, Airville, Fairfax Co, Va. [Nr Centreville, Va.]

FRI OCT 3, 1817
Nt'l Intell accounts are in the hands of Mr Franis Coyle, our old collector.

Mrd: on Sep 25, at Fredericksburg, Va, by Rev S Low, of Norfolk, Wm F Gray to Miss Mildred Stone, d/o Wm Stone.

Application for renewal of Military Land Warrant, 2061, dt'd Jan 25, 1816; same being lost or destroyed. -John Gidelman, late a pvt in the 5th reg U S Infty.

Notice-my wife, Mary Fronk, left my bed & board without any cause, I am determined to pay no debts of her contracting from this day. -Lewis Fronk

SAT OCT 4, 1817
Mrd: on Oct 2, by Rev Mr M'Cormick, Mr Jas B Holmead, merchant, of Wash City, to Miss Susan Stettinius, d/o Mr Saml Stettinius, dec'd.

Mrd: on Sep 25, at the residence of Mr Thos Riggs, by Rev Mr Linthicumb, Mr Philemon Griffith, to Miss Sarah H Riggs, all of Montg Co, Md.

$100 reward for runaway negro man, Chatham Brown, about 30 yrs old. -Wm Wells, of Geo, nr Mt Pleasant Ferry, PG Co, Md.

MON OCT 6, 1817
Newspapers-as early as 1736 a nwspr was established at Wmsburg, by W Parks. Clarkson & Davis began a nwspr at Wmsburg in Apr 1778.

Obit-died: on Sep 15, in his 42d yr, Elr Brown; for sometime a resident of Auburn, N Y; author of *History of the late War*, in two vols.

TUE OCT 7, 1817
Candle & Soap Manufactory, Canal Wharf. -Clement T Coote [Local ad]

For sale-land formerly occupied by Mr Chas Bennet, in Loudoun Co, Va; 312 acs. Will be shewn by Philip C Jones, who resides at Solomon Littleton's farm.

Notice-intending to remove to the country during the winter, I will rent my hse on 11th st. -Henry M'Pherson

Ladies with ltrs in the Wash P O, Oct 1, 1817:

Asher Mary	Attemus Miss Maria	Bran Madame
Burr Mrs Eliza	Bradley Miss Ann	Bryan Mrs Susanna
Braiden Eliz	Boyd Mary	Bray Miss Mary
Bellemain Miss L C	Claborne Jane	Clarke Mrs Eliza
Creighton Mrs Anna	Coolidge Mrs Mary	Denkler Mrs Ann
Dorsett Mrs Amelia Y	Davis Mrs M W D	Freeman Miss M A
Ferret Madame S-2	Green Mrs Mary	Gordon Martha
Goodrich Mrs	Greenfield Susanna	Hogan Mrs Sarah
Herbert Mrs Sally	Hawkins Miss E	Johnes Mrs Sandy
Jones Mrs Julian	Johnson Miss Susan	Jones Eliz L
Kalbfus Mrs C	King Eliz	Latourell Madame
Lee Miss Mary Ann	Maley Grace	McKim Miss Eliz

McCoy Miss Ann	McCardy Mrs Mary	McWaters Mrs Mary
Nelson Mrs Frances H	Nally Mrs Charity	Pemiliers Mrs
Power Miss Sarah Ann	Ptulan Madame	Purnell Mrs Nancy
Perry Miss Amelia	Rogers Mrs Lloyd	Smallwood Eliza
Shaw Mrs Elena	Sims Miss Ann	Shields Mrs Sarah
Taiter Mrs Sarah	Tippet Miss Sally	Tamson Mrs Eliz
Tidyman Mrs Susan	Vanderhader Mrs R	Wilson Mrs Sarah
Wert Lucinda		

WED OCT 8, 1817

Died: on Oct 5, after a short illness, Thos Rutter, Mrshl of Md Dist, in his 56th yr.

Died: on Oct 3, at his residence on Elk Ridge, Mr Henry McCoy, in his 54th yr.

Mrd: on Oct 7, by Rev Mr Ryland, of Gtwn, Mr Stephen Lancaster to Miss Sarah Beck, both of Wash City.

THU OCT 9, 1817

$200 reward for runaway negro man, Abram King, about 29 yrs of age; sawyer by trade. -J Tongue, nr Tracey's Landing, A A Co, Md.

Notice-pblc sale at the residence of Mr Geo Burns, Capitol Hill, a Hay Steelyd, with weight, chains, etc, seized to satisfy taxes due the Wash Corp. -Wm Ingle, Coll 3d ward.

Mrd: on Oct 5, by Rev Mr Kohlman, of Gtwn, Dennis Magruder to Miss Frances Fitzgerald, both of PG Co, Md.

Application for renewal of Military Land Warrant #7, dt'd Jul 27, 1815; lost or destroyed. -Geo Rowland, late Fife Maj in 36th regt of infty. 2-Same for Jas Murphy, land warrant #97, dt'd Aug 9, 1815, lost or destroyed. Late a pvt of the 14th regt U S infty. 3-Same for Robt Rawlins, late a pvt in the 36th regt U S infty; warrant #99, dt'd Aug 9, 1815.

Orphans Crt of Wash Co, D C. Sale at the late residence of Mrs Mary Peeling, dec'd, on N J av, nr the Capitol; all the prsnl est of dec'd. -John Carnes, adm.

FRI OCT 10, 1817

Died: on Oct 9, in Gtwn, after a long & distressing illness, Miss Adeline Peabody, age 1, d/o Gen John Peabody, of Gtwn. Funeral today from her fr's dwlg hse.

SAT OCT 11, 1817

To rent-3 story brick dwlg hse on Pa av, presently occupied by P D Stelle. Inquire of Mr Gideon Davis, or to John Knoblock, at the Glass hse. -Local

For sale-four young negro women. -Anthony Addison, First st, Gtwn.

Application for renewal of lost or destroyed Military Land Warrant; #135, dt'd Aug 14, 1815. Danl Doran, late a pvt of the U S Corps of Artl.

MON OCT 13, 1817
Sale of Curious Ware, at the hse oppo the Central Bank, Gtwn. -Vito Viti

Committed to the goal of Wash Co, DC; a black man, Wm Grason, 30 yrs old. His fr, N Grason, lives nr Fauquier C H, Va. -C Tippett, for W Boyd, Mrshl.

Died: on his passage from New Orleans to N Y in Sep last, Capt Thos Murray, of the Corps of Artl, U S army. Capt Murray was a ntv of Md.

TUE OCT 14, 1817
Died: on Oct 5, at *Harper's Ferry*, after a painful illness, Col Lloyd Beall, Military Store Kpr & Paymstr at that sta, & formerly an ofcr of the army.

Died: on Sep 29, at Augusta, Geo, Brvt Capt K McKenzie, of the corps of artl, U S army.

Died: on Sep 1, at New Orleans, Dr Jas Stephenson, Hosp Surg Mate, U S army.

Died: on Sep 5, at Pass Christian, Dr E L Allen, Hosp Surg Mate, U S army.

Wash Co, D C. Chas DeKrafft, insolvent debtor, confined in the prison bounds of Wash Co, for debt. -Wm Brent, clk.

Ladies shoe maker, Pa av, nr the Theatre, Wash. -Wm Morgan

R Darrah, dentist, has taken a rm next dr to Gen Peabody's on Bridge st, Gtwn.

WED OCT 15, 1817
Lines are written occasioned by the death of Miss Adeline Peabody, d/o Gen John Peabody, aged 19 yrs, who died after a long & peculiarly distressing illness, at Gtwn, D C, Oct 9, 1817.

Died: in Charlestown, Mass, on Oct 3, Col Nathl Hawkins, aged 69 yrs, ofcr of the Rev; ntv of R I.

THU OCT 16, 1817
Died: lately, at Agen, France, Madame Suzanne Toussaint-Louverture, of St Domingo, aged about 50 yrs. She has left 2 sons, Placide & St Jean Louverture; the latter is about 20 yrs of age. Another son, Isaac, the eldest of the 3, died about 12 yrs ago in Belle Island, to which place he had been exiled. -Jrnl du Commerce

Colonization Soc, Wash City. E B Caldwell, Sec.

Dr Elisha Harrison has relinquished the Drug & Med Store to Richd C Edgar; his whole attention will be to his professional pursuits; #5 Taylor's Row, Pa av, Wash.

FRI OCT 17, 1817
Wm W Bibb, late Senator in Cong from Ga, has rec'd the commission of Gov of the Terr of Ala, from the President.

Pblc sale; land in St Mary's Co, in Piney Point, formerly the prop of Stephen Lynch, late of said co, dec'd; sold to satisfy debt due on the mortgage to Alex'r Fenwick, of said Co. -G N Causin, trustee.

Creditors of Wm Eisenbeck are to render their claims by Nov 16. -G C Grammer, trustee.

SAT OCT 18, 1817
Land for sale-about 300 acs nr Trueman's Point, cld *Timber Neck*. -Geo Forbes, Hor C McElderby.

MON OCT 20, 1817
$50 reward for mulatto slave, Sally Dyson, age about 30 yrs; absconded from the svc of Dr Vowell, on Oct 4, & tk her 4 yrs old dght, Harriet Ann, with her. She was once the prop of the late Mrs Tabitha Jackson, of Nanjemoy, & may have gone to the plantation of Mr Ely Gray. She may have followed her late owner, Eleanor Jackson, bet this & Winchester, Va. -Jos Mandeville, Alexandria.

Val land prop for sale; of the est of the late Col T Lee, of Coton; 51 acs; 3 or 4 miles from Leesburg, Va; also lot adjoining with 360 acs; lot of 208 acs adj the land of Ludwell Lee; two lots oppo Mr L Lee's hse, one of 170 acs & the other of 125 acs. Apply to Mr John Mathias, srvyr of the county. R H Henderson, Leesburg, Va.

PG Co, Md. Stray horse colt came to my farm last spring. -Jas Scaggs

TUE OCT 21, 1817
Died: in Wash City, on Oct 11, Mrs Letitia Hamilton, wid/o F P Hamilton, of Wash City.

Died: at Sep 12, at the hse of Mr Thos Rowlet, Chesterfield Co, Va, Mr John Hulberd. He was a stranger, & came last from Charleston, S C. He arrv'd at Mr Rowlet's only 4 days before his death; stated he had travelled about 1,400 miles, & had a bro lvg in Wash City. Mr H left some prop [mostly money] in the hands of Mr R, which may be obtained by legal application.

For sale-land on which I reside, in PG Co, Md; about 100 acs. -Edmund Key

WED OCT 22, 1817
Died: Wm Marshall, a well known free mulatto man, suddenly on Oct 21, at Davis' Htl, Wash, by the burst of a blood vessel.

THU OCT 23, 1817

It is again asserted, that the Pope has dissolved the marriage bet Napoleon & Maria Louisa, & that their son is to be created Archbshp Primate of Ratisbone, & Arch Chancelor of the German Empire, as soon as he shall attain age for same.

Died: at Savannah, Ga, in Sep last, 1st Lt Wm Coffin, of the corps of artl, U S army.

Died: at his residence in Montg Co, Md, on Oct 19, Capt Henry O'Neale, in his 32d yr; of inflammatory rheumatism.

Died: on Oct 15, on board the U S ship *Independence*, after an illness of 3 days, Midshipman Delozier Higginbothom, of Balt, Md, aged 20 yrs.

FRI OCT 24, 1817

Superb French hats-oppo the Union Bank, Gtwn. -Henry Pyfer

Died: recently in Upper country, Col John Mercer, of Fredericksburg, Va; s/o Gen Mercer, who fell at Princeton, in the cause of American liberty. Col M was devoted to the same cause & principles for which his fr died.

Died: on Oct 4, Wm C Williams, of Woodstock, Shenandoah Co, Va; long at the bar of the Va Sup Crts.

SAT OCT 25, 1817

The City of Wash Gaz-commencement of this publication, will be deferred for a few days since materials have not yet arrived from Phil. -Jonathan Elliot

Furn by auction-at the late residence of Dr Wm Baker, in Montg st. -John Lockerman, trustee; D Mallory, auct.

Wash Co, D C. John Golding, insolvent debtor, confined in Wash Co prison bounds, for debt. -Wm Brent, clk.

For sale-val farm-328 1/2 acs in St Mary's Co, Md; with an excellent dwlg hse, etc. -Elder Wilder

St Mary's Co, Md, Chancery Crt, Aug Term, 1817. Ratify sale of rl est of Ignatius Thompson, dec'd, reported by Henry C Neale, trustee; $602. -Jo Harris, reg c c.

MON OCT 27, 1817

For sale-1,000 acs of Patuxent land, one side bounded by the rvr, the other by the main rd leading from Wash City to Annapolis, A A Co, Md. View same by calling on Mr Robt Fenwick, White Marsh. Terms-Francis Neale, Gtwn.

Died: on Sep 29, at his residence nr Vevay, Indiana, Mr Jean Piere Vairin, one of the late French emigrants, aged about 60 yrs. He has left a widow & 3 sons.

TUE OCT 28, 1817
Died: on Oct 24, at Balt, Md, Col Nathl Ramsay, naval ofcr of the Port of Balt; fought at the battle of Monmouth until he fell pierced with many wounds.

Edw Vidler, jr-Tailor, 7th st, Wash City. -Ad

Maj Jonathan Kearsley, who lost a leg in the late war, has been appt'd Coll of the Rev of the U S, for the Harrisburg Dist. -Lanc Intell.

Wants a situation in a pvt family, as a cook & mgr, widowed female, of middle age. Will do anything about the hse except washing & scrubbing. -Ann Riley, Alexandria.

WED OCT 29, 1817
Died: on Oct 20, at his residence in Isle of Wight Co, Va, in his 36th yr, Gen Francis M Boykin, ctzn & sldr.

Died: at his residence at the Miami Rapids, Maj Amos Spafford, Coll of the Customs for the port of Miami, in his 65th yr. [No date-recent]

Danl Simonds brought before me a stary mare, trespassing on his enclosures, nr Rock Crk Chr. -Jas M Varnum, J P for Wash Co.

THU OCT 30, 1817
Died: on Oct 3, the Rev Robt Finley, Pres of the Univ of Ga, after a painful illness of 18 days.

Wanted-a good salesman in a Grocery Store. Apply at the store of Mr Wm Good, oppo the P O, Gtwn.

Fountain Inn, Wash City-elegant & spacious hse, lately built by Benj G Orr, on C st, fronting Pa av; agreeable & comfortable. -Pendleton Heronimus.

Wash Co, D C. John P Maul, insolvent debtor, confined in the prison bounds of Wash Co, for debt. -Wm Brent, clk.

FRI OCT 31, 1817
Balt, Oct 29. John Lamarde, a Frenchman, was this day brought before the Judges of Balt City Crt for examination, chg'd with having murdered Andre Clement. Lamarde has been committed to prison for trial at the next session of the City Crt.

Orphans Crt of Chas Co, Md, Oct Term, 1817. Ordered that Enoch J Millard, adm with will annexed of the Rev Ignatius Baker Brooke, late of Chas Co, dec'd, give notice of same. -Humphrey Barnes, reg o/wills for Chas Co, Md. [Notice of same followed. -E J Millard, adm w a]

Mrsh'l sale-all the right, title, int, etc of Henry Dunlop in & to a second hand coachee with plated harness; at the suit of John Thompson, N Y, against said Henry Dunlop. -Wash Boyd, Mrshl.

For sale-two farms; 304 acs & 828 acs; wishing to remove to the south western country. Robt Taylor, Orange Co, Va.

SAT NOV 1, 1817
Mrd: in Wash City, on Oct 30, Mr Z C Chesley, merchant, to Miss Jane E B Thornton.

Mrd: on Oct 30, by Rev Mr Birch, Mr David Shoemaker to Mrs Tacy Bunson, both of Wash City.

Died: at New Orleans, on Oct 27, Maj Chas Wolstoncraft, of the Corps of Artl of the U S army.

I Chas Woodson, escheator for Pr Edw Co, Va, Jul 22, 1817: land to escheat to the Commonwealth; 75 acs, which the jury found John McMurray to have died seized, the land standing in the name of John Hubbard. One tract of 400 acs & another of 800 acs, by patents dt'd Aug 27, 1770, in the name of John Fisher, the jury find to escheat to the Commonwealth unconditionally. -Chas Woodson

Gardener wanted-apply to John H De Butts, Mt Welby, oppo Alexandria.

On Thu last the body of Mr Wm Maccubbin, aged about 19 yrs, s/o Moses Maccubbin, of this city, was found dead nr the Calverton mills; a victim of robbery while out fowling. Lg reward is offered. -Bal Fed Gaz.

MON NOV 3, 1817
$240 for stolen bank notes. -Thos Ragland, Balt, Md.

TUE NOV 4, 1817
Henry F Doyhar, fruit store & pastry cook, also dinner cook, Pa av, Wash City. He has lived in that capacity with Mr Madison, late Pres of the U S, Rufus King, & Nicholas Low, of N Y, etc.

Died: at Green Hill, nr Natchez, on Oct 31, Hon Josiah Simpson, one of the judges of the supreme crt, after a short & severe illness.

WED NOV 5, 1817
Museum of the Metropolis; in the hse formerly occupied by Gen Van Ness, Pa av, Wash. The subscriber take likenesses in oil or crayons; also will teach a few pupils in the art of painting & drawing. -Augustin De Milliere

Stolen on Mon, carpenter's tools; reward. -Aaron Nalley, Wash.

For sale-part of the prsnl est of David Beall, late of PG Co, Md, dec'd; plantation utensils, furn, etc. -Geo Page, adm.

THU NOV 6, 1817
Carving & gilding; shop on Pa av, Wash. -Ephraim Cilman

Army of the U S, Nov 1, 1817.
Ord Dept: 1st Lt Rufus LBaker to Capt, May 21, 1817, v Campbell, dismissed.
2d Lt John W Thompson to 1st lt, May 21, 1817, v Baker, promoted.
3d Lt Jas Simonson to 2d lt, May 21, 1817, v Thompson, promoted.
Corps of Engrs: 1st Lt Fred'k Lewis to Capt, Oct 1, 1817, v Cutbush, rsgnd.
2d Lt J L Smith to 1st lt, Oct 1, 1817, v Lewis, promoted.
Bvt 2d Lt R W Pooler to 2d lt, Oct 1, 1817, v, Smith, promoted
Corps of artl: 1st Lt John Farley to Capt, Jun 19, 1817, v Biddle, ast inspec gen.
2d Lt Jos P Prince to 1st lt, Jun 15, 1817, v Spencer, dec'd.
2d Lt Richd Bache to 1st lt, Jun 15, 1817, v Randall, rsgn'd.
2d Lt P J Neville to 1st lt, Jun 19, 1817, v Farley, promoted.
2d Lt M S Massey to 1st lt, Aug 5, 1817, v Goode, dismissed.
2d Lt T W Denton to 1st lt, Sep 30, 1817, v Coffie.
2d Lt Chas Anthony to 1st lt, Sep 19, 1817, v M'Kenzie, dec'd.
2d Lt W M'Clintock to 1st lt, Oct 24, 1817, v Lent, dismissed.
3d Lt Jas Monroe to 2d lt, May 2, 1817, v Roberts, dec'd.
3d Lt Robt C Brent to 2d lt, May 13, 1817, v Prince, promoted
3d Lt Geo A Washington to 2d lt, May 13, 1817, v Brown, dec'd.
3d Lt Robt J Scott to 2d lt, Jun 15, 1817, v Bache, promoted.
3d Lt Francis N Berrier to 2d lt, Jun 19, 1817, v Neville, promoted.
3d Lt Alex'r F Cochran to 2d lt, Aug 5, 1817, v Massey, promoted.
3d Lt Milo Johnson to 2d lt, Aug 5, 1817, v Dennis, dismissed.
3d Lt Robt M Forsyth to 2d lt, Sep 8, 1817, v Bosque, dropped.
3d Lt Thos W Lendrum to 2d lt, Sep 30, 1817, v Denton, promoted.
3d Lt Jas Spencer to 2d lt, Spe 29, 1817, v Anthony, promoted.
3d Lt Isaac A Adams to 2d lt, Oct 14, 1817, v Earle, dec'd.
3d Lt Wm M Graham to 2d lt, Oct 24, 1817, v Gigniliat, rsgn'd.
3d Lt Chas Dispenville to 2d lt, Oct 31, 1817, v Graffenviedte, rsgn'd.
1st Regt of Infty: 1st Lt Wm C Beard to Capt, May 1, 1817, v Baker, do.
1st Lt Wm Sumpter to Capt, may 31, 1817, v Butler, do.
2d Lt Waddy V Cobbs to 1st lt, Apr 15, 1817, v Ross, rsgn'd.
2d Lt Saml Houston to 1st lt, May 1, 1817, v Beard, promoted
2d Lt Wm K Paulling to 1st lt, May 31, 1817, v Sumpter, promoted.
2d Regt of Infty: 1st Lt W Browning to Capt, Nov 1, 1817, v Steele, rsgn'd.
2d Lt Robt M Harrison to 1st lt, Nov 1, 1817, v Browning, promoted.
3d Regt of Infty: 1s Lt John Garland to Capt, May 7, 1817, v Adair, rsgn'd.
2d Lt John B Clark to 1st lt, May 7, 1817, v Garland, promoted.
2d Lt Edw E Brooks to 1st lt, Jun 1, 1817, v Conway, rsgn'd.
4th Regt of Infty: 1st Lt John M'Gavock, jr to Capt, May 31, 1817, v Callis, do.
1st Lt Jas H Gale to Capt, Jul 31, 1817, v Neilson, rsgn'd.
2d Lt John C Wells to 1st lt, May 31, 1817, v M'Gavock, promoted.
2d Lt Francis W Brady to 1st lt, Jul 31, 1817, v Gale, promoted.

2d Lt John R Clark to 1st lt, Oct 31, 1817, v Randolph, rsgn'd.
5th Regt of Infty: 2d Lt Oliphant Martin to 1st lt, Jul 1, 1817, v Hovey, do.
7th Regt of Infty: 1st Lt Wm Bee, jr to Capt, Apr 30, 1817, v Armstrong, do.
1st Lt Jos J Clinch to Capt, May 31, 1817, v Bell, do.
1st Lt Thos Blackston to Capt, May 31, 1817, v Bailey, dismissed.
1st Lt Jacob Tipton to Capt, Jun 1, 1817, v Mallory, rsgn'd.
2d Lt Benj R Christian to 1st lt, Apr 30, 1817, v Bee, jr, promoted.
2d Lt Chas Betts to 1st lt, May 31, 1817, v Clinch, do.
2d Lt Daniel E Burch to 1st lt, Jun 7, 1817.
8th Regt of Infty: 1st Lt Thos Wright to Capt, Sep 25, 1817, v Mountjoy, rsgn'd.
2d Lt Nathl Young to 1st lt, Jun 26, 1817, v Hopkins, dec'd.
2d Lt Saml Riddle to 1st lt, Aug 13, 1817, v Whistler, dropped.
2d Lt John Maul to 1st lt, Aug 20, 1817, v Cuy, rsgn'd.
2d Lt Farly Eddy to 1st lt, Sep 12, 1817, v Stephens, dropped.
2d Lt Richd B Mason to 1st lt, Sep 25, 1817, v Wright, promoted.
Rifle Regt: 1st Lt Jos Calhoun, jr, to Capt, Mar 31, 1817, v Kean, rsgn'd.
1st Lt Jas H Ballard to Capt, Apr 22, 1817, v Shipp, dec'd.
2d Lt Jas S Gray to 1st lt, Mar 31, 1817, v Calhoun, promoted.
2d Lt Thos F Hunt to 1st lt, Jul 1, 1817, v Hamilton, rsgn'd.
2d Lt Wm S Blair to 1st lt, Jul 15, 1817, v Harrison, dropped.
2d Lt Horace Broughton to 1st lt, Jul 31, 1817, v Hollingsworth, rsgn'd.
Appointments: John Biddle to assist inspec genr'l, Jun 19, 1817.
Wm Baker, post surg, Jun 20, 1817.
Clajon Reiley, hosp surg's mate, Oct 31, 1817.
S C Muir, do, do.
Simeon Knight, battalion paymstr, May 16, 1817.
Jas Spencer, 3d lt corps of artl, Jul 17, 1817, promoted.
Isaac A Adams, do, do, do.
Wm M Graham, do, do, do.
Jas D Graham, do, do, do.
Chas Despinville, do, do, do.
John C Kirk, do, do.
John R Vinton, do, do.
Rich B Lee, do, do.
Fred'k L Griffith, do, do.
Edw I Lambert, do, do.
Wm G M'Neill, do, do.
Angus W M'Donald, do, do.
Henry Berryman, do, do.
Constantin M Eakin, do, do.
John D Orr, do, do.
Ethan A Hitchcock, do, do.
John M Washington, do, do.
Matthew A Patrick, do, Aug 18, 1817.
Jeremiah Yancey, do, do.
Wilson Whartley, do, Sep 4, 1817.
B Favrot, 2d lt 1st infty, May 8, 1817.
Wm Kerr, do, Aug 14, 1817.

Robt B Harney, do, Aug 18, 1817.
Richd Douglass, 2d lt 2d infty, Jul 14, 1817.
Michl F Vandeventer, do, Jul 22, 1817.
Geo W Stall, 2d lt 3d infty, Sep 4, 1817.
Wm F Taylor, 2d lt 4th infty, Aug 18, 1817.
M H Elliot, surg, 4th infty, Oct 31, 1817.
*Ephraim K Barnum, surg, 5th infty, Jun 11, 1817.
*Saml S Stacey, surg, 5th infty, Jul 22, 1817.
*Richd H Ashley, surg, 5th infty, Jul 30, 1817.
Henry Green, surg's mate, 5th infty, Jul 22, 1817.
Zalmo C Palmer, 2d lt, 6th infty, Jun 16, 1817.
Danl E Burch, 2d lt, 7th infty, Jun 15, 1817, promoted.
John B Hogan, paymstr, 7th infty, Sep 25, 1817.
Farly Eddy, 2d lt, 8th infty, Aug 11, 1817, promoted.
Richd B Mason, 2d lt, 8th infty, Sep 2, 1817, promoted.
Arthur Nelson, surg's mate, Oct 31, 1817.
Wm G Shade, 2d lt, rifle regt, May 22, 1817.
John Gantt, 2d lt, rifle regt, May 24, 1817.
Gabriel Field, 2d lt, rifle regt, May 24, 1817.
John Clark, 2d lt, rifle regt, Jun 20, 1817.
Chas Pentland, 2d lt, rifle regt, Oct 9, 1817.
By order, D Parker, Adj & Ins Gen.
[*Corr of Nov 7; E K Barnum & S S Stacey, & R H Ashley, are 2d lts in the 5th infty, & not surg's mates as stated in the Gen Order published yesterday.]

Mrd: on Oct 30, at Phil, by Rt Rev Bshp White, Col Athanasius Fenwick, of St Mary's Co, Md, to Miss Susan Howell, of that city.

Runaway German Redemptioners: Geo Hagin & his wife Gertrude, left my hse on Oct 27 last; the man is about 50 yrs old & the woman is about 30. -Thos W Pairo

FRI NOV 7, 1817
$240 reward for stolen bank notes; either in Richmond or Wash. -Thos Ragland, Balt, Md.

Land for sale-900 to 1,000 acs; the village of Centreville is part of this est; PG Co, Md. Apply to David M Forrest, atty at law, Wash City, or subscriber living on the premises. -John Darnall

Mrshl's sale: right, title, int, etc, of Ferdinando Fairfax, of lots in Wash City; seized at the suit of Geo Reynolds, against the said Fairfax, as special bail of Jas Hall.
-Wash Boyd, Mrshl, D C.

$100 reward for runaway negro, Frisby, prop of Col Gilbert C Russell; ran away from Union Town, Pa, on the march from Bowling Green, Va, to Wheeling, on the Ohio. Frisby is about 35 yrs of age; raised by Gov Bowie of Md; reads & writes a little; carpenter by trade; his wife belongs to Judge Key. Deliver to John Brandt & Co, New Orleans. -Gilbert C Russell, Marsham Jammison

SAT NOV 8, 1817
Died: on Nov 7, after a long & painful illness, Mrs Bridget Coltman, aged 51, w/o Mr Wm Coltman, of Wash City.

Mrd: at Phil, on Oct 28, by Rev Mr Carr, at the residence of Stephen Girard, Gen Henry Lallemand, to Miss Harriet Girard, niece of Stephen Girard. There were present, Messrs Cte de Survilliers, Mrshl de Grouchy & Son, Genrls Vandamme & Chas Lallemand, sen, & family & friends.

Mrd: at Utica, on Oct 20, by Rev Mr Dwight, Francis Granger, atty at law of Canandaigua & s/o the late Post Mstr Genr'l, to Miss Cornelia Van Rensselaer, eldest d/o Jeremiah Van Rensselaer.

Col Paul Bentalon is appt'd Mrshl of the Dist of Md, vice Thos Rutter, dec'd.

MON NOV 10, 1817
Orphans Crt of Wash Co, D C. Ltrs test on will & prsnl est of Lynde Elliot, late of said Gtwn & Wash Co, dec'd. -Statira Elliot, excx.

Mrd: on Oct 25, at the country seat of his excellency Hyde de Neuville, nr New Brunswick, N J, M Angelucci, his most christian majesty's cnsl for Balt, to Mademoiselle L Villaret.

Died: on Oct 25, nr Danville, Ky, Col Saml McDowell, in his 85th yr. Whig during the Rev war; one of the first settlers of Ky; crct Judge. He has left more than 100 descendants.

TUE NOV 11, 1817
Elbridge Gerry, s/o the late Rev patriot of that name, has been appt'd Srvyr of the port of Boston.

For sale-celebrated horse Florizel; on the Capitol Sq in Richmond, Va; by order of Mr Thos Ball, adm of Wm Ball, dec'd. -Thos Taylor

Mrd: on Oct 25, in Lincoln Co, N C, Hon Daniel Morgan Forney, mbr of Cong from that state, to Miss Harriet Brevard.

WED NOV 12, 1817
P Cassisi, Taylor, F st, Wash; experience in the finest hses in Europe.

On Sun, as the steam boat *Surprise* was returning from Annapolis, Mr Rich Sears, a promising young man of this city, fell overboard & drowned. -Balt Pat.

Mrd: on Nov 6, by Rev Mr Allen, at *Val Ambrosia*, Jefferson Co, Va, the seat of Nathl Craghill, Francis Lowndes, of Gtwn, to Miss Angeletta Craghill.

Orphans crt of Fred'k Co, Md. Prsnl est of Thos Gist Murray, dec'd, late Capt of artll in the U S army. -Henry Steiner, adm.

Eliz Oliver, sen'r, is opening her store in Gtwn; hair caps, frizets, kill beaux, etc.

Balt, Md. Caesar A Rodney, of Dela, John Graham, of Wash, & Theodorick Bland, of Balt, appt'd Comrs to proceed to So America, relative to the independence of that country; & H M Brackenridge, of Balt, will go as Sec.

For sale-*Spring Mills*, nr Winchester, Fred'k Co, Va; 200 acs. Excx of the est of Jona Hollingsworth, dec'd, living on the premises. -Hannah Hollingsworth

Wash Co, D C. John Mulloy, insolvent debtor, confined in the prison bounds of Wash Co, for debt. -Wm Brent, clk.

Died: on Oct 8, at Camden, S C, Mr Bryant Spradley, sr, in the 80th yr of his age. Mr S was born & always lived in Camden or its neighborhood.

Cheap hats for sale; next dr to Mrs Jolly, in the hse formerly occupied by Wm O'Bryan: Navy yd, Wash. -Benj Strong

THU NOV 13, 1817
PG Co, Md. Peter Jo Brightwell, brought before me a stray mare. -Daniel Rawlings, J P.

Died: at St Thomas, West Indies, Mr Geo Gozler & Philip Gozler, brothers, & sons of Mr John Gozler, of Gtwn. Mr Geo Gozler had been lately united to a lady on the island & his bro was on a visit; both were seized with fever.

FRI NOV 14, 1817
Wm Wirt, of Va, appt'd the Atty Gen of the U S.

Wm M'Guire, an ofcr of the Rev army, is appt'd Military Storekpr at Harper's Ferry, vice Col Lloyd Beall, dec'd.

SAT NOV 15, 1817
$20 reward for runaway negro man Thornton, aged about 18 yrs. -Edm'd Denney, Fairfax Co, Va Woodland.

Henry & Geo Miller, jr, will open a stable on 13th st, Wash City.

MON NOV 17, 1817
Wanted-in a small family, a svt women; plain cooking, washing, etc. -Toppan Webster

Notice-I have applied to the Judges of the Crt of Common Pleas of Cumberland Co, Pa-act of insolvent debtors. Creditors to appear at the Crt hse in Carlisle, on Dec 22. -John Sommer

J H Poor & Miles, auct'rs #2 Lorman Row, nr Gadsby's, Hanover st, Balt, Md.

Mrd: on Nov 13, by Rev W H Wilmer, Dennis M Lyles, of PG Co, Md, to Miss Eliza W Seaton, of Alexandria.

TUE NOV 18, 1817
PG Co, Md. A stray gelding came to my plantation on Oct 15. -Colbert Williams, lvg nr Magruder's tvrn.

Appointments:
Joshua Barney, of Md, appt'd Naval Ofcr for the port of Balt.
Thos Jenkins, of Va, Coll o/Direct Taxes & Int Duties for the 20th Coll Dist of Va.
Henry Boswell, of Md, Coll for the Dist of Nottingham.
Jas Brobson, of Dela, Mrshl in & for the Dist of Dela.
John Heath, of Va, Cnsl of the U S for the Island of Teneriffe.
John T Mason, of Ky, Mrshl for same.
Wm W Bibb, of Ga, Govnr in & over the Ala Terr.
Jonathan Kearsley, of Pa, Coll of Dir Taxes-for 10th Coll Dist of Pa.
Martin T Morton, of Mass, Coll & Inspec of Rev for the Port of Nantucket.

Justices of the Peace for Wash Co, DC:

Robt Brent	Thos Peter	Wm Thornton
Thos Corcoran	Thos Fenwick	Saml N Smallwood
Richd Parrott	John B Kirby	John Ott
Saml H Smith	Danl Rapine	Nicholas Young
John Threlkeld	Danl Reintzel	Jas M Varnum
Jos Cassin	Wm Waters	
Wm Waters		
Jos Forrest		

For sale-*Lawnville*, bet 5 & 600 acs, in Pr Wm Co, Va; subscriber will be on the farm. -G R A Browne

Wash Co, D C. 1-Handley Price, insolvent debtor, confined in Wash Co prison, for debt. 2-Wm Price, same. -Wm Brent, clk.

Tallyho! Tallyho! An extraordinary Bag Fox will be let loose at Upper Marlboro on Dec 4. Every comfort will be provided, & a nice premium given for the brush, by B Bowling, owner.

WED NOV 19, 1817
Mrd: at *Rosedale*, nr Wash City, on Nov 13, by Rev Mr Hawley, Lt John Tayloe, U S N, to Miss Maria Forrest, y/d/o the late Gen Forrest.

Mrd: on Nov 7, by Rev Mr Garnett, Mr Thos H Herndon, late of Wash City, to Miss Eliz Brock, d/o Capt Jos Brock, of Madison Co, Va.

Died: in Baton Rouge, La, on Sep 27, Maj Geo C Allen, of the hse of Vail & Allen, New Orleans, formerly Capt in the 7th regt U S Infty.

Died: in Pendleton Dist, on Nov 16, Mr John Gilleland, aged 116 yrs, 85 of which he had lived in America. He was born in Ire, County of Antrim; left a numerous offspring of chldrn & grchldrn, supposed to be upwards of one hundred.

THU NOV 20, 1817
Eulogy on Hon John Wheelock, L L D, late Pres of Dartmouth Univ, who died Apr 4, 1817, pronounced in the Univ Chapel Aug 27, 1817, by Saml C Allen. Pres W was 2d s/o Dr Eleazer Wheelock, founder of this institution; b at Lebanon, Conn, 1754; 1771 grad of the first class; appt'd lt Col in the svc of the U S; cont'd in svc until the death of his fr in 1779. [Notes-Hon Bezaleel Woodward-Prof of Math & Phil, died in 1804; Rev Sylvanus Ripley, Phillips Prof of Theology, died in 1787; Rev John Smith, S T D, Prof of Learned Languaged, died in 1809.]

Trustee's sale of all the lands of the late Richd Henderson, dec'd, in PG Co, Md; 6 to 700 acs, nr Bladensburg. -Colin Auld, trustee.

Land for sale-under the will of the late Bailey Washington, of Stafford Co, Va; 330 acs in said Co. -J Macrae, adm with will w a. Dumfries, Va.

Died: on Nov 17, at Annapolis, Mr John Munroe, an old & respected ctzn of Annapolis, & long the Post Mstr of that city.

Proposals for printing by subscription, the life of Jos Wheaton, who srv'd during the whole Rev war; afterwards 18 yrs as Sgt at Arms to the Hse o/Reps; acted in the Q M Gen's Dept in 5th & 8th Military Dists, during the last war with Gr Britain.

Pblc sale of sq 41, in Gtwn, of which Saml Craig, late of Alexandria, died seized. Also, all the right, title, int & est of the said Saml Criag, dec'd, existing under a contract entered into with Wm Stewart of Gtwn, in a lot on Cherry alley, Gtwn, with val brick dwlg hse, & which it appears was cnvyd by Elisha O Williams to said Stewart. -John G Ladd, trustee.

Remv'd from Capitol hill, & quit business there; settle with John Pic, Capt hill. I shall keep an oyster hse oppo the Centre Mkt Hse, in a blue hse. -Francis Pic

FRI NOV 21, 1817
The ofcrs of the 5th regt U S army, have resolved to do honor to the memory of Lt John Brooks, [s/o the late Govn'r of Mass,] late of the Marine corps, who fell in the contest in Lake Erie, by collecting his remains, which were buried on a remote island, & reinterring them, over which a monument is to be erected. The remains of Maj Holmes was likewise suggested by Gen Macomb. -Balt Pat.

Balt, Md, Nov 19. Trial pending since Fri, brought by Rev Geo Dashiell against Chas Worthington & wife, for words spoken of the plntf, tending to injure him as mnstr of the gospel; jury returned a verdict for the dfndnts.

Mrd: on Nov 19, by Rev Mr Balch, Mr Wm Markward to Miss Sarah Allen Tyler, all of Wash City.

Wanted-2 boys for the baking business. -Philip Hotte, nr the Navy Yd, Wash.

Died: in Plattsburg, N Y, Capt Elijah Boardman, of the 6th regt U S Infty. [No date-recent]

Died: in Stafford Conn, Dr Robt Stanton, aged 109 yrs, according to the account he has given of himself. -Con Pap.

SAT NOV 22, 1817
Mrd: on Nov 20, by Rev Mr Hawley, Mr Henry M Morfit, of Norfolk, Va, to Miss Cath Campbell, d/o the late John Campbell, of Wash City.

MON NOV 24, 1817
Mrd: on Oct 30, by Rev Mr Townshend Dade, at his seat in Montg Co, Md, Chas Bordley Ross, of Fred'k, to Miss Parthenia Ann Dade.

Teacher wanted; communications addressed to either Dr John Spence, Mr Jas Reid, Mr David Boyle, or Mr Jno Macrae, will be attended to. -Dumfries, Va.

TUE NOV 25, 1817
Mrd: on Nov 19, Thomson F Mason, of Alexandria, to Miss Eliz C Price, of Leesburg, Loudoun Co, Va.

Died: at Fayetteville, N C, a few days ago, Alex'r McMillan, lately elected Mbr of Cong from that Dist.

Two or three journeymen tailors will find employment by applying to Jas Druett, oppo the Seven Bldgs, Pa av, Wash.

Hardware & cutlery by auction; order of Orphans Crt of Wash Co, DC; entire stock in trade of the late Thos Robertson. -D Mallory, auct.

Pblc sale of 473 acs, 3 miles of Upper Marlboro, PG Co, Md; of which Edw Willett, sen, died siezed. -John Hodges, of Thos.

WED NOV 26, 1817
On Wed last Mr John C Price, of Coecil Co, Md, drowned while crossing Bohemia rvr in a boat; 3 negro men & a girl also drowned. -Fed Gaz.

$20 reward for negro man Solomon, prop of Ann Rochester; ranaway on Oct 12th from the farm of John McPherson, Jeff Co, Va. Apply to Jas S Ferguson, Rock's Ferry, Jeff Co, Va.

Died: on Nov 9, of a lingering illness, at Pittsfield, Mass, Col Simon Larned, aged 66; long a ctzn of Berkshire Co; an ofcr during the rev & the late war; formerly a rep in Cong from Mass.

THU NOV 27, 1817
Notice-I have appt'd Mr Jos Brooks my agent to rent & collect the rents of my hses in Gtwn. -John Cox

FRI NOV 28, 1817
Mrd: on Nov 25, by Rev Robt Angier, Mr John Hughes, of Wash City, to Miss Maria Gardiner, of Chas Co, Md.

$100 reward for runaway negro woman, Barbara, belonging to Mrs Ann Key, of D C. She is about 44 yrs old & one of the best female cooks in the country. -Thos Plater, Gtwn.

SAT NOV 29, 1817
Mrd: on Nov 27, at Alexandria, by Rev Mr Baxter, Mr Robt Fulton, of that place, to Miss Ann Maria O'Brien, of Wash City.

Died: on Nov 28, at the hse of her fr, nr the city, Miss Mary Ann Bradley, d/o Dr Phineas Bradley, in her 21st yr; leaving her parents, her sister, & her bros.

Died: on Mon night, of a burn rec'd the night before, by his night dress of cotton taking fire from a candle, Jas L McKenney, 2d s/o Mr Wm McKenney, of Gtwn, aged 4 yrs.

In Chancery, Mont co Crt, Md, Nov Term, 1817. David Porter vs Richd Lansdale. On Sep 26, 1816, Porter purchased of Lansdale, then a resident in Montg Co, 3 tracts of land, viz; *Yorkshire*; the resurvey, on part of the *Jas & Mary*; & another part of the latter. Deed was executed but not recorded; dfndnt hath since remv'd out of this state. -Upton Beall, clk

F Ronckendorff, confectioner, crnr of Pa av & 6th sts, Wash City.

MON DEC 1, 1817
Mrd: on Nov 27, in Gtwn, by Rev Francis Neale, & at his residence, Mr Walter Stewart to Miss Frances Compton, all of Gtwn.

Died: on Nov 30, Mr Alex'r L Joncherez, in his 45th yr; ntv of France, but for many yrs a ctzn of Gtwn. Funeral from his late dwlg on Bridge st, Gtwn, today.

In Chancery, Montg co Crt, Md, Nov Term, 1817. Francis C Clopper vs Monica Trail, Henry Trail, *Eliz Trail, *Ann Trail, David Trail, Archibald Trail. Bill is to have a deed recorded, executed by Archibald Trail in his life time, in favor of the cmplnt, cld *Rock Head*, Montg Co, Md. *Reside in D C. -U Beall, clk.

TUE DEC 2, 1817
Mrd: on Nov 20, at *Spring Hill*, the residence of Thos T Somervell, of PG Co, Md, by Rev Mr Willaston, John Marbury, of Gtwn, to Miss Eliz Somervell.

Ladies with ltrs in the Wash P O, Nov 30, 1817:

Alexander Mrs Eliza	Anderson Miss Jane
Boyd Mrs Archibald	Blagge Cath L
Baden Mrs N	Bright Miss Ann
Coolidge Mrs Mary	Coolidge Miss Mary
Cord Miss Amy	Clesaung Miss Sarah
Carricoe Mrs Jane	Fairfax Mrs Isabellak-3
Gilliam Mrs Henry	Hipkins Mrs Sally
Heronimus Miss J Ann	Hall Miss Eliza
Harridan Mrs Susan	Hamilton Miss Charlotte
Jarrett Mrs Louisa	Jones Miss Eliz
Jarrad Mrs Louisa	Jones Mrs Julian
Lie Mrs Eliza	Lowry Mrs Mary
Munsen Miss Rachael	Muse Miss Mary
McClung Mrs Susan	McCale Miss Ann
McRim Mrs Elizabeth	McCall Miss Ann
McDonald Mrs Anna	Mein Miss Eliz
Maupain Madame	Paidel Mrs Julren
Perry Miss Sarah	Rollins Mrs Eliz
Robinson Mrs Mgt	Somos Miss Rientom
Stook Betsey	Smith Mrs Anna M
Stephenson Mrs C	Trash Mrs Rebecca
Watson Mrs Eliz C	Wardrobe Mrs A
White Mrs Mary	White Miss Mary
Yates Miss S M	

WED DEC 3, 1817
The Woollen Factory of Mr Richd Crowninshield, nr Salem, Mass, was destroyed by fire on Tue; loss at $50,000.

Meeting of the Gtwn Dancing Assembly; Mgrs for the season:

John Mason	John Peter	Walter Smith
John Cox	Wm Whann	John Lee
Robt French	C T G Worthington	Jas B Beverly
Danl Randall		

Land for sale; order from Chas co Crt, Md; the whole of the rl est of Walter Brook, sen, dec'd, in Chas Co, Durham Parish, on the Potomac rvr at Brooks' Ferry, oppo Quantico crk; 330 acs. -Francis E Duddington, Isaac Maddox, Wm Greer, comrs- Alexandria.

Genrl hrdware, cutlery, grocs, etc. -Adam Baer, Capitol Hill, Wash.

THU DEC 4, 1817

Boston, Nov 29. We regret to announce the death of Capt Geo Crowninshield, cmder & owner of the vessel *Cleopatra's Barge*, & bro of the Sec of the Navy. We are indebted to him for the removal from Halifax of the remains of the lamented heroes Lawrence & Ludlow. We also learn that Saml Curwen Ward, who accompanied Capt C, confined at his home, died at Salem the same day. [No date-recent] {Dec 5 paper-Mr C was b in Salem on May 28, 1766; senior bro of Capt Richd Crowninshield, who lost his factory at Danvers, the preceding day.}

Mrd: on Nov 24, at Chambersburg, Pa, Robt Munro, of Gtwn, D C, to Miss Cath H Crawford, d/o Edw Crawford, of the former place.

Mrd: on Dec 2, by Rev Mr McCormick, Mr Jos Pope to Miss Mary Marshall, both of PG Co, Md.

Died: on Nov 26, at his seat in Nanjemoy, Chas Co, Md, after a long & severe illness, in his 49th yr, Massey Simms, Srvyr of the port of Nanjemoy & P Mstr.

Died: on Nov 11, at Westfield, Mass, Gen Wm Shepherd; ofcr of the rev.

Stone seal engraver, 65 So Third st, Phil, Pa. -R Lovett

Brdg Hse-Mrs Stanard can accomodate 10 to 12 mbrs of cong, with or without their families, the ensuing session. Her hse is on the main st, directly at the new bridge, is large, commodious, & very neatly furnished. Gtwn.

FRI DEC 5, 1817

Appt'd comrs of the U S to So America: Caesar Augustus Rodney, John Graham & Theodorick Bland.

Mrd: on Dec 2, by Rev Mr Matthews, Mr Peter Roux to Miss Rosa Mgt Julien, both of Wash City.

Died: on Dec 4, at a very advanced period of life, Mrs Jane Graham, relict of Richd Graham, late of Dumfries, Va, & the d/o Geo Brent, of Woodstock, Stafford Co, Va. Funeral today from Mr Andrew Ramsay's.

Pblc sale-order of PG Co crt, Md; all the rl est of John Jackson, dec'd; *Holdfast & Addition to Holdfast*, 25 acs. -Thos Pattison, Robt Chew, Thos Bowie, comrs.

SAT DEC 6, 1817

Died: lately, in Charleston, Dr Jos Kirkland, a most highly respected ctzn.

Died: about Nov 15, at his seat in King & Queen Co, Gen Henry Young, an old Rev ofcr, in his 76th yr.

MON DEC 8, 1817
Jas Preston is re-elected Govn'r of Va for the ensuing yr.

Died: on Nov 24, at Savannah, Capt Adrian Niel, of the corps of Artl, U S army.

TUE DEC 9, 1817
PG Co, Md, Crt, Dec term, 1817. Ratify sale reported by Benj Brookes, trustee, for sale of hse & lot, part of the rl est of John S Brookes, dec'd; sum-$1,005. -Edmund Key. -J R Magruder, clk.

Died: on Dec 8, after an illness of about 20 days, Silas Armstrong, aged 23 yrs, a Chf of the Dela tribe of Indians; one of the svr'l tribes which came to Wash City on pblc business a month ago.

Died: in Wash City, on Dec 6, after a long & distressing illness, Mrs Polly Beck, relict of the late Jos Beck, of Gtwn. She was a mbr of the Meth Episc Chr for many yrs.

More new goods, merchant tailor, Pa av, Wash City. -Richd Ballard

WED DEC 10, 1817
Died: on Dec 9, Lt Geo A Washington, of the Corps of Artl. Funeral this evening, from the residence of T L Washington, on Capitol hill, adj the Bell Tvrn.

Notice. I forbid all persons from harboring or trusting any person belonging to the ship *Lorenzo*, of N Y, now lying at the Navy Yd, Wash, on her account. -Absalom Savage.

Orphans Crt of Wash Co, D C. Ltrs of adm on the will & prsnl est of Laetitia Hamilton, late of said city, dec'd. -Thos Hughes, adm with will annexed.

THU DEC 11, 1817
Lines-written on the death of Wm Thompson, who departed this life on Dec 2, 1817, after an illness of a few hrs, at Dumfries, Pr Wm Co, Va. [Poem unsigned.]

Louis Le Preux, confectioner & distiller, I st, Wash.

PG Co Crt, Sep Term, 1817. Wm Dixon & Martha his wife, Leonard Wall & Thos Wall, for the division of the rl est of Wm Wall, under act to direct descents. Comrs appt'd on petition of Wm Dixon & others, for division of rl est of Wm Wall, state that the est cannot be divided; some reps reside out of state. -John Magruder, clk PG Co, Md.

FRI DEC 12, 1817
Wanted to hire, a female servant, liberal wages. -Lewis Machen

Orphans Crt of PG Co, Md, Feb Term, 1816. Ordered that Jos Edelin & Nicholas Stonestreet, excs of Dr Jas Edelin, give notice required by law. -Trueman Tyler, reg. [Same followed; signed by above excs.]

SAT DEC 13, 1817
Orphans Crt of Montg Co, Md. Prsnl est of Susannah B Magruder, late of said co, dec'd. -Wm Turnbull

Pblc sale of the late Col Henry Gaither, of the following prop, viz: *Exchange*, 827 acs in Montg Co, with spacious brick manion hse, etc. *Labyrinth*, 37 acs, adj the farm of Mr Thos Simpson, & has been occupied by him. -Benj Gaither, Trustee.

Pblc sale-order of Montg co Crt; comrs to divide the rl est of Lewis Bealmean, late of said co, dec'd; parts of *Valentine's Garden*, enlarged, & *Two Bros*, in the whole, about 240 acs; & dwlg hse. -Richd Anderson, Wm Wilson, Baker Waters, comrs.

MON DEC 15, 1817
Robt Keyworth, clock & watchmkr; Pa av, Wash.

Taken up, bright bay mare; person coming forward, & proving prop & paying chgs, may have the same by applying to. -Allison Richardson, nr the Navy Yd.

Sale by auction, the prsnl est of the late Thos Turner, at his late residence in Gtwn. -John Tyler, Trueman Tyler, excs. John Travers, auct.

TUE DEC 16, 1817
Lots in Wash City will be given in exchange for Military Bounty Lands in Ill Terr. -Wm Prout, nr the Navy yd.

WED DEC 17, 1817
Fredericksburg, Dec 13. The Mansion Hse, at Willis Hill, the seat of Byrd C Willis, nr this town, was totally destroyed by fire on Wed.

The Charleston Patriot, of Nov 27, states that Tho Loughton Smith, of that city, fell from the 3d story of a hse in Broad st, & died five hrs later.

Found-on Dec 15, a horse with saddle & bridle, tied to a tree, before my door. -David Appler, tvrn kpr.

Crct Crt of Wash Co, D C, Crt of Chancery. Sale of the prop of Geo Thompson, dec'd: 3 story brick bldg on Pa av; 2 unimproved lots on Fred'k st, Gtwn; one half of tract of 113 acs in Loudon Co, Va, the tract held by Geo Thompson & Geo Smith, of Dumfries, Va, & which said Thompson's part was purchased by Geo Magruder, at a former sale of Jan 9, 1816, & is now resold by order of said crt. -Wm Morton, trustee.

THU DEC 18, 1817

Mrd: on Dec 15, at Brooklyn, L I, by Rev Hugh Smith, Lt G W Hamersley, of U S Navy, to Miss Phoebe Boerum, of Brooklyn.

Mrd: on Dec 11, by Rev Neale H Shaw, Mr Zadok W Beall, late of PG Co, Md, to Miss Susan R G Morton, d/o Mr Saml Morton, of St Mary's Co, Md.

FRI DEC 19, 1817

Died: on Nov 23, at New Orleans, with the liver complaint, Wm C C Claiborne, late Govn'r of La, & recently chosen Senator of the U S from that state.

Died: on Dec 17, in Wash City, Mrs Ann Boyd, wid/o Archibald Boyd. Funeral this day from the hse of Mr E B Caldwell.

Committee appt'd on Mar 11 last, on the contemplated Southern Naval Depot, held in Leonard Town, Md, on Dec 10, 1817:

St Mary's Co, Md-

Barton Tabbs	Philip Key	John R Plater
Wm C Somerville	Athanius Fenwick	John Leigh
Gerard N Causin	Raphael Neale	H G S Key
Jas Forrest	Enoch J Millard	Archibald Binney
Lewis Ford		

Chas Co, Md-

John Campbell	Jas Fenwick	Clement Dorsey
John Barnes	John T Stoddert	Geo Parnham

PG Co, Md-

Robt Bowie	Jos Kent	Wm Beans
Wm Hebb	Henry Ashton	Edmund Key

Stephen Ormsby is chosen Pres of the Branch Bank at Louisville, Ky, & Wm Cochran cashier.

SAT DEC 20, 1817

Crct Crt of Wash Co, D C, in Chancery. Wm Prout vs John Vint. Foreclose on a mortgage of a certain lot, in Wash City, executed by said Vint to said Prout; Vint does not reside within D C. -Wm Brent, clk.

Mrd: on Dec 18, by Rev T Balch, Mr Jas Melvin, jr, of Gtwn, to Miss Mgt C Swett, of Newburyport, Mass.

Died: at New Orleans, a few wks ago, Chas G Boerstler, lately a Lt Col in the U S Army. He had engaged, since the peace, in mercantile business.

MON DEC 22, 1817

Mrd: on Dec 16, by Rev Mr Wyat, Mr Wm Cox, merchant of Wash City, to Miss Mary Ann Dawson, of Balt, Md.

Died: after a short but severe illness, [St Anthony's fire] in his 34th yr, Mr Thos Brereton, of Montg Co, Md.

$50 reward for runaway negro girl, calls herself Ann Higgins, age about 20 yrs. -Hosea Edmonston, Montg Crthse, Md.

Carriage for sale-F A Russell & Co, Gtwn.

TUE DEC 23, 1817
Notice to non-residents, that taxes for the yr 1817 become due to the Wash City Corp, payable on Jan 1, 1818. Geo Adams, coll for 4th ward.

Ashworth Chas S	Atchison Gustavus
Brady Nathl	Berry Zachariah
Bryden Jas	Bower John
Bullus John, Dr	Bowie Wash
Bowhay Wm	Ball Jos
Brice John-heirs	Carcaul David
Cocke Buller	Cooper Robt
Crowley John	Craven Tunis
Cranch Wm	Carson Geo
Duvall Edw	Dye Reuben
Dobbyn John	Elliot Bernard-heirs
Evans Philip, sen	Fuller Oliver
Frye John	Fox Josiah
Farrington Lewis-heirs	Ford & Herbert
Gray Wm-heirs	Gilmore Helen
Hunter John	Hebb Wm
Herbert Jas	Hayre John
Hitchburn Benj	Hebron Abigail
Hart Bernard	Hamden Wm-heirs
Jackson Isaac I I	Jones Chas
Ingerham Nath	Ingle Edw
King John	Keith Wm
Kreamer Henry-heirs	Kalkman Chas F
Lard & Mason	Lewis Jos S
Laight E W	McKim Jas-heirs
Maddox Notley	Moscross Henry
Marshall Saml	Minifie Chas
Otis Saml A	O'Hair Christopher
Pickman John	Potts Jas B
Parry Edw	Perry Caleb
Randle John, jr	Roach Mahlon
Reed Jas	Slater David
Stephenson Jas S	Simms Henry
Stoddert Bent-heirs	Spalding-heirs
Slater Jona-heirs	St Clair Arthur
Somerville, H V	Smith Wm
Spalding Philip	Scholfield Mahlon

Sands Francis	Smith Andrew	
Steel John	Thomas Richd	
Talbot Lewin	Teakle Littleton D	
Truxton Thos	Thompson Eliza S	
Toussard Lewis	Voss Nicholas	
Vint John	Walker Geo-heirs	
Wilson David	Westcoat Jas D	
Wickham Jas	Walker Jas jr	
Willink & Wilham	Wheeler Eliz	
Ward John	Walker & Wheeler	
Wilson Wm	Wheatley Bernard	
Young Saml W	Young Saml's widow	
Young Chas	Young Abraham-heirs	Young Thos
Young Susan	Young Wm	Young John
Young Morduit	Young Mary	Young, Ann

Mont co Crt, Md, in Chancery, Mar Term, 1817. Absalom Thrift & Jane his wife, Geo W Offut & Cassandra his wife, Thos B Scott & Mary his wife & Colmore Offutt, against John Wade & Eliz his wife, Baruch Offutt & Velinda his wife, John Cartenhour & Sarah his wife, Singleton Offutt & Clarissa his wife, Chas C Jones & Agatha Jones, Edmund Jones & Thos Jones, heirs at law of Rebecca Jones. Decree for the sale of the rl est in Montg Co, of Mordecai B Offutt, of said co, dec'd. Offutt willed the use of said rl est to his 2 youngest dghts, Mary Offutt & Clarissa Offutt, & Absalom Thrift & his wife & family, until his said dghts should die or marry; in which case he willed that all said land should be divided amongst his chldrn, Eliz Wade, Rebecca Jones, Cassandra Offutt, Verlinda Offutt, Sally Cartenhour, Jane Thrift, Mary Offutt, Clarissa Offutt, Colmore Offutt, to them & their heirs forever. Clarissa Offut mrd Singleton Offutt, in the left time of the testator, & that Mary Offutt has mrd Thos B Scott, since the death of the testator. -Upton Beall, clk of Montg co crt, Md.

Died: yesterday evening, Capt Saml Speake, a sldr of the rev, & an old inhabitant of Wash City.

Marshal's sale of the *Grange*, about *800 acs*, whereon Col Francis Newman now lives. Also *Benfield*, 900 acs, the prop of Newman. -Paul Bentalou, Marshal Dist Md. [Chas Co, Md, Dec 22, 1817]

WED DEC 24, 1817
Died: on Nov 23, suddenly, Miss Elvira Cooper, step-dght of Wm Lemon, of Cinc; it was to be her wedding night. -Gaz

Wash Co, D C. Alpheus J Hyatt, insolvent debtor, confined in Wash Co prison, for debt. -Wm Brent, clk.

THU DEC 25, 1817
Mrd: on Thu evening, by Rev J Chalmers, Mr Benj Wilson to Miss Mary Halsel, both of PG Co, Md.

$150 reward for delivering to me at my residence nr Leesburg, Loudon Co, Va, negro Ned, about 22 yrs of age. -H Gunnell, jr.

Wash Co D C. Alex'r Dickson, insolvent debtor, confined in Wash Co prison, for debt. Wm Brent, clk.

SAT DEC 27, 1817
Mrd: in Wash City, on Dec 21, by Rev Mr Brown, Mr Daniel Dejarnate to Miss ___dah Colemen, both of Caroline Co, Va.

Mrd: on Dec 25, by Rev Mr McCormick, Mr Aman Woodward to Miss Sarah Martin, both of Wash City.

Mrd: on Dec 25, by Rev Mr Burch, Mr John Connell to Miss Rebecca Parrott, both of this place.

A request-the subscriber requests Mr Chas F *Fuehrer, formerly Maj in the svc of the U S, to make him acquainted with his place of abode, as he has info from his sister Mary Jane Louisa *Biscamp nee *Fuhrer. -Lewis *Biskamp, 202 Mkt st, Balt, Md. [*2 splgs.]

MON DEC 29, 1817
Election to be held at the hse of Mrs Kortright, on Sat, for one mbr of the City Cncl to fill the vacancy occasioned by the resignation of Christian Hines. -Jos Brumley, W Worthington, jr, Saml McIntire. [Local Item]

Laborers wanted-J & D Bussard, Gtwn.

TUE DEC 30, 1817
Died: on Dec 18, at Newton, Sussex Co, N J, Col Chas Pemberton, in his 60th yr; served with credit during our Rev war.

For sale-the farm on which I reside, in Montg Co, Md; 294 acs. -Michl Connelly

Application for renewal of Land Warrant lost or destroyed; dt'd Aug 23, 1815. -John McAnall, late a pvt in the 30th regt infty. 2-Same for Wm Morris, late a pvt in the 38th U S Regt; dt'd Oct 4, 1815.

WED DEC 31, 1817
Resolution-to present an elegant sword to the infant & only s/o the late Col Benj Forsythe, who fell at Odletown, in Canada, Jun 23, 1814; & $250 annually for 7 yrs for his education, was passed at the late session of the Leg of N C.

Wash Co, D C. Abraham Landes, insolvent debtor, confined in Wash Co prison, for debt. -Wm Brent, clk.

—A—

Abbot, 229, 254
Abell, 143, 164
Abercrombie, 133
Abernathy, 56
Aborn, 25
Abraham, 3, 54
Achman, 123
Ackerman, 101
Ackey, 305
Ackland, 148
Adair, 237, 325
Adams, 9, 12, 17, 25, 39, 42, 44, 73, 76, 114, 118, 120, 122, 130, 145, 152, 172, 182, 183, 188, 195, 196, 200, 203, 205, 217, 222, 241, 242, 259, 277, 280, 296, 297, 301, 325, 326, 339
Adamson, 55, 151, 185, 309
Addicks, 46
Addison, 2, 2, 8, 19, 66, 106, 113, 124, 158, 181, 196, 204, 220, 234, 242, 247, 260, 274, 298, 319
Addition to Brook Grove, 270
Addition to Brooke Grove, 285
Adgate, 158
Adie, 261
Adkerson, 81
Adlum, 229
Ager, 310
Agonst, 273
Aird, 115
Aisquith, 87
Akins, 76
Albert, 76, 248
Albridge, 181
Albright, 248
Alburts, 183
Aldridge, 164
Alexander, 5, 6, 9, 20, 29, 49, 103, 172,
173, 177, 219, 235, 252, 303, 309, 312, 315, 334
Alexandria, 202, 221
Alexis, 93
Alfred the Great, 121
Allen, 4, 5, 29, 39, 51, 52, 53, 92, 118, 126, 129, 136, 144, 160, 162, 179, 192, 201, 215, 231, 238, 242, 248, 263, 272, 279, 320, 328, 331
Allison, 129, 242
Allmand, 183
Allston, 207, 265
Almeda, 133
Almeida, 304
Alston, 103, 156, 222
Alvason, 39
Alvord, 2
Amadeaus, 30
Ambaruse, 15
Ambrosia, 328
Ambush, 242
Ames, 98
Amick, 59
Ample Grange, 153
Amsterdam, 164
Analostan Island, 284
Anderson, 3, 9, 19, 36, 39, 47, 58, 67, 71, 88, 93, 94, 100, 112, 119, 121, 133, 149, 155, 176, 177, 183, 209, 211, 247, 256, 268, 274, 279, 285, 286, 298, 302, 334, 337
Andre, 260
Andrews, 21, 29, 39, 60, 97, 99, 101, 102, 106, 109, 113, 161, 181, 191, 205, 216, 218, 242, 247, 257, 274, 298
Angelucci, 328
Anger, 221, 312
Angier, 333
Anguie, 157
Angus, 197
Anner, 17

Annin, 112
Ansart, 178, 190, 213, 217, 222, 233
Anscut, 145
Ansley, 161, 271
Anthony, 325
Antoinette, 30
Anwright, 54
Appler, 136, 146, 337
Appleton, 40, 129, 181, 242, 247, 248, 274, 276, 298
Appling, 69, 78, 202, 274
Archer, 14, 103, 173, 219, 229, 235, 252, 257, 264
Archer's Purchase, 118
Ardrey, 76
Arickson, 22
Arlis, 271
Armistead, 57, 146, 183, 248
Armitage, 179, 239, 272
Armitead, 70
Armstead, 242, 276
Armstrong, 3, 36, 40, 50, 76, 160, 161, 197, 220, 224, 242, 276, 326, 336
Arnold, 3, 85, 89, 144, 267
Arny, 227
Arrel's Folly, 164
Arridah, 179
Asbury, 185
Ash, 247, 308
Ashby, 20, 271
Asher, 318
Ashes, 213
Ashford, 58
Ashley, 20, 137, 202, 327
Ashton, 16, 36, 112, 120, 298, 316, 338
Ashworth, 75, 270, 339
Askins, 183
Aspinwall, 77
Atchison, 339
Atkinson, 54, 248, 257
Attemus, 318

342

Auchmuty, 95, 280
Auckland, 45
Auford, 38
Aukerd, 235
Auld, 331
Aulic, 93
Ault, 168
Aults, 242
Austin, 69, 124, 144
Averill, 90, 91
Avery, 27, 34, 103
Avidesh, 239
Ayres, 40

—B—

Babbitt, 83
Bache, 76, 220, 325
Backman, 179, 239
Backster, 92
Backus, 91, 253, 260
Bacon, 16, 32, 47, 67, 78, 94, 129, 138, 179, 215, 247, 274, 298
Bacot, 47, 88, 94
Baden, 70, 100, 200, 334
Bader, 59
Baer, 92, 229, 335
Bagnell, 40
Bailes, 84
Bailey, 8, 23, 26, 54, 96, 106, 109, 143, 191, 202, 232, 242, 243, 269, 290, 326
Bailey's Retirement, 290
Bailly, 116
Baily, 39
Bain, 7
Bainbridge, 93, 153
Baine, 99
Baird, 220
Bakelow, 85
Baker, 2, 20, 38, 39, 91, 99, 126, 129, 134, 137, 144, 146, 172, 179, 183, 202, 207, 218, 239, 267, 271, 293, 309, 322, 325, 326

Balch, 84, 133, 147, 156, 199, 200, 202, 226, 237, 241, 256, 258, 314, 332, 338
Balderston, 124
Baldwin, 9, 20, 62, 130, 161, 165, 187, 191, 206, 257, 292
Ball, 78, 105, 137, 173, 181, 219, 224, 225, 233, 235, 241, 243, 248, 252, 296, 328, 339
Ballard, 23, 103, 114, 119, 197, 309, 314, 326, 336
Balls, 56
Balmain, 309
Balson, 54
Baltimore, 77, 124
Baltzell, 54
Baltzer, 126, 248
Baltzers, 7
Bancher, 66
Banday, 214
Bankhead, 300
Banks, 29, 177
Barber, 27, 38, 133, 212, 268
Barbour, 37, 56, 103, 263
Barclay, 43, 64, 170, 179, 217, 239, 243
Barcley, 272
Bard, 96, 145
Barge, 37, 58, 214
Barisford, 58
Barkelow, 89
Barker, 39, 115
Barkesdale, 274, 298
Barkley, 304
Barksdale, 239, 243
Barlow, 38, 58, 187, 248
Barnes, 9, 20, 112, 147, 156, 171, 177, 181, 187, 191, 193, 234, 243, 247, 254, 274, 292, 296, 298, 306, 323, 338
Barnet, 230
Barnett, 55, 103, 243
Barnewall, 93

Barnewell, 39
Barney, 1, 49, 59, 89, 95, 112, 113, 271, 330
Barnham, 12
Barnhouse, 317
Barnitz, 32
Barns, 22, 214
Barnum, 267, 327
Barnwell, 46, 198
Barrett, 200
Barrette, 277
Barrie, 248
Barroll, 34, 204
Barron, 243, 255, 284, 312
Barrott, 116
Barrows, 38
Barry, 70, 90, 104, 146, 182, 228, 241, 243, 247, 252, 256, 273, 283
Barslett, 39
Bart, 22
Bartle, 146, 173
Bartleman, 243
Bartlett, 11, 243, 290
Bartly, 178, 281
Bartnuc, 46
Barton, 90, 163, 256, 312
Bary, 241
Bascom, 13
Bashaw, 121
Basil, 200
Basil Warring's Lot Enlarged, 238
Basse, 257
Bassell, 247
Bassenheim Est, 257
Basset, 38, 298
Bassett, 57, 243, 274
Bassford, 311
Bast, 104
Basti, 248
Bateman, 90, 243, 277, 280, 300, 301
Batemen, 143
Bates, 1, 18, 21, 44, 47, 51, 53, 58, 66, 67, 68, 71, 78, 92, 103, 109, 123, 130, 132, 141, 147, 151, 155,

343

161, 172, 236, 278, 281, 285, 299, 310
Bathgate, 214
Battaile, 144
Baugh, 20
Baum, 256, 261
Baury, 93
Baxley, 54
Baxter, 51, 308, 333
Bay, 223
Bayard, 132, 165
Bayer, 239
Bayles, 301
Bayley, 46, 83, 124
Bayly, 8, 35, 68, 229, 257, 266, 313
Bayne, 89, 253
Beach, 191, 206
Beaden, 39
Beale, 91, 133, 195
Bealer, 23
Beall, 1, 2, 18, 38, 46, 48, 53, 56, 63, 67, 80, 91, 92, 109, 115, 117, 129, 135, 142, 164, 167, 175, 179, 183, 194, 200, 203, 210, 217, 220, 232, 234, 238, 239, 242, 243, 247, 259, 269, 272, 278, 284, 285, 289, 293, 300, 303, 312, 320, 325, 329, 333, 334, 338, 340
Beall's Pleasure, 238
Bealmean, 337
Bean, 181, 191, 243, 247, 274, 298, 308, 313
Beanes, 62, 136
Beans, 157, 338
Bear garden, 290
Beard, 62, 325
Beasley, 264
Beastall, 314
Beatman, 183
Beatty, 6, 58, 80, 89, 183, 220, 222
Beaumont, 141
Beck, 69, 130, 154, 174, 199, 237, 248, 294, 319, 336

Beckley, 40, 181, 243, 248
Beddo, 272, 297
Bedford, 188
Bedinger, 183
Bee, 326
Beebe, 54
Beeding, 76, 199, 294, 306
Beelen, 257
Beeler, 109, 161
Beesley, 3
Beeson, 55
Beidler, 182
Belknap, 57, 71, 103
Bell, 22, 50, 59, 66, 87, 90, 101, 150, 163, 206, 285, 326
Bell Air, 72
Bellassise, 134
Belle Field, 114
Belle Plain, 295
Belle Vue, 85, 104
Bellemain, 318
Bellevue, 47, 94, 279
Bellows, 22
Bellville, 266
Belman, 183
Belmont, 261, 303
Belsches, 198
Belt, 2, 3, 23, 56, 58, 74, 136, 167, 175, 196, 200, 207, 215, 224, 242, 250, 264, 290, 292, 297, 312
Belton, 68
Belvider, 59
Bender, 247
Bendy, 38
Benett, 116
Benfield, 260, 312, 340
Bennet, 54, 59, 83, 298, 318
Bennett, 52, 89, 102, 203, 204, 217, 268, 317
Bennett's Creek, 287
Benoit, 19
Benson, 56, 114, 174, 248, 276, 289
Bent, 206
Bentalon, 328
Bentalou, 340

Bently, 102, 243
Berard, 107
Bergh, 212, 304
Bernard, 161
Berrien, 155
Berrier, 325
Berry, 9, 22, 30, 55, 68, 107, 145, 149, 151, 169, 177, 183, 194, 197, 269, 277, 280, 286, 301, 303, 311, 312, 313, 339
Berryman, 74, 326
Berthier, 135
Bessent, 119
Bessett, 41
Bestor, 62, 248, 276, 298
Betterton, 38
Betton, 3
Betts, 124, 232, 326
Bevan, 181, 247
Bever, 242
Beveridge, 88
Beverley, 239, 251
Beverly, 19, 185, 196, 250, 251, 334
Bibb, 14, 310, 321, 330
Bickley, 286
Biddle, 42, 51, 70, 93, 181, 243, 247, 274, 298, 325, 326
Bidgood, 142
Bigelow, 10
Biggs, 144
Billings, 232, 254
Billingsley, 48
Billingsly, 121
Billmier, 273
Billmyer, 178
Bines, 103
Bing, 166
Bingham, 5, 284
Binney, 338
Binns, 219
Birch, 120, 324
Birchett, 45, 129
Birckhead, 8, 278
Bird, 38, 41, 42, 150, 274, 298
Birdsall, 51, 70
Birney, 144
Biscamp, 341

344

Biscoe, 96, 274, 286
Bishop, 22, 144, 177
Bishop of Asaph, 221
Bissell, 15, 66
Bixby, 31, 142, 179, 280
Black, 13, 35, 38, 60, 160, 252
Blackburn, 52
Blackney, 274, 298
Blackston, 326
Blackstone, 285
Bladen, 137
Blagden, 28, 43, 45, 47, 106, 139
Blagdon, 131
Blagg, 182, 241, 243
Blagge, 317, 334
Blahany, 71
Blair, 3, 141, 223, 326
Blake, 3, 6, 7, 25, 33, 36, 51, 99, 101, 138, 156, 210, 216, 225, 247, 271
Blakeley, 67
Blakely, 10, 93, 167
Blakesley, 57
Blanchard, 16, 22, 211
Bland, 243, 329, 335
Blaney, 12, 139
Blare, 201
Blaylock, 9
Bleak Hall, 262
Bledsoe, 101
Blenhelm, 52
Blershing, 293
Blocker, 214
Blodget, 84, 181, 249, 277, 280, 286, 301
Blodgett, 241, 242, 276
Bloodgood, 284
Bloodworth, 50
Bloomfield, 66, 221
Bloomsbury, 59
Blount, 136, 162, 242
Blunt, 124
Blythe, 145
Boardley, 181, 274
Boardman, 271, 332
Boaring, 252
Boarman, 21, 40, 44, 101, 207, 242, 243, 248, 264, 276, 296

Bodley, 238
Boerstler, 338
Boerum, 264, 338
Bogardus, 81
Boggess, 183
Boggs, 118
Bohrer, 80
Boisgervais, 263
Bole, 208
Bolles, 4
Bolling, 129
Bollinger, 15
Bolton, 79, 157
Bomford, 77, 80, 187, 256
Bonaparte, 21, 37
Bond, 65, 90, 95, 177, 278, 292, 298
Bonnel, 193
Bonnell, 12
Bonneville, 265
Boon, 53, 300
Boone, 10, 12, 22, 47, 48, 61, 94, 166, 243, 274, 277, 289, 298, 313
Booth, 44, 111, 251, 265
Boothe, 123, 213
Boots, 18
Borum, 192
Bosque, 95, 325
Bostick, 169
Bostwick, 43, 94
Boswel, 160
Boswell, 132, 135, 330
Boteler, 281, 307
Boughman, 146
Boughton, 8
Bourne, 9, 224
Boush, 188
Boutilher, 115
Bowan, 31
Bowell, 214
Bowels, 142
Bowen, 86, 125, 317
Bower, 339
Bowhay, 339
Bowie, 18, 19, 28, 131, 135, 141, 142, 160, 162, 173, 175, 181, 185, 194, 203, 204, 207, 215, 229, 240,

243, 247, 269, 274, 280, 294, 296, 298, 311, 312, 313, 327, 335, 338, 339
Bowles, 3
Bowling, 75, 133, 159, 212, 228, 236, 238, 252, 281, 284, 300, 303, 330
Bowly, 309
Bowman, 203, 225
Bowton, 152
Bowyer, 191, 264
Boyce, 58, 198, 260, 261
Boyd, 12, 17, 18, 20, 24, 27, 28, 34, 36, 40, 47, 61, 64, 66, 71, 73, 78, 85, 86, 95, 97, 99, 102, 111, 113, 114, 123, 128, 143, 144, 145, 149, 150, 151, 154, 195, 204, 210, 243, 286, 287, 297, 302, 308, 313, 318, 320, 324, 327, 334, 338
Boyer, 129, 179, 210, 243, 272
Boykin, 323
Boyle, 54, 74, 96, 172, 332
Boyton, 101
Boytt, 243
Brack, 105
Brackenridge, 206, 316, 329
Bradbury, 94
Braddock, 108
Braden, 179, 183
Bradford, 57, 181, 243, 247, 274, 294, 298
Bradford's Rest, 151, 241, 293
Bradley, 1, 19, 20, 45, 77, 102, 103, 185, 194, 273, 281, 311, 318, 333
Bradon, 4
Bradshaw, 154
Brady, 45, 107, 216, 241, 243, 248, 276, 290, 325, 339

Brahany, 85, 89
Braiden, 252, 318
Brailsford, 41, 94
Bran, 318
Branch, 4
Brandon, 82
Brandt, 328
Brannan, 228, 231, 287
Brant, 77
Branton, 58
Brashears, 20, 28, 29, 64, 73, 80, 112, 122, 132, 144, 184, 191, 205, 297, 313
Brashiers, 25
Brawner, 173
Brawner's Amendment, 173
Brawner's park, 173
Bray, 318
Brayne, 71
Brayton, 12
Brean, 211
Brearley, 66
Breckenridge, 30, 94, 146, 165, 170, 190, 194, 239, 240, 258, 285, 312
Breem, 15
Breese, 13, 197
Brenile, 203
Brenneman, 22
Brennock, 39
Brent, 1, 2, 4, 5, 8, 11, 12, 16, 20, 27, 28, 29, 31, 34, 36, 37, 38, 41, 42, 45, 47, 48, 51, 58, 59, 62, 64, 65, 66, 69, 70, 71, 72, 74, 75, 77, 79, 80, 81, 83, 88, 90, 91, 96, 99, 102, 111, 116, 117, 118, 120, 124, 125, 127, 137, 138, 143, 148, 149, 150, 155, 160, 162, 163, 169, 174, 178, 183, 186, 187, 188, 193, 194, 196, 201, 202, 204, 206, 210, 212, 215, 216, 217, 218, 219, 220, 222, 224, 225, 226, 227, 228, 230, 231, 235, 236, 239, 242, 246, 247, 249, 251, 254, 255, 256, 259, 261, 265, 270, 272, 276, 277, 280, 281, 282, 284, 285, 286, 289, 291, 292, 293, 294, 295, 296, 298, 299, 301, 302, 303, 305, 310, 312, 313, 315, 317, 320, 322, 323, 325, 329, 330, 335, 338, 340, 341
Brereton, 205, 339
Brevard, 328
Brevett, 248
Brewer, 161, 174
Brian, 88
Brice, 52, 86, 142, 243, 294, 311, 339
Brickell, 54
Bridges, 40, 102, 120, 160, 279
Briggs, 38, 195
Brigham, 173
Bright, 334
Brightwell, 329
Brinckerhoff, 144
Brinckle, 144
Brindige, 108
Bringhurst, 15
Bringman, 52
Briscoe, 43, 55, 95, 102, 133, 153, 197, 201, 247, 292, 316
Brishois, 115
Britt, 81
Britton's outlet, 228
Broadhead, 166
Broadus, 105, 126
Broadwell, 91
Brobson, 330
Brock, 331
Brockenbrough, 219
Brocket, 161
Brockman, 8
Brocks, 38
Brodeau, 130
Bronaugh, 131, 169
Brook, 77, 101, 334
Brook Piney Grove, 270
Brooke, 2, 3, 29, 31, 34, 44, 45, 47, 63, 65, 67, 95, 105, 112, 126, 145, 173, 196, 216, 219, 251, 257, 263, 276, 284, 286, 292, 323
Brooke Piney Grove, 285
Brookes, 83, 97, 243, 287, 295, 336
Brookfield, 96
Brooks, 5, 38, 58, 78, 88, 177, 209, 219, 285, 297, 325, 331, 333
Broom, 81, 279
Broome, 94
Broughton, 252, 326
Brown, 2, 8, 12, 13, 14, 25, 29, 31, 35, 37, 38, 39, 40, 43, 44, 45, 47, 48, 50, 53, 56, 57, 58, 59, 62, 63, 66, 86, 93, 99, 101, 102, 105, 106, 111, 118, 125, 126, 130, 139, 146, 150, 159, 160, 161, 164, 165, 170, 177, 181, 183, 187, 204, 206, 207, 224, 229, 233, 243, 247, 248, 252, 256, 258, 267, 268, 271, 273, 278, 280, 281, 285, 287, 288, 300, 318, 325, 341
Browne, 40, 47, 163, 214, 243, 330
Brownell, 143
Browning, 23, 325
Brownlow, 47, 94
Broxton, 216
Bruce, 3, 9, 100, 142, 160, 192
Bruff, 185, 237, 253
Brumley, 23, 28, 111, 129, 180, 205, 225, 230, 236, 240, 272, 288, 341
Bruner, 295
Brush, 68, 224, 272
Brush creek, 290

Bryan, 60, 141, 148, 210, 252, 318
Bryant, 29
Bryden, 127, 241, 243, 259, 339
Bryson, 215
Buchan, 15, 274, 298
Buchanan, 54, 96, 99, 179, 203, 237, 294, 297
Buchannan, 266
Buchannon, 181
Bucis, 241
Buck, 7, 126, 220, 263, 304
Buck Lodge, 188
Buck Range, 173
Buckey, 129, 179
Buckley, 268
Buckley's Tract, 317
Buckmaster, 5, 263, 268
Buckner, 141, 220
Budd, 93
Buddick, 261
Buel, 57
Buford, 97
Buisson, 116
Bull, 74, 113
Bullett, 256
Bullus, 339
Bumbury, 9
Bunce, 3
Bundy, 102
Bunson, 324
Bunyie, 62, 157
Bur, 296
Burch, 2, 68, 88, 106, 141, 164, 187, 207, 231, 232, 243, 252, 274, 285, 288, 289, 305, 307, 316, 326, 327, 341
Burchan, 243
Burchmore, 94
Burden, 152, 290
Burdick, 235
Burdine, 102, 254
Burdy, 58
Burford, 12, 35, 169, 315
Burgain, 3

Burgess, 20, 113, 142, 162, 165, 195, 230, 237
Burk, 96, 115, 305, 306
Burke, 132, 154, 248, 299
Burkey, 272
Burn, 66, 151, 246
Burnam, 228, 234
Burnel, 2
Burnes, 313
Burneston, 14
Burnet, 20
Burnett, 185, 256, 303
Burnham, 89
Burns, 32, 45, 47, 124, 220, 226, 276, 319
Burnside, 263, 285
Burr, 318
Burrall, 190
Burrish, 95
Burroughs, 305, 316
Burrows, 36, 99, 146, 234, 243, 248, 276
Burton, 1, 38, 40
Burwel, 169
Burwell, 105, 240
Busharie, 151
Bushby, 23, 28, 88
Bushell, 243
Bushfield, 116, 213
Bussard, 10, 86, 92, 230, 234, 243, 270, 341
Bussier, 177, 219
Bustic, 243
Butler, 2, 3, 11, 17, 32, 38, 44, 54, 72, 88, 94, 124, 126, 143, 164, 195, 218, 298, 310, 325
Butterfield, 213, 280
Butts, 113, 190, 312
Buzzard Island, 121
Byers, 188
Byon, 156
Byrd, 220, 283
Byrne, 44, 133, 177, 196, 207, 304

—C—

Cabeen, 214

Cabel, 219, 235
Cabell, 173
Cabin Point, 28
Cackley, 26
Cadot, 292
Cadwalader, 144
Cadwallader, 13
Caffray, 243, 276
Cafterton, 9
Cagely, 224
Cain, 164
Cairn, 91
Cairns, 110
Calagan, 133
Calaghan, 44, 304
Calder, 126, 248, 285
Caldwell, 36, 50, 64, 66, 82, 84, 89, 114, 129, 164, 179, 190, 198, 231, 233, 237, 239, 243, 264, 320, 338
Calet, 89
Calhoon, 42
Calhoun, 180, 211, 216, 240, 283, 314, 326
Callaghan, 212, 300
Callahan, 243, 272
Callan, 29, 109, 206, 215, 233
Callaway, 210
Callighan, 84
Callis, 325
Calvert, 38, 294
Calwell, 243
Cambridge, 141
Cameron, 6, 248
Cammach, 248
Cammack, 276
Camp, 12, 34, 171
Campbell, 4, 8, 21, 30, 35, 47, 48, 82, 89, 92, 102, 104, 106, 117, 118, 134, 137, 139, 140, 149, 155, 160, 161, 178, 179, 181, 190, 195, 196, 207, 208, 212, 213, 219, 233, 236, 237, 239, 243, 246, 247, 248, 254, 255, 264, 271, 274, 276, 298, 325, 332, 338

Cana, 158, 235
Canby, 113
Cannon, 18, 82, 101, 151, 258
Canter, 171
Capel, 58
Capron, 4
Carabe, 55
Carbery, 176, 187, 312
Carcaul, 339
Carcud, 182
Card, 218
Carden, 175
Carety, 99
Carey, 20
Carleton, 115
Carlilse, 257
Carlin, 69, 71
Carlisle, 54, 174
Carlon, 191
Carlton, 247, 275, 299, 316
Carmack, 129, 179
Carmichael, 208, 214, 243
Carmick, 236, 243
Carmicle, 296
Carnap, 243
Carne, 73
Carnes, 315, 319
Carns, 79
Caroll, 299
Carpenter, 78, 96, 187
Carr, 20, 62, 101, 131, 155, 163, 200, 206, 222, 252, 274, 298, 328
Carrell, 208
Carrere, 2
Carricoe, 334
Carrier, 267
Carrol, 40, 274, 298
Carroll, 2, 4, 6, 14, 36, 41, 78, 85, 88, 91, 93, 102, 103, 104, 117, 125, 140, 156, 158, 178, 181, 198, 243, 247, 248, 252, 275, 281, 292, 294, 298, 299, 304
Carroll's Manor, 157
Carrolls, 178

Carson, 5, 13, 54, 241, 339
Cartenhour, 340
Carter, 6, 52, 54, 76, 96, 132, 144, 179, 197, 198, 206, 214, 239, 254, 264, 267, 271, 273
Carter's Green, 65
Carvell, 204
Carver, 214
Carway, 214
Cary, 99
Case, 99
Casenave, 59, 209
Cashell, 34
Casner, 243
Cassady, 35, 267
Cassanave, 76, 249
Cassanove, 276
Cassimer, 39
Cassin, 28, 43, 93, 103, 120, 152, 166, 225, 251, 282, 289, 330
Cassisi, 328
Cassmann, 185
Caster, 166
Castile, 89
Cathcart, 187, 279
Catlett, 50, 103
Caton, 281, 290
Caucaud, 243
Causin, 223, 321, 338
Cavenaugh, 153
Cavender, 8
Caver, 148
Cavyico, 28
Cawood, 113, 147, 190, 312
Cazeau, 263
Cazenove, 196, 234
Cecil, 83, 187, 282, 307
Ceohagan, 87
Chace, 39, 88
Chafer, 242
Chaffin, 45
Chalks, 284
Chalmers, 89, 125, 296, 340
Chambers, 12, 30, 48, 77, 99, 204, 229
Champion, 103

Champlain, 181, 245, 249, 276
Champlin, 93
Champney, 36
Chance, 137
Chandler, 129, 167, 179, 181, 239, 247, 256, 273, 275, 298, 308
Chanson, 76
Chantelin, 84
Chapan, 246
Chapin, 98, 152
Chapline, 81
Chapman, 1, 54, 68, 72, 85, 89, 101, 114, 151, 157, 181, 236, 239
Chapu, 191
Charles, 268
Charlotte, 185, 202
Charlton, 107, 161
Chas & Benj, 185
Chas Borough, 292
Chas III, 138
Chas IV, 138
Chas Town, 233
Chase, 59, 91, 94, 103, 181, 205, 232, 243, 247, 280
Chases, 298
Chatelin, 178
Chauncy, 280
Cheeny, 76
Cheevers, 9
Chembers, 12
Cheshire, 316
Chesletine, 99
Chesley, 9, 54, 207, 218, 244, 259, 324
Chesney, 218
Chester, 111, 112, 181
Cheswell, 239
Cheves, 10, 32, 77
Chew, 26, 28, 47, 193, 215, 244, 335
Chew's Folly, 231
Chick, 152, 186, 302
Child, 1
Childress, 111
Childs, 57, 304
Chilton's Outlet, 265
Chism, 263

Chiswell, 179, 243, 259
Chittim, 193
Chotard, 126
Chrisman, 129
Christian, 326
Christie, 35, 133, 198
Christopher, 39, 128
Christy, 14
Chrystie, 279
Chub, 296
Chunn, 70, 112
Church, 99, 264
Churchill, 99
Cilly, 213
Cilman, 325
Cintra, 59
Cissel, 127, 219
Cissna, 70
Cist, 181, 243, 248
Claborne, 318
Clabourn, 252
Clack, 93
Clagett, 92, 121, 153, 163, 181, 204, 211, 213, 219, 223, 239, 243, 247, 275, 298, 315
Claggett, 25, 55, 129, 179, 216
Claiborne, 155, 338
Claney, 243
Clapham, 271
Clapp, 43
Clark, 8, 38, 43, 44, 74, 85, 99, 103, 106, 129, 144, 174, 176, 177, 179, 192, 235, 255, 265, 274, 286, 300, 325, 326, 327
Clarke, 2, 53, 73, 77, 81, 91, 93, 99, 102, 121, 126, 129, 134, 141, 147, 151, 156, 170, 171, 207, 239, 248, 261, 276, 318
Clarkson, 318
Clarl, 243
Claude, 59
Claxton, 68, 75, 295
Clay, 35, 117, 171, 175, 183, 189, 252
Clayland, 223
Clayton, 3, 62, 159

Clean Shaven, 254
Cleggett, 218
Clement, 2, 323
Clements, 155, 197, 252, 306
Clementson, 165, 230
Clemm, 55
Clendenen, 214
Clendenin, 67
Clendining, 201
Clephan, 131
Clephane, 291
Clesaung, 334
Clifton, 263
Clinch, 36, 326
Clingan, 258
Clingansmith, 64
Clinton, 39
Cloakey, 298
Cloaky, 71
Clopper, 333
Clopton, 222
Cloud, 35, 164, 218, 312
Clouden, 11
Clubb, 76
Cluff, 252
Coale, 34
Coalter, 219
Coan Mill, 233
Cobb, 62, 282, 288
Cobbett, 283
Cobbs, 325
Coburg, 204
Cochran, 13, 57, 185, 247, 248, 325, 338
Cochrane, 97, 102, 181
Cocke, 32, 36, 45, 77, 141, 173, 283, 339
Cockey, 204, 278
Cocking, 265
Codd, 72
Coe, 271
Coffee, 88, 206
Coffie, 325
Coffin, 322
Cohagan, 179, 295
Cohart, 183
Cohen, 55, 109
Coit, 261
Cokendorfer, 233
Cole, 3, 9, 39, 54, 152, 171, 236, 266, 291

Coleman, 5, 54, 140
Colemen, 341
Coles, 10, 81
Coles Point, 32
Collard, 172
Collet, 64
Collett, 99
Collings, 52
Collins, 54, 102, 177, 192, 209, 224, 237, 240
Collomy, 267
Colquhoun, 93, 140
Colston, 97
Colt, 180
Colter, 90
Coltman, 328
Coltmon, 59
Colton, 118
Comb, 261
Combe, 113
Combs, 44, 53, 139, 207
Commus, 183
Compton, 97, 124, 134, 150, 183, 333
Comstock, 235
Conard, 177
Concord, 40
Conden, 119
Condit, 103, 255
Cone, 173
Conger, 192
Conkling, 52
Conn, 172, 310
Connel, 154
Connell, 243, 275, 299, 341
Connelly, 183, 224, 341
Conner, 174
Conningham, 13, 239
Connino, 224
Conover, 264
Conrad, 179, 206, 219, 271
Contee, 134, 160, 207, 221, 254, 272
Contest Farm, 120
Conway, 94, 181, 234, 247, 325
Cook, 39, 52, 59, 90, 157, 161, 179, 193, 247, 252, 284, 287

Cooke, 19, 78, 143, 187, 232, 233, 268, 302
Cookendorfer, 294
Cool Run, 65
Cool Stream Farm, 201, 262, 270
Cooledge, 181, 243, 247
Coolege, 247
Coolidge, 89, 114, 181, 275, 298, 318, 334
Coombe, 53, 108
Coombs, 155
Coomes, 206
Coomes' Park, 128
Cooms, 122
Cooners, 76
Coones, 123
Cooper, 4, 9, 71, 93, 104, 210, 248, 252, 266, 275, 287, 339, 340
Coote, 318
Cope, 216, 248, 277, 280, 301
Copley, 157
Corbett, 189
Corbin, 31, 32, 102, 193
Corcoran, 19, 59, 330
Cord, 334
Corlass, 248
Corles, 124
Cormick, 227
Cornwallis, 136
Cornwallis' Neck, 21
Cornwell, 20
Corrie, 243
Corry, 65, 222
Corson, 183
Costigan, 310
Cottrel, 140
Couch, 54
Coulter, 194
Council, 214
Courtnay, 189
Courtney, 126
Courts, 98, 300
Cousins, 99
Covachiah, 224
Covachichi, 181, 248
Covington, 30, 83, 125

Cowan, 30, 40, 58, 101
Cowell, 39, 43
Cowman, 309
Cowper, 130, 194
Cox, 40, 53, 82, 96, 104, 116, 118, 119, 126, 144, 162, 177, 179, 191, 219, 240, 248, 253, 270, 277, 280, 290, 301, 310, 333, 334, 338
Coxe, 71, 162
Coyle, 28, 113, 168, 317
Coyles, 265
Cozens, 20, 58, 303
Crabb, 47, 94, 179, 289
Craddock, 114
Crady, 76
Crafton, 82
Craghill, 328
Crago, 273
Craig, 113, 181, 243, 247, 274, 298, 331
Craighton, 46
Craik, 8, 101
Crain, 151
Cramford, 88
Crampersey, 175
Cramphin, 126
Cranch, 182, 241, 339
Crane, 12, 93, 293, 300
Cranston, 153
Crary, 31
Craven, 130, 144, 182, 241, 272, 339
Crawford, 12, 20, 22, 120, 130, 141, 149, 158, 160, 181, 183, 224, 235, 237, 238, 239, 263, 272, 275, 289, 298, 302, 335
Craybourn, 13
Creager, 129, 136, 146
Crease, 176, 236
Creaver, 73
Crebs, 218
Creery, 18
Creighton, 19, 103, 197, 318
Cremer, 304
Cres, 96
Cretcher, 190

Crews, 12
Crimm, 126
Crips, 95
Crocker, 157
Crocket, 3
Croghan, 11, 291
Croll, 271
Cromer, 26
Cromwell, 78, 209, 299, 308
Cronge, 152
Crooker, 69
Crookshank, 243
Croom, 160
Crosbie, 80, 196
Crosby, 57, 82, 194, 267
Crosdale, 227
Cross, 24, 73, 142, 161, 198, 204, 259
Crossdale, 243, 293
Croteau, 211
Crouch, 99, 149
Crouse, 188
Crow, 147
Crowinshield, 153
Crowley, 67, 76, 94, 160, 182, 339
Crown, 215, 243, 247, 281
Crowninshield, 121, 334, 335
Crozet, 265
Cruikshank, 235, 258
Cruirshane, 226
Crump, 126, 271
Cruse, 110
Crutenden, 292
Cruzat, 268
Cubbon, 183
Cuffee, 315
Culbreth, 203, 229
Culpeper, 103
Culver, 133, 174, 209, 212, 303, 306
Cumming, 34
Cummingham, 94
Cummings, 30, 142
Cunningham, 8, 40, 119, 179, 243, 272
Curran, 181
Currell, 7
Currie, 189

Curry, 228
Curtenius, 271, 273
Cushing, 94, 104
Cushwa, 38
Cussein, 85
Custis, 164, 167, 179
Cutbush, 211, 325
Cuthbert, 103
Cutler, 23, 177
Cutting, 24, 143
Cutts, 103, 256, 306
Cuy, 326

—D—

Dabney, 173, 219
Dade, 49, 56, 200, 204, 207, 218, 332
Dagnet, 151
Daingerfield, 97, 307
Dale, 22, 248
Dallas, 57, 254, 255, 264, 266
Dallum, 253
Dalton, 243, 247, 275, 289, 299
Dane, 299
Dangerfield, 264
Daniel, 68, 112
Daniels, 22, 101
Darby, 195
Dare, 244
Darnall, 27, 40, 90, 102, 119, 181, 208, 238, 248, 327
Darnell, 243
Darnes, 309
Darrah, 168, 227, 320
Darrick, 144
Daschkoff, 67
Dashiel, 93, 289
Dashiell, 23, 114, 232, 278, 310, 332
Dashner, 9
Daughtery, 82
Dausy, 306
Davenport, 3, 26, 148, 215
David, 57, 160
Davidson, 36, 40, 41, 43, 44, 52, 96, 101, 137, 155, 170, 179, 181, 189, 201, 237,
239, 243, 248, 272, 276
Davie, 25
Davies, 220
Davis, 2, 11, 19, 20, 21, 28, 30, 38, 39, 54, 55, 58, 59, 72, 73, 76, 81, 99, 101, 115, 125, 126, 141, 145, 146, 148, 152, 155, 157, 178, 184, 192, 203, 224, 225, 226, 231, 242, 253, 254, 278, 287, 288, 293, 318, 319
Davison, 154, 192
Daviss, 268
Davisson, 154
Davy, 167
Dawe, 9
Dawes, 7, 95, 97, 173
Daws, 272
Dawson, 2, 18, 37, 217, 299, 338
Day, 6, 54
De Bell, 316
De Blois, 27
De Butts, 324
De Castanado, 263
De France, 45
de Grandpre, 47
De Groot, 59
de Grouchy, 328
De Krafft, 128, 148, 255, 270
De Laverre, 16
De Mestu, 43
De Milliere, 324
De Montalet, 37
de Neuville, 328
De Reenhart, 292
De Rumford, 280
De Russy, 78
de Survilliers, 328
de Tousard, 175
De Vilette, 6
de Villiers, 263
De Witt, 105
Deacon, 40, 93
Deagle, 44
Deakens, 129
Deakin, 181, 243, 249, 276
Deakins, 18, 20, 179
Dean, 75, 81, 94, 261, 303
Deane, 212, 256
Dearborn, 32, 50, 65, 275, 299
Dearborne, 243
Dearnborn, 247
Deary, 201
Deavor, 194
Deblois, 32, 77, 243
Debois, 7
Debutts, 277
Decatur, 27, 149
Decenta, 6
Deck, 160
DeCourcey, 146
Deer Park, 268
Degrushe, 235
Dehon, 307
Deitrick, 9
Dejarnate, 341
DeKrafft, 27, 102, 124, 320
DeKraft, 59
Delaborde, 148
Delacy, 72
Delancy, 271
Delany, 181
Delary, 212
Delespine, 214
Delino, 268
Delius, 129, 179, 181, 243
Delphy, 51, 92
Dempsey, 44
Dend, 224
Deneale, 103, 111, 234
Denholm, 127
Denison, 184
Denkler, 318
Denmore, 182
Denney, 142, 329
Dennie, 192
Dennis, 180, 240, 246, 325
Dennison, 76, 208, 243
Denny, 124, 278
Densley, 106
Dent, 35, 41, 116, 143, 200, 202, 243, 248, 253, 285
Denton, 119, 325

Derby, 121
Deringer, 52
Dermot, 41
Derrick, 2
Desbrow, 191
Desha, 51, 70, 280
Despinville, 326
Deveny, 139
Devereux, 250
Deverges, 268
Devourix, 192
Dewees, 3, 167, 175, 248, 258
Dewes, 179, 239
Dewey, 232
Dewis, 272
Dexter, 93, 193, 195, 208, 281
Dick, 96, 181, 184, 214, 275, 299
Dickerson, 150, 255
Dickins, 300
Dickinson, 125, 142, 204
Dickson, 26, 43, 46, 115, 341
Didier, 309
Diehl, 218
Difficult Darnhse, 173
Digbeth, 134
Digby, 35
Digges, 49, 88, 107, 133, 159, 252, 261, 270, 284
Digges' Settlement, 233
Diggs, 18, 155, 182, 212, 243, 247, 275, 299
Dill, 2
Dillahunty, 295
Dillard, 123
Dillon, 8, 259
Dina, 229
Dinmore, 209
Dinnies, 44, 133, 212, 304
Dinsmore, 152, 164
Dirickson, 294
Discover, 83
Diser, 59
Dispenville, 325
Dix, 259, 280

Dixon, 2, 8, 16, 26, 63, 67, 76, 83, 105, 152, 154, 161, 173, 178, 212, 219, 227, 235, 336
Dobbin, 114, 169, 176, 248
Dobbins, 3, 258
Dobbyn, 71, 115, 150, 182, 241, 339
Docker, 308
Dodd, 22
Dodge, 19, 109, 123, 185, 292
Doe, 75
Dogan, 9
Doherty, 267
Dohrman, 263, 266
Doill, 146
Dolboy, 271
Doleman, 32
Doll, 179, 239, 272
Dolman, 271
Dolph, 194
Donaher, 261
Donaldson, 48, 51, 57, 96, 152, 269
Donavan, 241
Donelson, 310
Donlevy, 212, 304
Donsett, 120, 125
Doran, 320
Dorfe, 59
Dorland, 3
Dorman, 29
Dormas, 40
Dornall, 13
Dorsett, 125, 134, 135, 149, 208, 251, 283, 318
Dorsey, 20, 54, 108, 126, 142, 174, 186, 204, 211, 223, 248, 269, 280, 294, 338
Dorsey's Manor, 269
Dotson, 114, 127
Dougherty, 11, 54, 83, 86, 103, 151, 210, 290
Doughlass, 124
Doughty, 36, 45, 52, 105, 123, 148, 202, 217

Douglas, 33, 39, 92, 107, 125, 163
Douglas Hill, 302
Douglass, 62, 145, 247, 327
Douse, 214
Dove, 148
Dove's Mill, 109
Dowel, 8
Downes, 42, 264
Downey, 220
Downs, 46, 192, 273
Dowson, 23, 222, 243
Doyar, 305
Doyhar, 221, 324
Doyle, 15, 44, 133, 208
Doyne, 168, 184
Dozier, 100
Dr Blake's, 201
Drake, 1, 147, 256
Drane, 189, 204, 237, 277, 312
Drayton, 52, 89, 261
Dresser, 28
Drish, 29
Drodly, 133
Druett, 268, 332
Drummond, 90, 314
Drury, 94, 296
Dryden, 18
Du Peron, 193
Du Pont, 307
Du Val, 297
Dublin, 58
Ducker, 22
Duckett, 170, 186, 200, 212, 291, 311
Duddington, 334
Dudn, 85
Duer, 179, 239
Duffey, 305
Duffin, 288
Duffy, 212
Dugan, 22, 134
Duggins, 56
Dugoure, 133
Duigenan, 211
Dukchart, 59
Duke of Calabria, 138
Duke of Wellington, 290
Dulan, 276
Dulancy, 310

Dulany, 20, 27, 93, 164, 247, 265
Duley, 185
Dunbar, 93
Duncan, 13, 33, 71, 94, 100, 123, 213, 280
Duncanson, 35, 179
Duncler, 296
Dunham, 239
Dunkin, 268
Dunlap, 30, 31, 37, 96, 177, 225, 251
Dunlop, 104, 229, 247, 270, 275, 299, 324
Dunn, 97, 148, 214, 231, 283, 289, 303, 315
Dunning, 262
Dupont, 119
Duport, 158
Dupuy, 99, 104, 155, 201, 248
Durand, 300
Durell, 129, 193
Durkee, 44, 133
Durkin, 129
Dusenberry, 46
Duval, 6, 10, 42, 156, 163, 184, 259, 300
Duvall, 2, 40, 44, 46, 47, 48, 56, 70, 73, 95, 103, 107, 175, 182, 203, 207, 233, 241, 247, 300, 339
Dwarigen, 184
Dwight, 253, 328
Dyal, 311
Dyckman, 261
Dye, 195, 241, 339
Dyer, 31, 113, 131, 226, 296, 305
Dyson, 31, 56, 66, 68, 321

—E—

Eagling, 252
Eakin, 156, 326
Eames, 89
Earl, 160
Earl of Waldegrave, 136
Earle, 39, 58, 182, 243, 247, 275, 298, 299, 325
Early, 154, 311
Eastburn, 171, 245
Eastman, 52
Easton, 68, 140, 164
Eaton, 106, 128
Ebsworth, 225
Eccleston, 89, 204
Echols, 210
Eddy, 326, 327
Edelen, 5, 21, 282
Edelin, 95, 168, 280, 337
Eden, 243, 275
Edes, 86
Edgar, 320
Edglin, 58
Edmenston, 42
Edmondson, 193, 205
Edmonson, 109, 243, 297
Edmonston, 3, 31, 53, 69, 122, 159, 169, 185, 223, 261, 339
Edmunds, 141, 214
Edson, 31
Edward, 229
Edwards, 4, 7, 51, 59, 81, 82, 92, 94, 146, 179, 181, 200, 243, 248, 311
Eggert, 51, 92
Ehrenzeller, 243
Eichelberger, 309
Eimerson, 218
Eisenbeck, 321
Elbers, 293
Elbert, 3, 106
Elder, 296
Eldredge, 279
Electius, 127
Elford, 220
Elgar, 45, 145, 205
Elger, 297
Elgin, 220
Eliason, 131
Elieson, 184
Ellerey, 18
Ellersli, 124
Elles, 58
Ellicott, 2, 98, 107, 278
Elliot, 94, 137, 153, 160, 182, 225, 277, 280, 301, 322, 327, 328, 339
Elliott, 92, 130, 238, 241, 243, 257, 286, 304
Ellis, 3, 119, 124
Elliston, 19
Elmore, 207
Elton, 10, 264
Elwell, 214
Elwes, 212
Elwis, 44
Ely, 108
Emack, 43, 279
Emanuel IV, 30
Emmet, 214
Emmory, 274
Emory, 298
Empie, 107
English, 95, 143, 206, 237, 255, 267, 280
Ennis, 308
Enniss, 124
Eno, 39, 85, 157, 226, 243
Enos, 18
Entris, 148
Entwisle, 115, 126, 291
Epinette, 302
Erving, 86
Erwin, 20
Esby, 71
Esenbeck, 80, 284
Eskridge, 264
Espey, 312
Essex, 221
Estee, 256
Estep, 142, 292
Estes, 90
Esteubueu, 184
Etting, 41, 179, 276, 309
Euler, 52
Eustis, 243
Evans, 20, 27, 58, 86, 114, 137, 155, 165, 197, 214, 215, 218, 220, 282, 284, 314, 339
Eveleth, 106, 253, 284

353

Everett, 38, 141, 219, 225
Everitt, 1
Eversfield, 10, 61, 118, 286
Everson, 88
Ewell, 6, 9, 89, 247, 275, 299
Ewing, 237
Exchange, 337

—F—

Faber, 251
Fabie, 59
Fackenthall, 177
Faddon, 93
Fagan, 120, 213, 307
Fahy, 5
Fail, 3
Fain, 22
Fairall, 208, 282
Fairbrother, 23
Fairfair, 108
Fairfax, 39, 142, 182, 200, 243, 297, 315, 327, 334
Fairhill, 270, 285
Fairlie, 5
Fairman, 3
Faiussy, 63
Falconer, 307
Falls, 167
Fango, 101
Fanning, 22, 51, 70
Faragut, 94
Farehill & Addition, 160
Farington, 277
Farish, 27, 158
Farley, 325
Farm, 49, 258
Farmar, 5
Farmer, 45, 137
Farnum, 11
Farragret, 40
Farrall, 308
Farre, 41, 312
Farrell, 111, 150, 207
Farrer, 194
Farrington, 182, 241, 243, 280, 301, 339
Farris, 163

Farrow, 110, 112, 126
Faulkner, 212
Favour, 210
Favrot, 326
Faw, 63, 154, 179, 239
Fawcett, 134
Fawn, 183
Fearon, 98
Feedin, 146
Felius, 291
Fellows, 177
Felps, 174
Feltus, 33
Fendall, 142, 144
Fennel, 178, 248
Fennell, 185, 202
Fenton, 192
Fenwick, 38, 41, 57, 59, 64, 89, 133, 181, 182, 189, 212, 243, 246, 247, 248, 249, 250, 256, 260, 266, 275, 299, 306, 313, 321, 322, 327, 338
Feran, 261
Ferdinand IV, 138
Ferguson, 130, 223, 309, 333
Fernald, 110
Fernandez, 44
Ferral, 107, 166
Ferrall, 70, 203
Ferrell, 39
Ferrell's Neglect, 128
Ferret, 318
Ferris, 252, 273
Fessenden, 110
Field, 129, 141, 198, 215, 226, 327
Fielding, 8
Fields, 39, 295
Fifehill, 52
Finagan, 99, 102
Findlay, 256
Findley, 159
Findly, 51
Finigan, 44
Finlay, 92
Finley, 3, 323
Finney, 14
Finnigan, 164
Fischer, 264

Fisher, 4, 54, 122, 182, 243, 247, 252, 324
Fisk, 103
Fitch, 8
Fitzgerald, 88, 160, 171, 243, 319
Fitzham, 13
Fitzhugh, 7, 74, 137, 198, 220, 278, 297, 299
Fitzpatrick, 98
Fitzsimmons, 191
Fitzwhylsonn, 274
Flannery, 40
Flaut, 243
Fleck, 179
Fleetwood, 52
Fleming, 23, 57, 296
Flemming, 76
Fletcher, 170, 214, 243, 247, 248, 275, 288, 298, 299
Fleury, 124
Fleytas, 34
Flick, 243
Flores, 284
Flournoy, 55
Floyd, 8, 117, 215, 239
Foley, 231
Folk, 4
Folks, 59
Folson, 262
Fontaine, 65, 99
Foote, 10, 29
Foots, 6
Forbes, 162, 260, 286, 321
Ford, 4, 25, 58, 75, 94, 102, 128, 157, 181, 228, 235, 248, 278, 280, 287, 308, 338, 339
Forde, 47, 95
Fordyce, 54
Foreman, 303
Fores, 134
Forest, 9, 178, 260, 288
Forest of Sherwood, 134
Forget, 210
Forney, 328
Forrest, 7, 37, 41, 43, 62, 93, 96, 98, 123,

144, 145, 164, 191,
216, 224, 264, 273,
289, 302, 327, 330,
338
Forrest of Sherwood,
178
Forster, 1
Forsyth, 39, 40, 69,
279, 325
Forsythe, 341
Fort, 191
Fortune's Retreat, 253
Fortune Enlarged, 253
Forwood, 204
Foster, 3, 30, 70, 160,
173, 192, 219, 235,
257
Foulon, 58
Fountain, 49
Fouquet, 91
Fowke, 76
Fowler, 3, 63, 182, 243,
247, 271, 273, 275
Fox, 20, 59, 166, 167,
182, 210, 241, 339
Foxall, 72, 104, 119,
171, 270
Foxhall, 248
Foyles, 32, 202, 224,
231
Fraham, 275
Fraize, 223
Francis, 40, 41, 116,
118, 137, 181, 209,
245, 276
Frank, 55, 58, 60, 203
Franklin, 76, 181, 221,
222, 243, 265, 269,
294, 307
Franks, 116
Franzoni, 101, 106
Fraser, 41, 77
Frazer, 89, 90, 101, 288
Frazier, 95, 204
Frederick, 73, 202
Freeman, 47, 94, 131,
133, 178, 233, 239,
264, 272, 279, 318
Freligh, 91
French, 48, 188, 208,
240, 243, 272, 290,
334
French's Discovery, 83

Fribeau, 160
Frick, 251
Friend, 112, 129, 288
Friendship, 109, 185
Frisbie, 192
Fritchie, 128
Frog-land, 96
Fronk, 318
Frost, 76, 97, 132, 186,
209, 230, 243
Frothingham, 162
Fry, 238, 241, 243, 301
Frye, 55, 102, 297, 339
Frye's Choice, 153
Ftizhugh, 219
Fuehrer, 341
Fugate, 191
Fuhrer, 341
Fuller, 191, 339
Fullington, 110
Fulsen, 139
Fulton, 88, 333
Funk, 295
Furguson, 81

—G—
Gable, 40
Gadd, 193
Gadsby, 141, 330
Gadsden, 88
Gaillard, 77, 171
Gaines, 15, 49, 51, 55,
70, 111, 136, 152,
232
Gaither, 102, 109, 122,
125, 159, 162, 179,
189, 228, 249, 312,
314, 337
Gaitier, 75
Galaher, 312
Gale, 39, 47, 95, 141,
148, 160, 217, 279,
325
Gales, 1, 19, 68, 102,
148, 163
Gallagher, 296
Gallaher, 248
Gallasby, 99
Gallaspy, 99
Gallatin, 86
Gallaway, 121
Galley, 27

Galloway, 182, 243,
247
Galt, 153
Galvin, 207
Gamble, 3, 14, 42, 47,
54, 93, 94, 197, 253,
266, 279, 296
Gambra, 155
Gambray, 15
Gangeware, 243
Gannan, 248
Gannon, 272, 298
Gano, 256
Gansevoort, 144
Gant, 126
Gantt, 32, 89, 92, 121,
140, 182, 223, 227,
234, 243, 277, 280,
301, 327
Gardiner, 39, 47, 51,
102, 133, 184, 244,
249, 276, 282, 333
Gardner, 1, 2, 18, 53,
92, 93, 94, 95, 112,
139, 141, 181, 196,
222, 225, 244, 265,
271, 272
Garey, 218
Garity, 35
Garland, 325
Garner, 138, 175, 201,
214
Garnet, 78
Garnett, 331
Garrad, 188
Garrard, 95, 141
Garrison, 100
Gary, 4, 26, 129
Gassaway, 56, 197,
268, 269, 270, 312
Gaston, 220, 304
Gates, 62
Gatt, 288
Gatton, 209, 229, 236,
255
Gaugh, 44
Gaunt, 264
Gaw, 152
Gaylor, 59
Gaylord, 103
Gearvis, 281
Gee, 214
Geers, 40

Geisinger, 93
Geissenheiners, 305
Geohagan, 87
George, 170, 243
Geouges, 247
Gerard, 110
German, 103
Gerrard, 244
Gerrish, 94
Gerry, 67, 233, 328
Gettings, 54, 135, 309
Getty, 100
Getzendaner, 234
Geyer, 177, 219
Gholson, 208
Gibbon, 184
Gibbons, 134
Gibbs, 94, 108, 126, 153, 184
Gibson, 8, 12, 26, 28, 40, 52, 57, 126, 142, 159, 161, 210, 243, 251, 252, 292, 309, 316
Gidelman, 318
Gigniliat, 325
Gilbert, 22
Giles, 188, 214, 234, 271
Gilham, 243
Gill, 54, 154
Gill's Land, 306
Gillam, 310
Gilleland, 331
Gillespie, 75, 105, 126, 214
Gillet, 160
Gillett, 192
Gilliam, 93, 334
Gilliland, 177
Gillip, 144
Gillis, 45, 60, 97, 99, 248
Gilliss, 113, 184, 244, 289
Gilman, 25, 37, 102
Gilmore, 339
Gilpen, 239
Gilpin, 243
Ginison, 244
Girard, 328
Girardin, 115
Gird, 226, 282, 291

Gist, 49
Gitt, 104
Gittings, 91, 164, 218
Given, 159
Givison, 160, 181, 248
Glascock, 72
Glass, 163
Glasscan, 39
Glassco, 233
Glasscock, 293
Glassell, 47
Glazier, 191
Gleason, 70
Glebe Land, 111
Glen, 121
Glendy, 194, 234
Glenn, 121, 164, 213, 224, 252, 256
Gloster, 170
Glover, 8, 38, 41, 126, 255, 267, 289, 293
Gobert, 48
Goddard, 52, 109, 241
Godefroy, 202, 248
Godfrey, 101
Godwin, 133
Gody, 168, 253
Goil, 129, 243
Goins, 58
Golden, 95
Golden Anchor Tvrn, 197
Golding, 322
Goldsborough, 7, 39, 80, 92, 105, 229, 255, 301
Goldsbrorough, 189
Goldsby, 8
Goldsmith, 144
Goldthwaite, 243
Gomegys, 16
Good, 323
Good Luck, 300
Good Will, 109
Goodall, 297
Goode, 213, 325
Goodhue, 118
Goodman, 12, 46
Goodrich, 136, 160, 191, 252, 282, 318
Goodrick, 59
Goodrum, 160
Goodwil, 176

Goodwin, 38, 309
Goodwyn, 183, 265
Goodyear, 77
Goolsby, 192
Gorden, 43
Gordon, 16, 82, 93, 96, 118, 318
Gore, 244
Goshen, 132, 293
Goswick, 59
Goszler, 96, 203
Gouch, 296
Gouges, 179, 181, 182, 244
Gough, 133, 212, 300, 304, 307
Gould, 241
Goulding, 174, 179, 239, 243, 244, 250, 272
Gover, 111, 136
Gowan, 248
Gowen's Adventure, 212
Gozler, 308, 329
Graeff, 239
Graff, 287
Graffenviedte, 325
Graham, 10, 25, 36, 38, 45, 65, 99, 115, 129, 158, 165, 182, 210, 243, 247, 256, 264, 276, 325, 326, 329, 335
Gramma, 182
Grammar, 129
Grammer, 8, 102, 248, 321
Granberry, 243
Granbery, 222
Granbury, 248, 276
Grandpre, 94
Grange, 260, 340
Granger, 52, 190, 328
Grant, 243, 245, 292
Grason, 320
Grassi, 50, 128, 133, 220
Grassie, 287
Grassy, 43
Grasty, 161

356

Graves, 19, 41, 72, 137, 165, 173, 184, 219, 235
Gray, 10, 20, 54, 55, 90, 91, 115, 124, 192, 238, 304, 318, 321, 326, 339
Grayham, 257, 273
Grayson, 47, 94, 126, 136, 194, 279
Greaves, 152
Greeley, 178
Green, 2, 13, 20, 22, 32, 37, 39, 46, 72, 91, 95, 109, 123, 126, 128, 133, 139, 144, 146, 160, 197, 217, 242, 243, 263, 280, 318, 327
Green's Forest, 128
Green Hill, 70
Green Spring, 5
Greene, 17
Greenfield, 1, 8, 31, 96, 104, 134, 135, 207, 318
Greenleaf, 20, 131, 202, 205
Greenleaf's Point, 43, 62, 70, 78, 87, 100, 120
Greenvelott, 244
Greenway, 28
Greenwell, 128, 143, 264, 308, 316
Greer, 8, 161, 205, 214, 276, 286, 334
Greerson, 209
Greetham, 34
Greeves, 110
Gregg, 33
Gregory, 26, 93, 191, 214
Greiner, 160
Grendall, 280
Gressum, 91
Grettin, 267
Grey, 136
Grierson, 240
Griffin, 54, 91, 122, 160, 179, 184, 199, 205, 243, 297, 298

Griffith, 13, 25, 112, 182, 244, 249, 311, 318, 326
Griffiths, 251
Griggs, 108
Grigneaus, 116
Grim, 162
Griswold, 76, 140, 209
Griyn, 296
Grizel, 59
Groce, 40
Groenveldt, 248
Groff, 179, 239, 243, 272
Groomslot, 133
Grooves, 47
Gross, 20, 224
Grosvenor, 96, 159, 280, 295
Grove, 173
Grundy, 204, 227, 243, 293
Grynn, 262
Guedron, 151
Guelph, 204
Guess, 243
Guest, 41, 125, 248, 253
Guillard, 224
Gulick, 84
Gummore, 3
Gummow, 31
Gunn, 171
Gunnell, 315, 341
Gunston Hall, 153
Gunton, 102
Gurnee, 192
Gustine, 28, 175
Guthrie, 192
Guyton, 35, 63
Gwinn, 197
Gwynn, 212, 218, 304
Gwynne, 11, 273
Gyrma, 34

—H—

H_narie, 12
Haas, 206
Hacket, 179, 239
Hackett, 244
Hackley, 265
Hackott, 272

Haddaway, 93, 294
Hadfield, 51, 53
Hadley, 214
Hadrick, 129, 179, 244
Haff, 153
Hagerty, 74, 208, 255
Hagin, 192, 327
Hagner, 30, 193, 210
Hagrer, 263
Haile, 267
Haines, 144
Hale, 54, 57, 242
Haley, 248
Haliday, 289
Halkar, 184
Hall, 2, 16, 25, 39, 44, 47, 48, 51, 63, 66, 70, 89, 93, 94, 95, 99, 141, 142, 158, 165, 172, 174, 182, 184, 202, 212, 223, 228, 244, 247, 257, 261, 275, 299, 303, 304, 311, 316, 317, 327, 334
Hallet, 39
Hallett, 12
Halloway, 3
Hallowell, 89
Hallum, 248
Halsel, 340
Halsey, 295
Ham, 179, 206
Hambleton, 38
Hamden, 109, 339
Hamer, 41, 91, 136, 146, 272
Hamersley, 91, 198, 338
Hamilton, 4, 11, 27, 39, 59, 70, 72, 76, 83, 92, 100, 124, 128, 129, 134, 154, 155, 160, 163, 168, 189, 192, 193, 208, 211, 229, 230, 252, 265, 303, 321, 326, 334, 336
Hamm, 221, 239, 244
Hammond, 17, 261
Hampleton, 164
Hampton, 76, 208, 244
Hamson, 110

Hana, 256
Hance, 261, 293
Hancock, 3, 4, 111, 142
Hand, 202
Hander, 273
Handey, 268
Handshaw, 99
Handy, 23, 76, 128, 153, 228, 237, 292
Haney, 267
Hanna, 47, 94
Hannah, 177, 193
Hannemon, 54
Hansborough, 104
Hansbrough, 66, 72
Hanson, 13, 26, 54, 66, 79, 96, 102, 110, 136, 159, 165, 209, 229, 230, 259, 266, 268, 280
Hanson's Trifle, 128
Hapiner, 305
Haraden, 110, 197, 230
Harbaugh, 18, 20, 113
Harbin, 55, 143, 147
Harcum, 307
Hard Bargain, 124, 173
Hard Struggle, 109, 307
Hardcastle, 142
Hardey, 117
Hardin, 117
Hardinge, 270
Hardy, 176, 224, 252, 304
Hare, 118
Hargate, 157
Hargreaves, 155
Harkness, 272
Harlan, 204
Harmon, 12
Harney, 327
Harold, 44
Harpelieth, 184
Harper, 10, 64, 81, 195, 206, 277
Harper's Ferry, 22, 39, 320, 329
Harral, 110
Harridan, 334
Harrington, 4
Harris, 4, 12, 25, 27, 32, 47, 52, 55, 58, 70, 76, 80, 95, 104, 109, 124, 133, 156, 186, 187, 189, 190, 200, 227, 235, 266, 268, 278, 279, 281, 308, 322
Harrison, 9, 13, 17, 31, 32, 40, 43, 68, 69, 72, 79, 102, 116, 137, 142, 151, 156, 161, 166, 177, 180, 184, 189, 205, 219, 244, 255, 268, 269, 272, 275, 294, 296, 299, 302, 315, 320, 325, 326
Harriss, 211
Harrod, 17, 38
Harry, 92, 205
Harryman, 142, 204
Hart, 4, 95, 130, 182, 241, 244, 277, 280, 301, 339
Hartnett, 271
Hartwell, 40
Harvey, 41, 83, 190, 230, 234, 290
Harwood, 121, 184, 218, 222
Hasbrouck, 103
Hasell, 148
Hasey, 71
Haskell, 192
Haskins, 87
Haslett, 263
Hass, 239
Hass_n, 186
Hastings, 192
Hasty, 99
Haswell, 198
Hatch, 284
Hathaway, 41
Hattan, 56
Hatton, 261
Hauptman, 289
Haushberger, 299
Haw, 21, 88, 126
Hawes, 103, 168
Hawker, 244
Hawkins, 22, 25, 38, 97, 99, 100, 103, 192, 204, 230, 252, 253, 281, 309, 318, 320
Hawks, 116
Hawley, 193, 273, 287, 296, 297, 330, 332
Haxall, 129
Hay, 29, 178
Hayden, 190, 292
Haylands, 252
Haymaker, 296
Hayne, 40, 126, 283, 310
Haynes, 42, 100, 214
Hayre, 339
Hays, 3, 12, 192, 213
Haywood, 3, 117
Hazard, 143, 291
Hazel, 257, 287
Hazelton, 4
Hazen, 39
Hazle, 150, 160
Heacock, 119
Head, 195
Healey, 160
Healy, 85
Heard, 207, 267
Hearn, 228
Heath, 7, 35, 38, 47, 55, 61, 62, 69, 83, 94, 114, 123, 124, 153, 177, 190, 197, 209, 214, 216, 248, 291, 330
Heathcoate, 181
Heathcote, 248, 276
Heaton, 30, 54
Hebb, 101, 127, 183, 241, 265, 294, 300, 308, 338, 339
Heblethweatt, 80
Hebron, 76, 152, 241, 244, 339
Hedges, 118, 186
Heichler, 24, 26
Heidelbach, 54
Heighe, 244
Heise, 68, 258
Heiskell, 112
Heit, 28
Hekenwalder, 257
Helen, 296
Hellen, 38, 150, 157, 184, 244

Hellrigles, 248
Helm, 139
Hembler, 244
Hembree, 82
Hemersley, 244
Hemmersley, 129
Hemmersly, 182, 247
Hemphill, 148, 154, 169, 172
Hempstead, 313
Hemsley, 50, 298
Henderson, 82, 85, 129, 142, 156, 159, 165, 179, 184, 191, 244, 247, 262, 275, 279, 321, 331
Hendley, 179, 195, 210
Hendly, 227
Hendrick, 267
Hendricks, 271
Henkle, 105
Henley, 67, 93, 184, 264
Henner, 188
Henning, 217, 247
Hennon, 19
Henry, 8, 20, 40, 54, 55, 95, 144, 156, 263, 282, 285, 302
Henshaw, 200
Hensley, 271
Henson, 208, 225, 236
Hepburn, 114, 144, 164, 169, 244, 247, 275, 299
Hepburne, 244
Herbert, 6, 86, 145, 229, 231, 318, 339
Hereford, 172
Herefordshire, 128
Herford, 57, 64, 80, 102, 115, 122, 132, 179, 186, 301, 306
Herin, 214
Herman, 71
Herndon, 86, 331
Heronimus, 15, 123, 125, 135, 139, 302, 323, 334
Herring, 54
Herriot, 213
Herrity, 55, 267
Herron, 128

Herty, 25, 29, 109, 247, 275, 299
Hess, 30
Hester, 177
Hestetter, 177
Heth, 226
Heugh, 167, 229
Heughes, 249
Hewett, 226
Hewitt, 28, 31, 33, 79, 91, 125, 126, 132, 205, 297
Hewlett, 19
Hewlit, 191
Hewss, 48
Heyer, 146, 200
Heyle, 181, 248
Hickey, 34
Hickman, 39, 169, 250, 258
Hicks, 8, 26, 207
Hicock, 79
Hider, 3
Higden, 208
Higdon, 41, 73
Higgenson, 62
Higginbothom, 322
Higgins, 122, 339
High, 118
Hilborn, 252
Hilderedle, 188
Hildreth, 78, 151
Hildt, 234
Hill, 10, 39, 63, 121, 124, 153, 158, 164, 182, 189, 197, 206, 208, 244, 247, 266, 267, 270, 275, 285, 287, 289, 290, 299, 305, 307
Hill Top, 231
Hillard, 248, 295
Hillary, 245
Hilleary, 69, 127, 202, 239, 250
Hillhouse, 170
Hilliary, 129, 179
Hillyar, 39
Hillyer, 144
Hinde, 168
Hindman, 3, 70, 179, 239, 244

Hines, 123, 137, 226, 289, 341
Hinkle, 307
Hinkson, 267
Hipkins, 209, 262, 284, 286, 334
History of Virginia, 138
Hitchburn, 182, 241, 277, 280, 301, 339
Hitchburne, 244
Hitchcock, 326
Hite, 75, 242
Hitechew, 188
Hithrington, 197
Hixson, 195
Hoban, 28, 140
Hobart, 118, 265, 291
Hobbs, 3, 40, 47, 119
Hodge, 144
Hodges, 19, 29, 76, 126, 134, 160, 164, 166, 175, 202, 207, 221, 229, 302, 332
Hodgson, 161, 186, 244
Hoff, 142
Hoffman, 9, 42, 46, 59, 91, 94, 96, 134, 178, 179, 234, 264, 309, 311
Hogan, 53, 318, 327
Hoge, 237, 239, 250
Hogpen Enlarged, 137
Holbert, 90, 146
Holbrook, 204
Holbrooks, 59
Holcomb, 259
Holcombe, 297
Holdfast & Addition to Holdfast, 335
Holiday, 59
Holker, 65
Holland, 40, 184, 185, 262, 268
Holland's Addition, 185
Holliday, 186, 244, 247, 275, 299
Hollingshead, 184
Hollingsworth, 127, 214, 309, 326, 329
Hollins, 127
Hollis, 307
Holly, 267

Holman, 309, 310
Holmead, 4, 141, 179, 239, 318
Holmes, 40, 69, 173, 206, 219, 235, 263, 269, 331
Holstein, 244
Holt, 60
Holtzman, 86, 122, 203, 241, 303, 310, 314
Homans, 36, 131, 304
Homer, 244
Honeywood, 97
Hooe, 5, 6, 100, 129, 153, 244, 247, 275, 299
Hoof, 239
Hooff, 179
Hook, 22
Hoomes, 29, 61
Hooper, 170, 199
Hoopes, 166
Hoot, 99, 213
Hoover, 186, 303
Hope Park, 109
Hopewell, 173
Hopkins, 12, 21, 129, 136, 158, 180, 304, 326
Hord, 258
Horde, 46
Horn, 167
Horn Point, 142
Horne, 162
Hornell, 12
Horner, 87, 103, 165
Horrell, 82, 207
Horry, 88
Horsely, 219
Horsley, 124, 313
Horvel, 61
Hoskinson, 42, 69
Hossack, 204, 227, 293
Hotchkess, 12
Hotte, 332
Hough, 138, 228, 263, 269
Housman, 276
Houssey, 46
Houston, 12, 325
Houtchens, 253
Hoventon, 93
Hovey, 326

How, 19, 185
Howard, 41, 54, 58, 59, 99, 117, 128, 146, 164, 182, 201, 208, 224, 241, 244, 277, 278, 280, 282, 289, 301, 312
Howe, 38, 92, 120, 162, 244
Howell, 83, 95, 103, 327
Howes, 214
Howland, 59
Howle, 280
Howsar, 263
Howse, 270
Hoy, 20, 181
Hoye, 92, 131, 182, 204
Hubbard, 3, 5, 52, 192, 324
Huber, 138, 312
Hubley, 28
Huddleston, 81, 159, 196, 272, 278
Huddleton, 21
Hudson, 12
Huet, 275
Huffington, 59
Huffman, 225
Huffsteller, 82
Hufty, 31
Hughes, 17, 18, 41, 61, 142, 168, 187, 210, 230, 239, 262, 306, 333, 336
Hugster, 244
Huie, 191
Huissy, 58
Hulberd, 321
Hulbert, 315
Huling, 145
Hull, 10, 93, 156, 169
Hume, 244, 248
Humphrey, 52
Humphreys, 13, 52, 126
Humphries, 40
Hungerford, 270
Hunt, 43, 55, 99, 217, 256, 306, 326
Hunter, 2, 30, 85, 103, 228, 241, 244, 309, 314, 339
Huntington, 145, 298

Hunton, 90
Huntt, 10, 156
Hurdle, 99
Hurlbert, 89
Hurlburt, 71, 77
Hurley, 99, 158, 209, 244
Husler, 275
Husses, 179
Husson, 177
Huston, 195
Hutchens, 58
Hutcheson, 64
Hutchins, 2
Hutchinson, 4, 12
Hutton, 160
Huyck, 206
Huyett, 207
Huzza, 54
Hyames, 124
Hyar, 317
Hyatt, 76, 102, 127, 176, 199, 259, 340
Hyde, 40, 47, 94, 126, 213, 306
Hylan, 181
Hyland, 244, 276
Hyles, 79
Hynum, 89

Ibric, 145
Iler, 59
Ingals, 215
Ingerham, 241, 339
Ingersoll, 1, 141
Ingham, 79, 103
Ingle, 64, 122, 132, 138, 186, 205, 247, 274, 280, 297, 298, 314, 319, 339
Ingles, 160
Inglis, 105, 271
Ingraham, 130, 182, 244
Inlet, 292
Innerarity, 161
Innis, 97, 224
Inskeep, 133, 220
Irish, 143
Irvin, 79, 92
Irvine, 238, 255

Irving, 5, 128
Irwin, 210, 235
Isaac, 40, 303, 308
Isaacs, 40, 46, 87, 264
Ishum, 41
Izard, 65, 268, 273

—J—

Jacaway, 191
Jack, 50, 114, 189
Jackar Strinactim, 176
Jackson, 8, 9, 13, 23, 28, 31, 33, 39, 58, 86, 96, 101, 111, 112, 117, 119, 126, 168, 174, 182, 193, 197, 203, 210, 215, 241, 244, 266, 268, 277, 280, 298, 301, 307, 309, 310, 321, 335, 339
Jackson's Improvement, 307
Jackson's Mount, 203
Jackson's Necessity, 203
Jacobs, 164, 206
Jacques, 177
James, 76, 113, 128
Jameson, 44, 133, 212, 264, 304
Jamieson, 191, 212, 244
Jamison, 287
Jammison, 328
Janifer, 275, 299
Janney, 212, 278
Jarboe, 80
Jarrad, 224, 334
Jarrett, 334
Jarvis, 89
Jas & Mary, 333
Jay, 152
Jeffers, 81, 240
Jefferson, 45, 47, 77, 133, 172
Jeffery, 101
Jeffries, 12
Jemmison, 183
Jenifer, 14, 24, 218, 247
Jenikins, 82

Jenkins, 16, 17, 22, 89, 101, 105, 112, 136, 144, 157, 165, 244, 273, 304, 330
Jenner, 314
Jenners, 39
Jenney, 149
Jennifer, 162, 182, 244
Jennings, 39, 103, 217, 244
Jennison, 262
Jentching, 123
Jepson, 52
Jessup, 45
Jewett, 41
Jinkins, 257
John's Last Sh_f, 309
John's Trouble, 173
John Brewer, 4
Johnes, 318
Johns, 34, 41, 43, 92, 97, 129, 142, 144, 183, 207, 225, 234, 239, 244, 264, 272
Johnson, 1, 2, 7, 11, 20, 21, 27, 33, 35, 39, 41, 47, 54, 58, 59, 60, 75, 83, 84, 94, 96, 101, 103, 112, 117, 123, 124, 125, 131, 133, 135, 143, 144, 145, 146, 150, 157, 158, 161, 182, 183, 184, 193, 204, 205, 208, 212, 217, 228, 229, 239, 244, 247, 248, 253, 257, 258, 259, 260, 267, 275, 276, 287, 298, 299, 318, 325
Johnson's Tvrn, 170
Johnston, 10, 67, 84, 95, 143, 146, 167, 207, 225, 235, 244, 252, 294
Johson, 41
Joice, 61
Jolley, 61
Jolly, 329
Joncherez, 44, 67, 133, 157, 178, 185, 212, 244, 333

Jones, 3, 7, 11, 13, 23, 24, 25, 29, 36, 38, 39, 47, 48, 49, 51, 53, 54, 65, 80, 84, 91, 92, 94, 99, 103, 117, 129, 130, 132, 136, 141, 144, 152, 156, 170, 173, 174, 179, 182, 184, 210, 212, 213, 214, 216, 219, 221, 225, 235, 239, 241, 244, 247, 252, 267, 273, 289, 296, 297, 298, 304, 318, 334, 339, 340
Jordan, 3, 51, 58, 92, 113, 186, 257, 291
Joseph, 118
Joy, 112, 204
Judge, 92
Judy, 316
Julien, 335
Junkin, 86
Jupee, 296

—K—

Kain, 24, 187, 262
Kalbfus, 318
Kale, 244
Kalkman, 339
Kalorama, 187
Kanah, 76
Kanall, 99
Kananagh, 233
Kantzow, 58
Karnap, 38
Karney, 76
Karthaus, 305, 306
Kaufman, 54
Keadle, 17
Kealy, 225
Kean, 107, 186, 204, 326
Keane, 52
Kearsley, 70, 87, 323, 330
Keech, 4
Keeling, 39
Keen, 135, 160
Keene, 115
Keeney, 29
Keisler, 244

Keith, 12, 339
Kell, 142
Kelland, 244
Keller, 283, 300
Kellog, 94
Kellogg, 47, 279
Kelly, 2, 20, 99, 184, 222, 281
Kemp, 107, 129, 142, 167, 174, 180, 184, 208, 239, 244, 272
Kendall, 263
Kendelsperyer, 191
Kendle, 184
Kendreb, 2
Kendrick, 214
Kenedy, 230
Kennedy, 39, 44, 60, 95, 139, 264, 306
Kenner, 70
Kenniston, 282
Kent, 35, 45, 49, 50, 62, 65, 90, 103, 129, 138, 142, 148, 171, 178, 196, 205, 208, 257, 260, 284, 338
Kent Island, 208
Keogly, 168
Kerr, 91, 99, 131, 146, 152, 180, 192, 239, 326
Kerry, 162
Kersenar, 22
Kershner, 142
Kesler, 129, 180, 239
Kessler, 54
Kesterson, 190
Ketcham, 70
Ketchum, 51, 217
Ketland, 129, 239
Kettell, 123
Kettle Run, 312
Keveny, 292
Key, 37, 84, 104, 131, 132, 146, 180, 184, 186, 239, 241, 251, 292, 293, 294, 321, 328, 333, 336, 338
Keys, 256, 272
Keyser, 34
Keyworth, 337
Kidd, 181, 248, 276
Kilgour, 226

Kilgrue, 36
Killinger, 293
Kilty, 35, 38, 130, 204, 269
Kim, 239
Kimball, 27
Kimberly, 18
Kincaid, 3, 184, 213
Kindell, 208
King, 11, 13, 22, 23, 25, 41, 53, 64, 67, 76, 92, 94, 96, 101, 102, 109, 137, 138, 147, 156, 162, 170, 173, 178, 182, 187, 190, 196, 211, 213, 219, 220, 231, 235, 241, 244, 248, 252, 253, 256, 260, 268, 270, 276, 277, 279, 280, 281, 282, 295, 301, 318, 319, 324, 339
King of Bavaria, 135
Kingsbury, 39, 66
Kingsley, 200
Kinsingen, 39
Kirby, 63, 182, 194, 244, 247, 275, 330
Kirk, 48, 180, 239, 244, 248, 272, 326
Kirkland, 335
Kirkpatrick, 144, 272
Kirkwood, 225
Kitchell, 160
Kitchen, 113
Kitchley, 244
Kitlan, 180
Kleiber, 18, 113, 237
Kline, 67
Klinger, 180, 244, 272
Knap, 29, 125
Knapp, 102
Kneller, 74, 110
Knight, 20, 326
Knoblock, 319
Knock, 137
Knott, 266
Knotts, 195
Knowles, 31, 41, 143, 156, 172, 186, 248
Knowlton, 92
Kohl, 110

Kohlman, 319
Kollock, 144
Kolp, 184
Koones, 115, 310
Koontz, 180, 239
Korn, 295
Kortright, 341
Kortwright, 111, 288
Krafft, 293
Kramer, 244
Kreamer, 277, 280, 301, 339
Kreemer, 149
Kretschman, 306
Kripgans, 11
Kruger, 180, 244, 272
Kuhn, 279, 301
Kuhne, 47, 94
Kurtz, 21, 112, 180, 187, 196, 199, 239, 247

—L—

La Croix, 116
La Gouthrie, 115
Labille, 178
Labyrinth, 162, 164, 337
Lacey, 13, 264
Lackland, 199
Lacy, 137, 315
Ladd, 331
Ladille, 106
Laidler, 134, 168, 281
Laidler's Ferry, 168
Laigh, 182
Laight, 243, 339
Laird, 115, 199, 248, 307
Lake, 244
Lallemand, 328
Lamar, 203, 310
Lamarde, 323
Lamb, 52, 102, 193
Lambert, 56, 59, 161, 182, 326
Lamble, 244
Lamkin, 286
Lamont, 79
Lamotta, 141
Lanaro, 39

Lancaster, 44, 133, 207, 273, 306, 313, 319
Lancy, 110
Landes, 102, 110, 195, 341
Landman, 54
Landraft, 3
Lands, 296
Landsale, 184
Landsdale, 41, 249
Lane, 2, 7, 82, 92, 96, 109, 141, 184, 195, 197, 266, 271, 291, 309
Lang, 253
Langdon, 85, 195
Langle, 47
Langley, 17, 40, 129, 244, 275, 299
Lanham, 311
Lankin, 262
Lansdale, 41, 153, 181, 249, 277, 333
Lapham, 1
Larandar, 164
Laraway, 54
Lard, 182, 241, 339
Larkin, 288
Larkum, 240
Larned, 115, 180, 181, 258, 333
Lasrh, 34
Lassailer, 116
Latham, 123
Lathrop, 110, 215
Latimer, 94, 140
Latimore, 286
Latourell, 318
Latrobe, 138, 209, 212, 317
Lattimer, 101
Laub, 106, 121
Lauderdale, 41
Laughton, 94
Launville, 300
Laurence, 230
Laurie, 9, 60, 64, 74, 86, 99, 170, 180, 187, 285
Laury, 45
Lavake, 156
Laval, 14, 262, 263
Lavall, 126

Lavender, 313
Law, 20, 32, 77, 84, 93, 96, 114, 156, 196, 274, 314
Lawder, 39
Lawless, 54
Lawnderwas, 39
Lawnville, 330
Lawrence, 5, 58, 70, 92, 167, 176, 198, 263, 335
Lawrens, 262
Lawrie, 36
Laws, 179, 295
Lawson, 54, 137
Layhill & Beall's Reserve, 194
Le Chevalier, 94
Le Clerc, 156
Le Duc, 18
Le Moine, 164
Le Preux, 336
Leach, 78, 126, 194, 202
Leake, 275, 299
Lear, 80, 102, 226, 237, 256
Leary, 145
Leatch, 224
Leavenworth, 69
Leckie, 120
Ledan, 225
Leduc, 1
Ledyard, 12
Lee, 2, 5, 7, 8, 9, 27, 35, 38, 39, 61, 70, 76, 77, 92, 95, 111, 116, 118, 122, 124, 129, 133, 143, 146, 147, 152, 156, 160, 162, 164, 180, 184, 198, 206, 212, 213, 217, 218, 223, 225, 229, 234, 237, 239, 247, 254, 256, 264, 266, 272, 274, 286, 288, 298, 303, 304, 318, 321, 326, 334
Leek, 247
Leeke, 129, 182, 244
Leet, 195
Lefeon, 35
Lefever, 36

Lefevre, 130
Leford, 40
Legens, 301
Legge, 47, 94, 279, 313
Lehmann, 292
Leib, 8, 76
Leidler, 247, 275, 299
Leigh, 338
Leiper, 232
Leitch, 182, 247, 275, 299
Leith, 59
Lemley, 38
Lemmon, 165
Lemon, 340
Lendrum, 325
Lenman, 55
Lennard, 210, 214
Lenox, 43, 96, 99, 186
Lent, 325
Leonard, 63, 93, 110, 159
Lester, 29, 242, 267
Lettsom, 165
Level's Blue Plains, 173
Levely, 54
Levenworth, 45
Levingston, 72
Levy, 264
Lewis, 2, 10, 46, 54, 65, 71, 83, 93, 95, 99, 116, 146, 159, 172, 173, 184, 198, 210, 213, 241, 244, 247, 263, 325, 339
Lewson, 216
Leyland, 244
Libby, 124
Liddy, 180
Lie, 334
Ligan, 184
Lillingtons, 214
Lindenberger, 309
Linding, 184
Lindsay, 21, 29, 102, 108, 114, 151, 205, 288
Linen, 109
Lingan, 20, 196, 232, 239
Lingerfetter, 244
Lingham, 244

Linghan, 39
Linnard, 118
Linscott, 39
Linsted, 198
Linstid, 179
Lint, 261
Linthicum, 229
Linthicumb, 318
Linton, 95, 280
Linwell, 128
Lipscomb, 158
Lipssomb, 259
Lithgow, 156, 312
Little, 34, 142, 170, 217, 229, 230, 271, 289, 291, 313
Little Worth, 140
Littlejohn, 141, 271
Littleton, 8, 318
Liturage, 117
Livens, 296
Livingston, 291
Lizure, 56
Lloyd, 79, 142, 160, 208
Lobbett, 295
Lochhead, 129
Lock, 207
Locke, 74, 158
Lockerman, 240, 322
Lockland, 134
Lockwood, 192
Lodge, 60
Lofberg, 147
Lofland, 130
Loftin, 114
Logan, 32, 234, 237, 238, 249
Lomax, 161
Long, 251, 252, 264
Long Discovered, 309
Long Meadows, 40, 115, 215
Longden, 161, 234
Longstreet, 134
Looal, 110
Looker, 228
Lookingbeel, 38
Loomis, 183, 199
Lorain, 3
Lorandere, 146
Lord, 47, 94, 256, 279

Lorman, 108, 117, 181, 244, 249
Loughborough, 180
Louis XVI, 30, 45
Louis XVII, 30
Loundes, 276
Louverture, 320
Love, 40, 76, 108, 117, 143, 303, 313
Lovejoy, 102
Loveland, 11
Lovett, 96, 335
Low, 2, 115, 132, 154, 268, 318, 324
Lowe, 3, 8, 11, 116, 139, 154, 198, 295
Lowera, 99
Lowman, 192
Lowndes, 75, 85, 123, 128, 135, 181, 244, 248, 328
Lowrey, 38, 225, 298
Lowry, 20, 38, 57, 76, 244, 267, 296, 334
Loyd, 74
Lucas, 121, 143, 173, 230, 296
Lucket, 305
Lucus, 76
Lucy, 228
Ludlow, 33, 144, 181, 248, 276, 279, 335
Ludwig, 311
Lufborough, 9, 92, 95, 102, 167
Luffborough, 29, 239, 272, 302
Luke, 250
Lukeus, 252
Lundholm, 11
Lung, 206
Lux, 182, 247, 275, 299
Lyddane, 210
Lyles, 6, 29, 142, 157, 163, 174, 197, 201, 223, 230, 244, 247, 330
Lyman, 280
Lymbourn, 42
Lynch, 30, 41, 129, 181, 201, 212, 216, 244, 249, 273, 276, 304, 308, 321

Lynn, 81, 182, 209, 244, 247, 274, 275, 298, 299
Lynn & Little Lynn, 186
Lyon, 53, 208, 240, 254, 265, 267
Lyons, 286

—M—

M'Adam, 94
M'Annally, 267
M'Auley, 12
M'Cabe, 40, 212
M'Call, 10, 59
M'Callion, 172
M'Can, 96
M'Candlish, 5
M'Caney, 222
M'Cann, 124
M'Cantus, 184
M'Cargo, 4
M'Carthy, 46
M'Carty, 149, 168
M'Caula, 114
M'Cawley, 93
M'Clarthy, 12
M'Clarty, 3
M'Claskey, 83, 265
M'Cleery, 86
M'Clellan, 127
M'Clelland, 11, 205, 288
M'Clennon, 91
M'Clintock, 325
M'Closkey, 148
M'Closky, 38
M'Clure, 267
M'Collum, 115
M'Comb, 43
M'Connel, 96, 232
M'Connell, 4, 27, 144
M'Cormick, 42, 43, 60, 75, 92, 96, 99, 115, 126, 133, 148, 149, 159, 169, 172, 174, 178, 180, 181, 186, 198, 205, 207, 226, 228, 232, 247, 266, 274, 279, 318
M'Coskry, 145
M'Coy, 31, 141, 160, 219, 245

M'Cracken, 191
M'Crae, 40
M'Creery, 180, 272
M'Culloch, 93, 292
M'Cullough, 305
M'Curdy, 128
M'Cutchen, 101
M'Dermott, 146, 191
M'Donal, 296
M'Donald, 40, 54, 64, 66, 77, 116, 146, 150, 326
M'Donough, 49
M'Dowell, 147, 277
M'Elderry, 174, 212, 291
M'Farlan, 8
M'Farland, 45, 221, 245, 288
M'Gavock, 325
M'Gee, 10, 32, 150
M'Glassin, 78
M'Gowan, 53, 93, 99, 108, 155, 179, 186
M'Grath, 272
M'Gregor, 316
M'Guire, 100, 127, 206
M'Henry, 180, 272
M'Ilhenny, 237
M'Ilvain, 213
M'Intire, 12, 139, 145, 219
M'Intosh, 297
M'Isaacs, 39
M'Kann, 58
M'Kean, 294
M'Kechnie, 145
M'Kee, 9, 111, 127
M'Keever, 94
M'Kenley, 302
M'Kenna, 229
M'Kenney, 104, 159, 165, 185, 234, 270
M'Kensie, 41
M'Kenzie, 325
M'Keowin, 58, 103, 141
M'Kim, 9, 41, 68, 71, 75, 205, 279
M'Kinley, 108
M'Kinney, 89, 175
M'Kinsay, 39
M'Kissoch, 94

M'Knight, 42, 127
M'Lain, 82
M'Laughlin, 147
M'Lean, 6, 58, 99, 132, 160, 245
M'Lellan, 292
M'Lelland, 186
M'Leod, 49, 87, 102, 125, 219
M'Mahan, 88
M'Mahon, 92, 129, 223, 245
M'Millain, 9
M'Millan, 192
M'Mullen, 26
M'Murray, 170
M'Nantz, 1
M'Neale, 168
M'Near, 98
M'Neil, 45
M'Neill, 200, 326
M'Nickle, 257
M'Nulty, 192
M'Pherson, 11, 128, 231, 318
M'Phersons, 112
M'Quinn, 208
M'Ray, 184
M'Sherry, 44, 256
M'Williams, 124, 151
M'Clarey, 180
M'Cormick, 245
M'Kenny, 184
Maben, 155
Mac Lain, 214
Mac Rae, 147
Macarty, 40
Macauley, 119
Macbreery, 245
Maccubbin, 324
Macdaniel, 126
Macdonough, 93
Mace, 282
Macgill, 308
Machan, 95
Machen, 122, 132, 237, 336
Machesney, 76, 232
Machin, 90
Macilroy, 262
Mackall, 8, 82, 142, 199, 252, 261, 293
Mackay, 245, 281

Mackell, 239
Mackey, 100, 142, 181, 187, 196, 247, 265, 300
Maclary, 245
Maclean, 13
Macomb, 70, 91, 111, 331
Macon, 302
Macpherson, 152
Macrae, 15, 331, 332
Macubbin, 114
Maddox, 50, 78, 119, 155, 173, 182, 184, 247, 253, 308, 334, 339
Madison, 42, 77, 110, 131, 199, 227, 268, 324
Maffitt, 68
Magill, 206, 232, 278
Magrath, 176
Magruder, 4, 19, 21, 32, 62, 77, 83, 86, 93, 100, 104, 105, 109, 116, 133, 144, 164, 166, 169, 174, 179, 183, 185, 196, 211, 222, 229, 233, 236, 250, 266, 287, 288, 301, 319, 330, 336, 337
Magruders Tavern, 62
Maguire, 157, 249
Mahan, 40
Mahon, 145
Mahoney, 124
Mahonna, 273
Mahuny, 18
Main, 62, 157
Mains, 177
Mairs, 94
Maitland, 23
Malcolm, 260, 263
Males, 39
Maley, 318
Mallendorff, 200
Mallory, 7, 16, 131, 134, 135, 197, 251, 322, 326, 332
Malony, 54
Maloy, 177
Man, 117

Manac, 194
Mandeville, 12, 72, 112, 157, 174, 302, 321
Manners, 94
Manney, 268
Manning, 44, 124, 219, 310
Manor Land, 224
Mansfield, 106
Mansfield & Collins Comfort, 119
Mantz, 180, 239, 245
Manuel, 6
Mara, 87, 245, 249
Marble, 144, 177
Marbury, 104, 131, 162, 220, 233, 240, 334
Maria, 100
Maria Antoinette, 45
Maria Louisa, 322
Marion, 63, 88
Mariott, 52
Mark, 41
Markin, 171
Markward, 297, 332
Marleham, 94
Marlowe, 200, 230
Marquart, 2
Marquert, 166
Marr, 144
Marriott, 117
Mars, 22
Marshal, 39
Marshall, 11, 20, 97, 101, 112, 129, 153, 172, 180, 198, 218, 239, 245, 273, 321, 335, 339
Marsteler, 259
Marsteller, 73, 78, 112
Marston, 70
Martin, 24, 39, 41, 42, 49, 58, 59, 65, 67, 89, 95, 100, 109, 126, 142, 145, 180, 188, 195, 208, 222, 225, 239, 245, 249, 272, 275, 299, 326, 341
Martinburgh, 41
Martsteller, 62, 201

Mason, 5, 20, 24, 38, 41, 60, 102, 104, 126, 138, 153, 157, 181, 183, 185, 204, 207, 213, 231, 239, 240, 241, 247, 249, 256, 270, 275, 283, 284, 287, 290, 291, 298, 302, 326, 327, 330, 332, 334, 339
Massey, 142, 204, 227, 249, 325
Masters, 83
Mathers, 120
Mathews, 8, 133, 153, 240, 276
Mathias, 143, 321
Matlock, 158
Matthew, 38
Matthews, 1, 21, 33, 40, 44, 45, 53, 55, 88, 106, 116, 131, 140, 144, 180, 187, 201, 208, 209, 212, 213, 215, 217, 218, 239, 259, 260, 270, 290, 304, 307, 309, 312, 317, 335
Matthias, 239, 291
Mattingly, 33, 191, 308
Mattox, 241
Mattree, 245
Maul, 268, 323, 326
Maupain, 334
Maupin, 118
Mauro, 104, 135, 172, 179, 302, 304
Maury, 43, 93, 197, 274, 314
Mawe, 59
Maxwell, 1, 3, 31, 44, 58, 101, 135, 180, 226, 239, 267
May, 6, 102, 129, 226, 270, 299
Mayer, 8, 125, 132, 169, 239, 249
Mayfield, 39, 142
Mayhew, 208, 209, 236
Mayo, 94, 266, 286
Mayson, 182
Mazzei, 202
Mc Coy, 23

McAnall, 341
McBurney, 57
McCabe, 304
McCale, 334
McCall, 334
McCally, 52
McCardy, 319
McCarty, 29, 231, 274
McChesny, 297
McClan, 245
McClung, 334
McCobb, 66
McComb, 266
McCormick, 4, 33, 71, 222, 228, 229, 236, 239, 249, 257, 258, 259, 276, 284, 286, 311, 312, 315, 335, 341
McCoy, 319
McCreery, 239, 294
McCrimmin, 165
McCue, 100, 250
McCulloch, 22
McCulloh, 52
McDade, 245
McDaniel, 258
McDermot, 249
McDermothroe, 249
McDevitt, 295
McDonald, 52, 131, 245, 255, 289, 317, 334
McDowell, 58, 328
McDuell, 305
McElderby, 321
McEldery, 260
McElroy, 7
McEvoy, 213
McEwen, 76
McFarland, 196
McFeely, 66
McGlue, 283
McGonegal, 253
McGrath, 239, 245
McGrew, 76
McGruder, 236
McHenry, 47, 239, 245, 295
McIntire, 132, 256, 341
McIntosh, 235
McIntyre, 95
McKee, 114

McKeldin, 292
McKenney, 98, 264, 333
McKenny, 247
McKenzie, 129, 320
McKeowin, 198, 203, 205, 211
McKim, 43, 318, 339
McLaughlin, 100
McLeod, 92, 201, 262, 270, 311
McLoud, 256
McMahon, 91, 247, 269
McMillan, 332
McMurray, 324
McNamara, 72
McNeal, 69
McPhail, 249, 276
McPherson, 69, 154, 222, 269, 304, 333
McPhial, 245
McQuackin, 245
McRae, 64
McRea, 219
McRee, 69
McRim, 334
McWaters, 319
McWilliams, 45, 228, 232
Meacham, 3
Mead, 134
Meade, 304, 310
Meadows, 307
Meakin, 284
Meakings, 212
Means, 188
Mebane, 12
Mechlin, 45, 170, 251, 288
Meckle, 245
Meconikin, 142
Meddart, 239
Meigs, 13, 16, 62, 102, 131, 156, 289
Mein, 334
Melish, 264
Melsheimer, 42
Melvin, 212, 236, 304, 317, 338
Menard, 304
Mercer, 20, 41, 172, 181, 193, 245, 252, 288, 322

Merchand, 177
Merchant, 60
Merchant Mill, 236
Meredith, 54, 168, 261
Mereer, 249
Meriweather, 245
Meriwether, 235
Merran, 146
Merrea, 55
Merrell, 61
Merren, 225
Merrick, 66
Merrill, 32, 90, 237
Merryman, 271
Merryweather, 247
Merson, 56
Mervine, 94
Mesher, 22
Messenger, 196
Messer, 214
Mewburn, 245
Meyers, 228
Michael, 204
Michell, 121
Middart, 180
Middieton, 146
Middle Brook Mills & Estate, 55
Middlemore, 165
Middleton, 2, 11, 39, 105, 110, 127, 138, 146, 171, 177, 184, 200, 202, 231, 270, 306
Milburn, 39
Miles, 20, 58, 174, 206, 239, 300, 330
Miley, 39, 239
Mill Farm, 260
Mill Mont, 229
Mill Prison, 51
Mill Seat, 270
Millard, 207, 228, 278, 323, 338
Millen, 177
Miller, 12, 13, 20, 39, 40, 42, 47, 49, 52, 53, 54, 59, 69, 77, 81, 92, 94, 95, 108, 109, 111, 124, 128, 129, 131, 137, 142, 143, 155, 156, 159, 183, 186, 202, 207,

213, 231, 239, 245, 260, 267, 270, 295, 296, 329
Millford, 112, 298
Milligan, 32, 36, 47, 122
Mills, 31, 95, 139, 182, 191, 200, 241, 280
Milton, 25
Milwee, 81
Mims, 262
Minchin, 39
Miner, 160
Mines, 14
Minifee, 245
Minifie, 41, 182, 241, 339
Minitree, 14, 58, 160, 182
Minor, 1, 19, 110, 117, 120, 164, 180, 201, 209, 245, 246, 247, 266, 303, 310, 311
Mintrum, 249
Mintum, 245
Minturn, 181, 276
Mitchell, 3, 18, 20, 28, 35, 36, 39, 55, 69, 83, 126, 146, 166, 177, 199, 208, 220, 235
Mix, 93
Moale, 184
Mod, 225
Moffett, 267
Mohonny, 40
Moilan, 245
Molar, 177
Mollison, 12
Monday, 23
Monroe, 7, 25, 36, 56, 103, 114, 172, 199, 203, 219, 325
Montalbino, 59
Monteath, 94
Montegat, 47
Montegut, 94
Montgomerie, 9
Montgomery, 26, 43, 46, 59, 94, 103, 147, 238, 258
Montrieul, 263
Moody, 205, 214

Moon, 154
Mooney, 45, 304
Moore, 3, 10, 14, 17, 32, 40, 48, 54, 55, 56, 59, 66, 80, 85, 92, 102, 122, 124, 129, 136, 139, 150, 159, 166, 167, 175, 176, 180, 191, 196, 200, 205, 223, 225, 226, 232, 234, 239, 245, 253, 272, 273, 279, 297
Moores, 213, 214
Moran, 231, 254
Morarty, 296
Mordall, 249
More Fields Enlarged, 287
Morehead, 126
Moreland, 137
Moreton, 3
Morfit, 332
Morgan, 6, 59, 72, 88, 162, 165, 200, 213, 258, 320
Moriarty, 195, 278
Moriatta, 298
Morin, 160, 249, 292
Mork, 198
Morrell, 28, 175
Morress, 268
Morris, 6, 14, 20, 86, 116, 180, 181, 184, 198, 225, 231, 233, 245, 249, 265, 273, 276, 296, 306, 313, 341
Morrison, 245, 256
Morriss, 162, 296
Morrissett, 161
Morse, 164, 191
Morsell, 83, 121, 150, 244
Morsell., 97
Morte, 141
Mortee, 233
Mortimer, 126
Morton, 94, 110, 116, 122, 184, 256, 330, 337, 338
Moscrop, 111, 116, 180, 239

Moscross, 339
Moseley, 194
Mosely, 103
Mosher, 101, 131, 146
Moss, 299, 309
Mott, 32
Mott., 118
Mould, 180
Moulder, 289
Moulton, 51
Mount, 259
Mountfort, 78
Mountjoy, 326
Mountz, 186, 204, 295
Moxley, 74, 79, 229, 303
Moxly, 185
Moyer, 180, 245, 272
Moylan, 181, 249, 276
Mt Air, 88
Mt Pleasant, 234
Muckle, 245
Mudd, 9, 70, 76, 132, 174, 227, 249, 269, 296
Mude, 76
Mughon, 94
Muhlenberg, 28
Muir, 41, 73, 99, 108, 141, 147, 161, 196, 276, 326
Mulladey, 44
Mullender, 12
Muller, 300
Mullican, 56
Mulliken, 235
Mullikin, 158, 207, 285
Mullon, 12
Mulloy, 80, 329
Mumma, 49, 53
Muncaster, 111
Munday, 187
Mundell, 92, 163
Munn, 100, 202, 229
Munore, 296
Munro, 72, 335
Munroe, 37, 138, 184, 185, 202, 225, 226, 256, 273, 298, 331
Munsen, 334
Munson, 12
Murdo, 108

Murdoch, 30, 70, 153, 180, 186, 239, 258, 265, 272
Murdock, 76, 141, 239
Murphey, 230
Murphy, 3, 72, 305, 307, 319
Murray, 25, 54, 89, 96, 133, 144, 163, 214, 257, 281, 283, 320, 329
Murrel, 11
Murrell, 237
Murtland, 72
Muse, 199, 288, 334
Musgrove, 82
Muskett, 52
Muson, 249
Mustin, 139
Myer, 148, 180, 232
Myers, 2, 30, 34, 55, 85, 128, 129, 147, 176, 180, 182, 217, 226, 239, 245, 249, 267, 271
Myrick, 8

—N—

Nabb, 79
Nabours, 23
Nachy, 184
Naismith, 90
Nalley, 324
Nally, 238, 319
Napoleon, 322
Narano, 40
Nash, 5, 54
Navy, 87
Naylor, 82, 86, 209, 230
Neads, 32
Neafus, 72
Neal, 90, 114, 199, 235, 236, 247
Neale, 24, 74, 133, 146, 182, 187, 188, 203, 231, 245, 249, 277, 292, 304, 322, 333, 338
Near, 141
Neil, 22
Neill, 275, 299

Neilson, 265, 269, 325
Nekervis, 112
Nelson, 54, 99, 117, 136, 234, 271, 319, 327
Nesmith, 38
Nevett, 247
Neville, 257, 325
Nevitt, 40, 124, 138, 160, 206
Newberry, 267
Newbold, 48
Newell, 93, 305
Newgent, 189
Newland, 20
Newman, 48, 103, 260, 314, 340
Newton, 4, 23, 73, 74, 77, 84, 103, 169, 180, 203, 219, 235, 239, 245, 280
Ney, 157
Niblet, 151
Niccoll, 47
Nicely, 58
Nichlin, 249
Nicholas, 65, 159, 183, 245
Nicholds, 245
Nicholls, 92, 107, 180, 239, 263, 266, 275, 299
Nichols, 20, 39, 132, 185, 239
Nicholson, 20, 41, 50, 53, 55, 137, 180, 181, 188, 204, 245, 247, 249, 263, 264, 276, 280
Nicklin, 182, 245
Nicks, 202
Nicoll, 94, 117, 279
Nicolle, 215
Nicolson, 264
Niel, 336
Nieson, 41
Niles, 27
Niman, 24
Nimmo, 89
Ninsene, 296
Nixdorff, 231
Nixon, 100, 105
Noel, 215
Noell, 129
Noland, 271
Nooaheevah, 42
Noon, 30
Norberry, 54
Nordyde, 39
Norgren, 39
Norman, 78
Norris, 14, 24, 26, 52, 54, 69, 94, 101, 110, 118, 136, 163, 184, 193, 274, 295
North, 175, 247
Norton, 90
Norvell, 111, 294
Norwood, 137, 150, 311
Noud, 120
Nourse, 81, 84, 106, 134, 192, 259, 317
Nowell, 192, 280, 299
Nowell's Fancy, 300
Nowlan, 214
Nowland, 2, 39
Noyes, 171, 217
Noyle, 52
Nugent, 93, 308
Number Six, 300
Nye, 37

—O—

O'Bannon, 200
O'Boyle, 164
O'Brian, 3
O'Brien, 27, 76, 111, 158, 212, 241, 269, 333
O'Bryan, 329
O'Connell, 225
O'Conner, 245
O'Conway, 94
O'Donnell, 126
O'Donnell's, 134
O'Fling, 57, 77, 169, 189
O'Hair, 339
O'Harra, 245
O'Neal, 60, 141, 202
O'Neale, 5, 25, 114, 157, 167, 272, 289, 322
O'Neall, 19
O'Reilly, 124
O'Reily, 109
Oakland, 183
Oaklands, 263
Oakley, 6
Ober, 6, 31, 41, 43, 241
Obrien, 304
Odell, 260, 261
Oden, 41, 99, 160, 182, 207, 249, 275, 276, 294, 299
Odenheimer, 43, 46, 93, 154
Odien, 275, 299
Odlin, 48
Oehler, 305
Oellers, 10
Offut, 340
Offutt, 132, 200, 340
Ogden, 144, 283
Ogle, 142
Ohara, 239
Okely, 189, 284
Olcote, 47
Olcott, 94, 279
Oliver, 39, 123, 144, 170, 172, 249, 263, 306, 329
Olmstead, 30
Olmsted, 263
Onderdonk, 147
Oneale, 174, 180, 193, 236
Oneile, 245
Onis, 287
Orandor_, 129
Orandorf, 180, 239, 245
Orcotte, 35
Ordean, 52
Orford, 58
Organ, 278
Orme, 129, 189, 199, 239, 245, 259, 301
Ormsby, 3, 103, 338
Orne, 118
Orr, 58, 69, 85, 99, 103, 198, 223, 290, 323, 326
Orrick, 230
Orth, 273
Osbern, 20
Osborn, 12
Osborne, 129

Osbourn, 201
Osbourne, 240
Osburn, 90, 240, 261
Ossian Hall, 137
Oswald, 181, 249, 276
Otis, 23, 84, 182, 339
Ott, 85, 102, 104, 126, 135, 170, 179, 197, 226, 235, 270, 330
Ould, 75
Oveler, 214
Overton, 12, 126, 172
Owen, 8, 116, 214, 242, 263, 269, 309
Owens, 24, 31, 39, 40, 283, 290
Owing, 23, 163
Owings, 56

—P—

P_tman, 12
Pace, 88
Pachard, 193
Padgitt, 5
Page, 53, 142, 280, 283, 325
Pageot, 37
Paidel, 334
Paine, 29, 193
Paint Mills, 62
Pairo, 6, 26, 113, 130, 327
Paleskie, 181, 249
Paliski, 276
Palmer, 34, 76, 232, 327
Palmon, 252
Pannill, 42
Park, 247
Parke, 182, 275
Parker, 7, 11, 15, 20, 24, 37, 61, 65, 67, 70, 78, 99, 119, 141, 142, 161, 202, 213, 214, 221, 245, 256, 265, 299, 305, 327
Parkhurst, 220
Parkinson, 182, 245, 247, 275, 299
Parks, 191, 245, 318
Parmlee, 54
Parnham, 338

Parran, 278
Parrot, 124, 241
Parrott, 97, 182, 188, 256, 330, 341
Parrous, 40
Parry, 31, 55, 61, 73, 130, 164, 215, 274, 296, 339
Parsons, 98, 128, 170, 208, 216, 245, 277, 280, 296, 301
Partlett, 54
Partridge, 106
Pasquin, 189
Patchart's Tract, 317
Patillo, 277
Paton, 15, 87, 144, 182, 310, 311
Patrick, 326
Patrick Magruder's Mill, 236
Patterson, 3, 14, 93, 95, 105, 131, 153, 160, 180, 191, 192, 215, 228, 239, 249, 257, 262, 263, 271, 281, 316
Patterson., 177
Pattison, 335
Patton, 8, 12, 24, 91, 208, 212, 245, 247, 275, 299, 304
Paulding, 198, 245, 260
Pauling, 239
Paulling, 325
Pawling, 180
Paxton, 30
Payne, 131, 219, 238, 262, 286, 310
Peabody, 76, 126, 142, 179, 230, 270, 280, 313, 319, 320
Peache's Balance, 303
Peache's Meadows, 303
Peache's Triangle, 303
Peachy, 94
Peacock, 135
Peake, 100, 164, 217, 306
Pearce, 64, 94
Peare, 254
Pearl, 134, 214
Pearson, 232

Pease, 101, 306
Peatross, 316
Pechin, 234
Peck, 55, 215
Peckham, 106
Pedersen, 95
Peeling, 319
Peerce, 223
Pegram, 173, 219, 235
Peirce, 71
Peircy, 114
Pelham, 30, 264
Pelin, 315
Pell, 280
Peltz, 52, 66, 74, 102, 166, 187, 231, 258
Pemberton, 341
Pemiliers, 319
Pendleton, 4, 15, 80, 122, 257, 314
Penefill, 33
Penn, 39, 146, 166, 173, 219, 235
Penney, 76
Pennock, 195, 247, 271
Penny, 267
Penrose, 182, 245, 247, 275, 299
Pentland, 327
Percival, 93
Perdreauville, 294
Perine, 88, 89
Perkens, 208
Perkins, 38, 54, 58, 76, 84, 89, 181, 249
Perrie, 96, 300
Perroe, 55
Perry, 5, 37, 65, 92, 125, 132, 136, 140, 196, 229, 245, 258, 296, 319, 334, 339
Pervost, 245
Pescud, 129
Peter, 2, 9, 19, 34, 91, 96, 104, 135, 162, 185, 225, 229, 234, 240, 245, 270, 330, 334
Peter Hubert, 288
Peters, 62, 150, 208
Petty, 154
Petworth, 209
Peyton, 6, 299, 309

Pfund, 301
Phelps, 3, 13
Phifer, 111
Philips, 150, 154, 245, 247, 264, 265, 275, 299
Phillips, 23, 182, 331
Philpot, 288
Piatt, 22, 184, 256
Pic, 331
Pickens, 25, 310, 314
Pickett, 249
Pickman, 339
Pickrill, 245
Pidgeon, 52, 191
Pie, 79
Pierce, 12, 86, 134, 165, 180, 239, 245, 272
Piercy, 76, 275, 299
Piere, 126
Pierson, 276
Pike, 145
Piles, 150, 303
Pindell, 222
Pinkney, 45, 50, 107, 167, 187
Piper, 145, 170
Pise, 44, 133
Pitcher, 19
Pitman, 39
Pitt, 197
Pitts, 137, 245
Plagemann, 293
Plaister of Paris, 252
Plant, 55, 317
Plate, 128
Plater, 42, 64, 229, 234, 241, 249, 293, 333, 338
Platt, 91, 126, 144
Pleasants, 60, 67, 103, 181, 245, 249, 285, 298
Pleasonton, 100, 121
Pledman, 52
Plowden, 41, 181, 239, 245, 249, 276
Plumber, 121, 137
Plummer, 22, 46, 185, 238
Poel, 273
Pogue, 54

Poindexter, 26, 173, 219, 235
Polhemus, 161, 293
Polk, 76, 81, 82, 102, 178
Polkinhorn, 54, 181, 242, 247, 274
Pollard, 52, 245, 249, 276
Pollock, 17, 23, 41, 51, 171, 181, 245, 249, 276
Pomfet Fields, 308
Pomroy, 72
Ponsonby, 43
Pool, 19, 113
Pooler, 325
Poor, 330
Pope, 3, 161, 301, 322, 335
Popham, 290
Port Tobago, 161
Porter, 3, 18, 40, 42, 46, 75, 88, 93, 106, 129, 181, 193, 239, 245, 249, 333
Porterfield, 160
Portland Manor, 13
Posey, 58, 151, 217, 225, 300, 316
Post, 54
Poster, 39
Poston, 58, 253
Potash, 91
Potter, 139, 245
Potts, 86, 159, 182, 207, 241, 256, 339
Pousin, 265
Poverty, 128
Powel, 114
Powell, 9, 54, 129, 136, 180, 181, 190, 195, 203, 206, 239, 245, 249, 276, 296
Power, 254, 288, 292, 319
Powers, 91
Prather, 87
Pratt, 20, 41, 137, 181, 202, 245, 249, 276
Prentis, 129, 256
Prentiss, 169, 257
Pres of Gtwn Coll, 249

Prescott, 10
President, 142
Preston, 30, 102, 103, 219, 273, 278, 336
Prettyman, 54
Prevost, 51
Prevote, 147
Price, 12, 23, 25, 40, 106, 130, 284, 330, 332
Priestley, 156
Primus, 271
Prince, 3, 6, 325
Prince Regent, 202
Princess Sophia Frederica, 311
Prior, 1
Prittle, 118
Proctor, 4, 210, 315
Prosch, 273
Prosser, 65, 120
Prout, 24, 73, 98, 112, 131, 228, 245, 246, 288, 337, 338
Pryor, 12, 13, 173, 219, 235
Ptulan, 319
Pulis, 25
Pumfrey, 312
Pumphrey, 52, 56
Pumroy, 2
Punch, 286
Purcel, 53
Purcell, 140
Purcey, 78
Purdom, 45
Purdy, 66, 260
Purnail, 219
Purnal, 235
Purnell, 319
Purrill, 54
Puthuff, 11
Putman, 233
Pye, 44, 62, 147
Pyfer, 322
Pyne, 300

Quarles, 112
Quarrier, 66
Queen, 1, 2, 16, 17, 23, 29, 48, 57, 60, 72,

84, 102, 136, 154, 162, 171, 208, 227, 231, 270, 277, 313
Quinn, 110, 225

—R—

Rabbit, 35
Raborg, 180, 228, 240, 245
Race, 130, 245
Race Ground, 300, 309
Rackliffe, 23
Radcliff, 183, 200, 202, 226
Radcliffe, 127, 287
Ragan, 148, 180, 194, 240, 245, 272
Ragland, 324, 327
Rakestraw, 79
Raley, 190
Ralph, 62, 207
Ralston, 144
Ramage, 93
Ramsay, 70, 102, 109, 151, 264, 323, 335
Randal, 30
Randall, 12, 76, 142, 182, 249, 325, 334
Randell, 135
Randle, 241, 339
Randles, 76
Randolph, 51, 61, 70, 95, 138, 142, 177, 196, 197, 326
Ranson, 252
Rapine, 28, 137, 209, 238, 288, 296, 330
Rapp, 36, 63
Rappleye, 90
Rappleyea, 85, 89
Ratcliff, 180, 189, 240, 299
Ratcliffe, 115, 272
Ratree, 249
Rattle, 56
Rattree, 181, 245
Rawin, 245
Rawlings, 313, 329
Rawlins, 319
Ray, 5, 35, 92, 99, 101, 157, 229, 264, 290
Ray's Adventure, 270

Raymer, 180, 239
Raymond, 214, 271
Rays, 297
Rea, 9, 41, 177, 214
Read, 19, 25, 144, 173, 182, 197, 215, 219, 241, 245, 261, 294, 298
Reagan, 59
Reager, 225
Reardon, 135
Reclanier, 180
Reclenear, 239
Recover, 175
Recovery, 207
Rector, 69
Redgreave, 54
Redman, 296
Redmond, 18, 225, 273, 295
Rednover, 129, 180, 239, 245
Reed, 39, 75, 130, 167, 182, 208, 229, 268, 275, 277, 280, 296, 299, 301, 314, 339
Reeder, 180, 240, 245, 272
Reese, 174, 198, 225
Reeves, 5
Reicess, 40
Reid, 12, 37, 126, 137, 159, 168, 197, 209, 237, 252, 332
Reiley, 184, 326
Reily, 78, 142, 235
Reinagle, 158
Reintzel, 112, 127, 153, 186, 314, 330
Reintzell, 52, 135
Relaimer, 245
Rench, 180, 239, 245, 272
Renfrow, 82
Renner, 10, 20, 185
Rennie, 41
Renshaw, 93
Rentfroe, 19
Renwick, 12
Reput, 52
Requa, 261
Resurvey on Hanover, 114

Resurvey on Honesty, 34
Resurvey on Thos & Mary, 307
Reynolds, 23, 152, 173, 219, 235, 269, 327
Rhea, 103, 245
Rhodes, 23, 184, 192, 235, 291
Riafs, 8
Ricaud, 263
Ricaus, 258
Rice, 3, 12, 286
Rich, 28, 91, 126, 164, 170, 176, 197
Richard & Nathan, 185
Richardet, 49
Richards, 16, 20, 39, 85, 120, 131, 144, 181, 221, 227, 233, 273, 306
Richardson, 3, 26, 47, 59, 76, 94, 96, 136, 163, 164, 184, 192, 222, 279, 337
Rich-Hill, 290
Richison, 273
Richmond, 249, 252
Ricketts, 299
Riddle, 77, 181, 245, 249, 256, 265, 326
Rider, 128, 245
Ridgate, 168
Ridgeley, 263
Ridgely, 9, 27, 79, 93, 121, 269
Ridgeway, 64, 180, 221, 252, 264
Ridley, 182, 247, 275, 299
Ridout, 147
Riffle, 286
Rigal, 202
Rigden, 289
Riggen, 13
Riggs, 20, 76, 92, 106, 121, 180, 185, 239, 272, 278, 293, 318
Right, 146
Righter, 78
Riker, 147
Riland, 39, 284

Riley, 11, 170, 212, 287, 304, 323
Rimus, 36
Rind, 122, 184
Ringgold, 50, 103, 152, 156, 204, 227, 229, 275, 299
Ringold, 184, 245, 247
Ripley, 66, 111, 122, 331
Ripple, 39
Rippley, 39
Riston, 39
Ritchie, 86, 92, 122, 129, 197, 219, 302
Riter, 73
Rittenhouse, 37, 97
Ritter, 2, 160
Rivers, 184
Roach, 39, 76, 241, 277, 281, 301, 339
Roane, 103, 173, 219, 235
Robb, 41, 304
Robbe, 125
Robbins, 101, 286, 287
Robero, 54
Roberts, 23, 103, 110, 126, 164, 177, 218, 225, 312, 325
Robertson, 1, 19, 23, 37, 51, 56, 96, 97, 102, 132, 169, 208, 215, 219, 232, 252, 257, 288, 293, 305, 317, 332
Robeson, 81, 214, 220, 302
Robey, 40, 160
Robinett, 270
Robins, 12, 198
Robinson, 12, 29, 52, 59, 73, 76, 89, 96, 109, 113, 129, 180, 226, 240, 248, 262, 271, 334
Robison, 225
Rochester, 108, 333
Rock Head, 334
Rockwell, 28
Rocky Point Fortified, 309

Rodgers, 40, 58, 93, 110, 125, 126, 144, 197, 245, 270
Rodney, 311, 329, 335
Rodolph, 124
Roe, 160
Roebuck, 212, 304
Rogers, 40, 165, 175, 237, 249, 265, 269, 274, 319
Rogerson, 41
Roley, 18
Rollins, 334
Romer, 261
Romeyn, 253
Ronckendorff, 333
Root, 78
Rose, 2, 23, 107, 114, 122, 227, 238, 275, 298, 299
Rose Hall, 168
Rosedale, 62, 123, 260, 330
Ross, 20, 28, 51, 53, 61, 72, 80, 100, 102, 103, 114, 121, 144, 160, 182, 205, 247, 249, 256, 262, 263, 275, 283, 299, 325, 332
Rothwell, 155
Rousling, 245
Rousseau, 5, 101
Roux, 335
Rowan, 213, 214
Rowand, 28
Rowe, 47, 54
Rowland, 2, 26, 76, 138, 164, 319
Rowlet, 321
Roy, 84, 249
Royce, 109
Rozier, 146, 245, 247
Rsrvy on Brook Park, 270
Rsrvy on St Geo, 270
Rudgate, 181, 247, 274, 298
Ruffe, 39
Ruggles, 12
Ruminer, 192
Rumley, 268
Rumsey, 90, 230

Runkel, 219
Rush, 41, 103
Russel, 154, 173, 184
Russell, 3, 7, 12, 20, 39, 41, 57, 58, 119, 124, 146, 182, 184, 199, 219, 230, 235, 245, 247, 252, 274, 299, 305, 314, 327, 339
Rust, 96, 118
Rutherford, 17, 78, 168, 173, 219, 235
Rutter, 95, 101, 182, 245, 247, 319, 328
Ruypers, 2
Ryan, 129
Ryder, 44, 133
Ryland, 199, 249, 272, 319
Rynchart, 59
Ryneason, 90

—S—

Sabin, 268
Sachse, 273
Sackett, 119, 221
Sacks, 40
Saddus, 40
Sadler, 134
Sale, 26, 102
Saller, 40
Salmon, 146, 164
Salomon, 256
Salter, 93, 277
Salvadore, 41
Sam, 262
Sambre, 317
Saml, 296
Samuel, 139
Sanderford, 273
Sanders, 45, 162
Sanderson, 101
Sandford, 182, 241, 245, 277, 280, 301
Sand-hill, 254
Sands, 22, 89, 130, 181, 182, 241, 244, 245, 249, 276, 277, 280, 301, 340
Sanford, 154, 197
Sarcke, 271

Sargent, 119
Sasser, 120, 306
Satchell, 20
Satterwhite, 226
Saunders, 112, 124, 227, 238, 317
Savage, 18, 89, 91, 195, 263, 336
Savary, 108
Sawyer, 217, 228
Sawyers, 253
Sayer, 247
Sayrs, 208
Scaggs, 321
Scags, 68
Scarborough, 211
Scarlet, 41
Scars, 213
Scattudes, 40
Schaeffer, 61
Schaer, 289
Schell, 221
Schelman, 240
Schisler, 195
Schley, 188, 195
Schlossard, 40
Schmucker, 32
Schnebley, 6, 180, 240, 246
Schnebly, 142
Schneller, 133
Schnoeder, 167
Schofield, 65
Scholfield, 10, 125, 132, 149, 180, 182, 246, 275, 299, 339
Schoolfield, 247
Schoonover, 193
Schorus, 164
Schroeder, 245, 309
Schultz, 168
Schumacher, 276
Schutt, 69
Schuyler, 66
Sciler, 36
Sclosser, 8
Scolfield, 129, 180, 240
Scotland, 293
Scott, 14, 15, 18, 32, 36, 45, 46, 48, 61, 68, 69, 87, 93, 111, 115, 119, 140, 164, 177, 182, 188, 192, 193, 202, 232, 246, 247, 266, 296, 302, 310, 325, 340
Scoval, 2
Scovelle, 100
Scribner, 4
Searcy, 90, 264
Searl, 274
Searle, 317
Sears, 246, 328
Seaton, 6, 99, 102, 330
Seddon, 32
Sedwick, 37, 278
Seely, 12
Seemes, 317
Segwick, 195
Seippel, 273
Seixas, 217
Selby, 3, 86, 169, 246, 277, 317
Selden, 2, 12, 303
Selfridge, 206
Sellack, 54
Seller, 39
Sellman, 142, 204
Semmes, 17, 24, 43, 58, 66, 91, 96, 114, 118, 121, 134, 138, 178, 211, 234, 275, 299
Semms, 302
Senat, 93
Senter, 15
Sergeant, 219
Sergent, 12
Serra, 1
Serrin, 76
Sersey, 63
Serurier, 37
Sessford, 115, 297
Sevier, 47, 61, 73, 88, 94, 95, 149, 162
Sewall, 35, 49, 58, 102, 103, 109, 182, 242, 294, 310
Sewart, 208
Sewell, 5, 47, 124, 247
Sexton, 149
Seyler, 54
Seyller, 18
Seymour, 29, 56, 216, 271, 299
Shaaf, 285
Shaaff, 13, 63
Shade, 327
Shafer, 99, 190, 246
Shaff, 240, 246
Shaffear, 180
Shaffer, 240
Shanklin, 6
Shanly, 154
Shannon, 268, 312
Shannon Hill, 108
Sharon, 90
Sharp, 28, 54, 62, 145, 188, 246, 249
Sharpe, 126, 276
Shaub, 250
Shaw, 46, 120, 141, 147, 184, 192, 199, 214, 225, 245, 247, 252, 273, 303, 319, 338
Shead, 3
Sheckles, 107
Sheetz, 60, 300
Sheffey, 105
Shekells, 200
Sheldon, 191
Shell, 55, 129, 180, 240, 246, 272
Shellman, 180, 246
Shelton, 112, 271
Shepard, 228
Shephard, 142
Shepherd, 92, 99, 129, 180, 214, 240, 246, 335
Sheppard, 3, 32, 76
Sherlock, 76
Sherrerd, 144
Shields, 39, 278, 319
Shindle, 315
Shinn, 78
Shinnick, 14, 89
Shipp, 287, 294, 326
Shippen, 240, 246
Shippin, 129, 180
Shivers, 294
Shnebley, 272
Shoaff, 2
Shoemaker, 28, 83, 160, 165, 246, 324
Sholl, 289
Shommo, 265
Shore, 129

Short, 9, 25, 90, 104, 263
Shorte, 303
Shorter, 225, 246, 296, 301
Shorthand, 118
Shreve, 249
Shrieve, 181
Shroeder, 130
Shropshire, 169
Shrub, 246
Shubrick, 33, 250
Shuck, 22, 85, 105, 162
Shuckle, 246
Shultz, 89
Shumate, 192
Shurly, 126
Shute, 17, 106, 247, 280, 314
Shutley, 56
Sibley, 140
Sidebotham, 246, 247
Sidebothom, 180
Sidebottom, 182
Siffert, 200
Silver Hills, 66, 104, 233
Sim, 10, 18, 48
Simkins, 127, 288
Simmes, 15, 56
Simmeymon, 58
Simmons, 15, 101, 273, 288, 303
Simms, 151, 241, 312, 335, 339
Simonds, 66, 214, 323
Simonson, 325
Simpkins, 3
Simpson, 34, 35, 84, 88, 135, 162, 179, 186, 197, 211, 243, 272, 278, 287, 297, 315, 324, 337
Simpson's Choice, 285
Sims, 161, 163, 184, 188, 271, 279, 302, 319
Simson, 239
Simtson, 172
Sinart, 184
Sinclair, 255
Singerfilter, 180
Singletary, 95

Singleton, 87
Sinnickson, 288
Sisterson, 245
Sites, 90
Siverly, 4
Sivley, 38
Skam, 246
Skidmore, 225
Skinner, 89, 96, 101, 190, 228, 246, 283
Skipwith, 89, 143, 175, 258
Skyren, 240
Slade, 224, 237
Slago Branch, 135
Slate Ridge, 72
Slater, 41, 130, 148, 151, 153, 178, 182, 215, 241, 245, 260, 277, 280, 284, 301, 339
Slater's Benefit, 128
Slaughter, 227, 258
Slave, 76
Sleeker, 192
Sleeper, 291
Sleepy crk, 290
Sluby, 180
Sly, 249
Slye, 120, 246, 276
Small, 18, 34, 265
Smallwood, 36, 45, 78, 97, 108, 111, 131, 132, 231, 245, 246, 288, 319, 330
Smart, 54
Smether, 224
Smith, 3, 5, 7, 9, 10, 13, 17, 20, 26, 27, 28, 29, 30, 35, 39, 43, 44, 47, 51, 52, 54, 56, 58, 59, 61, 64, 66, 72, 76, 89, 93, 94, 95, 97, 100, 104, 105, 117, 124, 129, 131, 132, 133, 140, 141, 144, 147, 154, 158, 160, 161, 163, 167, 174, 175, 176, 180, 182, 185, 186, 190, 200, 202, 203, 205, 211, 212, 215, 228, 229, 240, 241, 244, 245, 246, 249, 252, 256, 261, 263, 265, 271, 274, 275, 276, 277, 278, 279, 280, 284, 290, 297, 299, 300, 301, 306, 307, 309, 325, 330, 331, 334, 337, 338, 339, 340
Smith's Chance, 128
Smith's Mount, 219
Smither, 93
Smoot, 69, 154, 197, 204, 225
Smothers, 8
Smull, 238
Smyth, 78, 172
Snapp, 225
Snell, 13, 122
Snelling, 12
Snellings, 67
Sniffer, 93
Snow, 19, 225
Snowden, 57, 95, 134, 176, 208, 231, 246, 276
Snowhill, 65
Snyder, 61, 220, 278
Society Hill, 61
Sollers, 53
Solomon, 249
Somers, 112, 182, 241
Somervell, 236, 334
Somerville, 59, 174, 284, 338, 339
Sommer, 219, 330
Sommers, 148, 315
Somos, 334
Soolee, 178
Soper, 60, 138, 169, 175, 207, 221, 246, 252, 257, 295
Sotheron, 292
Sothoron, 207
Sotterley, 234
Sotum, 184
Southall, 141
Southerland, 278
Southgale, 180
Southgate, 240, 246, 272
Spackman, 134
Spafford, 40, 323

Spalding, 83, 104, 118, 121, 182, 183, 216, 241, 277, 287, 301, 312, 339
Spaldings, 221
Spangler, 225
Sparks, 118, 137
Sparrow, 283
Speage, 76
Speak, 76
Speake, 48, 76, 84, 246, 340
Spear, 12, 242
Spears, 182, 247
Spedden, 93
Spellman, 258, 263
Spence, 93, 159, 332
Spencer, 3, 28, 56, 93, 124, 137, 188, 202, 325, 326
Speyer, 230
Spicer, 300
Spicknell, 18
Spiller, 98
Spilman, 214
Spindle, 131
Spooner, 76, 94, 246, 262, 271
Spotts, 126
Spradley, 329
Sprague, 139
Spratt, 215
Sprigg, 9, 19, 48, 75, 89, 105, 116, 121, 249, 307
Spring Hill, 334
Spring Landing, 147
Spring Mills, 329
Springer, 198
Sprung, 158
Spunaugle, 202
Squire, 20
St Clair, 74, 339
St Clare, 241, 256
St Giles, 308
St John, 2
St John's, 232
St John's Addition, 232
St Tucker, 206
Stabler, 285
Stacey, 327
Stackpole, 34
Stafford, 267

Stagg, 191
Stagton, 252
Stall, 240, 246, 272, 327
Stallings, 93, 101, 140
Stamp, 146
Stanard, 23, 335
Stanford, 185
Stanley, 121
Stansbury, 54, 142, 252
Stanton, 296, 332
Stapeler, 225
Staples, 67, 112
Stapleton, 34, 223, 276
Starbuck, 93
Stark, 264
Starrett, 228
Stedham, 54
Steel, 6, 41, 94, 182, 241, 245, 277, 280, 288, 301, 317, 340
Steele, 312, 325
Steiner, 240, 329
Stelle, 33, 77, 97, 222, 319
Stem, 296
Stephen, 205
Stephens, 54, 57, 95, 103, 180, 182, 214, 225, 255, 326
Stephenson, 182, 214, 245, 320, 334, 339
Steptoe, 277
Sterett, 108
Sterling, 221, 269
Sterne, 94
Sterrett, 129, 181, 245, 246, 249, 276
Sterritt, 180, 256
Stettinius, 318
Steuart, 96, 131, 142, 167, 182, 225, 249, 250
Stevens, 142, 184, 240, 247, 264, 265, 283
Stevenson, 130, 193, 204, 219, 241, 262, 267, 316
Steward, 55, 76, 78, 240, 246, 250, 252
Stewart, 2, 23, 26, 33, 34, 35, 86, 87, 100, 101, 107, 109, 113, 119, 123, 124, 144, 146, 177, 180, 181, 182, 184, 188, 191, 224, 240, 243, 245, 246, 247, 249, 263, 264, 272, 273, 275, 285, 289, 295, 299, 315, 331, 333
Stickney, 169
Stiles, 230
Still, 82
Stillings, 58, 124, 208
Stinchcomb, 255
Stith, 207, 301
Stivers, 180
Stock, 76
Stockslagel, 12
Stockton, 94, 141
Stockwell, 126, 130, 161, 182
Stoddard, 119, 241
Stoddart, 72
Stoddert, 6, 85, 89, 98, 123, 129, 180, 182, 240, 245, 246, 271, 272, 277, 280, 301, 338, 339
Stokely, 172
Stone, 39, 74, 91, 136, 245, 284, 295, 301, 310, 313, 318
Stonestreet, 21, 157, 259, 337
Stook, 334
Storer, 68, 238
Storms, 39
Story, 275, 299
Stout, 19, 41, 94, 237, 297
Stoutenburg, 40
Stowe, 222
Strachan, 274
Strange, 129, 179, 180, 247
Stranger, 246
Stratford, 155
Strats Never, 83
Strawberry Hill, 136
Street, 12
Stretch, 133, 172, 179, 285
Stricker, 245
Strife, 303

Stringfellow, 126
Stringham, 94
Strobel, 89
Stromatt, 42
Strong, 47, 94, 103,
 144, 256, 279, 329
Strope, 79
Strother, 105, 139, 221
Stuart, 109, 137, 142,
 173, 178, 184, 203,
 207, 208, 219, 229,
 235, 258, 296, 297
Stubbs, 48
Stull, 277
Stump, 309
Styll, 142
Suit, 32, 207
Sullivan, 74, 84, 309
Sully, 225
Summers, 172, 263,
 277, 280, 301
Summy, 81
Sumner, 19
Sumpter, 25, 325
Sunsberie, 166
Suter, 281, 296
Sutherland, 78, 104,
 216, 225, 256
Suttle, 247, 302
Sutton, 11, 39, 204,
 246, 247, 257
Svertchkoff, 18
Swaine, 283
Swam, 20
Swan, 246
Swank, 245
Swann, 84, 180, 234,
 240, 246, 256, 290,
 296
Swanson's Lot, 46
Sward, 76
Sway's Rsrvy, 153
Swayne, 74
Swearingen, 48
Sweeney, 33, 228
Sweeny, 40, 66, 90,
 102, 108, 138, 153,
 289
Sweeting, 34
Sweitzer, 23, 61, 64
Sweney, 145
Swett, 338

Swift, 44, 47, 94, 95,
 106, 120, 190, 192,
 275, 299
Swingle, 180, 240, 272
Swingly, 246
Sword, 38
Swortwout, 30
Sylleman, 27
Symes, 74
Symmes, 254
Syms, 284
Sypert, 192

—T—

Tabbs, 2, 33, 61, 171,
 180, 338
Tacket, 3
Taft, 263
Tait, 126
Taiter, 319
Talbert, 72, 132, 170,
 174, 249
Talbot, 101, 270, 340
Talbott, 2, 160
Talbotts, 193
Talbutt, 77
Taliaferro, 61
Tall, 59
Talley, 119
Talley's Point, 142
Tallmadge, 215
Talmadge, 66
Tandy, 90
Taney, 55, 134, 146,
 184, 221, 254, 308
Tannehill, 19
Tanner's Hole, 173
Tappan, 162
Tarbell, 156, 238
Tarlton, 269
Tarman, 259
Tarrant, 186
Tate, 212, 310
Taulburd, 146
Tayloe, 18, 29, 98, 126,
 193, 209, 210, 232,
 330
Taylor, 16, 25, 34, 40,
 52, 55, 90, 93, 102,
 103, 112, 119, 129,
 142, 146, 150, 154,
 158, 165, 167, 173,

 180, 183, 212, 219,
 235, 238, 240, 244,
 245, 246, 256, 259,
 264, 266, 271, 274,
 283, 302, 309, 311,
 324, 327, 328
Tazewell, 105, 172
Teackle, 23
Teakle, 241, 277, 281,
 301, 340
Tearing, 38
Tebbs, 163
Techam, 164
Tecumseh, 133
Telfair, 3
Templeman, 129, 180,
 182, 240, 246, 272,
 273
Templemon, 240
Ten Brook, 144
Ten Eick, 198
Tench, 164, 184, 225,
 240
Tennehill, 139
Tennison, 262, 282,
 294
Tenny, 163
Terrell, 22, 214
Terrett, 309
Terry, 39
Tewell, 246
Thacker, 267
Thaxter, 10
Think, 54
Thomas, 13, 20, 39, 41,
 42, 48, 79, 82, 91,
 107, 129, 130, 139,
 141, 144, 145, 146,
 180, 181, 182, 207,
 208, 221, 225, 240,
 241, 246, 247, 249,
 263, 265, 271, 273,
 277, 280, 301, 340
Thomason, 270
Thompson, 2, 4, 5, 8,
 23, 36, 37, 39, 41,
 59, 72, 76, 99, 101,
 103, 110, 111, 126,
 130, 137, 149, 156,
 164, 168, 173, 181,
 186, 192, 197, 198,
 199, 207, 210, 225,
 240, 242, 246, 249,

271, 272, 276, 277,
  292, 296, 302, 307,
  309, 316, 322, 324,
  325, 336, 337, 340
Thomson, 124, 186,
  243
Thorburn, 246
Thorn, 246
Thornton, 8, 41, 50, 51,
  53, 69, 100, 123,
  181, 240, 246, 249,
  258, 272, 273, 276,
  277, 283, 299, 301,
  302, 324, 329, 330
Thorpe, 83, 122, 171,
  284
Thorper, 77
Thorton, 234
Thos, 8
Thos Law, 280
Three Bros, 104, 233
Threlkeld, 63, 104,
  260, 270, 273, 330
Thrift, 340
Thruston, 1, 41, 96,
  248, 256
Thurston, 96
Thwing, 190
Tickner, 94
Tidball, 206
Tidyman, 319
Tienan, 309
Tiernun, 23
Tiffin, 19, 62, 130
Tilford, 232, 256
Tilghman, 92, 129, 152,
  182, 204, 246, 248,
  275, 299
Tilghmen, 299
Tilley, 107, 175
Tillotson, 155
Tilman, 49, 53, 188
Tilton, 103
Timber Neck, 321
Timothy's lot enlarged,
  176
Tims, 27, 34, 97, 114
Tingey, 7, 10, 24, 27,
  36, 50, 156, 157, 272
Tippet, 123, 319
Tippett, 17, 24, 36, 45,
  61, 73, 77, 85, 99,

102, 114, 128, 143,
  145, 151, 264, 320
Tipton, 213, 326
Tod, 13
Todd, 94, 156, 208
Toland, 246
Toler, 82
Tolman, 8
Tolmie, 38
Tolson, 11
Tomlin, 60
Tomlinson, 71, 142,
  198, 259
Tompkins, 11, 112,
  199, 203, 219, 246,
  260, 273
Tomson, 100
Toney, 284
Tongue, 319
Tood, 67
Tool, 249, 298
Tooly, 55
Tootell, 2
Tornton, 246
Torrence, 256
Toscan, 85
Totten, 78
Toulbat, 225
Toulson, 71
Tousard, 246
Toussaint-Louverture,
  320
Toussard, 340
Towers, 72
Towles, 233
Towlston, 315
Townley, 172
Townsand, 268
Townsend, 30, 233, 234
Towson, 69, 92, 224
Tracey, 319
Trail, 333
Trance, 20
Trant, 264
Trap, 187
Traquair, 309
Trasel, 252
Trash, 334
Travener, 296
Traver, 42
Travers, 71, 87, 160,
  164, 168, 184, 188,
  195, 200, 237, 249,

265, 275, 299, 305,
  337
Traverse, 100, 248
Travett, 119
Travis, 3
Treadwell, 216
Treat, 161, 209, 230
Trenchard, 264
Trent, 132
Trepany, 39
Tresby, 271
Trescott, 78
Trice, 145
Trimble, 60, 70, 134,
  238, 264
Trinida, 241
Triplett, 2, 27, 48, 161,
  249
Trobridge, 118
Trotter, 149
Trubat, 304
Truby, 160, 192
Trudeau, 231
Truhumon, 39
Truitt, 3
Trumbull, 151, 260
Truxton, 246, 340
Tschiffely, 102
Tuck, 94
Tucker, 6, 13, 187, 256
Tuckfield, 51
Tuell, 8
Tullaye, 217
Tunnicliff, 17, 159, 293
Tunstall, 94
Turberville, 116, 156
Turnbull, 337
Turner, 6, 18, 63, 69,
  78, 81, 90, 100, 151,
  171, 177, 178, 187,
  223, 225, 250, 267,
  305, 315, 337
Turney, 12, 56
Turton, 15, 208, 259,
  282
Tuttle, 27, 203
Tweedy, 110, 298
Twigg, 95
Twiggs, 47, 279
Two Bros, 337
Two Brothers, 309
Twycross, 212

Tyler, 6, 44, 46, 70, 92,
  94, 109, 112, 120,
  142, 158, 173, 174,
  178, 208, 215, 305,
  332, 337
Tyrie, 143

—U—

Ulmer, 192, 257
Umholt, 246
Uncle & Nphw, 128
Underhill, 12
Underwood, 4, 52, 87,
  102
Unsler, 186
Unthank, 181, 249
Upham, 188
Upsal, 223
Upton, 269
Urquhart, 108, 117

—V—

Vageler, 89, 249
Vail, 126
Vairin, 322
Valaperta, 264
Valence, 39
Valentine, 153
Valentine's Garden,
  337
Valet, 158
Valett, 188, 189
Vallet, 79, 137
Vallette, 93
Van Beuren, 212
Van Cortlandt, 28
Van Dreeson, 191
Van Hoffen, 153
Van Horn, 20, 31, 145,
  176, 262, 282, 308
Van Houten, 16
Van Lear, 92
Van Manick, 181
Van Mannick, 249
Van Ness, 10, 34, 53,
  71, 99, 111, 124,
  135, 210, 324
Van Rensselaer, 223,
  328
Van Rissick, 285
Van Swearengen, 92

Van Wart, 260
Van Zandt, 102, 306
Vanbibba, 273
Vanbibber, 182, 240,
  243
Vanbidder, 180
Vance, 4, 232
Vancleave, 94
Vandamme, 328
Vanderhader, 319
Vandermere, 54
Vandeventer, 220, 327
Vandyke, 144
Vanemiller, 59
Vanlamp, 101
Vansville, 145
Vant Tassel, 261
Vanzandt, 225
Varden, 19, 20, 29,
  104, 160, 164, 195,
  278, 298
Vardey, 214
Varner, 214
Varnum, 37, 43, 45, 60,
  99, 151, 275, 289,
  323, 330
Varon, 103
Vaughan, 249, 284
Vaughn, 246
Veach, 183
Veazy, 204
Veirs, 4
Veitch, 180, 182, 240,
  248, 275
Venable, 169
Verdier, 291
Vergennes, 257
Vermillion, 100, 162
Verner, 189
Vernes, 63
Vethake, 145
Vickers, 39
Victor, 129
Vidler, 323
Villard, 14
Villaret, 328
Villere, 263
Vincendon, 44, 133
Vineyard, 191
Vinson, 5, 38, 149, 223
Vint, 241, 338, 340
Vinton, 326
Violet, 286

Viti, 320
Vogeler, 181
von Doring, 273
Von Harten, 59
von Randorff, 273
Voorhees, 12, 93, 264
Voss, 86, 180, 182,
  241, 340
Vowell, 252, 321

—W—

Wadden, 40
Waddle, 3
Wade, 6, 12, 45, 93, 98,
  164, 277, 340
Wadsworth, 36, 180,
  197, 246, 273, 291
Wager, 265
Waggoner, 30
Wagner, 19, 126
Waigand, 305
Wailes, 12, 56, 164,
  184
Wainwrght, 279
Wait, 91
Waite, 212
Wakefield, 263
Walbach, 12, 31, 34
Waldron, 2
Walgamot, 180, 240
Walies, 238
Walker, 2, 3, 17, 44,
  60, 66, 71, 77, 106,
  124, 128, 129, 130,
  150, 172, 180, 181,
  182, 186, 202, 205,
  209, 212, 213, 214,
  216, 220, 230, 231,
  236, 240, 241, 246,
  249, 262, 273, 277,
  279, 281, 301, 310,
  340
Walkington, 22
Wall, 20, 83, 173, 218,
  227, 336
Wallace, 19, 47, 54, 57,
  64, 128, 236, 303
Wallach, 35, 73, 172
Wallack, 180
Waller, 78, 167
Wallert, 184
Wallis, 221, 307

Walljamotte, 246
Walnut Ridge, 268
Walsh, 107, 152, 194, 304
Walter, 88, 227, 233
Waltham, 208
Walton, 77
Wand, 41, 246, 276
Wanemiller, 103
Wannall, 107
Wannell, 214
Ward, 8, 17, 23, 28, 41, 64, 72, 73, 90, 101, 103, 111, 112, 113, 125, 129, 130, 155, 161, 170, 182, 240, 241, 246, 249, 251, 252, 264, 277, 281, 301, 335, 340
Wardell, 60
Warder, 151, 249
Wardle, 94
Wardlen, 212
Wardrobe, 334
Ware, 3, 238, 261, 267
Warfield, 40, 173, 233
Waring, 23, 25, 67, 76, 97, 129, 180, 182, 246, 248, 275, 277, 299
Warner, 3, 49, 60, 264
Warrel, 267
Warrell, 33
Warren, 57, 79, 103, 118, 148, 267, 276, 284
Warring, 42, 240, 246, 304
Warring's Discovery & Second Thought, 238
Warring's lot, 238
Warrington, 34, 93, 268
Warten, 261
Warthen, 209, 272
Wartling, 55
Washburn, 265
Washburton, 49
Washington, 1, 20, 22, 37, 55, 64, 68, 73, 89, 102, 108, 117, 119, 127, 146, 159, 162, 182, 183, 189, 208, 230, 246, 248,

255, 262, 275, 281, 286, 315, 325, 326, 331, 336
Waterman, 315
Waters, 28, 29, 66, 73, 93, 111, 122, 143, 144, 145, 147, 163, 167, 174, 186, 194, 200, 204, 205, 223, 237, 278, 288, 297, 330, 337
Waterston, 102
Watkins, 2, 3, 34, 56, 75, 118, 275, 299
Watmaugh, 70
Watson, 5, 47, 70, 92, 94, 108, 113, 117, 124, 181, 190, 258, 279, 334
Watterston, 123, 140, 273
Watts, 69, 106, 131, 134, 135, 197, 251
Waugh, 23, 88, 113, 130, 301
Way, 36, 45, 51, 86, 97, 99, 102, 147, 179, 259
Wayman, 180, 182, 240, 246
Wayne, 29, 56, 77, 314
Weath, 52
Weaver, 169, 184, 198, 226, 288, 292
Webb, 21, 77, 93, 166, 249, 252, 296
Webster, 1, 63, 86, 94, 112, 152, 173, 191, 220, 235, 237, 242, 280, 329
Wedding, 55, 82
Weed, 1, 280
Weeks, 27
Weem, 129
Weems, 25, 48, 82, 88, 121, 141, 162, 246, 260, 290
Weightman, 26, 33, 147, 161, 179, 189, 197, 210, 241, 256, 277, 288
Weir, 135, 136
Weisenfells, 124

Weiskopff, 190
Weiskoppff, 227
Weissenfels, 146
Weisskopff, 135
Weist, 262
Wellborn, 210
Weller, 29
Wells, 24, 26, 44, 54, 86, 89, 91, 94, 101, 225, 263, 266, 268, 278, 304, 318, 325
Welsh, 102, 268
Welty, 171
Wendell, 265
Went, 227
Werninger, 316
Wert, 238, 319
Werts, 40
Wertz, 28, 40
Wescott, 246
Wesselhooft, 273
West, 3, 149, 175, 207, 214, 245, 260, 294, 309
West Hatton, 124
Westbury, 288
Westcoat, 241, 340
Westcot, 182
Westcott, 191
Westerfield, 234
Westerman, 31
Westner, 171
Westover, 283
Westwood Manor, 292
Wethwell, 296
Wetsel, 314
Wetsell, 240, 273
Weyman, 273
Weysell, 286
Whalen, 160, 249
Whann, 68, 91, 131, 240, 334
Whartley, 326
Wharton, 21, 36, 71, 103, 149, 227, 246, 269, 279
Wheat, 55, 191, 246
Wheatley, 105, 126, 340
Wheatly, 38
Wheaton, 14, 26, 149, 220, 251, 285, 315, 331

Wheelen, 44
Wheeler, 130, 133, 181, 182, 206, 212, 228, 241, 246, 249, 277, 281, 292, 301, 340
Wheelock, 122, 278, 331
Whelan, 113
Whelpley, 145
Whetcroft, 126, 188, 205, 260, 297
Whetmore, 213
Whillers, 52
Whippey, 9
Whipple, 188
Whistler, 326
Whitaker, 305
Whitbread, 136
Whitchair, 180
White, 12, 16, 29, 34, 39, 43, 47, 51, 54, 55, 66, 74, 77, 79, 90, 92, 94, 96, 107, 118, 119, 126, 127, 146, 167, 171, 172, 175, 193, 198, 201, 206, 214, 237, 240, 246, 252, 279, 296, 298, 301, 327, 334
White Marshes, 104, 233
Whitehair, 240, 273
Whitehave, 164
Whitehead, 8, 246, 249, 276
Whitehill, 63, 143
Whiteridge, 141
Whitesall, 246
Whiteside, 32
Whitesides, 13
Whiting, 39, 265, 299, 311
Whitington, 121
Whitmore, 291
Whitney, 39, 54
Whittelsey, 198
Whittemore, 3
Whitten, 20
Whittington, 12, 94
Whittle, 74
Wible, 40
Wickham, 246, 340
Wicomico Fields, 124

Wiesenthal, 94
Wight, 150
Wightt, 249
Wignell, 129
Wikoef, 34
Wikoff, 144
Wilcos, 13, 190
Wilcox, 24, 40, 99, 258
Wilcoxen, 314
Wilder, 322
Wildman, 25
Wiley, 68, 84, 144, 160, 186, 204, 220
Wilham, 130, 340
Wiliams, 14
Wilkins, 257
Wilkinson, 25, 65, 84, 105, 121, 140, 204, 217, 224, 244, 250, 267
Will, 160
Willard, 22
Willaston, 334
Willcocks, 8
Willcox, 129
Willet, 282
Willett, 166, 176, 332
William, 39, 184, 249
Williams, 25, 30, 33, 35, 39, 40, 42, 49, 54, 63, 81, 84, 85, 90, 92, 100, 104, 111, 112, 113, 136, 142, 148, 149, 159, 162, 167, 177, 178, 180, 184, 185, 188, 190, 191, 192, 194, 208, 225, 234, 235, 240, 246, 249, 252, 253, 260, 263, 271, 277, 291, 294, 301, 307, 309, 312, 322, 330, 331
Williamson, 9, 22, 39, 102, 149, 198, 264, 310
Willing, 20, 224
Willington, 3
Willink, 130, 246, 277, 281, 301, 340
Willis, 60, 90, 142, 147, 149, 159, 202, 249, 337

Williston, 306
Willman, 124
Willock, 182, 246, 249, 276
Wills, 54, 145, 236
Willshire, 304
Willson, 215
Willup, 271
Willyard, 42
Wilmer, 6, 11, 39, 42, 63, 85, 115, 152, 154, 158, 233, 302, 330
Wilson, 23, 28, 35, 42, 54, 73, 81, 99, 100, 102, 105, 110, 122, 130, 135, 142, 147, 164, 176, 177, 179, 180, 182, 185, 197, 203, 214, 231, 239, 240, 241, 246, 264, 267, 268, 271, 273, 274, 277, 281, 287, 288, 290, 296, 301, 309, 319, 337, 340
Wilson,, 265
Wincett, 296
Winchester, 34, 302, 309
Winder, 49, 180, 240, 246, 273
Windsor, 2
Windsor Forest, 64
Wine, 39
Wineberger, 109, 154
Wingard, 164, 218
Wingfield, 37
Winn, 19, 103, 126, 160, 164
Winship, 54
Winslow, 143
Winstern, 284
Winston, 108
Winter, 93, 246
Winters, 180, 227, 240
Wirgman, 34
Wirt, 161, 178, 219, 263
Wise, 36, 59, 94, 161, 175, 276
Wish, 197
Wishart, 2, 295
Wished, 103

381

Wistar, 77
Witherall, 100
Withers, 2
Witherspoon, 145
Wm Cearn's, 195
Wm Frederick the 6th, 311
Wolbert, 101
Wolcott, 119
Wolstoncraft, 324
Womesly, 296
Wonts, 296
Wood, 36, 39, 54, 70, 102, 121, 137, 151, 194, 226, 233, 253, 283
Wood's Joy, 151
Woodbury, 228
Wooden, 143
Woodfort Farm, 117
Woodhouse, 197
Woodland, 262
Woodley, 37
Woodruff, 144
Woods, 19, 250
Woodside, 64, 279
Woodson, 12, 26, 324
Woodville, 127
Woodward, 72, 94, 153, 187, 246, 331, 341
Woodworth, 106, 120
Woodyear, 34
Wool, 78
Woolley, 139
Woolsey, 197
Wormley, 112, 246
Worrick, 226
Worth, 69, 256

Worthington, 57, 102, 104, 115, 116, 134, 144, 196, 199, 201, 220, 229, 240, 270, 332, 334, 341
Worthington's Beginning, 285
Wright, 5, 10, 13, 43, 52, 58, 73, 76, 99, 101, 103, 107, 110, 112, 132, 182, 212, 220, 224, 229, 233, 245, 249, 299, 304, 326
Wrighter, 175
Wrigley, 21
Wroth, 142
Wyat, 338
Wyer, 54
Wyman, 198
Wynkoop, 297
Wysham, 59

—X—

XVIII, 30

—Y—

Yancey, 14, 73, 219, 235, 326
Yarnall, 266
Yates, 19, 108, 117, 211, 246, 253, 334
Yearly, 82
Yeates, 141, 268, 277, 281, 301

Yeaton, 182
Yewell, 288
Yonge, 77
Yonts, 82
Yorkshire, 333
Yost, 180, 240
Young, 12, 19, 28, 32, 36, 38, 41, 44, 45, 58, 59, 74, 77, 90, 92, 93, 97, 99, 103, 120, 125, 130, 131, 133, 137, 144, 149, 162, 173, 175, 180, 182, 184, 194, 197, 198, 214, 221, 228, 231, 240, 241, 242, 246, 247, 249, 257, 261, 275, 276, 277, 279, 281, 283, 286, 289, 296, 299, 300, 301, 312, 316, 326, 330, 335, 340
Youngs, 69, 78

—Z—

Zanona, 31
Zantinger, 146
Zantzinger, 70, 251
Zanzinger, 94
Zechinder, 6
Zeigler, 148
Zeller, 180, 240, 247, 273
Zimmerman, 59
Zoeller, 107

Other Heritage Books by the author:

National Intelligencer *Newspaper Abstracts, Special Edition: The Civil War Years, 1861-1863*

National Intelligencer *Newspaper Abstracts 1846*

National Intelligencer *Newspaper Abstracts 1845*

National Intelligencer *Newspaper Abstracts 1844*

National Intelligencer *Newspaper Abstracts 1843*

National Intelligencer *Newspaper Abstracts 1842*

National Intelligencer *Newspaper Abstracts 1841*

National Intelligencer *Newspaper Abstracts 1840*

National Intelligencer *Newspaper Abstracts, 1838-1839*

National Intelligencer *Newspaper Abstracts, 1836-1837*

National Intelligencer *Newspaper Abstracts, 1834-1835*

National Intelligencer *Newspaper Abstracts, 1832-1833*

National Intelligencer *Newspaper Abstracts, 1830-1831*

National Intelligencer *Newspaper Abstracts, 1827-1829*

National Intelligencer *Newspaper Abstracts, 1824-1826*

National Intelligencer *Newspaper Abstracts, 1821-1823*

National Intelligencer *Newspaper Abstracts, 1818-1820*

National Intelligencer *Newspaper Abstracts, 1814-1817*

National Intelligencer *Newspaper Abstracts, 1811-1813*

National Intelligencer *Newspaper Abstracts, 1806-1810*

National Intelligencer *Newspaper Abstracts, 1800-1805*

www.ingramcontent.com/pod-product-compliance
Lightning Source LLC
Chambersburg PA
CBHW071949220426
43662CB00009B/1062